The Essential Guide t

MW00769737

The Essential Guide to Dutch Music

100 Composers and Their Work

JOLANDE VAN DER KLIS (ED.)

AMSTERDAM UNIVERSITY PRESS

MUZIEKGROEP NEDERLAND

Editorial Board: Louis-Peter Grijp, Pay-Uun
Hiu, Jolande van der Klis, Paul Op de Coul,
Elmer Schönberger
Editor-in-chief: Jolande van der Klis
Translators: Robert Avak, Robert Benjamin,
Ian Gaukroger (Muse Translations)
Editors English texts: Caecile de Hoog, Ian
Gaukroger
Editor of work lists, bibliographies and
discographies: Mieke van Heijster
Picture researcher: Ingrid van Gelderen, Dirk
Jan Timmer
Original title: *Het HonderdComponistenBoek*
(Gottmer, Haarlem 1997)

Cover design: Crasborn Grafisch Ontwerpers
bno, Valkenburg aan de Geul
Lay-out: Magenta, Amsterdam

ISBN 90 5356 460 8

© MuziekGroep Nederland / Amsterdam
University Press, Amsterdam, 2000

Contents

Foreword

When, in 1997, the *HonderdComponistenBoek* appeared, the publication of an English version, soon afterwards, was already planned. Moreover, the very idea of compiling a reference work on Dutch composers was designed, from the outset, to accommodate the growing international demand for such a publication. Centrum Nederlandse Muziek (an institute which, along with the specialist music publishing house of Donemus, is now part of MuziekGroep Nederland) in its efforts to promote Dutch music found itself increasingly confronted with a call for comprehensive, reliable background information.

A Board of Editors, made up of prominent Dutch musicologists, was given the task to select one hundred Dutch composers. Although this number was perfectly arbitrary, it appeared to produce a very manageable volume, whose publication, moreover, could be realised reasonably expeditiously.

Numbers aside, the Editorial Board had to cut a few more knots. It was decided that the emphasis in the publication would be on contemporary composing, without neglecting the earlier style periods. The first criterion for inclusion was the composer's Dutch citizenship, prolonged residency in the Netherlands, or a particular bond with the Netherlands. Hence, the renaissance composers of the so-called Dutch Schools were disqualified from inclusion, since, according to research, all appeared to originate from Northern France. Hence, the earliest composers included in this volume are Cornelis Schuyt and Jan Pieterszoon Sweelinck, whose works were published in the late sixteenth century. On the other hand, foreign composers such as Klas Torstensson, Henrico Albicastro and Christiaan Ernst Graaf were found to meet the above criteria, since all composed most of their works on Dutch soil.

After ample consideration, it was resolved that each composer be given an equal amount of space, irrespective the importance assigned to them, or the volume of their output. In this way, time-bound value judgements were avoided, while treating relatively obscure, hitherto undocumented composers with equal reverence. This explains, for instance, why Hendrik Focking (only six flute sonatas survive today) is portrayed as prominently as the world-famous Louis Andriessen.

Finally, concerning the listing of the works, it was decided to include only a brief inventory with each entry. For those seeking more detailed information in relation to specific entries, a bibliography has been included containing references to specialist literature on the subject. Although such information may not be available in English, this was not a consideration for excluding key references.

While the ink on these pages is still new, negotiations are under way for a publication featuring 150, perhaps as many as 200 Dutch composers. Encouraging reactions from Dutch readers, as well as the many names that regrettably were omitted in the present publication, amply justify a 'remake'. However, mindful of the numerous supplements already required to update the information on contemporary (living) composers, one might question the efficiency of a new, printed version. The new media – especially the Internet – possibly are a more dynamic and approachable avenue for documenting the organic process of contemporary composing.

While discussions on the subject continue, those craving for more information after reading this publication are invited to read about its planned sequence at: www.muziekgroep.nl.

Jolande van der Klis
Culemborg, the Netherlands, August 2000

Note on the systematics of listed works, bibliographies and discographies

All listings of compositions, bibliographic works and sound carriers in this publication are intended, first and foremost, as a service catalogue for readers wishing to obtain more information about a certain composer or composers. The listed works, bibliographies and discographies are selective. In preparing them, completeness was never aspired: the selection reflects the author's choice entirely.

In organizing the works of composers who lived and worked before 1800, a different method of description was used in comparison with the works of more recent composers. In the first category, the dates given are the dates as these appear on the first edition (or first-known edition) of the work or the surviving manuscript. Their publishers often adorned later editions with new titles. Thus, in the case of printed works, the title of the work, the instrumentation (as completely as possible), opus number and year of print are shown. Hence, the year shown in this category does not necessarily tell us when the work was composed, but only when it first appeared in print. In the case of manuscripts, however, the dates shown refer to the year in which the work was composed.

As concerns the second category (from 1800), the title given to the work by the composer has served to determine its date of origination. Unless specifically stated otherwise, the dates given in this category therefore refer to the year in which the work was composed. Abbreviations denote the instrumentation (see explanatory list). Because publishers and publication dates are not of importance in identifying the compositions in this category, the information has been omitted.

In the category dating before 1800, the 'Writings' section refers to both printed works and manuscripts. With the composers dating after 1800, this section appears under the heading of 'Publications'. The details shown in this section may appear differently from one composer to the next, depending on oeuvre, style period and author's choice.

Mieke van Heijster

List of abbreviations

31-tone org	31-tone organ
A	alto, contralto
a.o.	and others
acc	accordion
a-cl	alto clarinet
ad lib.	ad libitum
adapt.	adapted
a-fl	alto flute
amp.	amplified
anon.	anonymous
a-rec	alto recorder
arr.	arranged/arranger/arrangment
a-sax	alto saxophone
B	bass
b-acc	bass accordion
bamb-fl	bamboo flute
Bar	baritone
bar.org	barrel organ
B-Bar	bass baritone
bc	basso continuo
b-cl	bass clarinet
b-fl	bass flute
b-gui	bass guitar
b-hn	basset horn
bn	bassoon
boy S	boy soprano
b-rec	bass recorder
br-sax	baritone saxophone
b-sax	bass saxophone
b-trb	bass trombone
c	circa
car	carillon
cel	celesta
ch.choir	children's choir
ch.v	children's voice
chamb.	chamber
cl	clarinet

collab.	in collaboration with
cond.	conducted
cop.	copyright
corn	cornet
Ct	countertenor
db	double bass(es)
dbn	double bassoon
dist.	distributor/distributed
ed.	editor/edited/edition
eh	English horn
el.	electric
electr.	electronic(s)
enl.	enlarged
ens	ensemble
ep.	epilogue
et al.	et alii
et seq.	and what follows
etc	et cetera
facs.	facsimile
fin.	finished
fl	flute
flhn	flugelhorn
frag.	fragment
gui	guitar
h.v	high voice
harm	harmonium/reed organ
hn	(French) horn
hp	harp
hpd	harpsichord
hrsg.	herausgegeben/Herausgeber
i.e.	id est
instr	instrument/instrumental
introd.	introduction
keyb	keyboard
KVNM	Koninklijke Vereniging voor Nederlandse Muziek-geschiedenis
l.v	low voice
lt	lute
m.choir	male choir
m.v	male voice

mand	mandolin
mar	marimba
md.v	medium voice
Mez	mezzo soprano
mix.choir	mixed choir
nar	narrator
no.	number
ob	oboe
oba	oboe d'amore
obbl.	obbligato
op.	opus
orch	orchestra
orchestr.	orchestrated/orchestration
org	organ
orig.	original
p.	page
perc	percussion
pf 2h	piano 2-hands
pf 4h	piano 4-hands
pf 8h	piano 8-hands
pf lh	piano left hand
pf	piano
pic	piccolo
pist	piston
pr.pf	prepared piano
pref.	preface
print.	printed/printing
pseud	pseudonym
pt	part
publ.	publication/published/publisher
qnt	quintet
qt	quartet
rec	recorder
recit.	recitation
re-ed.	re-edited
repr.	reprint
rev.	revised/revision
S	soprano
s.d.	sine datum
s.l.	sine loco
s.n.	sine nomine
SATB	soprano-alto-tenor-bass

sax	saxophone
sel.	selection
sp.chorus	speaking chorus
sp.v	speaking voice
s-rec	soprano recorder
s-sax	soprano saxophone
str	string(s)
sxt	sextet
synth	synthesizer
T	tenor (voice)
tb	tuba
timp	timpani
toy pf	toy piano
tpt	trumpet
tra.fl	transverse flute
trad.	traditional
transl.	translated/translation
trb	trombone
t-rec	tenor recorder
tr-rec	treble recorder
t-sax	tenor saxophone
t-trb	tenor trombone
TVNM	Tijdschrift van de Vereniging voor Nederlandse Muziekgeschiedenis
unfin.	unfinished
v	voice
vc	cello
vibr	vibraphone
vl	violin
vla	viola
vlada	viola d'amore
vladg	viola da gamba
VNM	Vereniging voor Nederlandse Muziekgeschiedenis (later KVNM)
vol.	volume
w.choir	women's choir
w.v	women's voice

The Essential Guide to Dutch Music

Henrico Albicastro

BIESWANGEN, C.1660 – 1730 OR LATER

The name Giovanni Henrico Albicastro, one of the few pseudonyms in Dutch music history, is an Italianized form of the amateur composer's actual German name: Johann Heinrich von Weissenburg. Albicastro came from Bieswangen in central Bavaria, not far from Pappenheim, where he is believed to have been born around 1660. The family name probably refers to the village of Weissenburg, which is near to Bieswangen. Great interest in Albicastro exists among the Swiss – a consequence of Johann Walther's supposition in his *Musicalisches Lexicon* (1732) that Albicastro came from Switzerland. However, this information is uncorroborated, which makes the Swiss claim to this composer doubtful.

In 1686 Weissenburg arrived in the city of Leiden, in the Dutch Republic, where he registered at the university as a 'Musicus Academiae'. The title would seem to imply that he was employed by the university as a musician, or in other words that he was responsible for the academy's official music-making, particularly as part of public ceremonies, such as the inauguration of a new Rector Magnificus. The university archives make no mention of such activities, however. In any case, Weissenburg could not have held this position for very long, for shortly after 1690 others (François Koopman, Charles le Vray) were appointed to the post.

There is evidence that Weissenburg spent several years in the Spanish Netherlands. In 1696 a collection of twelve of his trio sonatas appeared, entitled *Il giardino armonico sacro-profano*, edited by Franchois Barbry and published in Bruges by Franchois van Heurck. Only the first six sonatas of this collection have survived; the complete title, incidentally, refers to the work as 'opus 3'. (No information has survived on the previous opp.1 or 2.) Barbry was an amateur musician of Bruges who in 1695 was granted a patent to publish the music of eight composers, collectively identified in the patent application as 'Italians'. On closer inspection, most of the compositions appear to have been non-Italian works. Weissenburg appears first in the list, most likely because he had some sort of relationship with Barbry. Then follows Sebastian Scherer, which can be no coincidence either. Scherer (1631-1712) was a Bavarian musician who spent his entire life as a 'music master' and organist in Ulm. Given that Ulm is situated near Bieswangen, that Scherer was a generation older than Weissenburg and further, that he had published a collection of Ital-

Oath taken as an officer in the State Army,
5 October 1708

ianate trio sonatas in Ulm in 1680, it
seems reasonable to conclude that
Scherer was Weissenburg's music
teacher.

In 1708 Weissenburg's career took
a radical turn when he was promoted
to the rank of cavalry captain in the
State army. Presumably he had already acquired military experience
prior to this, but no details have been
found. Johan Hendrik van Weissenburg – as he is referred to in military documents – fought in the last
years of the War of the Spanish Succession (1701-1713), and remained in
the army after the Peace of Utrecht
(1713). His name is mentioned for
the last time in the Dutch army's annual officers' roll of 1730. Nothing is
known of Weissenburg's life after
1730, which leads to the assumption
that he died not long afterwards.

Weissenburg was a fairly productive composer, but given the details of his life
it is not surprising that most publications of his music were issued within a
limited period, namely, the time immediately preceding his service in the
Dutch army. The pieces issued between 1701-1706 under the pseudonym Albicastro by the Amsterdam music publisher Estienne Roger are a rather compact series of nine opuses. They comprise collections of violin sonatas (opp.2,
3, 5, 6 and 9), trio sonatas (opp.1, 4 and 8), and string concertos (op.7) in a decidedly Italianate idiom (i.e. that of Corelli), but slightly more angular and
with occasionally more unexpected turns. The succession of movements almost always follows the 'church sonata' sequence, with four movements
arranged in the order slow, fast, slow, fast. First movements seem at times
somewhat capricious given their succession of short fragments in contrasting
tempos and characters.

Albicastro composed mellifluous and fascinating music of high quality. If
we consider him a Dutch composer – and his biography does give reason to do
so – then he ranks among the most important of the first quarter of the eighteenth century. He forms a link between his predecessor Carolus Hacquart and

the later composers Willem de Fesch, Pieter Hellendaal and Unico Wilhelm van Wassenaer. In Albicastro, Corelli imitation in the Dutch Republic reached its peak.

RUDOLF RASCH

COMPOSITIONS

Il giardino armonico sacro-profano di dodici suonate in due parti, parte I dell'opera terza continente VI suonate a tre stromenti col basso per l'organo. – Brugge, Francesco van Heurck, 1696

XII Suonate a tre, due violini et violoncello col basso per l'organo ... opera prima. – Amsterdam, Estienne Roger, [1701]

XII Sonate a violino solo col basso continuo ... opera seconda. – Amsterdam, Estienne Roger, [1702]
Lost

XII Sonate a violino e violone col basso continuo ... opera terza. – Amsterdam, Estienne Roger, [1702]

XII Suonate a tre, due violini e violoncello col basso per l'organo ... opera quarta. – Amsterdam, Estienne Roger, [1702]
Modern ed.: 12 sonatas for two violins, cello and keyboard : op. 4 / ed. Timothy Roberts. Vols. 1-4. London, Grancino, 1987 (Early Ensemble Series 7a-d)

Sonate a violino solo col basso continuo ... opera quinta. – Amsterdam, Estienne Roger, [1703]

Sonate a violino solo e basso continuo ... opera sesta. – Amsterdam, Estienne Roger, [1704]
Lost

XII Concerti a quatro, due violini, alto, violoncello e basso continuo ... opera settima. – Amsterdam, Estienne Roger, [1704]
Modern ed.: Zwölf Concerti a 4 : Op. 7 / hrsg. Max Zulauf. Basel, Bärenreiter, 1955 (Schweizerische Musikdenkmaler 1)

[XII] Sonate da camera a tre, due violini e violone col basso per l'organo ... opera ottava.– Amsterdam, Estienne Roger, [1704]
Modern ed.: Zwölf Triosonaten : Op. 8 / hrsg. Max Zulauf. Basel, Bärenreiter, 1974 (Schweizerische Musikdenkmaler 10)

XII Sonate a violino solo col violone o basso continuo ... opera IX. – Amsterdam, Estienne Roger, [1706]

IN MANUSCRIPT: *Coelestes angelici chori,* motet for soprano, four instruments and bc
Brussels, Royal Conservatory, ms FG3

BIBLIOGRAPHY
E. Darbellay: 'Giovanni Henrico Albicastro alias Heinrich Weissenburg : un compositeur suisse au tournant des XVIIe et XVIIIe siècles', *Schweizerische Musikzeitung* 116, 1976, p. 1-11

DISCOGRAPHY
Trio Sonata op. 8, no. 3. Trio Sonnerie (Teleac TEL 8901-8905)

Maarten Altena

AMSTERDAM, 22 JANUARY 1943

Maarten Altena's activities since the late 1960s as an improvising double bassist have formed the background of his work as a composer. Though from the very beginning composition has played a role in his improvisation, it was only in the 1990s that he became confident that he was following a clear path as a composer. Not one to work out his musical thoughts in the isolation of a study, Altena's ideas are polished during his frequent performances with his own ensemble. For him, performance participation is essential. The Maarten Altena Ensemble is a remarkable unit, bringing together musicians from widely divergent fields, from Baroque to pop music, thus enabling Altena to try out various combinations of composition and improvisation. Through this experimental approach to working together, Altena distances himself from what he abhors most: academics and what he refers to as 'musical bureaucracy'.

Since his conservatory days, Altena has performed in various existing and *ad hoc* ensembles, among them Willem Breuker's groups, the Instant Composers Pool, the ensembles of Theo Loevendie, the Netherlands Ballet Orchestra, Derek Bailey's Company, and Orkest de Volharding. During his formative years it was Breuker and Misha Mengelberg in particular who set the tone for a new form of improvisation: a playful, often theatrical, Dutch response to American jazz. Around 1975 Altena began giving solo concerts in which he improvised in self-devised idioms far removed from the jazz styles of the time. This became the basis for his later ensemble work.

During the same period he and Theo Joling put on the music-theater productions *Ploink, Willem de Zwijger* [William the Silent], *Raffia* and *Conifeer*. Joining forces with Michel Waisvisz, he also initiated a series of (historicizing and satirical) productions entitled *Avond over Jazz* [Evening with jazz], in which Hugh Davies, Steve Lacy, Moniek Toebosch and others took part. Another collaborative venture with Waisvisz was the organization of five Claxon Sound Festivals. These were continued in the Rumori concert series in which Altena was as active in providing compositions as he was in performing.

The development from bassist to composer taught Altena to approach improvisation from a composer's perspective. The requirement of being able to express oneself through notated music flowed inevitably from his experience as an improviser. After studying the double bass, Altena took lessons in harmony from Reinbert de Leeuw. In 1997 he also had private lessons in counter-

5

point from Gerard Blok. However, the decisive impetus came from his lessons in composition with Robert Heppener, from 1980 to 1985, a teacher who proved more than adequate in filling the gaps in the work of a student whose musical course was already fixed.

Altena continued performing throughout this apprenticeship, his ensembles forming landmarks along the road: the Quartet, formed in 1978, became the Octet two years later, ultimately evolving into the Maarten Altena Ensemble in 1985. The Maarten Altena Ensemble's repertoire includes the music of Altena and other members, along with the work of composers drawn by the many colors the ensemble offers. Altena stimulates the musicians to produce their own characteristic sound, the effect of which is amplified in some performances by dramatic impulses from outside the group: the poet Remco Campert, artist Marc Terstroet, and various theater directors have worked with the group.

Since his studies with Heppener, Altena has also composed for Dutch and foreign soloists and ensembles. Improvisation, notably, plays no role in these works, though Altena does study closely the musical personalities of the intended performers. The vocal color, for instance, of the singer Jannie Pranger served as the basis of his *Toonzucht* [Sigh of sound] (1991), and *Puls* (1993) was written to 'suit' the percussionist Johan Faber. Altena has also composed for the Netherlands Wind Ensemble, the Mondriaan Quartet, the Nieuw Ensemble, Array Music in Toronto, and for symphony orchestra. Characteristic of all these works is his clear preference for connecting with the individual sound of the performers involved rather than confining himself to a particular style or idiom.

Because of Altena's regard for the personal way each musician handles his instrument, each new piece may contrast starkly with preceding compositions. There are constants, however, the melodic element being the most important – harmony, in his work, follows from melody, and not vice versa.

Another recurrent feature, and one closely connected with the impulsiveness of his improvisation, is his disruption of rhythmic structures in a way that generates new structures. Within this dynamic process, structures always remain identifiable, regardless of how altered they may be. Altena takes care to avoid the 'grey mass' of the new complexity of the 1980s, striving instead to make his musical structures as clear as possible. He appreciates the ability of old masters such as Ockeghem and Josquin to compile interesting rhythmic layers in a simple manner; like them, he seeks to provide a musical discourse discernible to the 'naked ear'.

The deconstructivism of Altena's approach to musical material is reflected in the course of his development as a composer. In *Zig Zag* (1993), a music-theater co-production of the Maarten Altena Ensemble and Marc Terstroet, he broke the improvisatory tradition of his group with a long, through-composed piece whose structure explores the extremes of musical archetypes: extreme bareness, extreme contrasts between high and low notes, extremely long note durations.

Altena's work is based upon what he calls an 'arsenal of tone rows' or 'chromaticized modes'. Scales exceeding the octave are determinant and may be used as a matrix to filter the available potential sound material. Such an approach reveals that Altena, a product of his generation, came of age with a bent for serialism. Other forceful influences on his work are improvisation, jazz and pop music. As a result, his musical spontaneity has always kept pace with his increasing mastery of compositional technique. In Altena's view, technique should be a combination of craftsmanship and experience – and the experience he has acquired with musicians and audiences is a palpable force.

Though the Maarten Altena Ensemble plays an increasing amount of composed music, it remains essentially an improvisational group, engaging in musical conversation with all of the theatrical tension this entails. And, according to Altena, the full range of dramatic constellations has yet to be attempted. This continually evolving practice provides a steady flow of new impulses, inspires him and forms the framework that determines the effect of his music. The relationship between improvisation and composition notwithstanding, Altena considers each new piece a bold adventure.

MICHIEL CLEIJ

COMPOSITIONS

VOICE (WITH PIANO UNLESS OTHERWISE STATED): *Toonzucht*, v (1991); *Speech* (1994); *La belle dame sans merci* (Keats) (1994); *Minnaars* (Campert) (1996)

VOICE AND ENSEMBLE: *Three Songs* (Plath) (1986); *Figuur* (1989); *Stad* (Campert) (1990); *Bandrecorder eenvoudig* (Campert) (1990); *Fat City* (Campert) (1990); *ABCDE* (1992); *Lento* (1993); *Slow motion* (1993, rev. 1994); *Tik* (1994); *Dowlands* (Wyatt) (1995); *Trappel* (1995); *Code* (1995)

CHOIR: *Dance* (Williams) (1987)

CHAMBER MUSIC: *Muur*, vl (1985, rev. 1987); *Lijn*, db, pf (1986); *Roep*, t-rec (1986); *1. Pièce*, ob, vl, vla, vc, pf (1988); *Stave*, t-sax (1988); *Pitch*, str.qt (1990); *Puls*, perc (1993); *Figura*, vc (1993); *Bemidei*, b-cl, pr.pf (1995); *Fast-Slow-Fast*, vl, vc (1995-1996); *Puls II*, perc (1996); *Puls III*, perc (1996); *Language*, el.gui (1996); *Snapshot 1*, pf (1992)/*Snapshot 2*, pf (1997); *Melody?*, cl, tpt, vl, db, pf, 2 perc (1997)

ENSEMBLE: *Rif*, instr.ens (1987); *First Floor*, wind ens, 2 db, pf, perc (1989); *Speaking*, 6 perc (1990); *Signo*, instr.ens (1990); *Stijg*, instr.ens (1990); *Loop*, t-sax, pf, perc, b-gui (1991); *Mouthpiece*, 2 ob, 2 cl, 2 bn, 2 hn (1995)

ORCHESTRA: *Secret instructions* (1992, rev. 1993)

DRAMATIC VOCAL: *Zijdelings afgesproten* (texts F. vande Veire, compiled from lectures, monographs and letters of the Dutch philosopher and mathematician L.J.E. Brouwer), v, 4 actors, instr.ens (1996)

BIBLIOGRAPHY
H. Bunkers and D. Wuisman: 'Hartslag van de tijd : Maarten Altena Ensemble 15 jaar', *GroenLinks Magazine*, Apr. 1995, p. 14

M. Cley: 'Musical hunger', *Key Notes*, 28, no. 3, Sept. 1994, p. 17-19

J. Oskamp: 'De zakelijke aanpak van Maarten Altena', *Entr'acte*, Apr. 1990, p. 8

J. van Slooten: 'Oneindige muziek uit het hoofd van Maarten Altena', *Entr'acte Muziekjournaal*, no. 1, 1997, p. 24-26

K. Stevens: 'De muzikale ontwikkeling van Maarten Altena', *Jazzfreak*, Nov. 1990, p. 15

Chr. Tarting: 'Writing bass', *Impressions du Sud*, no. 30, 1991, p. 86

DISCOGRAPHY
America is Waiting (Angelica Festival Bologna 1995) (Caicaimusic)

Cities and streets. Maarten Altena Ensemble (Hat Art CD 6082)

City Music. Maarten Altena Ensemble (Attacca Babel 9373)

Code. Maarten Altena Ensemble (Hat Art CD 6094)

Conduction 35, 36 American Connection (Lawrence D. Butch Morris testament : a conduction collection) (New World Records, New York 1995)

Dowlands. Maarten Altena Ensemble (NM Classics 92063)

Hemispheres. Hemispheres (Artifact Music ARt008)

High, low and order. S. Lacy, M. Altena (Hat Art CD 6069)

Let it be. Aki Takahashi (TOCE-8021) (Japan)

Miere. Maarten Altena Quartet (Nato/Paris 235)

Op stap. Maarten Altena Quartet (Claxon 80.5)

Pisa. Maarten Altena Quartet (Claxon 82.11)

Quick step. Maarten Altena Octet (Claxon 86.16)

Quotl. Maarten Altena Ensemble (Hat Art CD 6029)

Rif. Maarten Altena Ensemble (Hat Art CD 6056)

Rondedans. Maarten Altena Quartet (Claxon 85.15)

Slow Motion (Unknown Public – The Netherlands Connection) (Londen)

Slow motion (version 1992 and 1994); *Tik; Figuur; Lento; ABCDE.* Maarten Altena Ensemble (Composers' Voice CV 49)

Tel. Maarten Altena Octet (Claxon 83.12)

Tik (Jaar van de Ensembles) (Polygram Classic & Jazz 454 058-2)

Veranda. Maarten Altena Quartet (Claxon 82.10)

Working on time. Maarten Altena Ensemble (NM Classics 92063)

Hendrik Andriessen

HAARLEM, 17 SEPTEMBER 1892 – HAARLEM, 12 APRIL 1981

Hendrik Franciscus Andriessen was raised in a culturally oriented family in which his musical talent naturally flourished. His mother, Gesina Johanna Vester (1857-1939), was a painter and his father, Nicolaas Hendrik Andriessen (1845-1913), was the organist of the St. Joseph Church in Haarlem, a conductor of various choirs, and a composer. His brothers Willem and Mari respectively became a concert pianist and a sculptor.

Andriessen received his first musical instruction from his father and brother. As the family's financial situation was not very secure, he first embarked on a career in journalism, working from 1909 to 1913 for the Catholic daily *Nieuwe Haarlemsche Courant*. During this time he took organ lessons from the Haarlem municipal organist, Louis Robert. Upon his father's death in 1913, Andriessen succeeded him as organist at the St. Joseph Church but he also continued to work as a music critic until 1922.

Among the first of his works to be publicly performed was the organ piece *Premier choral*, in which Andriessen elaborates upon the harmonic style of César Franck, and a *Veni Creator Spiritus* for six-part mixed choir and organ. In 1914 Andriessen enrolled in the Amsterdam Conservatory. Until graduating in 1916 he studied the organ with Charles de Pauw and composition with Bernard Zweers. Stylistically, however, Andriessen was much more influenced by Alphons Diepenbrock, with whom he became friends in 1917. They shared the Roman Catholic faith and a predilection for French music. Andriessen's affinity with Diepenbrock's music is especially evident in his sacred choir music, as for example the *Missa in honorem Ss. Cordis* (1918?).

Beginning in this period, Andriessen also performed as a pianist and accompanist, for example with the soprano Mia Peltenburg. They showed a distinct preference for the music of French composers. Andriessen knew some of these composers personally, among them Roussel, Pierné, and Milhaud. The music of Hugo Wolf – one of the few exponents of the German culture that Andriessen admired – also appeared frequently on their programs. Of his works, *Magna Res est Amor* (1919), *Fiat Domine* (1920/1930), and *Miroir de Peine* (1923/1933) proved particularly successful.

From 1927 to 1949 Andriessen taught music theory at the Amsterdam Conservatory and in 1930 he also became an instructor of the organ, improvisation and Gregorian chant at the Roman Catholic Church Music School in

Utrecht. In 1934 he was appointed organist/conductor at Utrecht Cathedral. Three years later he succeeded Jan van Gilse as director of the Utrecht Conservatory and became a professor of composition at the Amsterdam Conservatory. During World War II Andriessen was dismissed from most of these positions; because of his refusal to join the 'Kultuurkamer', the Nazi-controlled regulatory organization for the arts, and his participation in the so-called *Bruinboek*, a document criticizing the Hitler regime, the publication and performance of his music was forbidden and he was barred from teaching, lecturing and performing. He was able to continue as conservatory director and accompanist of church services, as these activities did not fall under the jurisdiction of the Department of Propaganda and Arts. During this period Andriessen composed a *Te Deum* that was premiered after the liberation of the Netherlands. He moved to The Hague and from 1949 to 1957 served as director of the city's Royal Conservatory. He resigned from his other positions when in 1952 he was offered a chair in musicology at the Catholic University of Nijmegen.

Andriessen greatly influenced later generations, not only as a composer and teacher, but also as an organist. Among his most important followers were Albert de Klerk, Herman Strategier and Jan Mul. Outside the field of Roman Catholic church music, however, his composition was less influential, though he did serve as a major inspiration to his sons Jurriaan and Louis. Andriessen also figured significantly in the field of amateur music. As conductor of the Amsterdam Student Music Society 'J. Pz. Sweelinck', from 1919 to 1924, he presented a highly diversified repertoire, and as the composer of music intended for amateur ensembles – such as the well-known *Kuhnau Variations* (1935) – he stirred the souls of many music lovers.

When in 1949 Andriessen composed the opera *Philomela*, he found a kindred spirit in the librettist Jan Engelman. The manner in which Engelman was able to articulate their musical ideals in their correspondence could serve as the credo of Andriessen's entire oeuvre: no superfluous experimentation and the fullest attention focused on the melodic aspect. Even Andriessen's forays into twelve-tone rows – as in the Symphony no.4 (1954) or the *Symfonische étude* (1952) – approached the technique in a well-defined tonal manner. Andriessen's four symphonies, moreover, are scored for what in effect is a Classical, mid-nineteenth century orchestra.

With these four symphonies, Andriessen earned his place as one of the first – and few – Dutch symphonists, certainly when one considers that the work of Matthijs Vermeulen was still unknown when Andriessen began his Symphony no.1 in 1920. Andriessen's symphonic – particularly the Symphony no.3 (1946) – and concertante music are distinguished by their neo-classical form.

In his Concerto for Organ (1950), such historical forms as the passacaglia and toccata are employed, and the contrapuntal passage after the introduction of the *Canzona per violoncello solo e orchestra* (1965) is written in the style of the sixteenth-century canzona. There is no sign of gratuitous virtuosity, the music rather displays an affinity with the more insouciant character of Fauré's or Duparc's work.

This penchant for the superficially lighter Latin music culture, also apparent in the commedia dell'arte figures in the symphonic fantasia *Mascherata* (1962), is even more forcefully present in Andriessen's extensive vocal oeuvre. Until 1915 he composed numerous songs to German texts, but subsequently favored Latin as the language of his sacred vocal music and French for his songs. In the latter genre, melody reigns supreme; the accompaniment consists mostly of chords, but is seldom subordinated to the vocal part. Text painting is rarely present and the text setting is primarily syllabic. In the roughly twenty masses Andriessen composed, too, the composer opts for a contemporary but simple musical style with frequent homophonic choral sections.

In addition to his sacred works and compositions for amateur ensembles and didactic pieces, Andriessen's writings also made a profound impression on a broad musical public. Most of his articles, published in books, originally appeared among the hundreds of newspaper articles he wrote over the years. Unlike his contemporaries Vermeulen and Pijper, Andriessen never attacked the subject under review, his writing tending to be more reflective. Still, in

Over muziek [About music] (1950), he wrote: 'All too often, northerners bury themselves in what they set out to immerse themselves in.' This has become one of his immortal quotes.

ONNO SCHOONDERWOERD

COMPOSITIONS

SACRED VOCAL: *Veni Creator Spiritus*, mix.choir, org (1913); *Missa in honorem Ss. Cordis*, choir, org (1918?); *O Sacrum Convivium*, S, org (1919); *Magna Res est Amor* (Thomas à Kempis), S/T, org (also version with orch, 1919); *Fiat Domine* (Thomas à Kempis), v, org (1920, version with str.orch 1930); *Missa in festo Assumptionis Beatae Mariae Virginis*, choir, org (1925); *Missa Simplex*, choir (1928); *Missa Diatonica*, choir (1935); *Missa Christus Rex*, mix.choir, m.choir, org (1938-1942); *Te Deum Laudamus*, mix.choir, org (1943; orchestr. 1946); *Te Deum I*, mix.choir, orch (1943, orchestr. 1946); *Psalm 150 'Laudate Dominum'*, mix.choir (1958, rev. 1967); *Veni Creator*, mix.choir, orch (1960); *Psalm IX*, T, mix.choir, orch (1961); *Te Deum II*, mix.choir, orch (1968); *Lux Jocunda*, T, mix.choir, orch (1968)

SECULAR VOCAL: *Harmonie du Soir* (Baudelaire), v, pf (1917); *Miroir de Peine* (Ghéon), S, org (1923, version with str.orch 1933); *Due madrigali*, mix.choir, str.orch (1940); *Tre canzoni*, mix.choir (1958)

OPERA: *Philomela* (Engelman) (1949); *De Spiegel uit Venetie* (Nolthenius) (1965); *Perséphone* (Nolthenius) (1967)

PIANO: *Sonata [I]* (1934); *Pavane* (1937); *Sonata II* (1966)

ORGAN: Four chorales (1913; 1916, rev. 1965; 1920; 1921, rev. 1951); *Sonata da chiesa* (1926?); *Passacaglia* (1929); *Sinfonia per organo* (1940); *Quattro studi per organo* (1953); *Suite* (1968)

CHAMBER MUSIC: *Sonata*, vl, pf (1915); *Sonata*, vc, pf (1926); *Sonata II*, vl, pf (1931); *Drie inventionen*, vl, vc (1937); *Quartetto in stile antico*, str.qt (1957); *Il pensiero*,

str.qt (1961); *Concert spirituel*, fl, ob, vl, vc (1967); *Sonata*, vla, pf (1967); *Quatuor à cordes l'Indifférent*, str.qt (1969); *Sonata per clarinetto e piano* (1971); *Divertimento a cinque*, fl, ob, vl, vla, vc (1972); *Sonata per flauto e pianoforte* (1974)

ORCHESTRA: Four symphonies (1930; 1937; 1946; 1954); *Variaties en fuga op een thema van Johann Kuhnau*, str.orch (1935); *Ricercare* (1949); *Mascherata, Symphonische Fantasia* (1962); *Chantecler Ouverture* (1972)

SOLO INSTRUMENT AND ORCHESTRA: *Variaties op een thema van Couperin*, fl, str, hp (1944); *Concerto per organo e orchestra* (1950); *Canzona per violoncello e orchestra* (1965); *Concerto per violino e orchestra* (1969); *Concertino*, ob, str.orch (1970); *Concertino*, vc, orch (1970); *Chromatische Variaties*, solo quartet (fl, hb, vl, vc), str.orch (1970)

PUBLICATIONS

César Franck. Amsterdam, Becht, [1943]
Over muziek. Utrecht [etc.], Het Spectrum, 1950
Muziek en muzikaliteit. Utrecht [etc.], Het Spectrum, 1952
Aspecten der Nederlandse muziek. Inaugural address at the Catholic University of Nijmegen 3 Oct. 1952. Nijmegen, Catholic University, 1952
De gedachtengang in de muziek. Farewell address at the Catholic University of Nijmegen 9 July 1963. Utrecht [etc.], Dekker van de Vegt, 1963

BIBLIOGRAPHY

Hendrik Andriessen en het tijdperk der ontluiking, ed. F. Brouwer [et al.]. Baarn, Gooi en Sticht, 1993 (Kerkmuziek & Liturgie, 6). Four lectures given at a symposium on 16 May 1992, organized by the Catholic University of Nijmegen

Th.J. Dox: *Hendrik Andriessen, his life and work*. Doctoral dissertation, University of Rochester, 1969

Th.J. Dox: 'Hendrik Andriessen – The Path to Il Pensiero'. *Key Notes*, 13, 1981/1, p. 16-24

Duizend kleuren van muziek : leven en werken van Hendrik Andriessen, ed. A. de Jager [et al.]. Zutphen, Walburg Press, 1992

B. Kahmann: 'Andriessen', *Biografisch woordenboek van Nederland III*. The Hague, Instituut voor Nederlandsche Geschiedenis, 1989

R. Koning: 'In Memoriam Hendrik Andriessen'. *Key Notes*, 13, 1981/1, p. 14

Hendrik Andriessen tachtig jaar, ed. J.H. Moolenijzer. Haarlem, Gottmer, 1972

P. de Vroomen: *De doler en het kind van God : brieven en documenten van de samenwerking tussen Hendrik Andriessen en Pierre Kemp in de jaren 1917-1921*. Baarn, De Prom, 1987

J. Wouters: 'Hendrik Andriessen', *Sonorum Speculum*, no. 7, 1961

DISCOGRAPHY

Ballade. M. Karres (ob), A. Karres (pf) (WVH 093)

Ballade. E. Rombout (ob), A. Bär (pf) (BFO A-2)

Complete Organ Works. A. de Klerk (Lindenberg LBCD 31/34)

Chromatische Variaties; Variaties en fuga op een thema van Johann Kuhnau; Variaties op een thema van Couperin; Fiat Domine; Magna Res est Amor; Miroir de Peine. Various soloists, Netherlands Radio Chamber Orchestra, cond. D. Porcelijn (NM Classics 92023)

Concertino for cello and orchestra; Concertino for oboe and orchestra; Canzona for cello and orchestra; Concerto for violin and orchestra. M. Müller (vc), T. Schmidt von Altenstadt (vl), H. Swinnen (ob), Netherlands Radio Chamber Orchestra, cond. Th. Fischer (NM Classics 92066)

Miroir de Peine. R. Alexander (S), Netherlands Radio Chamber Orchestra, cond. D. Porcelijn (NM Special 92093)

Miroir de Peine; Magna Res est Amor. E. Ameling (S), A. de Klerk (org) (Globe GLO 6018)

Laudes Vespertinae. Vrouwen Kleinkoor Orpheus, cond. A. Wissink (WVH 122)

Passepied; Pavane; Sonata [I]. A. Middelbeek (pf) (HGM CD 01)

Pavane, Menuet. R. Brautigam (pf) (NM Classics 92045)

Ricercare (arr.). Dutch Royal Military Band, cond. P. Kuypers (MBCD 31.1010.72)

Qui habitat. Netherlands Chamber Choir, cond. U. Gronostay (NM Classics 92065)

Secunda raccolta (from: Intermezzi). A. de Klerk (org) (NM Classics 92034)

Sonata da chiesa. P. Kee (org) (Chandos CHAN 9188)

Sonnet; Missa Sponsa Christi; Omagio a Marenzio; Missa in festo Assumptionis Beatae Mariae Virginis. Choir Project Rotterdam, cond. M. Michielsen (WVH 076)

Symphony no. 4; Ricercare. Residentie Orchestra, cond. E. Spanjaard (Olympia OCD 507)

Symphony no. 4; Ricercare; Variaties en fuga op een thema van Johann Kuhnau. Residentie Orchestra, cond. E. Spanjaard (Olympia OCD 5008)

Symfonische etude. Concertgebouw Orchestra, cond. K. Kondrashin (BFO A-6)

Thema met variaties. B. de Vroome (org) (Marcato VLS-VLC 0492)

Trois pastorales. M. Koningsberger (Bar), K. Grout (pf) (Sweetlove SLR 9401255)

Variaties en fuga op een thema van Johann Kuhnau. Residentie Orchestra, cond. F. Leitner (Olympia OCD 504)

Louis Andriessen

UTRECHT, 6 JUNE 1939

Louis Andriessen is the most influential Dutch composer of his generation, a man who since the 1960s has been a major influence both on Dutch music and musical life in the Netherlands. His music has been central to the development of a characteristically Dutch style of composition, which distinguishes itself by its economy, straightforwardness and peculiarly eclectic use of existing musical models, ranging from pop music all the way back to Perotin.

Andriessen, the youngest son of the composer Hendrik Andriessen, received his first musical instruction from his father, studying later with Kees van Baaren and subsequently Luciano Berio. With Reinbert de Leeuw, Peter Schat, Misha Mengelberg and Jan van Vlijmen, he was one of the five-member collective that in 1969 composed the renowned opera *Reconstructie* [Reconstruction]. During this period he was also active as a member of the 'Nutcrackers', the young composers' protest movement which sought to revitalize musical activity. His principled stance manifested itself in both word and deed; in 1970, for example, he decided never again to compose for symphony orchestra, and in the years that followed he repeatedly formed his own ensembles, in which he often took part as well. Two of these groups, Orkest de Volharding and Hoketus, proved vital enough to continue on their own after Andriessen's departure.

In the 1960s Andriessen quickly mastered the then current developments in contemporary music. He composed serial music, citation and collage works, dabbled in graphic scores and realized two electronic compositions. An important influence and catalyst in the acquisition of his own recognizable idiom was the minimal music of the 1970s. *De Staat* [The State] (1976) was considered from its appearance the work in which Andriessen reached full maturity. This piece, subsequently receiving frequent performances abroad, comprises a series of massive blocks with the repetitive quality of minimal music, but which are repeatedly derailed by brusque transitions.

In 1977 Andriessen offered a decisive response to American minimalists – whose music was gradually becoming more snug and aesthetic – with the pounding, earthy sounds of *Hoketus*. His subsequent work still shows minimalist traits – a tendency for homogeneous sound, tonal elements and additive rhythms, and melodies derived from well-tailored canon techniques – but these have been thoroughly incorporated into his own style. Though An-

14

driessen himself once stated that there is only one thing going on in his music at any time, there is hardly a single passage that does not present at least two forces. A simple example is his penchant for the hocket technique, in which two voices, instruments or groups of musicians sound a note or chord in turn, but in such a way that what is heard sounds like 'one thing', even though it can also be perceived as the sum, or even the composite of two factors.

In nearly all of his larger works, Andriessen transcends the domain of the strictly musical with the addition of sung or spoken texts. These he carefully chooses, showing a clear preference for philosophical (Plato, St Augustine, Nietzsche) and historical writings that delineate a personal experience. The large dramatic clout of pieces like *Mausoleum* and *De Materie* [Matter] can in part be attributed to the combination of two kinds of text – and the consequential musical contrasts.

The special demands Andriessen makes on singers – a tight, clear sound with a minimum of vibrato – emphasize all the more his ideal of placing vocal and instrumental elements on the same wavelength. His music-theater works of the 1970s were conceived for singing actors who, however primitively, were better able to approach his ideals than the classically trained vocalists of the time.

The series of strict, monolithic works starting with *De Staat*, followed by *Mausoleum* (1979), *De Tijd* [Time] (1981) and *De Snelheid* [Velocity] (1983) and culminating in the four-movement music-theater work *De Materie* (1989), are the backbone of Andriessen's oeuvre. These pieces, too, have established his name abroad and since the 1970s have lured a steady stream of aspiring foreign composers to the Royal Conservatory in The Hague, where he teaches.

Aside from these large, notorious works, however, Andriessen has a vast collection of other pieces to his name. He has often turned his hand to music for theater, ballet and film. Characteristically, he seldom if ever repeats himself, choosing instead new technical or stylistic premises for each piece, while nevertheless imprinting his unmistakable stamp on each. His smaller-scale works bear particular witness to his love for music as a 'game' of infinite possibilities. This light-hearted side of Andriessen's work is exemplified in the more than twenty short pieces on the CD *The Memory of Roses*. Alongside purely musical postulations, political, philosophical and scientific themes also serve as germinating premises.

The two large music-theater works, *De Materie* and the opera *Rosa* (1994), with a libretto by filmmaker Peter Greenaway, can be seen as the apotheosis of the compositional arsenal Andriessen had built up in preceding decades. *De Materie* is essentially a work by Andriessen the thinker: a strict piece ruled by measure and numbers, an edifice in which numerous extramusical ideas borrowed from the exact sciences, architecture, religion, history, philosophy, painting and literature, are united in the contrapuntal network of musical structural models. It is like an ode to the flight of the human mind and it conjures visions of universal beauty and a higher order in which everything is interrelated.

Compared to *De Materie*, *Rosa* is the work of a 'doer': it represents the earthy, impulsive, even capricious side of Andriessen's music. Like Greenaway, Andriessen indulges himself in allusions, pastiches and dramatic contrasts. But this music, too, is rock-solid. The notion of music as a vehicle for personal emotion is foreign to Andriessen; the effluent passion of *Rosa* has nothing to do with compassion, but is in essence a consequence of the music itself.

In his two ensuing major compositions, Andriessen showed that he was still capable of extending the boundaries of his idiom without going so far as to belie himself. The three-movement composition *De Laatste Dag* [The Last Day] (1996-97), based on texts that deal with the dividing line between life and death, contain moments of an astonishing, detached sparseness with enormous expressive charge. For the opera *Writing to Vermeer* (1999) Peter Greenaway wrote a libretto consisting entirely of fictitious letters. Like the paintings of Johannes Vermeer, Andriessen's music is serene and aesthetic with a palpable nod in the direction of Sweelinck. If *Rosa* was first and foremost the spiritual offspring of the stuntman Greenaway, it is Andriessen's music that takes the dramaturgical lead in *Writing to Vermeer*. After the first series of performances in Amsterdam, the production was repeated with great success in Adelaide and New York.

FRITS VAN DER WAA

COMPOSITIONS

VOCAL: *Nocturnen*, S, chamb.orch (1959); *Il Principe*, 2 choirs, instr.ens (1974); *De Staat*, 4 w.v, large ens (1976); *Mausoleum*, 2 Bar, large ens (1979, rev. 1981); *De Tijd*, w.choir, large ens (1981); *Dances*, S, perc, hp, pf, str (1991); *M is for Man, Music, Mozart*, v, instr.ens (1991); *De Laatste Dag*, 5 v, instr.ens (1996); *Tao*, pf, 4 w.v, orch (1996); *Dancing on the bones*, ch.v, instr.ens (1997)

OPERA, MUSIC THEATRE: *Reconstructie* (with R. de Leeuw, P. Schat, M. Mengelberg, J. van Vlijmen, H. Mulisch, H. Claus), v, 3 choirs, large ens (1969); *Mattheus passie*, 8 v, 2 ob, hammond org, str (1976); *Orpheus*, 8 v, lyricon, el.gui, el.b-gui, synth, perc (1977); *De Materie (I De Materie deel 1; II Hadewych; III De Stijl; IV De Materie deel 4)*, S, T, sp.v, 8 v, large ens (1989); *Rosa*, soloists, choir, orch (1994); *Trilogie van de Laatste Dag*, choir, orch, pf (1997); *Writing to Vermeer* (1999)

CHAMBER MUSIC: *Séries*, 2 pf (1958); *Melodie*, s-rec, pf (1972-1974); *Il Duce*, electr. music (1973); *La Voce*, vc, v (single performer) (1981); *Ende*, 2 a-rec (single performer) (1981); *Overture to Orpheus*, hpd (1982); *Disco*, vl, pf (1982); *Trepidus*, pf (1983); *Facing Death*, str.qt (1991); *Hout*, t-sax, mar, gui, pf (1991); *Zilver*, fl, cl, vl, vc, 2 perc, pf (1994); *Base*, pf (1994)

ORCHESTRA, CHAMBER ORCHESTRA, LARGE ENSEMBLE: *Ittrospezione III (Concept II)* (1965); *Anachronie I* (1966-1967); *Contra Tempus* (1968); *De Volharding* (1972); *On Jimmy Yancey* (1973); *Hoketus* (1975-1977); *Symfonie voor losse snaren* (1978); *De Snelheid* (1983, rev. 1984)

PUBLICATIONS

'De Staat, Il Principe, Il Duce, Hoketus', *Key Notes*, 6, 1977/2, p. 42-44

'Componeren: een les' (with E. Schönberger), *Muziek & Dans*, vol. 3, no. 1, 1979

Het Apollinisch uurwerk. Over Stravinsky (with E. Schönberger). Amsterdam, De Bezige Bij, 1983

BIBLIOGRAPHY

A. Apon and T. de Graaff: 'Louis Andriessen : esthetiek en techniek', *Skrien*, no. 95, March 1980, p. 8-15

R. de Beer: 'Mondriaans compositie met drie kleuren uitgangspunt voor De Stijl van Louis Andriessen', *Muziek & Dans*, vol. 9, no. 5/6, 1985, p. 2-6

J. Bons and Th. Derks: 'Héél hard schreeuwen', *Ssst! : nieuwe ensembles voor nieuwe muziek*. Amsterdam, International Theatre & Film Books, 1996

A. Coenen: 'Louis Andriessen's De Materie', *Key Notes*, 25, 1988/1989, p. 2-12

E. Desmedt: *Louis Andriessen : eerst muziek, dan politiek*. Doctoral dissertation, Gent, 1988

P. Janssen: '"The moment someone starts to sing it immediately becomes a lot more interesting" : Three composers in conversation about their new operas', *Key Notes*, 28, 1994/4, p. 18

R. Koopmans: 'On music and politics : activism of five Dutch composers', *Key Notes*, 4, 1976/2, p. 19-36

Louis Andriessen. Brochure Donemus, 1993

R. Oehlschlägel: 'Etwas anderes tun, als die Leute tun : ein Porträt des Komponisten Louis Andriessen', *MusikTexte*, no. 9, Apr. 1985, p. 16-31

W.-J. Otten and E. Schönberger: 'Louis Andriessen's Matthew Passion and Orpheus : two steps up from the Hades of the opera tradition', *Key Notes*, 7, 1978/1, p. 22-34

F. van Rossum [et al.]: 'Louis Andriessen : "after Chopin and Mendelssohn we landed in a mudbath" ', *Key Notes*, 28, 1994/1, p. 8-15

O. Schneeweisz: 'Tien dode componisten : Rosa, een opera in de traditie van Bertolt Brecht', *Mens en Melodie*, vol. 49, 1994, p. 652-656

E. Schönberger: 'Over het ontstaan van "De Tijd" : Elmer Schönberger in gesprek met Louis Andriessen', *De Revisor*, no. 2, 1981, p. 24-32

E. Schönberger: 'On the conceiving of time', *Key Notes*, 13, 1981/1, p. 5-11

De Slag van Andriessen, compiled by F. van der Waa. Amsterdam, De Bezige Bij, 1993

F. van der Waa: 'A skull, a spider and a scherzo'. *Key Notes*, 31, 1997/4, p. 10-14

D. Wright: 'Louis Andriessen : policy, time, speed, substance', *Tempo, a quarterly review of modern music*, no. 187, Dec. 1993, p. 7-13

M. Zegers: 'Werken, niet zwijmelen : Louis Andriessen over zijn Trilogie van de Laatste Dag', *Mens en Melodie*, vol. 53, 1998, p. 4-9

DISCOGRAPHY

Base. M. Worms (pf) (NM Extra 98014)

Facing Death. Aurelia Saxophone Quartet (NM Classics 92053)

Facing Death. Schönberg Quartet (NM Classics 92078)

De Materie. James Doing, S. Narucki (S), G. Thoma, C. Oswin, Schönberg Ensemble, Asko Ensemble, members of the Netherlands Chamber Choir, cond. R. de Leeuw (Elektra Nonesuch 7559 79367 2)

Mausoleum; Hoketus. Ch. van Tassel (Bar), D. Barick (Bar), Asko Ensemble, Schönberg Ensemble, cond. R. de Leeuw, Hoketus (Composers' Voice CV 20)

The Memory of Roses (23 short pieces). Various performers (VPRO Eigenwijs EW 9305)

Nadir & Zenit, improvisations by L. Andriessen (pf) and G. Bijma (v) on texts by Polet (BV Haast CD 9303)

Nocturnen; Ittrospezione III; Anachronie I; Contra Tempus; Anachronie II. Various soloists, Netherlands Ballet Orchestra, cond. H. Williams (Composers' Voice CV 54)

On Jimmy Yancey. Orkest de Volharding, cond. C. van Zeeland (NM Specials 92093)

On Jimmy Yancey; Dat gebeurt in Vietnam. Orkest de Volharding (NM Classics 92021)

Rosa: The Death of a Composer. Various soloists, Schönberg Ensemble, Asko Ensemble, cond. R. de Leeuw (Elektra Nonesuch 7559 79559 2)

Séries. C. van Zeeland and G. Bouwhuis (pf) (NM Classics 92074)

De Staat. Schönberg Ensemble, cond. R. de Leeuw (Elektra Nonesuch 7559 79251 2)

De Stijl; M is for Man, Music, Mozart. G. Thoma, Schönberg Ensemble, Asko Ensemble cond. R. de Leeuw; A. Seriese (v), Orkest de Volharding, cond. J. Hempel (Elektra Nonesuch 7559 79342 2)

De Stijl; Trepidus; Dances. Kaalslag, cond. R. de Leeuw, G. Bouwhuis (pf), C. McFadden (S), Netherlands Radio Chamber Orchestra, cond. G. Schuller (Attacca Babel 9375)

De Tijd. Schönberg Ensemble, Percussion Group The Hague, Netherlands Chamber Choir, cond. R. de Leeuw (Elektra Nonesuch 7559 79291 2)

Trepidus. I. Janssen (pf) (NM Classics 92028)

Peter van Anrooy

ZALTBOMMEL, 13 OCTOBER 1879 – THE HAGUE, 31 DECEMBER 1954

Peter van Anrooy was raised in Utrecht, where in 1890 he enrolled in the Toonkunst Music School. At the age of sixteen, he played 2nd violin in the City Concerts conducted by Richard Hol. One year later, while still at high school, Van Anrooy took his place with the 1st violins of the Utrecht Municipal Orchestra, which incidentally performed two works of his, among which his Andante for Winds. Not wanting his schoolmates to know he was the composer of these works, Van Anrooy told them that they were written by a cousin. During this period he studied the violin with Gerrit Veerman and composition and theory with Johan Wagenaar. For his farewell concert with the Utrecht Municipal Orchestra in 1898, Van Anrooy conducted Beethoven's Symphony no.5. He went to Moscow, via Dresden, where, around 1899, he studied composition for a year with Sergey Taneyev, a student of Tchaikovsky, and conducting with Willem Kes, who at the time was the director of the Moscow Philharmonic Orchestra.

After having worked as an orchestral violinist in Zurich and Glasgow, he returned to the Netherlands in 1905. He earned his living for a short time as a private tutor in Amsterdam, but was soon appointed conductor of the Groningen Orchestral Society. From 1910 to 1917 he conducted the Arnhem Orchestral Society, subsequently succeeding Henri Viotta as conductor of the Residentie Orchestra. In 1914 Van Anrooy was awarded an honorary doctorate by the University of Groningen, with the historian Huizinga serving as his promoter.

Van Anrooy was a born orchestral rehearser; the successes of many a renowned conductor with the Residentie Orchestra during the hectic Scheveningen Summer Series resulted from Van Anrooy's preparation of the orchestra. However, he was not thoroughly appreciated in The Hague; owing to his reserved nature, he generally fared poorly in the inevitable comparisons made between him and the flamboyant Willem Mengelberg. He did, however, win national recognition through the youth concerts he initiated in 1924. The works performed in these concerts were introduced by him in preliminary program notes distributed among the schoolchildren of The Hague.

Although Van Anrooy had the reputation of not liking modern music, works of Mahler, Pijper, Hindemith and other composers of the day were regularly programmed in his concerts. Van Anrooy also showed great concern for the individual interests of the orchestra's musicians, for example with regard to pension issues.

Van Anrooy resigned his post with the Residentie Orchestra in 1935, one reason being discord over his choice of repertoire. In 1940, after resigning as conductor of the The Hague Toonkunst choir, the local chapter of the Society for the Advancement of Music, he was prompted by political motives to withdraw from public musical life altogether. Owing to his open criticism of the Nazi occupying forces, the performance of his music was banned during World War II. But he re-emerged into public life in 1947 with a biweekly radio program, 'Introduction to musical understanding', drawing a broad range of listeners.

Peter van Anrooy's orchestral work is couched in a neo-Romantic style. He is the composer of the popular Dutch orchestral piece the *Piet Hein Rhapsodie* (1901), the result of Johan Wagenaar's suggestion that he experiment with the song *De Zilvervloot* [The treasure fleet], by Johannes J. Viotta. The composition created such a stir at its premiere in Utrecht that it thoroughly overshadowed a performance that same evening of Johan Wagenaar's opera *De Doge van Venetië* [The Doge of Venice]. The Utrecht Municipal Orchestra regularly programmed the work and in 1902 the music publishing house A.A. Noske released an edition of the orchestral score and a piano four-hand reduction, later followed by a version for a single pianist. Van Anrooy's treatment of the song bears witness to the breadth of his imagination, and the orchestration is impeccable. The climax of the work centres on the rather down-to-earth refrain of the song: after an introductory motif sounded first in the oboe's upper register and then presented again by a bassoon rumbling in the depths, the refrain is transformed into a *galante* minuet. The piece closes with a triumphant quotation from the Dutch song *Wien Neêrlandsch bloed* [Those whose veins are filled with Dutch blood...]. It is not unthinkable that Jan van Gilse was inspired to compose his *St. Nicolaas* variations, also based on a Viotta song, by Van Anrooy's success with the *Piet Hein Rhapsodie*.

Van Anrooy's Piano Quintet (1898) is composed in a Brahmsian style, while the incidental music he wrote for the fairy tale *Das kalte Herz* is more reminiscent of the late nineteenth-century North German school of composition. The atmosphere of the prelude to the second act, for instance, is somewhat akin to Bruch or Humperdinck.

Even today, Van Anrooy's eighteen variations on *Aan den oever van den snellen vliet* [On the bank of a rapid rivulet] are performed. In these variations, Van Anrooy touches on the styles and musical approaches of such composers as Handel, Haydn, Beethoven, Schumann, Brahms, Chopin, Bizet and Lalo.

WILMA ROEST

COMPOSITIONS
Andante, wind ens (1895); *Ballade*, vl, orch; *Piano Quintet* (1898); *Piet Hein Rhapsodie*, orch (1901); *Das kalte Herz*, orch; *Achttien variaties op het thema 'Aan den oever van den snellen vliet'*, pf

BIBLIOGRAPHY
J. de Geus: 'Dr. Peter van Anrooy als leraar', *Mens en Melodie*, vol. 10, 1955, p. 2-3
W. Paap: 'Dr. Peter van Anrooy', *Mens en Melodie*, vol. 10, 1955, p. 1-2

DISCOGRAPHY
Quintet. M. Bon (pf), members of the Netherlands Radio Chamber Orchestra (BFO A-1)
Piet Hein Rhapsodie. Netherlands Radio Symphony Orchestra, cond. K. Bakels (NM Classics 92060)
Piet Hein Rhapsodie. Residentie Orchestra, cond. A. Dorati (Fontana 6530 044)

Kees van Baaren

ENSCHEDE, 22 OCTOBER 1906 – OEGSTGEEST, 2 SEPTEMBER 1970

Cornelis Leendert van Baaren liberated Dutch post-war music from a certain indolent provincialism. The 'Schoenberg of the Netherlands' is remembered chiefly as the teacher of a new generation of composers. The morality-opera *Reconstructie*, the quintessential work of the late 1960s, was premiered shortly before his death. Five of Van Baaren's students were involved in its composition: Louis Andriessen, Reinbert de Leeuw, Misha Mengelberg, Peter Schat and Jan van Vlijmen. Other Van Baaren students also made names for themselves, among them Jan Wisse, who emigrated to Switzerland, the pianist/composer Theo Bruins, and the conductor/composer David Porcelijn.

There can be little doubt of Van Baaren's excellence as a teacher, but his importance as a composer has been overshadowed by his unmistakably stimulating influence on his students. Moreover, his oeuvre is quite modest: some twenty pieces each averaging ten minutes' duration. Van Baaren could all too easily be dismissed as a somewhat closed and introverted personality, a strict academic who compiled the questions of the Dutch national music examinations. On the contrary, he was an exuberant musician who from his early youth was drawn to all manner of instruments.

The son of a music dealer, Van Baaren had free rein in the shop after closing hours. He played the piano, cello, and the harmonica too. Initially, he was a Grieg admirer, but later it was Debussy who became his idol. He discovered Berg and Webern while he was in Germany, where he studied at the Sternsche Conservatory after completing high school. He took piano lessons with Rudolf Breithaupt and studied composition with the cellist/theoretician Friedrich Koch. From Boris Blacher, one of his fellow students, he acquired his predilection for manipulating mathematically ordered meters, and from Koch his orientation to strict, linear counterpoint. This was of importance for his own atonal counterpoint: the nineteenth-century harmonic idiom evoked unpleasant associations in him. In Berlin he met Willem Pijper, from whom he took lessons when he returned to the Netherlands.

Van Baaren played jazz and accompanied the 'Kabarett der Unmöglichen' to earn a living. The combination of his composition aesthetics and performing activities would seem grossly incongruous to an outsider, combining as they did dodecaphony and Gershwin. But then, he was anything but a fanatical dogmatist.

22

Van Baaren's career gained momen-
tum after the war. From 1945 to 1947
he taught at Pijper's stronghold, the
Rotterdam Conservatory, from 1948
to 1953 he directed the Amsterdam
Muzieklyceum, until 1956 the conservatory in Utrecht and up to 1970
he was at the helm of the conservatory in The Hague. He was widely
known as a teacher who gave his students the freedom to develop.

Van Baaren wrote a 'Musical Self-
Portrait' for the weekly *Elsevier's
Weekblad*, musing: 'First, there is a
twelve-tone atmosphere with variable
meter, then follows a melodic line
like Puccini's. I wonder which better
suits my personality.' Both elements
are recurrent in his work, the 'care-
fully plotted garden', and the linear-melodic, 'flowery' element. Van Baaren's
music invariably sounds neat and translucent. He was averse to what he called
massiveness: 'When I was eighteen I heard a radio broadcast of Wagner's *Tristan* that appalled me. Such devaluation, this massiveness.'

Tristan und Isolde set tonality adrift and it was only logical that composers
sought new means of anchoring their work. Pijper devised the basic-cell technique, but Van Baaren turned to dodecaphony. To his mind there was little difference between the two, and when he once remarked as much to his earlier
teacher, Pijper answered: 'You have a point, but I simply cannot keep my eye
on twelve notes at the same time.'

In the cantata *The Hollow Men* Van Baaren had less to keep his eye on. The
vocal part is marked by free tonality, the instrumental part by free dodecaphony. This cantata, composed for the Sweelinck student society and rewritten for
large orchestra, was the first of Van Baaren's works to draw attention following
the war. His choice of the poem by T.S. Eliot bears witness to his cultural pessimism. The halting final passage portrays the crumbling of the will; there is
no hope of renewed spiritual life, the world does not end with a roar, but in pathetic moaning. The associative treatment of the text includes quotations from
children's songs and the *St Matthew Passion* – some twenty years before musical quotations came into fashion.

A dodecaphonically generated serial style, ordering not only pitch but such other parameters as tone duration and color according to twelve-tone principles, was applied by Van Baaren in his *Variations* for orchestra composed in memory of Fux, the 'savior' of the strict counterpoint of Bach's day. The row is strictly symmetrical, just as the five variations form a mirrored duality in the overall structure. In 1963 the work was choreographed by Vitali Osins for The National Ballet.

In the 1960s Van Baaren composed a piano concerto (not to be confused with the unassuming *Concertino* in the style of Pijper, whose influence could still be heard in the Septet). Notable in this concerto is the effort made to treat the piano and the orchestra as equal partners. There are no introductory, accompanying or connecting passages or functions. Here, too, the mirror of the row is present and contains all of the intervals within the octave.

Van Baaren was drawn to this way of working. It figures in the self-portrait and the variations, as well as in the Second String Quartet – his oeuvre begins with the First String Quartet, as all of his compositions prior to 1933 were destroyed – the Wind Quintet and the *Muziek voor klokken* [Music for bells] the second version of which is his last completed work. *Muziek voor orkest* [Music for orchestra], his last piece for large ensemble, is a typical Van Baaren blend of strict and playful elements. About the second movement, he said: 'This is the most problematical to perform because of the *non espressivo*, which is difficult to maintain, musicians always wanting to *do* something with it. It is the basis for a very broad melodic approach, which – pay attention to the strings! – should sound somewhat faltering. All of this must be clear and very transparent; only near the end is there a distant murmuring.'

ERNST VERMEULEN

COMPOSITIONS

VOCAL: *Three Poems* (Dickinson), w.choir (1947); *Recueillement* (Baudelaire), v, pf (1947); *The Hollow Men* (Eliot), soloists, choir, orch (1948); *Alpejagerslied* (Van Ostaijen), m.choir (1952); *Ichnaton* (Marsman), m.choir (1952)

INSTRUMENTAL: *String Quartet no. 1* (1933); *Concertino*, pf, orch (1934); *Trio*, fl, cl, bn (1936); *Sonatina*, pf (1948); *Suite*, school orch (1951); *Septet*, fl, ob, cl, bn, hn, vl, db (1952); *The Hollow Men*, orch (1955); *Sinfonie*, orch (1957); *Variations*, orch (1959); *Partita*, concert band (1961); *String Quartet*

no. 2 (1962); *Quintet*, fl, ob, cl, bn, hn (1963); *Piano Concerto* (1964); *Muziek voor 72 klokken* (1964); *Muziek voor fluitsolo* (1965); *Muziek voor orkest* (1966); *Muziek voor orgel* (1969); *Muziek voor 47 klokken* (1969)

PUBLICATIONS

'Kompositionsunterricht und Theorieunterricht', *Kongressbericht der 3. Direktorenkonferenz*, Köln, 1960

'Over Entelechie nr. 1 van Schat en Costruzione van Van Vlijmen', *Sonorum Speculum*, no. 9, 1961, p. 8-17

'Kees van Baaren in gesprek met A.B.M. Brans', *Preludium*, Feb. 1968

BIBLIOGRAPHY

E. de Cock: 'Tussen kiemcel en toonklok : Kees van Baaren : leerling en meester', *Mens en Melodie*, vol. 51, 1996, p. 432-436

J. Hill: *The music of Kees van Baaren*. Doctoral dissertation, University of North Carolina, 1970

H. Kien: 'The composer Kees van Baaren : towards a revaluation of the sound material', *Key Notes*, 4, 1976/2

T. de Leeuw: 'New trends in modern Dutch music', *Sonorum Speculum*, no. 4, 1960, p. 124-133

H. Metzelaar: '"Musicians wrestle everywhere": Emily Dickinson and Dutch composers'. *Key Notes*, 30, 1996/4, p. 24-28

W. Paap: 'De Sweelinckprijs voor Kees van Baaren', *Mens en Melodie*, vol. 25, 1970, p. 34-37

E. Vermeulen: 'Kees van Baaren's Antischool', *Key Notes*, 26, 1992/1, p. 14-17

J. Wouters: 'Componisten aan het woord', *Mens en Melodie*, vol. 19, 1964, p. 1-10

J. Wouters: 'Kees van Baaren', *Sonorum Speculum*, no. 34, 1968, p. 17-23

DISCOGRAPHY

Piano Concerto. D. Kuyken (pf), Netherlands Radio Symphony Orchestra, cond. A. Vedernikov (NM Classics 92058)

The Hollow Men. H. Meppelink (S), H. de Vries (Bar), Netherlands Radio Choir, Netherlands Radio Chamber Orchestra, cond. E. Spanjaard. (BFO A-17)

Muziek voor orkest; Muziek voor orgel. Concertgebouw Orchestra, cond. B. Haitink, Ch. de Wolff (org) (DAVS 7273/2)

Partita. Koningin Wilhelmina Concert Band of Wamel, cond. H. Klerx (Composers' Voice CV 84025)

Piano Concerto. A. Kontarsky (pf), Concertgebouw Orchestra, cond. B. Maderna (DAVS 6603)

Piano Concerto. Th. Bruins (pf), Royal Concertgebouw Orchestra, cond. B. Haitink (Q Disc 97014)

Piano Concertino. D. Kuyken (pf), Netherlands Radio Chamber Orchestra, cond. E. Spanjaard (NM Classics 92044)

Recueillement. W. Bronsgeest (S), Th. Bollen (pf) (Globe GLO 6018)

Septet. J. Walta (vl), J. de Wit (fl), F. Minderaa (ob), A. Rozeboom (cl), K. White (bn), V. Zarzo (hn), P. Stotijn (db) (Olympia OCD 505)

Sonatina. Th. Bruins (pf) (Composers' Voice CV 7904)

Sonatina. R. Brautigam (pf) (NM Classics 92045)

Henk Badings

BANDUNG, 17 JANUARY 1907 – MAARHEEZE, 26 JUNE 1987

Henk Badings was born in 1907 in Bandung, the Dutch East Indies, the son of a Dutch officer. After his father's death, the eight-year-old Badings came to the Netherlands with his mother, who also died shortly thereafter. Badings was then taken into a clergyman's family. Having composed several violin sonatas at the age of fourteen, the idea of becoming a professional musician began to take shape while he was still in high school, but his guardian strongly objected. More or less against his will, he enrolled in Delft's University of Technology to study engineering.

Throughout his stay in Delft he remained intensely preoccupied with music, laying the basis for his extensive knowledge of music theory and composition. He supplemented this self-taught knowledge with several lessons in composition with Willem Pijper. Seeing that the student was already so advanced, Pijper encouraged him to enter a music competition. Badings submitted his First Symphony (later revised), which he had composed before he came into contact with Pijper. The piece was given its first performance in 1930 by the Concertgebouw Orchestra, conducted by Louis Marie George Arntzenius.

In 1931 Badings graduated *cum laude* as a mining engineer, and took up a post as an assistant instructor in historical geology and palaeontology at Delft University. Four years later he decided to devote himself entirely to music and he left the institute to become a professor of composition and music theory at the Amsterdam Muzieklyceum, one of the capital's conservatories. From 1937 he held a similar post at the conservatory in Rotterdam. By then the Concertgebouw Orchestra had already performed several of his compositions, among which the First Cello Concerto, in 1930, and his Second and Third Symphonies, in 1933 and 1935, conducted respectively by Eduard van Beinum and Willem Mengelberg.

The Nazi occupation of the Netherlands had far-reaching consequences for Badings' career. From the beginning, he was part of a small group of prominent people who sought to bring order to the chaos into which Dutch musical life had fallen. It was for this reason that he first became involved with, later becoming a member of, the Netherlands 'Kultuurkamer', an advisory cultural commission established by the occupying forces. In 1942 he was appointed director of the State Conservatory in The Hague – succeeding Sem Dresden,

who, as a Jew, had been forced to resign – by the Department of Propaganda and the Arts. As a result of
these activities, the post-war Council
of Honor banned Badings for ten
years from participation in any form
of public music making. Badings
lodged an appeal with the Central
Council of Honor. Meeting twice in
December 1946, the Council lifted
the ban on the performance of his
work and his activities as a teacher,
but until 5 November 1947 he was
not allowed to participate in any professional musical organizations or to
engage in editorial work for music
journals.

Badings' composition during this
post-war period is characterized by a fascination with experimental fields such
as micro-intervals and new tonal systems; especially notable are his experiments with the 31-tone system. He also delved into electronic music and the
large number of pieces he wrote in this genre drew widespread, and particularly foreign, attention. From 1961 to 1977 Badings taught acoustics and information theory at the University of Utrecht's Institute for Musicology. In 1962
he was appointed to a position at the Hochschule für Musik in Stuttgart.

Badings composed more than a thousand works. His international reputation
rested primarily on his orchestral works, particularly the Third Symphony, the
Symphonic Variations and the First Double Concerto for two violins and orchestra. Although the melodic construction and harmonic logic of these early
works seem not quite fully developed, they do bear witness to a personal musical language that despite its pluriformity maintained a high degree of continuity throughout his long career. Badings' music is identifiable largely by its frequent octatonic sonorities, classical forms, penetrating opening signals and
the fundamental role of overtones. It is additionally characterized by his penchant for experimentation with tonal systems, sound effects and new media.

This exploration of new possibilities, combined with his interest in the
physiology of music and acoustics, earned him a reputation as a musical tech-
nocrat. Nevertheless, even in his electronic music it was not so much a new
approach to materials and procedures that fascinated him as the enrichment

of the traditional sound world. This is clearly evident in the *Capriccio* for solo violin (1959), for example, in which the orchestra is replaced by two sound-tracks.

Early in his career, Badings developed the conviction that an artist bears responsibility not only to 'his art', but also to society at large. Hence, he composed not only for film (such as *The Flying Dutchman* in 1957), radio (*Orestes* in 1954), and carillon, but also wrote didactic music as well as music for amateur choirs and wind orchestras.

That he remained true to his self-taught vision provides some explanation as to the position he holds in Dutch music history. Badings kept his distance from schools of composers and, unlike Willem Pijper and Hendrik Andriessen, never built up a 'composition school' at a Dutch conservatory. Nonetheless, he exerted considerable influence on the younger generation, not only because many of these younger composers – Jaap Geraedts, Ton de Leeuw and Hans Kox among them – came to him for instruction, but also because the versatility of his extensive output and the consummate craftsmanship it displays inspired composers that followed. It is in particular the spiritual foundation of his work, his conviction that music is first and foremost an earthly pursuit meant to be a part of human life, that left an impression.

CASPAR BECX

COMPOSITIONS

PIANO: *Reihe kleiner Klavierstücke* (1939); *Roemeense reisschetsen* (1935); Six sonatas (1934, 1941, 1944, 1945, 1945, 1947); Four sonatinas (1936, 1945, 1950, 1958)

ORGAN: *Archi fonica*, 31-tone org (1952); *Preludium en fuga I* and *IV*, 31-tone org (1952, 1956); *Reihe kleiner Klangstücke*, 31-tone org (1957); *Suite*, 31-tone org (1954); Nine pieces for organ; Ten pieces for organ and instrumental ensemble

CARILLON: Two sonatas (1949, 1950); Four suites (1943, 1951, 1953, 1953)

CHAMBER MUSIC: Three sonatas, vl (1940, 1951, 1951); Two sonatas, vc (1941, 1951); *Cavatina*, vla, pf (1952); Two sonatas, vc, pf (1929, 1934); *Vier voordrachtstukken*, vc, pf (1946); *Capriccio*, fl, pf (1936); *Sonata*, ob, pf (1929); *La malinconia*, a-sax, pf (1949); Four sonatas, 2 vl (1928/ 1963, 1967, 1975, in 31-tone tuning); *Piano Quartet* (1974);

Four string quartets (1931, 1936, 1944, 1966 in 31-tone tuning); Nine pieces for violin and piano; Duets, trios and quintets for various combinations

ORCHESTRA: Eleven symphonies (1932, 1934, 1943, 1949, 1953, with mix.choir 1954, 1956, 1961, 1964, 1964, 1968); *Largo en allegro*, str.orch (1935); *Aria trista e rondo giocoso*, chamb.orch (1948); *Hora*, chamb.orch (1935); *Predilcova*, chamb.orch (1935); *Symphonietta*, chamb.orch (1971); *Pupazzetti azzuri*, chamb.orch (1950); Six overtures, orch (1937, 1937, 1942, 1942, 1954, 1961); Four symphonic variations, orch (1936, 1950, 1956, 1960); *Twentse suite*, acc.orch (1976); 42 pieces for wind orchestra (1951 to 1986)

SOLO INSTRUMENT(S) AND ORCHESTRA: Two concertos, pf, orch (1939, 1955); Four concertos, vl, orch (1928, 1935, 1944, 1947); Two concertos, vc, orch (1930, 1954); Two concertos, fl, orch (1956, 1963 with wind orch); Two concertos, org, orch (1952, 1966); *Concerto*, vla, orch (1965); *Concerto*, eh, wind orch (1975); *Concerto*, sax (1951); *Concerto*, hp, orch (1967); Five double concertos (2 vl, orch, 1954; bn, d-bn, wind orch, 1964; 2 pf, orch, 1964; vl, vla, orch, 1965; 2 vl in 31-tone tuning, orch, 1969); Two triple concertos (vl, vc, pf, orch, 1942; 3 hn, wind orch, tape, 1970)

OPERA: *Orestes* (radio opera) (Badings, Starink) (1954); *Asterion* (radio opera) (Van Wijk Louw) (1957); *De nachtwacht* (Bouws) (1942); *Liefde's listen* (chamber opera) (Badings) (1945); *Martin Korda D.P.* (Badings, Van Eyk) (1960); *Salto Mortale* (television chamber opera) (Badings, Belcampo) (1959)

FILM MUSIC: *The Flying Dutchman* (1957); *Secret Passion* (1964); *Tronfølgern i Latin Amerika* (1966); *Indifference* (1968)

ELECTRONIC MUSIC: *Countess Cathleen* (fragment) (1952); *Kain* (ballet) (1956); *Evolutionen* (ballet) (1958); *De hoorschelp* (1958); *Genesis* (ballet) (1958); *The Woman of Andros* (ballet) (1959); *Salto Mortale* (see opera); *Martin Korda D.P.* (see opera); *Pittsburgh Concerto* (1965); *Armageddon* (1968); *Kontrapunkte* (1970)

DIDACTIC MUSIC: *Arcadia*, vol. 1-8, pf (1945-1967); *The Fiddler and his Mate*, vl (1945); Three suites, rec (1950, 1958, with vl 1957); Cavatinas for various instruments and piano; *Trio-cosmos*, 3 vl (1980-1982)

PUBLICATIONS
De hedendaagsche Nederlandse muziek. Amsterdam, Bigot & Van Rossum, 1936
Tonaliteitsproblemen in de nieuwe muziek. Brussels, Koninklijke Academie van Wetenschappen, Letteren en Schone Kunsten, 1951
'Aantekeningen over enige fundamentele elementen in de muziek (I-IV)'. *Mens en Melodie*, vol. 41, 1986, p. 380-388, 452-453, 503-509, 547-551
Numerous articles in *Elseviers Weekblad* (1952/1953) and various journals

BIBLIOGRAPHY
R. de Beer: 'An odour of taboo. Henk Badings, 1907-1987'. *Key Notes*, 24, 1987, p. 28-29
C. Becx: *Symfonische blaasmuziek*. Utrecht, SAMO-Nederland, 1989
P.T. Klemme: *Henk Badings : a catalog of works*. Michigan, Harmonia Park Press, 1994
L. Samama: *Zeventig jaar Nederlandse muziek : 1915-1985 : voorspel tot een nieuwe dag*. Amsterdam, Querido, 1986

DISCOGRAPHY
Canamus, amici, canamus; Finnigan's Wake. Netherlands Chamber Choir, cond. U. Gronostay (NM Classics 92065)
Chansons Orientales. H. Meens (T), T. Keessen (pf) (Globe GLO 6018)
Concerto (1967). V. Badings (hp), Concertgebouw Orchestra, cond. D. Zinman (BFO A-6)
Double Concerto (1954). H. Krebbers and Th. Olof (vl), Residentie Orchestra, cond. W. van Otterloo (Composers' Voice CVCD 26)
Double Concerto (1964). E. Corver and S. Grotenhuis (pf), Netherlands Radio Symphony Orchestra, cond. K. Bakels (NM Classics 92058)
La Malinconia. H. de Jong (sax), P. Hermsen (pf) (Fidelio 8849)
Symphony no. 15 (Conflicts and Confluences). Dutch National Youth Wind Orchestra, cond. J. Cober (BFO-A-9)
Symphony no. 15 (Conflicts and Confluences). Concert Band of the Maastricht Conservatory, cond. S. Pijpers (Molenaar MBCD 31.1006.72)
Symphonic Wind Music. Various soloists, Concert Band of the Brabant Conservatory, cond. J. Cober (Mirasound 49.9025)
Symphonic Prologue (Overture, 1942). Residentie Orchestra, cond. E. Spanjaard (Olympia OCD 507)

Johannes Gijsbertus Bastiaans

WILP, 31 OCTOBER 1812 – HAARLEM, 16 FEBRUARY 1875

Johannes Gijsbertus Bastiaans was born on the De Bredelaar estate in Wilp, several kilometres south-west of Deventer. He received his first musical instruction at the age of ten, in Deventer, with organ lessons from Engelbert Biermann and violin and music theory lessons from the Deventer city musician Georg Wilhelm Röhner. When his father died in 1829, Bastiaans became a watchmaker to provide for himself. Forbidden by his guardian to become a musician, Bastiaans left for Rotterdam in 1832 where, from 1834 onwards, he studied harmony and counterpoint with Carel Ferdinand Hommert, a young musician who had studied with Friedrich Schneider in Dessau. Hommert urged Bastiaans to go to Dessau. Encouraged by the progress his ward had made under Hommert, Bastiaans' guardian was now prepared to finance the young man's musical education.

In April 1836 Bastiaans went to Dessau to study theory and harmony with Schneider and the organ with Friedrich Rümpler. He soon broke off these lessons, however, and in early 1837 went to Leipzig, probably on the advice of Johannes Verhulst. For several months he took lessons in composition with Felix Mendelssohn Bartholdy. In addition, he was taught the organ, hymnology and counterpoint by Carl Ferdinand Becker, who introduced him to the original chorale melodies and the organ works of J.S. Bach. Leipzig's rich musical life greatly enhanced his knowledge of the repertoire.

In June 1838 Bastiaans returned to the Netherlands. His submission of various organ, piano and choral pieces drew the immediate attention of the Society for the Advancement of Music. He hoped to find work as an organist and to begin a school for organists. Failing in this, he accepted a position on 1 January 1840 as the organist of the Zuider Church in Amsterdam, where he was not permitted to make personal use of the organ for concerts or lessons. Although he was neither pleased with the instrument nor his salary, he stayed at this position until late 1858. To supplement his income, he taught singing at the Amsterdam Institute for the Blind from 1842 to 1844. In 1850 he began teaching a private course in music theory and one year later received permission to use the church organ to give lessons. In 1853 Amsterdam's Toonkunst Music School incorporated the lessons given by Bastiaans and those of his colleague Johannes Albert van Eijken – another Mendelssohn student – into its curriculum. But after three years the school was closed owing to insufficient enrollment.

By then Bastiaans had gained national recognition as an organist and
composer. In 1848 he had given his
first concert at the Remonstrant
Church in Amsterdam, where Van
Eijken was organist, but it was not
until 1850 that Bastiaans attained his
greatest successes. First came the favorable reception of his Fantasie-
Sonate on the patriotic song called
Wien Neêrlandsch bloed [Those whose
veins are filled with Dutch blood...],
composed in honour of the coronation of King William III in 1849,
which he performed on the organ of
the Great Church in Haarlem during
the fifth General Music Festival of
the Society for the Advancement of

Music. Of more significance historically, however, was a performance he gave
on 29 July 1850 at the Wester Church in Amsterdam of eight preludes, fugues
and chorale preludes by Bach, Bastiaans being the first in the Netherlands to
perform such a program. In the program notes, he emphasized the importance of Bach as a composer of Protestant church music, the chorale preludes
in particular. In 1851 he gave a concert of music of 'the school of Bach', performing compositions by Kittel, Krebs, Mendelssohn, Van Eijken and himself.
Bastiaans was one of the first in the Netherlands to give concerts of organ
music alone, breaking with the tradition of interspersing vocal or instrumental intermezzos and arrangements. Bach's music for the organ remained an
important part of his programs, although he also included his own organ compositions, particularly the sonatas for organ. After founding the first Bach Society in the Netherlands in 1850 in Amsterdam, Bastiaans further sought to
promote the composer's work. He was also involved in founding a Bach Society in Haarlem (1867 and 1871) and in Rotterdam (1870).

In July 1858 Bastiaans was appointed city organist and carilloneur in Haarlem, permitting him at last to give organ concerts in a church of his own and
to provide better for his large family. As a highly respected expert on the instrument, he was from now on frequently asked to appraise new and restored
organs. In 1867 he studied pneumatic organ mechanisms in Paris; he was
also considered a leading expert on chorale melodies. From 1864 he served on
the board of the Netherlands Chorale Society and during the same period was

commissioned by the Dutch Reformed Church to compose new melodies for the *Vervolgbundel op de Evangelische Gezangen* [The sequel to the collection of Evangelical Hymns].

The historical significance of Bastiaans lies in the fact that he was one of the founders of what was to become a flourishing 'Bach culture' in the Netherlands. Inspired by Bach, he was untiring in his efforts to improve the quality of Protestant church music and communal singing. He actively propagated the introduction of multi-part choral singing and the singing of older chorales in their original form or on new melodies. Nine of his melodies, among which the well-known *De Heer is mijn Herder* [The Lord is my Sheperd] (1866), are included in the new *Liedboek voor de Kerken* [Book of Hymns].

As a composer, too, Bastiaans sought to build on the work of Bach, though largely in the manner of Mendelssohn and his contemporary Adolph Friedrich Hesse. His compositions for the organ and piano, his cantatas and multi-part chorales are thus composed for the most part in a harmonically determined polyphonic style in which themes are periodic in structure or, in a word, 'melodic'. Often, a chorale melody or song serves as their basis.

Bastiaans earliest large-scale work is his *Sechs Orgelstücke* (1838), a collection of preludes, fugues and chorale arrangements for which he received a reward from the Society for the Advancement of Music. Notable in the collection is the chromaticism, which at times foreshadows that of Franck. In some pieces the chromaticism leads to frequent use of the French sixth chord and occasionally even to strictly constructed music, like the canonic fugue *Harmonie der Spheren* [Harmony of the Spheres] (1850), which, like Bach's *Kunst der Fuge,* is not written for a specific instrument. The organ preludes on German chorale melodies are more fluid in construction. Bastiaans' sonatas for organ combine contrapuntal passages with homophonic andantes and virtuoso passages.

After 1850 Bastiaans' style became more sober; he dedicated himself to composing music for church services. His four-voice harmonizations of psalms and chorales, collected in chorale books, could serve as organ accompaniments to communal singing or as polyphonic vocal works. These works are based on triads, these alone, to Bastiaans' mind, being capable of portraying 'perfection'. Bastiaans laid out a theoretical foundation of this view in his book on harmony published in 1867, which is partially based on the dialectic of Moritz Hauptmann.

JAN TEN BOKUM

COMPOSITIONS

VOCAL: Motet *Herr und Herrscher* (c 1838), arr.
as cantata *Gods grootheid in de natuur* (c
1860); Cantata *Komt christnen knielt voor
Jezus neer* (c 1840); *Cantata* (Decker Zim-
merman) (1842); Cantata *Alle volken looft
den Heere* (Heije) (1851); Cantata *Wie maar
den goeden God laat zorgen* (1852); Cantata
Weemoed en troost; Seven choral pieces on
religious texts (two for m.choir) (from
1841); Five choral pieces (m.choir) (1841,
1851-1858, c 1870); Six short choral pieces
(mix.choir); Ten choral pieces (ch.choir) (c
1845 and c 1851); Seven canons; Four songs
(with pf) (from c 1852); *Feestlied Heiligerlee*

CHORALES COLLECTIONS: 24 Chorales (c
1840) (twelve published as op. 6); *Vierstemmig koraalboek*; *Vierstemmig psalmboek*;
Rhythmische koralen; *Melodieën voor de
Waalse kerk* (1858); Various chorale
melodies

ORGAN: *Sechs Orgelstücke* (1838); Five sonatas
(including *Fantasie-Sonate*) (c 1847-1856);
Two Phantasies (1857 and 1864); *Preludium
en fuga vierhandig* (c 1840); *Preludium en
fuga* (c 1850); *Adagio en fuga*; *Largo, fuga en
andante*; Eleven fughettas and seven
fugues (from c 1836); *Cantabile en canon
voor 4 klavieren*; Four chorale variations;
Twenty chorale preludes; Fourteen adagios,
andantes and trios; Introductions to and
arrangements of works by Bach, Nicolaï
and Schumann

PIANO: *Zes liederen zonder woorden*, op. 4
(1839-1840); *Phantasy*; *Drie paraphrasen*;
Adagio en andante; *Adagio en rondo*; *Sonata*;
Koraalbewerking; Cadenza for Piano Concerto KV 491 by Mozart; Introduction to
and arrangement of the ricercare from
Bach's *Musikalisches Opfer*, BWV 1079

CHAMBER MUSIC: *Allegro*, vl, vc, db, harm;
Koraalfuga, fl, str.qt; *Harmonie der Spheren*
(1850); Arrangements for strings and harmonium of Bastiaans' own organ sonatas
and of works by Bach

PUBLICATIONS
De Zangkunst. Amsterdam, Günst, 1864

De piano. Haarlem, Bohn, 1867
Harmonia. Rotterdam, Altmann, 1867
Het orgel. Haarlem, Bohn, 1868

BIBLIOGRAPHY
J.G.A. ten Bokum: *Johannes Gijsbertus Bastiaans (1812-1875).* Utrecht, Oosthoek, 1971
H. van Nieuwkoop: *Haarlemse Orgelkunst
van 1400 tot heden : orgels, organisten en orgelge-
bruik in de Grote of St.-Bavokerk te Haarlem.*
Utrecht, VNM, 1988

Benedictus à Sancto Josepho (Buns)

GELDERN, C.1640 – BOXMEER, 6 DECEMBER 1716

Benedictus à Sancto Josepho spent his life in a border region between the northern and southern Netherlands and the German Rhineland that in the seventeenth and eighteenth centuries was divided into numerous small territories falling under various jurisdictions. Most of these principalities were under Catholic rule or had a predominately Catholic population. A true border region, a variety of cultural influences converged on it.

The family name of the cleric Benedictus à Sancto Josepho was Buns; his original first name remains unknown. He was presumably born in Geldern, which today lies in Germany, but at that time was part of the Upper-Gelre province of the southern, Spanish Netherlands.

Nothing is known of Benedictus' early musical training. In 1659 he entered the Carmelite monastery in his birthplace and there received his clerical name. In 1666 he was consecrated as a priest. Around 1670 Benedictus presumably left Geldern for the recently established Carmelite monastery in Boxmeer. In those days Boxmeer was part of the Catholic dominion of Bergh. Although surrounded by Dutch Republic land, it did not fall under its jurisdiction. There, in 1679, Benedictus is thought to have succeeded Brother Hubertus à Sancto Joanne (1633-1679) upon his death as organist at the monastery. By that time Benedictus already had four substantial collections of sacred music to his name published in Antwerp. He continued as the monastery organist until his death on 6 December 1716.

Benedictus composed an extensive oeuvre of concertato music for the Catholic church. His work includes music in all liturgical genres, and particularly those intended for the mass, the vespers, and other services: motets to liturgical and 'free' texts, settings of Marian antiphons (for instance, the *Salve Regina*), sacramental hymns (*Tantum ergo*), litanies, masses, requiems, etc. Some of the titles of these collections refer to the composer's Carmelite background, though this does not mean that performance of the works was intended solely to take place within the Carmelite monastic order. Benedictus' music was intended for use by any seventeenth-century Catholic church that had the prescribed musical resources: a singing master (*phonascus*), adult singers, choirboys, instrumentalists and an organist.

The collections follow a pattern common in the second half of the seventeenth century: first come several pieces for a solo voice, then pieces for two, three, four, and possibly five singers, all with the instrumental accompaniment of an ensemble of five strings (1st and 2nd violin, alto and tenor violin and cello or viola da gamba) or three strings (1st and 2nd violin with a bass) and possibly bassoon. This type of setting was geared towards the musical resources of Catholic churches in the southern Netherlands, the archbishopric of Liège, and the Catholic dominions of the Elector Palatine of Düsseldorf. The first opus alone is polychoral, with soloists and a ripieno choir, in accordance with mid-seventeenth-century practice.

Benedictus also worked on the revision of Gregorian chant for Carmelite worship, as evidenced by the *Processionale juxta usum fratrum B.V. Mariae de Monte Carmelo* (Antwerp, 1711). His work here follows principles of the time in which rhythm is simplified and new melodies are added in a contemporary idiom.

Apart from his eight collections of music for the church, Benedictus also composed instrumental music: his op.8, entitled *Orpheus Elianus*. It is a collection of thirteen trio sonatas for the usual combination of two violins, viola da gamba and basso continuo. The sonatas adhere more closely to the earlier seventeenth-century style of short, alternating cantabile and canzona sections than to the more tightly organized Corellian 'sonata da chiesa' and 'sonata da camera'. The succession of keys in this collection is worth noting. The first six sonatas follow the circle of fifths in the minor mode, from C through G, D, A, and E to B. Sonata no.7 begins in F-sharp minor but modulates to E-flat major. Sonatas nos.8-13 continue through the circle of fifths, but in the major mode, from E-flat, through B-flat, F, C and G to D.

Benedictus was an able composer who greatly contributed to the repertoire for the Catholic church in the countries to the south and east of the Dutch Republic.

RUDOLF RASCH

COMPOSITIONS

Missae, litaniae, et motetta IV. V. VI. vocibus cum instrument. et ripienis ... opus primum. – Antwerpen, heirs of Petrus Phalesius, 1666
Two masses, three motets, two litanies, for 5 solo voices, four-part choir, instruments and bc

Corona stellarum duodecim serta, I. II. II. IV. vocibus et instrumentis ... [opus secundum], editio secunda aucta et emendata. – Antwerpen, heirs of Petrus Phalesius, 1673
First ed. (c 1670) has been lost. Seven motets, two masses, litany, Salve Regina, Tantum ergo, for 1-4 solo voices and bc

Flosculi musici ... opus tertium. – Antwerpen, heirs of Petrus Phalesius, 1672
Fourteen motets, for 1-4 solo voices, instruments and bc

Musica montana in monte Carmelo composita, cantata in monte Domini, 1. 2. 3. vocibus, & unum Tantum ergo. 4. voc. & 2.3. vel 5. instrumentis ... opus quartum. – Antwerpen, Lucas de Potter, 1677
Twelve motets, for 1-4 solo voices, instruments and bc

Completoriale melos musicum, II. III. & IV. vocibus, II. III. vel V. instrumentis decantandum ... opus quintum. – Antwerpen, Lucas de Potter, 1678
Seven motets, four Maria antiphons, litany, two Tantum ergo, for 2-4 solo voices, instruments and bc, Sonata finalis II choris (twice 4 instruments)

Encomia sacra musice decantanda 1. 2. 3 vocibus et 2. 3. 4. et 5 instrum. ... opus sextum.– Utrecht, Arnold van Eynden, 1683
Nineteen motets, one mass, for 1-3 solo voices, instruments and bc. Modern ed.: Motets for one and two voices with instrumental accompaniment : from Encomia sacra musice decantanda (Ultrajecti 1683) / ed. by Marinus Waltmans. [Amsterdam], VNM, 1983. Includes nos. 1, 6, 9 and 11

Orpheus gaudens et lugens, sive cantica gaudii ac luctus, a 1, 2, 3, 3 & 5 vocibus ac instrumentis

composita ... opus septimum. – Antwerpen, Hendrick Aertssens, 1693
Fifteen motets for 1-5 solo voices, instruments en bc, four masses for 4-5 solo voices, instruments and bc

Orpheus Elianus a Carmelo in orbem editus ... opus octavum, a 2 violinis et basso viola cum basso continuo ...– Amsterdam, Estienne Roger, [1698]
Thirteen trio sonatas, for 2 violins, viola da gamba and bc

Missa sacris ornata canticis ... [1. 2. 3. vocibus et 1. 2. 3. 4. et 5 instrumentis] ... opus nonum. – Amsterdam, Estienne Roger, [1699]
One mass for 3 solo voices, ten motets for 1-3 solo voices, instruments and bc

BIBLIOGRAPHY

J.H. van der Meer: 'Benedictus a Sancto Josepho van de Orde der Carmelieten (1642-1716)', *TVNM*, 18, 1958, p. 129-147
J.H. van der Meer: 'Benedictus a Sancto Josepho von Karmeliterorden', *Kirchenmusikalisches Jahrbuch*, 46, 1962, p. 99-120; supplement in no. 47, 1963, p. 123-124
Fr. Noske: *Music bridging divided religions.* Wilhelmshaven, Noetzel, 1989 (four motets (from opp. 1, 5, 6 and 9) transcribed in vol. 2)

DISCOGRAPHY

Magnificat, op. 5, no. 3; O sors optata, op. 6, no. 9; Salve regina, op. 1, no. 3. Ensemble Bouzignac, cond. E. van Nevel (Vanguard Classics 99126)

Quirinus van Blankenburg

GOUDA, 1654 – THE HAGUE, 12 MAY 1739

Quirinus Gideon van Blankenburg was born in 1654 in Gouda. His father Gerbrant, the son of a schoolmaster, was born around 1620 on the isle of Texel. From 1641 to 1648 he was the organist in Zevenbergen and then, until his death in 1707, the organist at Saint John's Church in Gouda. On 26 November 1652 he married Maria Pardanus, a union from which Quirinus was born about two years later.

Quirinus van Blankenburg received his first musical instruction from his father. In the preface to his *Elementa Musica*, a treatise on music theory dating from 1739, Van Blankenburg relates: 'On this I must recall here that my father, informed by music-lovers who had travelled in Italy, was aware that music there had reached a much higher degree of perfection, and set merchants to buying all the newest works in Venice and transporting them here along with their wares: these alone pleased him. And later, when I was to learn music in my youth, I was permitted no books other than these; from which my thoughts were filled; through which in consequence I could not bear any clumsiness.'

In 1670, at fifteen, Van Blankenburg was appointed organist to the Remonstrant Church in Rotterdam. Because of his tender age, the commissioners of the organ were instructed to 'keep watch over the organist and his lifestyle'. He resigned this post in December 1674 and from January 1675 to August 1679 was the organist and carilloneur at the Reformed Church in Gorinchem. During this period Van Blankenburg became involved in the design of a carillon that was to be cast by Pierre Hemony for Gouda's Saint John's Church. His advice to the city council that C- and D-sharp be included in the lowest bells raised strong objections from Dutch carillon experts, Hemony among them. Van Blankenburg defended the proposal in a pamphlet entitled *Van de nootsakelijkheid van Cis en Dis in de bassen der klokken* [On the necessity of C- and D-sharp in the lowest bells of carillons] (c.1677), prompting a rebuttal by Hemony and others entitled *De onnootsakelijkheid en ondienstigheid van Cis en Dis in de bassen der klokken* [On the unnecessariness and uselessness of C- and D-sharp in the lowest bells of carillons]. Unfortunately, Van Blankenburg's essay has not survived.

In November 1679 Van Blankenburg enrolled as a student of philosophy and medicine at the University of Leiden, perhaps because he was uncertain what a future in music would hold for him. What he actually studied there is not clear. Some sources report that, aside from medicine and philosophy, he also studied mathematics and chemistry. It is not known whether he earned a degree, although he did remain in Leiden until 1683 and ultimately decided upon a career in music.

Around 1684 he took up residence in The Hague and there married Catharina Clara de Guise in 1686; the couple had two daughters: Marie Anne (b.1694) and Katarina Klare (b.1696). In 1687 Van Blankenburg succeeded Cornelis Schol as organist at the Royal Chapel. On 12 November 1699, two years before the Jan Duyschot organ was installed in the New Church, Van Blankenburg became organist at this church. He held both posts until 1703 and remained at the New Church until his death.

Despite an ample salary as an organist (700 guilders a year) and supplementary earnings from teaching prosperous citizens and nobles, Van Blankenburg suffered chronic financial problems. He managed to stay one step ahead of bankruptcy by borrowing against his salary.

Van Blankenburg was often called upon to appraise organs and carillons. As a result he also became involved in organ examinations in The Hague (New Church), Amsterdam (Remonstrant Church and Old Church), Alkmaar (Laurens Church), and carillon examinations in Gouda (Saint John's Church) and The Hague (Great Church). He also was successful as an organ repairman (Royal Chapel), a builder and renovator of harpsichords, and as a dealer in keyboard instruments. In addition, he made a living by composing and writing works on music theory.

Throughout his life, 'with the attention of 60 years', as he wrote, he was an advocate of the Cartesian, rational approach to music and music theory. In the preface to his *Clavicimbel- en orgelboek* [Harpsichord and organ book] (1732), a collection of psalm settings suitable for church organists as well as amateurs, he expounds the earliest results of this interest in an lengthy essay. Shortly before his death, he was to expand on these thoughts in the *Elementa Musica of niew licht tot het welverstaan van de musiec en de bascontinuo* [Elements of Music or a new light to the comprehension of music and the basso continuo] (1739). Set against the ambitious objectives Van Blankenburg envisioned, namely the revelation of 'certain fundaments' of music, the book is somewhat disappointing. It was lambasted in 1762 by Jacob Wilhelm Lustig, who called it an unparalleled 'muddle'. This judgment is not entirely fair. Along with autobiographical information and a composition entitled *Fuga Obligata*, *Elementa Musica* contains a wealth of information on the latest developments in instruments and instrument building, as well as interesting ideas on the relative and absolute tonal system.

The 84-year-old Van Blankenburg thought himself underappreciated as a composer and noted with some bitterness: 'If over the course of several years I attempted to present a piece of music of my making, it was never valued; it had to come from afar to be of any worth; but if instead of signing it with my name, Van Blankenburg, I wrote Di Castelbianco (meaning the same) in Italian, it was thought excellent: this lasting until I removed the disguise, at which point the problem would begin anew.'

Johann Walther's *Musicalisches Lexicon* (1732) shows that Van Blankenburg did indeed compose under this Italian pseudonym. Listed under the entry 'Castelbianco (Quirino di)' are two ariettas with variations and a *Toccata voor clavier* [Toccata for keyboard].

It is difficult to form an appraisal of Van Blankenburg's work on the basis of the compositions that are known to have survived. Aside from the cantata *L'Apologie des Femmes* (c.1715) for bass, two violins, viola da gamba and basso continuo – a mature and important work in the context of its time – the aforementioned *Fuga Obligata* (1725), the *Clavicimbel- en orgelboek der Gereformeerde Psalmen en Kerkgezangen* [Harpsichord and organ book of Reformed Psalms and Church Hymns] (1732), and *De verdubbelde Harmony* [The doubled harmony] – a curious piece written for the occasion of the marriage of Prince Willem Carel Hendrik Friso and Princess Anna von Braunschweig – there remain only a few short instrumental and vocal pieces and arrangements of compositions by Handel, Destouches and Störl.

Van Blankenburg died on 12 May 1739 and was buried three days later. His student, the blind Frans Piton, who because of Van Blankenburg's advanced age served him from 1720 as assistant organist, was appointed as his successor.

REIN VERHAGEN

COMPOSITIONS

Clavicimbel- en orgelboek der gereformeerde Psalmen en kerkgezangen, ... – The Hague, Laurens Berkoske, 1732

[De verdubbelde Harmony]
  Duplicata Ratio Musices, ou La double Harmonie ... dont la basse et le dessus de concert, ... tous pour le clavecin. – The Hague, Laurens Berkoske, 1733

La Double Harmonie, Augmentee de plusieurs Fugues, Allemande, Courante, ... & autres pieces de Clavecin
  Announced reprint, 1739, possibly not published

L'Apologie des Femmes (c 1715)
  Cantata for bass, 2 violins, viola da gamba and bc

Two Ariettas with variations (1714-1726); *Toccata voor clavier* (1714-1726)
  Included in *Musicalisches Lexicon* by Johann Walther (1732)

Fuga Obligata (1725-1726)
  Included in *Elementa Musica*
  (see writings)

Marche (c 1713); *Airs à deux trompettes* (c 1713); *Air nouveau* (c 1713)

WRITINGS

Van de nootsakelijkheid van Cis en Dis in de bassen der klokken (c 1677). Lost

Elementa Musica of niew licht tot het welverstaan van de musiec en de bascontinuo (1739)

BIBLIOGRAPHY
D.J. Balfoort: 'Quirinus Gideon van Blankenburg', *Die Haghe Jaarboek*, 1938, p. 153-224

DISCOGRAPHY
L'Apologie des Femmes. M. Koningsberger (Bar), Academy of the Begynhof Amsterdam, cond. R. Shaw (Globe GLO 5055)
  L'Apologie des Femmes. Cantorij Amsterdam, Netherlands Chamber Choir, members of the Residentie Orchestra, various soloists, cond. T.

Koopman (Olympia OCD 500)
  Clavicimbel- en orgelboek... (selection). G. Oost (hpd) (Marcato Keyboard MCD 129202)
  Fuga Obligata. J. Ogg (hpd) (Globe GLO 5101)

Gerard Boedijn

HOORN, 19 NOVEMBER 1893 – HOORN, 23 SEPTEMBER 1972

Gerardus Hendrik Boedijn was born in 1893, the son of a gunmaker at the Hoorn garrison who also repaired the musical instruments of the Hoorn battalion band. Thus Boedijn was involved with music from his earliest youth. Apart from his first instrument, the violin, he took up other instruments as a child, among them the flute, the clarinet, and somewhat later the saxophone and various brass instruments as well. These skills, combined with his excellent musical ear, were of much use to Boedijn's father in his capacity as instrument repairer.

After studying for a time to become a primary school teacher, Boedijn enrolled at the Amsterdam Conservatory in 1909 to study the violin with Heinrich Fiedler and Felice Togni. There he also had lessons in counterpoint, harmony, composition and instrumentation with Bernard Zweers and Cor Kint, and later with Carl Smulders. Boedijn was strongly influenced by Smulders, whom he got to know when at 22 he began teaching the violin and music theory at a private music school run by Jenny Goovaerts in Maastricht.

In 1917 Boedijn returned to Hoorn and earned his living as a violin teacher, composer, music critic, and conductor of his first brass band, in the nearby village of Zwaag. From 1927 he served for five years as director of the music school in the northern town of Veendam.

Conducting his brass bands in the provinces, Boedijn was struck by how musically outdated they were. A firm believer that folk art would die out if failing to keep up with the times, Boedijn decided to compose the music for these groups himself. His guiding principle was to build up a well-written and original repertoire for amateur orchestras. It is because of this that Boedijn may rightly be considered a pioneer in the field of modern wind music.

Around 1938 his *Gammatique* march from 1933 appeared with publisher Piet Molenaar in Wormerveer. This was the beginning of an extensive oeuvre of original music for concert and brass band. At first Boedijn's music, which was considered quite modern at the time, met with resistance, but he soon gained an international reputation as a composer of music for winds. His *Halewijn* (1940) is widely regarded as the crowning achievement of his music for wind orchestra.

To avoid his personal style drawing too great attention, as well as the too frequent incidence of his name on concert programs, Boedijn followed his publisher's advice and composed a number of lighter – and, from an artistic point of view, less commendable – pieces under the pseudonym Jack Harvey.

During this period his music for combinations other than winds alone was performed increasingly; on 10 December 1946 his Partita for double string quartet was premiered by the Rotterdam Philharmonic Orchestra, conducted by Piet van Mever. From the 1950s onwards, he frequently received commissions for (principally) music for winds.

In 1959 he was knighted in the Order of Orange-Nassau, in recognition of his local and national accomplishments, particularly with regard to the development of Dutch music for concert and brass band and his activities as a member of music juries. He also received the National Award from the Department of Education and Sciences for his *Landelijke suite* [Rural suite] op. 123 (1951), and the ANV-Visserneerlandia Prize for his *Introduzione rhapsodique* (1960) for carillon and orchestra.

Boedijn composed primarily for the choirs and bands he conducted. He never gave this up, even when commissions for new works flowed in. Hence, the majority of his work was written with the amateur musician in mind, and for this reason it was not always taken seriously by composers of music for professionals. Boedijn's reaction was that amateur music-making (particularly music for winds) was an integral part of Dutch musical life, not only from a social viewpoint, but also because it was precisely through these ensembles that many amateur musicians made their way to the ranks of professional orchestras.

Several of the principles Boedijn adhered to in writing for wind orchestras are worthy of attention here. First, he was opposed to arranging symphonic music for wind band. All too often, in his opinion, this led to a situation in which the symphonic character of the piece would be destroyed, while the result would scarcely suit the wind ensemble either. Instead, he believed, a personal style had to be developed that was geared towards the specific composition of the wind bands. Examples of this are the more prominent role allotted to percussion instruments, a section that previously often served merely to provide a metrical foundation, and the provision of musically and technically interesting parts for the inner voices. Boedijn was also convinced that folk music should play a major role in music for bands. Hence his penchant for both Dutch and foreign folklore, innumerable examples of which can be found in his work.

Finally, Boedijn had a strong pedagogic drive as a composer, focusing on particular rhythms, harmonies, meters and the like in order to teach the performers how to handle them.

Most of the more than 500 works he composed for widely divergent instrumental combinations are forgotten today. This is not the case with his works for wind band, although some of these pieces too are rather dated. Nonetheless, it is in this genre that Boedijn's significance lies. Like the composers Paul Gilson and Marcel Poot in Belgium, Boedijn – along with several other composers, including Meindert Boekel – provided Dutch wind bands in the first half of the twentieth century with original repertoire. His extensive knowledge of music for the concert, brass and marching bands – as revealed, for example, in his refined instrumentation for these forces – both directly and indirectly influenced others. Many composers who tried their hand at music for winds turned to Boedijn for advice, even the likes of Henk Badings, whose roots lay in the symphonic arena.

CASPAR BECX

COMPOSITIONS

SONGS: *Twee liedjes in de volkstoon*, v, pf (1919); *In nachtschaduw*, Bar, orch (1940); *Twaalf Westfriese liederen in de volkstoon*, v, pf (1944); *Ons lied van Noord-Holland*, 3 v, pf (1954); *Messchaerthymne*, Bar, orch (1972)

CHOIR: *Oogst*, m.choir (1924); *Regenboog*, m.choir (1933); *De dorschers*, m.choir (1935); *Maskendans*, mix.choir (1936); *Het spinstertje*, m.choir (1936); *E.M.K.-lied voor Enkhuizer mannenkoor*, m.choir (1951); *Motet*, S, m.choir (1972); *Geboorte*, m.choir; *Greeting*, w.choir; *Hymne aan den zang*, mix.choir

WIND BAND: *Gammatique* (1933); *Halewijn* (symphonic poem), op. 87 (1940); *Partita symphonique*, op. 100 (1942); *Symfonische schets*, op. 112 (1948); *Rossiniana : ouverture naar Italiaanse trant*, op. 114 (1948);

Hephaistos, concertouverture, op. 115 (1949); *Caesar en Cleopatra*, op. 122 (1950); *Landelijke suite*, op. 123 (1951); *Vijf epigrammen naar 'De Schoolmeester'*, op. 126 (1952); *Vier West-Friese schetsen*, op. 134 (1954); *Ladingen*, op. 143 (1955); *Bevrijdingshymne 'Aan het Nederlandse volk'*, op. 140 (1955); *Noordhollandse paneeltjes*, op. 152 (1957); *The Harp of Wales*, op. 158 (1959); *Esquisse triomphale*, op. 161 (1960); *Jan Klaasen en Katrijn : ouverture voor de poppenkast*, op. 173 (1962); *A chain of British songs*, op. 176 (1963); *Promenades*, op. 187 (1965); *Ballet astrologique*, op. 184 (1965); *De argonauten* (overture), op. 190 (1967)

CARILLON: *Gavotte* (1936); *Kwarten arabesk* (1940); *Tango* (1940); *Folkloristische suite 'Oud Hoorn'* (1941); *Partita* (1952); *Introduzione rhapsodique*, car, brass band (1958)

OTHER INSTRUMENTAL WORKS: *Folkloristische suite*, fl, ob, pf (1937); *Lyrische suite*, str.orch, pf (1937); *Poëtische suite*, ob, str.orch, timp (1941); *Hollandse rhapsodie* (1943); *Mei sinfonietta* (1943); *Partita*, 2 str.qt, orch (1944)

DISCOGRAPHY

Caesar en Cleopatra. Dutch Royal Military Band, cond. J. van Ossenbruggen (Molenaar MBS 31.004.63)

Caesar en Cleopatra. Musique Divisionaire du 6° Génie (Art et Musique AM 103/8606)

Divertimento. Netherlands Brass Orchestra (OMEGA 145.538-45 EP)

Gammatique. Dutch Royal Military Band, cond. P. Kuypers (Molenaar MBCD 31.1027.72)

Halewijn. Fanfare band Na Lang Streven (CAPRI CA 62-H)

Happy Time suite. Fanfare band St. Cecilia Steenbrugge (MDM Records 46824)

The Harp of Wales. Fanfare band St. Lambertus Gemonde (Eurosound ES 46.665)

Irish suite. Royal Scoutsharmonie Brugge (MDM Records 46824)

Michiel Adriaenszoon. Dutch Royal Military Band, cond. J. van Ossenbruggen (Molenaar MBS 31.0013.63)

Partita picola (part 3). Jugendkapelle Überlingen – Bodensee (EOM 12443)

Pastorale suite. Concert Band of the Brabant Conservatory, cond. J. Cober (Molenaar MBCD 31.1030.72)

Plechtige ouverture. Andel Fanfare band, cond. H. Klerx (Eurosound ES 46.344)

Rossiniana. Muziekvereniging Lamoraal van Egmond (Mirasound SP 241)

Sinfonie concertante. Band of the Netherlands Royal Airforce, cond. L. van Diepen (Molenaar MBCD 31.1014.72)

Konrad Boehmer

BERLIN, 24 MAY 1941

Konrad Boehmer was born in Berlin in 1941. He studied composition, sociology, philosophy and musicology in Cologne and gained a doctorate at the age of 25. He settled in Amsterdam in 1966, after having spent three years working at the WDR Electronic Studio, during which time he attended the Darmstädter Ferienkurse, where he took lessons with Boulez, Pousseur and Stockhausen. Until 1968 he worked at the Institute for Sonology in Utrecht, which was led by his former composition teacher Gottfried Michael Koenig. He wrote for the weekly magazine *Vrij Nederland* from 1968 to 1973, and has taught at the Royal Conservatory in The Hague since 1972. As a teacher of composition and conductor of his own music, he has traveled extensively within Asia and Latin America. In 1972, 1973 and 1978 he taught at the Cursos Latinoamericanos in Uruguay and Brazil. Among the many administrative positions he has held are the chairmanship of Geneco (the Society of Dutch Composers), board-membership of the Dutch Music Copyright Agency Buma, and chairmanship of CIAM (Conseil International des Auteurs de Musique). In 1985 he was awarded the Pierre Bayle Prize for music criticism.

In his doctoral thesis, *Zur Theorie der offenen Form in der neuen Musik*, Boehmer explores not only the open form of the 1960s, but also investigates exhaustively the flexible forms found in the works of such diverse composers as Guido de Arrezzo, Ockeghem and Mozart. Rather than aiming to construct a watertight theory of open form, his technical analyses and critical reflections approach the works on their own terms.

Nearly all of the ideological writings presented by the so-called 'Nutcrackers' – a group of young composers, who in the sixties sought to revitalize public music making in the Netherlands – were the work of Konrad Boehmer, the group's ideologist. Despite his commitment to the public at large, Boehmer resisted the vulgarization of music, following in this respect the example of Luigi Nono.

Apart from purely electronic compositions such as *Aspekt* (1966), awarded at the Fifth Bienniale in Paris, he has also written works for tape and large ensemble, (*Position*, 1961), tape and percussion (*Schrei dieser Erde*, 1979), and tape with four percussionists, two pianos and three pop singers (*Apocalipsis cum figuris*, 1984). In 1974 Boehmer embarked on a tryptich that explores the

sociological function of music from a political standpoint, consisting of the works *Canciones del Camino* (1974), which incorporates protest and folksongs of the Third World integrated into the orchestral score; *Lied aus der Ferne* (1976), to texts by Ho Chi Minh, for chamber orchestra, piano and soprano; and the aforementioned *Schrei dieser Erde*, whose tape part contains the voices of Colombian Indians, Varèse and Lenin. Apart from the neo-Expressionism of Cologne, another important model for Boehmer has been the composer Varèse. However, Boehmer regards sound not so much as an object, but rather as a process that is the foundation of the composition. He has also found inspiration in the character of Faust, as portrayed in Thomas Mann's *Doktor Faustus* (1947). His opera *Doktor Faustus*, awarded the Rolf Liebermann Prize in 1983, as well as *Apocalipsis cum figuris*, underline the downfall of this idealistic hero.

While the composition *Apocalipsis cum figuris* is difficult to define – exploring a region bordered by pop music, oratorio, radio drama and absolute music – Boehmer's theater piece *Woutertje Pieterse* (1988), after Multatuli's book and composed on the occasion of this major Dutch author's centenary, is no less complicated. The composer speaks of a 'cruel, serial children's operetta', permanent alienation at its most extreme in a strongly alternating scene, dreamed and vulgar, as loftily 'intellectual' as it is childishly naive. These extremes, in a broad spectrum ranging from seriousness to irony, are characteristic of this composer.

ERNST VERMEULEN

COMPOSITIONS

VOCAL: *Position*, v, tape, orch (1961); *Jugend*, 16
v, 12 instr (1967-1968); *Lied aus der Ferne*,
S, pf, orch (1976); *Je vis – je meurs*, S, fl,
perc; *Doktor Faustus* (opera) (1980-1983);
Malgré la nuit seule, S, 3 instr (1983-1984);
Apocalipsis cum figuris, tape, 4 perc, 2 pf, 3
pop singers (1983-1984); *Woutertje Pieterse*
(comic tragedy) (1988); *Menschenblut*, B, pf
(1987); *Vindurinn*, S, pf (1989); *Canto in
modo Nono*, ch.choir (1990-1991); *Voor-
vaderen*, S, pf (1994); *Orfeo demagico*
(opera) (1996-....); *Logos Protos*, tape, voices, perc (1996)

INSTRUMENTAL: *Klangstück I*, pf (1959); *Potential*, pf (1961); *Zeitläufte*, chamb.ens
(1962); *Information*, 4 perc, 2 pf (1964-
1965); *Aspekt*, tape (1966); *Atem*, fl (1975);
Sestina, ob (1977); *Schrei dieser Erde*, tape,
perc (1978-1979); *In illo tempore*, pf (1979);
Fingerspitzengew(f)ühl, pf (1979); *Fluit
douceur*, rec (1980); *Tango deslavado y mo-
roso*, pf (1984); *Chant de départ*, vc (1986);
Nomos Protos, instr.ens (1986-1987);
Kinderlied zu Dresden, pf (1990); *Da Ciri*, fl,
cl, vibr, vl, vc (1991); *Et in Arcadia Ego*,
str.qt (1991-1992); *Kronos Protos*, instr.ens
(1995); *Qadar*, fl, cl, vl, vc, pf (1997); *Nuba*,
fl, hp, vlada (1997)

ORCHESTRA: *Variationen*, orch (1959-1960);
Canciones del Camino, orch (1973-1974);
Konzert-Ouverture 'Doktor Faustus', orch
(1983); *Il Combattimento*, vl, vc, orch (1989-
1990); *Modern irony*, concert band (1993-
1994)

PUBLICATIONS

Zwischen Reihe und Pop. Vienna, 1970
Hanns Eisler : muziek en politiek, ed. K.
Boehmer and J.F. Vogelaar. Nijmegen, SUN,
1972
Gehoord en ongehoord : opstellen over muziek.
Utrecht, Oosthoek, 1974
'A chair that is not a work of art is not a
chair: Gottfried Michael Koenig, recipient of
the 1987 Matthijs Vermeulen Prize', *Key Notes*,
24, 1987, p. 55-56
'Poor old Darmstadt : The sanctification of
misapprehension into a doctrine', *Key Notes*,
24, 1987, p.43-47

Das böse Ohr : Texte zur Musik : 1961-1991.
Köln, DuMont, 1993
'Open the future', *Key Notes*, 30, 1996/2, p.
4-8
*Is er nog toekomst voor de Nederlandse
muziek?* Lecture at the Jan van Gilse Gala 8
September 1998, Beurs van Berlage Amster-
dam. Hilversum, Centrum Nederlandse
Muziek, 1998 (also published in Mens en
Melodie vol. 53, Oct. 1998, p. 401-410)

BIBLIOGRAPHY

R. de Beer: 'Dr. Faustus – A cynical opera
by Konrad Boehmer', *Key Notes*, 20, 1984/2,
p. 18-23

DISCOGRAPHY

Aspekt (BVHAAST 9011)
Atem. R. de Reede (fl) (BVHAAST 014, BS-
0193)
Canciones del Camino. Rotterdam Philhar-
monic Orchestra, cond. K. Boehmer
(BVHAAST 014)
Canto in modo Nono. Netherlands Chamber
Choir, cond. H. Kerstens (NM Classics 92025)
Et in Arcadia Ego (BVHAAST 9615)
*Je vis – je meurs; In illo tempore; Nomos Pro-
tos*. E. van Lier (S), L. Arends (fl), M. de Roo
(perc), G. Madge (pf), K. Becker (pf), Ensem-
ble Köln, cond. H. Platz (BVHAAST 9008)
Schrei dieser Erde; Apocalipsis cum figuris
(BVHAAST 9011)
Sestina. E. Rombout (ob) (BFO A-2)
Woutertje Pieterse; Lied aus der Ferne. Vari-
ous soloists, Rotterdam Philharmonic Orches-
tra, Netherlands Wind Ensemble, cond. L. Vis
(BVHAAST 9401/2)

Jan Boerman

THE HAGUE, 30 JUNE 1923

Jan Boerman studied the piano with Léon Orthel and composition with Hendrik Andriessen at the Royal Conservatory in his native city of The Hague. Boerman is one of the pioneers of electronic music in the Netherlands and, unlike many other composers, he has continued to explore the possibilities offered by the medium. While still a student, he composed a handful of instrumental pieces (chamber and orchestral music), but from 1959 he focused his attention for nearly twenty years almost exclusively on electronic music in the narrow sense of the term, i.e. tape compositions. His first electronic pieces were created in a studio at the University of Technology in Delft. He also worked in Utrecht at the Institute for Sonology. Beginning in 1962, he and Dick Raaijmakers assembled an electronic studio of their own in The Hague, which later formed the basis of the electronic studio of the Royal Conservatory, where all of his later electronic pieces were created. Since 1974 Boerman has taught electronic music and piano (as supplementary subject) at this conservatory.

Boerman has always held a rather isolated position, in part because of his somewhat withdrawn personality, but also because he has encountered few soulmates of his generation. Nonetheless, his music has always attracted a small circle of fervent followers. In 1962 his *Alchemie* was performed at a concert of the Mood Engineering Society (an alliance of young avant-gardists, including Willem de Ridder, Louis Andriessen and Peter Schat). Inspired by this, Rudi van Dantzig created two chorcographies to Boerman's music: *Monument voor een gestorven jongen* [Monument for a boy who died] (1965), based on *Alchemie*, and *The Ropes of Time* (1970), based on *De Zee* [The Sea].

The first recording of Boerman's work appeared in 1977. Although this LP issued by the Dutch music publisher Donemus (*Jan Boerman. Composition 1972, Alchemie 1961, De Zee;* CV 7701) was soon sold out and never rereleased, it laid the foundation for widespread recognition of Boerman's unique ability to transform an electronic medium which at first sight seems so sterile, into organic and immensely expressive worlds of sound. This general appreciation was reaffirmed in 1982 when Boerman was awarded the Matthijs Vermeulen Prize for his entire oeuvre. Despite his lifelong fascination with electronic music, Boerman always referred to his work in this medium as 'experiments' and repeatedly maintained that the entire genre amounts to no more than a

transitional phase. As early as the 1970s, he also worked on a number of pieces for two pianos, three of which were released for performance in 1980. In the mid-1970s he began to experiment with settings combining tape with live musicians. In the early 1980s he joined forces with a group called Het Nieuwe Leven [The New Life]. This collaboration yielded the 'material-music' *Weerstand* [Resistance], for electric guitar and tape, and two works entitled *Ontketening* [Unleashing], for percussion and tape.

Other works for tape and live sounds are his *Maasproject* (a spatial project, created in collaboration with the architect Jan Hoogstad, to be performed near the Rotterdam Euromast), and his large choral piece *Die Vögel* (1989). It was only in 1991 that Boerman first composed a large-scale instrumental piece without tape: *Muziek* for percussion and orchestra. Although this work reaffirms his affinity with corporeal, instrumental sound, he has continued to create purely electronic compositions. But this 'purely' must not be taken all too literally: his *Kompositie 1989*, for example, has unmistakable piano sounds. Boerman has never been an unswerving dogmatist.

Asked to name his favorite composers, Boerman, dropping his characteristic reserve, shoots back Debussy (for the 'color'), Monteverdi ('for the drama') and Bruckner ('for the panoramic element, but not only that, of course'). These characteristics are equally evident in Boerman's own work. When it first appeared, Boerman described his *Alchemie* (1961) as 'an attempt to derive musical form from moving tone color', an attempt, incidentally, that he considered not entirely successful. Nevertheless, passages of this work are based on a structural principle that he was later to use in his electronic (and some instrumental) pieces: the temporal aspect of sectioning determined by the Golden Section (the division of a line or a unit of time into two unequal parts so that the whole is to the greater part as that part is to the smaller part). Golden Section proportions are in evidence down to the smallest detail of Boerman's work. Though it has no influence on pitch, it is a crucial element in the layout of and relationship between structures, and thus for the unity of the composition. On a smaller scale, the Golden Section is clearly recognizable in proportional canons, and manifests itself on a larger scale in altered recapitulations.

Boerman described the technique in 1983 as 'a means of constructing a breakwater in the endless stream of sound generated in electronic music.' But the Golden Section in Boerman's music, like other techniques, could not be likened to a ready recipe for composition. Though the special qualities of his music may indeed be partially determined by initial planning and calculation, they are founded on the ear and intuition of the composer. At least equally essential is the material – the sound pigment – with which he works. The often sensual and spatial sounds alone lend his music a warm glow that is all too often lacking in electronic music. As most of Boerman's compositions rely on and reprocess material he has collected over the years, his pieces, however diverse, show a clear, 'genetic' relationship. Although the modern developments of the synthesizer and sampler technology have not gone unnoticed by Boerman, he remains in essence a craftsman of the old school: 'With the old techniques, tape cutting and such, you can do things much more quickly, if you know precisely what it is you want', he said in 1991.

Boerman's compositions, whether generated by loudspeakers or musicians, are equally strong in emotion and structural force. Nevertheless, his unmistakable musical identity comes most vividly to the forefront in his purely electronic music, of which *Kompositie 1972* remains his *chef d'oeuvre*. The most conspicuous aspect of this piece is that without being tonally oriented it is consistently based on the interval of the fifth – something that in instrumental music and in the hands of another composer could quickly sound trivial. Although this piece, unlike *De Zee*, which principally employs colored noise, is thus preoccupied with pitch, here too transitions in sound from tone to colored noise play an important role. The plastic, sometimes floating and then forceful language and forms Boerman uses to achieve balance in his musical architectures are difficult to put into words in other than associative terms. In an article in 1986, Roland de Beer described Boerman's sounds as 'Rocklike combinations of octaves, fifths and fourths that ring out, flicker like sheet lightning, or disappear as in a trio for organ, cymbalon and aeolian harp from another Brobdingnag.' It is a fitting characterization, for he who ventures into Boerman's world soon imagines himself a Lilliputian, gripped by the same feelings of awe and a sense of insignificance in the face of grand and inescapable natural violence. 1998 saw the release by Donemus of *The Complete Tape Music of Jan Boerman* in a set of five discs. To add even more lustre to this crowning achievement, Boerman was awarded an Edison in the category of 'performing musicians' in 1999, an honor that was greatly appreciated by the composer.

FRITS VAN DER WAA

COMPOSITIONS

INSTRUMENTAL, VOCAL (WITH OR WITHOUT
TAPE): *Zonnesteen* (declamatorio), v, tape
(1968); *Weerstand*, el.gui, tape; *Ontketening
I*, perc, tape (1983); *Ontketening II*, perc,
tape (1984); *Die Vögel*, choir, brass, tape
(1989); *Muziek voor slagwerk en orkest*, perc,
orch (1991); *Cortège en Scherzo*, 2 pf (1992-
1993); *Introductie en Fuga*, 2 pf (1996)

MUSIC FOR THEATRE AND BALLET (ELEC-
TRONIC): *Rhinoceros* (Ionesco) (1960); *Een
groot dood dier* (Schierbeek) (1964); *Alchemie : Monument voor een gestorven jongen*
(1965); *De Zee : The Ropes of Time* (1970)

ELECTRONIC MUSIC (2 OR 8 TAPES):
Musique concrète (1959); *Alliage* (1960); *Alchemie* (1961); *De Zee I* (1965); *De Zee II*
(1968); *Kompositie 1972*; *Kompositie 1979*;
Maasproject I (1984); *Maasproject II* (1995);
Kompositie 1989; *Tellurisch* (1991); *Vocalise
1994*; *Kringloop II* (1994); *Kringloop III*
(1995)

BIBLIOGRAPHY

R. de Beer: 'The voltage-controlled emotions of Jan Boerman', *Key Notes*, 18, 1983/2, p.
12-19

R. de Beer: 'Ik voel mijn geluiden niet als
een persoonlijk eigendom', *Haagse Post*, 4 June
1983 (another version of the article in *Key
Notes, 18*)

R. de Beer: 'Mythical shores in the king-
dom of tape', *Key Notes*, 23, 1986, p. 11

R. Gieling and M. Waisvisz: 'Een beschei-
den ontketening', *Wolfsmond* 13/14, 1985

D. Raaijmakers: 'Jan Boerman and electronic composition', *Key Notes*, 5, 1977/1, p. 45-
49

D. Raaijmakers and J. Boerman: *Applied
technique*. Sleeve notes CV 7701 (see discography)

B. Spaan: 'Pioniers in elektronica : Dick
Raaijmakers en Jan Boerman op bezoek bij de
Concertzender', *Mens en Melodie*, vol. 53, 1998,
p. 253-257

F. van der Waa: 'Mijn geluiden staan allemaal op elkaars rug', *De Volkskrant*, 14 June
1991

P.J. Wagemans: Sleeve notes CV 8603 (see
discography)

DISCOGRAPHY

Composition 1972; *Alchemie*; *De Zee* (Com-
posers' Voice CV 7701)
Kompositie 1972; *Kompositie 1979*;
Ontketening II (Composers' Voice 8603)
Musique concrète (Composers' Voice CV
7803)
The Complete Tape Music of Jan Boerman (cd
box, Composers' Voice NEAR 4/5/6/7/8)
Vlechtwerk; *Kompositie 1989*; *Tellurisch* (NM
Classics 92032)

Willem Frederik Bon

AMERSFOORT, 15 JUNE 1940 – NIJEHOLTPADE, 14 APRIL 1983

Willem Frederik Bon was an outsider among the avant-garde. A student of Kees van Baaren, he broke with all expectations in neither wishing nor feeling compelled to conform to strict dodecaphony. Willem Frederik Bon, 'Peke' to his friends, was the fourth child of a musical family. His brother Maarten became a concert pianist and composer, and his two half-sisters Marja and Charlotte became respectively a concert pianist and a violinist. After leaving grammar school, Bon studied the clarinet with Klaas de Rook in Amsterdam, which prompted him to compose the twelve etudes for clarinet, op.1. In 1964 he began studying composition with Kees van Baaren and orchestral conducting with Louis Stotijn, both of whom worked at the Royal Conservatory in The Hague. Between 1967 and 1971 he followed various conducting courses, in the Netherlands and abroad, with Milan Horvat, Jean Fournet, Dean Dixon and Herbert von Karajan.

For his final examination in 1971, Bon conducted the Residentie Orchestra in his second symphony, *Les Prédictions*. His first symphony, *Usher*, had been premiered two years previously at the Holland Festival.

Bon taught composition at the Groningen Conservatory, conducted the Amsterdam Sinfonietta from 1972 onwards, was assistant conductor of the Amsterdam Concertgebouw Orchestra from 1973 through 1975, and from 1977 was affiliated with two Norwegian orchestras. Several of his compositions, such as the Requiem and the Concertino for piano and orchestra (in a revision by his brother Maarten), were performed posthumously.

Bon composed the Requiem for mixed choir, string orchestra and piano while still a conservatory student, though it was only in 1984 that he submitted the work to the Dutch Music Copyright Agency Buma. The appended note, 'For the victims of World War II', speaks for itself: the subject fascinated the composer, who was born in the first months of the Nazi occupation of the Netherlands. His composition of a Roman Catholic mass is more surprising, considering his anti-clerical (though not anti-religious) upbringing. In the Sanctus, the chanting of the syncopated rhythms is an allusion to the student revolution, to 'Provo', the Dutch flowerpower movement, and to the anti-Vietnam demonstrations; Bon was one of the protesters who threw a smoke bomb at the royal coach during the wedding procession of Princess Beatrix and Prince Claus, his act being captured by television.

It was between 1976 and 1979 that Bon wrote his largest work, *Les Quatre Saisons de Verlaine* for soprano, mezzo-soprano, baritone, tenor and orchestra, a piece that can be performed in its entirety or in separate movements.

From 1975 onward, Bon took an interest in music for children, a pursuit that gave rise to one of his most popular compositions, *Eriks wonderbaarlijke reis* [Eric's miraculous journey] based on the book by Godfried Bomans. His interest in the educational role of music had found expression in family concerts he organized years earlier. Bon became acquainted with the phenomenon of youth concerts in the 1950s, when Eduard van Beinum, then recovering from his first coronary, conducted the orchestra while sitting down. Although at the time schoolchildren were much better behaved than in later years, the fact that Bon's setting of Bomans' tale for reciter and orchestra commanded their rapt attention throughout its forty-five-minute duration can be considered remarkable.

Bon never joined the ranks of serialists, though he did from time to time freely employ tone rows in his music. Influenced by Stravinsky, one could call his work neo-classical. In addition there is a certain somberness and a kinship with the early Anton Webern, while the influence of Alban Berg (*Lulu*) is evident in some of his pieces for string orchestra. This mixture of neo-classicism and expressionism, in a concise, typically Dutch form that is never markedly extravert, is in line with the tradition of Pijper, Badings and Orthel. The frequently changing moods create a searching, indefinite character, philosophical perhaps, and melancholic. Characteristic is the plaintive atmosphere of the Oboe Concerto, brought about by the use of a curious combination of solo instruments: English horn, heckelphone, oboe d'amore and oboe. Bon always considered timbre an important element of composition.

In Bon's view music was the expression of a poetical idea and extra-musical elements dominate in his work, as demonstrated by the two symphonies. He thus embarked on the composition of an opera based on the prose of Edgar Allen Poe. This work became the First Symphony, its title *Usher* referring to Poe's *The Fall of the House of Usher*. Classical antiquity was another source of inspiration, as evidenced by his *Circe, Prelude for orchestra*, based on the tenth book of Homer's *Odyssey*. The spell Circe casts on Odysseus to hold him prisoner is symbolized by the harp, vibraphone, celesta and piano and, in the middle movement, by the first and second violins and the oboe. It was as a sound colorist that Bon was at his best.

ERNST VERMEULEN

COMPOSITIONS

VOCAL: *Requiem*, mix.choir, str.orch, pf (1966-1967); *Trois poèmes de Verlaine*, Mez, fl, vc, pf (1967); *Missa brevis*, 4-part choir, winds (1969); *Jadis en Naguère*, Mez, cl, vl, pf (1970); *Quatre prophéties de Nostradamus*, S, orch (1973); *Le Grand Âge Millième : quatre quatrains de Nostradamus*, m.choir (1974); *L'Été*, A, orch (1976); *L'Automne*, Bar, orch (1977); *Le Printemps*, S, orch (1978); *Silence* (Poe), Mez, wind qnt, pf (1978); *Dag : vier liederen op tekst van Paul van Ostaijen*, Mez, perc (1979); *Eriks wonderbaarlijke reis*, sp.v, orch (1979, rev. 1980); *L'Hiver*, T, orch (1979); *Songs of Nature. Five Poems by W. Wordsworth*, Bar, pf (1982); *Erik* (opera) (Bomans) (unfin., 1977-1982)

INSTRUMENTAL: *Concertino*, pf, orch (1962-1964, rev. by M. Bon 1986-1988); *Wind Quintet no.1* (1963-1966); *Sonata*, vc, pf (1966); *Sonata*, ob, pf (1966); *Sonatina*, fl, pf (1966); *Miniaturen*, pf (1966); *Dialogen en monologen*, pf, orch (1967); *Cinq tours de passe-passe*, fl, pf (1967); *Nocturnes*, str.orch (1968); *Sketches*, instr.ens (1968, rev. 1975); *Symphony no. 1 : Usher*, orch (1968-1970); *Wind Quintet no.2* (1969); *Variaties op een thema van Sweelinck*, chamb.orch (1969); *Concerto*, str.orch (1970); *Games*, orch (1970); *Petite trilogie*, tr (1970); *Sans paroles*, cl, b-cl, vl, vla, vc (1970); *Sonata*, bn (1970); *Symphony no. 2 : Les Prédictions*, orch (1970); *Riflessioni*, fl, hp (1971); *To Catch a Heffalump*, orch, tape (1971); *Aforismen*, 15 str (1972); *Allégro*, hp (1972); *Circe*, orch (1972); *Passacaglia in Blue*, db, wind orch (1972); *Allégorie pour harpe, d'après Paul Verlaine*, hp (1972); *Oboe Concerto*, ob (also eh, heckelphone, oba), str (1974); *Trois gnossiennes* – Satie, orchestr.(1976); *Préludes*, pf (1959-1979); *Sonata (Drie monogrammen)*, vl, pf (1981); *Trio Saturnien*, vl, vc, pf (1981); *Symphony for Strings* (1981-1982)

BIBLIOGRAPHY

S. Smit: 'Eriks wonderbaarlijke reis : of een kruistocht voor de jeugdconcerten', *Muziek & Dans*, Dec. 1981

DISCOGRAPHY

Concerto for String Orchestra. Caecilia Consort, cond. D. Porcelijn (Attacca Babel 8844-2)

Eriks wonderbaarlijke reis. L. Lutz (sp.v), Brabant Orchestra, cond. W.F. Bon (Philips 6423 503)

Oboe Concerto (1974). F. van Koten (ob), Netherlands Radio Chamber Orchestra, cond. E. Bour (Paladino CD 002)

Le printemps. R. Alexander (S), Concertgebouw Orchestra, cond. B. Haitink (BFO A-5)

Quatre Propheties de Nostradamus. G. de Vink (S), Netherlands Radio Philharmonic Orchestra, cond. W.F. Bon (Muz.O.W. Stereo 24)

Cornelis de Bondt

THE HAGUE, 9 DECEMBER 1953

Cornelis de Bondt began composing relatively late in life. At 18 he wrote slow, Satie-like piano pieces. His family showed little interest in music, however, aside from Dutch Reformed congregational hymns, which the composer's father would accompany on the harmonium. At the Royal Conservatory in The Hague De Bondt studied composition with Jan van Vlijmen and later with Louis Andriessen, and music theory with Hein Kien, Ineke Kien-Vermaas and Diderik Wagenaar. At his graduation in 1984 he was awarded the prize for composition. Since 1988 he has been teaching music theory at the Royal Conservatory.

In the 1970s, and in part due to Van Vlijmen's influence, De Bondt experimented with the expressive atonality of Schoenberg's twelve-tone technique. It was through the hocket technique of *Bint* (1980), for two equal groups of five players, that he made the transition to the anti-Romantic aesthetics of Andriessen, who in the mid-1970s succeeded in blending Stravinskian montage techniques with the process-derived, repetitive music of the United States. This Dutch, more intellectual counterpart to American 'minimal music' is with its characteristically jagged rhythms less tonally oriented, mellifluous and swinging than the American variety. *Bint* is based on a matrix of two pulses in which De Bondt applied his own version of Steve Reich's phase-transition technique. Through its suggestion of tonality and its construction in a single, large form, *Bint* is a harbinger of De Bondt's later fascination with Beethoven's music.

In the 1980s De Bondt wrestled to free himself of the influence of his teachers, while nevertheless acknowledging that avant-garde serialism and American minimal music had left their mark on his own music. His fascination with nineteenth-century tonal harmony, however, goes far beyond that of the serialists and minimalists and he is not one to shy away from using exact quotations. For example, the entire structure of one of his most successful compositions, *De deuren gesloten* [Doors Closed] (1985) – the second part of *Het gebroken oor* [Broken Ear], for large ensemble – is based upon two quotations: the funeral march from Beethoven's Symphony no.3 and Dido's aria 'When I am laid' from the opera *Dido and Aeneas* by Henry Purcell.

De Bondt is almost painfully aware of music history and he notes that the concept of musical unity has been lost, mainly owing to the abandonment of the

hierarchical guiding principle of tonality. According to him, Mozart and
Haydn possessed 'musical ears', composing their music in relation to real
time, improvising as it were on the principles of tonality. Beethoven was the
first to turn away from 'real time' composition. His central musical message
lies in the synthetic developmental form, the dramatic, causal narrative of the
composition. In order to compose this way, he had to set time still; the piece is
constructed outside of its time scale. Since then the relationship between the
duration of the compositional process and that of the composition itself has
been distorted. A composer may work for months to construct a mere few
minutes' worth of music. Since Beethoven, De Bondt believes, the 'western
composer's ear has been broken'. In this context, the quotation of the funeral
march is significant. This march symbolizes for De Bondt the burial of tonality as *the* guiding principle.

The next historical step, he believes, was made by Stravinsky, who with his
neo-classical principles of composition does not tell his own tale but alludes to
other music that has become alienated from its sources. Schoenberg dealt the
final blow to the already seriously ailing tonality, and his twelve-tone technique marks the beginning of an absolute self-reliance on musical parameters
that reached a peak in the work of the serialists in the 1950s. What fascinates
De Bondt is the tension that arose when Schoenberg sought to fuse his new
tonal order with existing forms based on tonality.

The four-part cycle *Het gebroken oor* is the musical result of this personal interpretation of music history. The basic material of *Het gebroken oor* (part I,
1984), for thirteen instruments, is a quotation from Schoenberg's *Kammer-
symphonie*, op.9. The second part, *De deuren gesloten*, based on the *Dido and Aeneas* aria and the funeral march, assigns a special role to the Aries melody
from *Tierkreis* by Karlheinz Stockhausen. This melody is ingeniously linked to
the famous song 'As time goes by' from the film *Casablanca*.

The basic structure of the third part, *La Fine d'una Lunga Giornata* (1987),
for large ensemble, consists of eighteen chords from a fugue by Bach. De
Bondt creates an abstraction of the harmonic, melodic and rhythmic aspects
of this material in various pulse layers that can be superimposed upon each
other, as in *Bint*. Using computers and self-designed software, he creates a
composition from this material. He had used this software previously in
Karkas [Carcass] (1983), for large ensemble. In the fourth part of *Het gebroken
oor*, *Grand Hotel* (1985-1988), for piano solo, De Bondt looks not so much at
the method of composition as musical performance itself.

The *Het gebroken oor* cycle gives rise to associations with post-modern aesthetics, but it goes much further in that the composer attempts to create a
hierarchic layering of musical parameters without falling back on those characteristic of tonal composition. De Bondt attempts to create a coherent musical dimension by unraveling existing music down to its basic pulse and then
reconstructing it into a new composition with the aid of mathematical and
digital resources.

In 1992 De Bondt developed an electronic system that could hold live-per-
formed intervals for any desired length with the aid of various digital reverberation processors (Lexicon PCM 70) operated by pedals. *De namen der Goden*
[The Names of the Gods] (1993), for two pianos and electronics, closes with a
'chorale'. It is a canon on the *Dies Irae* melody, sounded in low, prolonged
tones in the pianos.

In *De tragische handeling* [Actus Tragicus] (1993), for five musicians and
electronics, De Bondt turns his attention, as he did in *Bint*, to the structural
principles of a 'ritual act'. Here he uses digital reverberation processors, doing
so again in *Dame Blanche* (1995). Although the sound world of *De namen der
Goden* and *De tragische handeling*, differs from that of previous works, in part
because of the use of electronic instruments, the dialogue (though here perhaps broken out into a battle) with music history is still present. However unflagging De Bondt's attempts are to free himself from history's shackles, he
comes time and again to the inevitable conclusion that it is impossible to definitively disregard the past.

MICHAEL VAN EEKEREN

COMPOSITIONS

VOCAL: *Harlekijn* (Van Ostaijen), T, Bar, B, instr.ens (1978); *Guillotine : een politieke cantate* (Lumumba, Luxemburg, Allende, Munzer, Saint Just) (with H. de Vriend and J. Rispens), m.choir, large ens (1978-1981); *Dipl'ereoo* (Empedocles), mix.choir, instr.ens (1990)

MUSIC THEATRE: *Gefrorne Fall, für Dick. Ein kleines holländisches Winterdrama*, Mez, pf, electr. (1992); *Beethoven is doof*, actor, mime player, electr. (1993), *Ivegenea* (1998)

CHAMBER MUSIC: *Wind Quintet* (1975); *Klein strijkkwartet* (1976); *Bint*, small ens (1979-1980); *Grand Hotel (Het gebroken oor*, part IV*)*, pf (1985-1988); *De namen der Goden*, 2 pf, electr. (1992-1993); *De tragische handeling*, small ens, electr. (1993)

ORCHESTRA, LARGE ENSEMBLE: *Kompositie voor blazers en strijkers* (1976); *Konsert*, bn, wind orch (1977); *Karkas*, large ens (1981-1983); *Het gebroken oor* (part I), 13 instr. (1983-1984); *De deuren gesloten (Het gebroken oor*, part II*)*, large ens (1984-1985); *La Fine d'una Lunga Giornata (Het gebroken oor*, part III*)*, large ens (1987); *Dame Blanche*, rec, chamb.orch, electr. (1995); *Singing the Faint Farewell*, large ens (1996)

PUBLICATIONS

C. de Bondt and P. Termos: 'Kind regards : a musical correspondence', *Key Notes*, 23, 1986 'Beethoven is Doof', *Programmaboek 'Confrontaties IV'*, 3-8 Nov. 1993 in Rotterdam

BIBLIOGRAPHY

R. de Beer: 'The awesome symphony orchestra : Kaalslag – presenting four premières in the Holland Festival', *Key Notes*, 21, 1985/1, p. 26-32

R. de Beer: 'Vier gesprekken : Cornelis de Bondt', *Programmaboekje Kaalslag (Musica '85)*, p. 30-40

H. Bosma: 'Composers and computers in The Netherlands', *Key Notes*, 25, 1988/1989, p. 51- 52

P. Luttikhuis: 'De mathematische blokken van componist De Bondt', *NRC Handelsblad*, 8 Dec. 1990

P. Luttikhuis: 'De koele passie of de voltrekking van het mechanisch ritueel', *Programmaboek Confrontaties IV*, 3-8 Nov. 1993 in Rotterdam

E. Schönberger: 'Bint van De Bondt : tien jaar na de dood van Stravinsky', *Vrij Nederland*, 25 April 1981

F. van der Waa: 'Zin in dat tevreden gevoel', *de Volkskrant*, 15 Feb. 1991 (interview with C. de Bondt, G. Janssen, W. Jeths and M. Padding)

L. van der Vliet: 'Operatie Het gebroken oor : de gemanipuleerde tonaliteit van Cornelis de Bondt', *Mens en Melodie*, vol. 53, 1998, p. 212-217

F. van der Waa and E. Wennekes: 'Love, death and the pencil sharpener', *Key Notes*, 30, 1996/3, p. 12-16

DISCOGRAPHY

Bint. Hoketus (Composers' Voice CV 8101)

Canon Perpetuus Perforatus, for music box (VPRO Eigen Wijs EW 9413)

De deuren gesloten. Kaalslag live (Attacca Babel 8738-1 & 8739-2)

Het gebroken oor; De deuren gesloten; La Fine d'una Lunga Giornata; Grand Hotel. Singing the Faint Farewell. Schönberg Ensemble, cond. M. Hamel, Netherlands Wind Ensemble, cond. Th. Fischer, Orkest De Volharding, cond. J. Hempel, Percussion Group The Hague, G. Bouwhuis (pf) (Composers' Voice CV 70/71)

De tragische handeling. Loos (Composers' Voice CV 58)

Henriëtte Bosmans

AMSTERDAM, 6 DECEMBER 1895 – AMSTERDAM, 2 JULY 1952

Henriëtte Hilda Bosmans was born into a very musical family. Her father, Henri Bosmans (1856-1896), was the solo cellist of the Concertgebouw Orchestra of Amsterdam; he died before Henriëtte's first birthday. Her mother, Sara Benedicts (1861-1949), was a piano teacher at the Amsterdam Conservatory for over forty years. Bosmans took piano lessons from her mother and at seventeen was awarded her diploma *cum laude* from the Society for the Advancement of Music.

Early on, Bosmans began performing regularly as a soloist at the Amsterdam Concertgebouw under the baton of such conductors as Willem Mengelberg, Ernest Ansermet and Pierre Monteux. She showed little interest in teaching. When, in 1943, Willem Pijper invited her to teach at the Rotterdam Conservatory, she declined. A free spirit with no desire to tie herself to scheduled lessons, she carefully guarded her independence.

Bosmans' first works were composed for the piano and date from 1914. Around this time she was taking harmony and counterpoint lessons from J.W. Kersbergen, and from 1921 to 1922 she studied instrumentation with Cornelis Dopper. In 1919, together with the violinist Ferdinand Helmann, she gave the first performance of her Sonata for Violin and Piano at the Stedelijk Museum in Amsterdam. Because of her close friendships with the cellists Marix Loevensohn and Frieda Belinfante, she composed extensively for this instrument, producing for example the Sonata for Cello and Piano, two cello concertos, and *Poème* for cello and orchestra.

Seeking a more contemporary idiom, Bosmans studied with Willem Pijper from 1927 to 1930. These were prolific years in which she composed, among other things, a string quartet and a Concertino for Piano and Orchestra. She performed the latter work in 1929 at the seventh festival of the International Society for Contemporary Music in Geneva. In 1932 Bosmans won a Concertgebouw composition prize with her Concert Piece for Flute and Chamber Orchestra.

Together with the violinist Francis Koene, Bosmans gave the Dutch premiere of Alban Berg's *Kammerkonzert für Klavier und Geige mit dreizehn Bläsern*. In 1934 she and Koene announced their engagement and Bosmans composed the Concert Piece for Violin and Orchestra as a gift to her fiancé. Koene fell ill, however, suffering from a brain tumor, and died the following

year, never having performed the
work. Overcome with grief, Bosmans
composed very little until the end of
World War II. Being half-Jewish, she
was barred from giving public performances from 1942, though she
did often perform in private.

After the war Bosmans resumed
composing. Initially she wrote two
songs celebrating the liberation and
subsequently a song with orchestral
accompaniment, *Lead, kindly light,*
which was premiered by the vocalist
Jo Vincent and the Concertgebouw
Orchestra, conducted by Sir Adrian

Boult. Her concert appearances picked up again, and she accompanied,
among others, the English tenor Peter Pears. Bosmans corresponded with
Pears' partner, the composer Benjamin Britten, who sent her a copy of Olive
Schreiner's text *The Artist's Secret,* which she set to music. Her activity in other
musical endeavors also increased. She became a member of the Dutch Music
Publishers Donemus' selection committee and wrote articles on music for various dailies and periodicals. She also had a close bond with the composer
Matthijs Vermeulen: each was enthusiastic about the other's work, and Ver-
meulen's interest was a great stimulant to Bosmans.

In 1948 she formed a duo with the French singer Noémie Perugia. The
friendship she developed with Perugia led to a creative outburst, and Bosmans
composed many songs dedicated to her.

In 1950 Bosmans fell ill; later she was diagnosed as having stomach cancer.
However, this did not prevent her composing *Verzen uit Maria Lécina* [Verses
from Maria Lécina], a ballad based on texts by Werumeus Buning, which was
posthumously performed. In 1951 she was knighted in the Order of Orange-
Nassau. In October of that year she was the soloist in a performance of her
Concertino with the Residentie Orchestra and in April 1952 she gave her last
concert with Perugia. Two months later Bosmans died at the age of 56. An in
memoriam concert of her music was organized by the Holland Festival the
following year.

Although she died relatively young and for ten years of her life composed very
little, Bosmans managed nevertheless to write ten pieces for orchestra, a large
body of chamber music, and forty-four songs.

Her early chamber music, such as the Trio for Piano, Violin and Cello (1921), is Romantic in character and based on Classical formal principles. Under the influence of Pijper, Bosmans' music became more compact and forceful, but remained clearly identifiable as her own. In no way did she imitate Pijper. New elements she introduced to her style at this time were polytonality and polymeter. Of the instrumental chamber music she composed during this period, the String Quartet (1927) occupies a prominent place. The work is composed in an Impressionistic idiom, with oriental themes in the first movement, and lively rhythmic motifs (polymeter) in the third.

The Concertino for Piano and Orchestra (1928) is one of her best known works. The first performance, with Bosmans as the soloist and the Concertgebouw Orchestra conducted by Pierre Monteux, was given on 10 January 1929. The piece, in four short uninterrupted movements, has an arresting opening with alternating 4/8 and 5/8 meters. Even today, the Concertino is highly regarded. Leo Samama wrote of this piece in *Zeventig jaar Nederlandse muziek* [Seventy Years of Dutch Music] (1986): 'This sparkling music has lost nothing of its playful character and power of musical persuasion after more than a half century. Bosmans, contrary to most of her colleagues, demonstrates a finely tuned ear for harmonic color.'

In Bosmans' Concert Piece for Flute and Chamber Orchestra (1929), alternating meter also plays an important role. The work closes with a catchy tango based on an ostinato motif, a favorite technique in Bosmans' arsenal. The Concert Piece for Violin and Orchestra (1934) has a more rhapsodic style.

In 1945 Bosmans composed *Doodenmarsch* [March of the Dead] for reciter and orchestra. This declamatorio, a genre popular in the Netherlands after the war, poignantly decries the war's violence and the ruins left in its wake. The influence of French impressionism, and that of Debussy in particular, is evident in this piece.

Bosmans' songs demonstrate her highly individual imagination and her ability to transform a wide range of poetical moods into music.

HELEN METZELAAR

COMPOSITIONS

SONGS: *Mon rêve familier* (Verlaine) (1921); *Drie liederen op Duitse tekst* (Tu Fu, Li T'ai Po, Bierbaum) (1927); *Die heil'gen drei Könige aus Morgenland* (Heine) (1935); *Im Mondenglanze ruht das Meer* (Heine) (1935); *Le diable dans la nuit* (Fort) (1935); *Dit eiland* (A. Roland Holst) (1947); *Drie brieven* (Werumeus Buning) (1947); *In den regen* (A. Roland Holst) (1947); *The artist's secret* (Schreiner) (1948); *Méditation* (Géraldy) (1948); *Les deux enfants du roi* (Verhaeren) (1949); *Dix mélodies* (1949-1951); *Chanson des escargots qui vont à l'enterrement* (Prévert) (1950); *La comtesse Esmérée* (Moréas) (1950); *Verzen uit Maria Lécina* (Werumeus Buning) (1950); *Pour toi mon amour* (Prévert) (1950); *On frappe* (Prévert)

(1950); *Aurore* (Verdet) (1950); *La chanson du chiffonnier* (Jouy) (1950); *Je ne suis pas seul* (Eluard) (1950); *Rondel* (Ponchon) (1951); *Das macht den Menschen glücklich* (Heine) (1951); *On ne sait rien* (Vacaresco) (1951)

PIANO: *Zes Préludes* (1916-1917); *Fantasie over de wals van Johann Strauss 'Geschichten aus dem Wienerwald'* (1938, manuscript); *Vieille chanson* (included in the collection *Hommage à Willem Pijper*) (1914)

CHAMBER MUSIC: *4 Voordrachtstukken*, vl, pf (1917); *Sonata*, vl, pf (1918, manuscript); *Sonata*, vc, pf (1919); *Trio*, vl, vc, pf (1921); *3 Impressions*, vc, pf (1926); *String Quartet* (1927); Cadenzas to Mozart's violin concertos KV 216 and 219

SOLO INSTRUMENT OR VOICE WITH ORCHESTRA: *Concerto no. 1*, vc, orch (1921); *Concerto no. 2*, vc, orch (1923); *Poème*, vc, orch (1923); *Concertino*, pf, orch (1928); *Concert Piece*, fl, chamb.orch (1929); *Concert Piece*, vl, orch (1934); *Belsazer* (Heine), Mez, orch (1935); *Lead, kindly light* (Newman), h.v, orch (1945, manuscript); *Doodenmarsch* (Eggink), sp.v, orch (1945)

BIBLIOGRAPHY
N. van der Elst: 'Henriëtte Bosmans als liederencomponiste', *Mens en Melodie*, vol. 7, 1952, p. 173-175

E. Looyestijn: 'Henriëtte Bosmans', *Zes vrouwelijke componisten*, ed. H. Metzelaar [et al.]. Hilversum, Centrum Nederlandse Muziek / Zutphen, Walburg Press, 1991

H. Metzelaar: 'Postwar Eggs from Holland : Benjamin Britten and Henriëtte Bosmans', *Muziek & Wetenschap, Dutch Journal for Musicology*, 6, 1997/98, p. 223-237

H. Metzelaar: 'Who sent Benjamin Britten Hundreds of Eggs from Holland? A somewhat one-sided friendship', *Key Notes*, 31, 1997/3, p. 17-21

W. Paap: 'Henriëtte Bosmans', *Mens en Melodie*, vol. 2, 1947, p. 72-76

DISCOGRAPHY
Chanson des escargots qui vont à l'enterrement; Complainte du petit cheval blanc; Les médisants. M. van Egmond (Bar), C. Canne Meijer (Mez), Th. Bollen (pf) (Globe GLO 6018)

Chanson des escargots qui vont à l'enterrement; Een lied voor Spanje. A. Haenen (S), T. Hartsuiker (pf) (CBS LSP 14514)

Concert Piece; Poème; Concertino. J. Zoon (fl), D. Ferschtman (vc), R. Brautigam (pf), Netherlands Radio Chamber Orchestra, cond. J. van Steen and E. Spanjaard (NM Classics 92095)

Concertino. R. Brautigam (pf), Netherlands Radio Chamber Orchestra, cond. E. Spanjaard (NM Classics 92044)

Three Songs on German Texts. N. Raphael-Tours (Mez), A. Gosman (pf) (Attacca Babel 8104)

Songs on French Texts; Ave Maria; Concertino; Concert Piece. N. Perugia (v), H. Bosmans (pf), V. Beths (vl), J. Boogaart (pf), H. Henkemans (pf), Netherlands Radio Philharmonic Orchestra, cond. L. Vis and J. Stulen (Attacca Babel 8314-4 & 8315-5)

Poème. D. Ferschtman (vc), Netherlands Radio Chamber Orchestra, cond. E. Spanjaard (NM Classics 92040)

String Quartet; En Espagne (from: 3 Impressions). Raphael Quartet, J. Decroos (vc), D. Dechenne (pf) (BFO A-1)

Verses from Maria Lécina. R.A. Morgan (Mez), F. van Ruth (pf) (NM Classics 92018)

Henriëtte Bosmans and her circle. Lieder by H.Bosmans, W.Pijper, L. van Delden, B.Frensel Wegener-Koopman. J. Bronkhorst (S), M. Hillenius (pf) (Globe GLO 5183)

The Brandts Buys family

The Brandts Buys family produced at least five successive generations of musicians. Most of them were organists, choral conductors, composers and teachers, but they also numbered two operatic composers and two musicologists.

LUDWIG FELIX (WILLEM CORNELIS) BRANDTS BUYS
Deventer, 20 November 1847 – Velp, 29 June 1917

Ludwig Felix Brandts Buys was the first of the family to be named after composers, in his case Beethoven and Mendelssohn Bartholdy, both idols of his father. He also owed his musical education to his father, who taught him singing, the piano, the organ and music theory. He received violin lessons from the Deventer violinist Frans Stroober. From an early age Ludwig Felix made public appearances, performing as a violinist at the church concerts of his brother Marius in the 1860s and 1870s. Apart from arrangements of popular arias and orchestral pieces, he also introduced original works from the Baroque era; as early as 1868 he performed a sonata and a concert by G. Tartini, the basso continuo part of which he had written out himself. He composed his first original piece in 1865: *Heidenröslein* for mixed choir. To earn a living he gave piano lessons in Deventer and Zutphen and played the violin in his father's orchestra.

Between 1868 and 1874 Ludwig lived with his brother Marius, for whom he occasionally filled in as organist/carillonneur in Zutphen. In 1873, Marius founded a Toonkunst choir in Zutphen, the local chapter of the Society for the Advancement of Music. But since illness prevented him from leading it, Ludwig became its first conductor. In 1874 he left for Rotterdam to become organist of the Walloon Church. But it was as conductor of the local Rotte's Male Choir, a post he held between 1874 and 1891, that Ludwig became a figure of national renown. He wrote many works for this choir, not only to German and Dutch lyrics, but also to a Latin psalm text (op.24). In his early years in Rotterdam he also became conductor of Euphonia, a mixed choir. In addition, he led the Toonkunst choir in Schiedam from 1877 to 1899. Because of his broad choral experience, Ludwig Brandts Buys was often invited as a member of juries of competitions in the latter years of his life. He composed special works

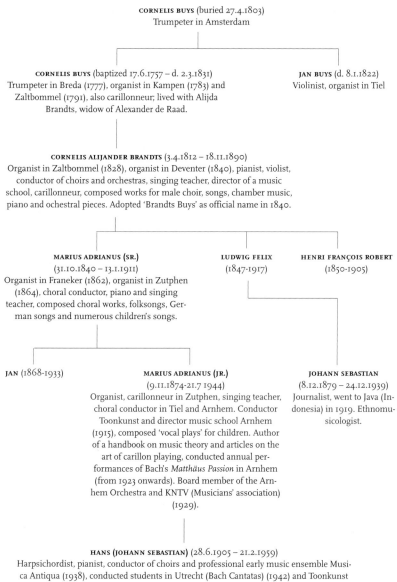

CORNELIS BUYS (buried 27.4.1803)
Trumpeter in Amsterdam

CORNELIS BUYS (baptized 17.6.1757 – d. 2.3.1831)
Trumpeter in Breda (1777), organist in Kampen (1783) and
Zaltbommel (1791), also carillonneur; lived with Alijda
Brandts, widow of Alexander de Raad.

JAN BUYS (d. 8.1.1822)
Violinist, organist in Tiel

CORNELIS ALIJANDER BRANDTS (3.4.1812 – 18.11.1890)
Organist in Zaltbommel (1828), organist in Deventer (1840), pianist, violist,
conductor of choirs and orchestras, singing teacher, director of a music
school, carillonneur, composed works for male choir, songs, chamber music,
piano and ochestral pieces. Adopted 'Brandts Buys' as official name in 1840.

MARIUS ADRIANUS (SR.)
(31.10.1840 – 13.1.1911)
Organist in Franeker (1862), organist in Zutphen
(1864), choral conductor, piano and singing
teacher, composed choral works, folksongs, German songs and numerous children's songs.

LUDWIG FELIX
(1847-1917)

HENRI FRANÇOIS ROBERT
(1850-1905)

JAN (1868-1933)

MARIUS ADRIANUS (JR.)
(9.11.1874-21.7 1944)
Organist, carillonneur in Zutphen, singing teacher,
choral conductor in Tiel and Arnhem. Conductor
Toonkunst and director music school Arnhem
(1915), composed 'vocal plays' for children. Author
of a handbook on music theory and articles on the
art of carillon playing, conducted annual performances of Bach's Matthäus Passion in Arnhem
(from 1923 onwards). Board member of the Arnhem Orchestra and KNTV (Musicians' association)
(1929).

JOHANN SEBASTIAN
(8.12.1879 – 24.12.1939)
Journalist, went to Java (Indonesia) in 1919. Ethnomu-
sicologist.

HANS (JOHANN SEBASTIAN) (28.6.1905 – 21.2.1959)
Harpsichordist, pianist, conductor of choirs and professional early music ensemble Musi-
ca Antiqua (1938), conducted students in Utrecht (Bach Cantatas) (1942) and Toonkunst
Arnhem, the local chapter of the Society for the Advancement of Music (1945). Director
Hilversum Conservatory (1951), composer of choral works, film music (first Dutch 'talkie'
Terra Nova, 1931), music for radio plays, publications about Bach's Wohltemperirtes Clavier
(1942), Bach (1950) and the Passions (1950). Research on works by P. Hellendaal (edition
of concerti grossi op.3, 1959); prepared editions of works by C.Ph.E. and W.F. Bach,
D. Buxtehude, S. van Noordt and R. Popma van Oevering

for these choral competitions, including psalms for male choir.

Ludwig was also a teacher of merit. In 1883 he was appointed singing teacher at the Rotterdam Toonkunst Music School and in 1897 he became organ teacher there as well. In addition, he gave private tuition in singing, the piano and theory. In 1907 he moved to Velp, and returned to conducting Toonkunst Zutphen between 1909 and 1912.

Ludwig Felix mainly wrote small-scale vocal works, mostly with piano accompaniment only. He started with German songs, but from 1870 onwards confined himself to the Dutch language. His national, march-like folksongs, in the style of J.J. Viotta and his father, earned him his early successes, such as *Sta pal mijn dierbaar vaderland* [Stand firm my beloved fatherland] op.4 (1870), which refers to the Franco-Prussian war. In the collection *Zingzang* [Singsong], with folksong melodies by himself and his brother Marius, which was published in 1870, Ludwig's contributions are diverse: he proved his aptitude not only for the traditional, this time Flemish-nationalist marching song, but also for the 'Lied' in the style of Mendelssohn, and the children's song such as Catharina van Rennes was to take up later. The much-reprinted *Mijne moedertaal* [My mother tongue] op.13 (1874), to a text by Frans de Cort, is a mixture of patriotic pride and subtle lyricism. His affinity with Schumann comes to the fore in, for example, the women's choir op.14 (1871) and op.20 no.1, a short piano piece inspired by *Kinderszenen*. In the years 1874-1875 Ludwig Brandts Buys devoted himself entirely to writing children's songs.

Genuine, fully fledged art-songs can be found in the collection *Sieben Lieder* op.21 (1876-1877). Written in a traditional, mainstream German style, they display a lyrical expressiveness quite uncommon in the works of Dutch composers at that time. Occasionally he uses a polyphonic phrase. Lyricism, a traditional, sometimes slightly chromatic style of harmony and carefully handled polyphony characterize many of his works for male choir, in particular the unaccompanied psalms, of which *Deus nostra spes* (1879) is the first.

HENRI FRANÇOIS ROBERT BRANDTS BUYS
Deventer, 20 April 1850 – Ede, 16 October 1905

Henri François Robert Brandts Buys studied the piano with his father Cornelis Alijander. Having worked for some years as a choral accompanist in Deventer and Zutphen, he became a conductor. During the season of 1868-69 he deputized for his father as conductor of the mixed Toonkunst choir Swelingh. A royal grant then enabled him to go to Cologne to further develop his skills as a pianist and composer. In 1876 he became the conductor of a mixed choir in

Lochem and the Deventer Male Choir which he expanded to include a mixed choir in 1877. He held the position until 1880. Meanwhile he spent another season (1877-1878) conducting Toonkunst Zutphen. He also directed Erato, a mixed choir in Nijmegen.

In 1878 Henri was appointed conductor of the Amstel Male Choir in Amsterdam, where he remained until 1885. In the meantime he was also the conductor of Oefening Baart Kunst [Practice makes perfect] and Musis Sacrum, both in Amsterdam as well. He conducted several major concerts such as the aubade to celebrate William III's seventieth birthday in 1887, when 5000 primary schoolchildren sang 'national' songs written by members of the Brandts Buys family: *De Nederlandsche Vlag* [The Dutch flag] op.8 by Ludwig Felix, *'t Is plicht dat iedre jongen* ['Tis each boy's duty ...] by Cornelis Alijander and Henri's own *Jubelgroet* [Joyous greeting]. In his final years his failing health prompted him to move to Ede.

Henri, too, wrote songs and choral music for male choir in the style of his family, but more important is the 'concertdrama' *Albrecht Beiling* from 1881. He shared Ludwig's appreciation of Wagner's innovations, but, unlike his brother, he actually adopted them in his compositions. This goes in particular for the modulatory-chromatic chord progressions in the orchestral writing, but less so for his treatment of the voices, which involve many text repetitions. Henri later turned the work into a genuine opera, which was performed in 1891 in the Amsterdam Park Theater.

JAN (WILLEM FRANS) BRANDTS BUYS
Zutphen, 12 September 1868 – Salzburg, 7 December 1933

Jan Brandts Buys received organ and piano lessons from his father, Marius Adrianus Sr. His uncle Ludwig Felix, who until 1874 lived with the family, probably had a hand in his musical education as well. Whatever the case may have been, Jan began to compose when he was six years old. As there was a lot of music-making in the home, he became acquainted not only with piano music but with the chamber music repertoire as well. Of the major composers, Beethoven and Mendelssohn, but also Grieg, were his favorites. He gave public performances as a pianist and organist from 1882 onwards, publishing his first composition in 1883: *Sechs Lyrische Stückchen und Variationen*, which he dedicated to his grandfather Cornelis Alijander.

From 1884 until 1889 Jan Brandts Buys was organist of the Broederen Church in Zutphen, the only official post he was to hold during his entire life. Irresistibly drawn to music, he had given up his grammar school education.

From left to right: Marius Adrianus Sr., Ludwig Felix, Henri François Robert and Cornelis Alijander

In 1889 he left for Frankfurt where, at the Raff Conservatory, he studied the piano with Max Schwarz, a pupil of Liszt and Von Bülow, and theory and composition with Anton Urspruch, another pupil of Liszt. Jan's fondness for both Slavic music and the music of Brahms presumably stemmed from this time, as Frankfurt had a rich musical life to offer. In Frankfurt he published his first German songs and a piano trio, and he started numbering his works anew.

Back in Zutphen, he enjoyed success with the performances of his works. In early 1892 he performed his *Konzertstück* for piano and orchestra op.3 with the Concertgebouw Orchestra. Shortly afterwards he went to Vienna to report on the International Exhibition for Music and Theater as correspondent of daily newspaper *Het Vaderland*. He stayed there, intending to compose. Some difficult years ensued. He earned his living as a corrector for various music publishers. In 1899 his Concerto op.15 won second prize at the Bösendorfer Competition for piano concertos, leading to a performance by the Vienna Philharmonic. From 1901 he worked for the newly founded publishing house Universal Edition, preparing piano reductions of many collections of Classical and early-Romantic orchestral and operatic works. One year later he began to work for publisher Doblinger, preparing piano editions of chamber music works of Ernö Dohnányi. These activities prompted Brandts Buys to compose several chamber music works, which Rudoph Fitzner and his string quartet performed soon afterwards. In 1907 the Wiener Konzertverein gave the first performance of the overture of his opera *Das Veilchenfest* and commended him for his *Illyrische Ballade* op.24.

The opera itself was premiered in Berlin's Komische Oper in 1909, but it was unsuccessful. In 1910 the composer travelled to Siffian, Tirol, in the hope of drawing inspiration from nature. Here he worked on a new opera which was performed in Dresden in 1913. In the same year Brandts Buys signed a contract with the Viennese publisher Josef Weinberger, who was to publish several of his compositions. He could now make a living as a composer and returned to Vienna in 1914. In 1916 his opera *Die Schneider von Schönau* became a resounding success. Until World War II this opera was to be performed in seventy European theaters. However, Viennese audiences did not like the work; they regarded Jan Brandts Buys as no more than a genial though consummate craftsman. In 1817 he dismissed his only pupil, Alois Hába, who was interested in modern music, after a few composition lessons. By the end of the war, his longing for nature returned and in 1920 he moved to Loznica, near Dubrovnik.

He found no peace there, however, as he had to travel long distances to attend rehearsals of his operas. His inspiration began to wane. He found a new place to live, this time in Central Europe, settling in Salzburg in 1928. There Bernard Paumgartner performed some of his new orchestral pieces. But his last two operas were not to be performed during his lifetime. He died in 1933, suffering from cancer of the bladder.

Beethoven, Brahms, Grieg and, to a lesser extent, Borodin and Dvořák, remained his examples throughout his life. Occasionally his music is reminiscent of Fauré (*Glockenspiel*, Suite op.43) or even Ravel (String Quartet op.28). On the whole, Brandts Buys expressed himself negatively about the music of his contemporaries. On the other hand, dance as well as non-authentic, Romantic versions of old Scandinavian, Dutch and eastern European folk songs inspired him. He sometimes translated his love of nature into a personal style: a mixture of clarity and exoticism within simple, small forms. Almost all of his operas are set in a remote, idealized German past or a dreamworld. In these works, the small forms are connected by reminiscence themes or key relationships.

Jan Brandts Buys integrated folk songs into his work to make it more accessible; his aim was to write music 'which will make serious musicians snigger, and which "ordinary people" will enjoy' (letter from 1933 to critic and composer Joseph Marx). In that sense the opera *Die Schneider von Schönau* is a good example of his writing and a successful work too. Although Jan Brandts Buys concentrated on opera, he was no dramatist. Most of his operas fall within the genre of comical 'Spieloper' and are lyrical works. In that respect he is related to contemporaries such as Julius Bittner and Leo Blech. Songs are of major importance within his oeuvre. While several of his early compositions were still related to the march-like Dutch folksong, most of his songs belong to the tradition of the Romantic song, although the melodic line is short. The piano usually serves merely as an accompaniment; only in the songs with strings and with solo flute (op.20) is there any depiction of atmosphere.

Brandts Buys is most progressive in his chamber music, particularly the string quartets. These works contain instances of modality (*Weihnachtsquintett* from 1903), blurred tonality (op.25 from 1908) and dissonant harmonic turns (op.28 from 1912). Major sevenths and related dissonants create the atmosphere of his serious opera *Der Eroberer* (1917). Fourth chords occur in his Violin Sonata (op.26 from 1909) and in *Die Schneider*.

Jan Brandts Buys' most inspired works were created between 1907 and 1915. Subsequent to 1920 the simple triad is predominant and during this period his music became increasingly static. The large number of operas as well as the instrumental concert repertoire making up his oeuvre set him apart from the other members of his family.

JAN TEN BOKUM

LUDWIG FELIX BRANDTS BUYS

COMPOSITIONS

SONGS (WITH PIANO UNLESS OTHERWISE STATED): *An die Natur*, op. 1 (1869); *In 't zonnige hoveken*, op. 3; *Sta pal* (Heije), op. 4; *Petrus Klage* (Tiedge), with orch, op. 5; *Zingzang* (five songs by Ludwig Felix, seven by Marius Adrianus), op. 7; *De Nederlandsche vlag* (Werndlij), op. 8; *Two Songs*, op. 9; *Two Songs* (Heije), op. 10; *Het klooster* (De Cort), op. 11; *Mijne Moedertaal* (De Cort), op. 13 (1874); *Kinderleven* (Goeverneur), op. 15; *Eroticon*, op. 16 (1874); *Two Songs*, op. 17 (1875); *Sechs Lieder*, op. 19; *Sieben Lieder*, op. 21 (1876-1877); *Six Songs*, op. 22; *Four Songs*, op. 27 (1885); *Four Songs*, op. 28 (incl. op. 22, no. 5 and 6); *Four Songs*, op. 29; *Transvaal en Nederland*, op. 31a; *Four Songs*, op. 33; *Gethsemane*, with orch, op. 34 (1899-1901); *Danklied*, op. 36; *Two Songs*, op. 38; *Three Songs*, op. 42; *Muizeke* (Antheunis), op. 44; *Koekoek 't is in de mei* (Assche), op. 48 no. 1; *Six Songs* (1866-1870); *Song*, with str.orch (1868); *Wiegenliedchen*, with vl and pf (1868); *Nine songs from 1875 to 1901*

CHOIR: *Three Songs*, w.choir, op. 6; *De vier jaargetijden*, m.choir, op. 12; *Uit duister tot licht*, w.choir, orch, op. 14 (1871-1874); *Het woud*, v, mix.choir, op. 18 (1875); *Das Singenthal*, v, mix.choir, orch, op. 23 (1878); *Deus nostra spes*, m.choir, op. 24 (1879); *Welkomstgroet*, m.choir, op. 25 (1879);

Hulde aan het onderwijs, v, m.choir, ch.choir, orch, op. 26; *Deus est nostra lux*, m.choir, op. 30; *Pro jure et libertate*, m.choir, op. 32; *'n Stem in Rama*, mix.choir, op. 35; *In 't woud*, m.choir, op. 37; *Super flumina Babylonis*, m.choir, op. 39; *Drie koren*, m.choir, op. 40; *Twee koren*, mix.choir/m.choir, op. 41; *Droeve tijden*, m.choir, op. 43 (1907); *Zegepraal*, m.choir, op. 45; *Het schrijverke*, mix.choir, op. 46 (1910); *De ruïne*, m.choir, op. 47 (1910); *Avondrood*, m.choir, op. 49; *Brautgesang*, w.choir; *Ahasverus*, soloists, mix.choir, orch (1873); *De Nederlanden*, m.choir (1875); *Nederland en de zee*, mix.choir (1880); *Ave Maria*, mix.choir (1898); Cantata *Waterloo*, m.choir (1890); *Gloire à toi*, m.choir (1890); *2 cantiques*, mix.choir (1875); 14 pieces for mixed choir (1865, 1874, 1875 (2x), 1881, 1885, 1903, 1904, 1912, 1916); 15 pieces for male choir (1872, 1874, 1875, 1877, 1878 (2x), 1879 (2x), 1882, 1904 (3x))

INSTRUMENTAL: *Kindes Freud' und Leid*, pf, op. 2; *Six Piano Pieces*, op. 20; *Albumblad*, pf; 8 short piano pieces (1866, 1867, 1868 (3x), 1881, 1890 (2x)); *Orgelvariaties en sonate* (1870); *Wien Neêrlands bloed*, str.orch (1895); Arrangements for small orchestra of compositions by Tartini and Martini

DISCOGRAPHY

Sag' ich liess sie grüssen; Wenn dermaleinst des Paradieses Pforten; Ich will meine Seele tauchen (from *Sieben Lieder*, op. 21). H. Meens (T), M. van Nieukerken (pf) (BFO A-1)

HENRI FRANÇOIS ROBERT BRANDTS BUYS

COMPOSITIONS

SONGS (WITH PIANO): *Levenslied*, op. 1; *Lieder für dich : 3 Gedichte* (Warkotsch), op. 2; *Six Songs*, op. 3; *Ik zing het lied der jeugd* (Coopman), op. 12 no. 1; *Winterabend* (Heine); *Jubelgroet*

CHOIR: *Een stem aan het strand*, m.choir, orch, op. 5; *Zomeravond*, m.choir, op. 7; *Albrecht Beiling : concertdrama*, soloists, choir, orch, op. 8 (1881); *Serenade*, choir (1879); *Lentekoningin*, soloists, choir, orch; *Cantata*, m.choir, concert band; *Kies mij*, m.choir; *'s Menschen bestemming*, m.choir; *Alaert Beiling : opera*, soloists, choir, orch

INSTRUMENTAL: *Ballträumereien*, vl, pf, op. 4; *Intermezzo*, str.orch (1889); *Romance*, vc, pf; *Scherzo*, pf; Various overtures

JAN WILLEM FRANS BRANDTS BUYS

COMPOSITIONS

SONGS (WITH PIANO UNLESS OTHERWISE STATED): *Sechs Lieder*, op. 2 (1890); *Sechs Lieder*, op. 18; *Drei Lieder*, with fl and pf, op. 20 (1900-1905); *Vier Lieder* (Welleminsky), op. 22; *Sechs Lieder* (Eichendorff), op. 30; *Drei Lieder*, with str.qt, op. 33 (1912); *Sechs Hafislieder*, op. 38 (1913); *Vier Basslieder*, op. 42; *Wanderer*, op. 47 (1927); *Bergpsalmen*, with orch op. 52; *Drei Lieder*, with str.qt, op. 54 (1932); *Three Songs* (1885-1888); *Six Songs*; *Ten hemelweg*; *Twee Franse liederen* (1889); *Three Songs* (1889-1890); *Two Songs* (1891); *Vier nachtliedjes* (Van Eeden) (1891); *Ten Songs* (1894-1904); *Der Abend kommt*; *Seufzerlein*; *Sieben Gedichte* (Zimmermann); *Frühzeitlicher Frühling* (Goethe), with str (1930)

CHOIR: *Ons Hollandsch lied*, op. 2; *Die Liebe*, v, choir, orch, op. 6 (1893); *Zwei Frauenchöre* (1927); *Chor der Toten*, op. 45 (1929); *Dem aufgehenden Mond*, op. 53 (1930); 5 choral pieces from 1885 to 1891

DRAMATIC VOCAL: [Spanish fragment] (1st act fin.) (1898); *Das Veilchenfest* (Heindl) (1905); *Glockenspiel* (Warden, Welleminsky) (1912); *Die Schneider von Schönau* (Warden, Welleminsky) (1914-1915); *Der Eroberer* (Warden, Welleminsky) (1917); *Der Mann im Mond* (Warden, Welleminsky) (1918); *Micarême* (Warden, Welleminsky) (1919); *Traumland* (J. Brandts Buys) (1927); *Hero und Leander* (Grillparzer) (1929); *Ulysses* (Solander) (1932); *Schluck und Jau* (Hauptmann)

PIANO: *Sechs lyrische Stückchen und Variationen*, op. 1; *Aus dem Lande Rembrandt's*, op. 5; *Drei Klavierstücke*, op. 9 (1893); *Fünf Characterstücke*, op. 11; *Moderne Studien*, opp. 13 and 14; *Tänze und Weisen*, op. 17; *Drei Klavierstücke*, op. 29; *Ave Samobor*, op. 37 (1913); *Sonata in b*; *Variationen über ein volksthümliches Thema* (1890); *Vier kleine stukken* (1885-1890); *Capriccio fugato* (1913); Three pieces (including *Liebliche Grazie*) (1912-1921)

ORGAN: *Orgel en Harmonium (with nine original pieces)*, op. 3; *Nieuw leven*, op. 4 (1888); *Hochzeitsmarsch*, op. 34 (1912); *Patria*, op. 36 (1912); *Onze koraalboeken*; *Toccata en fuga* (1891); *Choral* (1915)

CHAMBER MUSIC: *Piano Trio*, op. 1 (1890); *String Quartet*, op. 19 (1906); *Suite im alten Stil*, str.qt, op. 23 (1908); *Romantische Serenade*, str.qt, op. 25 (1908); *Sizilianische Serenade*, str.qt, op. 28 (1912); *Sextet*, 3 vl, 2 vla, vc, op. 40 (1913); *Suite*, vl, pf, op. 43 (1924); *String Quartet*, op. 49 (1928); *Herfstzang*, vla, pf (1889); *String Quartet* (1892); *Lied*, str.qt (1893); *Drei Variationen* (1915); *Quintet*, fl, str.qt (1903); *Sonata*, vl, pf (1909); *Quintet*, pf, str.qt (1913)

ORCHESTRA: *Konzertstück*, pf, orch, op. 3 (1890); *Des Meeressang*, op. 4 (1892); *Ode*, hp, hn, str.orch, op. 7 (1897); *Violin Concerto*, op.10; *Carnavalsouverture*, op. 12 (1896); *Piano Concerto*, op. 15 (1898); *Kaiserouvertüre*, op. 16 (1899); *Illyrische Ballade*, op. 24 (1907); *Oberon : romance*, vc, orch, op. 27 (1909); *Tancred*, vc, orch, op. 35 (1912); *Totenopfer*, op. 46 (1924-1928); *Festliche Musik*, op. 48 (1930); *Poetischer*

Spaziergang, op. 50 (1930); *Salzburger Serenade, op. 51* (1930); *Aus der spanischen Reitschule, op. 55; Diptychon, op. 57* (1930); *Serenade, op. 58* (1925); *Piano Concerto* (fragment) (1889); *Bilder aus dem Kinderleben* (1922); Final composition for orchestra (1933)

ARRANGEMENTS for piano and piano 4h of compositions by Beethoven, Dohnányi, Goldmark, Handel, Mendelssohn, Mozart, Schubert, Schumann and Weber; Collections of overtures with compositions by Adam, Auber, Balfs, Beethoven, Bellini, Boïeldieu, Cherubini, Donizetti, Gluck, Hérold, Kreutzer, Lortzing, Mendelssohn, Marschner, Meyerbeer, Mozart, Nicolai, Reissiger, Rossini, Schubert, Schumann, Spohr, Wallace, and Weber

BIBLIOGRAPHY
G. Verhey and G. Schlimme van Brunswijk: *Jan Brandts Buys, een Zutphens laatromanticus in het internationale muziekleven.* Zutphen, Van Someren & Ten Bosch, 1980

DISCOGRAPHY
Drei Klavierstücke, op. 29. J. de Bie (Schwann CD 310077 H1)
Sizilianische Serenade, op. 28. Raphael Quartet (BFO A-1)
Tänze und Weisen (sel.). F. van Ruth (pf) (Vara Gram VCD 477181-2)

Johannes Bernardus van Bree

AMSTERDAM, 29 JANUARY 1801 – AMSTERDAM, 14 FEBRUARY 1857

In his youth, Jo(h)annes Bernardus van Bree received violin lessons from his father Frans. It also seems that he studied music theory with Georg Bertelman for a short time. In about 1812 his family moved to Leeuwarden, where Van Bree tuned pianos and assisted his father in accompanying dance lessons. His violin playing was by then so advanced that he came to the attention of Baron C.E. Collot d'Escury, who around 1815 appointed him music teacher of his children at his home at Minnertsga near Sexbierum. During this period Van Bree also gave several performances in Leeuwarden as a violin soloist. He remained with the baron for four years but returned in 1820 to Amsterdam to become a violinist in the orchestra of the French Theater. In Amsterdam he continued to pursue a career as a violin soloist but most of his time was spent in giving violin and piano lessons.

In 1828 he turned to conducting, first with a mixed choral society. In 1829 he also conducted the symphonic portions of the concerts of the Felix Meritis Society and, after the departure of Antoine Fodor in 1830, he conducted the entire repertoire of the Felix Meritis Orchestra, which made him a leading figure in the musical life of the capital. Despite initial resistance from some of the amateurs who performed with the orchestra and the fact that few rehearsals were held, he was able to forge it into one of the best ensembles in the Netherlands. The orchestra gave twenty concerts per year, their programming consisting largely of accompaniments to virtuosic solo works. Van Bree also conducted various entertainment orchestras as well as choral societies of the French, Krijtberg and Mozes and Aäron Churches.

Van Bree gradually gained fame as a composer; he was required to write a new orchestral piece for the Felix Meritis Orchestra each year. In 1832 he received an honorable mention from the Society for the Advancement of Music for his Mass in A-flat for soloist, mixed choir and orchestra. Several of his war-songs, occasioned by the Belgian Rebellion, also met with success and captured him the title of National Composer. Van Bree was also active as a composer and conductor of opera: in 1834 his *Saffo* was given no less than fifteen performances within a single month. In 1835 he conducted Rossini's *Guillaume Tell* and his own *Le Bandit* at the French Theater in Amsterdam.

When in 1836 the Society for the Advancement of Music planned a big music festival, Van Bree was asked to conduct it. He was also appointed con-

ductor of the Amsterdam Toonkunst choir, the local chapter of the Society for the Advancement of Music. In the 1840s he conducted various music festivals put on by the Society. His repertoire included not only the oratorios of Handel and Schumann but also (in 1850 and 1851) earlier music such as sixteenth- and seventeenth-century motets and madrigals, as well as *Jesu, meine Freude* by Bach.

In 1840 Van Bree was appointed conductor of the orchestra of Amsterdam's City Theater but was forced to resign after one season when the National Opera was closed. In 1841 he co-founded the Caecilia Society, whose orchestra consisted entirely of professional musicians. This made it possible to rehearse more frequently, and thus attain a higher level of musicianship than with the Felix Meritis Orchestra. With this new orchestra, which eventually grew to some seventy musicians, he was required to give just two concerts per year. Thus he could concentrate on the works of Beethoven, Mendelssohn, Mozart and Weber, music that was not frequently performed at that time. The string quartet Van Bree founded in 1844, in which he played first violin, was also an accomplished ensemble. Here, too, Van Bree pioneered the music of Beethoven in the Netherlands. Particularly in the 1840s he conducted the choir of the Mozes and Aäron Church in performances of Haydn masses. In 1853 he conducted a performance of Beethoven's *Missa Solemnis.*

Towards the end of his life much of Van Bree's time was taken up with his administrative and teaching posts, although he also continued his work with orchestras and choirs. In 1847 he joined the board of directors of the Society for the Advancement of Music and in 1849 he was appointed its chairman. From 1853 to 1856 he was director of the Society's Music School, where he also gave lessons in music theory, violin, piano and singing.

Together with Johann Wilhelm Wilms, Van Bree was one of the most important musicians in the first half of the nineteenth century in the Netherlands, although both confined their activities to Amsterdam.

Van Bree composed some 200 pieces in every genre except the oratorio. As a conductor he attempted to counter as much as possible the light French cavatinas, romances and galops and virtuoso variations on well-known operatic themes that were so popular with the public, though in his own compositions he often employed similar styles. This holds particularly for his cantatas and festival overtures. Only in the string quartets, symphonic movements, masses and several piano pieces did he turn to the German-Austrian Classical-Romantic style. His works are melodically innovative but strictly homophonic and show little motivic development. With his predilection for modulations, Van Bree adhered to the then modern chromaticism such as is found in the works of the German violinist-composer Louis Spohr, whose music Van Bree frequently performed.

The *Allegro für vier Streich-Quartette*, composed by Van Bree in 1845 for the thirty strings of the Caecilia Orchestra, and first performed by them, is highly reminiscent of Spohr's double quartets. The allegro does reveal some motivic development, but the four quartets never engage in any polyphonic complexity. The influence of Mendelssohn is strongly felt in his other quartets. Van Bree's *Trois nocturnes* for piano reveal the influence of Field and Schubert, who at that time were scarcely known in the Netherlands. He tried to accommodate a variety of tastes.

Van Bree's opéra comique *Le Bandit* makes use of dramatic effects and motivic allusions, procedures he was able to acquaint himself with through the frequent performances of new works given by the German and French Theaters. In all of his works for theater (so-called 'zangspelen') spoken dialogue plays an important role.

JAN TEN BOKUM

COMPOSITIONS

SONGS: *Zes Liederen voor Noord Nederlandsche schutterijen; Adolf aan het graf van Maria* (Foppe); *Romance* (Vautrel); *Denk aan Van Speijk; Aan mijn kunst- en menschenminnend vaderland* (Foppe); *Two Songs; Koningslied; Lied* (Heije); Seven duets; Five children's songs (Heije) (c 1845); *Lied voor 5de eeuwfeest Mirakel van Amsterdam* (1845); *Aria*

CHOIR: *Engelenzang* (1831); Two motets (1830-1831, 1836); *Mis in As*, v, mix.choir, orch (1831); Two Laudates (1835, 1836); Five masses, 3 m.v, org; *Missa festiva*, soloists, mix.choir, orch (1840); Mass (on the occasion of the inauguration of the Mozes and Aäron Curch in Amsterdam), soloists, mix.choir, orch (1841); Benedictus for six masses by Haydn and one mass by Beethoven; *Requiem*, m.choir, org; *Mis*, 2 m.v, org; *Psalm 84* (Heije), v, mix.choir, orch (1851); *Responsoriën* (1855); *Psalm 149 en Laudate Dominum*, m.choir, org; *Magnificat*, soloists, mix.choir, org; *Feestcantate* (Heije), v, choirs, pf; Two secular cantatas, choir, orch; Two arias; Nine pieces for m. choir (including *Muggendans*)

MUSIC FOR THE THEATRE: *Neemt U in acht* (Foppe) (vocal play); *De Heldendood van J.C.J. van Speijk* (Kinker) (declamatorio) (1831); *Ja Neerlands Volk* (declamatorio) (1832); *De Mensch* (Foppe) (declamatorio); *Saffo* (Van Lennep) (vocal play) (1832-1834); *Toneelmuziek bij Esmeralda; Toneelmuziek bij Het feestvierend Nederland; Le Bandit* (Margaillan, after Theaulon) (comic opera)

PIANO: *Trois valses brillantes; Trois nocturnes; Haarlemmer spoorwegwals; Promenade champêtre : fantaisie; 3 scherzi; Impromptu; Sonata; 2 galops; Feestmarsch*

CHAMBER MUSIC: *Allegro für vier Streich-Quartette* (1845); Four String Quartets; *Souvenir d'Auber : Trois petites fantaisies*, vl, pf; *Air varié*, vl, pf or str.qt; *Quodlibet*, fl, 2 vl, 2 vla, vc, db; 33 violin duets for beginners; Six walzes, gui

ORCHESTRA: Two Symphonies; *Fantaisie en forme de symphonie* (on the occasion of the inauguration of the new concert hall Felix Meritis in Amsterdam) (1845); Four overtures (B minor, E-flat major, C major, D major); *Feestouverture*, choir, orch (1836); *Potpourri national (Quod libet)*; Five Violin Concertos; *Concertant*, 2 vl, orch; *Variations*, vl, orch; *Fantaisie Freischütz*, vl, orch; *Horn Concerto; Scène*, hn, orch; *Fantaisie Saffo*, hn, orch; *La Dame Blanche*, hn, orch; *Concertino*, bn, orch; *Fantaisie*, cl, orch; *Variations*, vl, orch; *Duo concertant*, 2 fl, orch; *Trois pas redoubles*, military orch (1832, 1833); *Introductie en marsch triomphale* (on national folk songs), military orch (c1832)

ARRANGEMENTS: *Symphony no. 2* – Spohr, str.sxt; *Joseph* – Méhul, str.qnt; *Octet op. 20* – Mendelssohn-Bartholdy, instr.ens (1841); *Mis op. 86* – Beethoven, m.choir; Arrangements of own compositions for quartet or piano

Concert Overture in B minor, Overture Le Bandit. Netherlands Radio Symphony Orchestra, cond. J. van Steen (NM Classics 92090)
Nocturne no. 2. M. Krücker (pf) (NM Extra 98011)
String Quartet no. 3. Nomos Quartet (NM Extra 98010)

BIBLIOGRAPHY
F.C. Kist: 'Necroloog', *Caecilia*, 14, 1857, p. 225-229
E. Reeser: *Een eeuw Nederlandse muziek : 1815-1915*. Amsterdam, Querido, 1950, 2/1986

DISCOGRAPHY
Allegro (4 str.qt). Members of the Residentie Orchestra, cond. F. Leitner (Olympia OCD 502)
Allegro (4 str.qt). Viotta Ensemble, cond. V. Liberman (NM Classics 92035)

Willem Breuker

AMSTERDAM, 4 NOVEMBER 1944

In Willem Breuker's earliest memories, droning street organs combine with mandolin orchestras and marching bands, trumpets, flutes and blaring fire engine sirens. His musical ideal is the convergence of 'high' and 'low' art: uncompromising experiment and musical enjoyment for all. Breuker puts all kinds of sounds and musical genres to work. His own musical pursuits are equally jumbled. Whether composing, playing the saxophone, leading his band or directing his CD company, Breuker has a stimulating effect on music and concert life; and he does so on his own terms while drawing a highly diversified audience.

Music has always been Breuker's driving passion. As a youth he devoured the records at the music library and scanned the radio in search of the most 'bizarre music' he could find. At his local music school he learned to play the clarinet. Later, with the Tuindorp-Oostzaan Concert Band, he played the bass clarinet and tenor saxophone. He shunned formal music theory and had no patience for practising. It was through playing, improvising, listening and experimenting that he became the Breuker he is today. He is of the generation that shook music to its foundations in the 1960s. The jazz world offered the most suitable launching pad for his work and it was here that he first made a name for himself.

His earliest surviving piece dates from 1960. In 1964 he entered the FAMOS Jazz Competition and won the soloists prize, a feat he repeated the two following years. In 1965 he joined the five-piece Free Jazz Incorporated band. This ensemble entered the commercially dominated Loosdrecht Jazz Competition, but failed to reach the finals. They went to Berlin and took part in a film. Breuker soon left, however, finding his colleagues not so much interested in music as in a lifestyle of communal living. Moreover, they would not – or could not – play his music.

Breuker re-entered the preliminary rounds of the Loosdrecht Jazz Competition in 1966 with a 24-piece orchestra and a noisily chaotic piece: *Litanie voor de 14e juni, 1966* [Litany for the 14th of June, 1966], a musical comment, breaking with all accepted jazz norms, on the notorious police action taken against Provo, the Dutch flower-power movement. The orchestra was spread over three stages, improvising not only music, but dance and declamation as well. The television broadcast of the final round, in which they performed a

different piece, *Time signals and sound density III*, established Breuker's reputation as the Netherlands' *enfant terrible*. He played with Boy Edgar's big band
a few times, but the band members disliked the individualistic idiom of his
music and refused to play his pieces. Breuker was more in his element in the
Gunter Hampel orchestra. With this ensemble he traveled the world and established contacts with likeminded spirits abroad.

In 1967, in a bid for independence and to forge a fusion of composition
and improvisation as well as maintain control over the release of recordings,
Breuker founded the Instant Composers Pool (ICP) with percussionist Han
Bennink and composer Misha Mengelberg. Although this afforded him his
first opportunity to give shape to his music-theatrical ideas, he withdrew in
1973. The democratic musicians' cooperative Orkest de Volharding, which he
founded with composer Louis Andriessen, was not radical enough for him
either. In 1974 he was asked to leave. He did so, forming the Willem Breuker
Kollektief.

This became, and still remains, the ideal group for him: a business-like
professional orchestra free of hierarchic structure and as independent as possible from subsidizing organizations and bureaucracy. Each member con-
tributes his own ideas and is given more or less free musical rein. The repertoire takes account of each musician's individual expertise and qualities, and
the concerts offer unorthodox 'music for human beings', as entertaining as it

is serious. The Kollektief has won great popularity both in the Netherlands and abroad.

Breuker's annual New Year's Eve festival, *De Klap op de Vuurpijl,* has been particularly successful since its inception in 1976. Equally characteristic of his non-conformist approach is BVHAAST, a company he set up for the production and distribution of the Kollektief's and his own CDs, as well as those of similarly minded composers and musicians ill-suited to working with commercial labels.

Breuker's eclectic idiom draws from the widest range of genres and, because of its directness and commenting nature, is especially suited to film, television and the theater, for which he has composed extensively since 1966. Any device is allowed: stylistic quotations, jokes, improvisation, sketches, sentimentality and protest – all these follow each other in quick succession. Original compositions rub shoulders with arrangements of Gershwin, Weill, Satie, Beethoven and Morricone. Breuker's music bursts at the seams with extra-musical associations, and therefore defies labelling. Though he is one of the most productive Dutch composers, he rarely has time simply to write music: he is continually performing as well. Breuker's music is meant to be played and is not art for art's sake. He once suggested that the quality of his work is a product of its quantity.

Breuker's inclination to 'derail' music is deeply ingrained. He composes instinctively and through association. When not writing for the Kollektief his music, like the work of a traditional tradesman, is made to order, though not necessarily to fit. 'Good music', he once stated, 'must be cocksure. Cheeky, against the grain, and emotional. It must have something to say and its intention must always be to make somebody cry.'

'There is no name for my music', Breuker once said. 'It is music for human beings. It is for everybody, for young and old. That's how I've always wanted it to be.'

FRANS VAN ROSSUM

COMPOSITIONS

A comprehensive list of compositions and discography (up to 1994) is included in the monograph by Françoise and Jean Buzelin (see bibliography)

INSTRUMENTAL: *Denk toch aan moeder,* orch (1972); *BVHAAST Symfonie,* orch (1974); *Export Vivaldi,* orch (1978); *Aanpakken en wegwezen,* orch (1986); *Bob's Gallery,* large ens (1986); *Heibel om een niemendalletje,*

large ens (1989); *Han de Vries,* ob, s-sax, orch (1992); *For Yo-Yo Ma,* vc, large ens, str (1992); *Waakvlam,* hpd, chamb.orch. (1993); *Psalm 122,* large ens, str, GK, bar.org (1996)

FILM MUSIC: *Sigaar 70* (1966); *De nieuwe IJstijd* (1974); *De platte jungle* (1987); *Twee vrouwen* (1979); *De illusionist* (1983)

INCIDENTAL MUSIC: *Baal* (Brecht) (1973); *Rit over het Bodenmeer* (Handke) (1974); *Getrommel in de nacht* (Brecht) (1975); *Het Koninkrijk* (Engelander) (1977); *Kees de Jongen* (Thijssen) (1993)

MUSIC THEATRE: *Kaïn en Abel* (L. de Boer) (1972); *La Plagiata* (Breuker) (1975); *Anthologie* (L. de Boer) (1975); *Wolkbreuk* (Boomsma) (1982); *Deze kant op, Dames* (I. Meijer) (1992)

BIBLIOGRAPHY

B. Andriessen: 'Op zoek naar het rake idee : Willem Breuker en zijn filmmuziek', *Mens en Melodie* vol. 53, 1998, p. 455-461

B. Andriessen: *Tetterettet : interviews met Nederlandse improviserende musici*. Ubbergen, Tandem Felix, 1996

F. and J. Buzelin: *Willem Breuker*. Paris: Éditions de Limon, 1992

F. and J. Buzelin: *Willem Breuker : maker van mensenmuziek*. Hilversum, Centrum Nederlandse Muziek / Zutphen, Walburg Press, 1994 (Dutch transl. by M. Nakken of the French monograph (see above)

Th. Derks: 'Spelen zal je!', *Ssst! Nieuwe ensembles voor nieuwe muziek*. Amsterdam, International Theatre & Film Books, 1996

G. Giddings: 'William Breuker Battles the Bourgeoisie', *Key Notes*, 10, 1979/2, p. 46-48

R. Koopmans and Orkest de Volharding: *10 jaar Volharding : tien jaar werken in een progressieve muziekpraktijk*. Amsterdam, Van Gennep, 1982

K. Whitehead: *New Dutch Swing*. New York, Billboard Books, 1998

DISCOGRAPHY

Baal Brecht Breuker Handke. Various performers, Studio Orchestra, cond. W. Breuker (BVHAAST CD 9006)

Bertolt Brecht : The Resistable Rise of Arturo Ui. De Samuel Falkland Show/Herman Heijermans. Willem Breuker Kollektief (BVHAAST CD 9003)

Export Vivaldi op. 156. Amsterdam Philharmonic Orchestra, cond. A. Kersjes (EMI 1A 051-2633 1 and Entr'acte CD2)

Heibel / Der Kritiker. Willem Breuker Kollektief, G. Bijma (v), L.L. Trytten (vl) (BVHAAST CD 9102)

De Illusionist. Various performers (Ariola 205.717 and BVHAAST CD 9205)

Kees de Jongen. Various performers, cond. W. Breuker (Clarison SKW 53343)

Kurt Weill (BVHAAST CD 9808)

Litany for the 14th of June. Various performers (Relax 33004)

Lost Ground (sel.). J. Raas (org). (NM Classics 92034)

Metropolis. Willem Breuker Kollektief, Mondriaan Strings, Toby Rix (BVHAAST CD 8903)

De Onderste Steen. Various performers (Entr'acte CD2)

Overtime/Überstunden. Willem Breuker Kollektief (with music by Breuker a.o.) (NM Classics 92042)

Pakkepapèn (BVHAAST 9807)

Parade. Willem Breuker Kollektief (with music by Breuker a.o.) (BVHAAST CD 9101)

Psalm 122 (BVHAAST CD 9803)

Sensemaya. Willem Breuker Kollektief, Mondriaan Strings, H. de Vries (ob), G. Kauffeld (v), L.L. Trytten (vl) (BVHAAST CD 9509)

Emile von Brucken Fock

KOUDEKERKE, 19 OCTOBER 1857 – AERDENHOUT, 3 JANUARY 1944

The third son of Henri Dignus von Brucken Fock (1817-1874), a Middelburg
civil servant, and Johanna Caland (1819-1891), Abraham Emilius von Brucken
Fock was born at the family's country estate Ter Hooge in Koudekerke, in the
province of Zeeland. He took piano lessons with Simon Verwijs, organist of
the New Church in Middelburg, and cello lessons with Abraham de Jong, concertmaster of Middelburg's local orchestra. De Jong helped his student become acquainted not only with chamber music, but also with the orchestral
repertoire by allowing him to join the orchestra during performances.

After leaving Middelburg, Von Brucken Fock rounded off his musical education by studying, it is said, Ernst Friedrich Richter's *Lehre der Harmonie* and
Henri Viotta's *Lexicon der Toonkunst* [Encyclopedia of Music]. Despite his musical talent, however, he kept to the family tradition of pursuing a career in the
military, and in 1875 enrolled in the Royal Military Academy in Breda. There
he led the cadet music group Sempre Crescendo, for which he also made
arrangements and wrote original compositions. He frequently took part in private concerts in and around Breda and, during this period, composed two festive cantatas, thereby coming to the attention of a wider public. In 1878 Von
Brucken Fock completed his studies and shortly thereafter married Samuela
Adriana Cornelia Pické, the couple producing two sons.

A period followed in which he was frequently transferred by the military. In
Utrecht, from 1881 to 1884, he wrote columns on music for the daily
Utrechtsch Dagblad. For the next two years he was stationed in Den Helder,
where he composed *Nachtlied* [Nocturnal song] for string orchestra, and *Concertwals* [Concert waltz] for orchestra. He was back in Breda from 1886 to
1891, during which time he composed several songs, among other works,
which were published in Germany. He then returned to Utrecht and remained
there until 1896. Two of his best-known compositions date from this period:
the *Koninginne-Marsch* [Queen's march], a symphonic poem based on a poem
by Holda (the pseudonym of Adriana Jacoba Francisca Piepers) and the one-
act music drama *Seleneia.* The libretto of this work was written by Holda's
daughter, Maria Constance Antoinette Snijders van Wissekerke-Clant van der
Mijll, who, not surprisingly, wrote under a pseudonym, namely M. Constant.
The first staged performance of *Seleneia* was held on 5 March 1895 in Amsterdam's City Theater, with Von Brucken Fock conducting. In mid-1894 he began

working on his second music drama, *Elaine und Lancelot*, but only completed one fragment of the work, entitled *Elainens Tod*.

In 1896 he was stationed in Arnhem for a second time and made the acquaintance there of Abraham Noske, who was later to be his publisher. During this time he published reviews in the daily *Arhemsche Courant* and occasionally conducted performances of his work with the Arnhem Orchestral Society. While in Arnhem, Von Brucken Fock maintained a close relationship with the orchestra and was even for a time the chairman of its board of directors.

After 1900 he was transferred four times before retiring to Aerdenhout in 1917. His musical activity had been severely restricted by the burden of his military duties since 1900, and it was only in the 1920s that he took up composing again. Among the works that followed is his only known chamber music piece, the string quartet *Sérénade fantastique* (1924). His performances were limited to private concerts. Von Brucken Fock died in Aerdenhout on 3 January 1944.

Any attempt to summarize Emile von Brucken Fock's music is made more difficult by the fact that a large portion of his work – including his unpublished music (among which, op.1-13) – has been lost. Some of his orchestral pieces, moreover, have only survived in piano reduction.

It is clear, however, that like many of his contemporaries, Von Brucken Fock was thoroughly influenced by the work of Richard Wagner. Even the earliest surviving compositions, the songs op.14 and op.16, reveal as much. Several of these songs, it is true, follow in the Schumann and Robert Franz Lieder tradition, but the sway of Wagner is demonstrably present in the others. The piano takes the lead in the unfolding of the musical material while the singer's role is more declamatory, and the harmonies highly chromatic. The piano parts are orchestrally conceived, their textures hardly discernible from the piano reductions Von Brucken Fock made of the orchestral scores of his music dramas.

The music dramas themselves are the most clearly indebted to Wagner's work. Their orchestral parts are based on a number of elementary motifs and the orchestration is calculated to accommodate the 'sunken' position of the orchestra in the Bayreuth theater. The vocal parts are declamatory and the orchestra unfolds characteristically Wagnerian 'unendliche Melodien'. The idiom of Von Brucken Fock's orchestral pieces is identical. Most of these are supplied with rather detailed programs.

Von Brucken Fock failed to develop an identifiably personal style, but in a period in which many Dutch composers (grudgingly or otherwise) fervently admired Wagner without going so far as to allow his ideas to play a role in their music he, like few others in the Netherlands, succeeded in according these new ideas a role in his music, in particular between the years 1890 and 1900.

JEROEN VAN GESSEL

COMPOSITIONS
* lost
** surviving only in vocal score

VOCAL: *Feestcantate* (for Heinrich Umland's 40th anniversary as a composer) (1877)*; *Feestcantate* (on the occasion of the 50th anniversary of the Koninklijke Militaire Academie) (1878)*; *Erstes Lied jung Werners*, T, pf (c 1885); *Drei Lieder*, op. 14 (c 1890); *Vier Lieder* (Bodenstedt, Sylva, Roell), v, pf, op. 16 (c 1890); *Seleneia* (Constant), S, A, T, orch (1892-1893)**; *Elainens Tod* (fragment) (1894-1895)**; *Zwei Lieder* (Hoeppl, Mörike), v, pf (c 1900); *Längst verwelkte Blumen blicken*, A, pf (c 1895)**; *Acht Gesänge*, v, pf (c 1900); *Frühling* (Rust), S, orch (c 1920)

INSTRUMENTAL: *Polka en mazurka*, pf (c 1870)*; *Nachtlied*, str.orch (c 1885)*; *Concertwals*, orch (c 1885)*; *Scène de Carnaval*, pf, op. 15 (c 1890)*; *Koninginne-marsch*, orch (1891); *Deutscher Triumph-Marsch*, orch (1894?)* *La lune blanche*, S, pf (1902?);); *Erinnerung*, vl, orch (1922?); *Wilhelmus-feestmarsch*, orch (1923); *Sérénade fantastique*, str.qt (1924); *Preghiera*, org, orch (1925?)*

BIBLIOGRAPHY
H. Nolthenius: *Gids door het muziekdrama in een bedrijf Seleneia*. Amsterdam, 1895

Onze musici : portretten en biografieën. Rotterdam, Nijgh & Van Ditmar, 1898
E. van Zoeren: *De Muziekuitgeverij A.A. Noske, (1896-1926): Een bijdrage tot dertig jaar Nederlandse muziekgeschiedenis*. Haarlemmerliede, Van Zoeren, 1987

Gerard von Brucken Fock

KOUDEKERKE, 28 DECEMBER 1859 – HEEMSTEDE, 15 AUGUST 1935

Gerardus Hubertus Galenus von Brucken Fock was born at Ter Hooge, a country estate outside Koudekerke near Middelburg. As a youth on the island of Walcheren he developed a love for nature and an aversion to life in the city, where his well-to-do family usually passed the winter. As a boarding school pupil in Kampen (1871-1873) he came to love the music of Chopin, and particularly this composer's *Bolero* op.19, played by one of the schoolmasters. His interest in music continued to grow when he returned to Middelburg. Stimulated by the music making of both his brothers – Henri played the piano, Emile the violin and the cello – Von Brucken Fock began taking viola lessons with Abraham de Jong. Together with his teacher and brothers, he would play piano quartets; meanwhile, he taught himself to play the piano.

Devoting his time to composing and drawing, Von Brucken Fock did not complete secondary schooling. In 1877 he went to study harmony with Richard Hol and the piano with Theo van der Wurff in Utrecht. It was through the concerts he attended in this city that he became fascinated by the music of Brahms. In 1879 he went to Berlin to study counterpoint at the conservatory with Friedrich Kiel. He quickly found the lessons dry, however, and he began taking composition lessons with Woldemar Bargiel instead. Both teachers based their instruction on the music of Brahms. Nevertheless, the theoretical side of music disappointed him, and he ended his studies, returning to the Netherlands. While in Berlin, however, he composed the *Sechs Clavierstücke* op.1.

The move back to his native land opened a forty-year period in which, driven by his restless nature, he continually travelled, changed residences, and was plagued by indecision as to whether he should pursue a career in music or drawing. At times, too, he would turn his back on the arts altogether to immerse himself in religious pursuits. In 1884 he journeyed to Dresden, Vienna, the German island of Borkum, and Paris, meanwhile composing, drawing and writing a travelogue for the daily *Handelsblad*. In 1885 Von Brucken Fock returned to Middelburg, but he spent the years 1887-88 in Paris trying his luck as a pianist.

He lived in Amsterdam from 1888 to 1891, where he occasionally wrote music criticism and led the choir of the Remonstrant Church. During this period he began reading Tolstoy and became increasingly doubtful about the validity of a life dedicated to the arts. Distressed by his idleness, he went to Leipzig in 1891 to work as a piano teacher, but he soon tired of the monotony of this existence. He then found work as an agricultural laborer on Walcheren, but this, too, failed to assuage his doubts. After this experience he once again turned his attention to composition.

From 1892 to 1895 Von Brucken Fock was in Paris, now a salvationist who limited his artistic output to the harmonization and playing of salvation hymns. In 1895 he left for Royan, in France, and there composed the op.12 'sea preludes'. From 1895-1904 he was back in Amsterdam and there (from 1899) he conducted the choir of the Free Evangelical Church. For this choir he composed the *Drie geestelijke liederen* [Three religious songs] op.14, and two cantatas. During a brief sojourn on Walcheren, in 1900, he wrote the op.15 series of *24 préludes* for piano, music that earned Grieg's praise. On the advice of Julius Röntgen, Von Brucken Fock began orchestrating the cantatas and, soon after that, Rudolf Mengelberg's Netherlands Music Festival of 1902 inspired him to turn his attention to larger-scale works for orchestra. He composed the oratorio *De Wederkomst van Christus* [The second coming of Christ] from 1904 to 1906. In 1901 he also began painting, and through this made the acquaintance of the painter Jan Toorop.

Living in Aerdenhout from 1904 to 1912, Von Brucken Fock composed various songs (1905 and 1906) and gave performances of his own music in Amsterdam, Rotterdam and Berlin, with the violinist Carl Flesch and conductor Daniël de Lange, among others. In 1912 he returned to Paris to concentrate on painting and also began sketching models. While there, he made the acquaintance of the painter Isaäc Israëls. Gerard von Brucken Fock lived in Laren from 1913 to 1917, where he devoted again much of his time to religion, though when Willem Mengelberg performed his French orchestral songs he returned to music. From 1917 to 1920 he lived in Katwijk and in 1920 moved to Heemstede. In the last years of his life he composed numerous orchestral impressions of his journeys through France, Switzerland and Germany.

The music of Gerard von Brucken Fock often consists of musical impressions of themes from nature, the sea in particular being a source of inspiration. Many of his orchestral works lean towards the music of the French impressionists and bear French titles. But owing to the gaps in his theoretical background, Von Brucken Fock seldom was able to work out his ideas to their full potential; because the motivic material is scarcely developed, the orchestral suites remain no more than brief, orchestrated impressions.

Central in his oeuvre are the 224 preludes for piano. Here, too, impressions of the sea are to be found: the op.8 no.5 and nr.10 pieces (1890), with their augmented triads and metric changes, for example, or *Laag water aan de Schelde* [Low tide on the Schelde river] (1901). More important in this genre, however, are the melodically forceful op.15 no.16 (1901) and op.16 no.7 (1902), with its continuous switching between major and minor keys. The *24 préludes*, op.15 (1900-1901), which bear a strong Chopinesque influence, became the best known of his preludes. Von Brucken Fock's music also shows an affinity with the music of Brahms, and at times that of Franck. The Brahmsian element is clearly evident, for example, in the first movement of the sonata for viola and piano, op.5; the setting of this work, incidentally, is very unusual in Dutch music. Von Brucken Fock's later work is more virtuosic, but somehow flatter.

Together with Daniël de Lange and Alphons Diepenbrock, Gerard von Brucken Fock was one of the first Dutch composers to write French songs.

JAN TEN BOKUM

COMPOSITIONS
Some opus numbers are used twice

SONGS (WITH PIANO UNLESS OTHERWISE STATED): 29 songs (1892-1930); 24 songs, v, orch (including nine songs to French texts); *Fourteen songs*, op. 18 (1905); *Five songs* , op. 22 (1906); *Seven songs*, op. 28; *Four songs*, op. 30

CHOIR: *De Schelde* (1899); *Psalm 1*, op. 11; *Drie geestelijke liederen*, mix.choir (1899); *Psalm 23* (1903); *Acht geestelijke liederen*; *Kerst-, Paasch- en Pinkstercantate* (1900-1903); *22 geestelijke liederen*, op. 17 (1905); *De Wederkomst van Christus*, op. 19 (1904-1906); *Zeven koralen*, op. 31; *De Opwekking van Lazarus* (1920-1921); *De komende Christus* (1930); *De nacht is voorbijgegaan; Requiem* (1888-1933)

DRAMATIC VOCAL: *De geparfumeerde zakdoek* (prologue) (1889); *Sing-Sang* (vocal play) (1890); *Jozal* (music drama) (unfin., 1910-1911)

PIANO (PIANO 2H UNLESS OTHERWISE STATED): 26 short pieces (1876-1932); 4 sonatas (1878, 1878, 1882, 1886); *Sechs Klavierstücke*, op. 29 (c.878-1889); *Valses*, op. 1; *Sechs Clavierstücke*, op. 1 (1885); *Spanische Tänze*, op. 3 (1884); 224 preludes (of which published: op. 2, op. 4 (1886), op. 8 (1890), op. 9 (1891), op. 12 (1891-1895), op. 15 (1900-1901), op. 16 (1902-1903), op. 20 (1906)); *Serenata*, op. 10; *Cinq moments musicaux*, op. 11 (1891); *Drie Spaansche dansen*, op. 13 (1898); *Ballade*, op. 21 (1906); *Ballade* (1918); 22 piano pieces (op. 24 to 27); *Preludium en fuga op G.H.B.F.* (1918); Dances and marches for piano 4h (1881-1886)

CHAMBER MUSIC: *Sonata*, vl, pf, op. 1 (1877); *Sonata*, vla, pf, op. 5 (1885?); *Elegy*, vl, pf, op. 7; *Sonata*, vl, pf (1881); *Sonata*, vl, pf (1889); *Stücke & Tänze*, vl, pf (1889); *Sonata*, vl, pf, op. 23; *Sonata*, vc, pf (1884/1931)

ORCHESTRA: *Piano Concerto* (1884-1888); *Tragische Ouverture*, op. 8 (1885); *Ouverture De Watergeuzen*, op. 10; *Gnomentanz*, op. 13 (1891); Nine suites (of which 5 *Impressions du Midi*); *Aus dem Süden*, op. 32; *Symphonisch gedicht* (1902); *Twee liederen van de Zee* (1906); *Twee impressies (Maannacht op zee, Côte sauvage)* (1916); Three symphonies

BIBLIOGRAPHY

G.H.G. von Brucken Fock : een mens van twee werelden. H.I.C. Dozy-de Stoppelaar [et al.]. Zeist, De Haan, 1959

Elias Brunnenmüller

?, c.1665 – ?, 1762

The biography of Elias Brunnenmüller (the name appears in other spellings, such as Brunmüller and Bronnenmuller) has yet to be written, as is the case with many other Dutch composers of the seventeenth and eighteenth centuries. It is known for certain that around 1690 he was Mattheson's teacher in Hamburg and that around 1710 he issued three collections of music for various instrumental combinations in Amsterdam. Other information – such as his descent, education, where he lived, when he died – are at best only known from unverifiable references in the literature.

The year of his birth can be calculated to have been about 1665, based on the dates of his publications. It is possible that the dedication of his op.1 to Paulus Friedeborn, tax commissioner of the Elector of Brandenburg in Cleves and the county of Mark, could indicate that he was born in one of these areas, but this is mere speculation. According to historical sources, Brunnenmüller studied with the Italian composers and violinists Alessandro Scarlatti, Carlo Ambrosio Lonati (or Lunati) and Arcangelo Corelli, though there is no documented confirmation of this either. If this supposition is factual, Brunnenmüller must in any case have traveled through Italy by the end of the seventeenth century. It seems conceivable that he took up residence in the Dutch Republic shortly after 1700 – according to sources, in The Hague in 1706 and around 1710 in Amsterdam. He is also said to have become a citizen of both these cities, though the respective rolls of citizens make no mention of him.

The patent granted Brunnenmüller by the States General as a 'burgher of Amsterdam and music-master', on 21 June 1709, for the publication of a number of compositions still remains the first verifiable fact of his life. He soon made use of this privilege and in August 1709 published his op.1, a collection of six trio sonatas in the Italian (Corellian) style. The edition was distributed by booksellers in various places in the Dutch Republic. The engraving of the plates was almost certainly done at the workshop of the Amsterdam music publisher Estienne Roger. Yet Brunnenmüller's chief distributor was not Roger, but the Amsterdam bookseller and printer François Halma, to whom Brunnenmüller transferred his patent on 20 April 1710.

Halma, who had by then moved to Leeuwarden and was printer of the States of Friesland, was the publisher of Brunnenmüller's op.2, a collection of pieces for keyboard instruments and other instrumental combinations enti-

tled *Fasciculus Musicus.* This collection is generally thought to have appeared in 1711.

A third opus was published by
Estienne Roger. It is a collection of
six sonatas for oboe and basso continuo (the last two are also suited to
the flute), dedicated to the gentleman
'C***'. The title page reports that as
the manuscript of the sonatas had
been stolen from the home of C***,
the immediate publication of the
work was the composer's only protec-
tion against a pirate edition. Brunnenmüller's op.3 is thought to have
appeared in 1712.

In 1713 François Halma put up
for sale the engraved plates, and
perhaps printed editions, from his
publishing house. Presumably, these

were bought by Estienne Roger, for Brunnenmüller's three opuses are listed
in Roger's catalogues in the following years. Several publications and adver-
tisements announce the impending publication of a music theory work by
Brunnenmüller entitled *De opregte en korte gronden der compositie* [The true
and short grounds of composition], but as far as is known this book was
never published.

Historical sources report Brunnenmüller's death to have been in 1762 (in
Amsterdam), no less than fifty years after the appearance of his op.3. There is
no information on his life in the intervening period. It is possible, of course,
that Brunnenmüller lived to a ripe old age but did not compose in later years,
although documented confirmation of this would be very welcome indeed.

Brunnenmüller's music is Italianate in style and character with a hint of Ger-
manic polyphony and angularity, like much of the music written by his German colleagues in the early eighteenth century. The op.1 trio sonatas and
opp.2 and 3 solo sonatas for violin, oboe, recorder or flute strictly comply with
Italian models, though occasional deviations may be noted in the succession
of movements. Characteristic is their mixture of abstract movements (vivace,
allegro, andante) with dance movements (some oddly spelled, such as 'cyque'
and 'cavotte') within sonatas, thus practically negating the distinction between

the church and chamber sonata. The occasional use of rather extensive fore-shadowing of melodic motifs by the basso continuo seems a recurrent feature in Brunnenmüller's music.

Opus 2, *Fasciculus Musicus*, also contains three suites for harpsichord. These consist of an introductory toccatina followed by several dance movements. The toccatinas are in three sections, the first based on scale figures and comparable motifs, the second fugal in character, and the third written in a less strict, homophonic/polyphonic style. The dance movements do not follow the common pattern of allemande, courante, sarabande and gigue, but appear in shorter successions, such as allemande, menuet, ciaccona.

Brunnenmüller also included four ariettas to Italian and German texts with oboe ad libitum at the close of his opus 2. These are entirely in keeping with Italian examples of this genre.

A final, recurrent feature of Brunnenmüller's music that merits attention here is his predilection for the descending, chromatically filled fourth, a figure he employed in all musical genres. It is so pervasively present that it could be said to serve as his musical signature.

RUDOLF RASCH

COMPOSITIONS

Sonate a due violini e violoncello col organo ... opera prima. – Amsterdam, Franciscus Halma, [1709]
Modern ed.: Six sonatas for two violins, cello and keyboard : opus 1 / ed. by Timothy Roberts. Fullerton CA, Grancino, 1986 (Early Ensemble Series 5a-b)

Fasciculus Musicus sive Tabulae varii generis modorum ac concentuum musicorum notis consignatae et compositae ... [opus secundum]. – Leeuwarden, Franciscus Halma, [1711]
Includes three keyboard suites, one oboe sonata, one recorder sonata, one violin sonata and four ariettas with oboe ad lib. Facs. ed.: introduction by Rudolf Rasch. [Utrecht], VNM, 1991 (Dutch Music Facsimiles 8). Modern ed. of the keyboard works: 3 suites voor klavier / ed. W.H. Thijsse, The Hague, Albersen, [c 1950]

VI sonates à un haubois ou violon & basse continue dont les deux dernières sont bonnes pour la flûte traversière. – Amsterdam, Estienne

Roger, [1711-1712]
Modern ed. of the last sonatas for flute: Two sonatas for flute and figured bass, 1712 / ed. by R.A. Rasch. Utrecht, Diapason Press, 1985

DISCOGRAPHY

Suite op. 2, no. 1. Trio Sonnerie (Teleac TEL 8901-8905)

Pieter Bustijn

?, 1649? – MIDDELBURG, BURIED 22 NOVEMBER 1729

Pieter (Pierre) Bustijn was a descendant of the French-speaking 'Bustyn' or 'Bustin' family that had emigrated to the Netherlands and quickly acclimatized itself to the new surroundings. Although the family expanded enormously in the seventeenth century, it died out completely in the eighteenth century.

Presumably, Bustijn was baptized on 25 July 1649 as 'fils de Jean' in the Walloon Church in Middelburg. Around 1685 he married Apollonia van Fuyrden, whose grandfather Cornelis had been a friend of the famous poet Jacob Cats (1577-1660). In the year of his marriage Bustijn bought a handsome house on Middelburg's Nieuwstraat, where he lived for the rest of his life. This house, in the immediate vicinity of the New Church, still stands at 19 Nieuwstraat.

It is not known for certain whether Bustijn was trained in music, but it is possible that he did receive some instruction from Remigius Schrijver. Not long after Schrijver's death in 1681, Bustijn succeeded him as organist at the New Church and as carillonneur at the adjacent convent tower, the 'Long John'. During this period he completed the work begun by Schrijver, namely the setting to music of *Uitbreidinge over het Bouk der Psalmen tot de hondert* [Expansions on the Book of Psalms to a hundred], poems written by the physician Matthias van Westhuyse and published in 1682. No copies of this publication are known to have survived. It is conceivable that Bustijn also took over the direction of the Middelburg collegium musicum, an ensemble that had existed since 1622 and was previously led by Schrijver.

Bustijn was asked to advise on the renovation of various organs in the province of Zeeland. In 1700, for example, he proposed that two registers be added to the organ of the Walloon Church in Middelburg. On another occasion, in 1711, he was paid more than eight pounds for appraising the organ of the Great or Maria Magdalen Church in Goes. The additions made to this instrument by the organ builder Cool show clear parallels with the renovations made several years previously on the organ of Middelburg's New Church. There are various indications that Bustijn, although for years organist on a Dutch instrument, was aware of developments made by the German school of organ builders. The most important features of the so-called 'Werk Prinzip', which reached a high point in the period from 1700 to 1750, were the contrast between a full, round great organ and a thin-sounding, piercing positive division, thoroughly autonomous pedals with solo registers, and a clear, direct sound throughout the instrument. The alterations made on the organs in Middelburg and Goes show that Bustijn had these characteristics in mind and was well abreast of the latest developments.

On 1 august 1712 the wooden upper section of the Long John tower and the carillon it housed were destroyed by fire. On 24 March 1714 the treasurers of Middelburg entered into a contract for the forging of a new instrument with one of the leading bell-founders of the day, De Grave and Van Noorden of Amsterdam. The carillon, which was to meet the strictest demands, was to be approved by a panel of 'the best and most experienced masters and musicians that the gentlemen contractors should wish to choose and to employ.' City records of 1715 show that Pieter Bustijn and Abraham de Coup, organist at the Walloon Church and carillonneur at the market tower, were selected for this panel. According to various sources, the new carillon was of excellent quality.

Around 1712 an edition of Bustijn's *IX Suittes pour le Clavessin* was issued by the well-known Amsterdam music publisher and printer Estienne Roger. The work was dedicated to Pieter de Huybert, sire of Burgh and councillor of the Court of Flanders. It is conceivable that De Huybert acted as a patron of Bustijn's and financed the printing of the collection. As one of the very few examples of early eighteenth-century Dutch suites for the harpsichord that have survived, this work holds a special place in Dutch music history and is of enormous historical significance. The suites are deliberately arranged according to key. The almost entirely balanced arrangement is reminiscent of the axial-symmetrical ordering of musical cycles that reached its peak in the work of J.S. Bach. The suites are composed in a unique style that foreshadows the keyboard compositions of Bach and Handel and also reveals the influence of French music. Several passages show a striking resemblance to passages composed by Bach.

Bustijn's suites apparently gained popularity in the first half of the eighteenth century. Not only were they listed in Dutch catalogues, they were also known abroad. In an anthology of music for keyboard instruments compiled by Johann Gottfried Walther (1684-1748) we find Bustijn's *Suite VIII* – copied by Johann Tobias Krebs (1690-1762) – alongside compositions by J.S. Bach, D. Buxtehude, J.L. Krebs and an important group of French composers. Quite possibly, Walther came to know Bustijn's work through Prince Johann Ernst von Sachsen-Weimar (1696-1715). This gifted student of Walther's returned to Weimar in 1713 after spending two years in the Netherlands, where he had studied at the University of Utrecht. It was expected of him that he would bring French and Italian music back from the Republic, given the international orientation of Amsterdam. It seems likely that on his return he brought the recently published suites by 'Pierre Bustyn' as well.

Walther also makes mention of these suites in his *Musicalisches Lexicon*. Bach is known to have maintained close contact with Walther in Weimar – Bach's mother and Walther's grandfather were siblings. Moreover, Bach had good relations with Prince Johann Ernst. The similarities between the works of Bustijn and Bach, combined with the fact that Bach was exceptionally well-acquainted with the work of other composers, lead to the assumption that Bustijn's suites drew Bach's attention. Unfortunately, this opus 1 collection is the only work of Bustijn to have survived.

From 1719 Benjamin Bouchart increasingly took over Bustijn's responsibilities at the organ and carillon and he was named Bustijn's successor at the composer's death in 1729. On 22 November of that year, Bustijn was buried at the New Church in Middelburg.

ALBERT CLEMENT

COMPOSITIONS

Uitbreidinge over het Bouk der Psalmen ... op Muzyk gestelt met drie stemmen en Bassus Continuus, begonnen door mr Remigius Schryver, ... *en voltrokken door mr Pieter Bustyn, ...* – Middelburg, wid. Schrijver, 1682

IX Suittes pour le Clavessin. – Amsterdam, Estienne Roger, [c 1712]
  Modern eds.: 1) Drie suites voor clavecimbel [G minor, A minor and A major] / ed. A. Curtis. Amsterdam, VNM, 1964 (Exempla Musica Neerlandica I); 2) IX suittes pour le clavessin / with an introd. and ed. by Albert Clement. Middelburg, Koninklijk Zeeuwsch Genootschap der Wetenschappen, 1992 (Exempla Musica Zelandica I). Facs. of the orig. ed.: Brussels, Royal Library Albert I, FETIS 2956 B mus.

BIBLIOGRAPHY

A. Clement: 'Pieter Bustijn : musicyn en organist', *TVNM*, 38, 1988, p. 81-99

A. Clement: 'Pieter Bustijn : musicyn en organist', *Zeeuws Tijdschrift*, 39, 1989/4, p. 143-150 (lightly rev. Dutch version of the above mentioned English article)

A. Clement: 'De Zeeuwse organist als componist in de 17e en 18e eeuw', *Het Orgel*, 89, 1993/8, p. 241-248; 1993/9, p. 281-286

DISCOGRAPHY

Suite in G major. T. Koopman (Philips 6514082)
Suite II in D major. B. Beekman (KZGW 6810 869)
Suite IV in C major. A. Clement (Jubal CD ZV 94172-2)
Suite V in G minor. B. van Asperen (Sony Classical SK 46349)
Suite VI in A minor. G. Dekker (Editio Laran ST 7072)
Suite VI in A minor. J. Ogg (Globe GLO 5101)
Suite VIII in A major. S.C. Jansen (Vivace 575)

Anna Cramer

AMSTERDAM, 15 JULY 1873 – BLARICUM, 4 JUNE 1968

In the first decades of the twentieth century, Anna Cramer gained a reputation as a composer of songs. Later, she was entirely forgotten, only to be rediscovered in the 1980s. The many uncertainties about her life led to the formation of myths about her. Her oeuvre consists of fifty-four songs in German, two operas and one piece for choir and orchestra. Many of these compositions have only survived in manuscript; they are housed in the Music Archives of the Gemeentemuseum in The Hague.

Anna Merkje Cramer was the eldest daughter of an Amsterdam merchant, but nothing is known about the conditions of her upbringing or her early musical education. From 1895 to 1897 she studied the piano and composition at the Amsterdam Conservatory, but the names of her teachers are unknown. Like many conservatory graduates of her time, Cramer went to Berlin after receiving her diploma in late 1897. There she had lessons with Wilhelm Berger and Max von Schillings.

In 1903 one of her lieder, *Wenn die Linde blüht*, was included in the publication of a collection entitled *Preislieder*. Cramer sent ten of her songs to the Middelburg music publisher A.A. Noske that year, but he declined to publish them.

The renowned German baritone Ludwig Wüllner included songs by Cramer in the program of his Dutch tour in 1906. These pieces were enthusiastically received; composer and music critic Daniël de Lange referred to the composer as 'an adornment' to Dutch art. In the following year the first publication of collections of songs by Cramer were issued by Fürstner in Berlin: *Fünf Gedichte von Klaus Groth*, op.1, settings of humoristic poems; and *Fünf Gedichte von O.J. Bierbaum,* op.2, five lyrical miniatures. A publication of fourteen *Volkstümliche Lieder*, op.3, was issued in 1908 by Heinrich Lewy in Munich, where Cramer had gone to study from 1907 to 1908. She visited Rotterdam, The Hague and Amsterdam in 1909 on a recital tour in which she accompanied three Dutch vocalists in performances of her songs.

In 1910 Cramer's *Sechs Lieder für eine Singstimme und Klavier*, op.4, was published in Berlin. There is much uncertainty about her life in the following years. In 1917 she was entered into the population register of Munich, her occupation being listed as 'Musikerin', and eight years later she took up residence in Vienna. It is almost certain that she composed from 1910 to 1925, but none of her works were published after the opus 4 collection. Presumably dating from this period are the opus 7 *Gedichte aus 'Die ewige Hochzeit'*, songs in manuscript to texts by the German playwright Max Dauthendey, and the 10 *Gedichte,* to texts by Detlev von Liliencron.

Cramer's stay in Vienna made a great impact on her work, particularly her acquaintance with the vocalist, poet and *Wiener Lied* composer Walter Simlinger (1889-1976). Cramer and Simlinger entered into close collaboration, producing in 1926 four songs on Simlinger texts. Two opera librettos were created in the following years, *Der letzte Tanz* and *Dr. Pipalumbo*. Cramer completed a piano reduction of *Der letzte Tanz* in 1927 and orchestrated several movements from the opera. Of *Dr. Pipalumbo* she realized the piano reduction and the orchestration of the introductory movement probably many years later. Though neither of the operas were performed, Simlinger played a major role propagating Cramer's songs. He was co-founder of an organization called 'Vereinte Kunst' that organized concerts in which Cramer's music was also performed. Of her Viennese songs and three arias, five pieces were premiered in 1927 in Vienna and two others in Dresden the following year. It was also in Vienna that she composed the large-scale *Zigeunerlied*, for violin, tenor, mixed choir and orchestra.

At the end of the 1920s Simlinger moved to Berlin and while in Germany he attempted without success to arrange performances of Cramer's operas. During this period Cramer suffered from constant financial problems because she had given up teaching and was not earning through composition. Her mother sent her a monthly sum from the Netherlands to pay for the essentials. In 1930, however, this was stopped. As a result Cramer fell into a psychological crisis and was committed to a psychiatric clinic for two months. She returned to Amsterdam in 1934 and lived in isolation. From letters she wrote to Simlinger we learn that she did not write nor play any music between 1931 and 1947. From 1947 onwards, she worked extensively on revisions of her compositions and on the piano score of *Dr. Pipalumbo*.

In 1958 she deposited her manuscripts, many in revised duplicate, in a vault at the Dutch Trading Company. Because of her advanced age and possibly chronic mental instability, it is unlikely that she wrote any more music. In 1960 she was admitted to the geriatric ward of the Hoog Laren psychiatric hospital in Blaricum and there she died, forgotten, on 4 June 1968.

Cramer revised almost all of her compositions, including the songs already published prior to 1911. It is not possible to precisely date her undated manuscripts because they were repeatedly revised with new sections covering the original passages.

Cramer's work shows characteristics of the German late-Romantic style. Many of the songs are intensely emotional, in part through the harmonies used in the accompaniment. The medium is chromatic, with a wealth of unresolved secondary subdominant-dominant progressions and other secondary functions, as well as regular excursions to other keys that are not actual modulations. The drama and expression of the piano parts – soloistic and at times with orchestral tendencies – and the recitative-like vocal parts often lean toward the operatic. Only the *Volkstümliche Lieder*, op.3, are somewhat different; these folk-song-like pieces are on the whole more symmetrical in structure and have simpler melodies.

In the compositions after 1910 and the revisions of previously published work, dissonance is increasingly used to add color and drama. Anti-metrical figures become more common. The works composed during Cramer's time in Vienna reveal impressionistic qualities and the influence of cabaret music.

Through an unfortunate set of circumstances, Cramer and her music sank into oblivion. Most of her works, however, have survived and, in part through the efforts of the late Willem Noske, the great promoter of the Dutch musical heritage, interest in her music has revived.

JEANINE LANDHEER

COMPOSITIONS
Year of orig. publ. between [ ], year of composition / time of development between ( )

SONGS (WITH PIANO): *Mädchenlied* (c 1896)(lost); *Vöglein wohin so schnell* (c 1896) (lost); *Wenn die Linde blüht* [1903]; *Abendfrieden* (Busse) (before 1907) (manuscript); *Fünf Gedichte von Klaus Groth*, op. 1 [1907]; *Fünf Gedichte von O.J. Bierbaum*, op. 2 [1907]; *14 Volkstümliche Lieder*, op. 3 [1908]; *Schlafliedchen für's Peterle* (Busse) (before 1909) (manuscript); *Sechs Lieder* (Bierbaum, Stieler, Hölty, Busse), op. 4

[1910]; *7 Gedichte aus 'Die ewige Hochzeit'* (Dauthendey) (after 1910?) (manuscript); *Episode* (Rosenfeld) (after 1910?) (manuscript); *10 Gedichte* (D. von Liliencron) (after 1910?) (manuscript); *Geheimnis aus der Zyklus 'Vom Kommen Werden und Vergehn'* (Simlinger) (c 1926) (lost); *Troubadour-Ständchen* (Simlinger) (c 1926-1927) (manuscript); *Zwei Notturnos* (Simlinger) (c 1927) (manuscript); *Serenata aus der Oper 'Der letzte Tanz'* (Simlinger) (c 1927) (manuscript: vocal score)

CHOIR: *Zigeunerlied* (Zaleski, transl. from the Polish), vl, T, mix.choir, orch (1926-1930) (manuscript: text, piano reduction, full score)

OPERA: *Der letzte Tanz : Oper in einem Aufzug* (Simlinger, after Giese-Itzenplitz) (c 1926-1927) (manuscript: libretto, piano reduction, full score of 'Serenata' and 'Tanzlied'); *Dr. Pipalumbo : komischer Oper in 3 Aufzügen u. einen Nachspiel* (Simlinger) (c 1926-1928) (manuscript: piano reduction)

BIBLIOGRAPHY

J. Landheer: *Anna Cramer: mythe en werkelijkheid.* Doctoral dissertation University of Utrecht, 1995
Archive Anna Cramer. The Hague, Gemeentemuseum, Music Archives

DISCOGRAPHY

Anna Cramer : liederen. R.A. Morgan (Mez), M. Benoist (pf) (Globe GLO 5128)
Flieder; Weisst du noch; Glück im Traum; Waldhornklänge. R.A. Morgan (Mez), T. Crone (pf) (Sweetlove SLR 9401255)

Lex van Delden

AMSTERDAM, 10 SEPTEMBER 1919 – AMSTERDAM, JULY 1988

Lex van Delden, born Alexander Zwaap, began teaching himself to compose when he was eleven years old. His first compositions he later acknowledged (among which, *L'amour* (1937), op.1, for voice, flute, clarinet, violin, viola and cello) date from the late 1930s. Van Delden studied the piano with Cor de Groot and medicine at the University of Amsterdam. As a Jew, he was forced to break off his education during the Nazi occupation of the Netherlands. He joined the Resistance and took the name Lex van Delden, which he later made his legal name. An exploding carbide lamp so seriously injured one of his eyes that he was forced to abandon his study of medicine for good.

Van Delden now focused on music, composition in particular, but he was also a prolific author on music, and he played an important role in the professional composer's organization Geneco and also the Buma, the Dutch music copyright agency. He was chairman of both organizations for a considerable time.

Not one to close himself off in an ivory tower, Van Delden kept close contact with the music-loving public and day-to-day musical life, especially with performers. His style shows the strong influence of Willem Pijper and the French composers; regarding harmony, bitonal elements play an important role. Rhythm in his music is on the whole quite lively; an expressive lyricism is characteristic of his slow pieces. The scoring of his orchestral music bears witness to consummate craftsmanship.

Van Delden's oeuvre of 114 opuses covers nearly all genres, with the exception of opera. Of interest is that his music often requires unusual forces, at times in compliance with the wishes of particular performers, but also in keeping with his own ideas. The harp holds a special place in his instrumental pieces. Van Delden was in close contact with Phia Berghout, the 'grande dame de la harpe', who succeeded in interesting a number of Dutch composers in the instrument. The acquaintance with Berghout also led to the composition of the first Dutch work for twelve harps. At her request, Van Delden and Marius Flothuis composed a *Kleine suite* [Small suite] in celebration of the sixtieth birthday of harpist Rosa Spier. The first and fourth movements of this suite (Prelude and Fughetta) were written by Flothuis, the second and third (Allegro and Valse lente) by Van Delden, who also composed the Finale, alla marcia, to which Flothuis contributed the Trio.

Van Delden's musical idiom remained relatively consistent throughout the years, although his early penchant for octatonic constructions
made way later for a freer approach to
tonal material. More importantly, his
later work shows broader expressiveness without sacrificing its characteristic playfulness. Examples of this
may be found in *Tomba* (1985), op.112,
for saxophone quartet, composed in
memory of his wife, who died that
year, and his last composition, the second Trio (1988), op.114.

Worth mentioning here of the orchestral works is *In Memoriam* (1953),
op.38, composed in memory of the
victims of the flood that swept the
southern Netherlands that year. The Third Symphony, *Facetten* (1955), op.45,
consists of a series of movements in different tempos played without a break,
that have no connection with traditional formal principles. These movements,
like those of the later *Musica Sinfonica* (1967), op.93, are developed from a limited array of tonal material presented in continually new forms.

For Phia Berghout, Van Delden composed his Harp Concerto (1951), op.32,
and for Hubert Barwahser the Flute Concerto (1965), op.85. Both are scored
for a small orchestra. Surprisingly, Van Delden did not write out a cadenza for
the outer movements of the Flute Concerto, but the slow movement is improvisational in character and is entitled 'Cadenza'. As is the case with the aforementioned *Tomba* for four saxophones, even the scoring alone makes the *Musica notturna a cinque* (1967), op.90, for harp and four cellos, stand out as a
remarkable work in the chamber music genre.

Van Delden was inspired in the composition by *Being Beauteous*, for soprano, four cellos and harp, by Hans Werner Henze, which was performed in
1964 at the 38th festival of the International Society for Contemporary Music
in Copenhagen.

The *Sestetto per archi* (1971), op.97, commissioned by the Buma cultural
fund, is clearly the most original of Van Delden's compositions. The six-instru-
ment scoring gives rise to ingenious explorations of the number three. The
first movement (Lento, Allegro and Lento) presents the interchanging of three

groups of two instruments; in the slow, second movement there are two groups of three instruments; only in the last movement, in which clusters are continuously built up and then broken off, do the strings serve as a true sextet.

An important role is played in Van Delden's oeuvre by works for a cappella choir and various combinations of instruments and choir. The *Partita piccola* (1949), op.23, merits special attention in this regard. After Debussy, Ravel and Caplet introduced the combination of voices without text and instruments, Van Delden (following Daniel Ruyneman, who wrote the first textless, Dutch a cappella work in 1918: *De Roep* [The Call]) composed his five-movement choral piece. The text is limited to 'ah, la, bo, bom'. The third movement is entirely hummed. For *Rubbáiyát* (1947), op.19, Van Delden was awarded the Great Music Prize of the City of Amsterdam. The work is based on the texts of Omar Khayyám, in the suggestive English translation of Edward Fitzgerald, and is scored for the unusual combination of choir, soprano and tenor soloists, two pianos and percussion. The short texts give rise to frequent repetition; the choir is used to hum in the background while the solo vocalist interprets the text (no.2). The limited number of percussion instruments, which require only three players, is very subtly used.

The theme of *Icarus, a radiophonic oratorio* (1962), op.77, links up with the events of the time, in this case space travel. The libretto – news reports declaimed by a reciter – documents the successes of Russian and American astronauts. These reports are put into perspective with quotations from the Bible and various sources from Antiquity. Notable is that Van Delden not only employed radiophonic methods but also integrated electronic instruments in his score.

MARIUS FLOTHUIS

COMPOSITIONS

VOCAL: *L'amour*, S, fl, cl, vl, vla, vc, op. 1 (1939); *In nachtschaduw*, S, orch, op. 2 (1940); *A Cassandre*, B, pf, op. 5c (1941); *Mignonne*, B, orch, op. 7e (1944); *Drie gedichten*, sp.v, op. 10 (1945); *Drie gedichten*, sp.v, pf, op. 10b (1945); *Rubbáiyát* (Omar Khayyám, transl. by E. Fitzgerald), S, T, mix.choir, perc, 2 pf, op. 19 (1947); *Zingende soldaten*, m.choir, op. 20 (1949); *Partita piccola*, mix.choir, op. 23 (1949); *Een Amsterdamsch lied*, mix.choir, pf, op. 29 (1951); *Vocalise op 'a'*, Mez, pf, op. 29a (1951); *Zangerslied*, w.choir/m.choir/mix.choir, op. 37 (1952); *De stroom* (symphony in 5 parts), S,

mix.choir, 7 wind instr, perc, pf, op. 34 (1952); *De stroom* (2nd version, also as Symphony no. 1), S, mix.choir, orch, op. 40 (1954); *De goede dood*, Mez, pf, op. 47 (1955); *Drie sonnetten van Shakespeare*, A, pf, op. 72 (1961); *Icarus : radiophonic oratorio*, S, A, Bar, sp.v, mix.choir, orch, electr., op. 77 (1962); *Galathea*, 1/2 h.v, pf, op. 99 (1972)

CHAMBER MUSIC: *Suite*, vla, pf, op. 4 (1939); *Trio*, pf, vl, vla, op. 7d (1941-1944); *Two Pieces*, vl, pf, op. 17 (1947); *Sonata*, pf, op. 24 (1949); *Duo*, fl, hp, op. 27 (1950); *Kleine suite* (with M. Flothuis), 12 hp, op. 30 (1951); *Sonatina*, a-sax, pf, op. 36 (1952);

Concertino, 2 hp, op. 76 (1962); *Four Pieces*, pf, op. 41 (1954); *Notturno*, hp, op.42 (1954); *String Quartet no. 1*, op. 43 (1954); *Impromptu*, hp, op. 48 (1955); *Sonata a tre*, fl, eh, bn, op. 59 (1957); *Quartetto*, fl, vl, vla, vc, op. 58 (1957); *Sonata*, vc, op. 63 (1958); *Intrada e danza*, 6 hp, op. 70 (1961); *Sonata*, vl, pf, op. 82 (1964); *String Quartet no. 2*, op 86 (1965); *Musica notturna a cinque*, hp, 4 vc, op. 90 (1967); *Sestetto per archi*, op. 97 (1971); *Catena di miniature*, fl, hp, op. 98 (1971); *Trio*, pf, vl, vc, op. 95 (1969); *Nonetto per Amsterdam*, cl, bn, hn, pf, 2 vl, vla, vc, db, op. 101 (1975); *String Quartet no. 3*, op. 106 (1979); *Sestetto per gemelli*, fl, ob, pf, vl, vla, vc, op. 110 (1983); *Tomba*, 4 sax, op. 112 (1985); *Duetto*, vl, hp, op. 111 (1984-1985); *Trio no. 2*, pf, vl, vc, op. 114 (1988)

ORCHESTRA: *Concertstuk*, pf, orch, op. 12 (1943-1945) (unfin.); *Introduzione e allegro*, vl, pf, orch, op. 28 (1951); *Concerto*, hp, orch, op. 32 (1951-1952); *Symphony no. 2 (Sinfonia giocosa)*, op. 39 (1953); *In Memoriam*, op. 38 (1953); *Trio per orchestra d'archi*, op. 44 (1954); *Symphony no. 3 (Facetten)*, op. 45 (1955); *Symphony no. 4*, op. 56 (1957); *Symphony no. 5*, op. 65 (1959); *Concerto*, 2 ob, orch, op. 64 (1959); *Piccolo Concerto*, 12 wind instr, timp, perc, pf, op. 67 (1960); *Concerto*, pf, orch, op. 66 (1960); *Concerto per due orchestre d'archi*, op. 71 (1961); *Draaidans*, wind orch, perc, pf, db, op. 75 (1962); *Symphony no. 6*, op. 69 and 81 (1961-1963); *Sinfonia no. VII*, 11 wind instr, op. 83 (1964); *Sinfonia no. VIII*, str.orch, op. 84 (1964); *Fantasia*, 8 wind instr, hp, op. 87 (1965); *Concerto*, fl, orch, op. 85 (1965); *Musica Sinfonica*, op. 93 (1967); *Concerto*, 2 s-sax, orch, op. 91 (1967); *Bafadis*, op. 103 (1977); *Marcia pomposa*, wind orch, op. 109 (1982)

Music for 6 ballets, 7 plays and 2 films

BIBLIOGRAPHY
J. Koelewijn: 'Typisch een man voor wie je bloemen koopt', *Vrij Nederland*, 7 Oct. 1989
'Lex van Delden : Impromptu for harp solo, op. 48', *Sonorum Speculum*, no. 7, 1961, p. 25-27

W. Paap: 'Lex van Delden', *Mens en Melodie*, vol. 10, 1955, p. 175
W. Paap: 'Lex van Delden', *Music in Holland*. Amsterdam, 1960

DISCOGRAPHY
Bafadis. Amsterdam Philharmonic Orchestra, cond. A. Kersjes (EMI 1A 051-26331)
Flute Concerto (DAVS 7172/3)
Impromptu, op. 48; Duetto, op. 111; Trio, op. 95; Sonatina, op. 36; Sestetto, op. 97. Various performers (BFO A-11)
Marcia pomposa. Dutch National Youth Wind Orchestra, cond. J. Cober (NM Classics 92009)
Marcia pomposa. Symphonic Band of the Maastricht Conservatory, cond. S. Pijpers (MBS 31.0020.67)
Orchestral works. Royal Concertgebouw Orchestra, cond. B. Haitink, E. Jochum and G. Szell (Etcetera KTC 1156)
Ouverture voor een feestdag. Symphony Orchestra Con Brio, cond. I. Soeteman (recorded Waalse Kerk 1983)
Sonata for violin and piano, op. 82. I. van Keulen (vl), R. Brautigam (pf) (NM Classics 92043)
Trio per orchestra d'archi (DAVS 6301)

Alphons Diepenbrock

AMSTERDAM, 2 SEPTEMBER 1862 – AMSTERDAM, 5 APRIL 1921

Alphons Johannes Maria Diepenbrock was born to a Catholic, culturally inclined family. He began taking piano and violin lessons at an early age and
somewhat later singing lessons. Despite his natural musical talent, he decided
to study Classical languages and graduated with a thesis on Seneca. Inspired
by such literary fellow students as Frederik van Eeden, Jacques Perk and Albert Verwey – who soon gained acclaim as De Tachtigers [The eighties group]
– Diepenbrock began composing songs on a regular basis. For several years,
he worked for the group's literary journal, *De Nieuwe Gids*.

As a grammar school teacher in 's-Hertogenbosch, he developed a friendship with the painter Antoon Derkinderen, stimulated by a common interest
in Wagner and the culture of the Middle Ages and Renaissance. In the shadow
of this city's Saint John's Cathedral, Diepenbrock worked for more than a year
on his first large-scale composition, the *Missa*. Although all plans to have the
work performed ultimately failed, the score was published with illustrations
by Derkinderen in 1896.

Diepenbrock returned to Amsterdam and worked as a private teacher and
writer for the new weekly journal *De Kroniek*. His articles on a wide range of
cultural and philosophical topics often sparked controversy. He also drew attention with his reflections on the Wagner Society and Anton Averkamp's
Klein-Koor a Cappella. When this choir added Diepenbrock's *Stabat mater dolorosa* to its repertoire he began to make a name for himself as a composer. He
found staunch advocates of his work in the soprano Aaltje Noordewier-Reddingius and the alto Pauline de Haan-Manifarges. To them he dedicated,
among other works, the two *Hymnen an die Nacht,* which after a successful
premiere remained in the repertoire. Diepenbrock prepared the First Netherlands Music Festival of 1902 with Willem Mengelberg and Bernard Zweers.
This festival was devoted entirely to Dutch music. The first performance of
Diepenbrock's *Te Deum*, at the opening of this festival, was a monumental
event. Composer and music critic Daniël de Lange referred to the piece in a review as one of the most important works of modern times.

When Gustav Mahler came to Amsterdam in 1903, he and Diepenbrock developed a close friendship. Diepenbrock corresponded extensively with the
Utrecht philosopher Hondius van den Broek about Mahler, Richard Strauss
and Friedrich Nietzsche. Diepenbrock's *Im grossen Schweigen*, to a text by Niet-

zsche, together with his *Te Deum* and *Vondel's Vaart naar Agrippine* [Vondel's Journey to Agrippin], soon became his most frequently performed works.

Diepenbrock gradually turned away from German culture. His Verlaine and Baudelaire songs illustrate his growing interest in French culture, and the influence of Debussy is apparent in *Marsyas*, the first of his *Toneelmuzieken* [Music for the stage]. For theater director Willem Royaards he composed in 1912 incidental music for Vondel's play *Gijsbrecht van Aemstel*. Slightly later, embittered by the First World War, Diepenbrock withdrew from public life, although he re-emerged after 1917 with incidental music for Aristophanes' *De Vogels* [The Birds] and Goethe's *Faust*. Diepenbrock was in poor health, however, suffering from liver cancer.

Heartened by a commission to compose incidental music for Sophocles' *Elektra*, an opportunity the classicist in him could not turn down, he finished the score in the summer of 1920. Not long thereafter, on 5 April 1921, he died.

Diepenbrock composed songs, works for voice and orchestra, (sacred) choral pieces and incidental music. Almost entirely lacking are instrumental compositions. In composing he allowed himself to be led by a text and in choosing it he was very original; he was the first to set the poetry of De Tachtigers to music as well as the first in the Netherlands to compose songs to French poetry. Two factors were decisive in his development as a composer. Very early, Diepenbrock studied the scores of Wagner, as evidenced by the text declamation and harmony in songs like *Der König in Thule* and *Mignon* (1886). He was also fascinated by the revival of Early Music. A comment he made after a performance of Palestrina's *Missa Papae Marcelli* shows that vocal music was for him the highest form of musical art: 'If music is ever to become again what it was in Antiquity [...] and in the Middle Ages [...] than she must [...] rediscover the old vocal element, and singing as the foundation of music making instead of instruments.'

Diepenbrock's stepwise melodic construction is related to that of Gregorian chant. His a cappella choral works, and most especially the *Missa* for double male choir, tenor and organ, intended for performance in a church, hark back to sixteenth-century polyphony. But with such Wagnerian characteristics as leitmotif and chromaticism, it was thought too bold, and it was only in 1916 that the work was given official approval for church performance.

Diepenbrock also sought to broaden his resources as a composer of songs, for instance in his *Hymnen an die Nacht* setting of a Novalis text. He was drawn to the work of this German romantic poet, and the elements 'Hymne' and 'Nacht', so pervasive in the poet's work, are also conspicuous in that of Diepenbrock. The overwhelmingly melancholy character of his music is linked with these factors. Notable are the long drawn out preludes, interludes and codas in the orchestra. Even before Mahler's *Das Lied von der Erde*, Diepenbrock was exploring the new genre of 'symphonic song'. The degree to which his orchestration advanced is demonstrated by *Die Nacht*. Its exceedingly subtle instrumentation, evoking a nocturnal atmosphere, is at least as important as the vocal aspect. The score is remarkably transparent as a consequence of the prominent roles given to the harp, mandolin, solo violin and woodwinds. Here, we find the influences of Mahler and Debussy forged into new unity.

Diepenbrock's crowning achievement was *Elektra*. Here, as in the incidental music for *De Vogels* and *Faust*, the Dutch translation of the text is spoken rather than sung; neither pitch nor rhythm is notated for the reciters. New is the vehement, almost grim character of the music. A compelling sound-world is created by the ostinato motifs and modal progressions.

Diepenbrock held an unusual place in cultural life around 1900 as a prominent music critic and writer on music. A self-taught composer, he wrestled with uncertainty and was often regarded as an amateur. His perfectionism, in combination with certain failings in his technical foundation, made him continuously revise his work. He took little account of the practicalities of musical life but at the same time demanded the utmost from performers. Diepenbrock recognized early on the importance of Wagner and Renaissance polyphony. Later, he found inspiration in Mahler and French music, thus initiating a new compositional trend in the Netherlands. In a way, Diepenbrock served as mentor to many of his younger contemporaries, although no teacher-student relationship ever existed. Among the composers influenced by him were Jan Ingenhoven, Matthijs Vermeulen, Hendrik Andriessen and Willem Pijper.

DÉSIRÉE STAVERMAN

COMPOSITIONS

VOICE AND PIANO (some were orchestrated at a later date): *Dämmernd liegt der Sommerabend* (Heine); *De klare dag* (Van Eeden) (1884); *Avondzang* (Perk); *Maanlicht* (Verwey); *Meinacht* (Swarth) (1885); *3 Ballads* (1885); *2 Balladen von Goethe* (1886); *Mignons Verklärung* (Goethe); *Die Liebende schreibt* (Goethe) (1887); *Ave Maria* (1889); *Jesu dulcis memoria* (1889); *Es war ein alter König* (Heine) (1890); *O, Jesu, ego amo te* (St. Francis Xavier) (1893); *Hinüber wall' ich* (Novalis) (1897); *Ecoutez la chanson bien douce* (Verlaine); *Ik ben in eenzaamheid niet meer alleen* (Van Deyssel); *Lied der Spinnerin* (Brentano); *Clair de lune* (Verlaine); *Hymne* (Novalis) (1898); *Zij sluimert* (Perk) (1900); *Memorare* (St. Bernardus) (1902); *Kann ich im Busen heisse Wünsche tragen* (Günderrode) (1902); *Ballad* (Daniélou) (1903); *Les Chats* (Baudelaire) (1906); *Recueillement* (Baudelaire) (1907); *Celebrität* (Goethe); *Der Abend* (Brentano); *Liebesklage* (Günderrode) (1908); *Mandoline* (Verlaine); *Puisque l'aube grandit* (Verlaine) (1909); *En sourdine* (Verlaine) (1910); *Berceuse* (Lerberghe) (1912); *L'invitation au voyage* (Baudelaire) (1913); *Les Poilus de l'Argonne* (Rameau) (1915); *Incantation* (Gide) (1916); *Belges, debout!* (Puymaly) (1916)

VOICE AND ENSEMBLE OR ORCHESTRA: *2 Hymnen an die Nacht* (Novalis) (1899); *Vondel's Vaart naar Agrippine* (Thym) (1903); *Im grossen Schweigen* (Nietzsche) (1906); *Die Nacht* (Hölderlin) (1911); *Bruiloftslied* (Beukers) (1912); *Lydische Nacht* (Verhagen) (1913); *Wenn ich ihn nur habe* (Novalis) (1915); *Come raggio di sol* (1917)

A CAPPELLA CHOIR: *Stabat mater dolorosa*, mix.choir (1888/1896); *Stabat mater speciosa*, mix.choir (1896); *Caelestis urbs Jerusalem*, mix.choir (1897); *Chanson d'automne* (Verlaine), mix.choir (1897); *Carmen saeculare*, mix.choir (1901); *Den uil, Oud paaschlied*, mix.choir (1902); *De groote hond en de kleine kat* (Verwey), mix.choir (1903); *Vier vierstemmige liederen*, mix.choir (1906); *5 Gesänge* (Goethe), mix.choir (1884/1908); *Rouw om het jaar* (Verwey), w.choir (1886);

Tibur (Matthison), m.choir (1884); *Veni creator spiritus*, m.choir (1906); *Ecce quomodo moritur*, m.choir (1913)

MALE CHOIR AND ORGAN: *Missa* (1891); *Tantum ergo sacramentum* (1901); *Hymnus de Spiritu Sancto* (1906)

CHOIR AND ORCHESTRA: *Reizangen uit Gysbrecht van Aemstel* (Vondel) (1892/1895); *Missa, Kyrië en Gloria* (1913); *Te Deum laudamus* (1897/1908); *Les Elfes* (De Lisle) (1896); *Hymne aan Rembrandt* (Van Moerkerken) (1906)

MUSIC FOR THE THEATRE: *Marsyas* (Verhagen) (1910); *Gijsbrecht van Aemstel* (Vondel) (1912); *De Vogels* (Aristophanes) (1917); *Faust* (Goethe) (1918); *Elektra* (Sophocles) (1920)

INSTRUMENTAL MUSIC: *Academische Feestmarsch* (1882); *Hymne*, vl, pf/orch (1898/1917)

BIBLIOGRAPHY

Alphons Diepenbrock : brieven en documenten, I t/m X, ed. E. Reeser. Amsterdam, KVNM, 1950-1998

T. Braas: 'Ik heb nu eindelijk het orchestreeren zoowat geleerd', *Harmonie en perspectief : zevenendertig bijdragen van Utrechtse musicologen voor Eduard Reeser*, ed. A. Annegarn [et al.]. Deventer, Sub Rosa, 1988

T. Braas: 'The Verlaine Songs of Alphons Diepenbrock', *Key Notes*, 30, 1996/4, p. 16-20

W. Bronzwaer: 'Alphons Diepenbrock en de Missa in die Festo', *Muziek in de 20e eeuw*, ed. J. Nuchelmans. Baarn, Ambo, 1995

D. Krouwel: 'Het sonnet in de muziek : Richard Strauss en Alphons Diepenbrock', *Harmonie en perspectief : zevenendertig bijdragen van Utrechtse musicologen voor Eduard Reeser*, ed. A. Annegarn [et al.]. Deventer, Sub Rosa, 1988

W. Paap: *Alphons Diepenbrock : een componist in de cultuur van zijn tijd*. Haarlem, De Haan, 1980

E. Reeser: *Alphons Diepenbrock*. Amsterdam, Bigot en Van Rossum

E. Reeser: 'Alphons Diepenbrock', *Sonorum Speculum*, no. 12, 1962, p. 1-11

E. Reeser: *Een eeuw Nederlandse muziek :
1815-1915.* Amsterdam, Querido, 1950, 2/1986
D. Staverman: 'Diepenbrocks tekstbehan-
deling in zijn "Wilhelm Meister-liederen", *'Tijdschrift voor Muziektheorie*, no. 3, 1996, p. 148-155
D. Staverman: 'Het vel dat nooit paste :
rondom het melodrama in Diepenbrocks
Marsyas', *Harmonie en perspectief : zevenendertig bijdragen van Utrechtse musicologen voor
Eduard Reeser*, ed. A. Annegarn [et al.]. Deventer, Sub Rosa, 1988
*Verzamelde geschriften van Alphons Diepen-
brock*, ed. E. Reeser and Th. Diepenbrock.
Utrecht [etc.], Het Spectrum, 1950

DISCOGRAPHY
Academische feestmarsch. Dutch National
Youth Wind Orchestra, cond. J. Cober (NM
Classics 92080)
Auf dem See; Chanson d'automne. Nether-
lands Chamber Choir, cond. U. Gronostay
(NM Classics 92065)
*Alphons Diepenbrock, Vol. I. Orchestral
Works.* E. Verhey (vl), Residentie Orchestra,
cond. H. Vonk (Chandos Chan 8821)
*Alphons Diepenbrock, Vol. II. Symphonic
Songs.* L. Finnie (Mez), R. Holl (B), Chr.
Homberger (T), Residentie Orchestra, cond.
H. Vonk (Chandos Chan 8878)
Alphons Diepenbrock, songs, Vol. 1, 2 and 3.
R. Alexander (S), Chr. Pfeiler (Mez), J. van Nes
(A), Chr. Prégardien (T), R. Hol (B), R. Jansen
(pf), L. van Doeselaar (org), D. Esser (vc) (NM
Classics 92050, 92051 en 92052)
Avondschemer. D. Kuyken (pf) (NM Classics
92049)
Berceuse. E. Ameling (S), D. Baldwin (pf),
R. van der Meer (vc) (Globe GLO 6018)
Caelestis urbs Jerusalem. Netherlands
Chamber Choir, cond. U. Gronostay (NM Clas-
sics 92039)
Lydische Nacht. Residentie Orchestra, cond.
E. Spanjaard (Olympia OCD 507)
Memorare. W. te Brummelstroete (Mez), R.
Overpelt (T), B. Bartelink (org), Vocal Ensem-
ble Markant, cond. M. Versteeg (KRO 94009)
Missa in die Festo. R. Overpelt (T), B.
Bartelink (org), Missa-Mannenkoor, cond. M.
Versteeg (KRO 94008)
Die Nacht. J. Baker (Mez), Royal Concertge-
bouw Orchestra, cond. B. Haitink (Q Disc
97014)

*Symphonic suite Elektra; Hymne an die
Nacht; Ouverture De vogels.* A. Auger (S), Royal
Concertgebouw Orchestra, cond. R. Chailly
(Composers' Voice Highlights CV 50)
Te Deum laudamus. Various soloists,
Toonkunst Choir Amsterdam, Concertgebouw
Orchestra, cond. E. van Beinum (BFO A-4)

Bernard van Dieren

ROTTERDAM, 27 DECEMBER 1887 – LONDON, 24 APRIL 1936

Bernard Hélène Joseph van Dieren was the youngest of five children born to a family of French-Dutch descent. Because his father was not very successful as a wine merchant, his mother provided for the family with her earnings as a seamstress.

Van Dieren began his musical education with violin lessons, possibly with Louis Wolff, then a prominent musician in Rotterdam. Having difficulties in conforming to the educational system of the time, Van Dieren's highschool years were not always happy. This inability to adapt again proved to be a source of difficulties in later life.

Van Dieren began to compose seriously around 1907. Two collections of his songs were published in that year by the Rotterdam music dealer Lichtenauer. The first was dedicated to the Rotterdam musician Willy Kindler, whose daughter Frida was a student of Busoni and at an early age enjoyed a reputation as an excellent pianist. When Frida left for England in 1909 Van Dieren soon followed; on 1 January 1910 they were married in London. As in his childhood, it was the woman of the house who provided a regular income.

Van Dieren composed fairly prolifically during his first years in London, but this came to a sudden halt in 1912 when he was discovered to be suffering from a kidney ailment. He underwent a total of nine operations but the illness proved incurable and at times quite painful. Presumably as a result of his illness, various compositions he began in this period were only to be completed much later. Definitive dating of his works is therefore not always possible.

Van Dieren's versatile personality brought him into contact with a large number of artists. A meeting in 1915 with the sculptor Jacob Epstein was the beginning of a close friendship. Epstein made a bronze study portrait of Van Dieren, which was later purchased by the city of Rotterdam and placed in De Doelen concert hall. Van Dieren, in turn, dedicated one of his most important compositions – *Diaphony* – to Epstein. In 1920 he actually wrote a book about this sculptor. Van Dieren was also acquainted during this time with the composers Cecil Gray and Peter Warlock (pseudonym of Philip Heseltine). Together they undertook with alternating success the production of various operas and concert series in London.

Shortly after the end of World War I Van Dieren returned with his wife and children to the Netherlands; his String Quartet no.2 was premiered in London

Bernard van Dieren (seated right) in Donaueschingen in 1922 with Paul Hindemith
(seated center) and others.

during his absence. He did not remain long, however; the necessity of medical
treatment forced him to return to England in March 1921.

In the 1920s Van Dieren's music was frequently performed, various musicians including it in their repertoire and several publishing houses beginning
to show interest. In 1925, Oxford University Press published twelve songs and
the premiere of *Serenade* was followed by a concert with sections of his opera
The Tailor, conducted by John Barbirolli. Through the efforts of Peter Warlock,
the Oxford catalogue included several more of his works in 1927. That year the
Amar Quartet performed his String Quartet no.4 in Frankfurt. Willem Pijper,
who reviewed the concert for music journal *De Muziek*, was not particularly
impressed with the work.

Peter Warlock's death on 16 December 1930 came as an enormous shock to
the Van Dierens, who had been the last to have seen him alive that day. The
family had been very close to Warlock, and Van Dieren remained a strong advocate of his music.

In 1935 Van Dieren's music essays were published under the title *Down
among the Dead Men and other essays*. Of particular importance are the articles
dealing with the pianist and composer Busoni. In his final year Van Dieren
composed the overture *Anjou* and, to his surprise, two orchestras vied with
each other for the right to give the first performance. Around Christmas 1935
it became clear that Van Dieren did not have long to live. He died on 24 April
1936 at the age of 48.

Van Dieren's work falls into three periods: his formative years until 1910, in which late-Romantic tonality dominates; from 1910 to 1917, in which his music shows increasing influences of Busoni and Schoenberg – the *Sechs Skizzen* (1911), for piano, for example, lean towards Schoenberg's free atonality; and from 1917 until his death in 1936. During this last period Van Dieren's style became increasingly polyphonic and various works for small instrumental ensembles began to emerge.

His mature work is dominated by lyrical counterpoint. Although he inclined toward atonality, Van Dieren never totally abandoned a sense of key, not even in compositions without key signatures. He also developed enormous rhythmic freedom, thoroughly negating the significance of bar lines. These serve merely for visual orientation, as for instance in the String Quartet no.2.

Although Van Dieren composed the first sketches for his opera *The Tailor* in 1917, he only completed the score in 1930. It has never been performed in its entirety and survives only in a chaotic manuscript. However, sections of it were given a concertante performance in 1925.

Van Dieren made especially high technical demands upon performers. His music was not written with the amateur in mind, an artistic mentality he inherited from Busoni. He exerted a strong influence on the music of Peter Warlock and Cecil Gray, and to a lesser extent upon that of William Busch and William Walton.

WILMA ROEST

COMPOSITIONS
Lost compositions are not included

VOCAL: *Ave Maria* (4 v) (1917?); *Ave Maria* (5 v) (1921); *Deus, deus, meus, ad te de luce vigilo* (Psalm 63), mix.choir; *Belsazar*, Bar, orch (1911); *Chinese symphonie*, soloists, mix.choir, orch (1914); *Diaphony*, Bar, chamb.orch (1916); *Two Recitations*, sp.v, str.qt (1917?); *Two Songs*, v, str.qt (1917?); *Spenser sonnet*, T, 11 instr. (1921); *Hommages*, Bar, 7 instr. (1931); *The Tailor* (opera) (Nichols), soloists, chamb.orch (1930). Approximately 60 songs (to English, German, French and Dutch texts), half of them only survived in manuscript

PIANO: *Sechs Skizzen* (1911); *Toccata* (1912); *Three Studies* (1925?); *Tema con variazione* (1927?)

CHAMBER MUSIC: *String Quartet no. 1* (1912); *String Quartet no. 2* (1917); *String Quartet no. 3* (1919); *String Quartet no. 4* (1923); *Serenade*, 9 instr. (1925); *String Quartet no. 6* (1927); *Sonata*, vl (1928); *Sonata*, vc (1930); *String Quartet no. 5* (1931); *Twee Estemporales*, hp (1931)

ORCHESTRA: *Elegy*, vc, orch (1908); Symphonic epilogue for 'The Cenci' (1910); Introduction to 'Les Propous des beuveurs' (1921); *Anjou : komische ouverture* (1935); *Symphony in 3 dance movements* (unfin.)

PUBLICATIONS
Down among the Dead Men and other essays. London, Oxford University Press, 1935
Jacob Epstein. London, The Boldley Head, 1920

BIBLIOGRAPHY

A. Chisholm: *Bernard van Dieren : an intro-duction.* London, Thames, 1984

F. Tomlinson: *Warlock and Van Dieren.* London, Thames, 1978

DISCOGRAPHY

Songs. S. van Lier (S), P. Prenen (pf) (BVHaast 051)

Songs for high voice and string quartet; Estemporale no.1 and 2 for harp; Songs for high voice and piano; Sonata for solo violin; Piccolo Pralinudettino Fridato; Sonatina Tytoica (British Music Label BLM 001)

Sem Dresden

AMSTERDAM, 20 APRIL 1881 – THE HAGUE, 31 JULY 1957

Sem Dresden was undoubtedly one of the most versatile personalities in twentieth-century Dutch musical life. The dangers of such versatility are well known: an inner necessity to continually occupy oneself with various aspects of the profession can soon lead to the public not giving all of these activities their due attention and appreciation. In general, creative activity is put aside in favor of the more appealing pursuits of the conductor, pianist, teacher, examiner, critic and conservatory director. The Frenchmen Maurice Emmanuel and Charles Koechlin are among the most notorious examples of composers who became the victims of their own all-roundness. Dresden's versatility, however, was deeply rooted in his personality and is also reflected in his compositions.

From 1924 to 1937 Dresden was director of the Amsterdam Conservatory, and from 1937 to 1949 of the Royal Conservatory in The Hague. However, on account of his Jewish background, German occupying forces barred him from holding the position between 1940 and 1945. As conductor of the Madrigal Society and the Haarlem Motet and Madrigal Society, he continued to build on the fruitful work begun by Daniël de Lange, namely broadening the repertoire to include more a cappella music from various periods. Dresden's publications include *Het muziekleven in Nederland sinds 1880* [Musical life in the Netherlands since 1880] (1923) and *Stromingen en tegenstromingen in de muziek* [Movements and countermovements in music] (1953).

Dresden was born into a merchant family and received scarcely any musical training. The teachers to whom he eventually turned were either Germans (Hans Pfitzner) or Dutchmen whose music was oriented towards German styles (Frederik Roeske and Bernard Zweers). Neither this background nor his participation in the musical life of Berlin while he was a student seem to have had a lasting influence on his musical personality. What he did retain was a thorough musical knowledge, from which his later students Jan Mul, Jan Felderhof, Willem van Otterloo and Leo Smit profited.

Early on, Dresden felt himself attracted to the then new currents in French music embodied in the work of Gabriel Fauré, Claude Debussy and Maurice Ravel. This is apparent, for example, in a work such as the Sonata for flute and harp (1917), composed two years after Debussy's Sonata for flute, viola and harp, which gives rise to the question whether Dresden already knew of Debussy's piece. This is certainly possible, as Debussy's composition had been performed in the Netherlands by that time.

In his book *Zeventig jaar Neder-landse muziek 1915-1985* [Seventy Years of Dutch Music 1915-1985] Leo Samama wrote: 'It is lamentable that Dresden so infrequently allowed himself to be led by the charm of his musical ideas. His compositional style was primarily academic. He adds: 'That Dresden was capable of giving musical form to turbulent emotions is evidenced by, among other things, several very exciting moments in the opera *François Villon* (1957; orchestrated by Jan Mul) and

various movements of the *Dansflitsen* [Dance flashes], for orchestra.' This comment also holds for such a work as the impressive *Chorus tragicus* (1928), for mixed choir, five trumpets, two bugles and percussion.

Here Samama cites a view of Dresden's work often expressed, namely that much of it reveals a high level of (academic) ability, but at the cost of emotional content. The opera *François Villon* as well as the large-scale *Chorus symphonicus* (1944-1955) defy this assessment, showing off the all-round nature of his personality to great effect.

Compositions such as the *Vier vocalises* [Four vocalises], for mezzo-soprano and seven instruments, several chamber music pieces, based on Dutch folk songs, and the five-movement *Sinfonietta*, for clarinet and orchestra, offer instances of exceedingly ingenious and refined flights of imagination – several of which attain such heights as to make it unjust summarily to dismiss them as being merely 'academic'.

Vier vocalises and *Chorus symphonicus* may be considered to represent the two extremes of Dresden's creative range. Vocalises are vocal etudes, but they can transcend their limits in the hands of a gifted composer; the *Vocalise-étude en forme de habanera* by Ravel and both *Vocalises* by Roussel amply demonstrate this point. The absence of text, moreover, has the advantage that the vocal part may be performed by an instrument without a great deal of tampering with the score. This is not possible in Dresden's *Vier vocalises*, however, for the accompaniment consists of seven instruments: flute, clarinet, bassoon, violin, viola, piano and percussion (kettledrum, side-drum, gong, suspended cymbal, cymbals and triangle). The titles of the four movements – Canto spianato, Fiorette, Staccato and Portamento – clearly indicate that these are intended as vocal etudes. Dresden referred to the piece as 'four vocalises for mezzo-soprano and chamber orchestra', which is something of an overstatement for a group of seven musicians, but it seems likely that this was his way of making clear that he wished the performance of the work to be led by a conductor. This is how the piece was premiered in Amsterdam's Concertgebouw on 2 February 1936, Dresden himself conducting the Dutch Chamber Music Society with the vocalist Hans Gruys.

Chorus symphonicus is a classic example of the cultural 'hidden resistance' to the Nazi occupation, comparable to Rudolf Escher's *Musique pour l'esprit en deuil*. The piece could be regarded as a Dutch companion to Stravinsky's *Symphonie de Psaumes*. The choice of the psalm texts (Psalms 139, 69, 57 and 34) which, just as in the case of Stravinsky, are sung in Latin, would themselves have precluded performance of the piece during the occupation, even discounting the fact that the composer was Jewish.

Vier vocalises and this choral piece have one aspect in common, namely the 'economy' technique used by Dresden in so many compositions. The example of Debussy's *Pelléas et Mélisande*, in which the usual instrumental forces of a modern orchestra are only sporadically employed in their entirety, certainly left its mark on Dresden. In the *Chorus symphonicus* this technique is also used in the choral setting.

MARIUS FLOTHUIS

COMPOSITIONS

VOCAL: *Drie liedjes* (Perk), v, pf (1904); *Gefunden* (Bierbaum), v, pf (1904); *Liebster, nur dich seh'n* (Rückert), v, pf (1904); *Der lustige Ehemann* (Bierbaum), v, pf (1904); *De fluitspeler* (Schürmann), v, pf (1917); *Bij den vijver* (Schürmann), v, pf (1917); *Treurig, treurig* (Rensburg), v, pf (1919); *Oud spinet* (Schürmann), v, pf (1919); *Chorus tragicus*, mix.choir, 5 tpt, 2 flhn, perc (1928); *Vier vocalises*, Mez, fl, cl, bn, vl, vla, pf, perc (1935); *Kerstlied*, v, perc, str.orch (1939); *O kerstnacht schooner dan de dagen*, 3 trb, mix.choir, str.orch (1939); *Vier liederen* (Donker), v, pf (1942); *Chorus symphonicus*, soloists, choir, orch (1943-1944, rev. 1955); *Daar was e wuf ...*, 2 S, A, T, B (1950); *Beatus vir* (St. Antonius), m.choir (1951); *Saint Antoine : symphonie-oratorio* (Flaubert), soloists, choir, orch (1953); *Psalm 84*, soloists, choir, orch (1954); *De wijnen van Bourgondië*, mix.choir,

orch (1954); *Carnavals-cantate*, S, m.choir, orch (1955); *Sint Joris*, soloists, choir, 2 pf, perc (1955, version soloists, choir, orch 1956); *Catena musicale*, S, fl, ob, cl, bn, vl, vla, vc, orch (1956); *Rembrandt's Saul en David*, S, orch (1956)

DRAMATIC VOCAL: *Toto* (operetta) (1945); *François Villon* (Dresden) (opera) (instrumentation completed by J. Mul) (1956-1957)

INSTRUMENTAL: *Vijf kleine klavierstukken* (1905); *Kleine suite*, fl, ob, cl, bn, hn, pf (1913); *Thema met veranderingen* (1914); *Sonata no. 1*, vc, pf (1916); *Suite (Rameau suite)*, fl, ob, cl, bn, hn, pf (1916, rev. 1948); *Sonata*, fl, hp (1917); *Suite no. 3 (Sextet no. 3)*, fl (and pic), ob (and eh), cl, bn, hn, pf (1920); *String Quartet no. 1* (1924); *Concerto no. 1*, vl, orch (1936); *Sinfonietta*, cl, orch (1938); *Concerto*, ob, orch (1939); *Concerto*

no. 2, vl, orch (1941-1942); *Concerto*, pf, ob,
str.qt (1942); *Sonata no. 2*, vc, pf (1942);
Suite, vc (1943); *Sonata*, vl (1943); *Trio*, vl,
vc, pf (1942-1943); *Toccata, koraal en fuga*,
org (1941-1946); *Concerto*, pf, orch (1946);
Three Piano Pieces, pf (1947); *Concerto*, fl,
orch (1949); *Three Pieces*, schl.orch (1949);
Dansflitsen, orch (1951, version for 2 pf
1953); *Concerto*, org, orch (1952-1953)

PUBLICATIONS

*Gedenkboek Amsterdamsch Conservatorium
1884-1934.* Amsterdam, 1934
Het muziekleven in Nederland sinds 1880.
Amsterdam, Elsevier, 1923
S. van Milligen and S. Dresden: *Ontwikke-
lingsgang der muziek van de oudheid tot onzen
tijd.* Groningen [etc.], Wolters, 2/1923
S. van Milligen: *Algemene muziekleer.* 3rd
ed. rev. by S. Dresden
Stromingen en tegenstromingen in de muziek.
Haarlem, 1953

BIBLIOGRAPHY

H. Badings: *De hedendaagsche Nederland-
sche muziek.* Amsterdam, 1936
W. Paap: 'Nederlandsche componisten van
onzen tijd, dl. III Sem Dresden', *Mens en
Melodie*, vol. 1, 1946, p. 73-79
W. Paap: 'In memoriam Sem Dresden',
Mens en Melodie, vol. 12, 1957, p. 225-227
W. Paap: 'Composers', *Music in Holland*,
ed. E. Reeser. Amsterdam
P. Sanders: *Moderne Nederlandsche compo-
nisten.* The Hague, [1930]
E. van Zoeren: *De muziekuitgeverij A.A.
Noske : (1896-1926) : een bijdrage tot dertig jaar
Nederlandse muziekgeschiedenis.* Haarlemmer-
liede, Van Zoeren 1987

DISCOGRAPHY

Chorus tragicus. Collegium Musicum Am-
stelodamense, Residentie Orchestra, cond. D.
Masson (Composers' Voice CV 6810 986-7)
Daar was e wuf... ; Hymnus matutinus.
Netherlands Chamber Choir, cond. H. van den
Hombergh (CBS 71110)
Dansflitsen. Residentie Orchestra, cond. W.
van Otterloo (Composers' Voice CV 26)
Oboe Concerto (Donemus DAVS 7374/2)
Violin Concerto no. 2 (Donemus DAVS
6702)

Gerrit Jan van Eijken

AMERSFOORT, 5 MAY 1832 – LONDON, 22 MARCH 1879

Gerrit Jan van Eijken was not the only member of his family to pursue a career in music. His father Gerrit was organist and bell-ringer at the Great Church in Amersfoort and a city music master. It was here that Gerrit Jan – Gerrit Isak according to his birth and death certificates – was born. He received his first musical instruction from his father, who taught him to play the piano and the organ and gave him lessons in harmony and composition. His older brother Jan Albert assisted at these lessons.

In 1851 Van Eijken entered the conservatory of Leipzig. As it had been in the Netherlands, his unusual talent was soon noticed. That same year he received the Honorary Award from the Society for the Advancement of Music for two sonatinas he composed for piano 'for the use and edification of our dear youth'. When he left Leipzig in 1853 he brought with him commendations from prominent figures in music and from his teachers, among whom was Ignaz Moscheles. During a short stay in Dresden he studied the organ with the court organist Johann Schneider and singing with Ferdinand Böhme, both with remarkable results. It was during this time that his first songs opp.1 and 2, were published in Leipzig.

In 1853 he returned to the Netherlands and took up residence in Amsterdam but, after falling seriously ill, he returned to his parents in Amersfoort to recover. In 1855 he moved to Utrecht, marking the beginning of a very active period of his life. He gave organ and piano performances, conducted the Schutterij, the civic guard ensemble that was a forerunner to the Utrecht Municipal Orchestra, wrote music criticism (his writings appeared regularly in *Caecilia*; he was also on the editorial board of this music journal) and he composed. Although as a composer he was highly respected by leading figures both at home and abroad, his fame never really took hold in the Netherlands, which must have affected him greatly. In 1857 Van Eijken became organist to the Walloon community in Utrecht. His efforts to raise the local level of music making led him to found a music school in Utrecht. Despite J.N. van Hall's fiery plea for Van Eijken in a pamphlet entitled *Een 'question brûlante' op muzikaal gebied* [A burning question in the field of music] (1862), he was passed over for the position of city music master in Utrecht. Possibly in reaction to this, he moved to Rotterdam in 1863, but in 1865 he returned to Utrecht and soon after married Wilhelmina Petronella Wethmar, a soprano

from Amsterdam with whom he would give frequent performances.

Perhaps as a result of repeated disappointments, Van Eijken soon left Utrecht again, this time for England, where his two daughters were born. In his years there he was very active as a teacher and composer, producing large numbers of compositions, paraphrases, arrangements and transcriptions. It seems unlikely, however, that he gained recognition for his work in England.

He passed his final years as an organist in Dalston, a suburb of London, and died there in 1879 at the age of 46 of 'delirium tremens and pneumonia', according to the death certificate. He was buried at Abney Park Cemetery which has since become so run down that his grave is no longer discernible.

Van Eijken left behind what on first impression appears to be a remarkable oeuvre. His creative spirit awakened when he was about eighteen and waxed until it suddenly seemed to expire following the op.11 songs. In the three op.13 vocal pieces it flickered to life, never again to make itself felt. The enormous amount of music he composed subsequently held the middle ground between mediocrity and sheer puerility. His decline as a composer was most likely a consequence of the many disappointments he suffered and his ensuing indifference and alcoholism.

In 1859 Emanuel Klitzsch commented in the *Neue Zeitschrift für Musik* on works of Van Eijken, written while the composer was still in his prime: 'In this it speaks for itself that the composer is not reminiscent of any model; he stands so firmly on his own two feet that nowhere does one notice a foreign sound.' One may justly speak of a Van Eijken style. In as far as a relationship with any other composer may be observed it is either with his contemporaries or with composers yet to be born.

Notable in the songs of his most fertile period is vehement and sometimes dramatic expressiveness combined with a certain introversion. This is particularly the case in *Der schwere Abend*, op.8/1, *Drei Lieder*, op.6 and *Fünf Gedichte*, op.11. Foreshadowing the music of Fauré and of Richard Strauss, the floating harmonies of *Mit deinen blauen Augen*, op.7/1, show a strong propensity toward unresolved progressions. Typical Debussian sounds emerge in *Die Sonne sank*, op.6/3, and *Wenn ich in deine Augen seh*, op.7/3. The cycle *Töne der Liebe*, op.10, to poetry by G.F. Daumer based on the biblical Song of Songs, may rightly be considered Van Eijken's greatest monument, the composer exploring the broadest scale of divergent and at times extraverted emotions. Some of his works show the sensibilities of a true opera composer, such as *Drei Balladen*, op.9. An actual opera composed by Van Eijken, *Het Kroningsfeest van Keizer Karel V te Bologna* [The coronation feast of Emperor Charles V at Bologna], dating presumably from c.1860, has been lost.

Of the instrumental works written when Van Eijken was in his prime, two compositions are worth closer inspection: *Deux sonatines pour le pianoforte*, op.3 and the Sonata for piano and violin, op.5. The outer movements of the *Deux sonatines* take their cue from the Classical style, with well-crafted development sections. In the middle movement of the second sonatina, the two variations are composed in a two-voice polyphonic elaboration on the theme, which could be seen as a review of the Dutch/North German style of keyboard music of the Baroque era.

The Sonata for piano and violin is like a volcanic eruption. The first movement is passionate and virtuosic, with a contrapuntally conceived development section combined with surprising modulations. The middle passage of the second movement foreshadows the music of Brahms. The third movement, alternating between lyricism and passionate outpourings, seems the work of an obscure Teutonic Chopin. It is also reminiscent of Schumann, however, as well as Fauré in many of its progressions.

RENÉ RAKIER

COMPOSITIONS

* lost

VOCAL: *Drei Lieder*, v, pf, op. I; *Sechs Lieder*, v, pf (manuscript); *Der Wunder Ritter*, v, pf, op.2*; *Entsagen*, v, pf, op. 4; *Drei Lieder*, v, pf, op. 6; *Drei Gedichte von Heinrich Heine*, v, pf, op. 7; *Zwei Gedichte von Nicolaus Lenau*, Bar, pf, op. 8; *Drei Balladen von Heinrich Heine*, B, pf, op. 9; *Töne der Liebe, aus dem Hohen Lied von G.Fr. Daumer*, v, pf, op. 10; *Fünf Gedichte*, v, pf, op. II; *Twee geestelijke liederen* (included in: *Caecilia*, 19 July 1867); *La Vénitienne : chant national* (Dufriche)*; *Drie 2-stemmige zangstukken*, op. 13; *Fünf Lieder*, v, pf*; *Gedicht von Heine*, T, pf*; *Ballade von Heine*, v, pf*; *Het Krooningsfeest van Keizer Karel V te Bologna* (opera)*; *De ridder van St. Jan*, v, pf (included in: *Swelingh, Jaarboekje aan de toonkunst in Nederland gewijd : 1859-1860*); *I Sorrow no more*, v, pf; *The Gift*, v, pf

PIANO: *Deux sonatines*, op. 3; *8 vierhändige Clavierstücke*, op 12; *Feest marsch : ter gelegenheid van het XLVIe lustrum der Utrechtsche Hoogeschool*; *Zwei Clavierstücke*, op. 16; *Autumn Song*, pf/harm; *Fairy Dances*; *Deux impromptus*; *Spinnlied*, op. 37; *The Happy Mountaineer*; *Marsch voor het Muzyk-korps der dienstdoende Schutterij van Utrecht*; *Marche triomphale*; *Trois aquarelles*; *Drie noveletten*; *Trois pensées musicales*; *Six Characteristic Pieces*, pf/org; *Twee polka-mazurka's*; *Prussian War March*; *Chant guerrier*; *Der Postillion*; *Sea Sheen*; *The Rivulet*; *El Hildage*; *Grand March, Nasr*

Eddin; *La fête de la reine, gavotte*; *Loure*; *Feu follet*; *Frage?*; *The Prince Imperial*; *Barcarole**; *Castanet Waltz**; *Cavalry March**; *Champagne galop**; *Cavalcade**; *Chant baccique**; *Evening Prayer**; *Festmarsch**; *Fête villageoise**; *Flying Leaves**; *Forest Murmuring**; *Frühlingslied**; *Gaité : mazurka**; *Galop**; *Gighardo*; *Hunters Farewell**; *Hunting Song (Jagdlied)**; *Maiden's Fanciers : valse caprice**; *Marche funèbre, and Lied ohne Worte**; *Papa's Birthday : March**; *Three Pieces**; *Serenade**; *Sérénade Bohémienne**; *Spring Song**; *Temple of Glory : Gavotte**

OTHER INSTRUMENTAL WORKS: *Sonata*, vl, pf, op. 5; *Serenade*, vl, pf; *Concertsonate*, org*; *Suite*, org; *Larghetto in C*, org*; *Cathedral Processional March*, org; *Organ Fugue*; *Ouverture voor het Blijspel van Pieter Langendijk: 'Don Quichot of de Bruiloft van Camacho'*, orch*

BIBLIOGRAPHY

'G.J. van Eijken': *British Library Catalogue of printed music to 1980*

'G.J. van Eijken', *Neue Zeitschrift für Musik*, vol. 51, July-Dec. 1859

Gerrit Jan van Eijken, 1832-1879 (biography and list of works). The Hague, Musica Neerlandica.

N. van Hall: *Een 'question brûlante' op muzikaal gebied*. Utrecht, De Bruyn, 1862

F. Pazdírek: 'G.J. van Eyken', *Universal-Handbuch der Musikliteratur aller Zeiten und Völker*

F. Stieger: 'Gerrit Jan van Eijken', *Opernlexikon*. Tutzing, Schneider, 1975

H. Viotta: *Lexicon der toonkunst.* Amsterdam, Van Kampen, 1883

R. Warren: *G.J. van Eijken in Engeland.* Report of a study tour to London, 7-16 Feb. 1986

DISCOGRAPHY

Songs, op. 7 and op. 9. H. Meens (T), L. Visser (B), L. van Doeselaar (pf) (Teleac TEL 8904)

Sonatina op. 3, no. 1. J. de Bie (pf) (Koch Schwann CD 310077)

Töne der Liebe aus dem Hohen Lied, op. 10; Fünf Gedichte, op. 11 (sel.); Drei Lieder, op. 6 (sel.); Zwei Gedichte, op. 8. A. Grimm (S), G. Smits (B), M. Reijans (T), F. van Ruth (pf) (NM Classics 92072)

Rudolf Escher

AMSTERDAM, 8 JANUARY 1912 – TEXEL, 17 MARCH 1980

The earliest memories and first school years of Rudolf Escher are connected with Java, the former Dutch East Indies, where his father worked as a geologist from 1915 to 1920. It was from his father that he received his first musical instruction. As a highschool student, Escher began to realize that he would like to be a composer, although he also felt drawn to painting and poetry. In 1931 he enrolled at the conservatory in Rotterdam, where he studied composition with Willem Pijper (from 1934 to 1937), and counterpoint with the organist J.H. Besselaar. In addition he learned to play the piano and the cello. During this period he also wrote his first reviews for the daily *Algemeen Handelsblad*. At 26 he drew attention with the book *Toscanini en Debussy, magie der werkelijkheid* [Toscanini and Debussy, the magic of reality] in which he provided penetrating analytical insights into Debussy's *La Mer*.

Escher lost nearly all of his compositions, poems, paintings and practically his entire library in the May 1940 bombardment of Rotterdam where he had lived from 1935. During the war his living conditions were less than comfortable owing to his refusal to join the 'Kultuurkamer', the cultural regulatory organization installed by the German occupation forces.

The liberation of the Netherlands changed his life. He became the art and music reviewer of the weekly periodical *De Groene Amsterdammer* and became part of the administration of the Netherlands Opera Foundation and the Foundation for Dutch Musical Interests (NMB). Success as a composer came in 1947 with the orchestral piece composed during the war *Musique pour l'esprit en deuil* in which his characteristic idiom came to the fore. Central in this is his predilection for a polymelodic, linear approach, together with harmonically derived structures that yield charged, complex and yet clearly comprehensible contrapuntal textures. The music of Pijper and Vermeulen was an unmistakable influence in this, though equally important were the influences of Gregorian chant and the Flemish polyphonists, early Monteverdi, Debussy, and, regarding the orchestration, Mahler and Ravel. This style reached a peak in the orchestral piece *Hymne du Grand Meaulnes* (1950-1951), in which melody, harmony and rhythm coalesce in a song of controlled ecstasy.

The essence of Escher's conception of composition lay in his painstaking search for clarity and optimal comprehensibility of the musical processes he set in motion. As a result, he mostly worked very slowly. Not infrequently he

119

found it necessary to make one or more revisions after the first performance of a piece (particularly expansive works with large forces) if the first version did not meet his expectations. The most extreme example of this is the Symphony no.2 (1958), which underwent three revisions (1964, 1971 and 1980). The other extreme is the *Trio à cordes* (also 1958), which was composed in barely a month, exceptionally quick for Escher. *Le vrai visage de la paix* (1953, rev. 1957), *Songs of Love and Eternity* (1955), *Ciel, air et vents* (1957) and the later *Three poems by W.H. Auden* (1975) are among the best choral works ever written by a Dutch composer.

The symphony and trio date from a period in which Escher made an intense study of the music of the youngest generation of avant-garde composers (Stockhausen, Boulez and others). This orientation toward serial music not only stemmed from curiosity but also from Escher's belief that he had reached a standstill with structural models that he had come to see as outdated. A visit to Pierre Boulez in Basel, in which the two composers analyzed a part of Boulez's *Pli selon pli*, reaffirmed this realization. Upon his return, Escher removed seven compositions from his list of works as he could no longer support their premises.

Seeking new impulses he later briefly explored the possibilities of electronic music at the Electronic Music Studio in Delft and began composing with twelve-tone rows. This ultimately proved the wrong direction because the anti-tonal implications of serialism integrated poorly with his tonally anchored basic premises. Nearly all of the compositions Escher undertook in the first half of the 1960s remained unfinished, including an ambitious project for two orchestras and electronics entitled *Summer Rites at Noon*, which after a long process of writing and revising finally reached the stage of a short score in 1971; Jan van Vlijmen orchestrated the work in 1988 and it came to be recognized as one of the most valuable pieces in Escher's oeuvre.

In 1964 Escher was appointed senior researcher at the University of Utrecht's Institute for Musicology, a position he held until 1977. There he conducted audio-physiological research, seeking a scientific foundation to his belief that atonal music conflicted with the natural tonal orientation of human hearing. He also taught a course on 'criteria of structure and form in the music of the twentieth century' in which the music of Boulez and Debussy was closely studied. Debussy's technique of generative interval manipulation proved especially influential on Escher's compositions.

Escher emerged as reborn with the *Quintetto a fiati* (1966-1967), a work in which the constructivist principles of serialism are intriguingly interwoven with his inalienable polymelodic style. This development continued to impressive heights in his later compositions, making the *Sinfonia per dieci strumenti* (1973-1976), *Sonata for clarinet solo* (1973), *Sonata per flauto e piano* (1976-1979), and his last composition, the Trio for clarinet, viola and piano (1978-1979) – his swan song – highlights of Dutch music.

ERIK VOERMANS

COMPOSITIONS

VOCAL: *Nostalgies* (Levet), T, chamb.orch (1951); *Chants du désir* (Labe), Mez, pf (1951); *Strange meeting* (Owen), Bar, pf (1952); *Le vrai visage de la paix* (Eluard), mix.choir (1953, rev. 1957); *Songs of Love and Eternity* (Dickinson), mix.choir (1955); *Ciel, air et vents* (Ronsard), mix.choir (1957); *De Perzen* (1963); *Univers de Rimbaud, premier cycle*, T, orch (1969-1970); *Three Poems by W.H. Auden*, mix.choir (1975)

CHAMBER MUSIC: *Sonata no. 1*, pf (1935); *Passacaglia*, org (1937); *Trio d'anches*, ob, cl, bn (1939, rev. 1941-1942); *Sonate concertante*, vc, pf (1943); *Arcana musae dona*, pf (1944); *Sonata*, 2 fl (1944); *Habanera*, pf (1945);

Sonata, vc (1945-1948); *Non troppo*, pf (1949); *Sonata*, fl (1949); *Due voci*, pf (1950); *Sonata*, vl, pf (1950); *Sonatina*, pf (1951); *Le tombeau de Ravel*, fl, ob, vl, vla, vc, hpd (1952, rev. 1959); *Air pour charmer un lézard*, fl (1953); *Allard's bruiloftswijsje* (1954); *Trio à cordes* (1959); *Hoggy – Woggy*, vl, pf (1960); *Quintetto a fiati* (1966-1967); *Monologue for flute* (1969); *Sonata*, cl (1973); *Sonata*, fl, pf (1976-1979); *Trio*, pf, cl, vla (1978-1979)

ORCHESTRA: *Musique pour l'esprit en deuil* (1941-1943); *Concerto*, str.orch (1947-1948); *Hymne du Grand Meaulnes* (1950-1951); *Symphony no. 1* (1953-1954, rev. W. Boogman 1991); *Symphony no. 2* (1958, rev.

1964, 1971, 1980); *Summer Rites at Noon* (1962-1969, orchestr. J. van Vlijmen, 1988); *Sinfonia per dieci strumenti* (1973-1976); *Six épigraphes antiques* – Debussy, orchestr. (1976-1977)

PUBLICATIONS
Toscanini en Debussy : magie der werkelijkheid. Rotterdam, Van Sijn, 1938
Debussy : actueel verleden, compiled and arr. D.J. Hamoen and E. Schönberger. Buren, Knuf, 1985
'Debussy and the Musical Epigram', *Key Notes,* 10, 1979/2, p. 59-63

BIBLIOGRAPHY
R. de Beer: 'Bleeding chunk', *Key Notes,* 24, 1987, p.24
B. Escher: *Rudolf Escher. Het Oeuvre: catalogue raisonné.* Amsterdam, KVNM, 1998
Het kunstwerk als daad : Rudolf Escher (1912-1980). Collaborative project of the Rudolf Escher Comité, the Utrecht University Museum and Music Center Vredenburg. Utrecht, Rijksuniversiteit, 1985
W. Markus: 'Een notitie over Rudolf Escher', *Mens en Melodie,* vol. 48, 1993, p. 88-94
H. Metzelaar: '"Musicians wrestle everywhere" : Emily Dickinson and Dutch composers'. *Key Notes,* 30, 1996/4, p. 24-28
Peter Schat-Rudolf Escher : brieven 1958-1961, ed. E. Voermans. Hilversum, Centrum Nederlandse Muziek / Zutphen, Walburg Press, 1992
Rudolf Escher en M.C. Escher : beweging en metamorfosen : een briefwisseling. Amsterdam, Meulenhoff/Landshoff, 1985
Rudolf Escher 1912-1980 : de boekenkasten van het Singel, compiled by B. Escher-Jongert and M. van der Kuijp. Documentation of books and scores collected from 1940 to 1980
E. Schönberger: 'Rudolf Escher : thinking in and about music', *Key Notes,* 5, 1977/1, p. 3-17
E. Schönberger: 'Hersenschim en blinde vlek', *De wellustige tandarts & andere componisten.* Amsterdam, De Bezige Bij, 1985

DISCOGRAPHY
Air pour charmer un lézard; Sonata for flute and piano. J. Zoon (fl), B. Brackman (pf) (NM Classics 92059)
Arcana suite. R. Brautigam (pf) (NM Classics 92045)

The Choral Works of Rudolf Escher. Netherlands Chamber Choir, cond. E. Spanjaard (NM Classics 92057)
Debussy – Six Épigraphes Antiques, orchestr. R. Escher. Royal Concertgebouw Orchestra, cond. B. Haitink (Q Disc 97014)
Hymne du Grand Meaulnes. Rotterdam Philharmonic Orchestra, cond. E. de Waart (Teleac TEL 8905)
Musique pour l'esprit en deuil. Concertgebouw Orchestra, cond. H. Vonk (BFO A-7/Composers' Voice CV 10)
Musique pour l'esprit en deuil; Concerto for Strings; Summer Rites at Noon. Royal Concertgebouw Orchestra, R. Chailly (NM Classics 92048)
Sonata concertante; Sonata per violino e pianoforte; Sonata per violoncello solo; Arcana Musae Dona; Trio à cordes. Various performers (Composers' Voice CV 8403)
Symphony no. 2; Sonata for Clarinet Solo; Quintetto a fiati; Nostalgies; Sinfonia per dieci strumenti. Various soloists, Rotterdam Philharmonic Orchestra, cond. R. Dufallo, Netherlands Radio Chamber Orchestra, Ph. Langridge (T), cond. L. Vis (Composers' Voice CV 7704)
Sonata. P. Wispelwey (vc) (Globe GLO 5089)
Le tombeau de Ravel (fragments). J. Zoon (fl), B. Schneemann (ob), R. Hoogeveen (vl), Z. Benyacs (vla), D. Ferschtman (vc), G. Wilson (hpd) (NM Special 92093)
Le tombeau de Ravel; Six épigraphes antiques; Largo; Hymne du Grand Meaulnes. Ensemble Alma Musica, Rotterdam Philharmonic Orchestra, cond. P. Daniel and J. Tate, Concertgebouw Orchestra, cond. L. Vis (Composers' Voice CV 22)
Le tombeau de Ravel; Trio à cordes; Trio for Clarinet, Viola and Piano. J. Zoon (fl), B. Schneemann (ob), R. Hoogeveen (vl), Z. Benyacs (vla), D. Ferschtman (vc), G. Wilson (hpd), H. de Boer (cl), F. van de Laar (pf) (NM Classics 92026)
Univers de Rimbaud, cinq poèmes. J. Giraudeau (T), Residentie Orchestra, cond. F. Leitner (Olympia OCD 506)
Le vrai visage de la paix; Songs of Love and Eternity; Ciel, air et vents; Three Poems by W.H. Auden. Netherlands Chamber Choir, cond. H. van den Hombergh (Composers' Voice CV 8104)

Jacob van Eyck

?, c.1590 – utrecht, 26 march 1657

Jacob van Eyck was probably born in the garrison town of Heusden in the Dutch province of Brabant. Both his father, Goyart van Eyck, and mother, Heilwich Bax, were of noble birth. Jacob was one of five children. The precise date of Van Eyck's birth is not known; on 23 January 1628 he swore before a Utrecht notary that he was 'about thirty-eight years old'. The fact that he was blind might explain why he lived with his mother until 1625.

In Heusden Van Eyck honed his skills as a carillonneur and became an expert in the field of bells. Heusden had one carillon in the tower of the town hall. On 1 January 1622 Van Eyck assumed responsibility for changing the pegs of the bell's mechanical drum and at times he played the carillon. Undoubtedly, the opportunities in Heusden were too limited to allow him to fully develop his talents. After making several visits to Utrecht, Van Eyck was appointed carillonneur at the city's Dom Church in 1625. He later held similar positions at Utrecht's John's Church and Jacob's Church. In 1628 he was entrusted with the technical supervision of the bells of all Utrecht parish churches and its town hall, thus gaining the title of 'Director of the bell-works'. The many improvements van Eyck brought about bear testimony to his powers of persuasion and authority.

Van Eyck played an important role in the development of the carillon. It was he who discovered the tone structure of bells, and how it can be influenced through its shape. Applying his knowledge of the principles of resonance, he was able to produce five separate partials. His findings were reported by various intellectuals including Isaac Beeckman, René Descartes and Constantijn Huygens. His discovery was put into immediate practice by the bell foundry of François and Pieter Hemony.

It is owing to his recorder playing that Van Eyck's compositions are still known today. It was first mentioned in 1640 by the poet Regnerus Opperveldt in an ode extolling the Saint John's churchyard in Utrecht. Van Eyck's first compositions were printed in 1644. In the spring of 1649 he completed *Der Fluyten Lust-hof* [The flute's garden of delight]. It is possible that in issuing these publications he wished to show that recorder playing was more than just a pastime to him: almost immediately after the completion of *Der Fluyten Lust-hof*, on 17 May 1649, the Chapter of Saint John's raised his salary from 80 to 100 guilders 'on condition that on occasion in the evening he would entertain

DER

FLUYTEN LUST-HOF,

Beplant met Pſalmen, Pavanen, Allmanden, Couranten, Balletten, Airs, &c.
En de nieuſte voizen, konſtigh en lieflyk gefigureert, met veel veranderingen.

Door den Ed. Jʀ. Jᴀᴄᴏʙ *van* Eʏᴄᴋ, *Muſicyn en Direĉteur*
vande Klok-wercken tot Uitrecht, &c.

Dienſtigh, voor alle Konſt-lievers tot de Fluit, Blaes en allerley Speel-tuigh.

T W E E D E  D E E L.

t'Aᴍsᴛᴇʀᴅᴀᴍ, by*Paulus Matthyſz,* in de Stoof-ſteeg in de Boek drukkery gedrukt, 1646.

the people strolling in the churchyard with the sound of his little flute.'

Van Eyck's finances during his first years in Utrecht were strained. Initially, he accepted a modest salary of 350 guilders. His efforts were rewarded in 1645, however, with a salary of 600 guilders. Van Eyck's final years were marked by declining health. On 25 February 1654 he had his will drawn up and on 8 October 1655 Johan Dix was named to replace him as carillonneur of the Dom Church 'during his disposition'. Probably one of Van Eyck's students, Dix served as his deputy, executor of his will and as his chief heir.

Van Eyck died on 26 March 1657 and was buried the next day at the Orphan's Church, a short distance from where he had lived. For three hours, the bells of the Jacob's Church and the Dom Church were tolled in his memory. Lambertus Sanderus and Lodewijk Meijer wrote elegies on the death of the 'Utrecht Orpheus' and Sanderus composed a four-line verse inscribed on Van Eyck's gravestone.

Der Fluyten Lust-hof was intended for the 'handflute', today known as the soprano recorder. The collection is in two volumes, the first was issued in 1644 under the title *Euterpe oft Speel-goddinne I* [Euterpe or The playing Muse I], the second in 1646 as *Der Fluyten Lust-hof II*. When in 1649 a revised and greatly enlarged reissue of *Euterpe* appeared, it was called the first volume of *Der Fluyten Lust-hof*. Various printings appeared up until Van Eyck's death, all produced by Paulus Matthysz. in Amsterdam. The two volumes were dedicated to the secretary at the Dutch court and composer Constantijn Huygens, a distant relative of Van Eyck. There are approximately 150 compositions in *Der Fluyten Lust-hof* (depending on how repeated pieces, for example, are counted). Most are sets of variations to popular melodies, Genevan psalms and foreign airs. Among the best-loved pieces today are the variations on *Doen Daphne* [When Daphne], Giulio Caccini's *Amarilli mia bella*, John Dowland's *Pavane lachrymae* and the *Engels nachtegaeltje* [English nightingale]. The variation technique was called 'breecken' (breaking), and involved the division of notes from the theme into groups of shorter note values (diminution). This process leads to increasing virtuosity: whole notes being divided into halves, then quarter notes, eighth notes, etc. It is a practice comparable to the keyboard (Sweelinck) and lute variations (Vallet) of the time, with the exception that Van Eyck was limited to monophony. Therefore, the style of the variations is ornamental and is related to the Italian art of improvised diminutions. Van Eyck was not the only Dutch composer who wrote solo variations for the recorder: similar works were composed by Jacobus van Noordt, Pieter de Vois and Johan Dix.

There is no demonstrable stylistic development in *Der Fluyten Lust-hof*. The works probably continued to evolve as Van Eyck played them over the years until they were finally solidified when written out. Thus, *Der Fluyten Lust-hof* could be interpreted as a survey of what Van Eyck collected and developed during his career, more a state of affairs than a retrospective.

Paulus Matthysz. also published other pieces by Van Eyck in anthologies printed at the same time as *Der Fluyten Lust-hof*. One piece, entitled *Stemme nova*, was for lack of space transferred from *Euterpe* to *Der Goden Fluit-hemel* [The Gods' flute heaven], where it appeared anonymously. A variation piece by Pieter de Vois on the melody *Je ne puis eviter*, which appeared in *'t Uitnement Kabinet* [The excellent cabinet] (1646), contains ten bars by Van Eyck.

Five duets were added to *Der Fluyten Lust-hof I* in 1649, the upper part taken from existing solo variations in most cases. These duets are demonstrably not the work of Van Eyck and can be attributed with near certainty to Paulus Matthysz., who was a composer and recorder player as well as publisher and bookseller.

THIEMO WIND

COMPOSITIONS

Der Fluyten Lust-hof ... eerste deel. – Amsterdam, Paul Matthysz, 1/1644 [*Euterpe oft Speel-goddinne*], 2/1649, 3/c 1656
Facs. and modern ed.: see vol. 2

Der Fluyten Lust-hof ... tweede deel ... – Amsterdam, Paul Matthysz, 1/1646, 2/1654
Facs. ed. of vol. 1, 2nd ed. 1649 and vol. 2, 2nd ed. 1654: ed. Kees Otten. Amsterdam, Groen. Modern ed.: ed. Thiemo Wind. Naarden [etc.], XYZ, 1986-1988

Stemme nova, included in *Der Goden Fluithemel*. – Amsterdam, Paul Matthysz, 1644
Facs. ed. of *Der Goden Fluit-hemel*: ed. Thiemo Wind. Utrecht, STIMU, 1993

Ten bars added to *Pieter de Vois' variaties over 'Je ne puis eviter'*, included in *'t Uitnement Kabinet I*. – Amsterdam, Paul Matthysz, 1646

BIBLIOGRAPHY

R. van Baak Griffioen: *Jacob van Eyck's Der Fluyten Lust-hof (1644-c.1655)*. Utrecht, 1991
D. van den Hul: *Klokkenkunst te Utrecht tot 1700, met bijzondere aandacht voor het aandeel hierin van Jhr. Jacob van Eyck*. Zutphen, 1982
R. Rasch: 'Some mid-seventeenth century Dutch collections of instrumental ensemble music', *TVNM*, 22, 1972, p. 160-200
Th. Wind: 'Chain variations in van Eyck's "Der Fluyten Lust-hof"', *The American Recorder*, vol. 28 no. 4, 1987, p. 141-144
Th. Wind: 'Die Psalm-Variationen Jacob van Eycks : Geschichte, Analyse, Interpretation', *Tibia* 90/1, p. 22-32.
Th. Wind: 'Jacob van Eyck and his "Euterpe oft Speel-goddinne"', *The American Recorder*, vol. 27 no. 1, 1986, p. 9-15
Th. Wind: 'Jacob van Eyck's Der Fluyten Lust-hof : composition, improvisation, or...? : consequences for performance practice', *Proceedings of the International Recorder Symposium Utrecht 1993*. Utrecht, STIMU, 1995
Th. Wind; "Je ne puis eviter" : 17de-eeuwse blokfluitvariaties van een Nederlandse 'groupe des trois', *Musica Antiqua*, 10/3, p. 104-111
Th. Wind: '"Some mistakes or errors..." : searching the authentic intentions of Jacob van Eyck', *The Recorder Magazine*, vol. 11, no. 3, 1991, p. 82-86
Th. Wind: '"Stemme Nova" : eine neuentdeckte Komposition Jacob van Eycks', *Tibia*, 93/2, p. 466-469
Th. Wind: 'Why the duets from Der Fluyten Lust-hof are not by Jacob van Eyck', *The Recorder Magazine*, vol. 16, no. 2, p. 44-48

DISCOGRAPHY

An extensive discography up to 1988 is included in the monograph by Van Baak Griffioen (see bibliography)

Der Fluyten Lust-hof (sel.), M. Verbruggen (rec) (Harmonia Mundi France, HMU 907072)
Jacob van Eyck & Dutch songs of the Golden Age, S. Coolen (rec), Camerata Trajectina (includes fifteen pieces and their vocal models) (Philips 442 624-2)
Onder de linde groene, Bravada, Doen Daphne d'overschoone maeght. Trio de L'Oustal, L. Swarts (vc) (NM Classics 92101)
Preludium ofte Voorspel; Den Lustelycken Mey; Preludium & Echo. M. Miessen (rec) (BFO A-2)
Rondom Jr. Jacob van Eyck (c 1590-1657) : diminutiekunst in de 17e eeuw. C. Bremmers (rec), Ensemble Giardino (Includes: *Pavane Lachrymae; Een Schots Lietjen; Blydschap van myn vliedt; Amarilli mia bella*, and other compositions) (Sonclair Records, JB 109074)

Willem de Fesch

ALKMAAR, 1687 – LONDON, C.1760

Willem de Fesch was born in Alkmaar in 1687. His parents were natives of Liège and shortly after his birth they returned to this city. In the first years of the eighteenth century De Fesch arrived in Amsterdam, where he remained until 1725. It is not known what he did for a living, but this undoubtedly would have involved giving lessons and concerts. Early in life De Fesch gained fame as a violin virtuoso. Also unclear is the nature of his relationship to the Flemish violinist Carel Rosier (1640-1725). De Fesch presumably studied with him, for in 1711 he married Rosier's daughter Maria Anna. However, Rosier had no influence on De Fesch's compositional activities, though dozens of editions of the latest Italian music published in Amsterdam by Roger did leave their mark. The early sonatas and concertos by De Fesch bear unmistakable witness to this fact. In 1725 De Fesch was appointed kapellmeister to the cathedral in Antwerp, the only permanent position he is known to have held. His years at this post were overshadowed by conflicts with chapel musicians and the church authorities: church archives show De Fesch to have been a stubborn, temperamental personality. In 1731 he resigned and emigrated with his family to England.

In London, De Fesch built a career as a freelance musician – a lifestyle that apparently suited him better than holding a steady (church) position. In Handel's shadow, he complied with the prevailing musical tastes of London and became a valued addition to the city's cultural life. He regularly performed as a soloist and took part in important productions in London. For example, he led the orchestra in a performance of Handel's *Occasional Oratorio* in 1746 and from 1748 was concertmaster at Marylebone Gardens. In addition, he gave lessons and was active as a composer. On several occasions he attempted to make a name for himself with large-scale compositions, including two oratorios. Some years before his death he also tried his hand at comic opera. However, De Fesch gained much more acclaim as a composer of sonatas and songs, which throughout his life were published in London. He died around 1760.

De Fesch made his debut as a composer in a genre that would only gain popularity later in the eighteenth century; his op.1 (1716) was a collection of six violin duets, instead of the usual solo and trio sonatas. Both parts are written in a remarkably virtuoso style. De Fesch's Amsterdam period, incidentally, was dominated by the violin and instrumental music, the concerto in particular. Apparently impressed with the Italian concerto style, so popular in the Amsterdam of his day, he published no less than three collections of six concertos each (opp.2, 3 and 5). The influence of Torelli, Corelli and Vivaldi is evident in these works.

The op.3 concertos (c.1718) seem modeled after the renowned Vivaldi concertos of the same opus number, *L'Estro Armonico* (1711). Vivaldian themes and ritornellos are found in each of De Fesch's three collections, though in their form and instrumentation the works are closely related to Corelli's concerti grossi. The solo violin figures prominently, often with lengthy passagework. The last op.3 concerto is a true concerto for violin, with a written out virtuoso cadenza at the close of the first movement. A northern element is discernible in the use of solo woodwinds in several of the opp.3 and 5 concertos.

This element is also in evidence in the op.10 concertos, which De Fesch published in London in 1741. The concerti grossi of Corelli and his successor Geminiani were exceptionally popular in this city and Handel published his own highly original concertos (op.6) one year prior to De Fesch. De Fesch's concertos follow in the footsteps of these works. They are more introverted and mature than his work of the Amsterdam period.

De Fesch published another collection of six violin sonatas (op.4a) in Amsterdam; the last of these is an especially idiomatic, virtuoso piece with numerous double stops. Later sonata collections – the solo sonatas of op.6 and the first half of op.8a, as well as the opp.7 and 12 trio sonatas – turn away from this predilection for the violin and are suited to a range of melody instruments. In these collections, an increasing simplicity of the musical idiom is noticeable. In the sonatas of the London period (opp.8 and 12) in particular, De Fesch creates a more translucent, somewhat 'galant' style. A strong preference for dance forms is characteristic of his style of sonata composition.

A similar trend is evident in De Fesch's duets. It is no coincidence that he made his debut with a duet collection, for this genre became his specialty. Two collections, opp.9 and 11, were composed for the transverse flute, a very popular instrument in London at the time. The latter halves of opp.4 and 8a contain six sonatas for the original combination of two cellos. Later, two more collections appeared, each with six sonatas for cello and continuo (opp.8b and 13). Because of these, De Fesch should be counted among the major composers of music for the cello of his time.

It is likely that De Fesch first tried his hand at vocal compositions in Antwerp. A cycle of lamentations has been lost, but an Easter mass and a motet have survived. He adapted easily in England, composing numerous songs and several English-language oratorios. Although the music of his oratorio *Judith* (1733) apparently has not survived, the score of his second oratorio *Joseph* (1743) was rediscovered several years ago. The work reveals Handelian influence, particularly in the arias. The work as a whole casts light on De Fesch's melodic talent and his ability to convey strong emotions in music that is rich in contrast.

De Fesch's output is of international stature. Not one of his eighteenth-century compatriots could compete with him in versatility and productivity. But his music does have its limitations, especially with regard to harmony and rhythm. His mastery of counterpoint was also scant. Hence the predominance of two-voice writing in his composition; it is in his songs, solo sonatas and duets that his talent for graceful melody and simplicity of expression reached its full potential.

PIETER DIRKSEN

COMPOSITIONS

VI Duetti a due violini ... opera prima. – Amsterdam, Jeanne Roger, 1716

VI Concerti a quattro violini, alto-viola, violoncello e basso per l'organo ... opera seconda. – Amsterdam, Jeanne Roger, [c 1717]
For 2 violins, cello, strings and bc

VI Concerti ... opera terza. – Amsterdam, Jeanne Roger, [c 1718]
Three concertos for 2 violins, cello, strings and bc, two concertos for 2 oboes, bassoon, strings and bc, one concerto for violin, strings and bc

XII Sonate in due libri, il primo: 6 a violino, violone e cembalo, ed il secondo: 6 a due violoncelli ... opera quarta. – Amsterdam, composer, 1725

VI Concerti, li quattro primi sono a due flauti traversieri, due violini, alto viola e basso per l'organo; li due ultimi, a quattro violini, alto viola, violoncello e basso per l'organo ... opera quinta. – Amsterdam, Michel Charles Le Cène, [c 1725-1730]
Four concertos for 2 flutes, strings and bc; two concertos for 2 violins, cello, strings and bc

VI Sonate a violino, o flauto traversiero, col basso, per l'organo ... opera sesta. – Brussels, Joseph Vicidomini, [c 1730]

X Sonata a tre, due flauti a traverso o due violini, e violoncello o basso continuo ... opera settima. – Amsterdam, Gerhard Friedrich Witvogel, [1733]

XII Sonatas, six for a violin, with a thorough bass ... and six for two violoncellos ... op. 8. – London, Benjamin Cooke, [1733]

Six sonatas for a violoncello with a thorough bass for the harpsichord ... opera ottava. – London, John Johnson, [1733]

VI Sonata's for two german flutes ... opera IX. – London, John Simpson, [1739]

VIII Concerto's in seven parts. Six for two violins, a tenor violin, and a violoncello, with two other violins, and thorough bass, for ye harpsicord, one for a german flute with all the other instruments, and one with two german flutes, two violins, tenor violin, violoncello and thorough bass for the harpsicord ... opera the tenth. – [London], s.n., [1741]

Thirty duets for two german flutes, consisting of variety of aires in different movements compos'd for the improvement of young practitioners on the german flute ... opera XI. – London, John Walsh, [1747]
Previously published without opus number as *Musical amuzements*. London, author, 1744

*Twelve sonatas for two german flutes, or two violins; with a bass for the violoncello or harpsichord...*opera XII. – London, John Walsh, [1748]

VI Sonatas for a violoncello solo, with a thorough bass for the harpsichord ... opera XIII. – [London], s.n., [c 1750]

Canzonette ed arie a voce sola di soprano, col basso continuo: e da potersi suonare con violino o flauto traversiero. – London, John Simpson, [1739]
Seventeen Italian songs for soprano and bc, some with obbligato violin or flute part

XX Canzonette a voce sola di soprano, col basso continuo, da potersi suonare con violino, flauto traverso e mandolino ... the second collection. – London, for the author, [c 1745]
Twenty Italian songs for soprano and bc, some with obbligato violin, flute or mandolin part

The songs in the Tempest or the Enchanted Isleland. – London, William Smith, [1746]

Five songs for soprano, oboe and strings: *While you here do snorling lie, Where the bee sucks, Ere you can say, Oh bid you faithfull Ariel fly* and *All fancy sick*

VI English songs with violins, and german flutes, and a through bass for the harpsichord. – London, John Walsh, [c 1748]
For voice and bc, some with two violins or two flutes

Mr. Defesch's songs sung at Marylebon-Gardens. – London, John Walsh, 1753

Approximately 40 English songs, published in periodicals or separately

IN MANUSCRIPT:
Apis amata, motet for alto, 2 violins and bc. Brussels, Royal Conservatory; *Missa paschalis* (1730), Antwerp, Archive of the Antwerp Cathedral; Concerto in A minor for 2 violins, ripieno violin and bc (1738), Amsterdam, University of Amsterdam; *Joseph*, oratorio (1745), London, Royal Academy of Music; Missa Brevis in G major. Amsterdam, Toonkunst Library

LOST:
Five Lamentations (1726); *Judith*, oratorio (1733) (the libretto and a song, published as *A favorite song in the oratorio Judith by mr. De Fesch*, London, s.n., s.d., have survived); Bassoon Concerto (1743); *Love and Friendship, a New English Pastoral Serenata* (1744) (only the libretto has survived); *The London Prentice* (comic opera) (1754)

BIBLIOGRAPHY
F. van den Bremt: *Willem de Fesch (1687-1757?) : Nederlands componist en virtuoos : leven en werk*. Brussels, Royal Belgian Academy, 1949
H. O' Douwes: 'De cellocomposities van Willem de Fesch', *Mens en Melodie*, vol. 14, 1959, p. 40-42
Willem de Fesch (1687-c. 1760) : voordrachten gehouden in Alkmaar, september 1987. Alkmaar, Stichting Feschtival, cop. 1987. With contributions by I. Cholij, M.L. Göllner, W. Noske, G. Spiessens a.o.

DISCOGRAPHY

6 Concertos, op.5. J. Wentz (tra.fl), Musica ad Rhenum (NM Classics 92054)

Concerto op. 3, no. 2. Residentie Orchestra, cond. T. Koopman (Olympia OCD 500)

Concerto op. 10, no. 2. Musica ad Rhenum (NM Classics 92037)

Concerto op. 10, no. 2. Musica ad Rhenum (Vanguard Classics 08 5077 71)

Sonata op. 6, no. 1. R. Kanji (rec) a.o. (Globe GLO 5101)

Sonata op. 7, no. 4. Amsterdam Baroque Ensemble, cond. T. Koopman (WVH 010)

Sonata op. 8, no. 3 and no. 5, Sonata op. 12, no. 6. Trio de L'Oustal, L. Swarts (vc) (NM Classics 92101)

Marius Flothuis

AMSTERDAM, 30 OCTOBER 1914

Marius Flothuis studied the piano with Arend Koole, music theory with Hans Brandts Buys and musicology with Albert Smijers at the University of Utrecht, and later with Bernet Kempers at the University of Amsterdam, where he received his doctorate in 1969 with a thesis on *Mozarts Bearbeitungen eigener und fremder Werke*. Flothuis has played a role in Dutch and international music life, fulfilling a number of official posts. From 1937 to 1942 he was assistant artistic director of the Amsterdam Concertgebouw Orchestra. He was summarily dismissed from this position after refusing to apply for membership of the 'Kultuurkamer' (a regulatory cultural agency installed by the German occupying forces during World War II), his wife being half-Jewish. From 18 September 1943 to 4 May 1945 he was held in German captivity.

In 1953 Flothuis resumed his duties with the Concertgebouw Orchestra and from 1955 to 1974 he was its artistic director. He has worked as a music journalist for *Het Vrije Volk* (1945-1953), has been a librarian at the publishing house and library of Dutch music Donemus (1946-1950), a professor of musicology at the University of Utrecht (1974-1982) and chairman of the Zentral-Institut für Mozart-Forschung in Salzburg (1980-1994).

As a musicologist, Flothuis worked on the preparation of the collected works of Gluck, Mozart and Debussy, and the *Hommage aan Willem Pijper* collection of piano pieces by Dutch composers; he also prepared editions of works by Haydn and Belle van Zuylen. Among his many publications are the books *Hedendaagse Engelse componisten* [Contemporary English Composers] (1949), *Notes on Notes, selected essays* (1974), and *Denken over muziek* [Thinking about music] (1993), *Mozarts Klavierkonzerte* and *Mozarts Streichquartette* (both 1998), as well as program notes and articles in newspapers and Dutch and foreign music journals. His areas of special interest include the composers Monteverdi, Schubert and Mahler, French music from 1880 to 1920, and women composers. Flothuis is known as a leading authority on Mozart, in whose music he admires the balanced instrumentation' and the equilibrium between form and content'.

These are qualities he also seeks in his own work. He has a predilection for an open and translucent instrumentation; compound sonorities and tutti passages are rare in his music. His orchestral and chamber music is characterized by its transparency and, like Mozart, he places the strings and woodwinds at the core of the orchestra. Examples of this approach are his *Concertouverture, Symfonische muziek* (awarded a prize by the former Ministry of Education, Arts and Sciences), and the *Canti e giuochi*. Rather than taking the form of a heroic battle between individual and collective, the concertos follow a Mozartian pattern of dialogue between a solo instrument and a rather large chamber ensemble. Examples of this may be found in the Piano Concerto (1948) and the Flute Concerto no. 2, *Per sonare ed ascoltare* (1971); in the last movement of the latter work the orchestra is silent, yet even here the soloist does not get the chance to dazzle the audience.

Flothuis' ideal of transparency is even more pronounced in his chamber music than in his orchestral music through its clear distinction of melody from accompanying instruments. Because of this, the music is more harmonically than contrapuntally conceived, but even in pieces where timbre and polyphony are emphasized (such as the *Quattro invenzioni per quattro corni*, 1963), or in compositions with unusual settings, balance and clarity predominate.

Aside from Mozart, others have influenced Flothuis, for example, Schubert in the *Valses sentimentales* for piano four hands (1944); the Suite for harpsichord (1953) is reminiscent of Baroque suites; and Boulez left his mark on the instrumentation of *Hymnus* (1965), for which Flothuis received an award from the Johan Wagenaar Foundation.

Rhythmically, Flothuis' music is characterized by a certain homogeneity, particularly in swift closing movements, for example in the two pieces entitled *Sonata da camera* – the first for flute and piano (1943) and the second for flute and harp (1950). Despite the many changes of meter, the music conveys a clear sense of metrical and rhythmic continuity, supported by a tonally oriented harmonic-melodic approach and clearly profiled form. These classical premises are also expressed in a Debussyian idiom, for instance in the tryptich *Preludio, notturno e capriccio* for string trio (1989) and the Sonata for oboe, French horn and harpsichord (1985), the setting Debussy envisioned for his uncomposed fourth sonata. The *Fantasia* for harp and orchestra, *Canti e giuochi, Per sonare ed ascoltare,* and the String Quartet no.2 show Flothuis experimenting with form, despite the classical details in, for example, their harmony.

Flothuis usually composes just a single work per genre, but there are exceptions. For example, after the String Quartet – which he considers one of the best things' he has composed and which won him the Van der Leeuw Prize – he did not abandon the genre. A second string quartet came forty years later. And more than 25 years after the first Flute Concerto he composed a second – for Hubert Barwahser on the occasion of his retirement from the Concertgebouw Orchestra. He has also dedicated compositions to other musician friends: *Pour le tombeau d'Orphée,* to the harpist Phia Berghout, *Poème* for harp and orchestra to Manja Smits, *To an old love* to Kathleen Ferrier, and some works to students while he was a professor.

Flothuis' oeuvre consists largely of vocal and chamber music, including solo pieces and piano works intended for performance in small concert halls. The vocal pieces, and in general the works composed up to about 1946, are often more extravert in expression. Examples of this are his compositional debut, the *Vier liederen* op.3 [Four songs], (1938-1939), *Sonnet,* op.9, the *Dramatische ouverture* [Dramatic overture], not a vocal work as such but originally intended as the overture to an uncomposed opera, and especially *Hymnus.* The reserve, nuance and subtlety shown in Flothuis' music gives rise to comparisons with the music of Fauré.

Flothuis' music and writings are concise and concentrated. Longer works consist mostly of series of shorter movements that at times are thematically related. With the exception of opera, he has composed in every genre.

EMANUEL OVERBEEKE

COMPOSITIONS

VOCAL: *Four Songs* (Morgenstern), S, pf, op. 3 (1938); *Sonnet* (Toller), Mez, orch, op. 9 (1940); *Bicinia* (Fort, Gossaert, De Vries, Demoustier), w.choir, op. 20 (1944); *Cantata Silesiana* (Silesius), w.choir, fl, str.qt, hpd, op. 29 (1946); *To an old love* (Marsh), Mez, orch, op. 32 (1948); *Four Trifles* (Townsend Warner, Teasdale, Raine), l.v, pf, op. 33 (1948); *1945* (two songs) (Aafjes), mix.choir, op. 36, no. 4 (1952); *Odysseus and Nausikaa* (Rieu, after Homeros), S, A, T, Bar, hp, op. 60 (1960); *Hymnus* (Bachmann), S, orch, op. 67 (1965); *Hommage à Mallarmé,* m.v, fl, vc, pf, op. 80 (1980); *Vrijheid* (Kazantzakis, Luxemburg, Toller, Sartre, Bloem), Mez, 2 sp.v, mix.choir, fl, str.orch, op. 83 (1983); *Santa Espina* (Aragon), Mez, orch, op. 88 (1986)

CHAMBER MUSIC: *Nocturne,* fl, ob, cl, op. 11 (1941); *Sonata da camera,* fl, pf, op. 17 (1943); *Aria,* tpt, pf, op. 18 (1944); *Valses sentimentales,* pf 4h, op. 21 (1944); *Duettino pastorale,* 2 vl, op. 23, no. 2 (1944); *Pour le tombeau d'Orphée,* hp, op. 37 (1950); *Partita,* vl, pf, op. 38, no. 1 (1950); *Kleine suite* (with L. van Delden), 12 hp (1951); *String Quartet,* op. 44 (1952); *Quattro invenzioni,* 4 hn, op. 64 (1963); *Partita,* 2 vl, op. 69 (1966); *Sonate,* ob, hn, hpd, op. 85 (1985); *Preludio, notturno e capriccio,* str.trio, op. 91

(1989); *Quartetto II (Fantasia)*, str.qt, op. 94 (1992); *Quintet*, fl, vl, vla, vc, hp, op. 95 (1995)

ORCHESTRA: *Concerto*, fl, orch, op. 19 (1944); *Concerto*, hn, orch, op. 24 (1945); *Dramatische ouverture*, orch, op. 16 (1946, rev. 1951); *Concerto*, pf, orch, op. 30 (1948); *Concerto*, vl, small orch, op. 39 (1951); *Fantasia*, hp, small orch, op. 51 (1953); *Concertouverture*, orch, op. 56 (1955); *Concerto*, cl., orch, op. 58 (1957); *Symfonische muziek*, orch, op. 59 (1957); *Espressioni cordiali*, str.orch, op. 63 (1963); *Canti e giuochi*, wind qnt, orch, op. 66 (1964); *Per sonare ed ascoltare*, fl, orch, op. 73 (1971); *Poème*, hp, chamb.orch, op. 96 (1993)

PUBLICATIONS
Hedendaagse Engelse componisten. Amsterdam, Becht, 1949
Pianomuziek. Bilthoven, Nelissen, 1958
Mozarts Bearbeitungen eigener und fremder Werke. Salzburg, Bärenreiter, 1969
Notes on Notes, selected essays. Buren, Knuf, 1974
Taken van de hedendaagse musicoloog. Buren, Knuf, 1974
'Marius Flothuis on himself', *Key Notes*, 4, 1976/2, p. 57-59
Traditie en verzet. Utrecht, Joachimsthal, 1982
Brieven in opmaat. Utrecht, Veen, 1990 (sel. of letters to Flothuis with commentary)
Denken over muziek. Kampen, Kok Lyra, 1993
'...exprimer l'inexprimable...' – essai sur la mélodie française depuis Duparc. Amsterdam, Rodopi, 1996
Mozarts Klavierkonzerte. München, Beck, 1998
Mozarts Streichquartette. München, Beck, 1998

BIBLIOGRAPHY
K. Jansen: 'Marius Flothuis neemt afscheid als hoogleraar muziekwetenschap', *NRC Handelsblad*, 26 Dec. 1982
T. de Leur: 'De componist Marius Flothuis', *Preludium*, Dec. 1986, p. 2-5
E. Mulder: 'Marius Flothuis 70 jaar', *Preludium*, Oct. 1984, p. 12-14

W. Paap: 'Composer's gallery : Marius Flothuis', *Sonorum Speculum*, no. 6, 1961, p. 2-8
W. Paap: 'Nederlandse componisten van deze tijd', *Mens en Melodie*, vol. 6, 1951, p. 4-9
L. Samama: *Zeventig jaar Nederlandse muziek : 1915-1985 : voorspel tot een nieuwe dag*. Amsterdam, Querido, 1986

DISCOGRAPHY
Canti e giuochi. Concertgebouw Orchestra, cond. B. Haitink (Composers' Voice DAVS 6504)
Hymnus. E. Spoorenberg (S), Concertgebouw Orchestra, cond. B. Haitink (BFO A-5 / Composers' Voice CVCD 8)
Hymnus; Per sonare ed ascoltare. H. Barwahser (fl), Concertgebouw Orchestra, cond. B. Haitink (Composers' Voice CV 7603)
Pour le tombeau d'Orphée. S.A. Claro (hp) (Funix Musik Forlag FMF CD 1007)
Pour le tombeau d'Orphée. M. Smits (hp) (Vanguard Classics 99035)
Sonnet, op. 9. J. van Nes (Mez), Royal Concertgebouw Orchestra, cond. B. Haitink (Q Disc 97014)
String Quartet op. 44. Raphael Quartet (Olympia OCD 508)
Symfonische muziek. Concertgebouw Orchestra, cond. E. van Beinum (Composers' Voice Highlights CV 26)

Hendrik Focking

DANZIG, 17 AUGUST 1747 – AMSTERDAM, 7 APRIL 1796

The Mennonite couple Cornelis Focking and Trijntje Cornelis Nollen, as yet childless, left Haarlem in 1739 to join the Mennonite community in Danzig. On their return to the Dutch Republic in 1752 they took up residence in Amsterdam; the family then had four children, of which Hendrik was the third. Nothing is known of Hendrik Focking's youth in Amsterdam. He was blind, a circumstance which, also considering the posts he held in his later life, suggests that he may have been a student of the then well-known Jacob Potholt (1720-1782), who was also blind. Potholt was from 1765 to 1782 organist at the Old Church and carillonneur of the tower of the town hall.

In any case, on 31 January 1769 Focking was appointed carillonneur at the Old Church Tower and Reguliers Tower (now known as the Munt Tower), a position he held until his premature death at the age of 49 in 1796. The combined appointment yielded him 210 guilders per year, a reasonable salary for a musician in the eighteenth century. Shortly after taking up this post (15 October 1769) he married Anna Lodewijks (1740-1809), born in Danzig and also a Mennonite. The couple had three children.

In 1780 Focking was appointed organist of the combined Mennonite congregations 'Near the Lamb and Near the Tower' (the 'Near the Lamb' congregation was named after a nearby brewery, The Lamb on the Singel, and the 'Near the Tower' congregation after the nearby Jan Rodenpoorts Tower). Worship at Mennonite churches was traditionally rather austere, but even there the introduction of the organ into the church and organ music to church services proved inevitable in the end. In 1777 the 'Near the Lamb' church installed an organ built by the Amsterdam organ builder Johannes Stephanus Strumphler. The church's first organist, Johan Adam Remmers, resigned in 1780 to become the organist at the Walloon Church in Amsterdam, apparently considered an improvement of position. Although a number of organists applied for the post, the church council did not organize the customary auditions but chose Hendrik Focking as Remmers's successor in a secret ballot. Possibly Focking's Mennonite faith played a role in this. When in 1786 a Strumphler organ was placed in the other church of the community 'Near the Tower', Focking was presumably the organist there, too.

Focking was the teacher of the blind organist and carillonneur Daniël Brachthuyzer (1779-1832), who was to become quite famous, as well as of his

own eldest son, Cornelis Focking, born in Amsterdam on 9 November 1770. After Hendrik Focking's death, Cornelis Focking applied to the Mennonite community to be appointed his successor, naming his experience as his father's replacement and as organist at the Lutheran Church in Rotterdam. However, he was turned down and the church appointed a certain J. Andriessen instead. Focking's posts as carillonneur at the Old Church Tower and Reguliers Tower went respectively to J.H. Warninck and his pupil Daniël Brachthuyzer.

Hendrik Focking is known in particular for his six sonatas for flute and basso continuo, which he published himself. As the title page makes no mention of his various positions, the work presumably appeared in 1769, shortly before his appointment as carillonneur. The flute sonatas follow the mid-eighteenth-century north-German sonata model for melody instrument and basso continuo as established by C.Ph.E. Bach, J.Ph. Kirnberger. J.G. Müthel, and others. (It is uncertain whether Focking's early youth in northeastern Germany played a role in this.) Such sonatas are in three movements, the first in a moderate tempo (for instance an andante), the second fast (allegro), and the last a menuet or air, often with variations. The style is galant and more lively than the flute sonata of the first half of the eighteenth century. Focking's work is less capricious and inventive than the sonatas of C.Ph.E. Bach. Nevertheless, his flute sonatas are well written and technically challenging but at the same time quite playable, and thus much appreciated by flutists.

RUDOLF RASCH

COMPOSITIONS

VI Sonates pour la flûte traverse solo avec une basse continuo ... oeuvre première. – Amsterdam, [composer], [c 1765-1769?]
Facs. ed.: epilogue Kees Otten. Amsterdam, Groen, 1986. Modern ed.: Sonata a flauto traverso e basso continuo in sol maggiore : opera prima no. 2, ed. H. Schouwman. Amsterdam, Heuwekemeyer, 1956

DISCOGRAPHY

Sonata no. 5. Amsterdam Baroque Ensemble, cond. T. Koopman (WVH 010)
Sonatas nos. 1, 2 and 3. P. van Houwelingen (rec, tra.fl) a.o. (WVH 078)

Jan van Gilse

ROTTERDAM, II MAY 1881 – OEGSTGEEST, 8 SEPTEMBER 1944

Jan Pieter Hendrik van Gilse was born into a family that produced many journalists and theologians. His father was editor-in-chief of the daily *Arnhemsche Courant* and from 1897 to 1901 a member of the Dutch parliament. Van Gilse received his schooling in The Hague and Rotterdam and then studied composition and conducting with Franz Wüllner at the Cologne Conservatory. His First Symphony (1901) was awarded a prize by the 'Verein Beethovenhaus', his Second Symphony was performed by the Concertgebouw Orchestra, conducted by Willem Mengelberg, and his cantata *Sulamith* was premiered in Arnhem in October 1903.

In 1902 Van Gilse went to Berlin to complete his studies under Engelbert Humperdinck. His most important work of this period is the large-scale cantata *Eine Lebensmesse*, based on a text by Richard Dehmel. In 1905 he went to Bremen to work as répétiteur and third conductor of this city's opera. During this period he composed his Third Symphony (1907), for which he was awarded the German 'Prix de Rome'. Before leaving for Rome, he worked for a time for the North Netherlands Opera. After spending a year in Rome Van Gilse took up residence in Munich. There he composed his first opera, *Frau Helga von Stavern* (to his own libretto), which was never performed, the song cycle *Gitanjali* (to translations of texts by Rabindranath Tagore), and the Fourth Symphony.

In 1916 he moved to Amsterdam and in 1917 was appointed conductor of the Utrecht Municipal Orchestra, a position in which he broke new ground, both musically and socially. The financial situation of the orchestra was greatly improved through his efforts and a pension fund was formed for the musicians. As a conductor, he introduced many new compositions to Utrecht audiences, particularly those of the contemporary and French repertoires.

Van Gilse was greatly appreciated by the public and the musicians. In 1919, however, the young composer Willem Pijper became the music critic of the daily *Utrechts Dagblad*. Pijper regularly panned Van Gilse's conducting, a situation that ultimately led to a conflict in which Van Gilse demanded that Pijper be barred from his concerts. The orchestra's board of directors initially granted this demand, but when it became apparent that they had gone back on their decision, Van Gilse, deeply disappointed, resigned in 1921.

Van Gilse left Utrecht and after passing through Switzerland went to

Berlin. He had composed very little while in Utrecht; during his 'years of banishment', as he referred to the period from 1922 to 1933, he composed a second song cycle based on texts by Rabindranath Tagore (1923) – the *Dansschetsen* [Dance sketches] for piano and orchestra (1926) – and an ambitious cantata in four movements, *Der Kreis des Lebens* (1929), to texts by Rainer Maria Rilke. He also wrote two parts of his memoires during this period.

Van Gilse's organizational activities made a great impact on musical life in the Netherlands. Together with several prominent colleagues, he founded in 1911 Geneco, the Society of Dutch Composers, and in 1913 the Dutch Music Copyright Agency Buma. He was chairman of Geneco from 1926 to 1942 and of Buma from 1917 to 1942. In 1935 he also founded the NMB, a Foundation for Dutch Musical Interests, an organization whose purpose was to promote Dutch music. After World War II the Buma Fund and the Donemus Foundation, two organizations concerned with the advancement of Dutch music, evolved from the NMB.

In Berlin Van Gilse felt increasingly uncomfortable with the growing incidence of Fascism. In June 1933 he was appointed director of the Utrecht Conservatory, but his period here (1933-1937) was a constant source of annoyance for him. He ultimately resigned to dedicate himself to composing, performing as a guest conductor and continuing his Buma activities. It was during this period that he worked on his second opera, *Thijl*, based on the Tijl Uilenspiegel character from the book by the Flemish author Charles de Coster.

World War II halted Van Gilse's career. His consistent rejection of the German regime led him to become increasingly involved in the artists' resistance group and finally forced him to go underground. His music was barred from performance and his scores were confiscated. Living in hiding at various addresses, Van Gilse edited the illegal newspaper *De vrije kunstenaar* [The free artist], but he had to give this up because of his repeated moves. His sons, both active in the resistance, were executed in 1943 and 1944 respectively, a loss he never recovered from. While lodging at his eighteenth underground address, the home of composer Rudolf Escher, Van Gilse fell ill. He died at the

Oegstgeest hospital, where he had been admitted under a false name, on 8 September 1944.

As a composer Van Gilse was no pioneer and he took a relatively long time to develop an individual style. The influence of his education in Germany clearly affected his early work. Until 1916 his music was very much under the influence of the German-Austrian tradition, the work of Gustav Mahler in particular. The intensive study he made of the music of Debussy, Ravel, Roussel and their contemporaries prompted him to introduce French elements into his work. Typical, for instance, is his use of short motifs, augmented chords, parallel harmony and a penchant for multi-colored, translucent instrumentation. Exemplary of his work during this period are the unfinished String Quartet (1922), *The Gardener/Der Gärtner* song cycle for soprano and orchestra (1921-1923), and the three *Dansschetsen* for piano and orchestra (1925-1926).

Van Gilse eventually blended the German Romantic atmosphere of his early work with French Impressionistic influences of the 1920s. While the *Prologus brevis* (1928), for orchestra, could still be regarded as a transitional work, the synthesis was truly attained in the cantata *Der Kreis des Lebens* (1928-1929), composed immediately after *Prologus brevis*, in the opera *Thijl* (1938-1940), and in the unfinished declamatorio *Rotterdam* (1942). In these last-named compositions Van Gilse's personal style emerges, in which he refrains from adopting the anti-Romantic element characteristic of the French style. Moreover, in *Thijl* and *Rotterdam* elements of folk music are added.

HANS VAN DIJK

COMPOSITIONS

Van Gilse did not provide his works with opus numbers
* unpublished

SONGS: *De waterlelie*, Mez/A, orch (1899)*; *Waldnacht*, S/T, pf (1901?); *Entweihung*, S/T, pf (1901); *Geheimnis*, S/T, pf (1902); *Minnelied*, S, orch (1903); *Mein Herz ist wie ein See so weit*, S, orch (1903)*; *Eine Weise*, A, pf (1903)*; *Frieden*, A, pf/orch (1905); *Das Königslied*, A, pf/orch (1905); *Herbststurm*, A, pf/orch (1905); *Abend*, A/Bar, pf (1905); *Een poezenidylle*, A, pf (1906)*; *Alles was blühen will* [fragment], A, pf (1906)*; *Requiem*, A/Bar, pf (1906); *Neergebrand*, A/Bar, pf (1908); *Auf eine Hand*, A/Bar, pf (1908); *Die Eigensinnige*, S/T, pf (1908); *Lied der h. Jungfrau*, A/Bar, pf (1908); *Auf* *einer grünen Wiese*, A/Bar, pf (1908); *Hans der Schwärmer*, S/T, pf (1908); *Säntis*, S/T, pf (1909); *Ein kleines Lied*, A/Bar, pf (1911?); *Der Schlaf, der auf Kindesauge ruht*, S, pf/orch (1915); *Bring ich dir buntes Spielzeug*, S, pf/orch (1915); *Ich weiss, da ist nichts als deine Liebe*, S, pf/orch (1915); *Lied auf dem Flusse*, S/T, pf (1922-1926); *Der junge Prinz*, S, pf/orch (1923); *Wenn ich Nachts zum Stelldichein gehe*, S, pf/orch (1921); *Sag mir, ob das alles wahr ist*, S, pf/orch (1923); *Der Reisebecher*, A/Bar, pf (1927); *Auf dem Canal Grande*, A/Bar, pf (1927); *Eingelegte Ruder*, A/Bar, pf (1927); *Schnitterlied*, A/Bar, pf (1927)

OTHER VOCAL WORKS: *Sulamith* (cantata), S, T, Bar, mix.choir, orch (1902); *Eine Lebensmesse* (cantata) (Dehmel), S, A, T, B, choirs, orch (1904); *Frau Helga von Stavern* (opera) (Van Gilse) (1913); *Gitanjali*, S, orch; *The Gardener* (Der Gärtner), S, orch (1921-1923); *Der Kreis des Lebens* (cantata) (Rilke), S, T, mix.choir, orch (1929); *Thijl* (opera) (1940); *Rotterdam* (declamatorio) (fragment) (1942)

CHAMBER MUSIC: *Zilveren feestmarsch*, pf 4h (1896)*; *Sonata in F minor* (fragment), vl, pf [?] (1896)*; *Trio in E-flat major* (fragment), vl, vc, pf (1896)*; *Sonata in C minor* (fragment), pf (1899)*; *Variaties over een St. Nicolaasliedje*, pf 4h (1910); *Nonet*, ob, cl, bn, hn, 5 str.instr (1916); *String Quartet* (fragment) (1922); *Sonata* (fragment), vl, pf (1922)*; *Drie dansschetsen*, 2 pf (1927); *Trio*, fl, vl, vla (1927)

ORCHESTRA: *Concertouverture in C minor* (1900); *Symphony no. 1 in F major* (1901); *Symphony no. 2 in E-flat major* (1903, rev. 1928); *Vorspiel 'Eine Lebensmesse'* (1903); *Symphony no. 3 in D minor*, S, orch (1907); *Variaties over een St. Nicolaasliedje* (1909); *Symphony no. 4 in A major* (1910*; rev. 1915); *Symphony no. 5 in D major* (fragment) (1922)*; *Drie dansschetsen*, pf, orch (1926); *Prologus brevis* (1928); *Preludium 'Der Kreis des Lebens'* (1928); *Kleine wals* (1936); *Treurmuziek bij den dood van Uilenspiegel* (1940); *Andante conmoto* (fragment) (1935?)*

BIBLIOGRAPHY
Archive Jan van Gilse. The Hague, Gemeentemuseum, Music Archives
H. van Dijk: *Jan van Gilse : strijder en idealist : een bijdrage tot de kennis van de Nederlandse muziekgeschiedenis in de periode 1900 – 1944.* Doctoral dissertation University of Utrecht, 1980. Abridged version: Buren, Knuf, 1988

DISCOGRAPHY
Concert Overture in C minor. Netherlands Radio Symphony Orchestra, cond. J. van Steen (NM Classics 92090)
Drie liederen uit R. Tagore's 'Gitanjali'. A. van Wickevoort-Crommelin (S), Maastrichts Stedelijk Orkest, cond. H. Hermans (Marl 098803) (recorded 19 Oct. 1941 in the Dominican Church in Maastricht in the composer's presence)
Drie liederen uit R. Tagore's 'Gitanjali'. E. Lugt (S), Concertgebouw Orchestra, cond. B. Haitink (Donemus DAVS 6405)
Drie liederen uit R. Tagore's 'Gitanjali'. M. Kweksilber (S), Residentie Orchestra, cond. E. Bour (Phonogram 6814.781/786)
Nonet; String Quartet (1922, unfin.); Trio (1927). Viotta Ensemble, Ebony Quartet (NM Classics 92056)
Symphony no. 2 in E-flat major (rev. version). Gelderland Orchestra, cond. G. Octors (Donemus CVS 1985/1)
Treurmuziek bij den dood van Uilenspiegel. Utrecht Symphony Orchestra, cond. P. Hupperts (Donemus DAVS 6405)
Treurmuziek uit de dramatische legende 'Thijl'. Concertgebouw Orchestra, cond. B. Haitink (BFO A-5)
Treurmuziek uit 'Thijl'. Residentie Orchestra, cond. E. Spanjaard (Olympia OCD 507)
Trio. M. Schneemann (fl), M. Blankestijn (vl), G.J. Leuverink (vla) (Donemus / De IJsbreker CVE 1)

Various recordings in the archive of the Dutch Broadcasting Company (NOB)

Christiaan Ernst Graaf

RUDOLSTADT, 30 JUNE 1723 – THE HAGUE, 17 JULY 1804

In the Netherlands, his home for over half a century, Christiaan Ernst Graaf adapted his first and last names to the Dutch spelling, using two a's instead of one. His father, the violinist and composer Johann Graf, was concertmaster and, from 1739, kapellmeister at the court of Schwarzburg-Rudolstadt in the principality of Thüringen. Of his seven musical sons, some were members throughout their lives of the Rudolstadt court chapel, while others sought their careers abroad. Christiaan Ernst was the most talented. He probably received his first musical training from his father. The two counts of Schwarzburg-Rudolstadt contributed the considerable sum of several thousand German guilders to further his study of the violin. It is not known where Graaf received his musical education. When his father died, on 2 February 1750, he was a 'Cammer Musicus' in Rudolstadt. Christiaan Ernst, who had incurred large debts, went on a journey on 11 May 1750. He was given two month's leave, which was extended a couple of times, but Graaf quite carelessly exceeded the time permitted him. From Amsterdam, where he worked as a dance teacher, he applied in 1752 for a position as concertmaster in his birthplace, a post he had been promised twice in the past. However, nothing came of it and Graaf was dismissed by his angry patron, for whom he was still working, at least officially, as a chamber musician. Two years later he unsuccessfully applied for the position of kapellmeister in Rudolstadt. Graaf decided to remain in the Netherlands, but he never lost contact with his native land. His opp.12 and 13 as well as his passion-oratorio *Der Tod Jesu* (1802) are dedicated to members of the Rudolstadt nobility.

In Middelburg, he led the collegium musicum, to the members of which he dedicated his op.1 symphonies, published in 1756 or 1757. In 1758 he was appointed court composer in The Hague to Princess Anna, widow of William IV and Princess Regent to her underaged son William V. The eldest daughter of King George II of England, she had been the patroness (and student) of Handel in London, and of Jean-Marie Leclair in the Netherlands. Thus, Graaf was in the service of a true music-lover. After her death on 12 January 1759 he remained 'composer to the court of the prince of Orange-Nassau' until 1766, when he was appointed kapellmeister by William V who became Stadtholder in that year. In addition to the salary Graaf received as a member of the orchestra, William V paid him an annual one-thousand guilders from his private funds, a stipend that continued after he retired in 1790; when William V left for England in 1795 the new rulers continued this financing.

In the second half of the eighteenth century, the post of Kapellmeister to a Stadtholder was the most important musical position in the Netherlands. Of the orchestral and chamber music Graaf composed for the weekly court concerts at the Stadtholder's Chambers in The Hague, a significant number have survived in print. The composer also met and accompanied the many renowned soloists who visited the court, including Mozart and Beethoven, who in their early youth were engaged to perform (in 1765, 1766 and 1783, respectively)

for the Stadtholder's family. It was at this time, for William V's inauguration as Stadtholder, that Mozart composed his variations for harpsichord on Graaf's song *Op de installatie[...]* [To the installation ...] (KV 24). Just as Graaf did not perform in The Hague alone – he also gave concerts elsewhere in the Netherlands – he did not compose solely for the entertainment of the Stadtholder's family either. In 1781 he led the performance in the Frisian town of Bolsward of a large-scale work he had composed for the installation of a new organ in this city's Great Church; in 1802 Graaf, then 79 years old, conducted in The Hague an oratorio he had composed in celebration of the Peace of Amiens.

Christiaan Ernst Graaf's interests went beyond music; a self-portrait he painted in oil was in the possession of Carl Philipp Emanuel Bach, as was a portrait he painted of his younger brother, the flutist and composer Friedrich Hartmann Graf (who, incidentally, also worked in The Hague for several years under the name Graaf). According to his later biographer, Broekhuyzen, Christiaan Ernst Graaf was 'a practitioner of arts and sciences, a well-read man, a pleasant companion, and in the circle of his friends even voluble and cheerful, and gifted with such a talent for teaching, particularly to young people, that he was able to endow them with a taste for arts and sciences.'

Several of Graaf's students later played a prominent role in Dutch music; his pedagogical approach is crystallized in his theoretical treatise *Proeve over de natuur der harmonie* [Treatise on the nature of harmony] and the accompanying *Leçons pour la basse générale*. Graaf died of a stroke at the age of 81 and was buried in the Great Church in The Hague. His widow, Petronella Trimpont, died six years later.

Graaf's music exemplifies the galant style: concise, easily accessible, and with an illusion of natural simplicity. His instrumental music employs relatively simple motifs, rather than long melodic lines. His instrumentation was highly original, as evidenced by his duet for one violin played by two violinists, and his concerto for six kettledrums. Of historical interest is much of his chamber music of the 1760s and 1770s. The harpsichord and violin in his op.4, for instance, engage in an exciting dialogue in which they continuously reverse roles; each takes the lead, then accompanies, and later is the equal of the other. Also noticeably competing with each other are the parts in the op.15 string quartets, with occasional virtuoso passages for the cello in particular – all this before Haydn and Mozart composed their great works in the genre. With their melodic charm, most of Graaf's songs transcend the level of music for domestic use. Judging by the quality of the *Kerk-Gezangen* [Church Hymns] and *Der Tod Jesu* it is regrettable that so few of Graaf's large-scale vocal works have survived.

LUC VAN HASSELT

COMPOSITIONS

VOCAL:

Laat ons juichen, Batavieren. Op de installatie van Zyn Doorluchtige Hoogheid Willem den Vyfden... 1766. – Amsterdam, Johann Julius Hummel

Vingt cinq fables dans le gout de M. de la Fontaine, en musique pour le chant et clavecin ... tome premier, livre I, oeuvre XXI. – The Hague, Wittelaer
Also published as op. 18

Kleine gedigten voor kinderen van mr. H. van Alphen ... in muziek gezett. – Amsterdam, Markordt
Three volumes (vol. 1 1779, vol. 2 1780, vol. 3 without year)

IN MANUSCRIPT:

Kerk-Gezangen ter inwyding van het orgel in de Groote Kerk te Bolsward [28 June 1781] (text J.A. Backer, for soloists, choir, orchestra

and organ); *Der Tod Jesu* [1802] (text K.W. Ramler, for soloists, choir, orchestra and organ)

CHAMBER MUSIC:

Sei sonate a violino primo, violino secondo e basso... opera seconda. – The Hague, P. van Os, [1758]

VI sonate a cembalo obligato e violino... opera IV. – Amsterdam, Johann Julius Hummel, [1761]
3rd movement of no. 6 also published separate as *Ally Croaker*

Sei sonate a tre, due violino e basso continuo... opera quinta. – The Hague, s.n.

Sei quintetti a flauto traverso, violino, viola, violoncello e basso... opera VIII. – Amsterdam, Johann Julius Hummel, [1768]

Six sonates à deux violons et violoncello... oeuvre X. – The Hague, s.n
Three sonatas for 2 violins and cello, three sonatas for 2 violins and bc

Sei quartetti a flauto, violino, viola e basso... opera XII. – Amsterdam, Johann Julius Hummel, [1772]

Trois sonates pour le clavecin avec l'accompagnement d'un violon et de la basse... oeuvre XIII. – The Hague, s.n., [1774]

Sei quartetti per due violini, alto e violoncello obligato... [opus 15]. – Paris, Mme Bérault, [1776]
Different nos. 4 and 5 occur in other editions of this work

Six quatuors à deux violons, taille et basse... oeuvre XVII. – Berlin, Johann Julius Hummel; Amsterdam, au Grand Magazin de Musique, [1777]

Six sonates pour le clavecin ou forte et piano avec un violon... oeuvre XIX. – Berlin, Johann Julius Hummel; Amsterdam, au Grand Magazin de Musique, [1779]

Duo économique pour un violon à deux mains et deux archets... oeuvre XXVII. – The Hague, s.n
Also published as op. 31

II Sonates pour le clavecin à quatre mains... oeuvre XXIX. – The Hague, s.n., [1787, 1788]

[10] Petites pièces aisées pour le clavecin à quatre mains. – oeuvre XXX. – The Hague, s.n.

Leçons pour la basse générale suivant l'ordre des degrez de ses accords en sonatines pour un violon avec la basse chiffrée. – Amsterdam, A. Olofsen, [1790 a.f.]

Three menuets (keyboard notation with figured bass), included in *L'Écho*. – Liège, Benoît Andrez, 1758

ORCHESTRA:
Sei sinfonie a violino primo, secondo, viola, e basso... opera 1. – Middelburg, S. Mandel-green, [c 1756]

Sei sinfonie a violino primo e secondo, viola, basso e cembalo, con due oboe, flauti traversi e corni ad libitum... opera terza. – s.l., s.n., [1759]

Six sinfonies à deux violons, taille et basse, deux hautbois ou flutes trav. et deux cornes ad libitum... oeuvre sixième. – The Hague, s.n.

Six simphonies à deux violons, taille & basse, deux hautbois et deux cornes de chasse ad libitum... oeuvre VII. – Amsterdam, Johann Julius Hummel, [1766]

Six simphonies à deux violons, taille & basse, deux flutes & deux cornes de chasse... oeuvre IX. – Amsterdam, Johann Julius Hummel, [1769]

Six simphonies à deux violons, taille, basse, deux flutes et deux cors de chasse... oeuvre XI. – Amsterdam, Johann Julius Hummel

Six sinfonies à deux violons, taille, basse, deux hautbois ou flutes et 2. cors de chasse... oeuvre XIV. – Berlin, Johann Julius Hummel; Amsterdam, au Grand Magazin de Musique, [1776]
Previously published as *Symphonies périodiques*, 1774

Six simphonies à diverses instruments... oeuvre XVI. – Berlin, Johann Julius Hummel; Amsterdam, au Grand Magazin de Musique

Trois simphonies à grand orchestre... oeuvre XX. – Berlin, Johann Julius Hummel; Amsterdam, au Grand Magazin de Musique

IN MANUSCRIPT:
Cello Concerto; Five symphonies; *Winter-symfonie; Grande simphonie Hollandoise en deux choers, sur les evenements de l'année 1787*

WRITINGS
Proeve over de natuur der harmonie in de generaal bas, benevens een onderricht eener korte en regelmaatige becyffering. – The Hague, Wittelaer, 1782

BIBLIOGRAPHY

G.H. Broekhuyzen: *Over het leven en de werken van eenigen der voornaamste toondichters in de onderscheidene vakken der compositie.* Manuscript in the Theater Instituut Nederland, Amsterdam

A. Clement: Preface to the facs.ed.: *C.E. Graf, Sei sinfonie à violino primo ... op. 1*, Middelburg, Koninklijk Zeeuwsch Genootschap der Wetenschappen, 1994 (Exempla Musica Zelandica, 2)

P. Gülke: *Musik und Musiker in Rudolstadt.* Rudolstadt, Sonderausgabe der Rudolstädter Heimathefte, 1963

L. van Hasselt: 'Beethoven in Holland', *Die Musikforschung*, 1965, p. 181-184

[L. van Hasselt]: 'Uitslag van de prijsvraag', *Mens en Melodie*, vol. 31, 1976, p. 289-292

L. van Hasselt: 'Violisten vóór', *Mens en Melodie*, vol. 31, 1976, p. 204-209

R.G. King: 'C.E. Graf's music on the occasion of the consecration of the Martinikerk organ at Bolsward (1781)', *TVNM*, 44, 1994, p. 115-131

D.F. Scheurleer: *Het muziekleven in Nederland in de tweede helft der 18e eeuw in verband met Mozart's verblijf aldaar.* The Hague, Nijhoff, 1909

Th. de Wyzewa and G. de Saint-Foix: *Wolfgang Amédée Mozart.* Paris, Desclée de Brouwer, 1936-1946

DISCOGRAPHY

Symphony in C major, op. 14 no. 4. Residentie Orchestra, cond. T. Koopman (Olympia OCD 501)

Hef aan! Bataaf! (Quintet op. 8 no. 1, Four songs). Ensemble Pont de la Virtue (Erasmus WVH 187/188)

Carel Hacquart

BRUGES, C.1640 – 1701?

Very little is known about the life of Carel Hacquart; indeed, information is only available about those few decades – from 1670 to 1690 – in which he was active as a composer. Hacquart was probably born around 1640 in Bruges and emigrated to the northern Netherlands around 1670. Like his brother the viola da gamba player Philip Hacquart (whose six suites for this instrument have survived), Hacquart worked as a freelance musician in Amsterdam. He was evidently very successful, for in 1674 he was able to finance the publication of his extensive op.1, a collection of ten concertante motets. The work was dedicated to the stadtholder William III of Orange; perhaps Hacquart was hoping for an appointment at his court in The Hague.

In the 1670s Hacquart came to the attention of the poet/author, composer and diplomat Constantijn Huygens, to whom he dedicated *De Triomfeerende Min* [Triumphant love] in 1680. In 1679 Hacquart took up residence in The Hague. There he earned his living as a music teacher to the 'beau monde' and organized public concerts, probably the first such concerts in the Netherlands. The then elderly Huygens, who praised Hacquart as 'ce grand maistre de musique', aided the brilliant musician in this undertaking. In 1686 two collections of Hacquart's instrumental music were published, the last of his known works. No information exists on Hacquart's life after 1689; perhaps he joined the retinue of William of Orange in England. In 1697, a 'Charles Hakert, native of Holland', possibly this composer, was given permission to return to the Netherlands. In 1702 the Amsterdam music publisher Estienne Roger gained possession of Hacquart's work, giving rise to the assumption that the composer must have died shortly before that.

Hacquart's surviving work is limited to four printed collections whose diversity and high quality, however, show him to have been an important composer. In the *Cantiones sacrae*, his most important work, Hacquart proves to have been aware of the advances made in the Italian motet of his time, though French influences are also evident. The *Cantiones sacrae* employ the common alternation of arias, ariosos, homophonic passages and fugatos. The solo passages demand a high degree of virtuosity from the vocalists. The texts are adapted from the psalms and from Thomas à Kempis' *Imitatio Christi*.

Hacquart's mastery is shown particularly in the varied vocal and instrumental combinations used in the collections. Of all seventeenth-century Dutch collections of vocal music, Hacquart's are the most variegated; no two pieces are composed for the same combination. His collection is systematically ordered in two halves, the first five motets being accompanied by continuo alone, the second five by two violins, a bass string instrument and continuo. The two to seven voices named in the title are systematically expanded, from the continuo duet of no.1 (*Miser es*) to the festive motet no.10 (*O Jesu splendor*) for vocal quartet and three-part string ensemble. In keeping with this de-

De Triomfeerende

M I N,

V R E D E S P E L.

Gemengt met Zang- en Snaarenfpel,
Vliegwerken, en Baletten.

Door

D. B.

'A M S T E R D A M,
By *Pſalm Matthyſ. gedrukt.*
Voor d'Erfgenamen van *Jacob Lefcailje*, op de Middeldam,
naaſt de Viſchmarkt, 1680.

sign, the first motet with obligato strings (no.6), the bass solo motet (*Ego sum*), is scored for three violins instead of the usual two, thus continuing the five-part setting of the no.5 continuo motet, *Erravi sicut ovis*. The traditional SATB and SSB vocal combinations appear only twice, both with and without violins. The remaining motets reveal the composer's liking for unusual combinations, such as the spectacular duet for basses (*Quis mihi det*), the aforementioned bass solo motet, or the splendid *Deus misereatur nostri* (Psalm 66), for three male voices (alto, tenor and bass) and strings, a combination evidently influenced by French music.

The printed edition of the incidental music for *De Triomfeerende Min*, issued without an opus number in 1680, contains the vocal and continuo parts but omits all instrumental parts; hence, the ballet music and overture are missing. This pastoral, written in collaboration with the poet Dirk Buysero, was composed in celebration of the Peace of Nijmegen (1678). Possibly the first Dutch opera, the work was performed in this century, although its production was hampered by the incomplete score and the fact that it is not an opera in the modern sense, but a pastoral with through-composed songs and dances.

In 1686 two of Hacquart's instrumental collections were published. *Harmonia parnassia*, op.2, was printed in Utrecht by Arnold van Eynden and dedicated to Count Willem van Hoogendorp, a student of Hacquart's. This is arguably the most important violin collection published in the Netherlands in the seventeenth century. Like opus 1, it contains ten pieces. The first six take the common form of trio sonatas for two violins and basso continuo, but with a viola da gamba playing a more embellished version of the bass part. The remaining four sonatas once again show Hacquart's preference for unusual combinations. Stylistically, *Harmonia parnassia* reveals the influence of the Italian trio sonata model as practised immediately before Corelli, exemplified in the work of Legrenzi, Bassani and Giovanni Battista Vitali. The role of virtuosity is negligible, with motivic and harmonic richness, contrapuntal consistency and cantabile instrumental lines serving as the chief focus. Hacquart's sonatas comply with the common alternation of fast and slow movements. Notable in this work are the fugal 'canzone', the 'bizarria' in a fleeting triple meter and the folk-like melody of the 'aria'.

Hacquart's op.3, *Chelys* (1686), comprises twelve suites for viola da gamba solo. There are indications that the work originally had a continuo part that has been lost (only one copy of the solo part has survived). Through the profusion of double stops and illusion of polyphony in the solo part, characteristic of contemporary French and German gamba music, the work is relatively complete harmonically, and therefore these suites are playable in their existing form. Only occasionally does the composer deviate from the standard pattern of movements of prelude-allemande-courante-sarabande-gigue. The suites show the influence of French music in terms of melody and harmony as well as that of the English school, particularly through their use of composed diminutions. Though Hacquart's *Chelys* has fared poorly in the repertoire, these suites for viola da gamba, within the limitations of the genre, hold a worthy place alongside the motets and sonatas.

PIETER DIRKSEN

COMPOSITIONS

Cantiones sacrae 2, 3, 4, 5, 6, 7, tam vocum quam instrumentorum ... opus primum. – Amsterdam, Paul Matthysz, 1674
Ten motets for 1-5 voices, 3-4 strings and bc

Harmonia parnassia, sonatarum trium & 4 instrumentorum ... opus secundum. – Utrecht, Arnold van Eynden, 1686
Ten sonatas for 3-4 strings and bc

Chelys ... opus tertium. – The Hague, author, 1686
Twelve suites for viola da gamba solo

De Triomfeerende Min. Vredespel. Gemengt met zangen, snaarenspel, vliegwerken, en baletten door D. Buysero. – Amsterdam, Paul Matthysz, Jacob Lescailje, 1680
Music for Buysero's play for 1-4 voices and bc

BIBLIOGRAPHY

P. Andriessen: *Carel Hacquart (c. 1640-1701?) : een biografische bijdrage : het werk.* Brussels, Koninklijke Academie voor Wetenschappen, Letteren en Schone Kunsten, 1974
E.H. Meyer: 'Die Vorherrschaft der Instrumentalmusik im niederländischen Barock', *TVNM*, 15, 1936, p. 56-83 and 264-281
F. Noske: *Music bridging divided religions.* Wilhelmshaven, Noetzel, 1989

DISCOGRAPHY

Domine, quae est fiducia tua, op. 1, no. 3; Domine, Deus meus, op. 1, no. 4; Sonate op. 2, no. 5. Ensemble Bouzignac (Vanguard Classics 99126)

Eravi sicut ovis, op. 1, no. 5. Ensemble dell'Anima Eterna, Vocal Ensemble Currende, cond. J. van Immerseel (Teleac TEL 8901-8905)

O Jesu splendor, op. 1, no. 10. Cantorij Amsterdam, members of the Residentie Orchestra, cond. T. Koopman (Olympia OCD 500)

Sonata op. 2, no. 10. Members of the Residentie Orchestra, cond. T. Koopman (Olympia OCD 500)

Sonatas op. 2, nos. 2 and 8. Trio Sonnerie (Teleac TEL 8901-8905)

Gerhardus Havingha

GRONINGEN, BAPTIZED 15 NOVEMBER 1696 –
ALKMAAR, 6 MARCH 1753

Gerhardus Havingha was born in the city of Groningen. His father was organist of various churches there, including the Martini Church, where Havingha
was baptized on 15 November 1696. In all likelihood, Gerhardus Havingha
and his brother Henricus – who became a preacher after a brief career as an
organist – were trained as organists by their father.

As a youth, Havingha often deputized for his father on the organ. His early
years in Groningen were especially important because it was there that he became acquainted with the German innovations in the organ through the instruments made by the master organ builder Arp Schnitger (1648-1719). In
the decades around the turn of the century, Schnitger either built or restored
the organs of nearly every church in the province of Groningen. Even the
Groningen collegium musicum, of which the city organists were also members, installed a small Schnitger organ.

Havingha's first position as an organist came in 1718 at Appingedam in
Groningen. In 1722 he left this north-east corner of the Dutch Republic to succeed the suddenly deceased Egbert Enno Veldcamps as city organist of Alkmaar.

Havingha's life in Alkmaar was typical of that of a city organist in the Dutch
Republic: he accompanied psalm singing in the church and played as the congregation left at the end of services, periodically gave organ recitals, maintained the instrument in good repair, appraised organs, gave music lessons
and led the city's collegium musicum. Through these activities, Havingha was
a central figure in the musical life of Alkmaar. The Laurens Church organ he
found upon his arrival, although not really of poor quality, was nonetheless
outdated, judged by the standards of 1722. Having been built around 1640 by
father and son Germer Galtuszoon and Galtus Germerszoon van Hagerbeer, it
had been the pride of Alkmaar ever since, not least because of its panels that
were painted by Jacob van Campen. Compared with the fine registrations and
balanced mixtures of the Schnitger organs Havingha had known in Groningen, the Hagerbeer organ was unwieldy, dated, and too weak at unexpected
moments to adequately accompany the congregation.

Almost immediately after accepting the appointment, Havingha proposed
that radical alterations be made to 'his' instrument, convincing the Alkmaar

city council to engage the son of Arp Schnitger, Franz Caspar, for the restoration. Schnitger began work in 1723, and made sweeping changes in the construction, the pipes and the registration of the organ and tuned the instrument to equal tempterament, which was still a novelty at the time. Havingha apparently feared that these alterations could lead to objections, for he kept the nature of the work secret even from his collegium musicum. It was only upon completion that the extent of the changes became clear. A storm of protest followed. The collegium musicum divided into pro and con factions. The city council, however, supported Havingha throughout the upheaval.

VIII SUITES

Gecomponeerd voor de
(*Clavecymbal off Spinet*
Bestaande
in
Ouvertures, Preludien, Allemanden
Couranten, Sarabanden, Airs
Gavotten, Entrées, Marschen
Menuetten, en Gigs
Opgedraagen
aan de
EDELE GROOT ACHTBAARE HEEREN BORGEMEESTEREN
der Stad
ALKMAAR
door
GERHARDUS HAVINGHA
Opera Prima

T' AMSTERDAM
by
Michel Charles le Cene
Muzyk en Boekverkooper

Several works were published during the controversy, the most important being Havingha's explanation of the issue. In his book *Oorspronk en voortgang der orgelen, met de voortreffelykheit van Alkmaars groote orgel, by gelegenheit van deszelfs herstellinge* (1727) [Origins and development of the organ, with the excellence of Alkmaars large organ, on the occasion of this instrument's restoration], Havingha extensively explains the background, principles and execution of the restoration of the instrument. Havingha's publication, an important document in the history of organs, provoked two rebuttals: Jacob Wognum's *Verdediging tegen de lasterende voorreden over de oorspronk en voortgang der orgelen* (Alkmaar, s.a.) [Defense against the libellous exposition on the origins and development of the organ], and Aeneas Egbertus Veldcamps' *Onderrichtinge ... wegens eenige perioden tegens hem uytgegeven in het boek genaamt Oorspronk en voortgang der orgelen* (Alkmaar, 1727) [Instruction ... because of some passages against him in the book named Origins and development of the organ]. Wognum was a member of the Alkmaar collegium musicum, and on good terms with Havingha, at least before the organ controversy. Veldcamps was the son of Havingha's predecessor in Alkmaar and was organist of the Jacob's Church in The Hague at the time of the commotion; he had been asked by Havingha's critics to come to their aid. Both writers rejected the Havingha-Schnitger innovations made to the construction, disposition and tuning of the organ. Nevertheless, the organ remained as Schnitger restored it in 1723.

The controversy surrounding this organ is of more historical significance than it may seem at first. The introduction of equal temperament opened unprecedented possibilities, particularly regarding the use of previously unpractical keys with more than three sharps or flats. Havingha utilized these keys in his only surviving set of compositions, the *VIII Suites* (1724), which were published in Amsterdam. The suites of this collection open with a movement rather diverse in character (overture), in most cases followed by dance movements such as the allemande, courante, sarabande and gigue. Some of the suites contain other types of movements such as arias. Havingha's style of writing for keyboard instrument leans more to the Italian-German traditions than the French. Some movements are ornately embellished. Worth noting is the succession of keys – D-minor, E-major, B-flat-minor, A-major, A-sharp-minor, E-flat-major, D-minor and F-major – which can only be played in equal temperament. The collection shows Havingha to have been a very capable composer.

Other pieces he wrote for the collegium musicum – including solo sonatas for flute or violin and basso continuo, trio sonatas, and sonatas for three violins and basso continuo – were not published and have presumably not survived. Havingha did undertake the publishing of a second book: David Kellner's *Treulicher Unterricht im General-Bass* (Hamburg, 1732) was issued in Havingha's Dutch translation in 1740 as *Korte en getrouwe onderrigtinge van de generaal bass or bassus continuus*.

After the controversy surrounding the Schnitger organ, Havingha returned to a more peaceful existence. He remained the city organist of Alkmaar until his death in 1753.

RUDOLF RASCH

COMPOSITIONS

VIII Suites, gecomponeerd voor de clavecymbal off spinet, bestaande in ouvertures, preludien, allemanden, couranten, sarabanden, aire, gavotten, entrées, marschen, menuetten, en gigues ... opera prima. – Amsterdam, Michel Charles Le Cène, [1724] Facs. ed.: with an introd. by Clemens Romijn. Utrecht, STIMU, 1990. Modern ed.: Werken voor clavecimbel / publ. by Jos. Watelet. Antwerpen, Vereniging voor Muziekgeschiedenis te Antwerpen, 1951. Reprint: Amsterdam, Swets & Zeitlinger, 1971 (Monumenta Musicae Belgicae 7)

WRITINGS

Oorspronk en voortgang der orgelen, met de voortreffelykheit van Alkmaars groote orgel, by gelegentheit van deszelfs herstellinge. Alkmaar, Jan van Beyeren, 1727 Facs. ed.: ed. and with introduction by Arend Jan Gierveld. Buren, Knuf, 1985 (Bibliotheca Organologica 13)

Korte en getrouwe onderrigtinge van de generaal bass of bassus continuus. Amsterdam, Gerhard Fredrik Witvogel, 1740 Transl. after David Kellner (1732)

BIBLIOGRAPHY
J.W. Enschedé: 'Gerhardus Havingha en
het orgel in de Groote- of Sint-Laurenskerk te
Alkmaar', *TVNM*, 8, 1908, p. 181-261
A.J. Gierveld: Preface to the facs. ed. of
Oorspronk en voortgang (see writings)
M.A. Vente: 'Aeneas Egbertus Veldcamps,
drager van oudhollandse orgeltradities (1686-
1741)', *TVNM*, 20, 1967, p. 249-264

Pieter Hellendaal

ROTTERDAM, I APRIL 1721 – CAMBRIDGE, 19 APRIL 1799

Pieter Hellendaal was born in Rotterdam and baptized as a son of Johan Hellendaal and Neeltje la Croix. In 1731 the family took up residence in Utrecht, where the ten-year-old Hellendaal immediately became the organist at the Nicolas Church, albeit under the supervision of his father, a schoolmaster who apparently had musical talents. Hellendaal continued as an organist in Utrecht until the family moved to Amsterdam in 1737. He must also have learned to play the violin, considering his stay around 1740 in Padua with Giuseppe Tartini at the master's *Scuola delle nazioni*. Prior to this excursion abroad, Hellendaal may have had lessons in Amsterdam with the violinist/composer Pietro Antonio Locatelli, though there is no evidence of this. Upon returning to Amsterdam Hellendaal gave frequent concerts as a violinist. It was during this period that he published his first collections of violin sonatas: opp.1 and 2, each comprising six sonatas, issued in 1744 and 1748 respectively.

On 8 January 1749 Hellendaal enrolled at the University of Leiden in order to work in an academic environment. He also continued to perform as a concert violinist, for example at the 'New Vaux-hall' summer concerts in The Hague, and was also for a time assistant organist at the Mare Church.

Around the beginning of 1752 he left for London, where he soon gained fame through his numerous performances as a violinist. He also gave lessons and traded in sheet music. 1758 saw the publication of his *Six grand concertos for violins &c.* (op.3), a collection of concerti grossi in the Italian-English style of Handel and Geminiani. However, the security of life as an organist also appealed to Hellendaal: he became the organist at King's Lynn in Norfolk in 1760. After moving to Cambridge in 1762 he was appointed organist at Pembroke Hall Chapel (1762-1777) and, subsequently, at Saint Peter's College (1777-1799). His appearances as a concert performer gradually diminished, but he continued to compose, for string instruments in particular. Around 1765 he published a collection of six sonatas for violin and basso continuo (op.4), in 1780 a collection of eight sonatas for cello and basso continuo (op.5), and around 1790 *Three grand lessons* for keyboard instrument with violin and cello accompaniment (op.6).

During his later years in Cambridge, Hellendaal's son Peter Hellendaal Jr. began making a name for himself as a musician, though details of his life and

Concert in Cambridge, 1767 (Hellendaal is at the far left); engraved by Abram Hume

work have not survived. Hellendaal Sr. died in Cambridge on 19 April 1799 at the age of 78.

Structurally speaking, Hellendaal's sonatas for violin – which, with 29 works, form the bulk of his music – are in keeping with the work of the generation of Tartini and Carl Philipp Emanuel Bach. The majority are in three movements, the first slow or moderate in tempo (usually a largo or andante), the second in a fast common time, and the third also fast, but usually lighter in character and in triple meter. Several of the violin sonatas follow the traditional 'sonata da chiesa' pattern of a slow, introductory movement, a fast, 'serious' movement in common time, a slow 'affettuoso' movement, and a brisk last movement, often marked rondo, pastorale or allegretto. Hellendaal's violin sonatas have a virtuoso character with profuse ornamentation, rapid passages and double stops. The Cambridge sonatas that have survived in manuscript contain a number of virtuoso cadenzas and capriccios, apparently inspired by those in Pietro Antonio Locatelli's *L'arte del violino* (1733).

The op.5 cello sonatas breathe the same cantabile yet virtuoso atmosphere as the violin sonatas. The last four of the eight cello sonatas are far more technically demanding for the soloist than the others. Although the cello sonatas were composed later than most of the violin sonatas, their structure follows the old-fashioned 'sonata da chiesa' scheme.

Hellendaal's concerti grossi, as was nearly inevitable for English works in the genre during this period, are strongly influenced by George Frideric Handel, who with his *Twelve grand concertos for violins etc. in seven parts*, op.6 (1740), had set the style. Hellendaal went so far as to even copy Handel's title almost verbatim, but there are more parts in Hellendaal's pieces because he adds a viola to his concertino (solo string ensemble), as did Francesco Geminiani and others before him. Hellendaal's concerti grossi are in five movements; the first four closely adhere to the 'sonata da chiesa' scheme of an overture, a fugue, a more contemplative movement and a finale. The fifth movement serves rather as an encore, a light piece in closing, such as a menuet, bourrée, march or pastorale.

Hellendaal's work is typical of mid-eighteenth-century music; the basso continuo still forms the foundation of the work, but the melody already leans toward the galant style. As he continued to use the figured bass principle up to his last compositions, he cannot be counted among the most progressive composers of his time. In fact, he continued to employ the style of his earliest pieces (1740-1750) up until his death at the close of the eighteenth century. But all of his music is skillfully composed, mellifluous and never boring. His solo sonatas are unique in their combination of cantabile atmosphere and virtuosity. Despite their orientation to the Handelian model, his concerti grossi also show a combination of musical and technical elements that is immediately recognizable.

RUDOLF RASCH

COMPOSITIONS

Sonate a violino solo e basso ... opera prima. – Amsterdam, [for the composer, engraved by J.Martin], [1744]
Six sonatas for violin and bc

VI Sonate a violino solo e basso ... opera seconda. – Amsterdam, composer, [1748]
Facs. ed.: introd. by Leendert Haasnoot, Marijke Carasso-Kok, Eduard Melkus. Utrecht, VNM, 1984 (Facsimilia Musica Neerlandica 2)

Six grand concertos for violins &c. in eight parts ... opera terza. – London, Walsh, for the author, [1758]
Six concerti grossi, with a concertino consisting of first and second violin, viola, cello, a ditto ripieno section and bc.
Modern ed.: Concerti grossi opus III / ed. H. Brandts Buys. Amsterdam, VNM, 1959 (Monumenta Musica Neerlandica 1)

Six solos for a violin with a thorough bass for the harpsichord ... opera quarta. – London, John Johnson, [c 1765?]
Six sonatas for violin and bc

Eight solos for the violoncello with a thorough bass ... op. Vta.. – Cambridge, author [engraved by Caulfield], [1780]
Eight sonatas for cello and bc. Modern ed.: Eight solos for the violoncello with a thorough bass, op. 5 / ed. by Rudolf Rasch.

Amsterdam, VNM, 1981 (Monumenta Musica Neerlandica 13)

Three grand lessons for the harpsichord or piano forte, with an accompanyment for a violin & violincello ... opera 6. – London, G. Goulding, [c 1790?]
Three sonatas for keyboard with violin en cello accompaniment. Survived incomplete

Hellendaal's celebrated rondo for the organ, harpsichord or piano forte, also for the violin and violoncello. – Cambridge, Morris Barford, [c 1790?]
Contrary to the title a rondo for violin and bc

A collection of psalms for the use of parish churches... compos'd & harmoniz'd by Peter Hellendaal senr., selected and arrang'd by Peter Hallendaal junr. – Cambridge, the editor, [c 1795?]
3- and 4-part arrangements of psalm melodies

IN MANUSCRIPT:
Sonate a violino e basso, Cambridge, Fitzwilliam Museum, Music MS 32-F-30, with eleven sonatas not included in opp. 1, 2 and 4; Various *canons*, *catches* and *glees* in manuscript and printed collections and single publications (information in Haasnoot's dissertation, see bibliography)

BIBLIOGRAPHY
L. Haasnoot: *Leven en werken van Pieter Hellendaal (1721-1799)*. Doctoral dissertation University of Amsterdam, 1983

DISCOGRAPHY
6 Concerti Grossi (op. 3). European Community Baroque Orchestra, cond. R. Goodman (Channel Classics CCS 3492)
Concerto Grosso op. 3, no. 1. Residentie Orchestra, cond. N. Harnoncourt (Olympia OCD 501)
Six Grand Concertos for Violins etc. in eight parts (op. 3). Combattimento Consort Amsterdam, cond. J.W. de Vriend (NM Classics 92019)
Six Grand Concertos for Violins etc. in eight parts (op. 3). Combattimento Consort Amsterdam, cond. J.W. de Vriend (NM Special 92097)

Six Solos for Violoncello and bc (from op. 5). J. ter Linden (vc) a.o. (NM Classics 92008)
Sonata op. 4, no. 3. Amsterdam Baroque Ensemble, cond. T. Koopman (WVH 010)

Oscar van Hemel

ANTWERP, 3 AUGUST 1892 – HILVERSUM, 9 JULY 1981

Oscar van Hemel was a contemporary of Hendrik Andriessen, Willem Pijper, Prokofiev, Honegger, Bartók, Milhaud and Poulenc. Although he was raised in the conservative surroundings of the Antwerp Conservatory, with its Romantic leanings, subsequent to 1930 he composed in a style that was influenced not only by the aforementioned contemporaries, but by Schoenberg, Webern, Stravinsky and Hindemith as well. Van Hemel created an extensive and diverse body of works, an oeuvre that shows great craftsmanship and occupies a place of its own in the history of Dutch music. Oscar van Hemel grew up in the atmosphere of his father's love of music. At fifteen he enrolled at the Royal Flemish Conservatory in Antwerp to study the violin with Jan Bacot, a proponent of the Belgian school of violin playing and former student of Eugène Ysaÿe. He also had lessons in harmony, counterpoint and composition with August De Boeck and Lodewijk Mortelmans. He left the conservatory in 1914 and, serving as a soldier at the outbreak of World War I that year, he was wounded during the bombardment and surrender of Antwerp. He fled to the neutral Netherlands and never returned.

Van Hemel went to Roosendaal and worked as a concert violinist and violin teacher. From 1915 to 1917 he lived in Amsterdam, and was employed as a violinist in the newly founded orchestra of the Netherlands Opera. In his frequent visits to the performances given by the Concertgebouw Orchestra during this period, he came to know the music of Richard Strauss, Debussy and Ravel. In 1918 he took up residence in Bergen op Zoom and became a teacher of the violin, piano and music theory at the local music school. It was during this period that his earliest surviving works – songs and piano music – were composed.

Until 1931 Van Hemel composed in a lyrical-Romantic style tinged with Impressionism, as evidenced by his setting of a text by Adama van Scheltema, *De Kudde* [The Flock], for alto and chamber orchestra. Through the conductor Eduard Flipse, who performed a fair amount of contemporary Dutch music with the Rotterdam Philharmonic Orchestra at the time, Van Hemel made the acquaintance of Willem Pijper, then director of the Rotterdam Conservatory and the most sought-after composition teacher in the Netherlands. He studied with Pijper from 1931 to 1933.

Van Hemel's Sonata for violin and piano was published in 1933. This piece, in effect the 'opus 1' of an entirely unknown 41-year-old composer, took the Netherlands by surprise. From then on, his output as a composer continued to grow. There followed, for example, his Symphony no.1, String Quartet no.2, Suite for flute and chamber orchestra, Piano Trio, and, during World War II, the cantata *Maria Magdalena*, the Concerto for piano and orchestra, *Ballade* for full orchestra, and the Violin Concerto no.1. Van Hemel's orchestral works were frequently performed by the Rotterdam Philharmonic Orchestra under Eduard Flipse. In *Resurrectio* (1941), Van Hemel portrayed the re- covery of the city of Rotterdam and

the Rotterdam Philharmonic Orchestra from the bombardment of 14 May 1940.

Van Hemel moved to Hilversum in 1949 and there composed numerous pieces, often on commission from the Netherlands Broadcasting Company, the KRO broadcasting company, the Dutch government, and the cities of Am- sterdam and Hilversum. He also worked as a music critic for the daily news- papers *Gooi- en Eemlander* and *Maasbode*.

Van Hemel won many awards. In 1946 his First Violin Concerto received the Music Prize of the city of Amsterdam and his *Ballade* for full orchestra won him the Dutch Government Prize. In addition, he received the ANV-Vis- serneerlandia Prize on two occasions: in 1958 for the cantata *Maria Magdalena* and in 1962 for his String Quartet no.6. The String Quartet no.4 was awarded the Professor Van der Leeuw Prize.

Arthur Honegger's description of the composer's task as a search for new ways of playing the same old game is certainly applicable to the music of Van Hemel. His development as a composer can best be gauged by reviewing the problems he tackled: structure (sonata, rondo, song and variation forms) and tonality (modality, free atonality, bitonality, twelve-tone technique and serial- ism). Because of the strength of his intensely musical, lyrical talent, he did not abandon the traditions of the Classical and Romantic past, but rather ab- sorbed them. At the same time, he was open to the latest developments of his time. His natural melodic orientation did not deter him from giving the greatest possible attention to form. As a result, Van Hemel's music became increasingly finely crafted over the years, the role of free counterpoint growing in importance. His inherently Romantic tonal conception, too, was rejuvenated from the 1950s onwards through an interest in pluritonal elements and various methods of serial composition. Van Hemel incorporated all of this seamlessly into his compositions.

Van Hemel could be described as a moderately modern composer who merged Classical forms such as the sonata, song and rondo with modern harmonies and melodies. He employed the basic cell technique, sonorities based on the fourth, bitonality, twelve-tone technique and serialism, but he continued to aim at a broad audience. It is no wonder that the works of Van Hemel were frequently performed between 1940 and 1970.

CLEMENS ROMIJN

COMPOSITIONS

Complete list of works is included in the monograph by C. Romijn (see bibliography)

SONGS WITH PIANO: *Liefdeliedje* (De Mont) (1919); *Schemerliedje* (Reddingius) (1920); *De Kudde* (Adama van Scheltema) (1923); *Gebed voor Ra* (1923); *Sluimer* (Perk) (1937); *Mensen van de hei* (Van Duinkerken) (1938); *Marschlied* (Sji King/Slauerhoff) (1939); *Holland / Wolkenstoeten* (H. Roland Holst) (1939); *Amarillis* (Van Ostaijen) (1942/1958); *Marialied 'Geboorte'* (Gezelle) (1947); *Gij badt op eenen berg* (Gezelle) (1950); *Brabants lied* (Asselbergs) (1955); *Idylle* (Nahon) (1958); *Toen trad de Dood binnen* (Aafjes) (1958); *Dat liet* (Nahon) (1958); *Aan de zee* (Engelman) (1958); *Liggen in de zon* (Andreus) (1958); *Door de avondwereld* (Adama van Scheltema) (1958); *Trittico liturgico* (1959)

SONGS WITH ORCHESTRA: *De Kudde* (Adama van Scheltema) (1923); *Sluimer* (Perk) (1937); *De mensen van de Hei* (Van Duinkerken) (1938); *Le tombeau de Kathleen Ferrier* (1955); *Trittico Liturgico* (1959)

A CAPPELLA CHOIR: *Jubelstadje* (Van Duinkerken), m.choir (1930); *Het slijpertje*, m.choir (arr.) (1945); *Magnificat*, m.choir (1945); *Copla's*, m.choir (1947); *Zing in de bomen*, w.choir (1947); *De Bierbroederkes*, ch.choir (1948); *De schalmei*, mix.choir (1951); *Ballade des pendus*, mix.choir (1951); *Kinderkruistocht*, w.choir (1952); *De welgeletterde knecht*, mix.choir (1958); *Isidorus*, mix.choir (1958); *Twee contrasten*, m.choir (1959); *Four Shakespeare Sonnets*, mix.choir (1961)

CHOIR WITH PIANO/ORGAN: *Mis 'COSMOS'*, m.choir, pf (1926); *Cantate 'Gij waart nog jong'* (Van Dam), w.choir, pf/hp (1938); *Jubileumcantate*, w.choir, pf/hp (1938); *Boerecharleston* (Van Ostaijen), mix.choir, pf (1941); *Drinklied* (Chesterton/Van Duinkerken), mix.choir, pf (1941); *Dorpsdans* (Perk), mix.choir, pf (1941); *Vaandellied*, w.choir, pf/hp (1945); *Marialied* (Van Duinkerken), m.choir, pf (1950); *Krans der middeleeuwen*, mix.choir, pf (1952); *Het lage landje bij de zee* (Nijsse), ch.choir, pf (1955); *Psalm CXVI Laudate omnes gentes* (Smit), ch.choir, pf (1955); *Kinderkruistocht* (Nijhoff), w.choir, pf/hp (1958)

CHOIR WITH ORCHESTRA: *Marialied 'Geboorte'* (Gezelle), ch.choir, orch (1947); *Hart van Nederland* (Aafjes), m.choir, orch (1952); *Passie voor de jeugd 'Jezus lijden en sterven'* (Galesloot, Kuitenbrouwer), ch.choir, orch (1954); *Van vreugden ons alle die kinderen zingen*, ch.choir, orch (1954); *Rondeau et Ballade* (Charles d'Orléans),

w.choir, orch (1959); *Song of Freedom*
(Socrates, Martin Luther King), mix.choir,
orch (1969); *Herdenkingshymne 1940-1945*
(Nijhoff a.o.), mix.choir, orch (1955/1970)

SOLOISTS, CHOIR, ORCHESTRA: *De Bruid*
(Prins) (1946); *Dat liet van Alionora*
(Boutens) (1946); *De Stad* (symphonic
poem) (Van Duinkerken) (1949); *Viviane*
(opera) (Lutz) (1950); *Ballade van Brabant*
(Van Duinkerken) (1952); *Canticum
Psalmorum* (1954); *Les Mystères du Christ,
Hymne symphonique* (1958); *Maria Mag-
dalena* (sacred cantata) (1941); *Ballade van
Kapitein Joos de Decker* (Werumeus Buning)
(1943); *Krans der middeleeuwen* (1952); *Te
Deum* (1958); *Tuin van Holland* (Stuiveling)
(1958); *Huwelijkscantate Beatrix – Claus*
(Rijnsdorp) (1966); *De prostituée* (opera)
(Van Hemel) (1978);

PIANO: *Kleine suite* (1934); *Humoreske* (1942);
Sonata no. 1 (1943); *Vier oorlogspreludes*
(1945); *Sonata no. 2* (1945); *Spleen* (1946);
Prelude (1946); *Burlesque* (1946); *Sonatine
'Zie de maan schijnt'* (1951); *Capriolen*
(1953); *Sonatina* (1954); *Tema con variazioni*
(1955); *Sonatine facile* (1958); *Herfststem-
ming* (1959); *Sonatine voor de linkerhand*, pf
lh (1959)

ORGAN, CARILLON: *Klompendans*, car (1939);
Meditatie, org (1952); *Variaties over 'Daar
was een sneeuwwit vogeltje'*

CHAMBER MUSIC: *Thema met variaties*, vl, pf
(1926); *String Quartet no. 1* (1931); *Sonata
no. 1*, vl, pf (1933); *String Quartet no. 2*
(1935); *Piano Trio* (1937); *Piano Quartet*
(1938); *Sonata*, vla, pf (1942); *Sonata*, vc, pf
(1943); *Sonata no. 2*, vl, pf (1945); *String
Quartet no. 3* (1947); *Suite*, vl, pf (1950); *Trio
à cordes* (1951); *Concertino*, tpt, pf (1953);
String Quartet no. 4 (1953); *Intrada*, wind
instr (1954); *Vier koperkwartetten*, wind ens
(1955); *Pastorale suite*, fl, pf (1956); *String
Quartet no. 5* (1956); *Pavane en gigue*, fl, ob,
hn, bn (1958); *Klarinetkwintet*, cl, str.qt
(1958); *Trio*, fl, ob, bn (1959); *Divertimento 2
per 12 strumenti a fiato e pianoforte* (1959);
Concerto per strumenti a fiato (1960); *Puck*,
vl, pf (1960); *España*, vl, pf (1960); *Capric-*

cio, cl, pf (1960); *String Quartet no. 6*
(1961); *Donquichotterie*, 4 trb (1962); *Sextet
per strumenti a fiato e pianoforte* (1962);
Suite, 2 vl (1967); *About commedia dell'arte*,
ob, vl, vla, vc (1967); *Wind Quintet* (1972)

ORCHESTRA: *Symphony no. 1* (1935); *Suite*,
chamb.orch (1935); *Resurrectio* (1941); *Ballade* (1942); *Divertimento*, schl.orch (1946);
Symphony no. 2 (1948); *Divertimento-ballet
uit de opera Viviane* (1950); *Feestelijke ouverture* (*Vivat Brabantia*) (1952); *Symphony no.
3* (*Sinfonietta*) (1952); *Tema con variazioni*
(1953); *Entrata festante* (1953); *Olof-suite*
(1953); *Moments symphoniques* (1960); *Symphony no. 4* (1962); *Three contrasts per strumenti a fiato e percussion* (1963); *Entrata per
orchestra* (1964); *Divertimento 3 per orchestra
d'archi* (1965); *Polonaise per orchestra*
(1966); *Divertimento 4 per orchestra e
pianoforte* (1974); *Symphony no. 5* (1964,
rev 1980)

SOLO INSTRUMENT WITH ORCHESTRA:
Thema met variaties, vl, orch (1926); *Violin
Concerto no. 1* (1944); *Intermezzo uit de
opera Viviane*, vl, orch (1950); *Concertino*,
vl, orch (1963); *Violin Concerto no. 2* (1968);
Violin Concerto no. 3 (1977); *Uilenspiegel 'for
ever'*, 2 vl, orch (1958); *Concerto*, 2 vl,
str.orch (1971); *Concerto*, vla, orch (1951);
Concerto, vc, orch (1963); *Suite*, fl,
chamb.orch (1937); *Concerto da camera per
flauto e strumenti ad arco* (1962); *Concerto*,
ob, orch (1955); *Serenade per orchestra
d'archi e trio a fiato* (1965); *Piano Concerto*
(1942)

BIBLIOGRAPHY

J. Juda: *Voor de duisternis viel : 1930-1940*.
Nieuwkoop, Heuff, 1978

P. van Moergastel and W. Riksen: *Oscar
van Hemel : catalogus orkestwerken, koorwerken,
kamermuziek, toetsinstrumenten en liederen*.
Tilburg, Brabant Conservatory, 1990-1991

M. Monnikendam: *Nederlandse componisten
van heden en verleden*. Amsterdam, Strengholt,
1968

Muzikale ommegang, ed. G. van Raven-
zwaaij. Amsterdam, Nederlandse Keur-
boekerij, 1948

C. Romijn: *Oscar van Hemel : componist*

tussen klassiek en atonaal. Alphen a/d Rijn,
Caneletto, 1992
    L. Samama: *Zeventig jaar Nederlandse
muziek : 1915-1985 : voorspel tot een nieuwe dag.*
Amsterdam, Querido, 1986
    W.H. Thijsse: *Zeven eeuwen Nederlandse
muziek.* Rijswijk, Kramers, 1949
    J. Wouters: *Nederlandse componisten galerij :
negen portretten van Nederlandse componisten,*
vol. 1. Amsterdam, Donemus, 1971

DISCOGRAPHY

Klarinetkwintet. Netherlands String Quar-
tet, J. D'hondt (cl) (DAVS 6204)
    *Krans der Middeleeuwen; Trittico Liturgico;
Kinderkruistocht; Four Shakespeare Sonnets;
Isidorus; De welgeletterde knecht; De schalmei;
Twee contrasten; Copla's; Jubelstadje; Geestelijke
cantate Maria Magdalena.* Various performers
(Marcato Keyboard MCD 219701)
    *Piano Trio; Sonatina for Piano; String Quar-
tet no. 4; Klarinetkwintet; About commedia dell'
arte.* Various performers (Marcato Keyboard
MCD 199602)
    Symphony no. 4. Netherlands Radio Phil-
harmonic Orchestra, cond. J. Fournet (DAVS
6601)
    *Violin Concerto no. 1 and 2; Ballade; Te
Deum.* Th. Olof (vl), Utrecht Symphony Orchestra, cond. P. Hupperts, H. Krebbers (vl),
Concertgebouw Orchestra, cond. B. Haitink,
Netherlands Radio Orchestra, cond. L.
Driehuys, R. Kroese (S), C. Hessels (A), B. van
't Hof (T), C. Niessen (B), Netherlands radio
Choir, Netherlands Radio Chamber Orchestra,
cond. A. Rieu (Marcato Keyboard MCD
139203)
    Violin Concerto no. 2. H. Krebbers (vl), Con-
certgebouw Orchestra, cond. B. Haitink
(DAVS 7374/2)

Robert Heppener

AMSTERDAM, 9 AUGUST 1925

Robert Heppener studied the piano under Jan Odé and Johan van den Boogert at the Amsterdam Conservatory. He later took lessons in composition with Bertus van Lier who, suprisingly, concluded after a time that Heppener would need to undergo psychoanalysis before he could ever become a composer.

Upon completing his studies, Heppener taught music theory for several years at the Rotterdam Conservatory and the Amsterdam Muzieklyceum, one of the capital's two conservatories. He then taught composition and music theory at the Amsterdam Muzieklyceum and served as the institute's assistant director, positions he later held at the Sweelinck Conservatory in Amsterdam. After this he taught these subjects at the Maastricht Conservatory. In 1979, Heppener abruptly resigned from his various positions, moved to South Limburg and stopped composing. Encouraged by his former student Joël Bons and the conductor Ed Spanjaard, he resumed in 1984, that year completing *Memento* for soprano and eight instruments, which he dedicated to Bons.

Heppener has been the recipient of all the major Dutch music awards. In 1969 he received the Fontein-Tuynhout Prize for *Canti carnascialeschi* (1966), in 1974 the Willem Pijper Prize for *Four Songs on poems by Ezra Pound* (1970), in 1993 the Matthijs Vermeulen Prize for *Im Gestein* (1992), and in 1996 the Johan Wagenaar Prize for his entire oeuvre.

Heppener never felt at ease with the group of politically motivated composers that joined forces to form the 'Nutcrackers', a young composers' protest movement which sought to breathe new life into public performances of music. Nor did he feel drawn towards the prevailing musical trends of the 1960s and 1970s. It was not so much that he objected on principle to avant-garde techniques, rather he encountered a certain physical resistance in attempting to employ these techniques.

An early, expressive work like the *Symphonie* (1952) is notable for its alternation of long, lyrical melodies with rhythmic passages as well as its harmonic style and octatonic construction, representative of Dutch music at that time. The orchestral song *Cantico delle creature di S. Francesco d'Assisi* (1952) for voice, harp and strings, reveals the influence of Britten and, in the vehement close of the middle movement, intentionally emulates the chromaticism of Matthijs Vermeulen.

Ten years later, Heppener achieved a more balanced orchestral style in *Eglogues* (1963), one of his most frequently performed compositions. Though still not an avant-gardist, Heppener strove in *Eglogues* to reform his harmonic idiom, taking as a model the music of Hans Werner Henze, which he greatly admired at that time.

Heppener has composed numerous vocal works. *Canti carnascialeschi*, for chamber choir, based on the Florentine carnival poetry of Lorenzo de' Medici, Niccolò Machiavelli and others, is one of his most virtuosic and varied compositions. In depicting the text he readily leaps from a choir divided in many parts to four- or eight-part madrigals, from solos to tuttis, from harmonic to polyphonic textures, from homophony to heterophony, and from spoken text to choral clusters. He clearly has less difficulty in employing experimental techniques in vocal compositions, for these are in a sense justified by the text.

Four Songs on poems by Ezra Pound for high voice and piano, is an intimate, personal composition. Heppener selected the texts from Pound's *Ripostes* collection because of the contrast they convey between life in the city and in nature. He evokes a surrealistic atmosphere of estrangement in the work, for example through the (sparing) use of 'Sprechgesang'.

Del iubilo del core che esce in voce (1974) for choir and 16 solo voices, and

Nachklänge (1977) for chamber choir, spatially divided into four groups, are the most modern of Heppener's compositions with regard to their notation and the vocal techniques they employ. Both exact notation (five-lined staff with clef and metrical signature) and approximate notation (three-lined staff, for high, middle and low, rhythms indicated in seconds and graphic lines for the 'melody') are employed. The use of such notation has enabled Heppener to broaden the range of his expressive possibilities. *Nachklänge* is a taut composition that focuses on sonority, while *Del iubilo* is more lively and playful.

In 1988 Heppener composed *Boog* [Arch], an orchestral work commissioned by the Concertgebouw Orchestra for its hundredth anniversary. In this piece the tension builds up very gradually, starting in the strings with a single interval generating more and more tones, both harmonically and melodically. As the complexity increases the various orchestral voices whirl around each other, reaching a climax at the end of the work. The effect is one of springing a bow. With the 'firing of the arrow' the tension is suddenly released and a slow, gentle coda ensues.

Heppener's music did not essentially change after his personal crisis in 1979. He is still a composer with a musical rather than cerebral ear. The current antidogmatic climate has had a beneficial effect on his work. Judging by *Spinsel* [Yarn] (1986) for piano solo, it even seems that he has integrated musical gestures from the post-serial idiom into his own musical language. Interest in his work has also increased. In 1994, the Nieuw Ensemble asked Heppener to compile a program centered around his music. He came up with a double-pronged program combining his compositions with the music of Guillaume Dufay, a composer he much admires. In 1996 Heppener completed an opera in three acts based on the novel *Een ziel van hout* [A wooden soul], by the Austrian author Jakov Lind.

MICHAEL VAN EEKFREN

COMPOSITIONS

Film music is not included

VOCAL: *Cantico delle creature di S. Francesco d'Assisi*, h.v, str.orch, hp (1952, rev. 1955); *Het derde land* (Nijhoff), mix.choir, orch (1962); *Canti carnascialeschi* (L. de' Medici, Machiavelli, Guggiola, Allamanni, Poliziano), mix.choir (1966); *Fanfara trionfale, per tre gruppi*, mix.choir, orch (1967); *Four Songs on poems by Ezra Pound*, S, pf (1970); *Del iubilo del core che esce in voce* (Jacopone da Todi), mix.choir (1974); *Hec*

Dies, 4 vocal and instr. groups (quadrofonic composition) (1973); *Nachklänge* (Celan), mix.choir (1977); *Memento*, S, instr. ens. (1984); *Tussen bomen* (Van Geel), B-Bar, pf (1985); *Hymn to harmony* (Shakespeare), S, Ct, rec, vladg, mar, tape (1987, rev. 1993); *Cadens* (Kusters), Mez, instr. ens. (1990, rev. 1993); *Bruchstücke eines alten Textes (Psalm 43)*, mix.choir (1990); *Colloque solitaire*, Mez (in: *Tien vocale minuten*) (1990); *Im Gestein* (6 songs) (Celan), mix.choir, instr. ens. (1992); *Een ziel van hout* (opera) (1996)

167 · Robert Heppener

CHAMBER MUSIC: *Nocturne*, pf (1953); *Septet*, fl, cl, bn, 2 vl, vla, vc (1958); *Arcadische sonatine*, 2 rec, vl (1959); *A fond de fleurettes*, str.qt (1961); *Quartetto*, a-fl, vl, vla, vc (1967); *Canzona*, sax.qt (1969); *Fanfare*, 3 tpt, 3 trb (1970); *Pas de quatre mains*, pf 4h (in: *Een suite voor de suite*) (1975); *Spinsel*, pf (1986); *Qu'amas l'aura*, fl (1986, rev. 1988); *Toonladder (Scale)*, a-rec (1991); *Telemann blow-up*, fl (in: *G. Telemann fantasias, with musical comments*) (1992)

ORCHESTRA, LARGE ENSEMBLE: *Symphonie*, orch (1952); *Derivazioni*, str.orch (1958, rev. 1980); *Sinfonietta*, orch (1961); *Cavalcade : ouverture-en-rondeau*, orch (1963); *Eglogues*, orch (1963, rev. 1980); *Scherzi per archi* (1965); *Hymns and conversations*, 28 hp (1969); *Air et sonneries*, orch (1969); *Muziek voor straten en pleinen*, orch (1970); *Sweelinck-fanfare*, orch (1977); *Boog*, orch (1988); *Hear hear*, instr.ens (1989); *Trail*, instr.ens (1993)

BIBLIOGRAPHY
J. Bons and N. Cornelissen: ' "Ik mocht alles, maar zij mochten niet" : interview met componist Robert Heppener', *Promskrant*, no. 2, Feb. 1994
L. van Delden: 'Een carrière in film-muziek : componist Robert Heppener (40) wil "verstaan" worden', *Het Parool*, 8 Jan. 1966
M. van Eekeren: ' "You have to dare to go with the flow" : the physical music of Robert Heppener', *Key Notes*, 30, 1996/4, p. 10-15
J. Geraedts: 'Robert Heppener : the liberation generation', *Key Notes*, 5, 1977/1, p. 26-31
R. Hazendonk: 'The composer's own truth : Robert Heppener's Memento, a dramatic scene for soprano and eight instruments', *Key Notes*, 22, 1985/2, p. 23-29
J. Oskamp: 'Robert Heppener componeert vanuit het onderbewuste : een stuk voor achtentwintig harpen, hoe kom je er op', *De Groene Amsterdammer*, 25 Apr. 1990
W. Paap: 'De componist Robert Heppener', *Mens en Melodie*, vol. 22, 1967, p. 39-43
P. Peters: ' "Na de seriële dictatuur is de vrijheid weer terug" : slingerbeweging in de muziek brengt Robert Heppener terug in de belangstelling', *NRC Handelsblad*, 11 Apr. 1994
H. Posthuma de Boer: 'Heppener over

"Boog": "Weten in de muziek doe je met je oren" ', *Preludium*, vol. 48, no. 2, 1989, p. 10-12
A. Schelp: 'Hec dies, een zang en een tegenzang : quadrofonisch koorwerk van Robert Heppener', *Mens en Melodie*, vol. 30, 1975, p. 201-203
E. Vermeulen: 'L'arc de Robert Heppener', *Septentrion*, vol. 19, no. 1, 1990, p. 81-82
J. Wouters: 'Robert Heppener – Eglogues', *Sonorum Speculum*, no. 24, 1965, p. 16-17

DISCOGRAPHY
Canti Carnascialeschi; Del iubilo del core che esce in voce; Nachklänge; Bruchstücke eines alten Textes. Netherlands Chamber Choir, cond. T. Kaljuste and D. Reuss (Composers' Voice)
Canzone. Netherlands Saxophone Quartet (Composers' Voice CV 8002)
Del iubilo del core che esce in voce; Nachklänge. Netherlands Chamber Choir, cond. H. van den Hombergh and F. Müller (Composers' Voice CV 7902)
Eglogues. Concertgebouw Orchestra, cond. E. Jochum (BFO A-7 / Composers' Voice CVCD10)
Eglogues. Limburg Symphony Orchestra, cond. D. Robertson (0029 275)
Eglogues; Muziek voor straten en pleinen. Royal Concertgebouw Orchestra, cond. B. Haitink and R. Benzi (Composers' Voice CV 8202)
Four songs on poems by Ezra Pound. R. Alexander (S), E. Spanjaard (pf) (CBS LSP 14514)
Four songs on poems by Ezra Pound. R, Alexander (S), E. Spanjaard (pf) (Globe GLO 6018)
Sweelinck fanfare. Amsterdam Philharmonic Orchestra, cond. A. Kersjes (EMI 051 26331)
Telemann blow-up. E. Pameijer (fl) (RN Classics 93003)
Trail; Memento; Boog. J. Manning (S), Nieuw Ensemble, Dutch National Youth Orchestra, cond. E. Spanjaard (Composers' Voice CV 62)
Tussen bomen; Spinsel; Four Songs on Poems by Ezra Pound. S. Narucki (S), W. Oosterkamp (Bar), S. Grotenhuis, T. Ehlen and E. Spanjaard (pf) (Composers' Voice CV 48)

Simeon ten Holt

BERGEN, 24 JANUARY 1923

Simeon ten Holt comes from a family of artists. His father was the painter Henri F. ten Holt, of Bergen, a coastal town north of Amsterdam with many artists among its residents. From 1935 Ten Holt, together with Nico Schuyt, studied music theory and piano with the Bergen composer Jacob van Domselaer (1890-1960), whose influence is clearly felt in Ten Holt's first pieces for the piano, *Kompositie I-IV, Suite* and *Sonate*. The death, early in 1945, of his friend Jaap van Domselaer – the son of his teacher – during an attempt to reach liberated territory by swimming across the Maas River, made a great impact on Ten Holt. From 1949 to 1952 Ten Holt lived in France, where he took lessons from Honegger and Milhaud at the Ecole Normale in Paris.

In 1954 he returned to Bergen and took up residence in a renovated World War II bunker. There he composed his important piano piece *Bagatellen* (1954). Reacting against the strict tonal influence of Van Domselaer, he developed his own method of coming to terms with the concepts of tonal and atonal music. This method, which he called 'diagonal thought', entails the simultaneous use of complementary keys at tritone intervals. The method led in the late 1950s to the composition of *Diagonaalsuite, Diagonaalsonate* (for piano) and *Diagonaalmuziek* (for strings).

Ten Holt's commitment to social issues, his philosophical nature and literary qualities found expression in articles he wrote about music from 1968 to 1973 for H.C. ten Berge's literary periodical *Raster*. ('The center-oriented tonal system is rooted in a relation-modality that, translated to its social aspect, perpetuates slavery and the abuse of power, privilege and injustice, and by virtue of its structure and origins is steeped in historical guilt. In a tonally composed piece we always hear a repressed memory, a bad conscience and the wish and desire to share in the power of a privileged group.')

In 1968 Ten Holt composed *..A/.TA-LON*, a music theater piece for mezzo-soprano and 36 playing and talking instrumentalists. Technically, this work is the culmination of a period in which serial principles prevailed. It was performed several times by the Asko Ensemble in 1978 and is considered one of Ten Holt's most important compositions. Also in 1968, Ten Holt founded the Bergen Study Group for Contemporary Music. For this group, which still exists, he organized concerts of contemporary music, first in the Bergen Arts Centre and later in the Ruïne Church. He has also performed as a pianist,

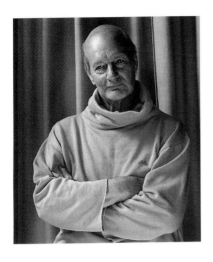

mostly in concerts of his own work.

Ten Holt's percussion piece *Tripti-con* was premiered at the 1969 Holland Festival. From 1969 to 1975, he worked at the electronics studio in his home and at the Institute for Sonology in Utrecht on various electronic pieces, including *Inferno I and II*, and *I am Sylvia but Somebody Else*. During this period he regularly attended the Warsaw Autumn Festivals and maintained contact with the Polish composer Zygmunt Krauze.

Ten Holt taught a course on contemporary music from 1970 to 1987 at the Arnhem Academy of Visual Arts. His experiments with group improvisation resulted in a form of theater in which every aspect of the work is determined by the students. From 1977 to 1979 he composed *Canto Ostinato*, for keyboard instruments. The number of performers, the duration of the piece and the number of repeats of the various sections comprising the work are variable. This freedom gives the performers a joint responsibility for the final result. *Canto Ostinato* is characteristic of a decidedly repetitive-music oriented style Ten Holt developed in the 1980s and 1990s in which tonality and repetition suggest a new aesthetic ('tonality after the death of tonality'). Other examples of this style are *Lemniscaat, Horizon, Incantatie IV, Soloduiveldansen II* and *III* [Solo Devil Dances] (for keyboard instruments), and *Palimpsest* (for strings).

Because of the variable duration of Ten Holt's compositions, performances of his work can be spectacularly long. In the longest performance, in 1983, a two-day marathon performance of *Lemniscaat* at a cinema in Bergen, pianists performed the work in two- to three-hour blocks, alternating with a tape recording.

Ten Holt explains: 'My compositions are created without a preconceived plan and are the result of a journey to an unknown destination, so to speak. Much time, patience and discipline are required to effectively produce a (genetic) code that determines the form, structure, duration, scoring etc. It's a laborious process because the vision of the generating code is repeatedly obscured by human shortcomings and personal will, while what is needed are moments of clarity and vitality. And then, the sea washes and polishes, time crystallizes.'

KEES WIERINGA

COMPOSITIONS

PIANO: *Kompositie* (1941); *Kompositie I-IV* (1942-1948); *20 bagatellen* (1954); *Allegro ex machina* (1955); *Journal* (1957); *Diagonaalsuite* (1957); *Muziek voor Pieter* (1958); *Diagonaalsonate* (1959); *Soloduiveldans I* (1959); *5 etudes* (1961); *Cyclus aan de waanzin* (1961); *Interpolations* (1969); *Natalon in E* (1979-1980); *Soloduiveldans II* (1986) *and III* (1990); *Eadem sed Aliter* (1995); *Soloduiveldans IV* (1998)

KEYBOARD INSTRUMENTS (VARIABLE NUMBER OF INSTRUMENTS): *Sekwensen* (1965); *Canto Ostinato* (1977-1979); *Lemniscaat* (1983); *Horizon* (1983-1985); *Incantatie IV* (1990); *Méandres* (1996-1998)

ENSEMBLE: *Suite*, str.qt (1954-1955); *Divertimento*, 3 fl (1957); *Diagonaalmuziek*, str (1958); *Tripticon*, 6 perc (1965); *String Quartet no. 2* (1965); *..A/.TA-LON* (Ten Holt), Mez, 36 playing and speaking instrumentalists (1967-1968); *Differenties*, pf, 3 cl, vibr (1969); *Palimpsest*, str.septet (1992)

ORCHESTRA: *Epigenese* (1964); *Centri-fuga* (1979); *Une musique Blanche* (1982)

ELECTRONIC MUSIC: *Kockijn : een kermiskroniek* (film music) (1966); *Sevenplay* (1970); *Inferno I and II* (1970-1971); *I am Sylvia but Somebody Else* (1973); *Aforismen*

BIBLIOGRAPHY

M. Aleven: 'De componist anno 1969 is een klankregisseur', *de Volkskrant*, 27 Sept. 1969
J. Eilander: 'Nostalgie van een vreemdeling', *de Volkskrant*, 24 Apr. 1994
R. Gieling: 'Een gesprek met Simeon Ten Holt', *Wolfsmond*, 13/14, 1986
R. Molengraaf: 'De doorbraak van een componist naar een nieuwe toonbeleving', *Jonas*, 8 Jan. 1987
E. Schönberger: '..A/.TA-LON : concreet in een album van Hergé', *Vrij Nederland*, 4 Feb. 1978
E. Vermeulen: 'Simeon Ten Holt', *Haagse Post*, 1 Jan. 1978

Television portraits:
By R. Gieling in *NOS-Beeldspraak*, 14 March 1987
In *Reiziger in Muziek*, VPRO, 14 Jan. 1996

DISCOGRAPHY

Canto Ostinato. G. Bouwhuis, G. Carl, C. van Zeeland and A. Vernède (pf) (Composers' Voice CVCD 2/3/4)
Canto Ostinato. K. Wieringa and P. de Haas (pf) (Emergo Classics EC3944-2)
Horizon. P. de Haas, Y. Abbe, F. Oldenburg and M. Krill (pf) (Composers' Voice CVCD 5/6)
Incantatie IV. F. Hommes, A. Middelbeek, S. Sittig and K. Wieringa (pf) (De Jongste Dag CDJD 18 SH)
Lemniscaat. E. Dijkhuizen, J. Brink, A. van Groningen à Stuling and K. Wieringa (pf) (Clarison CLAR 53317/53318/53319)
Méandres. P. de Haas, K. Wieringa, E. Dijkhuizen and F. Oldenburg (pf) (NM Classics 92106)
Natalon in E ; Cyclus aan de waanzin (De Jongste Dag CDJD 13 SH)
Soloduiveldans 2. K. Wieringa (pf) (Erasmus WVH 055)
Soloduiveldans 2 and 3. P. de Haas (pf) (Clavicenter PDH 25091)
Soloduiveldans 3, Eadem sed Aliter. K. Wieringa (pf) (Do records 003)

Anthon van der Horst .

AMSTERDAM, 20 JUNE 1899 – HILVERSUM, 7 MARCH 1965

Anthonie van der Horst came from a humble Amsterdam background. His talent for music began to manifest itself at a very early age. When he was four he would play with his father the symphonies of Beethoven in transcriptions for piano four hands. Two years later he composed his first piece, a work for tenor, male choir and orchestra, and by the time he was ten years old he was the organ soloist and accompanist in his father's ensemble.

Van der Horst studied at the Amsterdam Conservatory, where he had lessons in music theory with Anton Tierie, organ lessons with Jean Baptiste Charles de Pauw, and composition with Bernard Zweers. During his brief time at the conservatory, his teacher De Pauw offered him many opportunities to perform as a soloist on the Maarschalkerweerd organ in the Amsterdam Concertgebouw. Sketchbooks he kept bear evidence of the progress he made in composition under Zweers' tutelage. From a late-Romantic German style he gravitated towards a French Impressionist one in which he soon showed a liking for unusual meters, rhythms and bitonality.

In 1917, upon completing his studies, Van der Horst was the first in the Netherlands to be offered the opportunity to acquire a 'Prix d'Excellence'. On 14 June 1919 the young organ virtuoso presented himself at the organ of the Amsterdam Concertgebouw before an international jury.

Van der Horst then worked for several years as an organist and pianist. He performed with such leading vocalists as Jo Vincent, Louis van Tulder, Max Kloos, Suze Luger, Ilona Durigo and Ali Khan. Together with Aaltje Noordewier-Reddingius, he was the first non-Englishman to record for Colombia in London (1929). He was also the organist at the English Reformed Church in the Amsterdam Begijnhof from 1919 to 1944, and from 1954 at the Great Church in Naarden.

Van der Horst began his career as a conductor in 1920 with the Christian Oratorio Society in Utrecht, with which he remained affiliated until 1938. In 1921 he became rehearser and organist to the Dutch Bach Society and in 1931 he succeeded Johan Schoonderbeek as its conductor. From 1931 to 1949 he conducted the Royal Oratorio Society in Amsterdam and from 1937 to 1957 the Excelsior Royal Choral Society in The Hague.

Van der Horst married Elisabeth van Schevichaven in 1922 – her mother was Johan Schoonderbeek's sister-in-law. Van Schevichaven, who had studied

the piano with Willem Andriessen, performed as a piano accompanist early in her career and later also wrote program notes and performed as a reciter. Her subtle spirituality influenced the Van der Horst family, to which three sons were born.

Apart from his activities as a performing artist, Van der Horst was also a music teacher. In 1919 he taught music theory at the Music School of the Society for the Advancement of Music in Bussum, of which Schoonderbeek was the director. When Schoonderbeek founded the Gooi Music College in Hilversum in 1923, he employed Van der Horst as a teacher there as well. But Van der Horst was most influential in his work at the two music institutes in Amsterdam. From 1921 to 1937 he taught music theory, composition and the organ at the Amsterdam Muzieklyceum, in those days known for its innovative approach to education. In 1935 he succeeded Cornelis de Wolf as professor of the organ at the Amsterdam Conservatory, where from 1936 he also taught choral and orchestral conducting. Many of his students later became important figures in Dutch musical life, among them Albert de Klerk, Piet Kee, Herman Nieland, Meindert Boekel and Charles de Wolff.

As an organist, conductor and organ teacher, Van der Horst always sought to gain a better understanding of music. He ultimately did much of the pioneering work in the Netherlands in the field of historical performance practice, publishing the results of his research in a book entitled *Bach's Hoogmis* (1941), about Bach's B minor Mass. With the viola da gamba player Carel van Leeuwen Boomkamp, he sought out original Baroque instruments. In 1948 he received an honorary doctorate from the University of Groningen.

Despite these many pursuits, Van der Horst was first and foremost a composer. His sensitivity to language motivated his musical preference for unusual meters, such as $2^{1}/2/4$ time, essentially a duple meter with an added eighth note. Although this seems akin to Messiaen's 'valeur ajouté', its linguistic origin sets it apart. This also holds for Van der Horst's 'modus conjunctus' tonal system which, although it is structurally identical to Messiaen's second mode, proceeds from an entirely different theoretical premise.

In Van der Horst's First Symphony (finished in 1939), the 'modus conjunctus', evolved from a loose approach to bitonality in his previous works, decisively influences the sound. The term appears in the titles of the larger organ and piano pieces that followed in the next decade. He began to apply the system with more freedom in the Second Symphony (1955), a move necessitated by the mystical vocal sound in the large symphonic/choral pieces of this period (*Choros II, La Nuit*), which called for greater freedom and a more impressionistic type of sound. These works also reveal his interest in eastern music.

Van der Horst composed in a wide variety of genres, although his works for symphony orchestra and orchestra with choir – many of which were given evocative titles and have programmatic content – are clearly the most important. Many of these works have rarely been performed. Van der Horst approached composition as though he were painting in sound and timbres. His orchestration places him in the tradition of the great nineteenth-century symphonic composers. His final work was a salute to Dutch music making: *Salutation joyeuse* (op.105), composed for the 75th anniversary of the Concertgebouw Orchestra.

GERT OOST

COMPOSITIONS
Complete list of works is included in G. Oost's monograph *Anthon van der Horst : leven en werken* (see bibliography)

VOICE WITH ACCOMPANIMENT: *Oratio Moysi*, S, org (1928, version S, orch, 1942); *7 Italiaanse liederen*, version S, pf, op. 21a, version S, chamb.orch, op. 21b (1935); *Hymne 'Blijdschap'* (Gezelle), S solo or with org/pf (1935); *Le ciel en nuit s'est déplié*, v, pf, op. 81a (1958)

OTHER VOCAL WORKS: *Choros (I)*, soloists, choirs, orch (1932); *Te Deum*, Bar, choirs, orch (1945); *Choros II (La Nuit)*, version choir, op. 63 (1953); *Choros II (La Nuit)*, version choir, orch, op. 67 (1954); *Choros VI (Wilhelmus van Nassouwe)*, choir, orch, op. 77 (1957); *Symphony [no. 3]*, soloists, choir, orch, op. 84 (1959); *Vondels Minnedeuntjes*, choir, pf (1961); *Hommage to the BBC*, choir, orch, op. 98 (1962)

ORGAN: *Suite in modo conjuncto* (1943); *Partite diverse sopra O Nostre Dieu* (Psalm 8) (1947); *Sonata in modo conjuncto*, version org/hpd, op. 51a (1948); *Suite*, 31-tone org, op. 60 (1953); *Variazioni sopra Christ lag in Todesbanden*, op. 64 (1953); *Etude de concert*, op. 104 (1963)

CHAMBER MUSIC: *Suite*, vc (1941); *Sonata in modo conjuncto*, version 2 pf, op. 51b, version fl, vl, vc, op. 51c (1948); *Thema met variaties in modo conjuncto*, pf (1950); *Thème, variations et fugue*, vl, fl, vla, op. 76 (1957)

ORCHESTRA: *Symphony [no. 1]*, op. 23 (1939); *Nocturne funèbre* (1950); *Concerto per organo romantico e orchestra*, op. 58 (1952); *Concerto spagnuolo*, vl, orch, op. 61 (1953); *Symphony no. 2*, (1955); *Concerto*, org, str.orch, op. 85 (1960); *Salutation joyeuse*, orch, op. 105 (1964)

PUBLICATIONS

Bach's Hoogmis (with G. van der Leeuw).
Wageningen, Holland, 1941
'Over de plaats en betekenis van het weten
in de wereld der muziek', *Mens en Melodie*, vol.
3, 1948, p. 297-302

BIBLIOGRAPHY

'Anthon van der Horst', *Biografisch woordenboek van Nederland*. The Hague, Instituut
voor Nederlandse Geschiedenis, 1979 et seq.
'Anthon van der Horst', *Die Musik in
Geschichte und Gegenwart*
G. Oost: 'Anthon van der Horst (1899-
1965) en de Nederlandse orgelkunst', *De
Orgelvriend*, 32, 1960, p. 6-11
G. Oost: *Anthon van der Horst : leven en
werken*. Alphen a/d Rijn, Canaletto, 1992
G. Oost: 'Onbekende kerkliederen van
Guillaume van der Graft en Anthon van der
Horst', *Organist en Eredienst*, 1990, p. 229-235
W. Paap: 'In memoriam Anthon van der
Horst', *Mens en Melodie*, vol. 20, 1965, p. 99-103
W. Paap: 'Nederlandse componisten van
deze tijd : dr. Anthon van der Horst', *Mens en
Melodie*, vol. 14, 1959, p. 171-178
J. Wouters: 'Anthon van der Horst', *The
New Grove dictionary of music and musicians*
J. Wouters: 'Composers' gallery : Dr. Anthon van der Horst (1899-1965)', *Sonorum
Speculum*, no. 23, 1965, p. 1-17

DISCOGRAPHY

Choros II (La Nuit), op. 67. Ifusagi Müverszegyüttes Choir, cond. A. Medveczky, Residentie Orchestra (Olympia OCD 505)
Choros II (La Nuit), op. 63. Netherlands
Chamber Choir, cond. H. van den Hombergh
(CBS 71110)
Dialogo (from *Suite in modo conjuncto*). J.
van Dommele (org) (NCRV 9087/90)
Improvisatie (1947); Concerto, op. 58; *Choros
VI*, op. 77, *Dialogo* (from *Suite in modo conjuncto*). A. van der Horst (org), A. de Klerk (org),
Noordholland Philharmonic Orchestra, cond.
A. Vandernoot, various soloists and choirs,
Netherlands Radio Orchestra, cond. A. de
Klerk (Marcato MCD 119201)
Songs and Organ Works. I. Maessen (S), G.
Oost (org) (Marcato MCD 169501)
Organ Works. Ch. de Wolff (org) (JQZ QCD
31062)

Partita diverse on psalm 8. J. Jongepier (org)
(Lindeberg LBCD 11)
Reflections sonores, op. 99. Residentie Orchestra, cond. H. Vonk (Het Residentie Orkest
6814 781/78)
Reflections sonores, op. 99. Royal Concertgebouw Orchestra, cond. B. Haitink (Q Disc
97014)
Variazioni sopra Christ lag in Todesbanden.
H. van Nieuwkoop (org) (NM Classics 92034)

Wouter Hutschenruyter Sr.

ROTTERDAM, BAPTIZED 28 DECEMBER 1796 –
ROTTERDAM, 8 NOVEMBER 1878

According to the archives of the Old Catholic Church on Rotterdam's Slijk wa-
terway, Wouter Hutschenruyter was baptized on 28 December 1796. At the
age of seven he began taking lessons with the master violinist Dahmen and
three years later gave a much-acclaimed performance on this instrument.
Hutschenruyter was also so accomplished on the trumpet that at an early age
he became a trumpeter with the orchestra of the flourishing Saturday Concerts. In 1809 he was named first trumpeter of the city's civic guard ensemble.
He later learned to play the natural horn and was reputed to have been an excellent organist and singing teacher. Though he worked in Rotterdam,
Schiedam, Delft, Leiden, The Hague and Gouda, he remained a resident of his
native city throughout his life.

Concerts at the beginning of the nineteenth century were an elite form of
entertainment. Starting in 1824, Hutschenruyter sought to remedy this situation by organizing inexpensive concerts. These performances, given by professional musicians, were very successful and ultimately drew competitors: when
the Harmonic Society was founded in 1826 it also sought to popularize concerts. Hutschenruyter was contracted as first hornist in the new orchestra, for
which he received six guilders per concert and admittance to post-perfor-
mance balls. Some years later, a more professional orchestral society, Eruditio
Musica, was founded. In 1829 Hutschenruyter became its first director, a post
he held until 1865. In 1842 he was appointed choral director of Toonkunst
Rotterdam, the local chapter of the Society for the Advancement of Music. He
also taught singing at the Music School opened by this Society in 1844.

When Robert Schumann visited Rotterdam during the 1853-1854 concert
season, he noted in his diary: 'Very capable orchestra that plays with great enthusiasm. The music director Hutschenruyter [...] Excellent performance of
my compositions [...].'

In 1854, Rotterdam held its Grand Music Festival in celebration of the twenty-
fifth anniversary of Toonkunst, for which Hutschenruyter composed a *Feest-ouverture* [Festive overture]. The daily *Nieuwe Rotterdamsche Courant* called it 'a
masterly work'. It also elicited the praise of Franz Liszt and Anton Rubinstein,
who attended the festival as well. Hutschenruyter paid much attention to emerging musical talents, Dutch as well as foreign. He assisted Richard Hol at every

opportunity and, perhaps more no-tably still, arranged performances for Hermina Amersfoordt-Dijk, a pianist-composer from Amsterdam. He con-tinued conducting into old age.

Almost entirely self-taught as a com-poser, Hutschenruyter has some 150 works to his name, many of which unfortunately have been lost. His work covers a wide range of genres and includes cantatas, concertos, a declamatorio, songs, military music, masses, overtures, symphonies, and even an opera. He arranged many operas for the civic guard ensemble, a common practice at the time. He also composed a number of pieces for this ensemble, in celebration of the Dutch liberation from French rule in 1813. In 1814 he composed his first Concerto for horn and it was followed by four oth-ers, although only one has survived intact. It is a melodious and virtuoso piece with many Mozartian broken triads and seventh chords and Romantic ap-pogiaturas. The first movement is marked by a surprising transition to a minor key; the second passes via a seventh chord and a short cadenza to the lively finale.

As far as is known, he composed four symphonies, including the military-band symphony *La bataille de Waterloo* (1815). A panel of judges from the Society for the Advancement of Music thought the Symphony no.1 (1837) rem-iniscent of the music of Spohr, Haydn and Beethoven. They called the Sym-phony no.2 (1840), published by Schott & Söhne in Mainz, 'a finely crafted, beautiful and effect-filled orchestral piece, bearing evidence to [the compos-er's] talent and knowledge, skill and grace in orchestration.' For both works, he received 25 golden ducats. His Symphony no.3, the *Symphonie Triomphale* from 1854, was dedicated to 'HM the King of Belgium', which earned him a gold medal.

Hutschenruyter composed seven overtures, a popular genre at the time. The Society for the Advancement of Music awarded two of them with twenty golden ducats. His five cantatas were composed for specific occasions. Though he had written sacred music from an early age, the four masses, among them the richly instrumented *Missa Solemnis* (1850), for orchestra, choirs and soloists, were works of his later years.

The declamatorio *Iwan en Pauleska* (1835) is program music dealing with the Polish revolt against Russia in 1830. Tender themes are overshadowed by heroic blasts of horns, while surprising changes of meter and key create a fitful impression. The work bears unmistakable traces of Rossini and evokes reminiscences of Weber, Mendelssohn and Schumann.

In tribute to the composer for his 'truly great masterpiece', his only opera, *Le Roi de Bohème*, given a concertante performance in 1852, Hutschenruyter was given a laurel wreath and serenaded. But a review in the music journal *Caecilia* was more ambivalent: 'It is practically written, well-crafted and excellently orchestrated and contains much that is new. However it is too drawn out and often commonplace; too seldom does one hear thoughts indicating the presence of inspiration.'

His songs include one of the most popular of the time, *Het Breistertje* [The knitting maiden] to a text by Nicolaas Beets. This song was even issued in a German translation. Popular, too, was the sacred song *Het Land der Zaligen* [The land of the blessed], which in harmonic terms is much more daring. He also composed children's and patriotic songs.

Wouter Hutschenruyter was a significant figure in the history of Rotterdam. As a teacher he inspired many young people to pursue careers in music and he was the first to open the concert hall to the common man. Hutschenruyter was a tireless worker who was much appreciated in his day.

TILLY JUMELET-VAN DOEVEREN

COMPOSITIONS

SONGS (FOR VOICE AND PIANO UNLESS OTHERWISE STATED): *Aanroeping* (Heye) (1815); *Chant patriotique* (Durand), v, pf/gui (1830); *Zegelied voor den Prins van Oranje en Hoogstdeszelfs Broeder* (Van Someren) (1831); *Een kruis met rozen* (De Genestet) (1840); *Het Land der Zaligen* (Heye) (1840); *Des Heeren huis* (Heye) (1845); *Tranen* (Heye) (1845); *Verlangen* (Heye) (1846); *Vergeet mij niet* (Heye) (1847); *De blijde toekomst* (Van der Hoop), ch.choir, pf (1850); *Lied der Koningin* (Hofdijk) (1853); *Vier kinderliederen* (Parson, Dusseau) (1857); *'s Konings jaardag* (Peypers) (1861); *Vier geestelijke liederen*, soloists, mix.choir, pf; *Des Heeren zegen* (Heye); *Niet alleen* (Van der Hoop); *Waar de liefde woont, woont God*; *Hemelsche engel, verlaat ons toch niet* (Van der Hoop); *Gebed*, 3 v; *Sluimerlied* (Heye); *Het Breistertje* (Beets); Various 2-part children's songs

CANTATAS: *Cantate ter feestviering van de vereeniging der beide schilderkunstige maatschappijen te Rotterdam* (Harderwijk), soloists, mix.choir, orch (1826); *Cantata* (Vernée), mix.choir, orch (1834); *Cantata* (Tollens), v, mix.choir, orch (1854); *Cantate bij het 25 j.* [i.e. 40 j.] *jubilée van Prins Frederik der Nederlanden als Grootmeester Nationaal* (Van Lennep), m.choir, org, orch (1856); *Cantate bij het 100 j. bestaan der Loge De Drie Kolommen te Rotterdam* (Maronier), v, mix.choir, orch (1867); *Heft aan, heft aan, o feestgenoten*, m.choir, pf

DRAMATIC VOCAL WORKS: *Iwan en Pauleska* (declamatorio) (Van der Hoop) (1835); *Le Roi de Bohème* (opera) (Saint-Georges) (1852)

SACRED VOCAL WORKS: *Missa solemnis* (1850); *Missa* (1860); *Missa tribus vocibus virilibus in Festa Sancti Laurentii* (1867); *Missa Decima Missarum in festis solemnioribus decantandarum* (1869); *Te Deum Laudamus; Ecce panis angelorum;* Various catholic church hymns, 5 Tantum-Ergo's, various songs

SYMPHONIES, OVERTURES: *Ouverture potpourri op nationale melodieën* (1814); *La bataille de Waterloo : simfonie de grand orchestre,* op. 6 (1815); *Overture* (1820); *Overture,* wind orch (1829); *Overture* (1832); *Overture* (1834); *Ouverture van het Declamatorium Iwan en Pauleska* (1835); *Symphony no. 1* (1837); *Symphony no. 2* (1840); *Symphony no. 3 (Symphonie Triomphale)* (1854); *Feest-ouverture* (1854)

SOLO INSTRUMENT(S) AND ORCHESTRA: *Concerto,* hn, orch (1814); *Concerto,* 8 timp, orch (1833); *Concertino,* tpt, orch (1833); *Concertino,* hn, orch (1838); *Concertant,* 2 hn, orch (1841); *Concertino,* trb, orch (1841)

MILITARY MUSIC: *Zes marschen voor vier cornetten* (1811); *Adagio* (1813); *Marche funèbre* (1813); *Twee marschen* (1815); *Zes marschen* (1822); *Groote fantaisie militaire De Zegepraal bij Leuven* (1830); *Standaardmarsch* (1849); *Feest-marsch* (1850); *Inweidings-marsch* (1852); *Marsch* (1853); *Metalen Kruis defileermarsch* (1863); *Feest-marsch* (1859)

BIBLIOGRAPHY

T. Jumelet-van Doeveren: *Eene inrigting voor grondig en min kostbaar onderwijs : 150 jaar muziekscholen in Rotterdam 1844-1994.* Rotterdam, Donker, 1995

T. Jumelet-van Doeveren: *Leven en werken van Wouter Hutschenruyter sr. uit Rotterdam 1796-1878.* Doctoral dissertation University of Utrecht, 1988

DISCOGRAPHY

Ouverture van het Declamatorium Iwan en Pauleska (arr. for wind band 1841). Dutch National Youth Wind Orchestra, cond. J. Cober (NM Classics 92080)

Constantijn Huygens

THE HAGUE, 4 SEPTEMBER 1596 – THE HAGUE, 27 MARCH 1687

Constantijn Huygens was born into a wealthy family, active in the highest circles of the civil service: his father, Christiaan Huygens Sr., was secretary of the Council of State. Huygens received a broad education, studying as a child such subjects as languages, mathematics, music and drawing, initially under his father's instruction, though later he was taught by private tutors. From 1616 to 1617 he studied at the University of Leiden. In the years that followed he traveled extensively (four trips to England between 1618 to 1624, and one to Venice in 1620), often as part of diplomatic delegations of the Dutch Republic.

In 1625 he was appointed secretary to the Stadtholder of the Dutch Republic, Prince Frederik Hendrik, a post he also held under William II. From 1630 he was a member of the 'Domain Council', an agency that managed the House of Orange's possessions, and through this post he remained affiliated with the family throughout his long life. After the death of William II in 1650 he made several journeys as an envoy of the Royal household, for example to Brussels (1656-1657), Paris (1661-1665) and London (1662-1663). The last years of his life he spent quietly in The Hague and at his small country house 'Hofwijck' just outside the city.

Huygens is known particularly for his literary work and verse, leaving upon his death a large body of poems in Dutch, French, Latin, Italian, English, Spanish, Greek and German. In his poetry Huygens shows himself to be erudite and sharp-witted, but his style is often artificial and complicated.

Huygens was an avid amateur musician. During his youth he was taught to play a number of instruments, such as the lute, viola da gamba, harpsichord and organ. He studied the lute with Jeronimus van Someren (1580-1651) of The Hague, and keyboard instruments with Pieter de Vois (c.1580-1654), organist at the Jacob's Church in The Hague. Later, around 1640, he also took up the theorbo, and in his later years (he was over seventy) he learned the guitar, an instrument that was then becoming fashionable. Huygens also composed for all of these instruments, presumably mostly short pieces like allemandes, sarabandes, gigues, pavanes and airs, grouping them together in manuscripts. By his own account, these pieces ultimately numbered around 900. Apart from pieces for one instrument he also composed a number of trios for viola da gambas. The manuscripts of his instrumental works have been lost; only an Allemande for viola da gamba has survived in a copy.

Constantijn Huygens surrounded by his children

His vocal music was more fortunate. A collection of pieces for voice and basso continuo entitled *Pathodia sacra et profana* was printed and published in 1647 by Robert Ballard in Paris. It contains twenty Latin psalms, twelve Italian airs and seven French airs. The psalm texts (several verses each) were taken from the Vulgate, the Italian texts were mostly written by the poet Marino, and the French were by Huygens himself. These songs are concise, like the instrumental works, and are printed on facing pages. They are lively and declamatory, oriented more to the Italian style than the French. Although initially written with lute accompaniment, the printed edition includes a basso continuo accompaniment, and as such it is the first example of its kind ever to have been published in France. Not only was the edition of *Pathodia* a mark of recognition of the quality of his music, but Huygens seems also to have considered it the ideal gift; years after publication he still distributed copies among his family, friends and business relations, regardless of whether they were professional musicians or amateurs, or whether they were interested in music at all.

It is certain that Huygens also composed other vocal works, most likely in his early years. But the number of these works cannot be ascertained as a large majority has been lost.

Huygens maintained contact with many amateur and professional musicians in the Dutch Republic and abroad; among the first group were the priest Joan Albert Ban (Haarlem), the scholar Marin Mersenne (Paris), the Duarte family (Antwerp), Utricia Ogle (who was of mixed English and Dutch descent and had lived in The Hague, Utrecht and Hamburg; the *Pathodia* was dedicated to her), Maria Casembroot (a friend from The Hague), Béatrix de Cusance (the Duchess of Lorraine, who lived for a time in Antwerp and Brussels), and Sébastian Chièze (an aristocrat from Orange who later served as William III's envoy to Madrid).

Among the professional musicians with whom he was acquainted or corresponded were Jacques Gaultier and Nicholas Lanier (both court musicians in London), Thomas Gobert (court kapellmeister in Paris), the De la Barre family (court musicians in Paris), Henri Dumont (organist and court chapelmaster in Paris), Jacques Champion de Chambonnières (court harpsichordist in Paris), and Johann Jacob Froberger (former imperial organist, later in Mainz and Héricourt). Huygens regularly met with some of these musicians to play music, while with the others he maintained a correspondence. These letters, many of which (though not all) have survived, provide a veritable treasure trove of information on seventeenth-century music making.

On only one occasion, in 1641, did Huygens make his views on a musical issue publicly known. In the pamphlet *Gebruyck of ongebruyck van 't orgel in de kercken der Vereenighde Nederlanden* [Use and non-use of the organ in the churches of the United Netherlands] he voiced his support for organ accompaniment of congregational singing in the church. Although this pamphlet stirred controversy, it seems not to have had a direct influence, even though Huygens' ideas ultimately prevailed.

As an amateur composer, Huygens could permit himself to entertain strictly personal ideas on music. His songs do not fit any of the seventeenth-century currents of composition. He collected elements from different styles and genres (such as the French 'air de cour' and the Italian monody and aria) and forged them into a unique musical expression. It is thus not surprising that his music remained chiefly confined to personal use and did not draw followers. Nonetheless, the *Pathodia sacra et profana* are frequently performed today.

RUDOLF RASCH

COMPOSITIONS
Pathodia sacra et profana. – Paris, Robert Ballard, 1647
Twenty Latin psalms, twelve Italian airs and seven French airs for voices and bc. Modern ed.: Pathodia sacra et profana / ed. Frits Noske. Amsterdam, Noord-Hollandse Uitg. Mij., 1957 (repr.: Amsterdam, Groen, 1975)

WRITINGS
Gebruyck of ongebruyck van 't orgel in de kercken der Vereenighde Nederlanden. Leiden, Elzevier, 1641
Facs. ed.: introd. and comments F.J. Zwaan. Amsterdam, Noord-Hollandse Uitg. Mij., 1974

BIBLIOGRAPHY
De briefwisseling van Constantijn Huygens (1608-1687), vol. 1-6, ed. J.A. Worp. The Hague, Nijhoff, 1911-1917
T. Crawford: 'A composition for viola da gamba by Constantijn Huygens', *Veelzijdigheid*, 1987, p. 79-88
L.P. Grijp: 'Melodieën bij teksten van Huygens', *Veelzijdigheid*, 1987, p. 89-107
C.L. Heesakkers: *Constantijn Huygens : mijn jeugd.* Amsterdam, Querido, 1987. Dutch transl. of Huygens' autobiography
Musique et musiciens au XVIIe siècle : correspondance et oeuvres musicales de Constantin Huygens, ed. W.J.A. Jonckbloet and J.P.N. Land. Leiden, Brill, 1882
F. Noske: 'Rondom het orgeltractaat van Constantijn Huygens', *TVNM*, 17, 1955, p. 278-309
F. Noske: 'Huygens, de musicus : enkele aspecten', *Veelzijdigheid*, 1987, p. 129-140
S.D. Post: 'Constantijn Huygens' Musicae : achttiende-eeuws handschrift werpt nieuw licht op Huygens' nagelaten composities', *De zeventiende eeuw*, 8, 1992, p. 275-283

R.A. Rasch: 'Constantijn Huygens : een muzikale heer van stand', *De zeventiende eeuw*, 3, 1987, p. 99-114
Veelzijdigheid als levensvorm : facetten van Constantijn Huygens' leven en werk, ed. A.Th. van Deursen [et al.]. Deventer, Sub Rosa, 1987

DISCOGRAPHY
Pathodia sacra et profana (sel.). Camerata Trajectina (Globe GLO 6013)

Jan Ingenhoven

BREDA, 19 MAY 1876 – HOENDERLOO, 20 MAY 1951

In 1904 Breda's Male Choir won first prize at the International choral competition in Rotterdam. Its conductor was the 28-year-old Jan Ingenhoven, who
for two years had been leading this choir, in addition to several other choirs
and orchestras in Breda and Dordrecht. Until that time, Ingenhoven was almost entirely self taught. In his childhood he learned to play the clarinet and
also performed as a singer. His first compositions date from 1902, a period in
which he had taken some lessons from Ludwig Felix Brandts Buys. In 1906 he
moved to Munich and there studied composition with Felix Mottl.

Ingenhoven remained in Munich for seven years. As conductor of the
Münchener Orchester Verein and the Philharmonisches Orchester, he was a
strong advocate of contemporary music. His programming was unique to the
city: in his very first year he organized at his own cost concerts of Dutch music
with the works of Johan Wagenaar, Alphons Diepenbrock, Charles Smulders
and his own compositions. Also in 1906 he introduced Debussy's *Prélude à
l'après-midi d'un faune* in Munich. His Festival of French Music in 1910, with
harpsichord works by Rameau and Couperin and contemporary pieces by
Chabrier and Debussy, created a sensation. Ingenhoven composed several
pieces for large orchestra during this period, including the *Symphonische Tonstücke* and *Brabant und Holland*.

From 1909 to 1912 he led the Münchener Madrigal-Vereinigung, a choir of
about fifteen professional singers whose repertoire ranged from Palestrina
and Monteverdi to Brahms and Debussy. They soon became well known in
Germany, Switzerland and Italy. The insights Ingenhoven gained into Renaissance polyphony with this choir strongly influenced further development of
his style.

In 1913 Ingenhoven decided to withdraw from conducting so that he could
dedicate his energies to composition. At the outbreak of World War I he took
up residence in Paris. Between 1911 and 1913 several of his compositions, including the Wind Quintet, were premiered in Amsterdam. 'An ingenious
composer', wrote the music critic Matthijs Vermeulen of the creator of this
frequently performed piece. But Ingenhoven's music was not often programmed during World War I, and this adversely influenced his creativity.

From 1919 to 1922 he composed a series of new works, beginning with two
violin sonatas and two cello sonatas. Ingenhoven was well aware that his

183

strength lay in chamber music. He was then living in Thun, Switzerland. Although various of his works were published, his music was seldom heard in the Netherlands after 1918. Deeply disappointed at this neglect, he called his fatherland 'a sad country for music'. In 1925 a chamber music evening dedicated to his music was held in Germany. He composed several new pieces after this, for example *Kamermuziek* [Chamber Music] for clarinet and string trio, but these were to be his last. After the death of his wife in 1929 he sank into depression. He returned to the Netherlands, where for another twenty years he lived in isolation in Hoog-Soeren.

Ingenhoven's music is characterized by a spirit of independence that manifests itself in a fundamental disdain of accepted rules. The individual voices generally seem oblivious to one another, each emerging as a strong character in its own right. Melodically and rhythmically, his music is complicated and often experimental. Its long melodic lines are reminiscent of Gregorian chant.

In 1906 he composed *Zarathustras Nachtlied* for voice and orchestra, to a text by Nietzsche; he had not yet heard Mahler's Symphony no.3, which uses the same text. Its theme, the freedom of man, had deep personal meaning to him and his treatment of the text indeed offers a very personal interpretation. Another early work, the *Symphonisches Tonstück 2* (1907), not only begins without a time signature but also in a key that is entirely unclear. Like many composers of his generation, Ingenhoven was striving at the time to expand the tonal system. In a letter to Diepenbrock in 1906 he speaks of the possibilities afforded by a quarter-tone system. Equally experimental is the harmonic palette of his a cappella choral piece *Nous n'irons plus au bois* (1909), which balances on the edge of atonality.

Ingenhoven composed no large-scale works after 1910. His extensive experience with Renaissance polyphony led him to turn his attention to chamber music. In the string quartet, he found a pendant to the a cappella choir. His *Drei Sätze für Streichquartett* (1908) were well received at their premiere in 1912 and are particularly notable for their highly nuanced rhythm. In his book

Zeventig jaar Nederlandse muziek 1915-1985 [Seventy years of Dutch music 1915-1985], Leo Samama dubs the second movement 'a symphonic poem in a chamber setting'.

Characteristic of both the Wind Quintet and the *Streichquartett in einem Satz* (both composed in 1911) is the translucence of texture despite the polyphonic writing. Ingenhoven himself had a preference for this quartet because of its improvisatory character. The Wind Quintet, also in one movement, breathes the spirit of Classical chamber music. Ingenhoven was greatly attracted to the sound of the clarinet, his own instrument, and the many recitative-like solo passages in this quintet illustrate the point. Also remarkably playful and free of ponderousness is an unpublished wind quintet with piano dating from 1914. The reminiscences of Debussy in the slow middle movement evoke the atmosphere of impressionism while the exuberant finale seems more inspired by Richard Strauss.

The two violin and two cello sonatas composed after World War I call for quasi-improvisational performance; the second cello sonata even bears the inscription 'quasi una fantasia'. These four sonatas were later associated with the four seasons, the withdrawn and sober character of the second cello sonata in one, rhythmically regular movement being the winter.

Ingenhoven's pioneering work as a conductor was acknowledged and appreciated, but he suffered many disappointments as a composer. Through its lack of clearly delineated themes and harmonic foundation, his music seems to float weightlessly. Herein lies the source of the frequently voiced criticism that his music lacks form. Around 1920 no other composer in the Netherlands worked in a similar idiom. Ingenhoven's idividualism contributed to his isolation. He was aware that the complexity of his music was unusually demanding for musicians but he was seldom prepared to make concessions. A third of his roughly sixty opuses is still waiting to be published. As early as 1938, the composer Daniel Ruyneman observed that Ingenhoven's music had been unjustly neglected. His explanation was that music that even 'slightly deviates from the norm is not accepted in our musical culture.'

DÉSIRÉE STAVERMAN

COMPOSITIONS

VOICE AND PIANO: *Blumenlieder* : *7 Lieder* (1907); *Zwei Lieder*: 1. *Abendständchen* (Brentano) (1908), 2. *Der träumende See* (Mosen); *Avondzang* (De Vooys) (1909)

VOICE AND ORCHESTRA: *Zarathustras Nachtlied* (Nietzsche) (1906); *Klaus Tink* (Kopisch) (1909)

CHOIR: *Quatuors à voix mixtes*: 1. *O bone Jesu* (1903), 2. *Ave verum* (1908), 3. *Nous n'irons plus au bois* (Banville) (1909), 4. *Rondel* (D'Orléans) (1909); *St. Jans vier* (Gezelle), mix.choir (1909); *Nordische Landschaft* (Eick), soloists, m.choir, orch (1910); *Amor* (Brentano), w.choir (1911); *An die Nacht* (Brentano), w.choir (1911); *Mietje* (Gezelle), mix.choir (1913); *An die Nacht* (Brentano), mix.choir (1911); *De wilde wind* (Gezelle), m.choir (1926); *Welch ein Schweigen*, m.choir (1927)

CHAMBER MUSIC: *Drei Sätze für Streichquartett* (1907-1908); *Streichquartett in einem Satz* (1911); *Wind Quintet* (1911); *String Quartet no. 3* (1912); Two sonatas, vl, pf (1919-1920, 1921); Two sonatas, vc, pf (1919, 1922); *Sonatina*, a-cl, vl (1925); *Pièces pour trois instruments divers* (1912-1913, 1914-1915, 1918); *Kamermuziek*, cl, str.trio/str.orch (1926)

ORCHESTRA: *Symphonisches Tonstück nos. 1, 2 and 3* (1905, 1907, 1908); *Brabant und Holland* (1910-1911); *Vier Stücke*, 3 cl, 3 hn, timp, str (1924)

BIBLIOGRAPHY

M. Hoedeman: *Jan Ingenhoven*. Doctoral dissertation University of Utrecht, 1982. Supplement: contents archive Jan Ingenhoven

M. Hoedeman: 'Stylistic experiments in the songs of Jan Ingenhoven', *TVNM*, 34, 1984, p. 68-78

E. Reeser: *Een eeuw Nederlandse muziek : 1815-1915*. Amsterdam, Querido, 1950, 2/1986

E. Reeser: 'Jan Ingenhoven', *Die Musik in Geschichte und Gegenwart*

D. Ruyneman: *De componist Jan Ingenhoven : beschouwingen in het licht van de hedendaagsche muziek*. Amsterdam, De Spieghel

L. Samama: *Zeventig jaar Nederlandse muziek : 1915-1985 : voorspel tot een nieuwe dag*. Amsterdam, Querido, 1986

M. Starreveld-Bartels: 'Jan Ingenhoven', *The New Grove dictionary of music and musicians*

DISCOGRAPHY

Various recordings in the archive of the Dutch Broadcasting Company (NOB). No CD-recordings of Van Ingenhoven's works exist.

Guus Janssen

HEILOO, 13 MAY 1951

Guus Janssen once referred to his parents' record collection – a jumble of Classical music, jazz, operetta and the popular music of the day – as the harbinger of his future. He still has fond memories of the yodelling he would listen to on a worn-out 45 rpm record. The instinct for the ambiguity of divergent musical material is a constant in Janssen's music. His compositions always probe the borders between abstract and concrete, between tonal and atonal elements, between the accessible and the esoteric. It is the music of a clever and discerning omnivore.

Janssen took his first piano lessons from Piet Groot, who one day in 1965 let him hear a recording of the *Concerto da camera* by Peter Schat. 'I am going to do that, too', thought Janssen. Through his older brothers, he became acquainted with jazz, from Dixieland to Miles Davis and Willem Breuker, and together with them he practised self-devised, free improvisational forms. He also accompanied church services on the organ. Although his encounter with soul music amounted to a minor revelation, he was mostly oblivious to the popular music of the 1960s. The other important discovery was the music of Charles Ives, whose work seemed perfectly to symbolize the tangle of music in his thoughts.

After completing high school, Janssen studied the piano with Jaap Spaanderman and composition with Ton de Leeuw at the Amsterdam Conservatory. He played the piano with a number of groups including the Asko Ensemble which performed several of his works. Composition and improvisation, however, remain his primary occupations.

Since 1973 he has performed with various improvisational groups. In the ensembles he has formed, ranging from a trio to a modest orchestra, his brother Wim (percussion) and reed player Ab Baars have been the most constant factors. In addition, Janssen has drawn attention with his solo improvisations which, since the late 1980s, he has performed on the harpsichord as well as the piano. His idiosyncratic style of music making earned him the Boy Edgar Prize for Jazz and Improvised Music in 1981. Three years later, the other facet of his double talent gained recognition with the Matthijs Vermeulen Prize, awarded for his chamber piece *Temet*.

The composer and the improviser in Janssen, in as much as there is a difference between the two, have always kept pace with each other. At the end of the 1970s he gained acclaim with such compositions as the cross-grained

concerto for piano and wind instruments *Dans van de malic matrijzen* [Dance of the malic molds] (1978), *Toonen* (1980) for orchestra, which was also performed at Donaueschingen, and especially with the string quartet *Streepjes* [Dashes] (1981).

Over the years Janssen has composed for a broad spectrum of Dutch soloists, ensembles and orchestras, ranging from the recorder player Walter van Hauwe to the Concertgebouw Orchestra, from carillon, gamelan and ballet music to his opera *Noach*, which was premiered at the 1994 Holland Festival, directed by Pierre Audi and with scenery by Karel Appel. *Noach* was a resounding success, in part owing to the felicitous combination of seemingly opposing forces: the wild animal fantasies of Appel set against the organizing hand of Audi; the bitter irony of Friso Haverkamp's measured, cataloguing texts set against the playful irony of Janssen's alternately furious and tranquil music; and above all, owing to the precision shown by the composer in positing 'open spaces' in the score where the improvisers taking part in the performance free themselves of exact notation to demonstrate their special qualities.

From the very beginning, Janssen's work has been distinguished by quasitonal structures, carefree excursions and references to a wealth of sometimes trivial kinds of music, qualities that initially gave rise to criticism in the serially shaded musical climate of the early 1970s. However, especially when the comparatively speaking 'wild' adventures of his earliest compositions gradually gave way to an atmosphere of elegant economy, audiences became more receptive to Janssen's original and spiritual plays on tones and traditions.

In this respect, the string quartet *Streepjes* is a perfect, eight-minute specimen of 'Janssen in a nutshell'. Janssen transforms the four separate instruments of the Classical string quartet into a single instrument of sixteen open – some of them retuned – strings that play almost exclusively harmonics. In this way a melody is often put together by the four players tone by tone. The 'streepjes' are delicate squiggles, like arpeggios on a glass harmonica. The music is chromatic but continuously opens up tonal paths. Within this texture, little 'trap-doors' pop open from time to time from which emerge, like the cuckoo from a Swiss clock, Classical string chords played with a heavy vibrato. The overall effect gives no indication of the degree of precision and effort demanded of the musicians. Awkward sounding moments do arise, but these are, as it were, 'played'.

Streepjes is exemplary of the main characteristics of nearly all of Janssen's compositions, which return time and again in varied forms. He continuously plays with the perception of musical 'laws'. Tonal forces are conjured up, often in overtone structures, but they are invariably derailed. Rhythmic constancy is created only to be scattered by abrupt changes of tempo or disrupting lengthening or shortening tactics.

A 'ready-made' element (a fragment consisting of a rhythm, a chord or – as in *Streepjes* – a 'sound') is found in many works, usually in combination with montage technique. And even the montage technique tends to undermine the flow on the most immediate level; in the large structure of the work, however, this device provides coherence. But however topsy-turvy the chunks of music stand in immediate relation to each other, they are strung together in a way that creates logically coherent sentences, formulas and cadences. The overall form in Janssen's music can almost always be termed Classical: almost invariably, there is a three-part structure functioning as exposition, development section and recapitulation, or a chain of variations.

Janssen names the Flemish painter Roger Raveel as his most important model. Like Raveel's ideal of seeing the world with 'eyes that do not know what they see', and thereby creating an intriguing mixture of abstraction and realism, Janssen seeks to hear with an untrained ear, one that stands open to all musical realities, finding eclectic combinations of elements that bring about a new, adventurous order through which not only a poetic undertone sounds, but often a seemingly guileless humor as well.

These qualities are all the more pronounced in *Noach* and *Hier*^{O}, both theatrical works that Janssen brought to fruition together with Friso Haverkamp and stage director Pierre Audi. *Noach*, a grotesque inversion of the bible story in which the hero is a symbol for mankind's endeavor to destroy God's creation, was such a success at its premiere in 1994 that it was repeated five years later. The composer's ensuing opera *Hier*^{O}, premiered in January 2000, deals partly with the city of Amsterdam's folie de grandeur and includes an appearance of the Holy Trinity in the shape of three female Chinese vocalists, for whom the composer concocted a spicy brew of his own and Peking Opera idioms.

Haverkamp's litany-like summaries, his association-rich language and his phantasmagorical inversions of the received order combine magnificently with Janssen's partly through-composed, partly improvised music, music which is honed to the qualities of the ensembles he himself put together.

FRITS VAN DER WAA

COMPOSITIONS

VOCAL: *Overture Aanvallen van uitersten* (Toebosch), sp.v, orch (1983); *Zonder* (Haverkamp), mix.choir (1986); *Garni*, Bar, 10 instr. (1990); *Dodo's groove*, B, instr.ens (1991); *Wening*, S, cl, str.qt, tape (1992); *Faust's licht* (Haverkamp, after Stein), Mez, sp.v, str.qt (concert version) (1994); *Dodo : kleines Bestiarium Noachs* (Haverkamp), B-Bar, instr. ens (1996)

OPERA: *Faust's Licht* (chamber opera) (Haverkamp, after Stein), Mez, 4 sp.v, str.qt (1985-1986, rev. (1988); *Noach* (Haverkamp) (1991-1993); *Hier⁰* (2000)

CHAMBER MUSIC: *Muziek voor 6 houtblazers* (1972); *String Quartet no. 1* (1973-1975); *Brake*, pf (1974); *Met spoed*, b-cl, pf (1975); *Muziek voor geëlectrificeerde hobo*, el.ob (1975); *Octet*, 5 wind instr, 3 str.instr (1978); *Vijf kreukels*, 1-3 acc (1979); *Ritmische etude*, bar.org (1979); *Streepjes* (String Quartet no. 2) (1981); *Juist daarom*, ob, cl, s-sax, pf, vc (1981); *Danspassen*, cl/b-cl, mand, gui, vc, db (1982); *Dik en dun*, car (also version for pf) (1982); *Ut, re, mi, sol, la*, wind qnt, str.qnt, pf (1982); *Temet*, fl (also b-fl and pic), vl, vc, hp (1983, rev. 1984); *Sprezzatura*, b-cl (1984); *Wandelweer*, 3 gui (1984); *PF*, pf, a-sax, perc (1985); *Voetnoot I*, pic (1987); *Voetnoot II*, Zwaanenburg a-fl (1988); *Functional*, pf (1988); *Pogo 3*, hpd (1989); *Largo*, rec (1989); *Voetnoot III*, 2 fl (1990); *Ijoh*, t-sax (1990); *Veranderingen*, 2 pf (1990); *Zangbodem*, rec.qt, pf (1990); *Echo's en fantasieën*, org (1991); *Bah Rock*, fl (1992); *Klotz*, vl, hi-hat, cl, b-hn, b-cl, gui, db (1994); *Mikado*, vl, vc, pf (1995); *Tapdance*, hp, perc (1995); *Blauwbrug*, pf (1996)

ORCHESTRA, CHAMBER ORCHESTRA, LARGE ENSEMBLE: *Gieter* (1973); *Dans van de malic matrijzen* (1976-1977); *Toonen* (1980); *Woeha* (1984); *Bruuks* (1985); *Deviaties* (1986); *Keer* (1988); *Concerto*, pic, wind orch (1991); *Winter* (1991); *Zoek* (1993); *Passevite* (1994); *Toestand* (1995)

BIBLIOGRAPHY

H. Bosma: 'Composers and computers in the Netherlands', *Key Notes*, 25, 1988/89, p. 51-54

E. de Cock: 'Een uitdijend heelal : de achteloze muziek van Guus Janssen', *Mens en Melodie* vol. 53, 1998, p. 63-69

E. Schönberger: 'String quartet or "string quartet" ', *Key Notes*, 23, 1986, p. 13

F. van der Waa: 'Guus Janssen and the skating-on-thin-ice feeling', *Key Notes*, 28, 1994/3, p.8

DISCOGRAPHY

Bah rock. E. Pameijer (fl) (Attacca Babel 9478)

Blauwbrug. M. Worms (pf) (NM Extra 98014)

Brake. G. Bouwhuis (pf) (Composers' Voice CV 8703)

Chamber & Solo. Various soloists and ensembles (includes: *Streepjes, Voetnoot I, Veranderingen, Temet, Octet, Klotz*) (Composers' Voive CV 61)

Dancing series. Guus Janssen and his orchestra (includes: *Hip hop; Slow fox; Pogo 1 en 2; Jojo jive; Incourante; Passepied; Mambo*) (Geestgronden CD GG1)

Dans van de malic matrijzen. G. Janssen (pf), Residentie Orchestra, cond. L. Vis (Olympia OCD 506)

Guus Janssen, harpsichord (includes: *Preludium; Ostinato 1, Vrij naar LT; PF; Cha tsja; One bar; Pogo 3*) (Geestgronden CD GG7)

Klankast. G. Janssen (pf) (includes: *Mikstuur; Ostinato1; Scheel; Ostinato 2; Klankast; Hi-hat-Koprol; Functional; Dik & dun*) (Geestgronden CD GG9)

Noach. Various soloists, Tuvan singers, Nieuw Artis Orchestra, Mondriaan Quartet, cond. L. Vis (Composers' Voice CV 42/43 / Geestgronden CD GG13)

Pok. G. Janssen (pf), P. Termos (a-sax), W. Janssen (perc) (Geestgronden CD GG3)

Sprezzatura. H. Sparnaay (b-cl) (Attacca Babel 8945-1)

Wandelweer. Amsterdam Guitar Trio (Composers' Voice CV 8701)

Woeha. Orkest de Volharding, cond. C. van Zeeland (NM Classics 92021)

Zoek. E. Pameijer (pic), G. Janssen (hpd), Nieuw Sinfonietta Amsterdam, cond. L. Markiz (NM Classics 92041)

Willem Jeths

AMERSFOORT, 31 AUGUST 1959

As a boy of fourteen Willem Jeths would improvise atonal music at the piano. When he was about sixteen, he began carefully to notate his musical fantasies. Nevertheless, even after completing high school he did not immediately decide to study composition. He enrolled instead in the teacher-training program of the Sweelinck Conservatory in Amsterdam, although he felt slightly out of place. It was during this period that he composed for the Arti theater group in Amsterdam, giving his first performances with a small orchestra in Amsterdam's Theater De Balie. He also worked as a pianist in the one-man theater productions of comedian Paul Haenen.

In 1982 Jeths began studying composition with Hans Kox, completing his training in 1988 with Kox's successor at the Utrecht Conservatory, Tristan Keuris. From 1983 to 1991 he also studied musicology at the University of Amsterdam.

With *Novelette* (1986), for violin and piano, Jeths first freed himself from the influence of his teachers. Although he continued to develop an individual style from this time on, his manner of composing does show three significant similarities with the work of his former teacher Keuris: firstly, there is the principle of exploring every facet of the musical material, secondly, he tends to highlight certain sections or passages of pieces with a modal or harmonic 'color', and thirdly, he always strives to create an appealing musical result. This latter aspect manifests itself in Jeths' predilection for clarity of structure and in his economic use of material.

Novelette is based from beginning to end on a fourth chord. This chord is usually sounded in the piano part, while the violin mostly emphasizes the sevenths intervals in the chord. While there is not a single triad or other more traditional chord in the piece, the musical progression is clear and accessible to the listener through the unity of the harmonic structure and the regular return in both instruments to 'anchor notes' in the same octave. For Jeths, atonality is not derived from an extra-musical, academic system of composition or avant-garde concept, but is a product of its own musical logic. The appeal of his music is also generated by the creative attention he gives to possibilities of timbre, both of individual instruments and of ensembles. The violin parts in *Novelette* and his violin concerto *Glenz* require unusual playing techniques that give rise to new timbral gradations.

Mythos (1992), for harpsichord, offers a good example of Jeths' method
of working. To compose this piece,
he had a two-manual harpsichord installed in his house and, through improvisation and experimentation, became fascinated with the timbral
possibilities that arise from coupling
the manuals. When, for example, a
key is slowly depressed, the two
strings of the different manuals
(tuned an octave apart) sound in
quick succession. Jeths utilized this
effect for further manipulations of
sound color, such as the muting or
retuning of strings, thus bending the

octaves to other intervals and providing the basis for a new idiom that is nevertheless still characteristic of the instrument. In the opening 43 measures of
A bout de souffle (1993) for clarinet, bassoon, horn and string quartet, subtle
white noise textures are sounded by the bassoon and horn together with repeating or long-held notes, harmonics, tremolos and notated trills. In his ex-
ploration of the possibilities of timbre, Jeths has unmistakably found an example in the music of György Ligeti.

   Glenz (1993) for violin and string orchestra shows traces of Ligeti's delicate
timbral structures in its division of the string orchestra into a scordatura
group and a tutti group. The scordatura group is tuned to provide a chromatic
range of open strings while the tutti group is scored almost entirely *divisi*. The
continuity of timbral textures, however, is repeatedly interrupted by aggressive
pizzicato chords, giving the work enormous rhythmic vitality. Within the often
complicated sound fields, certain tones or intervals repeatedly pop out like
markers.

   The large forces of the Piano Concerto (1994) include a wealth of unusual
instruments (such as washboard and referee's whistles) and the six percussionists play mostly metal instruments such as triangle, cymbals, crotales, ce-
lesta and glockenspiel. The orchestration of the first movement and the metal-
lic, hammering piano sounds are reminiscent of Messiaen's *Turangalîla
Symphony* and Ligeti's Piano Concerto. The second movement is more lyrical
and tranquil. The third evokes memories of Stravinsky's *Le Sacre du Printemps*. *Fas/Nefas* for harp and orchestra was composed in 1997. In this work
Jeths shifts his compositional focus from the development of musical material

to instrumental colors and sound-effects. In *Flux/Reflux* for orchestra (1998) he adds to this the spatial dimension of sound by placing the strings of the orchestra in a V-shape pointed to the audience. This enables him to let the sound move back and forth through the orchestra.

Jeths has already received various international prizes. In 1991 his *Arcate* (1990) earned him the honorary diploma of the Carl Maria von Weber Competition, and one year later he received a commendation for the same work (string orchestra version, 1991) from the Music for String Compositions Competition of the Oare String Orchestra in Kent, England. In 1996 he won second prize at the Vienna International Composition Competition for *Glenz*.

In 1994 and 1995 Jeths completed the first two arias (*I Go* and *Zjisszjiss*, to a libretto by Bertjan ter Braak) of an opera on Mathilde Willink, the wife of the Dutch painter Carel Willink.

MICHAEL VAN EEKEREN

COMPOSITIONS

VOCAL: *Les chats* (song cycle) (Baudelaire), S/Bar, pf (1982); *Chanson einer Dame im Schatten* (Celan), S, orch (1983); *Crimes glorieux* (Lautréamont), mix.choir, 2 pf, perc.ens (1990); *D'aprile e di maggio* (Da San Gimignano), S, Mez, Bar, fl, cl, bn (1992); *I Go* (aria from the opera *Mathilde Willink*), Mez, cl, str.qt (1994, version Mez, sax.qt, 1995); *Zjisszjiss* (aria from the opera *Mathilde Willink*), Mez, sax.qt (1995)

CHAMBER MUSIC: *Novelette*, vl, pf (1986); *Brezza*, fl, perc (1987, rev. 1988); *Raptim*, fl, a-cl/b-cl, pf (1988); *Arcate*, str.qt (1990); *Morpheus*, 2 vl (1991); *Epitheta*, pf (1991); *Mythos*, hpd (1992, rev. 1994); *A bout de souffle*, cl, bn, hn, str.qt (1993); *Chiaroscuro*, pf (1995); *Dwaallicht* (performance), fl (1995); *Chiaroscuro*, version instr.ens (1996); *...Un vago ricordo...*, str.qt (1996), *Vertooning*, hn (1997); *Onde*, wind qnt (1998); *Bella figura*, vla (1999)

ORCHESTRA: *Procurans odium* (1984); *Concerto*, a-sax, str.orch (1985, rev. 1987); *Arcate*, version str.orch (1991); *Glenz*, vl, str.orch (1993); *Concerto*, pf, orch (1994); *Meander* (1994); *Throb*, orch (1995); *Fas/Nefas*, hp, orch (also version pr.pf, orch) (1997); *Flux/Reflux*, orch (1998); *Falsa/Ficta*, vc, orch (1999)

BIBLIOGRAPHY

K. Arntzen: 'Dutch economy and an urge to expand horizons : Willem Jeths grants 'ugliness' a legitimate status'. *Key Notes*, 31, 1997/2, p. 22-24

I. van der Goot: 'Componist Willem Jeths aan het werk', *Concertkrant Culturele Raad Zuid-Holland*, Jan. 1995, p. 10

P.-U. Hiu: 'Klankbord voor de versnippering', *de Volkskrant*, 17 Dec. 1993

P. Janssen: 'Van Diepenbrock tot Willem Jeths (Nederlandse componisten en Mahler)', *Luister*, May 1995

E. Kempers: ' "Als componist moet je altijd je eigen manager zijn" : interview met C. Micháns en W. Jeths', *Utrechts Nieuwsblad*, 26 Jan. 1988

P. Luttikhuis: ' "Ik werd gepest en speelde orgel" : gesprek met componist Willem Jeths', *NRC Handelsblad*, 15 Feb. 1991

P. Luttikhuis: 'Strijkkwartetten van Nederlandse componisten : interview met G. Janssen, M. Padding en W. Jeths', *Mens en Melodie*, vol. 46, 1991

J.-P. Meijer: *De zoektocht naar muzikale grenzen. Esthetiek en compositietechniek bij Willem Jeths*. Doctoral dissertation University of Utrecht, 1997

N. Moritz: 'De analyse : Willem Jeths', *Entr' acte Muziekjournaal*, no. 10, 1996, p. 27-29 (analysis of *Glenz*)

B. van Putten: 'Een beladen waagstuk met

vier stemmen', *Het Parool*, 16 Feb. 1991

T. Ruijfrok: 'De nieuwe welluidendheid van Willem Jeths : première Introdans op werk van Nederlandse componist', *Nijmeegs Dagblad*, 28 Feb. 1992

F. van der Waa: 'Zin in dat tevreden gevoel : interview met C. de Bondt, G. Janssen, W. Jeths en M. Padding', *de Volkskrant*, 15 Feb. 1991

J. Zandbergen: 'Muzikale mooipraterij, daar houd ik niet van : Morpheus van Willem Jeths, speciaal gecomponeerd voor Introdans', *De Gelderlander*, 30 March 1992

DISCOGRAPHY

Glenz. P. Brunt (vl), Nieuw Sinfonietta Amsterdam, cond. L. Markiz (NM Classics 92041)

Mythos. A. de Man (hpd) (NM Classics 92038)

Raptim. Het Trio (Radio Nederland 1991)

Otto Ketting

AMSTERDAM, 3 SEPTEMBER 1935

Otto Ketting, son of the composer Piet Ketting, studied the trumpet at the Royal Conservatory in The Hague. From 1954 to 1961 he was a trumpeter with the Residentie Orchestra of The Hague and with various jazz and dance orchestras. From 1967 to 1974 he taught composition at the conservatories in The Hague and Rotterdam and from 1978 to 1991 he gave ensemble classes for contemporary music in Rotterdam. He also appeared as a conductor, and not only of his own music.

Ketting is a self-taught composer, although he did receive much advice from his father. His lessons in Munich with Karl Amadeus Hartmann in 1961-1962 hardly qualify as such; when Hartmann saw Ketting's Symphony no.1 he declared: 'There is nothing more I can teach you. You already know everything.' Ketting's description of Hartmann's music also applies to his own work: 'The slow movements are adagios of tremendous tension and expressiveness, the fast movements are mostly endowed with a hammering, motoric obsession, full of complicated manipulations, carved from granite.' Ketting was one of the first Dutch composers to turn to serial music. *Due canzoni*, two orchestral pieces which won him the Gaudeamus Prize in 1957, show the influence of Webern's op.6 and op.10 *Orchesterstücke*. In the Symphony no.1, the melody and instrumentation in particular bear witness to the influence of Alban Berg.

With these works, his fascination with the Second Viennese School of composers reached its temporary peak and conclusion. Ketting began to compose more than before for advanced amateur musicians in a tonal idiom scored principally for brass instruments: *Fanfares*, *Thema en variaties* [Theme and variations], *Intrada*, *Intrada festiva* and *Mars* [March]. He did not entirely abandon serial technique, but rather integrated it in a more dance-like idiom, as for example in *Pas de deux*. In 1962 he composed for Bert Haanstra's *Alleman* [Everyman] the first of his twenty film scores. He also composed ballet music. His collages, intended for various purposes and instrumental combinations, were reactions in particular to the seriousness of much dodecaphonic music. *Collage no.5* is intended for beginning pianists, and in *Collage no.9* Ketting pokes fun at the rituals of public performances.

Ketting countered the sumptuousness and complexity of the *Due canzoni* and Symphony no.1 in the late 1960s with the sobriety of *A Set of Pieces* (1967) for flute and piano and *A Set of Pieces* (1968) for wind quintet. *Monumentum* (1983) for brass instruments, piano and percussion, stands out for its sparse resources and its melodies constructed mostly from very long notes and large leaps. The structures change almost imperceptibly.

Both *A Set of Pieces* for flute and piano and a similarly-titled work for wind quintet proved very significant to his development as a composer. The technique of the almost imperceptible shifting of certain structures is also typical of *Time Machine* and *For Moonlight Nights*. Ever since writing these works, Ketting has been using this technique of melodic build-up in compositions for both small and large forces. In the latter, such as *Time Machine* and the *Symfonie voor saxofoons en orkest* [Symphony for saxophones and orchestra], he combines this melodic technique with short motifs that are repeated rapidly, as in minimal music. These repetitions yield a static effect, but are also frequently coupled with a characteristic shift of rhythm and orchestration in blocks.

Whereas the rapid figures in *Time Machine* and the *Symfonie* are scored mostly for the brass instruments and the slower figures for the strings, Ketting distributes these elements more equally in his works subsequent to 1980, for example in the *Capriccio* and the Piano Trio. Static melodic buildup dominates in *The Light of the Sun*, *Monumentum*, the opera *Ithaka*, *Summer Moon*, the adagios from the *Symfonie voor saxofoons en orkest*, and in smaller-scale works such as *Summer* and *Autumn*.

The abovementioned works are not tonal in the Classical sense of the word. *Time Machine* is based on a series of chords that are not diatonic, even though they display harmonic cohesion. The instrumentation, leaning heavily on objective wind instrument sounds and long-held chords played by the piano, vibraphone and/or marimba, betrays Ketting's admiration for Stravinsky.

Over the last twenty years, Ketting has consciously run counter to musical conventions in many compositions. *For Moonlight Nights* is not a traditional concerto for flute, but rather a musical reflection on the possible relationships between an individual and a group. The *Symfonie voor saxofoons en orkest* is not a concerto for four soloists and orchestra, but a symphony in which the quartet of soloists is gradually absorbed by the orchestra, though they do remain the guiding force. *Ithaka*, composed for the opening of the Music Theater in Amsterdam, is more a song cycle than an opera. The characters reflect on a dramatic climax that took place prior to the beginning of the opera. The *Capriccio*, a concerto for violin based on a capriccio by Paganini, is a work for ensemble with an obligato violin part in which Paganini's etude-like figures and their derivations are replaced by the repetition of typically 'Kettingesque' motifs. The Piano Trio is far removed from those 'in which the piano sets out a harmonic pattern in lush chords and the two strings, with a profusion of double stops, do their best to sound like a string quartet', in Ketting's words. The Symfonie no.3 has a Mahlerian adagio but never actually quotes Mahler.

Ketting also takes an unorthodox approach in the tetraptych *De overtocht* [The crossing], *De aankomst* [The arrival], *Het oponthoud* [The sojourn] and *Kom, over de zeeën* [Come, over the seas]. *De overtocht* (composed in 1992 for the Nieuw Ensemble, which has made a specialty of performing pieces with lively, soloistic-virtuoso passages for plucked and bowed strings in a high register) is a static piece, predominantly written in a low register. *Het oponthoud* (written in 1993 for Orkest de Volharding, which specializes in compelling wind music filled with jarring dissonants and jagged rhythms) is also a static composition that mostly employs the instruments in their low registers. *De aankomst* (written in 1993 for the Nieuw Sinfonietta Amsterdam, which mostly plays strongly melodic and lively Romantic music) is also a static piece, though harmonic development is nevertheless the dominating element. The piece ends with a bustling elaboration of a single chord. In *Kom, over de zeeën*, written for the Royal Concertgebouw Orchestra, Ketting plays with the contrast between solo parts or instrumental groups set against the entire orchestra.

Ketting has gained international recognition for *Time Machine*, which has frequently been performed in both Europe and the United Sates, the *Symfonie voor saxofoons en orkest*, winner in 1979 of the Matthijs Vermeulen Prize and the second prize at the Rostrum of Composers in Paris, and the Symfonie no.3, winner of the 1992 American Barlow Prize.

A volume of his essays on music was published in 1981 under the title *De ongeruste parapluie* [The anxious umbrella]. 1997 saw the publication of his autobiograpical book *Time Machine*.

EMANUEL OVERBEEKE

COMPOSITIONS

DRAMATIC VOCAL: *Dummies* (Schierbeek)
(1974); *O, gij, rhinoceros* (1977); *Ithaka* (Ketting, Hin) (1986)

CHAMBER MUSIC: *Intrada*, tr/hn (1958); *A Set
of Pieces*, fl, pf (1967); *A Set of Pieces*, wind
qnt (1968); *Mars*, 4 cl, 4/8 sax (1979); *Autumn*, hn, pf (1980); *Summer*, pf, fl, b-cl
(1985); *Pianotrio* (1988, rev. 1995); *Winter*,
a-fl, hp, vl, vc (1988)

LARGE ENSEMBLE: *Drie fanfares*, brass sxt
(1954); *Fanfares 1956*, 16 wind players, perc
(1956); *Divertimento festivo*, wind orch
(1960); *Intrada festiva*, 11 wind players,
perc (1960); *Time machine*, 16 wind players, perc (1972); *Monumentum*, 18/22 wind
players, pf, perc (1983); *Capriccio*, vl,
instr.ens (1987); *Preludium*, 12 sax (1989)

ORCHESTRA: *Passacaglia* (1957); *Due canzoni*
(1957); *Concertino*, 2 tpt, orch (1958); *Symphony no. 1* (1957-1959); *Pas de deux*
(1961); *Collage no. 9* (1963); *For Moonlight
Nights*, fl, orch (1973); *Symfonie voor saxofoons en orkest* (1978); *The Light of the Sun*,
S, orch (1978); *Symphony no. 3* (1990);
Summer Moon, S, orch (1992); *De overtocht* (1992); *Het oponthoud* (1993); *De
aankomst* (1993); *Kom, over de zeeën*
(1994); *Cheops*, hn, orch (1995)

PUBLICATIONS

*De ongeruste parapluie : notities over muziek
1970-1980*. The Hague, Ulysses, 1981
'Film Music: Finished one day, recorded
the next and usually forgotten the day after'.
Key Notes, 10, 1979/2, p. 20-27
'Schoenberg in Holland'. *Key Notes*, 13,
1981/1, p. 25-27
Time Machine, over en door Otto Ketting, ed.
M. Brandt and T. Hartsuiker. Amsterdam,
Donemus, 1997

BIBLIOGRAPHY

M. Brandt: 'De anti-opera Ithaka op platen',
Mens en Melodie, vol. 42, 1987, p. 12-14
E. de Cock: 'Doceren en doseren : composi-
tiedocent Otto Ketting', *Mens en Melodie*, Oct.
1997, p. 419-421
P. van Deurzen: 'Fanfares onder een doek :

analyse : Monumentum van Otto Ketting',
Mens en Melodie, vol. 48, 1993, p. 507-512
T. Hartsuiker: Sleeve notes Composer's
Voice CV 7601 (see discography)
L. Samama: 'Facetten van een symfonie als
référence : de Derde van Otto Ketting',
Entr'acte , no. 4, 1991, p. 12-16
L. Samama: 'Otto Ketting's Symphony for
saxophones and orchestra : elements of a tech-
nique', *Key Notes*, 10, 1979/2, p. 14-19
L. Samama: 'Aspects of a symphony as ref-
erence game', *Key Notes*, 26, 1992/1, p.9
E. Schönberger: 'Otto Ketting, his sym-
phonies, his film music and Dutch musical
life', *Key Notes*, 10, 1979/2, p. 10-14
L. van der Vliet: 'Programmeren is componeren : het muziekleven volgens Otto Ketting', *Mens en Melodie*, Oct. 1997, p. 414-418
E. Voermans: 'De opkomst van het Duys-
publiek', *Het Parool*, 20 March 1992

DISCOGRAPHY

Due Canzoni. Residentie Orchestra, cond.
H. Vonk (Olympia OCD 505)
Intrada. L. Leutscher (tr) (Mirasound
399113)
Intrada. R. Mase (tr) (Summit Records
DCD 148)
Intrada Festiva. Flexible Brass (World Wind
Music 500-037)
Ithaka. Various soloists, Netherlands
Opera Choir, Netherlands Philharmonic Or-
chestra, cond. L. Vis (Composers' Voice CVS
1986/4)
The light of the sun; Symphony no. 3. J.
Gomez (S), Netherlands Radio Symphony Or-
chestra, cond. K. Montgomery, Netherlands
Radio Philharmonic Orchestra, cond. O. Ket-
ting (BVHAAST CD 9105)
Mars (8 sax). Amsterdam Saxophone Quar-
tet a.o. (Sosta 35011-2)
Music for the films *Bij de beesten af, Alle-
man, Dr. Pulder zaait papavers*. Instrumental
ensemble cond. O. Ketting (BVHAAST 023)
Music for the film *De provincie* (sel.). Members of the Royal Concertgebouw Orchestra,
cond. O. Ketting (CineMusica SCCD 001)
Music for the films *Het theater van het
geheugen, De provincie, De Anna, Het archief*.
Instrumental ensemble, cond. O. Ketting, G.
Bouwhuis (pf), members of the Royal Concertgebouw Orchestra, cond. O. Ketting, A. van

Velsen (cl, t-sax), Ch. Levano (pf) (BVHAAST
CD 9504)
*De overtocht; De aankomst; Het oponthoud;
Kom, over de zeeën.* Nieuw Ensemble, cond. E.
Spanjaard, Nieuw Sinfonietta Amsterdam,
cond. L. Markiz, Orkest de Volharding, cond. J.
Hempel, Royal Concertgebouw Ochestra,
cond. R. Chailly (Composers' Voice CV 55)
Preludium. World Saxophone Orchestra,
cond. E. Bogaard (Ars Classicum/Dureco
1155502)
A Set of Pieces . A. de Quant (fl), R. Jansen
(pf) (Composers' Voice 8102)
A Set of Pieces. H. Starreveld (fl), R. Eck-
hardt (pf) (NM Classics 92068)
Song without Words. E. Pameijer (fl) (Attac-
ca Babel 9478)
Summer. Het Trio (NM Classics 92022)
Symphony no. 1. Concertgebouw Orchestra,
cond. B. Haitink (Composers' Voice CVCD
8/BFO A-5)
Symphony no. 3. Netherlands Radio Philharmonic Orchestra, cond. O. Ketting (RCA
Victor 74321/308892)
Time Machine. Bläserensemble des Inter-
nationalen Jugend-Festspieltreffen, cond. F.
van Koten (BFO 1013)
*Time Machine; A Set of Pieces (wind qnt);
For Moonlight Nights.* A. de Quant (fl), Netherlands Radio Philharmonic Orchestra, cond. O.
Ketting, Ardito Quintet (Composers' Voice CV
7601)
*Time Machine; For Moonlight Nights; Sym-
phony for Saxophones and Orchestra; Monumentum.* Rotterdam Philharmonic Orchestra,
cond. E. de Waart, A. de Quant (fl), Netherlands Radio Philharmonic Orchestra, cond. O.
Ketting, Netherlands Saxophone Quartet, Concertgebouw Orchestra, cond. B. Haitink, ensemble of the Rotterdam Conservatory, cond.
O. Ketting (Composers' Voice CV 21)

Piet Ketting

HAARLEM, 29 NOVEMBER 1904 – ROTTERDAM, 25 MAY 1984

Piet Ketting was a prolific composer who found the time to create an extensive oeuvre alongside his many activities as a teacher, organizer, journalist, chamber musician and conductor. Composing was essential to him. As a high-school student he was so often kept in after school that his father actually wanted to remove him; as it turned out, his perpetual detentions were merely a ruse by the boy himself, enabling him to go to a friend's house after school to compose. After the death of his father, the Ketting family moved to Bilthoven and Ketting received his mother's permission to pursue a career in music.

In 1926 he enrolled in the Conservatory in Utrecht, then directed by Anton Averkamp. There he took lessons in singing and choral conducting with Jan Dekker, orchestration with Evert Cornelis and, most influential on his musical development, composition with Willem Pijper.

Ketting wrote for various newspapers, the *Nieuwe Rotterdamsche Courant* and *De Telegraaf* among them. In 1930 the daily *Rotterdams Nieuwsblad* sent him to London to cover a week-long seminar on contemporary music. During this week the Wimbledon tennis tournament was being held, there was a world championship boxing match, and the Arsenal soccer team was playing a home game (Ketting himself, incidentally, made it to the third eleven of Rotterdam's Sparta soccer team). During his visit Ketting filed a series of sports columns until he finally received a telegram from his exasperated editor asking when his report on the seminar could be expected.

In 1930 he took up an appointment as an instructor of music theory, choral conducting and composition at the Rotterdam Conservatory, a position he held until 1956. From 1946 to 1949 he was also director of the Amsterdam Muzieklyceum. He subsequently conducted the Rotterdam Chamber Orchestra and Rotterdam Chamber Choir, until 1960. The Chamber Orchestra, founded by the city of Rotterdam as part of a project to help unemployed musicians, drew such large audiences that within two years it had become a formidable competitor to the Rotterdam Philharmonic Orchestra. When Ketting began conducting the symphonies of Brahms and Beethoven, he crossed into forbidden territory, in the view of Eduard Flipse, who was principal conductor of the Rotterdam Philharmonic Orchestra. Under pressure, the city dissolved the chamber orchestra.

It is said that while he was a conservatory student, Ketting would eavesdrop

on the rehearsals of the Haarlem Orchestral Society pressing his ear to an air vent half a meter above the moss-covered pavement. Aside from an earache, this practice cost him Pijper's support, who strongly objected to Ketting's passion for conducting, regarding him primarily as a composer. Their final falling out came in 1935.

That year Ketting, himself at the piano, formed a trio with flutist Johan Feltkamp and oboist Jaap Stotijn, an ensemble that toured the world for many years. Equally notable were his interpretations of the music of Bach, for example the controversial *St. Luke's Passion*, the *Art of Fugue*, the *Suites* and the *Brandenburg Concertos*.

In 1956 Henk Dieben, a Haarlem music-lover and expert on numerical symbolism, bequeathed to Ketting his Kabbalistic study of Bach's music. Although this research was never published, two Debussy biographies did find their way into print. After Ketting's death, his son Otto discovered among his things a trunk filled with notes and correspondence on Bach's works, reduced to reams of figures having mystic significance.

Like many students, Ketting sought to outdo his teacher. If Pijper composed short pieces, Ketting would write shorter ones. He was initially influenced by late Romantic music and the work of Debussy, although this changed when he studied with Pijper. The Lento from Pijper's Sonata seems to roam through Ketting's Trio sonata (1928), the connection transpiring when the work was performed in the year of his death. In the 1930s he drastically simplified his style, as evidenced by the terse Trio for flute, clarinet and bassoon. The Sonata for Flute combines strict contrapuntal style with complex polymeter and explores the technical resources of the instrument.

All of his experimentation notwithstanding, Ketting was above all concerned with the listener's perception of music, believing it unnecessary that listeners should be aware of the mechanics of a piece. In program notes to the Symphony no.1 (premiered in June 1931 in Utrecht, conducted by Evert Cornelis) Ketting included a remark rather reminiscent of a style frequently used in contemporary CD liner notes: 'the climaxes come 3, 7, 11 and 17 minutes after the beginning.' He then offered the audience a variant on Petrarch's dictum 'A joy other than learning I seek not', substituting the word 'enjoying' for 'learning'.

A characteristic comment was his remark on the *Sinfonia per violoncello e orchestra*: 'I must disappoint those who sit in wait for a cadenza played by the soloist.' In later works, perhaps owing to his increasing interest in vocal music, melody became more important and he tried to rid himself of the breathless style derived from Pijper.

Many of Ketting's compositions were commissioned: for example, *De havenstad* [The port] (to a text by Victor van Vriesland) for soloists, choir and orchestra, composed for the anniversary of the Rotterdam Student Society; and *De verheerlijkte Kokila* [The adulated Kokila] (to a text by Balthasar Verhagen) for the same forces, composed for an anniversary of an Amsterdam Student Society in 1937. This work was destroyed by fire during the bombing of Rotterdam at the beginning of World War II; however, a first version has survived.

The many pieces for a cappella choir and choir with orchestra date from the mid-1960s. He also composed a number of songs, to texts by Shakespeare and others, including the Dutch poets Vondel (1587-1679) and Nijhoff (1894-1953). He received the ANV-Visserneerlandia Prize in 1973 for the *Vier gedichten van Martinus Nijhoff* [Four Poems by Martinus Nijhoff] for mezzo-soprano and chamber orchestra.

Four piano sonatinas date from his earliest period: *Praeludium en fuga no.1* for piano and *Praeludium en fuga no.2* for two pianos. A piece with a characteristic title is the *Preludium, interludium en postludium per due pianoforti*, for which the Johan Wagenaar Foundation awarded him the Willem Pijper Prize. Three string quartets date from the period of the sonatinas. Piet Ketting further composed various trios and two concertinos, one for bassoon and the other for clarinet.

ERNST VERMEULEN

COMPOSITIONS

VOCAL: *De havenstad* (Van Vriesland), soloists, mix.choir, orch (on the occasion of the 5th anniversary of the Rotterdams Studenten Corps) (1933); *De verheerlijkte Kokila* (Verhagen), soloists, mix.choir, orch (on the occasion of the anniversary of the A.M.S.V.) (1937, rev. version lost); *Vier gedichten* (Nijhoff), Mez, chamb.orch; Choral works a cappella or with orchestra from the mid Sixties; Songs on texts by among others Shakespeare, Nijhoff, and Vondel.

INSTRUMENTAL: Four Sonatinas, pf (1926-1929); Three String Quartets (c 1926-1929); *Symphony no.1* (1929); *Praeludium en fuga no. 1*, pf (1940); *Praeludium en fuga no. 2*, 2 pf (1941); *Concertino*, bn (1968); *Preludium, interludium en postludium*, 2 pf (1971); *Concertino*, cl (1973); Works for various kinds of trios.

BIBLIOGRAPHY

H. Badings: *De hedendaagse Nederlandse muziek*, Amsterdam

G. van Barneveld: 'Muziek maakt rustig en verkwikt', *Rotterdams Nieuwsblad*, 17 Nov. 1979

W. Paap: 'De componist Piet Ketting', *Mens
en Melodie*, vol. 23, 1968

DISCOGRAPHY
*Praeludium en fuga, no. 1 and no. 2; Preludi-
um, interludium en postludium; Prelude en
fughetta.* G. Hengeveld, H. Lagendaal and J.
van der Meer (pf), K. Verheul (a-fl)) (DAVS
7475/4)
　　Three Sonnets (Shakespeare). E. Cooymans
(Mez), R. Jansen (pf) (CBS LSP 14514)
　　Trio Sonata. Het Trio (NM Classics 92022)

Tristan Keuris

AMERSFOORT, 3 OCTOBER 1946 – AMSTERDAM, 15 DECEMBER 1996

A striking characteristic of the music of Tristan Keuris is the harmonious combination of what in French is so neatly termed *l'artiste et l'artisan*, the artist and the craftsman. Keuris had a knack for couching his compositional innovations in finely wrought constructions whose highly idiomatic individual parts, largely free of unusual effects, are interwoven into very refined instrumentations. Composing, arranging and scoring are variants of the same creative process and can hardly be considered separately in Keuris' music.

Keuris studied composition with Ton de Leeuw at the Utrecht Conservatory, enrolling at the age of fifteen, having had lessons with Jan van Vlijmen in his native Amersfoort. Upon graduating in 1969 he was awarded the Prize for Composition. In 1975 he received the Matthijs Vermeulen Prize for the orchestral work *Sinfonia* and in 1982 the Culture Prize of the city of Hilversum, where he lived after 1976. Keuris became one of the Netherlands' leading and most versatile composers. His music is often performed by prominent orchestras and ensembles, both at home and abroad. Most of his works were written to commissions, from the Royal Concertgebouw Orchestra, the Houston Symphony Orchestra, the BBC, the Raschèr Saxophone Quartet, and others.

Keuris coupled his craftsmanship with an openness towards musical tradition. He made no secret of his admiration for Mahler, Webern and Stravinsky. In his vocal works, Keuris has shown that he was by no means deaf to Puccini and Verdi, although one cannot claim that he leant heavily on those illustrious predecessors. Keuris' idiom is original and recognizable. Its motivic, often athematic style of writing takes on a lyrical, even cinematic expressiveness, all incorporated into a logical and consistent musical discourse, rich in surprising turns and contrasts. Orchestral timbres are never degraded to mere decor, instead guiding the dialogue between horizontal and vertical elements.

For a long time Keuris had a predilection for seemingly traditional genres, as evidenced by such titles as *Quartet, Sonata, Concerto, Serenade, Fantasia, Divertimento*, and *Trio*, but, like Schoenberg, he breathed new life into these older forms. His attraction to the symphony and, by extension, the symphony orchestra is an example of this. The two-movement *Sinfonia* (1974) evokes associations with the past through its very title and *Movements* (1981) traces the contours of the Classical symphony through its four-movement form and tempo indications, including a scherzo and symphonic finale. *Laudi* (1993), in

an allusion to Mahler's *Lied von der Erde*, is subtitled 'A symphony'. This imitation of the Classical symphonic scoring and form reaches its peak in the four-
movement *Symphony in D* (1994-1995).

Disregarding the dozens of pieces he composed as a teenager, Keuris' oeuvre may be divided into three periods. From 1967 to 1977 he composed mostly
chamber music, strongly favoring wind instruments. The few orchestral
pieces he wrote during this period – the exceptions to the rule – offer an early
indication of what was to come. Initially, his writing in this period was characterized by a free atonal idiom, but more tonal elements gradually emerged. An
important work of this period is the *Sinfonia* for orchestra which, because it
earned him the Matthijs Vermeulen Prize and was also performed abroad,
marked his breakthrough as a composer. With a playing time of thirteen minutes and a score for comparatively large forces, the *Sinfonia* is also his most
mature work of the period. Particularly notable is the E-major theme at its
close.

Keuris entered a new phase with the *Capriccio* (1978) for wind ensemble.
While earlier works sometimes give the impression that the musical idea is
constrained by the smaller forces, his work became more balanced in this period. His gravitation towards tonal elements continued and his rhythms became simpler. Until 1988, Keuris composed exclusively instrumental music.

The number of his orchestral works grew steadily during this period and his pieces became increasingly longer, reaching a peak in the twenty-five-minute-long *Movements* (1981). In *Catena* (1988), for 31 wind instruments and percussion, Keuris forges a chain from twelve links of various lengths and musical content. The minor third from the tubular bell overtones is the cornerstone of the piling up of thirds, resulting in his characteristic seventh chord constructions.

Catena heralded the composer's final period, a phase superficially distinguished by its move away from formal titles. Of greater interest, however, is that Keuris began composing for the human voice, for example in *To Brooklyn Bridge* (1988) and *Three Michelangelo Songs* (1990). He often scored for solo voices, showing a particular preference for four- or six-part choral combinations. *L'Infinito* (1990) is dominated by an ensemble of five solo voices. Its last movement, which is essentially single-voiced, achieves depth by its steady alternation of voices, illustrating Keuris' growing tendency toward clearer and more peaceful writing. This development reaches its peak in *Laudi, Een symfonie*, in which use of the material remains at all times economical.

Laudi, to texts by Gabriele d'Annunzio, is Keuris' magnum opus. Not only is it his longest composition – forty-five-minutes in four, coherent movements – its scoring for large orchestra, two choirs and vocal soloists is of enormous proportions as well. One detail demonstrates the refinement of Keuris' composition, specifically his scoring. While both choirs and the orchestra work their way to a resounding climax, a single mezzo-soprano soars above the churning mass on a high G-sharp. This lone, fragile tone glitters like a sparkling diamond in an austere and solid crown of precious metals.

EMILE WENNEKES

COMPOSITIONS

CHAMBER AND ENSEMBLE MUSIC (SOME WITH VOICES): *Sonata*, pf (1970); *Saxophone Quartet* (1970); *Concertante muziek*, instr.ens (1973); *Muziek*, vl, cl, pf (1973); *Fantasia*, fl (1976); *Concertino*, b-cl, str.qt (1977); *Capriccio*, 12 wind instr, db (1978); *Acht miniaturen*, instr.ens (1980); *String Quartet* (1982); *Clarinet Quartet* (1983); *Piano Trio* (1984); *String Quartet no. 2* (1985); *Music for saxophones*, sax.qt (1986); *Clarinet Quintet* (1988); *To Brooklyn Bridge*, mix.choir, instr.ens (1988); *Intermezzi*, 9 wind instr (1989)

ORCHESTRA (SOME WITH VOICES): *Concerto*, a-sax, orch (1971); *Sinfonia*, orch (1974); *Serenade*, ob, orch (1976); *Concerto*, pf, orch (1980); *Movements*, orch (1981); *Violin Concerto* (1984); *Variations*, str.orch (1985); *Concerto*, sax.qt, orch (1986); *Symphonic transformations*, orch (1987); *Catena*, wind orch (1988); *Three Michelangelo Songs*, Mez, orch (1990); *Double Concerto*, 2 vc, orch (1992); *Concerto*, org, orch (1993); *Laudi, Een symfonie* (D'Annunzio), Mez, Bar, 2 mix.choir, orch (1993); *Three Preludes*, orch (1994); *Violin Concerto no. 2* (1995); *Symphony in D* (1995); *Arcade* (1996)

BIBLIOGRAPHY

R. de Beer: 'In gesprek met Tristan Keuris. Over het schrijven van muziek. Hoe componeert de componist, II', *De revisor,* June 1982, p. 30-39

R. de Beer: 'Movements by Tristan Keuris: "I must always feel: how the hell did you do that?"', *Key Notes,* 15, 1982/1, p. 1-13

M Cleij: 'Echt een man met romantische uitstraling', Programme guide to the 'Keuris orgel festival', June 1999. Hilversum [et al.], Centrum Nederlandse Muziek [et al.], 1999

P.-U. Hiu: 'Lofzang op een stalen constructie', *Entr'acte,* Febr. 1994, p. 16-19 (also included in the programme guide to the Keuris orgel festival, see above)

J. Kolsteeg: 'The sound of misty white', *Key Notes,* 29 [i.e. 28], 1994/2, p. 10-13

J. de Kruijff: 'Waardoor raakt iemand geïnspireerd? Gesprek met Tristan Keuris.', *Elsevier's Magazine,* 8 March 1986

P. Luttikhuis: 'Noten om jaloers op te zijn : Tristan Keuris : "Het seriële systeem geeft de componist te weinig vrijheid" ', *NRC Handelsblad,* 6 Jan. 1989

H. Posthuma de Boer: 'De opdracht. Tristan Keuris in gevecht met "Gods eigen accordeon" ', *Orgel Concertgebouw in ere hersteld.* Rotterdam, WYT Uitgeefgroep, 1993

A.-J. Roelofs: 'Rondom Tristan Keuris', *Opmaat,* June 1994, p. 25-28

L. Samama: 'Tegen de jaargetijden in componeren : het Klarinetkwintet en Catena van Tristan Keuris', *Preludium,* Jan. 1989, p. 8-10

L. Samama: *Zeventig jaar Nederlandse muziek : 1915-1985 : voorspel tot een nieuwe dag.* Amsterdam, Querido, 1986

E. Schönberger: 'Een mammoet op rolschaatsen', *De vrouw met de hamer & andere componisten.* Amsterdam, De Bezige Bij, 1992

E. Schönberger: 'Tonality reconsidered : Tristan Keuris : "Strive as you will after greater diversification, it all ends up sounding the same" ', *Key Notes,* 5, 1977/1, p. 18-25

H. Visser: ' "Van de mogelijkheden van het orkest raak ik lichtelijk opgewonden" ', *Stemmen uit de Nederlandse muziek van nu.* Utrecht, Joachimsthal Publishers, 1981

E. Wennekes: 'Tristan Keuris (1946-1996) : artist and craftsman', *Key Notes,* 31, 1997/1, p. 13-16

E. Wennekes: *Tristan Keuris : Kunstenaar en ambachtsman in één persoon.* Brochure Donemus, Amsterdam, 1997 (also included in the programme guide to the Keuris orgel festival, see above)

E. Wennekes: '"Nou, mijnheer, zo ellendig is dit stuk ook weer niet", Kanttekeningen bij dertig jaar Keuris-receptie', Programme guide to the 'Keuris orgel festival', June 1999. Hilversum [et al.], Centrum Nederlandse Muziek [et al.], 1999

DISCOGRAPHY

Arcade; Laudi. Netherlands Radio Philharmonic Orchestra, cond. D. Porcelijn (Emergo Classics 3933-2)

Aria. J. Zoon (fl), B. Brackman (pf) (NM Classics 92059)

Capriccio. Netherlands Wind Ensemble, cond. L. Vis (Composers' Voice CV 7804)

Catena. Members of the Rotterdam Philharmonic Orchestra, cond. E. de Waart (Teleac TEL 8905)

Catena. Stockholm Wind Symphony Orchestra, cond. D. Porcelijn (Caprice CAP21414)

Clarinet Quintet. G. Pieterson (cl), Orlando Quartet (Emergo Classics EC3955-2)

Music for Saxophones. Aurelia Saxophone Quartet (NM Classics 92053)

Music for Saxophones. The Nex Sax Project (Arsis Classics 95003)

Muziek voor viool, klarinet en piano. Eimer Trio (Dynamic CDS 60)

Oeroeg. The Alfabet of Dutch Film Music (Cinemusica SCCD 001)

Passeggiate. Amsterdam Loeki Stardust Quartet (CCS 8996)

Piano Concerto. R. Eckhardt (pf), Netherlands Radio Philharmonic Orchestra, cond. L. Vis (NM Classics 92070)

Piano Concerto; Movements. Th. Bruins (pf), Rotterdam Philharmonic Orchestra, cond. R. Dufallo, Concertgebouw Orchestra, cond. B. Haitink (Composers' Voice CV 8304)

Piano Trio; String Quartet no. 1. Mendelssohn Trio, Gaudeamus Quartet (Attacca Babel 8526-1)

Sinfonia. Royal Concertgebouw Orchestra, cond. B. Haitink (Q Disc 97014)

Sinfonia; Alto saxophone Concerto; Muziek voor viool, klarinet en piano; Concertante muziek; Fantasia. Various soloists, Rotterdam Philharmonic Orchestra, cond. E. de Waart, Nether-

lands Radio Philharmonic Orchestra, cond. D.
Masson (Composers' Voice CV 7703)

Sinfonia; Movements; Violin Concerto. Rotterdam Philharmonic Orchestra, cond. E. de
Waart, Concertgebouw Orchestra, cond. B.
Haitink, J. Berkhemer (vl), Netherlands Radio
Philharmonic Orchestra, cond. E. Howarth
(Composers' Voice CV 30)

String Quartet no 2. Raphael Quartet (Attacca Babel 8948-5)

To Brooklyn Bridge. Various soloists, Choir
for New Music, Aurelia Saxophone Quartet,
Quartet Nieuwe Muziek (Radio Nederland
Wereldomroep 1990)

Variations for Strings. Caecilia Consort,
cond. D. Porcelijn (Attacca Babel 8844-2)

Violin Concerto no. 2; Symphony in D. Y.
Toda (vl), Netherlands Radio Chamber Orchestra, cond. D. Porcelijn (Emergo Classics EC
3940-2)

Servaas de Konink

DENDERMONDE, BAPTIZED 9 OCTOBER 1654 –
AMSTERDAM, BURIED 15 JULY 1701

Servaas de Konink, the son of Petrus de Coninck and Josina Spanoghe (the spelling of his name is in keeping with convention in the Dutch Republic, differing from the Latinized and Flemish variants), began his musical education in 1663 as a choirboy under the tutelage of choirmaster Joannes van der Wielen at Saint Jacob's Church in Ghent, where he remained until 1665. Nothing is known of his movements during the ten years after he left Saint Jacob's Church and before he enrolled as a student in Leuven on 11 February 1675. It is most likely that in about 1683 De Konink moved to Brussels where he married Arnolda Hooymans. He left Brussels some time before 1688 to settle in Amsterdam, where he remained for the rest of his life.

In Amsterdam De Konink presumably led a typical musician's life, although few details are known. In any case, he was involved with the Amsterdam City Theater; he composed the music for the vocal play *De Vrijadje van Cloris en Roosje* [The courting of Cloris and Roosje], which was premiered there on 8 June 1688. This music, unfortunately, was lost when the City Theater burned to the ground in 1772. His opp.1 and 4 trios may well have served as opening and entr'acte music to the play, but this is pure speculation. Neither can the supposition be confirmed that he was a musician in the theater orchestra. The dedication to his incidental music for Racine's play *Athalie* suggests that he may have been a music teacher at the French school for girls of Lucie Quartier, a Huguenot living in Amsterdam.

In a remarkably short period, between 1696 and 1699, a series of seven collections of instrumental and vocal music by De Konink were published by the Amsterdam music publisher Estienne Roger. Their rapid succession suggests that at least some of them had already been composed by 1696. De Konink's position in Roger's catalog also suggests that he somehow assisted Roger in his publishing house. Whatever the case, these seven opuses show De Konink to have been a capable and talented composer who was well versed in a variety of styles and genres: instrumental and vocal music for the theater, the Catholic Church and for domestic use.

De Konink's instrumental music consists of the two previously mentioned collections of trios (short preludes, airs, allemandes, menuets, etc., for two descant instruments and basso continuo), the op.5 sonatas for two flutes, vio-

209

H O L L A N D S C H E
MINNE- EN DRINK-
L I E D E R E N,

Gecomponeert door Mr. SERVAAS de KONINK:

En van veele Fauten gecorrigeert door HENRICO ANDERS.

T' A M S T E R D A M,

By P I E T E R   M O R T I E R, op de Vygendam,

werd verkoft alderhande foorte van Mufique, zoo Italiaanfche, Franfche, Engelfche,
als Nederlandfche, twee derde beeter koop, als die by andere verkoft zyn geweeft,
en dan veel Correéter, beeter Druk, en Papier.

lins or oboes, and the op.6 solo sonatas for flute, oboe or violin and basso continuo. One would be justified in supposing that the last two collections are
musically identical, the second instrument in the op.5 collection being a trans-
position of the op.6 basso continuo part – a common practice around 1700.
This too, however, remains a point of speculation, as the op.5 collection has
been lost. In any case, op.5 is one of the earliest examples of sonatas for two
instruments unaccompanied by basso continuo.

De Konink's op.2 comprises the music for voice, two violins and basso continuo he composed for the final scenes of all of the acts (except the fifth and
last one) of *Athalie*, Racine's lengthy sacred drama. De Konink proves a skilled
craftsman in his use of the French language and his adaptation of the dramatic French style of Jean-Baptiste Lully.

In striking contrast to *Athalie* is De Konink's op.3, the *Hollandsche minne-
en drinkliederen* [Dutch love and drinking songs], music for one (sometimes
two) voices with basso continuo, intended for domestic performance. The
anonymous Dutch texts range from rather refined love songs to coarse and
rowdy drinking songs. According to the composer's directions it had been his
intention to include both the French and Italian styles in these pieces. To the
listener, however, it is the French style that dominates.

A stronger Italianate influence prevails in De Konink's *Sacrarum armoni-*

arum flores, 'flowers of sacred harmonies', a collection of motets to Latin texts for between one and four voices (sometimes grouped as soloists and tutti), two violins and basso continuo. These were intended for performance during the Catholic Mass and fall in the tradition of late-seventeenth-century Italian works in the genre, in particular those of the Ferrarese conductor Giovanni Battista Bassani. De Konink knew Bassani's music through reprints published in Amsterdam by Roger. A number of the texts in De Konink's settings were directly borrowed from collections of Bassani's music. De Konink dedicated the collection to the Benedictine nuns of his native Dendermonde; the abbess there was a first cousin on his mother's side. This dedication was a purely honorary tribute for the nuns, whose simple chapel had neither an organ, nor singers and choirmaster, could not possibly have performed the music.

Apart from the seven opuses, various isolated pieces by De Konink were issued in songbooks and collections published by Roger. Most are songs to French or Dutch lyrics, although there are also several cantatas to Italian texts. De Konink was a reasonably prolific composer who worked mostly in the French style. His music was composed shortly before the Dutch Republic was inundated with Italian and Italianate works in the early eighteenth century.

De Konink died in 1701, not yet 47 years old, and was buried on July 15. His son, Servaas de Konink Jr. (baptized in Brussels on 8 September 1682 and buried in Amsterdam on 13 February 1718), was also a theater musician and the two are often confused. Nothing is known of De Konink Jr.'s compositions. He did, however, edit several collections of airs (melodies without texts) under the title *Hollantsche Schouwburgh- en pluggedansen* [Dutch theater and folk dances]. Three collections were published from 1714 to 1716; later volumes were not published under his name.

RUDOLF RASCH

COMPOSITIONS

Trios pour la flûte, le violon, le hautbois et toutes sortes d'instruments ... premier oeuvre. – Amsterdam, J.L. Delorme & Estienne Roger, [1696]
30 mostly short pieces for two high instruments and bc. Probably written (as op. 4) as entr'acte music for the theatre. Partly modern ed.: Trios Opus 1 und Opus 4 (1696-1698), vol. 1-3. / ed. F. Noske. Locarno, Noetzel, 1988

Athalie, tragédie tirée de l'Écriture Sainte par Mr. Racine, avec les choeurs mis en musique. – Amsterdam, Estienne Roger, 1697

Complete text of Racine's play, the final choruses of acts 1-4 (not of act 5) with music for voice, 2 instruments and bc

Hollandsche minne- en drinkliederen. – Amsterdam, Estienne Roger, [1697]
Lost. The revised edition survived: *...'en van veele fauten gecorrigeert door Henrico Anders',* Amsterdam, Pieter Mortier, 1709
Twelve songs for voice and bc, of which two songs in dialogue form, two with 2 violins. Poet unknown. Modern ed. of two songs in Noske's article *Nederlandse liedkunst in de zeventiende eeuw* (see bibliography)

212 · Servaas de Konink

Trioos voor de fluyten, hautbois en violen ...
tweede trioos boek, vierde werk. – Amsterdam, Estienne Roger, [1698]
35 mostly short pieces. See annotation to op. 1

XII Sonates à deux flûtes, violons ou hautbois sans bass ... cinquième oeuvre. – Amsterdam, Estienne Roger, [1698]
Lost

XII Sonates à une flûte, violon ou hautbois ... sixième oeuvre. – Amsterdam, Estienne Roger, [1698]
Lost. The manuscript Wolfenbüttel, Herzog August-Bibl., Cod. Guelf. Vogel 139, is probably a copy of the print. Various sonatas have been published after this Wolfenbüttel manuscript.

Sacrarum armoniarum flores, una, 2, 3, et 4 vocibus et duobus instrumentis ... opus septimum. – Amsterdam, Estienne Roger, [1699]
The title page gives the fictitious indication 'Venetie, Giuseppe Sala'. Ten motets for 1-4 voices, 2 violins and bc

Various songs included in *Verscheide nieuwe zangen* (text Cornelis Sweerts). – Amsterdam, Cornelis Sweerts, 1697, and in *Boertige en ernstige minnezangen*. – Amsterdam, Joannes Strander, 4/1705, 5/1709

Various French airs, included in *Recueil d'airs sérieux et à boire ...* livre quatrième. – Amsterdam, Estienne Roger, 1697

Two Italian cantatas, included in *Cantate a I e II voci con tromba e flauti e sensa*. – Amsterdam, Estienne Roger, 1702

IN MANUSCRIPT:
Three suites for ensemble (dated 1700) in Wolfenbüttel, Herzog August Bibliothek

BIBLIOGRAPHY
F. Noske: 'Nederlandse liedkunst in de zeventiende eeuw : Remigius Schrijver en Servaas de Koninck', *TVNM*, 34, 1984, p. 49-67
F. Noske: *Music bridging divided religions.* Wilhelmshaven, Noetzel, 1989

F. Noske: 'Un caméléon musical : De Konink et la partition d'Athalie', *Athalie : Racine et la tragédie biblique*, ed. M. Couvreur, Brussels, Le Cri, 1992
F. Noske: 'Une partition hollandaise d'Athalie', *Mélanges d'histoire et d'esthétique musicale offerts à Paul Masson*, 1955, vol. 2, p. 103-111
R. Rasch: 'De Dendermondse componist Servaas de Koninck (1654-1701)', *Gedenkschriften van de Oudheidkundige Kring van het Land van Dendermonde*, fourth series, 10 (yearbook 1990), p. 5-35
R.Rasch: 'Servaas de Koninck et les représentations d'Athalie à Amsterdam', *Athalie : Racine et la tragédie biblique*, ed. M. Couvreur, Brussels, Le Cri, 1992

DISCOGRAPHY
Love and drinking songs of the Netherlands. Ensemble Dopo Emilio (includes the *Hollandsche minne- en drinkliederen* and some pieces from op. 1 and 4) (Emergo EC 3961-2)
Mortales sperate, op. 7, no. 6. Ensemble Bouzignac, cond. E. van Nevel (Vanguard Classics 99126)

Hans Kox

ARNHEM, 19 MAY 1930

Hans Kox has the reputation of being a reserved, even traditional composer, but this characterization is only partially accurate. Certainly, Kox is not one to seek the new for its own sake, although such trends as serialism have not passed him by unnoticed; his traditionalism finds expression in the crafts-manship he employs, regarding technique solely as a means to an expressive goal. In an article in the music journal *Key Notes*, the musicologist Bas van Putten wrote: 'Kox's beautifully manicured scores bear witness to an intense melodic talent – everything sings, even the instrumental works – and consum-mate technical refinement. His is a dynamic and restless music, with extreme contrasts between strict motion and hymnic lyricism, *ostinato* and *libera-mente*.'

Even so, Kox has thoroughly studied a wide range of contemporary tech-niques and trends in composition and put them to use in his own work. In contrast to the prevailing aesthetic conceptions of the first decades after World War II, these techniques were for him never more than a means to convey an emotional – and verbally inexpressible – message. His relaxed attitude to-wards the tools of composition shows him to be a flexible composer com-manding a domain hovering between extremes.

Like his brothers, the conductor Frits Kox and pianist Wil Kox, Hans Kox received his first music lessons from his father, who was the organist and con-ductor at the Church of Our Lady in Arnhem. From the age of nine he often deputized for his father, accompanying church services at the organ. After completing high school he began studying the piano in 1947. A year later he enrolled in the Utrecht Conservatory to study composition with Henk Ba-dings. Under the tutelage of Jaap Spaanderman, he passed the Netherlands State Examination in piano in 1951. During this period he succeeded Herman Strategier as organist at the Saint Walburgis Church in Arnhem.

In 1953, during the Gaudeamus Music Week, Kox made his debut as a com-poser, with the Trio no.1 for two violins and viola. In 1954 and 1955 he com-posed the Sonata no.1 for piano, and the String Quartet no.1; these playful compositions were praised for their astonishing formal cohesion. Kox also had success in 1954 at a composition competition that was part of the Haar-lem Organist Competition, receiving an award for his *Preludium en Fuga* [Pre-lude and Fugue]. Two years later he composed his first orchestral work, a piece

commissioned for Eduard van Beinum's twenty-fifth anniversary as a
conductor. This *Concertante muziek*
(1956) for three brass instruments
and orchestra marked the end of his
apprenticeship.

In 1957 Kox accepted an appointment as director of the Doetinchem
Music School, where he had been
teaching for some time. Under his
leadership the school became a
renowned institution that figured
strongly in the region. In 1970, resigning the post to devote himself
entirely to composition, Kox moved
to Haarlem. Until 1974 he served as
an advisor to the North Holland Philharmonic Orchestra and later, until
1984, as a staff member and teacher of composition at the Utrecht Conservatory. Among his important works of the 1980s and 1990s are the Symphony
no.3 (1985), the oratorio *Sjoah* (1989) and the opera *Das grüne Gesicht* (1991).
In the 1970s his work enjoyed great popularity, particularly abroad.

Kox has composed more than 130 pieces, covering every genre: symphonic
music, chamber music, opera, film music, oratorio, concertos and a cappella
choral music. In *Concertante muziek* (1956) for horn, trumpet, trombone and
orchestra, the influence of his teacher Henk Badings (Kox admired Badings'
craftsmanship) is still clearly audible. Classical structure and the harmonic influence of Mahler and Badings are characteristic of Kox's works during this
period; examples are the Symphony no.1 for string orchestra and the Symphony no.2 for orchestra, the Concerto for piano and orchestra and the Concerto
for violin and orchestra. Other important works of this time are the *Little Lethe
Symphony* and the *Concerto* for orchestra, which demonstrate his talent for
writing for specific ensembles or soloists. Composing for specific soloists, incidentally, has remained a constant in Kox's work, examples of which are the
pieces he has written for the saxophonist John-Edward Kelly.

Kox's music after 1963 has shown greater structural freedom. Instances of
this are provided by compositions from his series of *Cyclophonieën* (Cyclopho-
ny, 'the cycle of sound'), the first of which was written in 1964. Kox chose this
name for the pieces because, unlike the terms 'symphony' or 'sonata', it is free

of historical connotations and thus leaves room for personal interpretation of form. The *Cyclophonieën* are short pieces with a concert-like character and flexible structure. Their instrumentation varies greatly, ranging from very small (*Cyclophonie III*, for piano and tape) all the way to large orchestra (numbers II, IX and X). In May 1998 all fifteen *Cyclophonieën* were performed in Amsterdam.

Kox has not limited his experimentation to form alone. He has also composed, for example, in the 31-tone temperament of Christiaan Huygens/Fokker (*Three Pieces*, for solo violin, *Four Pieces*, for string quartet, and the *Serenade*, for two violins). Moreover, he has worked with gradually shifting timbres set in a static context (*Phobos*, for orchestra), and with graphic and proportional notation, as in *Requiem for Europe* and the opera *Dorian Gray*.

In 1969, for the twenty-fifth commemoration of the Battle of Arnhem, he composed *In those days* for choir and orchestra, for which he was awarded the Prix d'Italia in 1970. World War II is a recurrent theme in Kox's choral music and oratorios. In dramatic works such as *In those days*, *Requiem for Europe*, *Sjoah* and the *Anne Frank Cantate* he employs a style full of expressive tension. In the orchestral song cycles, such as *L'Allegria* (first-prize winner at the 1974 Rostrum of Composers) and *Gedächtnislieder*, his talent as a scenic composer comes to the forefront, as does his ability to let vocal parts grow into dramatic personages.

These qualities are also evident in the four operas composed by Kox, which are distinguished by their forceful theatrical impact and the tight unity between the music and drama. In 1975 he composed the opera *Dorian Gray*, based on the novel by Oscar Wilde. The work elicited strong criticism after its premiere that year, in particular for a perceived lack of stylistic unity. His opera *Das grüne Gesicht*, which he worked on from 1981 to 1991, has yet to be performed.

ANTHONY FIUMARA

COMPOSITIONS

VOCAL: *3 Coplas* (Werumeus Buning), Mez, pf (1955); *Chansons cruelles* (Louvier, Merz, Rilke), mix.choir (1956); *Stichtse kantate*, sp.v, mix.choir, orch (1958); *Amphion*, 2 sp.v, brass sxt, perc (1958); *Vues des anges* (Rilke), Bar, vl (1959); *Kantate van Sint Juttemis* (Gijsbers), T, Bar, m.choir, pf (1962); *3 Chinesische Lieder* (Tu Mu), Bar, pf (1962); *Zoo : een 'beestachtige' kantate* (Fop, pseud. of Stip), m.choir, orch (1964); *Litania*, w.choir, instr.ens (1965); *L'allegria* (Ungaretti), S, orch (1967); *In those days* (Livius, Erasmus, Churchill, Bible text), 2 mix.choir, orch (1969); *Puer natus est*, mix.choir, orch (1971); *Requiem for Europe* (Célan, Kox), 4 mix.choir, 2 org, orch (1971); *Gedächtnislieder* (Célan), h.v, instr.ens (1972); *De vierde kraai oftewel de kraaiende vier* (Fop, pseud. of Stip), m.choir, 2 tpt, 2 trb, perc (1972); *Dorian Gray* (opera) (Kox) (1973, rev. 1976); *Cyclophonie X* (Kox), mix.choir, str.orch (1975); *Het lied der arme klanten* (Van Eeden), m.choir, wind orch (1977); *Lord Rochester* (opera) (Elmer) (1978); *Anne Frank Cantate : a Child of Light*, S, alt, B, mix.choir, orch (1984); *Amsterdam cantate* (Kox, Dullaert, Van Langendonck, Adama van Scheltema), mix.choir, orch (1985); *Doulce mémoire ,* mix.choir (1988); *De schalmei* (Slauerhoff), mix.choir (1988); *Sjoah : oratorium* (psalm text), S, T, B, mix.choir, orch (1989); *Magnificat I en II* (Waaijman), S, A, T, Bar, B (or choir) (1990); *Das grüne Gesicht* (opera) (Kox, after Meyrink and Jacobowski, Ungaretti) (1981-1991); *Das Credo quia absurdum : cantata mystica* (Nietzsche, Rilke, Bible and Koran texts), S, B, mix.choir, orch (1995); *Cyclophonie XV* (Kuhlmann), Mez, instr.ens (1998)

CHAMBER MUSIC: *Sonata*, vl, pf (1952); *Trio no. 1*, 2 vl, vla (1952); *Sonatina*, hpd (1953); *Two Piano Pieces* (1954); *Aria*, pf (1954); *Preludium en Fuga*, org (1954); *Sonata no. 1*, pf (1954); *Sonata no. 2*, vl, pf (1954); *Trio no. 2*, 2 vl, vla (1954); *Sonata no. 2*, pf (1955); *String Quartet no. 1* (1955); *Trio no. 3a*, vl, vla, vc (1955); *Ballet diabolus feriatus*, 2 pf (1956); *Sextet*, fl, ob, vl, vla, vc, hpd (1957); *Sextet no. 2*, str.qt, hpd, pf (1957); *Sonatina miniatura*, a-rec, hpd (1957); *String Quintet*, 2 vl, 2 vla, vc (1957); *Kleine suite*, 2 tpt, trb (1958); *Drie stukken*, vl (31-t.st) (1958); *Quartet*, pf, vl, vla, vc (1959); *Sextet no. 3*, wind qnt, pf (1959); *Sonata*, vc (1959, rev. 1985); *Suite*, car (1959); *Barcarolle*, pf (1960); *Passacaglia en koraal*, 31-tone org (1960); *Sextet no. 4*, wind qnt, pf (1960); *3 etudes*, pf (1961); *Sonata no. 3*, vl, pf (1961); *Four Pieces*, str.qt (31-tone tuning) (1961); *Studies in contrapunt*, fl, hpd (1962); *Cyclophonie III*, pf, electr. sounds (1964); *4 didaktische stukken*, 2 tpt, trb (31-tone tuning) (1964); *Cyclophonie IV*, a-rec, str (1965); *Sonata no. 4*, vl, pf (1966); *Piano Quartet no. 2* (1968); *Serenade*, 2 vl (31-tone tuning) (1968); *Cyclophonie VII*, vl, pf, 6 perc (1971); *Cyclophonie VIII*, wind qnt, str (1971, rev. 1982); *Préludes*, vl (1971); *Capriccio*, 2 vl, pf (1974); *A Gothic Concerto*, hp, chamb.orch (1975); *The Jealous Guy Plays his Tune*, vl, pf (1975); *Melancholieën*, pf (1975); *Piano Trio* (1976, rev. 1991); *Suite*, 3 gui (1977); *Cyclophonie XII*, 8 vc (1979); *Sweerts de Landas-suite*, vl,

pf (1981); *Sonata*, t-sax, pf (1983); *Cyclophonie XIII*, 2 pf (1984); *Saxophone Quartet* (1985); *Sonata*, a-sax, pf (1985); *Sonata*, vc, pf (1987, rev. 1991); *Saxophone Quartet no. 2* (1987, rev. 1988); *Introduktie & allegro*, brass qt (1988); *Looks and Smiles for the Orgellas*, 2 pf 8h (1988); *The Three Chairs*, 3 sax (1989); *Four Studies*, db (1989); *Through a Glass, Darkly*, a-sax, pf (1989); *Asklepios*, wind ens (1990); *Partita*, pic-ob, wind ens (1991); *Cyclophonie XIV (The Birds of Aengus)*, vl, hp (1992); *The Stranger*, a-sax (1995); *String Quartet no. 2* (1996); *Galgentrio*, a-sax, vc, pf (1997)

ORCHESTRA: *Concertante muziek*, hn, tpt, trb, orch (1956); *Little Lethe Symphony*, orch (1956, rev. 1959); *Concerto*, fl, orch (1957); *Variatie*, 2 vl, orch (1958); *Concerto pour orchestre* (1959); *Symphony no. 1*, str.orch (1959); *Ballet spleen*, orch (1960, rev. 1994); *Concerto*, pf, orch (1962); *Concerto*, vl, orch (1963); *Concerto*, 2 vl, orch (1964); *Cyclophonie I*, vc, large ens. (1964); *Cyclophonie II*, orch (1964); *Cyclophonie V*, ob, cl, bn, str.ens (1966); *Music for Status Seekers*, orch (1966); *Symphony no. 2*, orch (1966); *Cyclophonie VI*, large ens (1967); *Concerto*, vc, orch (1969); *Concerto*, vc, 2 ob, 2 hn, str.orch (1969, new instrumentation 1981); *Phobos*, orch (1970); *Six One-Act Plays*, orch (1971); *Concerto bandistico*, school orch (1973); *Cyclophonie IX*, perc, orch (1974); *Sinfonia concertante*, vl, vc, orch (1976); *Vangoghiana*, wind orch, str.orch, perc (1977); *Concerto no. 2*, vl, orch (1978, rev. 1981); *Cyclophonie XI*, big band (1978); *Dorian Gray Suite*, orch (1979); *Concertino chitarristico*, 3 gui, orch (1981); *Irold's Youth*, orch (1983); *Notturno e danza*, pf, vl, vla, vc, str.orch (1983); *Maskerades*, school orch (1984); *Symphony no. 3*, orch (1985); *Musica reservata*, wind orch, orch (1986, rev. 1987); *Le songe du Vergier*, vc, orch (1986); *Sinfonia concertante*, 4 sax, orch (1988); *Ruach*, wind orch (1990); *Asklepios*, wind ens (1990); *Partita*, pic, ob, wind ens (1991); *Face to Face*, a-sax, str.orch (1992, rev.1993); *Concerto no. 3*, vl, orch (1993); *Orchester-Suite aus der Oper 'Das grüne Gesicht'* (1994); *Symphonie de Zampillon*, wind ens (1995); *The Waterbeggars*, wind orch (1995);

Virtual Visions, wind orch (1996); *Concerto no. 2 (An Odyssey)*, vc, orch (1997); *Das Lied des Exils*, ob, orch (1998)

BIBLIOGRAPHY
H. Adema: 'Das Credo quia absurdum',
Decorum, March 1997
W. Paap: 'De componist Hans Kox', *Mens en Melodie*, vol. 24, 1969, p. 35-42
B. van Putten: 'De wederopstanding van componist Hans Kox', *Vrij Nederland*, 2 Sept. 1995
B. van Putten: 'Hans Kox. Return to the critical mass', *Key Notes*, 29, 1995/4, p. 10-15
B. van Putten: 'Hans Kox', Brochure Donemus 1998
R. Starreveld: 'Hans Kox : Cyclophonies', *Sonorum Speculum*, no. 52, 1973
G. Werker: ' "In those days" by Hans Kox : a musical memory of the Battle of Arnhem', *Sonorum Speculum*, no. 43, 1970, p. 24-30

DISCOGRAPHY
L'Allegria; Cello Concerto; Violin Concerto no. 2; Concertino for Alto Saxophone and 10 Wind Players. Various performers (Attacca Babel 9262-1)
Cello Concerto. Q. Viersen (vc), Netherlands Radio Chamber Orchestra, cond. E. Spanjaard (NM Classics 92040)
Oratorium Shoah. K.-Y. Hee (S), N. van der Meel (T), L. Visser (B), Netherlands Radio Philharmonic Orchestra, Netherlands Radio Choir, cond. D. Porcelijn (TBI 1-93)
Spleen; Six One-Act Plays; Dorian Gray Suite; Orchester-Suite aus der Oper 'Das grüne Gesicht'. Tasmanian Symphony Orchestra, cond.D. Porcelijn (Koch Schwann)
The Three Chairs. Raschèr Saxophone Quartet (Caprice 21441)
Through a Glass, Darkly; Violin Sonata no. 4; Cello Sonata; Piano Sonata no. 2; String Quartet. Various performers (Attacca Babel 9374)
Through a Glass, Darkly. J.-E. Kelly (sax), B. Versteegh (pf) (Col Legno AU 31817)
Violin Concertos nos. 1, 2 and 3. S. Marcovici (vl), Netherlands Chamber Orchestra, cond. Ph. Entremont (Composers' Voice CV 68)
The Waterbeggars. Symphonic Band of the conservatories of Arnhem, Zwolle and Enschede, cond. D. Annema (Molenaar MBCD 31.1046.72)

Elisabeth Kuyper

AMSTERDAM, 13 SEPTEMBER 1877 – VIGANELLO, 26 FEBRUARY 1953

Elisabeth Lamina Johanna Kuyper was a socially conscious artist who throughout her life experienced discrimination against women in music. Many of her activities were undertaken in the hope of changing this situation.

Though Kuyper's family was by no means well off – her father was a civil servant – there was a piano in the home and music lessons were affordable. When Kuyper was seven, her music teacher announced there was nothing more he could teach her. At the age of twelve she enrolled in the Music School of the Society for the Advancement of Music, where she gained a professional education in music. At seventeen Kuyper was awarded a piano diploma and a grade-one teaching certificate with honors. At her final examination she performed her own Piano Sonata and *Preludium en Fuga* [Prelude and Fugue]. In 1895, when she was taking lessons in composition with Daniël de Lange, her one-act comic opera *Een vrolijke episode uit het Nederlandsche volksleven* [A merry episode from Dutch folklife] was performed in Amsterdam. Only a few arias and sketches of this work have survived.

Like many aspiring Dutch musicians, Kuyper decided to continue her education abroad. In 1896, she became the first woman to be admitted to the composition master class at the Königliche Hochschule für Musik in Berlin. Kuyper completed her studies there in 1900. She subsequently took composition lessons with Max Bruch, in whom she found the inspiring instructor she had missed at the Hochschule. The relationship with Bruch proved very significant for Kuyper. He stimulated and inspired her to compose, aided her in practical matters, and until he reached old age conducted the premieres of her work. Kuyper's lessons with Bruch proved to be productive. Among the works she composed between 1901 and 1905 are a Sonata for violin and piano, the *Ballade für Violoncello und Orchester* and the *Serenade für Orchester*.

Between June 1905 and July 1907, Kuyper received the Mendelssohn Staatsstipendium für Komposition, the first woman to be thus honored, and a stipend from the Dutch government. During this time she composed one especially large-scale piece, the Violin Concerto in B-minor, op.10, her most frequently performed work.

In 1908, in part through Bruch's intervention, Kuyper became the first woman to teach music theory and composition at the Hochschule. Six months later, she applied for and received Prussian citizenship, required for obtaining

The Berliner Tonkünstlerinnen-Orchester, with Elisabeth Kuyper as conductor.

a tenured position at the Hochschule. She did not receive it, however, until 1912. During this period she became a foreign music correspondent to the newspaper *Nieuwe Rotterdamsche Courant*.

Her career as a conductor began with the foundation of an amateur choir, with which she gave a well-received concert at the Internationale Volkskunst-Ausstellung of 1908. As women were not permitted in the ranks of the major symphony orchestras of that time, she founded in 1910 the Berliner Tonkünstlerinnen-Orchester. With this orchestra, during a concert on the theme 'Die Frau als Dirigentin', she presented the premiere of her *Festkantate* in 1912. Despite favorable reviews, the orchestra lacked the financial basis for success and it was disbanded one year later.

In 1919 Kuyper returned to the Netherlands to convalesce after undergoing a major operation. In her absence, she was dismissed from the Hochschule. The intrigues and the exertions of teaching had taken a heavy toll. She began composing again in 1920. Aside from a number of projects in which she collaborated with the novelist Frederik van Eeden, she composed the Sonata no.2 for violin and piano, and the *Symphonie*. She went to England, where the women's movement was stronger than in Germany, and founded and conducted the London Women's Symphony Orchestra. Unfortunately, this also failed because of insufficient funding. Undaunted, she went to New York in 1924 and founded The American Women's Symphony Orchestra. This project also ended in bankruptcy.

Disillusioned, Kuyper traveled to Switzerland in late 1925. In four years' time she had founded women's orchestras in three countries. Despite the enthusiasm with which these initiatives were met, financial backing for a professional women's orchestra proved everywhere unattainable.

Until 1939 she lived alternately in Switzerland and Berlin, composing, arranging and publishing works in a lighter genre, such as *Dreams on the Hudson Waltz* and *American Lovesong*. Later, she wrote mostly vocal works.

At the outbreak of World War II, and owing to her poor health, Kuyper moved to the Swiss city of Muzzano. Unable to reach an agreement with the Hochschule in Berlin on her pension, she lived in poverty. Her situation improved after 1947 when she found occasional employment with the Southern Swiss Radio as an assistant conductor.

Kuyper's music reflects the developments made in composition from 1880 to 1920, ranging from simple and functional tonal pieces to ones containing daring modulations, and an often virtuosic and strikingly dissonant character. While her body of compositions does not embrace such extreme contrasts as that of, for example, Arnold Schoenberg, she was definitely influenced by Richard Strauss, especially in the *Sechs Lieder für eine Singstimme und Klavier*, op.17, one of her best works.

Kuyper's style began to emerge as early as the Violin Sonata no.1 in A-major; her lyrical music builds on the sonatas of Mendelssohn, Schumann and Brahms, while adding many more modulations. Such harmonic volatility, also characteristic of Bruch, was considered a flaw by her early critics. The lyricism of the Violin Sonata is also evident in the orchestral work *Serenade*. Its atmosphere corresponds to Dvořák's and Tchaikovsky's works in this genre while its orchestration resembles the serenades of Brahms and Max Reger. The style is influenced by Baroque music as well as the modal melodies of folk music.

These influences are underscored by two other pieces for orchestra, the *Ballade für Violoncello und Orchester* and the Violin Concerto. The first is of a lighter sort and has something of the 'alla Zingarese' that was so popular in Central Europe around 1900. Unlike the lyrical virtuosity of the Violin Concerto, the themes used in the *Ballade* are lacking in variety. While the influence of Bruch and Dvořák is perceptible, Kuyper's personal style is still evident. The Piano Trio in D-major, op.13, is widely considered one of her best works. Though the influence of others is no less evident, its tone seems more authentic.

In 1953 Kuyper died in Viganello, asphyxiated in her home by a defective oil heater. By then, she had already been forgotten. That she never received the recognition she deserved in the Netherlands is probably because she worked abroad. Recently, several German publications have revived interest in her.

WILLEM JETHS

COMPOSITIONS

VOCAL: *Een vrolijke episode uit het Nederlandsche volksleven* (opera) (c 1895) (partly survived); *Festkantate*, soloists, w.choir, sp.v, orch (1912); *Eudoxia's zang*, S, org/pf (1921); *Sechs Lieder*, v, pf (1922); *Hymne an die Arbeit*, w.choir, S, orch or m.choir, T/S, orch (1922); *Ewig jung ist nur die Sonne*, m.choir (1941); *American Lovesong*, S/T, pf (c 1944)

PIANO: *Preludium en Fuga* (before 1895); *Piano Sonata* (before 1895); *Serenata Ticinese* (1928)

CHAMBER MUSIC: *Sonata*, vl, pf (1901); *Trio*, vl, vc, pf (1910); *Sonata no. 2*, vl, pf (1920-1925)

MUSIC FOR THE THEATRE: *Beati Pacifici* (c 1920) (lost); *De Broederveete* (c 1920) (lost)

ORCHESTRA: *Ballade*, vc, orch (1903); *Ouverture Willem van Oranje*, orch (before 1905) (lost); *Serenade für Orchester in fünf Sätzen* (1905, arr. for pf 4h, c 1905-1911); *Symphonie* (c 1920-1925) (lost); *Das Lied [von] der Seele*, 7 v, orch (with dance) (1923); *Dreams on the Hudson Waltz* (1925, arr. for pf, c 1928) (orig. version lost)

PUBLICATIONS
'Mein Frauenorchester'. *Allgemeine Musikzeitung*, Dec. 1919, p. 732
M. Seiffert: *Wat leeren ons de schilderijen en prenten der zestiende eeuw over de instrumentale begeleiding van de zang en den oorsprong van de muziekgravure* (transl. E. Kuyper). Amsterdam, 1925
Mein Lebensweg. Führende Frauen Europas, vol. 1. München, 1928

BIBLIOGRAPHY
W. Jeths and Ph. Lelieveldt: 'Elisabeth Kuyper', *Zes vrouwelijke componisten*, ed. H. Metzelaar [et al.]. Hilversum, Centrum Nederlandse Muziek / Zutphen, Walburg Press, 1991

S. Winterfeld: 'Elisabeth Kuyper, eine Holländische Dirigentin und Komponistin in Berlin', *Komponistinnen in Berlin : 750 Jahre Berlin*, 1987, p. 220-242

DISCOGRAPHY
Der Pfeil und das Lied; Marienlied; Ich komme heim aus dem Sonnenland; Zwischen dir und mir; Herzendiebchen (from op. 17) I. Maessen (S), R. A. Morgan (Mez), F. van Ruth (pf) (NM Classics 92018)

Daniël de Lange

ROTTERDAM, 11 JUNE 1841 – POINT LOMA, 31 JANUARY 1918

At the age of eleven Daniël de Lange, the son of a Rotterdam organist/carillon-neur, composed and conducted a piece for choir and soloists based on Psalm 137. His father taught him to play the piano and organ and he took cello lessons from Simon Ganz. He studied harmony and composition with Johannes Verhulst and Johannes Franciscus Dupont at the Rotterdam Music School. At fourteen he enrolled in the Brussels Conservatory, where Bernard Damcke was one of his teachers.

In 1858 De Lange went to Vienna with his elder brother, the pianist Samuel de Lange (1840-1911), and together they formed a cello-piano duo that made various concert tours to Poland and the Balkans. From 1860 to 1863 the two brothers taught at the conservatory of Lemberg (now Lvóv) in Poland. Upon returning to the Netherlands, De Lange was appointed successor to his late cello teacher Simon Ganz at the Rotterdam Music School but, discontented with this institute, left for Paris in 1865. There he became acquainted with Berlioz, Massenet, Lalo and Bizet. In Paris, he earned his living as organist to the Protestant Congregation, as a choral director, and by giving private lessons in composition, one of his pupils being Ernest Chausson.

De Lange was on vacation in Rotterdam when the Franco-Prussian War broke out in 1870. He decided to remain in Holland, accepting a teaching position at the Music School of the Society for the Advancement of Music in Amsterdam; he also founded a chapter of this Society in Leiden. His influence on music in the Netherlands reached a peak when he became secretary of the Society for the Advancement of Music in 1878. In this position, which he held until 1908, he focused in particular on improving Dutch musical education.

In 1884 he co-founded the Amsterdam Conservatory with Julius Röntgen, Frans Coenen and Johan Messchaert. The very fact that this institute was named 'conservatory' made its founding an important event, for at that time even the royal musical training center in The Hague had the status of a 'music school'. De Lange was director of the Amsterdam Conservatory from 1894 until 1912, when he was succeeded by Röntgen. In 1913 he moved with his second wife to Point Loma, California, a Mecca for theosophists, where he died in 1918.

De Lange undertook pioneering work as a choral conductor. Together with such leading Dutch singers as the baritone Johan Messchaert, the soprano Aaltje Noordewier-Reddingius and the tenor Johan Rogmans, he founded the Amsterdam A-Cappella Choir in 1881. This ensemble specialized in early Netherlands polyphony. In its first year it gave the first Dutch performance of Palestrina's *Missa Papae Marcelli*. The choir gained international acclaim with a performance at the International Music Exhibition in Vienna. De Lange dissolved the ensemble when he became director of the Amsterdam Conservatory in 1894, but the tradition it set in motion was continued by his former student Anton Averkamp. After a performance of Palestrina's *Stabat Mater* given by Averkamp's choir in 1893, the composer Alphons Diepenbrock wrote: 'It seems to me that this choir lacks the sophistication and casual elegance of De Lange's ensemble.'

De Lange also introduced many of the new works of his contemporaries to Dutch audiences. In 1882 he gave the first Dutch performance of the opera *La Damnation de Faust* by Hector Berlioz. His extensive experience as a musician abroad had given him what by Dutch standards was a broad view on musical developments in Europe.

De Lange did not compose a large body of works. 'He was not primarily driven by a compulsion to create', wrote the composer and music critic Sem Dresden, 'or then again, perhaps he wanted or needed to suppress this urge.' He composed symphonies, choral and piano works, chamber music, songs and several orchestral songs, to texts by Frederik van Eeden and Albert Verwey, poets belonging to De Tachtigers [The eighties group], the major literary movement of the time. De Lange dedicated his opus 1 to his former teacher Johannes Verhulst, with whom he maintained a warm friendship until the latter's death in 1891. Their views on music, however, grew increasingly apart as De Lange's music gravitated more and more towards Berlioz, Liszt and Wagner, composers Verhulst abhorred.

De Lange developed a style in which daring harmonies were employed alongside principles borrowed from early music, such as the double choir writing of Giovanni Gabrieli. In Paris he composed longer works, such as the Requiem, the *Symphonie en ut mineur*, op.4, dedicated 'à mon ami Edouard Lalo' and theater music for the entr'actes in Victor Hugo's *Hernani*.

For many years the Requiem lay untouched in the archives of the Gemeentemuseum in The Hague until it was discovered in 1972 by Willem Noske, a violinist and renowned researcher of Dutch music. Nevertheless, the manuscript was not prepared for performance nor was it published until 1992. The Requiem shows the influence of Renaissance polyphony combined with the chromaticism of De Lange's time. With two four-part choirs and two four-part soloist ensembles, the scoring resembles that of sixteenth- and seventeenth-century choral music. The Requiem was performed in 1993 by the Netherlands Chamber Choir and was very well received. The premiere was held in Paris, the city where De Lange composed the piece in 1868 and where he had received his most important musical impulses.

JOHAN KOLSTEEG/HUIB RAMAER

COMPOSITIONS

VOCAL: *Requiem*, 8-part mix.choir (1868); *Vor einzer Genziane*, v, pf, op. 7; *Lieder und Gesänge*, v, pf, op. 10; *De Roze* (Verwey), op. 12 (1885?); *Twee liederen* (Ritschl), v, pf; *Vijf liederen* (A. Roland Holst, Swarth, Kloos, Gutteling), v, pf; *Zes liedjes* (Lovendaal, Heije, Antheunis), v, pf; *Scene aus Hamerling's Venus im Exil*, v, pf; *Two Songs* (Hooft), v, vl, vladg/vc, hpd/pf; *De val van Kuilenburg* (opera); *Thränen* (Von Chamisso), v, pf; *Vijf gedichten van Jacques Perk*, v, pf

INSTRUMENTAL: *Varations et allegro fugué*, pf, op. 1; *Pièces*, pf, op. 2; Two symphonies; Entr'acte music for *Hernani*; *Vierstemmig koraalboek*, org/pf

DISCOGRAPHY

Requiem. Netherlands Chamber Choir, cond. U. Gronostay (NM Classics 92039)

Ton de Leeuw

ROTTERDAM, 16 NOVEMBER 1926 – PARIS, 31 MAY 1996

Ton de Leeuw is widely considered one of the most important Dutch composers since 1945. His individual interpretation of musical developments makes him a fascinating and exceptional personality.

De Leeuw, the son of musical parents, was raised in Breda and took private lessons during the war with Louis Toebosch, Everhard van Beynum and Henri Geraedts. In 1946 he passed the Netherlands State Examination in piano, music theory and music history. While studying with Henk Badings he composed *Treurmuziek in memoriam Willem Pijper* [Funeral music in memory of Willem Pijper] as a tribute to this composer, who died in 1947 and whom he took as a model. From 1949 to 1950 he studied in Paris with Olivier Messiaen and Theodore de Hartmann. It was there that he came to know the music of Webern. His work of this period, however, such as the Sonata for two pianos, still shows the influence of Hindemith in its motoric rhythms.

De Leeuw's interest in Webern and serialism was heightened by a visit to Darmstadt in 1953. By then, he had also become fascinated with non-Western music, with which he became acquainted while studying at the University of Amsterdam with the ethno-musicologist Jaap Kunst, a leading expert on Javanese gamelan music. De Leeuw's first pieces to explore non-Western elements are *Vier ritmische etudes* [Four rhythmic etudes] and *Drie Afrikaanse etudes* [Three African etudes].

In a musical and philosophical sense, the East became for De Leeuw a focal point and inexhaustible source of inspiration. His String Quartet no.1 (awarded the Prix des Jeunesses Musicales in 1958) is inspired by serial principles but refers in particular to Japanese music, which is characterized by a sobriety similar to that of Webern. Together with *Mouvements rétrogrades*, the String Quartet no.1 marks the beginning of a new phase in his development.

In 1961 de Leeuw was sent by the Dutch government to India to study the classical music of this country. Later, often under the aegis of UNESCO, he traveled extensively – for example to Japan, Indonesia, Hong Kong, Iran, and the Soviet Union – to lecture and give workshops on the relationship between Eastern and Western music. De Leeuw taught composition and electronic music at the Amsterdam (later Sweelinck) Conservatory from 1959 to 1986, and was its director from 1971 to 1973. His students included such widely differing composers as Jacques Bank, Bernard van Beurden, Margriet Hoenderdos, Guus Janssen, Tristan Keuris, Jos Kunst, Alex Manassen, Daan Manneke, Chiel Meijering, Wim de Ruiter, Joep Straesser, Paul Termos, Jan Vriend, and Sinta Wullur.

De Leeuw's experiences with Eastern classical music, which often springs from ethical and religious ideals, led him to voice well-founded criticism of the policies of Dutch orchestras and broadcasters. In 1967 he proposed the founding of a 'mobile ensemble' for modern music. The 'De Leeuw Plan', dating from 1968, in which he urged that a classical music radio station be established in the Netherlands, ultimately led to the founding of Radio 4.

In 1974, at the Queekhoven villa in Breukelen, De Leeuw organized a Musicultura seminar dedicated to East Asia. In his keynote speech to the gathering he proposed that the concepts of archetypes and the collective subconscious provide a common point of reference that might be tapped to reach mutual understanding between cultures. This Musicultura initiative grew into the biennial International Composers Workshop which, until his death, De Leeuw led with Dimiter Christoff. In 1986 De Leeuw moved to Paris.

Mouvements rétrogrades (1957) for orchestra was the first high point of De Leeuw's oeuvre. In an introduction to the piece, he quoted Jaap Kunst: 'Western music is filled with action and tension. Javanese music, in contrast, can best be described as time conveyed in music.' While *Mouvements rétrogrades* does not directly borrow from Javanese music in stylistic terms, it does show a similarity on a more abstract level, i.e. a cyclical element derived from repeating, rhythmic retrograde patterns. This cyclical element, in a variety of forms, is what binds De Leeuw's oeuvre. Its intellectual motivation lies in the search for balance, rather than dramatic contrast.

Symphonies of Winds directly reflects De Leeuw's experiences in India. It begins with an *alap*-like introduction (*alap* is a slow improvisatory prelude introducing the mood of an Indian composition/improvisation), a device he also used in the opening of many later works. With a quotation from Stravinsky's *Symphonies of Wind Instruments* De Leeuw expresses his great admiration for this 'first, great anti-Romantic'. Among other works that draw from his experiences in India are *Ombres* and *Nritta*.

In subsequent works the influence of Japanese culture dominated. In haiku-derived *Men go their ways* for solo piano, De Leeuw requires that the pianist approach the piece in a manner clearly derived from the Zen tradition: receptiveness, concentration on the moment, and the avoidance of explicit purpose.

The high point of this period is a work for soprano and orchestra, *Haiku II*, in which the soprano sings from various positions in the hall. Here, and in *Spatial Music I-IV*, De Leeuw gives an entirely personal interpretation to the con-

cept of spatial music that in its effect strongly differs from that of Stockhausen and Xenakis. *Lamento Pacis*, for choir and instrumental groups, also reflects De Leeuw's Japanese experiences. The second movement is dedicated to Zeami, one of the founders of Noh theater, and the character of the flute is related to No-kan.

Modality became increasingly important in the 1970s, as the titles *Mo-do*, a piece for harpsichord, and *Modal Music* indicate. In *Gending, a Western Homage to the Musicians of the Gamelan*, scored for the traditional Javanese gamelan, modality is already intrinsic to the instruments used. But there are also other elements derived from Javanese music: structural, in the way cyclical patterns unfold over larger time spans, and conceptual, in the conscious striving for non-dramatic music. De Leeuw specifically cited the northern Indian *dhrupad* style as the inspirational source of *Mountains*, for bass clarinet and tape. Without degenerating into imitation or exoticism, this influence is also recognizable in the recurrent bourdon.

De Leeuw was not only interested in the technical resources of modality – he even introduced a new concept: extended modality – but even more so in ethical factors traditionally connected with the concept of modality. An important work in his extended modality style is the trilogy *Car nos vignes sont en fleur*, *And They Shall Reign Forever* and *Invocations*. It was his desire to link with the great traditions of East and West that prompted him to use Biblical texts.

In his essay *Terug naar de bron* [Back to the source] De Leeuw exhaustively explains the backgrounds of his aesthetics and describes his pitch-duration model, a technique in which a modal set of tones is filtered through a temporal grid so that only a few tones are sounded at each repetition of the model. Unity manifests itself as plurality and vice versa. This technique reached full maturity in *Résonances*, an orchestral piece composed for the centennial of the Concertgebouw Orchestra.

In the 1980s De Leeuw wrote a number of pieces for a cappella choir or choir with instrumental accompaniment, a notable example being *Cinq hymnes* for mixed choir, two pianos and two percussionists. His renewed interest in vocal music culminated in the music drama *Antigone*, performed at the 1993 Holland Festival.

Shortly after his death, De Leeuw's *Three Shakespeare Songs* (1995), entitled *Nightmusic, No longer mourn* and *But time decays,* were premiered during the Holland Festival in Amsterdam's Concertgebouw. This work was commissioned by the Fund for the Creation of Music for the Holland Festival and Ensemble InterContemporaine. In 1996 De Leeuw was posthumously awarded the Matthijs Vermeulen Prize for the *Three Shakespeare Songs*.

JURRIEN SLIGTER

COMPOSITIONS

VOCAL: *Berceuse presque nègre* (Van Ostaijen), m.v, pf (1948); *Diablerie* (Engelman), S, pf (1948); *Goden en zangers* (A. Roland Holst), S, pf (1948); *Die Weise von Liebe und Tod* (Rilke), v, pf (1948); *De ueren van de bittere passie Jesu Christi*, l.v, pf (1949); *Vijf liederen op teksten van Lorca*, l.v (1950-1952); *Twee liederen op teksten van Gabriela Mistral*, S, pf (1953); *Missa brevis*, mix.choir (1953); *Vier koorliederen* (medieval text) (1954); *Prière* (Koran text), GK (1954); *De toverfluit* (Aafjes), S, fl, vc, pf (1954); *Acht Europese liederen*, m.v, pf (1954); *Vier liederen* (medieval text), v, 3 rec (1955); *Brabant* (Lau-

rey), Mez, orch (1959); *Haiku I*, S, pf (1963); *Psalm 118*, 3-part choir , 2 trb/org (1966); *Haiku II*, S, orch (1968); *Vocalise*, v (1968); *Lamento Pacis I, II, III* (Erasmus), mix.choir, instr.ens (1969); *Cloudy Forms* (Shi-T'ao), m.choir (1970); *The Magic of Music*, 2-part choir (1970); *The Birth of Music I* (text Indian myth), mix.choir (1975); *And They Shall Reign for Ever* (text Apocalyps), Mez, cl, hn, pf, perc (1981); *Car nos vignes sont en fleur* (text Song of Songs), mix.choir (1981); *Invocations*, choir, Mez, instr.ens (1983); *Chimères* (De Nerval), 2 Ct, T, 2 Bar, B (1984); *Les chants de Kabir*, 6 v (1985); *Transparence*, mix.choir, 3 tpt, 3 trb

(1986); *Cinq hymnes*, choir, 2 pf, perc
(1987-1988); *Natasja*, v (1990); *Three
Shakespeare Songs*, Mez, instr.ens (1994-
1995)

CHAMBER MUSIC: *Scherzo*, pf (1948); *Trio*, vl,
vla, vc (1948); *Introduzione e passacaglia*,
org (1949); *Sonatina*, pf (1949); *Sonata, fl,
pf* (1949); *String Quartet* (1949); *Sonata, 2
pf* (1950); *Four Preludes*, pf (1950); *Variations sur une chanson populaire française*,
pf/hpd (1950); *Cinq etudes*, pf (1951);
Sonata, vl, pf (1951); *Vier ritmische etudes*, pf
(1952); *Trio*, fl, cl, pf (1952); *Vijf schetsen*, ob,
cl, bn, vl, vla, vc (1952); *Danse lente*, pf
(1953); *Pastorale*, pf (1954); *Drie Afrikaanse
etudes*, pf (1954); *Lydische suite*, pf (1954);
Zes dansen, pf (1955); *Andante en vivace*, fl,
pf (1955); *Sonatina*, vl, pf (1955); *String
Quartet no. 1* (1957-1958); *Vioolstuk*, vl, pf
(1959); *String Quartet no. 2* (1964); *Schelp*,
fl, vla, gui (1964); *The Four Seasons*, hp
(1964); *Men go their ways*, pf (1964); *Night
Music*, fl (1966); *Music for violin* (1967); *The
Nine Rasas*, pf (1968); *Music for Oboe*
(1969); *Reversed Night*, fl (1971); *Spatial
Music II*, 4-9 perc, electr. (1971); *Midare*,
mar (1972); *Sweelinck-variaties*, org (1972-
1973); *Music for Trombone* (1973-1974); *Canzone*, 4 hn, 3 tpt, 3 trb (1973-1974); *Mo-do*,
hpd/el.clavichord (1974); *Rime*, fl, hp
(1974); *Linkerhand en rechterhand*, pf
(1976); *Modal Music*, acc (1978-1979); *Interlude*, gui (1984); *Apparences I*, vc (1987);
Apparences II, 4 cl (1987); *Les adieux*, pf
(1988); *Hommage à Henri*, cl, pf (1989);
Trio, fl, b-cl, pf (1990)

ORCHESTRA: *Concerto grosso*, str.orch; *Treurmuziek in memoriam Willem Pijper*, orch
(1948); *Symphonie*, str, perc (1950); *Symphonie voor strijkers* (1951); *Plutos-suite*, orch
(1952); *Suite*, youth orch (1954); *Mouvements rétrogrades*, orch (1957); *Nritta*, orch
(1961); *Ombres*, orch (1961); *Symphonies of
Winds* (1963); *De bijen*, orch (1964); *Syntaxis II*, orch (1966); *Spatial Music I*, un-
limited number of any instr. (1966); *Spatial Music III*, orch, tape (1967); *Spatial
Music IV*, 12 instr (1968); *Music for Strings*,
12 str (1970); *Gending : a Western Homage
to the Musicians of the Gamelan*, gamelan

(1975); *Alba*, chamb.orch (1982); *Résonances*, orch (1984-1985)

CONCERTOS: *Piano Concerto* (1948-1949); *Violin Concerto* (1953); *Violin Concerto no. 2*
(1961); *Music for Organ and 12 Players*
(1970-1971); *Concerto*, 2 gui, 12 str (1987-
1988); *Danses sacrées*, pf, chamb.orch
(1990)

OPERA: *Alceste* (television opera) (1962); *De
droom* (1963), *Antigone* (1991)

COMPOSITIONS WITH ELECTRONICS: *Job*
(1956); *Elektronische studie* (1957); *Anti-
phonie* (1977); *Syntaxis I* (1965-1966);
Mountains (1977); *The Magic of Music II*
(1977); *The Birth of Music II* (1978);
Chronos (1980); *Clair obscur* (1981-1982)

MUSIC FOR THE THEATRE: *Medeia* (Euripides), ob, v (1956); *Le bourgois gentilhomme*
(Molière) (1956); *De Trojaanse vrouwen*
(1957); *Wozzeck* (Büchner), electr. (1959);
J.B., electr. (1959); *Het spel van Adam*,
soloists, choir, orch (1960)

MUSIC FOR TELEVISION: *Alceste* (see above);
Krishna en Radha (television ballet), fl, hp,
perc (1964); *Litany of Our Time* (television
play), S, instr.ens, choir, tape, live electr.
(1969-1970)

MUSIC FOR RADIO DOCUMENTARIES AND
PLAYS: *Plutos*, orch, v (1951); *De laatste
dagen van Pompei*, orch (1955); *De stem van
de jeugd*, choir, orch (1955); *Het stenen hart*,
orch (1959); *Signalement van het ik*, vla, vc
(1962); *Helpers bij de drempel*, vla, vc (1962)

PUBLICATIONS

*Muziek van de twintigste eeuw : een onder-
zoek naar haar elementen en structuur*. Utrecht,
Oosthoek, 1964; Utrecht, Bohn, Scheltema,
1977 (3rd ed.)

Ton de Leeuw, ed. J. Sligter. Hilversum,
Centrum Nederlandse Muziek / Zutphen, Walburg Press, 1992. Includes articles by the composer previously published in various periodicals: *Mensen en muziek in India; Reisherin-
neringen uit Japan; Muziek in oost en west : een
sociaal probleem; Interactie van culturen in de*

hedendaagse muziek; Vragen, ideeën en verwachtingen; Terug naar de bron 'We live atop a volcano', *Key Notes*, 30, 1996/1, p. 4-7
Various articles in Dutch and international publications

BIBLIOGRAPHY

L. Domenick: 'Mode and movement in recent works of Ton de Leeuw', *Key Notes*, 17, 1983/1, p. 15-23
R. de Groot: 'Aspects of Ton de Leeuw's musical universe', *Key Notes*, 23, 1986, p. 17-31
R. de Groot: 'A wave chosen from the sea', *Key Notes*, 23, 1986, p. 10
R. de Groot: *Compositie en intentie van Ton de Leeuws muziek : van een evolutionair naar een cyclisch paradigma.* Doctoral dissertation University of Amsterdam, 1991
R. de Groot: 'The inspiration of Ton de Leeuw : Aspects of a life of listening', *Key Notes*, 30, 1996/3, p.4-7
W. Markus: 'Music and time : observations on Arnold Schoenberg and Ton de Leeuw', *Key Notes*, 23, 1986, p. 14-16
J. Kolsteeg: 'Antigone according to De Leeuw & De Leeuw', *Key Notes* 28, 1994/1, p. 4
B. Robindoré: 'Where there is no vision, the people perish', *Key Notes* 28, 1994/1, p. 20
L. Samama: *Ton de Leeuw : Terug naar de bron.* Brochure Donemus, Amsterdam, 1993
L. Samama: *Zeventig jaar Nederlandse muziek : 1915-1985 : voorspel tot een nieuwe dag.* Amsterdam, Querido, 1986
Ton de Leeuw, ed. J. Sligter. Hilversum, Centrum Nederlandse Muziek / Zutphen, Walburg Press, 1992
J. Wouters: 'Ton de Leeuw (1926)', *Nederlandse componistengalerij : negen portretten van Nederlandse componisten, vol. 1.* Amsterdam, Donemus, 1971
Various articles in Dutch and international publications

DISCOGRAPHY

Les adieux. P. de Haas (pf) (Clavicenter PDH 250902)
Antigone. M. Mahé (Mez), Netherlands Radio Chamber Orchestra, members of the Netherlands Radio Choir, cond. R. de Leeuw (NM Classics 92036)
Apparences II. Netherlands Clarinet Quar-

tet (CD 89-101)
Chamber Music. Het Trio, S. Douwes (cl), J. Gruithuyzen (pf) (NM Classics 92020)
Cinq hymnes. Netherlands Chamber Choir, G. Hommerson (pf), P. Prenen (pf), H. Halewijn (perc), G. de Zeeuw (perc), cond. R. de Leeuw (NM Classics 92025)
Cinq hymnes. Netherlands Student Chamber Choir, H. Adolfsen (pf), D. Bol (pf), D. de Graaf (perc), R. Kornet (perc) (WVH 158)
Danses sacrées. D. Kuyken (pf), Netherlands Radio Chamber Ochestra, cond. E. Spanjaard (NM Classics 92044)
Gending. Ensemble Gending, cond. J. Sligter (NM Classics 92062)
Interlude. W. Hoogewerf (gui) (Composers' Voice CVCD 8701)
Men Go Their Ways. I. Janssen (pf) (NM Classics 92028)
Modal Music. M. Dekkers (acc) (NM Classics 92013)
Mouvements rétrogrades. Concertgebouw Orchestra, cond. G. Szell (BFO A-7)
Mouvements rétrogrades. Residentie Orchestra, cond. E. Bour (Olympia OCD 505)
Night Music. H. Starreveld (fl) (NM Classics 92068)
Ombres. Royal Concertgebouw Orchestra, cond. B. Haitink (Q Disc 97014)
Prière. Netherlands Chamber Choir, cond. U. Gronostay (NM Classics 92065)
Sweelinck Variations. L. van der Vliet (org) (Composers' Voice CVCD 16)
Symphonies of Winds; Haiku II; Résonances. Rotterdam Philharmonic Orchestra, cond. E. de Waart; E. Vink (S), Residentie Orchestra, cond. E. Spanjaard (Composers' Voice CVCD 23)
Symphonies of winds. Rotterdam Philharmonic Orchestra, cond. E. de waart (Teleac TEL 8905)
Trouvaille; Tu m'as. J. Vindevogel (S), L. Kende (pf) (Vox Temporis Productions VTP CD 92 011)

Henk van Lijnschooten

THE HAGUE, 28 MARCH 1928

Hendricus Cornelis van Lijnschooten was one of the first youngsters to complete the general musical training course given by the well-known music pedagogue Willem Gehrels at the Public Music School in The Hague. As a child, he took lessons on the violin and clarinet at this school and at eight began playing the clarinet in the local concert band. At twelve, Van Lijnschooten began taking lessons with the composer Frits Koeberg, who for a lengthy period trained him in music theory and the basic principles of conducting, as well as encouraging him to compose. In 1946 Van Lijnschooten became a clarinettist and violinist with the Royal Military Band, which was conducted by Rocus van Yperen. He also studied conducting with Van Yperen and composition with Hendrik Andriessen at the Royal Conservatory in The Hague.

It was during this period that he began conducting amateur bands, among them the Forum Hadriani Youth Band, one of the first of its kind in the Netherlands. In 1956, one year after receiving his diploma in band conducting and clarinet, he succeeded Gijsbert Nieuwland as Captain Conductor of the Marine Band. Van Lijnschooten remained at this post until 1964, and subsequently dedicated his time to composition and teaching band conducting at the conservatories in Rotterdam, Utrecht and Arnhem. He also held various positions in the field of wind music.

From the 1970s Van Lijnschooten's activities spread to foreign countries. He often served as a jury member, gave courses and conducted in most European countries, the United States, Canada, Russia and Japan. In recent years he has been particularly active in international organizations, laying the groundwork, for example, for the establishment of the World Association for Symphonic Bands and Ensembles (WASBE). After 1970 he also published works under the pseudonyms Ted Huggens and Michel van Delft, giving him the freedom to compose in an unpretentious, entertaining style.

Van Lijnschooten has not only been instrumental in establishing specialized courses for band conducting at Dutch conservatories, he has also played a central role in developing group instruction for wind instruments, an initiative he developed in the 1960s with Hans Lussenburg at the Rotterdam Music School.

Van Lijnschooten is the recipient of various awards and distinctions; in 1985 he was made a Knight in the Order of Orange-Nassau, in 1986 he was

awarded the Netherlands Wind
Music Prize for his accomplishments in this field, and in 1994 he
received a commendation for his
many accomplishments in the advancement of amateur wind playing.

Most of Van Lijnschooten's compositions are in keeping with the didactic
goals he set. From his first experiences with conducting, in 1950, he
was aware that there was a lack of
repertoire suitable for amateur musicians – music geared toward their
level of understanding and at the
same time calculated to improve
their proficiency. To fill this void, Van
Lijnschooten initially made arrangements of other music, merely be-
cause this was more or less expected of him when he began conducting the
Marine Band in recordings for Phonogram. But he gradually came to focus
more on composing. For most of his earlier compositions, he found in – mostly Dutch – folk-song material the ideal vehicle for presenting his musical
ideas. His love of this music, stimulated by the Gehrels method, led to such
compositions as *Rapsodie over zeemansliedjes* [Rhapsody on Sailors' Songs] and
the *Nederlandse Suite*, written for the Marine Band.

Most of Van Lijnschooten's music is clearly recognizable by its blend of recurrent elements that upon closer examination are derived from a single pro-
cedure: the exploitation on every level of the basic musical material. On the
rhythmic and metrical level, for example, he subjects the material – often a
folk song – to elaborations based on changes of meter, shifting of accents, and
repetitions or gradual transformations of a given rhythmic figure. Melodically
and harmonically, this is achieved through inversions and the presentation of
the basic melody in block chords. Another recurrent element is the hocket-like
manner in which a theme is rapidly taken over by a succession of instruments
and instrument groups through all registers of the ensemble. Examples of his
use of these methods, which often result in technically difficult passages for
the musicians, may be heard in such compositions as *Overture for Fun* (1971),
Variations on a Japanese Folksong (1976), and *Three Caprices for Band* (1978).

Van Lijnschooten's influence on (amateur) music making in the Netherlands is not limited to his compositions, but is also a product of the many initiatives he has undertaken in this field. Through his sharp and critical insight into developments in this field over the years, and the guiding role he has served in areas he considered to be foundering, he has made an enormous contribution to the evolution of the wind band into becoming a valued facet of Dutch music.

CASPAR BECX

COMPOSITIONS

WIND BAND: *Mare Liberum-mars* (1960); *Rapsodie over zeemansliedjes* (1962); *Nederlandse suite* (1963); *De geuzen in de Bomlerwaard* (1965); *Hanselijn* (1966); *Kleine suite over volksliederen* (1967); *Kleine speelmuziek* (1968); *Vier impressies* (1970); *Overture for Fun* (1971); *Variations on a Japanese Folksong* (1976); *Three Caprices for Band* (1978); *Suite on a Hymn* (1978); *Junior Variations* (1979); *A Tribute to the Liberators* (1980); *Suite on Greek Love Songs* (1983); *Four Characters* (1985); *Interruptions* (1985); *Rhapsody Gelre* (1992)

ENSEMBLE: *December cantate* (1963) (manuscript); *Tweede rapsodie uit de Lage Landen*, mand.orch (1967) (manuscript); *Mini concert*, posthn, brass qt (1969) (manuscript); *Capriccio*, 2 rec (1969); *Drie rapsodische miniaturen*, acc.orch (1970); *Chorale prelude*, 4 hn (1980); *Valerius gedenckklanck*, m.choir, wind players (1990) (manuscript)

DIDACTIC COMPOSITIONS: *Acht klankstudies* (1969); *Muziek voor jonge blazers* (1969); *Ons eerste concert* (1971); *Ons eerste klarinetboek* (1971); *100 Warm-Ups* (1974); *Ons eerste trompetboek* (with J. Floore) (1975); *Acht adagio's* (1978); *20 Tune Up's* (1979); *100 takteeroefeningen* (1984); *24 mini etudes* (1985)

ARRANGEMENTS FOR WIND ENSEMBLE : *Karel Doormanmars* – Drukker (1960) (manuscript); *Hornpipe* – trad. (1965); *Koninklijke muziek* – Praetorius (1972); *Drie Friese liederen* – anon. (1975) (manuscript); *Gymnopedie nr.1* – Satie (1979); *Sacred Music* – Bruckner (1980); *Pomp and Circumstance no.1* -Elgar (1985)

DISCOGRAPHY

Overture for Fun; Nederlandse suite; Kleine speelmuziek; 4 impressies. Melomaan Ensemble, cond. H. Janssen and H. Lamers (Molenaar MBCD 31.1001.72)

Pietro Locatelli

BERGAMO, 3 SEPTEMBER 1695 – AMSTERDAM, 30 MARCH 1764

As a teenager Pietro Antonio Locatelli already held a position as a violinist in his native Bergamo. In late 1711, however, he left for Rome to further hone his skills. There he studied with Giuseppe Valentini and may also have taken lessons with the aged Arcangelo Corelli. From 1717 to 1723 he often performed at the palazzo of Cardinal Ottoboni. Like many of his Italian contemporaries, he came into contact around this time with the Amsterdam music publisher Roger, who arranged his debut as a composer. In 1723 Locatelli left Rome to tour as a violin virtuoso, visiting various courts in Italy and Germany. From 1725 to 1727 he also held a position at the court in Mantua. His contemporaries praised his violin playing for its precision, force and passion.

Locatelli's life took a new direction when in 1729 he gave up the life of a traveling virtuoso, moved to the merchant city Amsterdam, and turned his attention to composition. After revising his op.1 (1729), he composed seven further collections. The publisher Michel-Charles Le Cène, Roger's successor, acquired the rights to Locatelli's opp.1, 3 and 4 concertos; the opp.2, 5, 6, and 8 sonatas were published by Locatelli himself. He supplemented his earnings by giving lessons, conducting amateur ensembles, arranging private concerts, and acting as an advisor to Le Cène. His business acumen enabled him to live quite comfortably. He collected an extensive library of books on music theory, philosophy, theology, topography, history and ornithology, and a large number of paintings and drawings. These wide-ranging interests might explain why in the last twenty years of his life the flow of his publications all but halted. A few years before his death, on 30 March 1764, he published the op.9 collection of six concerti grossi, a work that has unfortunately been lost.

Locatelli clearly set his sights on creating a well-rounded body of instrumental compositions in the main genres of his time – the solo sonata, trio sonata, solo concerto and concerto grosso – the majority of which is for strings. It is unknown whether he composed vocal music and only a few of the many manuscripts attributed to him are authentic. The rest of his work has survived in impeccable publications. In all these matters, Locatelli shows himself a true successor of Corelli.

The op.1 concerti grossi, which he composed as a youth in Rome in 1721, fall directly in line with the work of Corelli. Like this master, Locatelli divided

the collection into eight serious church concertos (containing eleven fugues!), arranged according to a slow-fast-slow-fast pattern of movements, and four chamber concertos, couched principally in dance forms. Their able counterpoint, pithy themes and well-considered harmonies place them firmly in the Roman tradition. Standing apart in this conservative collection is the beautiful last concerto *da chiesa* which, in keeping with Corelli, is a Christmas concerto and closes with a *Pastorale*. It is not surprising that, of all Locatelli's works, it was this concerto of which Johann Sebastian Bach possessed a copy.

The seven collections that followed, from 1732 to 1744, share a common style that contrasts with the conservative op.1 concertos. In Italy, a new Baroque style with early Classical tendencies was emerging in which the upper voice(s) gained individuality at the cost of the independent bass. Locatelli, along with Tessarini, Sammartini, Tartini and Vivaldi, was one of its pioneers. Symbolic of the transition is that his first work in this 'galant' style, the op.2 sonatas dating from 1732, featured the quintessential solo instrument of the style, the flauto traverso. Aside from the strings, this is the only instrument for which he composed.

Locatelli's most famous work, *L'arte del violino* op.3, a group of twelve concertos for the violin, appeared the following year. This work is stylistically akin to Vivaldi's op.7 violin concertos. Though less original, Locatelli applies the new homophonic style more radically and demands greater virtuosity of the violinist – in particular in the 24 Capriccios added to the outer movements. These offer an entire compendium of violin technique: double stops, extremely high positions, large intervals, bariolage, arpeggios, staccato and other bowing techniques alternating at a dizzying pace. The Capriccios greatly contrast with the remaining movements of the concertos, which are thematically more introspective, emphasizing cantabile playing in the solo violin part. It is not least this juxtaposition of virtuosity and 'Empfindsamkeit' that makes the collection so fascinating.

Together with *L'arte del violino*, Locatelli's twelve op.6 sonatas for violin (1737) form his major contribution to the art of violin playing. Here too, unusual demands are made on the violinist's technique, though in a way much more integrated into the sonata form: a richly ornamented, slow opening movement, followed by a fast movement and closing with a lighter piece, in a moderate tempo, with virtuosic variations. Only the last sonata, a grave 'sonata da chiesa', deviates from the norm, having as an encore a 'Capriccio, prova del intonatione', an extremely virtuoso spin-off from *L'arte del violino*. Locatelli's op.8 contains six sonatas for violin in the same vein and four fascinating trio sonatas for two violins and basso continuo. The relative simplicity of the six op.5 trio sonatas shows that they were intended for a different audience.

The six *Introduttioni teatrali*, the first half of op.4, stand apart in Locatelli's work. These short, brilliant orchestral pieces are in the style of the Italian opera-sinfonia. The second half of this collection and the op.7 collection each comprise six concerti grossi, the last in each case breaking the pattern. Op.7, for instance, closes with the programmatic *Il Pianto di Arianna*, a violin concerto in disguise consisting of nine short contrasting movements crammed with colorful, opera-like effects.

On his engraved portrait, made by the Amsterdam painter Cornelis Troost, Locatelli reveals his artistic creed: part books from *L'arte del violino* mingle with the fugue of the op.1/8 concerto. Thus the message is conveyed of virtuosity tempered by compositional craftsmanship.

PIETER DIRKSEN

COMPOSITIONS

XII Concerti grossi a quattro, e a cinque ... opera prima. – Amsterdam, Jeanne Roger, [1721]
For 2 violins, viola, cello, strings and bc

XII Sonate a flauto traversiere solo e basso ... opera seconda. – Amsterdam, composer, [1732]

L'arte del violino. XII Concerti cioe, violono solo, con XXIV capricci ad libitum ... *violino primo, violino secondo, alto, violoncello solo, e basso* ... opera terza. – Amsterdam, Michel Charles Le Cène, [1733]
For violin, strings and bc. Facs.ed.: Amsterdam, Groen, 1981.

Opera quarta, parte prima, VI introduttioni teatrali, parte seconda, VI concerti, violino primo, secondo, alto e violoncello soli, violino *primo, secondo, alto e basso ripieni*. – Amsterdam, Michel Charles Le Cène, [1735]
For 2 violins, viola, cello, strings and bc

Sei sonate a tre, o due violini, o due flauti traversieri, basso per il cembalo ... opera quinta. - Amsterdam, composer, [1736]

XII Sonate a violino solo e basso da camera ... opera sesta. – Amsterdam, composer, [1737]
For violin and bc

VI Concerti a quattro ... opera settima. – Leiden, Adriano van der Hoeven, [1741]
For 2 violins, viola, cello, strings and bc

X Sonate, VI a violino solo e basso e IV a tre ...
opera ottava. – Amsterdam, composer,
[1744]
Six sonatas for violin and bc and four
sonatas for 2 violins and bc

Sei concerti a quattro ... opera nona. – Amsterdam, Johannes Covens, 1762
For 2 violins, viola, cello, strings and bc
Lost

IN MANUSCRIPT:
Two concertos (A major, E major) for violin,
strings and bc. Dresden, Sächsische Landesbibliothek
Concerto (G major) for flute, strings and bc.
Münster, Universitätsbibliothek
*Sinfonia a 2 violini, viola e basso composta per
l'essequie della sua donna che si celebrano in
Roma.* Only known in an early 20th century edition: *Trauersymphonie* : (sinfonia a 2
violini, viola e basso, composta per l'essequie della sua Donna che si celebrano in
Roma) / hrsg. von A. Schering. Leipzig,
Kahnt (Perlen alter Kammermusik
deutscher und italienischer Meister)
Trio Sonata (E-flat major), Paris, Bibliothèque
du Conservatoire
Trio Sonata (A major), Lund, Universitetsbiblioteket
Violin Sonata (F major), Rome, Biblioteca Musicale Santa Cecilia
Violin Sonata (G minor), Leufsta Bruk, De
Geer Collectie

BIBLIOGRAPHY
A. Dunning: *Pietro Antonio Locatelli : Der
Virtuose und sein Welt*. Buren, Knuf, 1981
A. Hutchings: *The Baroque concerto*. London, Faber and Faber, 1961, 3/1973
A. Koole: *Pietro Antonio Locatelli da Bergamo : (1695-1764)*. Doctoral dissertation University of Amsterdam, 1949
A. Loft: *Violin and keyboard : the duo repertoire, vol 1*. New York, Grossman, 1973
H.-J. Schulze: 'Ein apokryphes Händel-Concerto in Joh. Seb. Bachs Handschrift?',
Bach-Jahrbuch, 1980, p. 27-33

DISCOGRAPHY
6 Sonate a tre, op. 5. Musica ad Rhenum
(Vanguard Classics 99087)

L'arte del violino, op. 3. E. Wallfisch (vl),
Raglan Baroque Players, cond. N. Kraemer
(Hyperion CDA 66721/3)
L'arte del violino, op. 3, no. 1, 2, 5 and 6. J.
van Zweden (vl), Combattimento Consort Amsterdam (Sony Classical 32277)
  *Concerti grossi op. 1, no. 2, 5 and 12; Il pianto
d'Arianna, op. 7, no. 6; Sinfonia funebre*. L'Europe Galante, cond. F. Biondi (Opus 111 OPS
30-104)
  Flute Sonatas op. 2. J. Wentz (tra.fl), Musica
ad Rhenum (Vanguard Classics 99099)
  Flute Sonates op. 2. S. Preston and N.
McGegan (tra.fl), A. Pleeth (vc), Chr. Hogwood
(hpd) (L'Oiseau Lyre 436 191-2)
  *Introduzioni teatrali, op. 4a; Sonatas op. 5,
no. 2 and op. 8, no. 2*. Freiburger Barockorchester, cond. Th. Hengelbrock (Deutsche
Harmonia Mundi 05472 772072)
  Sonatas op. 6, no. 2, 6, 11 and 12. E. Wallfisch (vl), Locatelli Trio (Hyperion CDA 66363)
  *Flute Sonatas op. 2, no. 2 and 6; Violin
Sonatas op. 6, no. 12; Sonatas for flute, violin and
bc, op. 5, no. 1, op. 8, no. 7 and 8*. Schönbrunn
Ensemble (Globe GLO 5134)

Theo Loevendie

AMSTERDAM, 7 SEPTEMBER 1930

A late developer, Theo Loevendie enrolled in the conservatory in Amsterdam at the age of twenty-five, studying the clarinet and composition. Loevendie began his musical career as a jazz clarinettist and saxophonist, worked for several months in Turkey during the 1950s, and in the 1960s composed and arranged for the band of Boy Edgar. He has performed with his ensembles at various international festivals.

In 1961 Loevendie composed his first 'serious' piece, the String Quartet. This was followed eight years later by his first commissioned piece, *Scaramuccia*. In his own view it was because of his lack of affinity with the musical avant-garde of the 1950s that he began composing later in life. In this music he missed the spontaneity and unpredictability of jazz, considering serialism 'an excess of the rationalistic'. Nonetheless, over the years he has increasingly employed a wide variety of compositional methods, albeit ones that leave the composer much freedom and require some type of improvisation. To the eye, Loevendie's music looks a finely crafted construction, but it sounds playful and surprising.

His first large-scale compositions, written in the late 1960s and early 1970s, are pieces for soloist and orchestra: *Scaramuccia*, *Orbits* and *Incantations*. The solo parts, respectively for clarinet, French horn and bass clarinet, make use of the same type of figures typical of his jazz improvisations: not so much a melody above a fixed harmonic scheme in a steadily repeated meter as melodic embellishments based on a row chiefly characterized by its alternation of intervals. *Strides* (1976) for piano, consists of elaborations on the stride piano playing of the Harlem jazz pianists of the 1920s.

Loevendie also makes use of other elements foreign to Western practices. In *Timbo* for percussion ensemble the drums are beaten with the hand. Both African polyrhythm and medieval isorhythm find their way into the *Six Turkish Folk Poems*. In all of these works his conscious disregard of harmony is another non-Western element. Loevendie has long been uninterested in the conflict between tonal and atonal music; his melodies are modal by nature. The emphasis he places on the independence of different melodies and their rhythmic ordering is reminiscent of Turkish music. *Twee korte stukken* [Two Short Pieces] for piano illustrate his penchant for the carillon and repeated tones. He is also very fond of canons.

In the orchestral piece *Flexio* (1979), he first systematically employed his 'curve technique'. In his own description, this is a means of creating order based on 'augmenting and diminishing intervals while maintaining the melodic, harmonic and rhythmic shape of the "curve", the succession of intervals (small, large, largest) remaining fixed.' The freedom this technique allows the composer is in keeping with Loevendie's background as an improviser and his distaste for rigid systems.

Whereas the curve in *Flexio* is exclusively melodic in character, in *Music for flute and piano* Loevendie also employs rhythmic cells that can be shortened and lengthened as desired. Of the two movements of the Nonet (1980), the first is a rhythmic palindrome, the second is based on a row of pitches that gradually expands to include thirty-five tones. This row is subsequently compressed.

Loevendie often writes for instruments commonly used in jazz and plucked-string instruments, the latter finding expression in *De Nachtegaal* [The Nightingale], *Six Turkish Folk Poems* and *Back Bay Bicinium*. The remarkable combination of bass clarinet, mandolin, guitar, violin and percussion used in *Venus and Adonis* (music for a theatrical arrangement of Shakespeare's poem) is a reference to the consort music of Shakespeare's day and suggests at the same time a Turkish-sounding heterophony. It is his only composition in which the cullings of non-Western folk music are obvious. The performance of this work in 1980 led to the founding of the Nieuw Ensemble, which in turn has inspired many Dutch and foreign composers to write for these unusual forces.

The tension between freedom and order is also the theme of *Naima* (1985), Loevendie's first opera. The woman Naima leaves the inflexible 'Instituut' (the rulers) and joins a group of roving musicians, among them Hunchback, who marries Naima and makes her pregnant. Her child, Amian, later comes to power, slays the old ruler, and becomes equally tyrannical. Naima and the musicians refuse to follow Amian and leave. In *Naima*, Loevendie incorporates elements of Western operatic tradition, borrowed in particular from Verdi (*Otello*) and Handel. Stylistically, it is much like his earlier work. Here too he employs ostinatos, repeating tones and ornamented melodies, and he even integrates one of his earlier pieces, *Timbuktu* (1969), into the music for the roving musicians.

His earlier vocal and instrumental compositions, such as *De Nachtegaal* and *Six Turkish Folk Poems*, seem in retrospect to have a theatrical character. More of this was to follow. *Oh oor o hoor* [Oh ear o hear], for orchestra and vocalist to poetry by Lucebert, is alternately recited and sung. In *Gassir, the hero* (1990), his second opera, premiered in Boston, Loevendie applies his curve technique to the harmony and utilizes the freedom this affords him to employ other techniques.

Loevendie's third opera, *Esmée*, is based on a libretto by Jan Blokker. Premiered at the 1995 Holland Festival, this opera also deals with the relationship between freedom and order, as evidenced by the figure of Esmée van Eeghen, a member of the Dutch resistance during World War II who was suspected of spying for the Germans. The atmosphere of this opera (the Protestant environment of Dutch resistance fighters) moved Loevendie to make references to German art song, military brass bands, Protestant psalm melodies, chorale arrangements and café music.

Although Loevendie is primarily a composer, he is still active in the area of performance. In the 1970s he organized the STAMP concerts of the Alternative Music Performance Foundation: informal, small 'happenings' on Sunday afternoons in Amsterdam's Shaffy Theater in which various genres were presented alongside one another. These concerts laid the foundation for the present ensemble culture in the Netherlands. From 1983 to 1987 Loevendie was chairman of the Society of Dutch Composers. He currently teaches composition in the Netherlands as well as abroad and continues to perform as an improviser. His *Bons* [Boom] for improviser and chamber ensemble is an excellent example of the combination of composed and improvised music. The music is wholly written out for the ensemble, while the soloist improvises on melodic fragments from the score. In the *Atlantis Suite* for jazz ensemble and two female vocalists the situation is reversed: the vocalists have only a few passages where they, in the composers words, 'can work reasonably independently with the notes I have written down, based on what we [the ensemble] are doing at the moment.'

Loevendie is the recipient of many awards. In 1979 he received the Wessel Ilcken Prize for his work as a jazz musician, in 1984 the Koussevitzky Award for *Flexio*, in 1986 the Matthijs Vermeulen Prize for *Naima*, and in 1988 the 3-M Prize for his entire oeuvre.

In the 1990s Loevendie returned to his beginnings as a composer, with works for soloist and orchestra like the Concerto for Piano and Orchestra (1996) and the violin concerto *Vanishing dances* (1999). He is currently working on his fourth opera, *Johnny and Jones.*

EMANUEL OVERBEEKE

COMPOSITIONS

OPERA: *Naima* (1985); *Gassir, the hero* (1990); *Esmée* (1987-1994); *Johnny and Jones* (1999-...)

PIANO: *Toccata* (1965); *Twee korte stukken* (1976); *Strides* (1976); *Walk* (1985); *On the train* (1992); *Four Easy Pieces* (1993); *The Barpianist*, pf (1997)

CHAMBER AND ENSEMBLE MUSIC: *Aulos*, one or more instr. (1972); *Timbo*, 6 perc (1974); *Six Turkish Folk Poems*, S, fl, cl, hp, pf, perc, vl, vc (1977); *De Nachtegaal* (Andersen), sp.v, 7 instr (1979); *Music for flute and piano* (1979); *Nonet*, pic, cl, bn, hn, tpt, trb, pf, perc, db (1980); *Venus and Adonis*, b-cl, mand, gui, vl, perc (1981); *Dance*, vl (1986); *Back Bay Bicinium*, pic, cl, vl, vla, vc, perc, pf (1986); *Duo*, b-cl (1988); *Bons*, improvisator, instr.ens (1991); *Drones*, vl, pf (1991); *Cycles*, vl, cl, vc, pf (1992); *Lerchentrio*, cl, vc, pf (1992); *Trait d'union*, fl (1992); *Two Pieces on Canons by Guillaume de Machaut*, version 3 fl, a-fl (1993), version 4 sax (1994); *Laps*, 10 instr (1995); *Qué pasa en la calle?*, 4 tr (1996)

ORCHESTRA: *Scaramuccia*, cl, orch (1969); *Orbits*, hn, orch with 4 obbl. hn (1975); *Incantations*, b-cl, orch (1976); *Flexio* (1979); *Naima suite* (1986); *Oh oor o hoor* (Lucebert), Bar, orch (1987); *Concerto*, pf, orch (1996); *Concerto "Vanishing dances"*, vl, orch (1999)

PUBLICATIONS

'Existing gaps can be narrowed : autobiography and analyses', *Key Notes*, 5, 1977/1, p. 32-40

BIBLIOGRAPHY

J. Bernlef: 'I don't lie in my music' (interview), *Key Notes*, 28, 1994/2, p. 16

M. Brandt: 'Theo Loevendie : "Het elitaire ligt me van huis uit helemaal niet!" ', *Klank & Weerklank*, vol. 12, no. 5, 1990, p. 7-24

R. de Groot: 'Flexibility: Pitch organisation in recent works by Theo Loevendie', *Key Notes*, 14, 1981/2, p. 13-29

R. de Groot: *Het naamloze lied van Gassir, de Held*. Lecture at the Jan van Gilse Gala,

8 Sept. 1994, Beurs van Berlage Amsterdam. Hilversum, Centrum Nederlandse Muziek, 1994

P. Janssen: '"The moment someone starts to sing it immediately becomes a lot more interesting" : Three composers in conversation about their new operas', *Key Notes*, 28, 1994/4, p. 18

R. Koning: 'Free individual versus traditional institution – Theo Loevendie's first steps in the New World and the world of opera', *Key Notes*, 20, 1984/2, p. 16-17

E. Schönberger: 'Sjostakovitsj' nachtegaal en Loevendies patrijs', *Vrij Nederland*, 21 May 1994

E. Schönberger: 'Stukken uit één stuk', *De vrouw met de hamer & andere componisten*. Amsterdam, De Bezige Bij, 1992

E. Voermans: *Het verstandelijk gevoel en het gevoelig verstand*. Brochure Donemus, Amsterdam, 1994

Theo Loevendie : programmaboek : een project van het Hilversums Conservatorium 1-16 april 1992, ed. J. Röntgen

E. Voermans: 'Sympathy for the outcast', *Key Notes*, 29, 1995/2, p. 10

DISCOGRAPHY

The Barpianist. M. Worms (pf) (NM Extra 98014)

Chess. Theo Loevendie Consort (BASF 14-25180-2)

Gassir, the Hero. Various soloists, Asko Ensemble, cond. D. Porcelijn (Composers' Voice CV 35)

Mandela. Theo Loevendie Consort (Catfish 5C054-24152)

Music for Flute and Piano. K. Verheul (fl), J. van der Meer (pf) (Globe GLO 5130)

Music for Flute and Piano. J. Zoon (fl), B. Brackmann (pf) (NM Classics 92059)

De nachtegaal. L. Visser (sp.v), Ensemble M, cond. D. Porcelijn (Composers' Voice CV S 1981/1)

Nonet. Netherlands Radio Chamber Orchestra, cond. E. Bour (BFO A-17)

On the Train. M. Worms (pf) (BVHAAST 9403)

Orbits; Incantations; Flexio; Naima Suite. Rotterdam Philharmonic Orchestra, cond. R. Bradshaw and O. Ketting, H. Sparnaay (b-cl), Residentie Orchestra, cond. P. Eötvös, Nether-

lands Ballet Orchestra, cond. D. Porcelijn
(Composers' Voice CV 24)

Plus One. H. Starreveld (fl), H. Sparnaay
(b-cl), R. Eckhardt (pf) (Attacca Babel 9161-4)

Six Turkish Folk Poems. D. Dorow (S), Residentie Orchestra, cond. E. Bour (Olympia
OCD 506)

Strands. H. Starreveld (fl) (NM Classics
92069)

Toccata; Two Short Pieces; Strides; Walk. P.
de Haas (pf) (Clavicenter PDH 250902)

*Two Pieces on Canons by Guillaume de
Machaut.* Tibia Quartet (WVH 154)

*Venus and Adonis; Strides; Six Turkish Folk
Poems; Music for Flute and Piano; Two Songs;
Back Bay Bicinium.* R. Hardy (S), J. van Nes
(Mez), J. Snijders (pf), Nieuw Ensemble, cond.
E. Spanjaard (Etcetera KTC 1097)

Walk. I. Janssen (pf) (NM Special 92093)

Walk; Strides. I. Janssen (pf) (NM Classics
92028)

Tera de Marez Oyens

VELSEN, 5 AUGUST 1932 – HILVERSUM, 29 AUGUST 1996

Tera de Marez Oyens, née Wansink, showed an interest in music at an early age. She was raised in Hengelo and left high school at the age of sixteen to enroll at the Amsterdam Conservatory. There she studied the piano with Jan Odé, harpsichord with Richard Boer, violin with Jan Henrichs and Camille Jacobs, and conducting with Felix Hupka. She graduated from the conservatory at the age of twenty and shortly afterward married her former piano teacher, the pianist and composer Gerrit de Marez Oyens, whose surname she continued to use after their separation.

After graduating she took private composition lessons from Hans Henkemans, under whose tutelage she learned much about instrumentation in particular. In the 1960s she studied electronic music with Gottfried Michael Koenig at the Institute for Sonology in Utrecht. Fascinated by the new possibilities this medium afforded, she set up a modest electronic studio in her home in Hilversum. Of particular interest to her was the combination of electronic and acoustic instruments. De Marez Oyens was also interested in composing for schoolchildren and amateur ensembles. For many years she gave improvisation courses, to both adults and children. She published her ideas on this subject in *Werken met moderne klanken* [Working with modern sounds] (1978).

On 6 September 1975 De Marez Oyens became the first woman to conduct the Overijssel Philharmonic Orchestra. She often conducted performances of her works abroad as well. She taught for many years; in 1975 she was appointed at the Zwolle Conservatory to teach 'the practice of contemporary music' and later became a professor of composition at this institute, a position never previously held by a woman in the Netherlands. Her second marriage, to the political scientist and writer Menachem Arnoni, greatly influenced her work. From 1972 until his death in 1985 she was very productive. Arnoni's writings inspired many of her compositions, for example *From Death to Birth* (1975) for a cappella choir, and *The Odyssey of Mr. Goodevil* (1976-1981) for orchestra, four soloists, two narrators and two mixed choirs.

For many years she combined her career as a performer with making radio programs, teaching and composing, although she resigned her position at the Zwolle Conservatory in 1987 to devote more time to composition. De Marez Oyens was often invited to give improvisation courses in the Netherlands and abroad. She taught summer courses in Vienna and lectured on such subjects as electronic music, music education, the role of women in music, and her own works. She also served as a jury member in composition competitions and traveled extensively to congresses and symposia in for example South Korea, Alaska, Brazil and the United States.

During the last years of her life most of her works were composed to commission. Her extensive oeuvre comprises more than 200 pieces, including orchestral and choral works, chamber music, electronic music, and, dating from her early years, children's operas.

Much of her music reflects her social consciousness, as the titles of many works indicate: *Het lied van de duizend angsten* [The song of the thousand fears], *Litany of the Victims of War*, and *Sinfonia Testimonial* – which incorporates the testimony of Mexican and Chilean political prisoners.

Her early works are characterized by a mixture of Romantic and Impressionistic elements. One example is *Der Chinesische Spiegel* (1962), a piece in three movements for tenor solo and orchestra based on texts by Li Tai Po, for which she was awarded the ANV-Visserneerlandia Prize in 1964. Her style altered radically in 1966, with a predominance of short motifs and heightened tension through the frequent use of augmented octaves and minor seconds, although she continued to have a predilection for setting literary texts.

Like many composers, she turned to graphic notation in the 1960s and 1970s although, discounting her improvisation courses, she later returned to exact notation. Her late works are less programmatic and are based on somewhat loosely applied tone rows. In 1988 she composed a Cello Concerto for Maria Hol for five different instruments, employing scordatura (retuning of strings) to produce unusual sounds and chords. The cellist is directed to move from one cello to another, thus producing striking changes in timbre. The three-movement Concerto for Piano and Orchestra (1990) provides another example of her interest in new timbres. For the second movement of this work, she found inspiration in the Japanese sumi painting technique.

Among her last compositions are the Alto Saxophone Concerto (1992) and the *Linzer Concert* (1993) for accordion and orchestra. A visit to Korea inspired *Nam San* [Southern Mountain] for marimba. On 19 October 1995, the Rotterdam Philharmonic Orchestra performed the premiere of *UNISON*, a work commissioned by the National Committee for the 50th Anniversary of the United Nations. During the last months of her life, while she was suffering from cancer, De Marez Oyens was married to the author Marten Toonder.

HELEN METZELAAR

COMPOSITIONS

VOICE WITH INSTRUMENT(S): *Zuid-Afrikaanse liederen*, S/T, pf (1951); *And Blind She Remained*, v, keyb, perc (1978); *Three Hymns* (Arnoni), Mez, pf (1979); *Vignettes* (De Marez Oyens), S, fl, perc, pf (1986); *Shadow of a Prayer* (De Marez Oyens), S, fl, pf (1989); *From a Distant Planet* (De Marez Oyens), Bar/A/Mez, pf (1990); *If Only* (Welles) S, fl, perc, pf (1991)

CHOIR (MIXED CHOIR A CAPPELLA UNLESS OTHERWISE STATED): *Deposuit potentes de sede* (1970); *Canto di parole* (De Marez Oyens) (1971); *Bist du bist* (Mon) (1973); *From Death to Birth* (Arnoni) (1974); *Ode to Kelesh* (Arnoni), mix.choir, fl, ob, perc, pf, str (1975); *The Lover* (Arnoni) (1975); *Black* (De Marez Oyens) (1981)

OTHER VOCAL WORKS: *Der Chinesische Spiegel*, T, orch (1962); *The Odyssey of Mr. Goodevil* (Arnoni), orch, 4 soloists, 2 narrators, 2 mix.choir (1984); *Het lied van de duizend angsten* (Van Delft), orch, 2 soloists, 2 mix.choir (1984); *Sinfonia Testimonial*, orch, mix.choir, tape (1987); *The Narrow Path* (De Marez Oyens), S, fl, 2 gui (1996);

PIANO (PIANO 2H UNLESS OTHERWISE STATED): *Sonatina* (1961); *Sonatina*, 2 pf (1963); *Ballerina on a cliff* (1980); *Sentenced to Dream* (1990)

CHAMBER MUSIC: *Deducties*, ob, hpd (1964); *Mosaic*, ob, cl, hn, bn, pf (1979); *Contrafactus, String Quartet no. 2* (1981); *Lenaia*, fl (1982); *Octopus*, b-cl, perc (1982); *Möbius by Ear*, vla, pf (1983); *Trajectory*, sax.qt

(1985); *Valalan*, gui (1985); *Powerset*, sax.qt, slw (1986); *Gilgamesh Quartet*, 4 trb (1988); *String Quartet no. 3* (1988); *Mandala*, a-sax, pf (1988); *Dublin kwartet*, vl, vla, vc, pf (1989); *Nam San*, mar (1993); *Pradzky Hrand*, 2 gui (1993); *A Wrinkle in Time*, fl, vl, vc, pf (1994)

VARIABLE INSTRUMENTATION: *Sound and Silence II*, one or more instr, actress ad lib. (1971); *Takadon*, wind instr, voice(s), perc, gui, str, pf; *Music for a small planet*, 8 melody instr, v, perc (1988)

ORCHESTRA: *Introduzione*, orch (1969); *Litany of the Victims of War*, orch (1985); *Structures and Dance*, vl, orch (1986); *Symmetrical Memories*, vc, orch (1988); *Confrontations*, pf, orch (1990); *Interface*, str.orch (1990); *Linzer concert*, acc, orch (1993); *Alto Saxophone Concerto* (1992); *Squaw Sachem Symphony*, orch (1993); *Ceremonies*, orch (1993)

MUSIC FOR SCHOOL ORCHESTRA AND AMATEUR GROUPS: *Dolcinettes*, several rec (1952); *Bamboerijntjes*, several rec/bamb-fl (1957); *Partita for David*, school orch (1960); *Kerstcantate*, choir, school orch (1961); *Adventures in Music*, school orch (1970); *Suite for Pipers and Fiddlers*, school orch (1971); *Suite du petit prince*, school orch (1973); *Snapshots*, school orch (1979); *Free for All*, five instr (1986)

ELECTRONIC MUSIC WITH OR WITHOUT ACOUSTIC INSTRUMENTS: *Safed*, tape (1968); *Photophonie*, 4 track tape and 8 light sources (1971); *Mixed feelings*, 4 track tape, perc (1973); *Trio*, bass instr, perc, tape

(1974); *Dances of Illusion (verbosonic-electronic ballet)* (1975); *Concerto,* hn, tape (1980); *Charon's Gift,* pf, tape (1982); *Ambiversion,* b-cl, tape (1983); *Cello Concerto,* vc/5 instr, tape (1986)

PUBLICATIONS

Werken met moderne klanken : samenspel voor stemmen en instrumenten. Haarlem, De Toorts, 1978

BIBLIOGRAPHY

R. Himmelbauer: 'Landschaft der Klänge : in Erinnerung an die holländische Komponistin Tera de Marez Oyens', *Frau und Musik,* July-Sept. 1996, no. 39/96
'In memoriam Tera de Marez Oyens (1932-1996)', *IAWM Journal,* vol. 3, no. 1, Feb. 1997, p. 3-8
L. Knödler: 'De verbijsterde wereld van *Sinfonia Testimonial* – Tera de Marez Oyens, fulltime componiste.' *Muziek en Dans, vol 12.* March 1988, p. 24-26
K. Kuijpers: 'Koormuziek van Tera de Marez Oyens', *Dechorum,* March 1997, p. 7-9
H. Metzelaar: 'In memoriam Tera de Marez Oyens 1932-1996', *Key Notes,* 30, 1996/4, p. 29
H. Metzelaar: 'Tera de Marez Oyens', *The New Grove Dictionary of Women Composers,* ed. J.A. Sadie and R. Samuel. London, MacMillan, 1994, p. 312-313
E. Overweel: 'Tera de Marez Oyens', *Zes vrouwelijke componisten,* ed. H. Metzelaar [et al.]. Hilversum, Centrum Nederlandse Muziek / Zutphen, Walburg Press, 1991, p. 198-232
W. Paap: 'Een componistenechtpaar : Tera en Gerrit de Marez Oyens', *Mens en Melodie,* vol. 14, 1974, p. 66-69
M. Roegholt: 'Als een man zit te componeren, wordt hij niet door de melkboer gestoord', *Opzij,* Nov. 1985, p. 58-60
'Tera de Marez Oyens (1932-1996)', special issue of *De Nieuwsbrief,* Stichting Vrouw en Muziek, no. 12, Dec. 1996
M. Toonder: *Tera, autobiografie; epiloog.* Amsterdam, De Bezige Bij, 1998
H. Visser: 'In ieder geval heb ik niet de intentie de arbeidersklasse te verheffen', *De Tijd,* 22 Jan. 1982, p. 47-49

DISCOGRAPHY

Confrontations, Linzer Concert, Structures and Dance (Marcato Keyboard MCD 189601)
Contrafactus, String Quartet. Dufy Quartet (NM Classics 92018)
From Death to Birth; Ballerina on a Cliff; Ambiversion; Vignettes; Trio; Dreams of Madness. Various soloists, Netherlands Vocal Ensemble, members of the Netherlands Radio Choir, cond. M. Voorberg and T. de Marez Oyens (BVHAAST CD 9211)
Safed (Composers' Voice CV 7903)
Sinfonia testimonial; Charon's Gift; Litany of the Victims of War. T. de Marez Oyens (pf), Netherlands Radio Choir, Netherlands Radio Symphony Orchestra, cond. K. Montgomery and J. Stulen (Composers' Voice CVCD 8702)
Waves, Recurring Thoughts of a Haunted Traveller. I. Kappelle (S), Syrinx Saxophone Quartet (Erasmus WVH 164)

Johan de Meij

VOORBURG, 23 NOVEMBER 1953

Johan Abraham de Meij began as a trumpeter and cornet player in the Forum Hadriani wind band in his native Voorburg. A few years later he began playing the trombone, taking lessons from Anne Bijlsma Sr., the father of the famous cellist Anner Bijlsma. After high school he enrolled in a teacher's college and, upon completing his studies, he taught for several months. He then decided to change careers. During his military service he was a tuba player and trombonist in the Cavalry Military Band. In 1977 he became a tenor tuba player and trombonist in the Amsterdam Police Band and began studying conducting with Rocus van Yperen and Jan van Ossenbruggen, and trombone with Arthur Moore at the Royal Conservatory in The Hague.

De Meij took his first steps as a composer by making arrangements for, among others, the Dutch Brass Sextet, of which he was a member for fourteen years. Since 1978 an ever-growing number of highly varied arrangements of his have been published by Molenaar Edition Wormerveer. His works include transcriptions of film music and Broadway musicals, arrangements of Classical and popular music, and dozens of vocal and instrumental accompaniments for well-known soloists.

De Meij made his debut as a composer in 1979 with *Patchwork*, a short piece written for the Dutch Brass Sextet. A long silence ensued, until 1988 when he presented *The Lord of the Rings*, his grandly conceived Symphony no.1, for concert band, which he had been working on for about four years. Arie van Beek, with whom De Meij had been taking conducting lessons, had suggested that De Meij compose a work based on Tolkien's famous trilogy. The finished work is a suite in five movements – *Gandalf, Lothlórien, Gollum, Journey in the Dark* and *Hobbits*. Its premiere in Brussels in 1988, by the Great Concert Band of the Belgian Guides, was followed shortly afterward by the Dutch premiere, in Kerkrade by the Royal Military Band. Throughout this period the critics remained unanimous in their praise. In 1989 the success of *The Lord of the Rings* culminated when De Meij received the American Sudler Award, the most prestigious prize in the field of music for wind band. The composer was subsequently granted a stipend by the Fund for the Creation of Music.

In 1988 the Amsterdam Police Band, of which De Meij had been a member for eleven years, was dissolved. Since then he has devoted his time to composition and arranging, in addition to incidental appearances with such ensembles as Orkest de Volharding, The Netherlands Radio Chamber Orchestra and The Amsterdam Wind Orchestra. Most notable of the works he has written in this period is his second symphony, *The Big Apple*, subtitled 'A New York Symphony'. This work, commissioned by The United States Air Force Band in Washington D.C., received honorable mention from the jury at the 14th International Composition Competition in Corciano, Italy.

Since his success with *The Lord of the Rings*, De Meij has set up his own publishing firm – Amstel Music – managing the promotion of all its activities himself.

De Meij's first arrangements, of music by Barry Manilow, Abba and The Beatles, created the image that he worked solely in the popular genre. However, he selected these works not so much out of personal preference as from an unfailing intuition for the taste of the public. Other such examples are arrangements he made for wind orchestra of the music of Andrew Lloyd Webber, Ennio Morricone and John Williams.

In his own compositions, De Meij demonstrates that his heart lies with symphonic music, and he tries to build bridges to that world. He achieves this by casting his works in a symphonic mold while including obligato instruments such as the piano, harp, harpsichord and a large battery of percussion instruments. His orchestration itself adds to the effect.

Characteristic is his preference for programmatic subjects, the attention he gives to extra-musical touches – ranging from various effects to the city sounds he recorded for *The Big Apple* – his keen sense of scoring and his inventiveness. A good example of this is a passage in the third movement of *The Lord of the Rings* in which the soprano saxophone and trombone are paired as a single instrument in a lengthy solo, evoking the slippery nature of the Gollum character.

De Meij's long experience as an arranger of musicals and film scores remains an underlying element in his composition. Techniques often used in this genre – such as repeated short signal motifs in the orchestra, evocative tone fields in the woodwinds, melodic percussion, and heroic themes in the brass – abound in such mammoth compositions as *The Lord of the Rings* and *The Big Apple*. He makes no secret of his admiration for models such as Leonard Bernstein and John Williams, the music of Stravinsky functioning as a common denominator.

De Meij's strong influence on the world of wind band music – even though this did not make itself felt until his first symphony appeared – is a product of his efforts to win acceptance of the wind orchestra as the equal of the symphony orchestra. Because he composes purely from artistic considerations and as a composer feels responsible for the orchestra's make-up, he has given music for this medium a new impulse.

CASPAR BECX

COMPOSITIONS

WIND BAND OR ENSEMBLE: *Patchwork* (1979); *Symphony no. 1 'The Lord of the Rings'* (1988); *Loch Ness : a Scottish fantasy* (1988); *Pentagram* (1989); *Aquarium* (1991); *Symphony no. 2 'The Big Apple'* (1993); *Polish Christmas Music,* part I (1995); *T-Bone Concerto* (1996); *Continental Overture* (1996); *Madurodam (Miniatuur-suite)* (1997); *La Quintessenza* (1998); *Casanova,* vc, wind band (1998-1999)

ARRANGEMENTS

OF CLASSICAL MUSIC: *Chanson de matin* – Elgar (1987); *American Suite* – Dvořák (1988); *Jupiter Hymn from The Planets* – Holst (1989); *Romeo and Juliet* – Prokofiev (1991); *Aladdin Suite* – Nielsen (1992); *Ratatouille satirique* – Satie (1994); *Jazz Suite no. 2* – Sjostakovitsj (1995); *To my Country* – Zweers (1996); *Trois Rag-Caprices* – Milhaud (1996)

OF FILM MUSIC AND MUSICALS: *Moment for Morricone* – Morricone (1980); *The Pink Panther theme* – Mancini (1982); *James Bond 007* – Barry/Norman/Conti (1983); *Star Wars Saga* – Williams (1987); *The Phantom of the Opera* – Lloyd Webber (1988); *Out of Africa* – Barry (1991); *Highlights from the Musical Chess* – Ulvaeus/Andersson (1992); *Miss Saigon : a Symphonic Portrait* – C. Schönberg (1994)

OF ENTERTAINMENT MUSIC: *Abba cadabra* – Ulvaeus/Andersson (1978); *Copacabana* – Manilow (1979); *Beatles' Collection* – Lennon/McCartney (1981)

VOCAL AND INSTRUMENTAL / MUSICAL ACCOMPANIMENT: *Shoutin' Liza trombone* – Fillmore (1982); *This Nearly Was Mine (from South Pacific)* – Rodgers/Hammerstein (1984); *In the Mystic Land of Egypt* – Ketèlby (1985); *2 Songs from Porgy and Bess* – Gershwin (1993)

DISCOGRAPHY

Chess. Band of the Netherlands Royal Airforce, cond. J. de Meij (MBCD 31.1031.72)
Johan de Meij and Friends. Dutch Brass Sextet (DHR 5.001)
Loch Ness. Dutch Royal Military Band, cond. P. Kuypers (CD/MC KMK 002)
Miss Saigon – a Symphonic Portrait. Symphonic Band of the Brabant Conservatory, cond. J. Cober (MBCD 31.1036.72)
Moment for Morricone. Harmonie de la ville Du Havre (Cybelia CY 5003)
Pentagram. Dutch National Youth Wind Orchestra, cond. D. Oosterman (CD/MC Mirasound 399112)
Portrait of Johan de Meij. Dutch Royal Military Band, cond. J. de Meij (CD/MC KMK 003)
Ratatouille. Arnhem Symphonic Winds, cond. J. de Meij (Amstel Classics CD 9501)
The Scandinavian Connection. Danish Con-

cert Band, cond. J. Jensen, Harmonie St.
Michaël Thorn, cond. H. Friesen, Chr. Lind-
berg (trb) (Amstel Classics CD 9701)

Symphony no. 1'The Lord of the Rings'.
Dutch Royal Military Band, cond. P. Kuypers
(CD/MC KMK001)

*Symphony no. 1 'The Lord of the Rings'; Suite
from the ballet Romeo and Juliet.* Amsterdam
Wind Orchestra, cond. A. van Beek (CD JE
Classic 900101)

Symphony no. 1 'The Lord of the Rings'. The
U.S.Air Force Band Washington, D.C. (BOL-
9005C)

Symphony no. 2 'The Big Apple'. Amsterdam
Wind Orchestra, cond. H. Friesen (CD WWM
500.003)

Chiel Meijering

AMSTERDAM, 15 JUNE 1954

The Dutch composer Chiel Meijering has a number of un-Dutch characteristics: he is very prolific, finishing dozens of compositions every year, he is spontaneous, extravert and emotional. He regularly makes scathing comments on Dutch music. His position as a composer in the Netherlands is somewhat ambivalent: he leans too far towards the pop scene to be considered a 'serious modern' composer, but as a pop musician he is accused of being too Classical.

Meijering finds appealing the formula of the Dutch television program 'With a little help from my friends', in which pop musicians work together with the Metropole Orchestra. He has contributed various arrangements and compositions to this program. For the opening of the Ajax soccer team's new stadium on 25 August 1996, he made arrangements of *We are the Champions* and *We Will Rock You* by the rock band Queen. And for the commemoration on 28 May 1997 of the airlifting of aid to the Netherlands under the Marshall Plan, he was commissioned by the Ministry of Interior Affairs to write a work for the Netherlands Wind Ensemble, the vocalist Denise Jannah and the Resurrection Singers.

Born and raised in Amsterdam, he studied composition, piano and percussion instruments at the city's conservatory after completing high school. His composition teacher, Ton de Leeuw, was both as a person and as a composer his complete opposite and when the gulf between their ideas grew too large, Meijering decided to continue alone.

Meijering is a strong advocate of 'uncensored writing': directly notating the spontaneous idea without losing time over fitting it into a plan, which for him destroys the original impulse. Techniques of composition, he believes, alienate the composer from his emotions. Meijering not only works quickly, he is also open to all kinds of influences. A musical omnivore, he can accommodate elements from the widest range of genres and styles in his work: pop music, folk music, non-Western music, serial music, minimal music, and classical music.

Each composition is thoroughly different from preceding ones. The only thing they have in common is their broad stream of ideas aimed at continuously stimulating the listener's interest. Meijering seeks to entertain. His greatest fear is that the audience will become bored; he relies on a rule of thumb that anything lasting three minutes or more will be perceived as being long. Composers, he believes, should take this into consideration. For Meijering, good music follows a rate of change similar to that in pop music video clips.

To attract immediate attention,the titles of Meijering's compositions are often sexual allusions, such as *19 Centimeter* (1981); occasionally such titles are couched in a style hinting at pop music, for example *I Can't Get no Satisfaction* 1983, rev. 1984).

He is a practical composer and prefers to compose at the request of specific ensembles, thus assuring performance of the commission. *Are You Afraid of the Dark?* (1980), for three guitars, is the first in a series of more than twenty pieces that Meijering, himself a guitarist, has written for the Amsterdam Guitar Trio. These pieces are among his best work and with them the Amsterdam Guitar Trio has become one of the strongest advocates of Meijering's music.

In his music for larger ensembles, Meijering tends to be a bit more heavy-handed and to employ more academic techniques of composition. *Bedouin Caravan in the Desert* (1977), for orchestra, is written according to a strictly conceived plan; Meijering found the actual writing out of the notes a tedious exercise in notation.

To hold the listener's attention, Meijering employs an aggressive style with instrumental virtuosity and eruptions of motion. *I Like Rats, but I don't Like Haydn* (1981, rev. 1983), for saxophone quartet, is an energetic jazz/funk composition whose Stravinskian chain structure passes through a shining mosaic of tiny blocks, including Ellington-like motifs, dark, reiterated chords, ostinato figures and swinging solos.

Meijering's music is not always merely energetic, however. A series of pieces for three guitars, viola and tape, *No Rhyme no Reason* (part 1, 2 & 3, 1987) and *Another Day Dies on a Gull's Cry* (1988), shows him to be receptive to influences of meditative New Age music and World Music. The tapes made for these pieces include the sound of gulls and breaking waves, Ghanaian singing and drumming, and the screams of a furious crowd. These are blended with lyrical viola melodies and acoustic guitar.

Alongside the continuous stream of chamber music composed during the first half of the 1990s, Meijering also produced a number of orchestral works – *Evocation* (1990), for violin and orchestra, *Hypomania* (1991) – and a number of pieces primarily for wind ensemble – *Walkover* (1990), *Het ontblote feit* [The bare fact] (1991), *Street Chicks* (1991), *Macho* (1992), *Flying Buddhas* (1993). In 1994 he also composed his first full-length opera, *St. Louis Blues*, for seven solo voices and wind ensemble. Based on the book *Voyage of the Damned* by Gordon Thomas and Max Morgan, the libretto, by Paul Binnerts, is about the tragic sea voyage made in 1939 by 937 Jews on the passenger ship St. Louis in the hope of starting a new life in Cuba or the United States. His opera *Gershwin in Blue* was premiered in 1998.

MICHAEL VAN EEKEREN

COMPOSITIONS

VOCAL: *Why Don't You Think of the Children* (Meijering), S, vl, pf (1981); *Spiegels* (Terhorst), mix.choir (1982); *'n Grote keel om mee te drinken* (Meijering), Mez, a-sax, pf, perc (1988); *Give Me a Break*, S, instr.ens (1992); *De jeuk is erger dan de pijn* (Du Perron, Rantzig), Mez, 3 acc, b-acc (1994)

OPERA: *St. Louis Blues* (1994); *Gershwin in Blue* (1998)

CHAMBER MUSIC: *Cycle of Time*, 6 cl (1990); *Elle a chaud au cul*, a-sax, mar, synth, b-gui (1990); *You Can't Keep a Good Man Down*, 6 b-cl or b-cl and tape (1991); *Nip in the Bud*, 4 sax (1991); *King of the Hill*, 6 vc (1992); *Suburbanality*, 4 sax, pf (1992); *Treklip*, fl, 2 hp, 2 pf (1993); *Was guckst du mir denn immer in die Bluse*, 2 hpd, el.gui (1993); *Pithycantropus erectus*, vla, pf (1994); *Wind at Will*, acc, b-cl (1994); *Kruipfloxen*, acc, vl, db (1994)

ENSEMBLE: *1 miljard billen*, wind ens (1981, herz. 1982); *De neusgaten van Sophia Loren*, instr.ens (1983, rev. 1984); *Achterlangs*, gamelan, 5 brass instr, perc (1989); *Sax-Sux*, 11 sax (1991)

INCIDENTAL MUSIC: *Ter hand genomen* (film music) (1984); *Ahnung des Endes* (ballet music) (Meijering), mix.choir, orch (1985); *Ur-Faust* (music theatre) (Goethe), soloists, mix.choir, chamb.orch (1986)

ORCHESTRA: *The end of a specimen*, orch (1981, herz. 1982); *De geur blijft hangen*, 3 gui, orch (1982); *De grootte*, str.orch (1984); *Mogadon*, orch (1985); *Onderwerping*, a-sax, orch (1986); *Neo-geo*, bn, orch (1987)

BIBLIOGRAPHY

R. Hazendonk: 'Opera van Chiel Meijering beleeft première in Arnhem : "Eigentijdse muziek is eigenlijk ouderwets" ', *De Telegraaf*, 10 March 1995

K. Jansen: 'Chiel Meijering : "een orkest moet stomen"', *NRC Handelsblad*, 26 Jan. 1979

B.-H. van Lambalgen: 'Componist Meijering over St. Louis Blues : opera over Exodus via Hamburg-Amerikalijn', *Het Parool*, 9

March 1995
Ch. van der Leeuw: ' "Nederlanders zijn
boerenpummels, en dat hoor je in hun
muziek" : groepsinterview met D. Manneke,
Ch. Meijering, C. de Bondt, G. Janssen en K.
de Vries', *De Tijd*, 13 June 1986, p. 76-81
P. Luttikhuis: 'Componist Chiel Meijering
over de saaiheid van de concertwereld :
"Moeilijk doen kunnen we allemaal" ', *NRC
Handelsblad*, 13 Dec. 1991
D. Nagan: 'Oorlogsdrama op muziek', *Algemeen Dagblad*, 9 March 1995
F. van der Waa: 'Overstelpend aanbod
eigentijdse Nederlandse muziek : ' "Wij zijn
de nieuwe bevrijde generatie" : groepsinterview met B. Tarenskeen, Ch. Meijering en H.
van der Meulen', *de Volkskrant*, 10 Jan. 1986

DISCOGRAPHY
La belle dame sans merci. P. Wispelwey (vc)
(Channel Classics CCS7495)
A Birds Eye View. A. in 't Veld (acc), A.
Tönkö (vl) (NM Classics 92013)
Electric Blue. Netherlands Radio Chamber
Orchestra, cond. E. Bour (NOS 1980)
Hypomania. Ricciotti Ensemble (BVHaast
CD 9110)
*I Like Rats, but I don't Like Haydn; 'n Haar
op 'n hoofd*. Amsterdam Saxophone Quartet
(Sosta 35011-2)
A Lady Shaves her Legs. R. Westerheide
(gui), A. de Man (hpd) (WVH 072)
No Pain, no Gain. Novair Duo (Globe 5138)
Het ontblote feit. Ensemble De Ereprijs
(Klimop 004)
Parrots in Tunesia – Urfassung. K. Verheul
(fl), J. van de Meer (pf) (Globe 5130)
The Pizza – connection. H. de Jong (sax), P.
Hermsen (pf) (Fidelio 8849)
Sitting Ducks. Amsterdam Loeki Stardust
Quartet (Channel Classics CCS8996)
Two Men and a Lady. Amsterdam Guitar
Trio (Includes: Are you afraid of the dark?; Two
Men and a Lady; No Rhyme No Reason; Miss
Garcia doesn't Ring Anymore; Another Day
Dies on a Gull's Cry; The Insects are Coming)
(RCA Victor Red Seal RD 60165)
Zou het pijn doen. Ensemble De Ereprijs
(BVHaast CD 8901)

Misha Mengelberg

KIEV, 5 JUNE 1935

Few Dutch composers have been able to build such a huge reputation on the basis of such relatively infrequently performed compositions as has Misha Mengelberg – that is, if a composition is defined as a score containing 'suggestions on how a group of musicians, to which one does not necessarily belong, is to play', as once formulated by this composer/improviser/ pianist. Since the end of the 1950s, Mengelberg has been composing such pieces, but their number falls far short of the astronomical number of his improvisations, which he also considers compositions. The debate about the difference in status and artistic value between composition and improvisation is beginning to wind down, not least because from the very beginning Mengelberg has considered both pursuits as equal.

For Misha Mengelberg, a scion of the renowned music dynasty that also produced the conductor Willem Mengelberg (1871-1951) and the composer Karel Mengelberg (1902-1984), composition, music making, improvisation, and activism for the betterment of musical life are all part of one, larger purpose seeking to demonstrate that even without the musical establishment or generally recognized methods of composition, worthy music is still possible. Worthy music, he holds, requires 'fiddling around as well as perfect discipline' and a straight-from-the-shoulder effect. Tradition and experiment, avant-garde and jazz go hand in hand. Mengelberg's work is one large series of surprises; he has an enormous reservoir of styles and idioms at his disposal and the attitude that sooner rather than later 'it's time for something different'.

His interests have always overlapped and complemented each other. After a brief period as an architecture student, he began studying music theory in 1958 with Kees van Baaren. At that time he already had a trio that chiefly played improvised music. In September of that year, he was present in Darmstadt when John Cage introduced 'a certain casualness in music that at this time was anything but expected.' Although the casualness appealed to Mengelberg, the underlying theory did not. He was equally repelled by Cage's 'Eastern mumbo-jumbo', as well as his plan 'to ban literature from music'.

Mengelberg began to compose, leading to the then unheard-of situation when in 1959, together with his trio he won the Loosdrecht Jazz Competition for his improvising. As a composer, he subsequently had his Quartet for trumpet, bassoon, viola and percussion premiered during the Gaudeamus Music

255

Week. Two years later, in 1961, while the Misha Mengelberg Quartet was taking Dutch jazz by storm ('Holland's best and most creative jazz band', according to the press), he submitted to the Gaudeamus Music Week his *Musica per 17 strumenti*, a composition in which each musician plays just one tone. Mengelberg considered it 'a tease', but the jury (with Stockhausen, Ligeti and Krenek) were so impressed they awarded it the Prince Bernhard Fund Prize for the best Dutch composition. Mengelberg also participated on occasion in the counter-culture Fluxus events, including the 1964 Rotterdam Flux Festival in which his *In Memoriam Hans van Sweeden* was performed, a work consisting of endless repetitions of just a few notes. *Spel* [Play] was a conceptual piece, the composer doing nothing more than stare at a watch lying on the piano.

While Mengelberg and others of his generation such as Louis Andriessen, Reinbert de Leeuw, Jan van Vlijmen and Peter Schat demonstrated both openly and behind the scenes to make Dutch musical life more democratic (for example, the so-called Nutcracker Protest of 17 November 1969, which disrupted a performance in the Amsterdam Concertgebouw), his compositions took issue with the national policy toward the arts (*Omtrent een componistenactie* [On a composers' demonstration]) and imperialism (*Vietcong*). In the year the jazz world awarded him the Wessel Ilcken Prize (1967), Mengelberg, the percussionist Han Bennink (with whom he had been making music since 1961), and composer/wind player Willem Breuker (at that time also a member of the Misha Mengelberg Quartet) founded the Instant Composers Pool (ICP). The name of the organization effectively conveyed its message: the musician's improvisations in ICP concerts (and on their recordings) amounted to instant composition. The name of the organization forced everyone – composers and musicians, subsidizers and public – to judge the music on its own merits and not as something half way between composed music and jazz. Mengelberg was also a part of the collective (two authors and five composers) that in 1969 succeeded in having the opera *Reconstructie* [Reconstruction] performed. The improvisational moments in this piece should be considered his signature.

Mengelberg also focused on other matters than the democratization of music. In the first half of the 1970s he combined his ideas and approach with those of Wim T. Schippers in a pair of astonishingly complex theater works (among which, *Bugpeh expé*, 1974, and *Een behoorlijk kabaal* [A considerable racket], 1975) that were improvisationally composed, written and performed, and because of their disciplined – one could say literary – nonsense and fiddling, left the Fluxus movement far behind.

In 1974 the population of improvising musicians was growing so fast that the Association of Improvising Musicians (BIM) was founded. Amsterdam's Bimhuis became its podium and headquarters and Mengelberg was appointed its first chairman. The move toward a more democratic subsidization of composers, accomplished by the founding of the Fund for the Creation of Music, was in part a consequence of Mengelberg's work with the Society of Dutch Composers (Geneco). For all of this, he was awarded the Bird Prize at the 1989 Northsea Jazz Festival.

In terms of improvisation and composition, Mengelberg's music channels thinking toward doing and vice versa. Fundamental is the premise that 'the idea dictates the method.' The fact that 'there is actually absolutely nothing to explain' is to him one of the most appealing aspects of music. Style and slogans are foreign to him, montage and collage are merely tools that reflect the speed with which our thoughts 'zap' from one thing to another. What is most important is the reasoning. 'Neither the results nor the methods applied are the most important part of music, but whether there is some thought behind it.' Mengelberg's music lives off the moment. Few of his notated pieces have made their way into the repertoire. Those that have done, however, are like paragraphs in a single, continuing narrative full of unexpected turns, supplements and deletions of which the listener catches occasional snatches and 'can take some of these home with him.' But it's only 'really fun', he believes, 'when you can connect actual poignancy with it.' This has always been the main issue: 'Whatever I happened to be doing, I thought it was fantastic at that moment.'

FRANS VAN ROSSUM

COMPOSITIONS

Quartet, tpt, bn, vla, perc (1959); *Musica per 17 strumenti* (1959); *3 pianopieces + pianopiece 4* (1961-1966); *Medusa,* str.qt (1962); *Viobum,* vl, pf (1964); *In Memoriam Hans van Sweeden* (1964); *Commentary,* orch (1965); *Omtrent een componistenactie,* fl, ob, cl, bn, hn (1966); *Vietcong; Exercise,* fl (1966); *Senanovi,* v, pf (1967); *Amaga,* gui, hawai-gui, b-gui, 5 loudspeaker units, 3 amplifiers, product modulator, amplitude modulator (1968); *Hello Windyboys,* 10 wind instr, electr. (1968); *Anatoloose,* orch, tape and w.v ad lib. (1968); *Reconstructie* (with L. Andriessen, H. Claus, R. de Leeuw, H. Mulisch, P. Schat and J. van Vlijmen), v, 3 choirs, large ens (1969); *Met welbeleefde groet van de kameel,* orch (1971-1973); *Onderweg,* orch (1973); *Bugpeh expé* (1974); *Een behoorlijk kabaal* (1975); *Dressoir,* 10 wind instr, pf (1977); *Weter Klok's Waardengang : musico-drama,* fl (1978-1979); *Borneose brij,* wind orch (1979); *3 intermezzi,* 12 wind instr, db (1980); *Concerto,* sax, orch (1982); *Zeekip ahoy,* orch (1984); *Enige ervaren zeekippen tegen een achtergrond van gezanten voor sour cream,* 3 rec (1985); *Impromptus,* pf, v (1988); *Bospaadje Konijnehol I en II,* orch; *Gooi vang,* Mez, B (1991); *Telemann nee, fantasie ja,* fl (1992); *Wat volgt,* pf (1997)

BIBLIOGRAPHY

B. Andriessen: *Tetterettet : interviews met Nederlandse improviserende musici.* Ubbergen, Tandem Felix, 1996

J. Bernlef: 'Vrijheden en verboden : een gesprek met Louis Andriessen en Misha Mengelberg', *Raster,* no. 19, 1981, p. 88-105

J. Corbett: *Extended play : sounding off from John Cage to Dr Funkenstein.* Durham/London, Duke University Press, 1994

R. Koopmans: 'Composers' Voice Special – Misha Mengelberg', *Key Notes,* 16, 1982/2, p. 34

H. Ruhé: 'Misha Mengelberg', *Fluxus, the most radical and experimental art movement of the sixties.* Amsterdam, 'A', 1979

B. Vuijsje: *De nieuwe jazz.* Baarn, Bosch & Keuning, 1978

DISCOGRAPHY

Bospaadje Konijnehol I. ICP Orchestra (ICP 028, dist. BVHAAST)

Bospaadje Konijnehol II. ICP Orchestra (ICP 029, dist. BVHAAST)

Dressoir. Orkest de Volharding, cond. C. van Zeeland (NM Classics 92021)

Impromptus. M. Mengelberg (pf and v) (FMP CD 7, dist. BVHAAST)

Wat volgt. M. Worms (pf) (NM Extra 98014)

Leo Michielsen

BATAVIA, 19 NOVEMBER 1872 – WASSENAAR, 30 MARCH 1944

Leonard Pieter Joseph Michielsen was born the son of Leonardus Johannes Ja-cobus Michielsen, a civil servant in the Dutch East Indies, and Suzette An-toinette Theodore Mijer. After leaving grammar school in Haarlem he studied law at the University of Amsterdam, graduating in 1901. Having been called to the bar he worked for the Board of Appeal (accident insurance department) until 1904, and subsequently, until 1913, as a lawyer in Arnhem. During this period he frequently wrote concert reviews for the daily newspapers *De Telegraaf* and *Het Vaderland* and for the music journal *Caecilia*. In 1913 he moved to The Hague and worked first as director of the Central Office of the Union of Credit Agencies and then, until 1926, for the Justice Department, as head of the Immigration Service and National Passport Office.

Leo Michielsen composed his first pieces while still at grammar school, and earned the respect of such contemporaries as Alphons Diepenbrock, Johan Wagenaar and Willem Landré with his songs and the *8 klavierstukken* [8 Keyboard pieces]. Between 1905 and 1940 his works were regularly performed in the Netherlands and abroad: first by Julia Culp, Tilia Hill, Anton B.H. Ver-hey and Willem Andriessen, among others, and later by Ilona Durigo, Julie de Stuers and Hans Schouwman. The Society of Dutch Composers (Geneco) named him a 'senior member' in 1917. From 1933 he served on the boards of Geneco and the Foundation for Netherlands Musical Interests and was a member of the General Assembly of the Music Copyright Agency Buma; he was co-founder of the – pre-war – Netherlands Chamber Orchestra, which was conducted by Otto Glastra van Loon. On the invitation of the Buma chairman, Jan van Gilse, Michielsen became a board-member of this organization in 1941 and, with Karel Mengelberg, worked to keep both Buma and Geneco out-side the sphere of influence of the Department of Propaganda and the Arts es-tablished by the German occupying forces during World War II. He had al-ready given ample evidence of his diplomatic abilities twenty years previously in his work with Dr. D.F. Scheurleer, chairman from 1921 to 1927 of the 'Union Musicologique', an international organization aimed at reuniting the musicological community, estranged during World War I.

The last years of his life were beset with difficulties. Apart from financial problems resulting from the bankruptcy of the Scheurleer Bank in the early 1930s, the Jewish background of his wife Dorothea J.F. Hijmans was a source

of mounting tension during the Nazi occupation. Michielsen and his wife died shortly after one another during a forced evacuation ordered by the Nazis in connection with the construction of the Atlantic Wall.

In all likelihood, Michielsen studied the piano with the Haarlem pianist and composer Leander Schlegel (1844-1913), but this composer's style made no noticeable impact on Michielsen's early work – a collection of songs to poetry by Heine, which are stylistically related to Schumann, and short, poetic, but sometimes rather virtuoso pieces for the piano. Though almost certainly a self-taught composer, in 1903 his *Adagio* for piano won him the annual prize awarded by the music journal *De Nederlandsche Muziekkalender*. He also composed quasi-naive pieces inspired by texts 'im Volkston'. In pieces such as *Veilchenduft*, the strikingly original *Chanson d'automne*, to a Verlaine poem, and *Sur la terre il tombe de la neige*, to a poem by Hérold, Michielsen demonstrated his natural gift for composing songs. From 1910 to 1920 *Sur la terre* was an exceedingly popular item at vocal recitals. Michielsen's best songs from these years are stylistically related to the late songs of Johannes Brahms and Richard Strauss. Still, he effectively avoided all too conspicuous imitation by expressing the language and meaning of the poetry in natural melodies optimally suited to the voice. In the Netherlands, he was considered a very promising composer of songs shortly before World War I. After drastically altering the style of his piano music in the somewhat eclectic *8 Klavierstukken* collection (1913-1916), his most magnificent compositions ensued, such as *Sechs Gesänge chinesischer Lyrik* (1914-1917) and unpublished settings for mixed choir of three Chinese poems in German translation. These works rank among the best composed in the Netherlands at that time. In the three choral settings, Michielsen gives a highly original interpretation of the mood and content of the texts using traditional harmonies. In the *Sechs Gesänge,* the voice and the piano are joined to create an intimate rendition of classical Chinese miniatures without falling into the pseudo-orientalisms so popular at that time or overly stated 'Weltschmerz'. A second collection, *Neue Gesänge chinesischer Lyrik*, published in 1930, failed to equal the success of the first.

JAAP VAN BENTHEM

COMPOSITIONS

SONGS: *Zwei Lieder* (Leander, Ernst); *Drei Lieder* (Geiger, Heine, Fischer); *Drei Lieder im Volkston* (Heine); *Vier kleine Lieder* (Ritter, Poschinger); *Lied* (Swarth); *3 romances* (repr.: *3 mélodies*); *Veilchenduft*; *Vier Lieder* (Mackay, Lingg, Essers, Monsterberg-Muenckenau); *Deux chansons* (Hérold, Du Bellay); *Sechs Gesänge chinesischer Lyrik*; *Neue Gesänge chinesischer Lyrik*; Approximately 30 songs, partly in private collections.
Several songs, incl. previously unpublished songs, collected in: *Leo Michielsen, Selected songs*, VNM, 1990 (Dutch Music Facsimiles, 6)

CHOIR: *3 koorwerken* (Tschan-Jo-Su, Khong-Fu-Tse, Lo-Tschan-Nai, German transl. H. Bethge)

PIANO: *Adagio*; *8 klavierstukken*; *Improvisatie voor D.F. Scheurleer* (in *Gedenkboek Dr. D.F. Scheurleer*, 's-Gravenhage, 1925)
Approximately 40 early piano pieces

BIBLIOGRAPHY
Archive Leo Michielsen. The Hague, Gemeentemuseum, Music Archives
J.B. van Benthem: 'Leo Michielsen', *Biografisch woordenboek van Nederland* I, 1979
J.E. Puite: "*Stukken van veel poëzie en klankschoonheid*" : *de piano-solo-werken van Leo Michielsen*. Doctoral dissertation University of Utrecht, 1993 (with extensive biography)
E. Reeser: *Een eeuw Nederlandse muziek : 1815-1915*. Amsterdam, Querido, 1950, 2/1986
E. Reeser: *Stijlproeven van Nederlandse Muziek : 1890-1960*, vol. I, p. 73-76

DISCOGRAPHY
8 klavierstukken. A. Middelbeek (pf) (HGM CD 01)
Moederken; Ueber allen Gipfeln ist Ruh. L. de Koning (S), J. van Benthem (pf) (Mirasound Musica 441983)

The Van Noordt family

Seventeenth-century music in Amsterdam was largely dominated by three families of organists: the Sweelincks, the Lossys and the Van Noordts. Three members of the Sweelinck family played the organ at the Saint Nicholas or Old Church, and two generations of Lossys were organists at the New Church before they were succeeded by the Van Noordts.

SYBRANDUS VAN NOORDT SR.
?, c.1590 – Amsterdam, buried 28 December 1654

The date and place of birth and parentage of Sybrandus van Noordt Sr., the patriarch of this musical family, remain unknown. In 1640, the year in which his wife Jannitgen Jacobs died, he was carillonneur of the five most important bell-towers in Amsterdam. Two of his four sons, Jacobus (born c.1616) and Anthoni (born c.1619), followed in his footsteps and became musicians.

No compositions of his are known, but the fact that the city of Amsterdam entrusted him with its five 'most capital towers' does bear witness to his musical ability. He died in late December 1654 and was buried in the Zuider Church.

JACOBUS VAN NOORDT
Amsterdam, c.1616 – Amsterdam, 29 December 1680

Jacobus van Noordt, Sybrandus' eldest son, probably received his initial musical instruction from his father. It is likely that the organist at the Old Church, Dirck Sweelinck, also played a role in his education. Upon the death of Willem Jansz Lossy in 1648, Jacobus van Noordt was appointed his successor at the Nieuwezijds Chapel. In 1652 he left this post to take the place of the recently deceased Dirck Sweelinck at the Old Church. According to Joan Dullaert's poem *Op 't klokkespel van Mr. Jacob van Oort* [To the carillon playing of Mr Jacob van Oort] (1659), he was also occasionally employed as carillonneur. In 1648 he married Elsje Corver, a Roman Catholic and daughter of a soap maker. They had nine children. One of them, Sybrandus Jr. (born in 1659), also became an organist.

His earliest known compositions probably date from 1648. Nine of his compositions for a solo instrument were published in *'t Uitnement Kabinet* [The excellent cabinet] (1649, reprint c. 1655), a collection of pieces for various instruments. His expertise on the organ extended to involvement in building and repairing various instruments.

Jacobus van Noordt was less successful in his personal life. Perhaps owing to his extravagant character, he fell into serious financial difficulties and was forced to borrow increasingly large sums, which he was subsequently unable to repay. On 19 November 1671 he was declared bankrupt. His home and possessions were sold and until 1673 his salary was put at the disposal of the 'Bureau of Insolvent Estates'.

Because of his advanced years and poor health he was 'named emeritus and excused from duties as organist at the Old Church' on 22 July 1679. His son Sybrandus was appointed his successor that same day. He died several weeks after his wife in 1680 and was buried in the New Church.

Although Jacobus van Noordt is believed to have been an excellent organist and according to Dullaert played the carillon 'with heavenly taste', he was a minor composer. His nine compositions for descant instrument published in *'t Uitnement Kabinet* are rather simple examples of the popular variation genre. Compared to the similar works (regarding form and style) of Jacob van Eyck, Jacobus van Noordt's compositions have marginal importance.

ANTHONI VAN NOORDT
Amsterdam, c.1619 – Amsterdam, buried 23 March 1675

Sybrandus van Noordt's second son, Anthoni, succeeded his brother Jacobus as organist of the Nieuwezijds Chapel in 1652. Twelve years later, on 20 August 1664, he became organist of the New Church. As Jacobus van Noordt was at that time organist at the Old Church, the Van Noordt family was to hold the most important organist positions in Amsterdam for over a decade. Anthoni van Noordt's compositions were published in 1660 in the *Tabulatuur-boeck van Psalmen en Fantasyen* [Tablature book of psalms and fantasias]. Anthoni van Noordt was called on to appraise organs in Amsterdam and Rotterdam.

Very little is known about his life. Like his brothers Joan the painter and Lucas, a preacher in Diemen, near Amsterdam, he never married. Owing to ill health, he was dismissed as organist at the New Church on 20 November 1673 although he did retain his salary. He died two years later and was buried in the Zuider Church in Amsterdam.

Anthoni van Noordt's only known compositions are published in the *Tabulatuur-boeck van Psalmen en Fantasyen*, but these alone make him a worthy successor to Jan Pieterszoon Sweelinck. Anthoni's preface includes an indirect reference to this effect. The collection contains ten psalms with variations and six fantasias for the organ. The psalm settings stand out for their ingenuity in conveying the meaning of the text. The work is intended for an organ with at least two manuals and pedals. Despite its importance, it did not bring the composer much success. The Secretary at the Dutch court and composer Constantijn Huygens, who understood better than Van Noordt the changes in public taste and the role of a church organist, was unconvinced that these compositions ('although good and masterly') would find much use in the Netherlands or abroad.

SYBRANDUS VAN NOORDT JR.

Amsterdam, baptized 10 August 1659 – Amsterdam, buried 25 February 1705

Sybrandus van Noordt, the eighth child of Jacobus van Noordt and Elsje Corver, was born in August 1659 and named after his grandfather. Judging from the inventory of Jacobus van Noordt's possessions, prepared at his bankruptcy in 1671, Sybrandus van Noordt was already being prepared for a career in music at the age of twelve. The document lists 'a harpsichord, staffs to play upon, as well as a table and slate to write upon and a small clavichord' standing in the child's room. The bankruptcy of his father put an end to Sybrandus van Noordt's training in music and cast a shadow on his future prospects. For four years he worked as a clerk in a notary's office. When Jacobus van Noordt's financial difficulties cleared and payment of his salary was reinstated in 1674, Sybrandus van Noordt resumed his study of music and in 1679 succeeded his father as organist at the Old Church.

The nature of this position underwent an enormous change when on 10 October 1680 the city and church councils of Amsterdam, in keeping with developments in many Dutch cities, approved the use of the organ for accompanying congregational psalm singing. Prior to this, organists such as Jacobus and Anthoni van Noordt – and the Sweelincks and Lossys before them – served solely as concert-giving city musicians whose duties in the church entailed playing the organ before and after church services and at other set times. It was in this tradition that Sybrandus van Noordt was raised. As a result of this change he later experienced much strife with city and church authorities as to the strict artistic and social limitations within which he was required to work.

Like his father and uncle, Sybrandus van Noordt was an expert on the organ; the role he played in an extensive renovation of the Old Church great organ (1686) spread the 27-year-old's fame throughout the land. From then on he was often contracted to appraise organs and carillons.

On 19 September 1683 he married Debora de Goijer from Diemen. The couple had three daughters, the first, Nisa, was born eleven months after the wedding. Debora de Goijer came from a reasonably prosperous family of farmers from whom she inherited a considerable sum of money. With this capital, added to his comparatively generous salary and extra earnings, Sybrandus van Noordt was an affluent man by around 1688-89. However, an Italian prince in Amsterdam, Mario Plati, lured the gullible organist into investing his entire capital in a 'wonder product' for cleaning pearls and Van Noordt lost everything in the swin-

SYBRANDUS van NOORD.

dle. He subsequently resigned as organist at the Old Church in 1692 to succeed Joan Dusart at the more lucrative post of organist and carillonneur at the Great Church in Haarlem.

His period in Haarlem proved disastrous. After he became embroiled in repeated conflicts with his employers over absences, drunkenness and fighting, the Haarlem city council forced his dismissal in 1694, whereupon the Van Noordt family returned to Amsterdam. All the city's organ positions were filled, however, and Van Noordt's reputation was so damaged that he never again received an appointment as organist. For the rest of his life he earned his living as a freelance organist, an appraiser of organs and carillons and as an inspector at the Amsterdam bell foundry.

Around 1701 Van Noordt composed the *Sonate per il Cimbalo appropriate al flauto & violino, opera Prima*. It was republished during his lifetime (1704-1705) under the title *Mélange italien* by Estienne Roger. This op.1 contains three sonatas for harpsichord and a transcription of the second sonata for violin duet. The sonatas are notated in such a way as to make them suitable for performance also by one melody instrument (recorder, violin) and basso continuo. These were the first Dutch sonatas for harpsichord; indeed, after Johann Kuhnau, Van Noordt was one of the first composers of harpsichord sonatas in all of Europe. The sonatas are distinguished by their broad melodic lines, lengthy sequential passages and the virtuosity of their passagework. The *Sonata a Cimbalo Solo* is by far the most interesting, and its idiom is close to that of Vivaldi.

Sybrandus van Noordt died in February 1705 and like his father was buried in the New Church. He was the last in the line of Van Noordts who distinguished themselves as musicians. Their place and importance in Dutch music history is imposing but at the same time difficult to trace. No students or successors of any stature are known. All that remains is a handful of attractive compositions and one masterpiece, Anthoni van Noordt's *Tabulatuur-boeck*.

REIN VERHAGEN

JACOBUS VAN NOORDT

COMPOSITIONS
[5] Petites Branles; Frere Frapar; Malle Symen; Preludium; Repicavan
For one instrument without bc. Included in: *'t Uitnement Kabinet ... Tweede deel.* – Amsterdam, P. Matthysz, [1649] (repr. *c* 1655)

BIBLIOGRAPHY
J.H. Giskes: 'Jacobus van Noordt (*c* 1616-1680) : organist van Amsterdam', *Amstelodamum*, yearbook 81, 1989, p. 83-124

ANTHONI VAN NOORDT

COMPOSITIONS
Tabulatuur-boeck van Psalmen en Fantasyen ... – Amsterdam, Willem van Beaumont, 1660

DISCOGRAPHY
Fantasia II. B. van Asperen (Sony Classical SK 46349)
Fantasia in G major; Psalm 38. J. Tuma (Supraphon Sup 0065-2)
Psalm 24. E. Roloff (MDG 319 0538-2)
Psalm 116. H. van Nieuwkoop (Canal Grande CG 9102)
Tabulatuur-boeck van Psalmen en Fantasyen (sel.). L. van Doeselaar (NM Classics 92024)

SYBRANDUS VAN NOORDT JR.

COMPOSITIONS
Sonate per il Cimbalo appropriate al flauto & violino ... opera prima. – Amsterdam, Henrico Anders, [*c* 1701]
Repr. as *Mélange italien ou Sonates à 1 flûte & 1 basse continue, à 2 violons sans basse & à un clavessin seul ...* opera prima. – Amsterdam, Estienne Roger, [*c* 1704/1705]

BIBLIOGRAPHY
R. Verhagen: *Sybrandus van Noordt : organist van Amsterdam en Haarlem (1659-1705)*. Amsterdam, Koninklijke Nederlandse Toonkunstenaars Vereniging, 1989

DISCOGRAPHY
Sonata. B. van Asperen (hpd) (Sony Classical SK 46349)
Sonata op.1, no.1. M. Miessen (rec), B. van Asperen (hpd), W. Möll (vc) (BFO A-2)

Cornélie van Oosterzee

BATAVIA, 16 AUGUST 1863 – BERLIN, 12 AUGUST 1943

Cornélie van Oosterzee moved with her parents from Batavia, the Dutch East Indies, to the Netherlands at the age of five so that her father could take up a position as president of the Dutch Trading Company. As a child, she took piano lessons from C.L.W. Wirtz at the Royal Music School in The Hague and later, theory lessons with W.F.G. Nicolaï. When her father died, she and her mother returned to Batavia, where she lived from 1883 to 1888, a period she considered unfruitful for her musical development.

Initially, Van Oosterzee was intent on pursuing a career as a concert pianist, but after consulting Clara Schumann, who thought her too old to set out on this path, decided to become a composer instead. Once back in the Netherlands, she resumed her studies with Nicolaï in The Hague and a short time later went to study in Berlin. After repeated disappointments in gaining admission to a conservatory, she was accepted by the Sternsches Konservatorium, where she studied with Rudolf Radecke. After two years in Berlin, she returned to the Netherlands to study counterpoint with Samuel de Lange. She then went back to Berlin and enrolled in Heinrich Urban's Meisterschule for instrumentation, according to whom 'she certainly did not compose like a woman'.

Shortly thereafter her music was regularly performed in the Netherlands and in Germany. In 1891 her Piano Quartet in C-sharp minor was played in public and, at the opening in 1894 of the new City Theater in Amsterdam, her first orchestral piece, *Jolanthe,* was performed by the Concertgebouw Orchestra under Willem Kes. In later years this overture was a regular fixture on orchestral programs.

In 1896 she conducted the Utrecht Municipal Orchestra in the premiere in Utrecht and Rotterdam of her *Königs-Idyllen,* a suite of four symphonic poems based on Tennyson's *Idylls of the King.* She also conducted successful performances of these symphonic poems in Leeuwarden, Nijmegen and Haarlem. *Königs-Idyllen* was later conducted by Arthur Nikisch in Berlin and Willem Mengelberg with the Concertgebouw Orchestra in Amsterdam.

On 11 October 1900 Willem Mengelberg led the Concertgebouw Orchestra in the Dutch premiere of Van Oosterzee's Symphony in F-minor. Around this time the weekly *Weekblad voor Muziek* wrote that this work 'must be counted among the very best orchestral works written by a Dutch composer.' Three

years later her piano sonata *Italia* won a competition organized by the journal *Nederlandsche Muziekkalender*.

While Van Oosterzee continued composing a number of small-scale pieces, she developed plans to write an opera. On 1 May 1910 her music drama *Das Gelöbnis* was premiered in the Court Theater of Weimar. Although German critics gave the work poor reviews, a review by S. Van Milligen in the music journal *Caecilia* spoke enthusiastically of 'the very evocative drama and the rich orchestral colors.' Van Oosterzee was conscious of her unusual position as a woman composer and participated in the women's suffrage movement. For the opening of the National Exhibition of Women's Work in The Hague in 1898 she composed and conducted a cantata for women's choir, soloists and orchestra. The libretto left no doubt as to her thoughts on the suffrage movement: women must fight for emancipation. In Berlin she chaired the music department of the Lyceum Club, an organization of women from the upper echelons of society that engaged in cultural activities and were active in political and social questions. In 1912 Van Oosterzee forcefully laid out her views on the development of women composers in the periodical *Toonkunst*: 'a development that slowly but calmly and courageously is taking to the field amidst the battalions of male pens, which scratchily insist and restate that in this regard there is nothing to develop in women, and consequently accuse nature of a most peculiar one-sidedness in her distribution of talents.'

Van Oosterzee wrote articles for various periodicals and newspapers. From 1895 to 1914 she was a correspondent with the daily *Algemeen Handelsblad,* writing a column entitled 'Letters from Berlin' in which she reported on the musical life of this city. From 1895 to 1906 she wrote a similar feature for the *Weekblad voor Muziek*, and worked for the music journal *Caecilia*.

At an early age (in 1897) Van Oosterzee was made a dame in the Order of Orange-Nassau. She also was an honorary member of the Bach Society in Haarlem, and in 1901 she was named a member of merit of the Society for the Advancement of Music.

Little is known about the last 25 years of her life. In 1926 the *Berliner Musiker Jahrbuch* made mention of her (listing her address as 19 Rankestrasse). In 1943, three days after her death, the *Algemeen Handelsblad* ran an article on her, referring to the waning interest in her music: 'Slowly, her orchestral and chamber music has disappeared from concert programs. The increasing interest in the compositions of young composers has caused less attention to be given to her work.'

Cornélie van Oosterzee, who admired the work of Wagner and Strauss, had a particular talent for drama and for conveying moods. Her largest work, the opera *Das Gelöbnis*, is in the style of the Italian *verismo*: murder and guilt are the *Leitmotifs* of the libretto. But she was also well grounded in the music of Brahms and Schumann. Wouter Hutschenruyter Jr. described the first movement of *Königs-Idyllen* as 'fresh and young, a powerful work with exquisite thematic development and excellent instrumentation'. Her previously mentioned cantata of 1898 was based on a libretto filled with contrast, well suiting her penchant for drama.

Aside from her larger works, Van Oosterzee composed chamber music ranging from simple pieces for piano four hands, in which reminiscences of her youth in Batavia emerge, such as *Javaanse Dans* [Javanese dance] and *Maleis Wiegenlied* [Malaysian lullaby] to German salon music of the 1920s such as *Zwei Phantasiestücke* for piano trio. Throughout her career she composed songs to Dutch, German and French texts in a late-Romantic style. Her German songs show the influence of Hugo Wolf and Richard Strauss, while her French songs reveal her acquaintance with the music of Berlioz.

Many of her larger-scale works, such as the symphonies and her opera, were never published and have never been located. They may very well have perished in the destruction of Berlin at the end of World War II.

HELEN METZELAAR

COMPOSITIONS

SONGS WITH PIANO: *Drei Lieder*, op. 3; *Tannhäuserlied*, op. 7; *Vier Gesänge*, op. 12; *Zwei Gesänge*, op. 19; *Zwei Stimmungsgedichte*, op. 21; *Drei Liebeslieder*, op. 22; *Vieux Airs de la Marquise*, op. 25; *Chansons sentimentales*, op. 54; *2 Lieder*, op. 59

CHOIR: *Te Bethlehem : uit de Legende van Jeschua ben Jossef* (De Mont), mix.choir, op. 14; *Cantata*, soloists, w.choir, orch, org (1898); *Droomevrouw, kom*; *Madonna*, mix.choir; *Berusting*, mix.choir; *Avond*, mix.choir

OPERA: *Das Gelöbnis* (premiered in 1910)

PIANO (PIANO 2H UNLESS OTHERWISE STATED): *'Italia' : sonate* (1903); *Fête costumée : 3 fantaisies*, op. 15; *4 petites valses capricieuses*, op. 23; *Sechs leichte Stücke*, pf 4h, op. 55; *Carnaval : 3 fantaisies*, op. 58; *Javaanse Dans*, pf 4h; *Maleis Wiegenlied*, pf 4h

CHAMBER MUSIC: *String Quartet* (*c* 1888);
Piano Quartet in C-sharp minor (*c* 1890);
String Quintet in B-flat major (*c* 1892); *Zwei
Phantasiestücke*, pf, vl, vc, op. 18

ORCHESTRA: *Jolanthe : lyrisch drama in één
bedrijf; Nordische Fantasie; Königs-Idyllen;
Symphony in F minor* (1900)

PUBLICATIONS
Autobiography, *Nederlandsche Muziekkalender*, vol. 3, 1994, p. 35-37

BIBLIOGRAPHY
W. Hutschenruyter jr.: 'Cornélie van Oos-
terzee', *Eigen Haard*, 20 Oct. 1896
H. Metzelaar: 'Cornélie van Oosterzee', *The
New Grove Dictionary of Women Composers*, ed.
J.A. Sadie and R. Samuel. London, MacMillan,
1994, p. 353
S. van Milligen: 'Das Gelöbnis : muziek-
drama van Cornelie van Oosterzee', *Caecilia*,
1910, p. 177-181
W.F.G. Nicolaï: 'Critische aankondigingen',
Caecilia, 51, 1894, p. [15]-16
H. Nolthenius: 'Cornélie van Oosterzee',
Weekblad voor Muziek, vol. 3, 1896, p. 319-320
and 329
Onze Musici : portretten en biografieën. Rot-
terdam, Nijgh & Van Ditmar, 1898
H. Smit: *Enige aspekten van de 'emancipatie'
van de Nederlandse vrouw in het muziekleven in
de periode 1889-1913*. Dissertation University of
Utrecht, 1983
H. V.: 'De Tentoonstellings-Cantate van
Cornélie van Oosterzee', *Caecilia*, 55, 1898, p.
128-130
E. van Zoeren: *De Muziekuitgeverij A.A.
Noske (1896-1926) : een bijdrage tot dertig jaar
Nederlandse muziekgeschiedenis*. Haarlemmer-
liede, Van Zoeren, 1987, p. 205-206

Léon Orthel

ROOSENDAAL, 4 OCTOBER 1905 – THE HAGUE, 6 SEPTEMBER 1985

At the age of sixteen Léon Orthel, who was born in Roosendaal, studied composition with Johan Wagenaar at the Royal Conservatory in The Hague. He was trained as a pianist by Everhard van Beynum at the same institute. A scholarship from the Dutch government enabled him to study in Berlin in 1928-1929 with the Russian-Swiss composer Paul Juon and the renowned musicologist Curt Sachs. Upon returning to the Netherlands he completed his musical education under Johan Wagenaar.

Orthel made his debut as a composer in 1930 with *Concertino alla Burla*, in which he performed as piano soloist. From 1947 until his retirement in 1971 he was a professor at the Royal Conservatory in The Hague. He also taught composition at the Amsterdam Conservatory (1949-1971) and was chairman of the composers' chapter of the Royal Netherlands Music Society (1947-1970) and the Johan Wagenaar Foundation (1952-1972). As a composer, however, Orthel had few followers.

Orthel's music is not often programmed, although the *Piccola Sinfonia* (Second Symphony) was performed quite frequently in the 1950s. After retiring he focused on chamber music, in particular songs with piano accompaniment, a genre he had avoided when he was younger. He found inspiration in the German and French poems of Rainer Maria Rilke. Orthel interwove melodies from children's songs in many of his works, out of pure nostalgia, according to his colleague piano teacher Cor de Groot. The *Kleine balletsuite* [Small ballet suite] (commissioned by the Residentie Orchestra) incorporates as many as seven of these songs and the *Piccola Sinfonia* adds a children's New Year song from the province of Brabant that 'suddenly sprang to mind'. Orthel composed the fifth Piano Sonatina, for the left hand, after learning that his colleague Cor de Groot was having problems with his right hand. Most of his orchestral works were premiered by the Rotterdam Philharmonic Orchestra under Eduard Flipse.

Orthel belonged to what has come to be known as the 'lost generation': composers educated in the 1920s and 1930s whose traditional style did not fit in with the modernistic and avant-garde tendencies of the 1950s. Notable in Orthel's music is his desire to take account of the public's capabilities of musical perception. Not that he shied away from experimenting with modern tech-

niques: his First Symphony (1931-1933) has a twelve-tone theme, and in later works, such as *Epigrammen*, he explored polytonal and atonal techniques. But he ultimately distanced himself from modernism and found inspiration in a Romantic style, which in the post-war modern clamor was received by some critics with a mixture of relief and unease.

This was the case, for example, with his Fourth Symphony, which music critic Wouter Paap described in the periodical *Mens en Melodie* (1950) as filled with 'pathetic fantasy' that arises from the often 'unexpected impulses in which the longing for virtuosity and the need for the dramatic conveying of feelings vie for prominence', although 'pathos seemed one of those qualities that modern music had unanimously abandoned.' Despite his positive words, Paap voiced concern that it was not entirely clear where Orthel's music 'was headed'. He saw in its pathos the danger of 'externalization'.

In retrospect, Orthel's best-known work, the Second Symphony (1939), reveals him to be a composer who was very conscious of the musical developments of his time. This piece, in six uninterrupted movements, seems written by someone who took insightful note not just of what his Dutch and French contemporaries were doing, but also of Shostakovich's music. The Second Symphony has a forward drive, leaving itself and the listener no time for reflection and, despite its slightly threatening atmosphere, certainly no reason for gloom. The Fourth Symphony – whose many surprising turns make it exciting from beginning to end, despite its great length, is different in this respect. Here, Orthel seems to have wanted to confirm his preference for dark colors. Notable characteristics are his liking for the 'al niente' close and extremely low pedal points; in the Second Symphony there is even a low A, which is held for a full hundred measures.

JOHAN KOLSTEEG

COMPOSITIONS

SONGS: *Three Songs* (Rilke), S/T, pf, op. 26
(1943); *Two Songs* (Rilke), S, pf, op. 30
(1946); *Two Songs* (Rilke), S, pf, op. 33 (1951);
Three Songs (Smelik), S, pf, op. 49 (1965);
Three Songs (Rilke), S, pf, op. 51 (1965); *Two
Songs* (Rilke), S, pf, op. 53 (1966); *Two Songs*
(Rilke), Bar, pf, op. 54 (1967); *Three Songs*
(Rilke), m.v, pf, op. 55 (1971); *Two Songs*
(Rilke), B-Bar, pf, op. 56 (1971); *Four Songs*
(Nijhoff), 2 for S/T, cl, and 2 for S/T, pf, op.
64 (1972); *Three Songs* (Rilke), S, pf, op. 74
(1975); *Four Songs* (Eyck, Oosterhuis, Sme-
lik), A, pf, op. 85 (1978); *Four Songs* (Bloem,
Van Eeden, Slauerhoff, Spijkerman), S, pf,
op. 86 (1980)

PIANO: Piano Sonatinas (op. 28; op. 36; op. 70,
op. 73; op. 78; op. 84; op. 90); *Hommage à
Ravel, en forme d'étude*, op. 40, no. 2 (1958);
Etudes caprices, op. 39 (1957); *Piano
Sonatina*, pf lh, op. 44 (1959)

CHAMBER MUSIC: *Cello Sonata no. 1*, op. 6
(1925); *Cello Sonata no. 2*, op. 41 (1958)

ORCHESTRA: *Scherzo*, pf, orch, op. 10 (1927 or
1929?); *Concertino alla Burla*, op. 12 (1930);
Symphony no. 1, op. 13 (1931-1933); *Epigrammen*, op. 17; *Symphony no. 2 (Piccola Sinfonia)* (1939); *Symphony no. 3* (1943); *Kleine
balletsuite*, op. 31 (1947); *Symphony no. 4
(Sinfonia concertante)*, op. 32 (1949); *Cello
Concerto no. 2*, op. 95 (1982)

BIBLIOGRAPHY
J. Geraedts: 'Léon Orthel : Scherzo no. 2',
Sonorum Speculum, no. 25. 1965, p. 20
C. de Groot: 'Wie vergeet een componist?
Het publiek of de uitvoerenden?', *Mens en
Melodie*, vol. 41, 1986, p. 298 – 307
W. Paap: 'Vierde symphonie van Léon Or-
thel', *Mens en Melodie*, vol.5, 1950, p. 411
P.Visser: 'In memoriam Léon Orthel', *Mens
en Melodie*, vol. 40, 1985, p. 445
J. Wouters: 'Léon Orthel : Piccola Sinfonia',
Sonorum Speculum, no. 6, 1961, p. 20

DISCOGRAPHY
Symphony no. 2 (Piccola Sinfonia). Residentie Orchestra, cond. W. van Otterloo (Composers' Voice CV 26)

Cornelis Thymanszoon Padbrué

HAARLEM, C.1592 – 1670

The composer, shawm player, harpsichordist and singing master, Cornelis Padbrué (or Patbrué) was born around 1592 in Haarlem and raised in a musical family. His grandfather, Jehan de Pattebruecq – known as 'Jenning the Singer' (of the choir of the Saint Bavo Cathedral in Haarlem) – originally came from Hainaut. Padbrué's father, Thyman Janszoon, was a braid worker and one of the City Shawm Players of Haarlem. A dozen or so compositions for lute by Padbrué's uncle David have been preserved in manuscript. Jan Thymanszoon, a brother of Padbrué who died young, was also a shawm player in the service of the city of Haarlem as well as a painter. The whereabouts of the portrait he painted of Padbrué are unknown.

When he was around 18 years old, Padbrué joined a four-member ensemble of city minstrels as a shawm player. In 1629 he became leader of the group, succeeding Jan Willemszoon Lossy, the former teacher of Jan Pieterszoon Sweelinck. In 1635, after 'longstanding disagreement and quarreling among these minstrels', Padbrué was dismissed from city service.

In 1631 his first madrigal collection – *Kusjes* [Kisses], to poetry by Jacob Westerbaen – was published. This collection became very well known, as indicated by the fact that numerous new texts were written to go with Padbrué's melodies, a practice known as contrafactum technique.

In the 1630s Padbrué probably entered into collaboration with the poet Joost van den Vondel. Around 1633 Van den Vondel wrote the verse *Deuntje, aen Mr. Cornelis Thymansz. Padbrué* in which he invites the composer to set his poetry to music ('Wil je zingen, ick wil rijmen,/O genoeghelicke Tymen' – Would you sing, I would rhyme,/O pleasant Tymen). It is thought that Padbrué composed the choruses for Van den Vondel's tragedy *Ghysbrecht van Aemstel* (1637), but of these only the melody of the chorus *O Kersnacht! schoonder dan de dagen* [O Christmas eve! more beautiful than the days] has survived. This melody became very popular and gave rise to many contrafacta until deep into the eighteenth century. It is still sung today in a version from the Dutch psalm book, the *Liedboek voor de Kerken*.

In 1640 Padbrué published a ten-section madrigal to Van den Vondel's poem *De Kruisbergh* [Calvary]. The choice of this text could be understood as a reference to his Roman Catholic sympathies. The collection also includes a madrigal cycle on a Van den Vondel text criticizing the divisions in the Christ-

KVSIES,
In't Latijn ghefchreven,
Door
IOANNES SECVNDVS,
Ende in duytfche vaerfen ghefteldt,
Door IACOB WESTERBAEN,
Beyde Haeghfche Pöeeten:

Nu eerft op Mufijck ghebracht, à *III. ende IIII. ftemmen:*
Met een BASSO CONTINVO.
Door
CORNELIS THYMANS PADBRVÉ,
Muficijn van Haerlem.

BASSUS.

Tot Haerlem,

Gedruckt by Harman Cranepoel, Boeck-drucker inde korte Bagijne-ftraet,
in't groene Kruys. *Anno M. D.C. XXXI.*

---

ian world (*Klaght over de Tweedraght der Christe Princen* [Complaint on the discord of the princes of Christ]) and some Latin motets.

After losing his position with the city, Padbrué composed various occasional works celebrating marriages of prosperous citizens of Amsterdam and Haarlem. Another indication of his social connections is the collection of madrigals and motets *'T lof van Jubal. Eerste vinder der musijcke* [In praise of Jubal, first finder of music] (1643), op.3, to texts by (presumably) Van den Vondel, Van Baerle, Cats and Westerbaen. The dedication of this collection to the city council members of Haarlem spurred a reconciliation: the council awarded him an inscribed silver platter. Encouraged by the enthusiastic response to this work and the recognition of his talent, Padbrué two years later published a sequel named *'T lof Jubals, tweede boeck* [In praise of Jubal, second book]. op.4.

In 1646 Paulus Matthysz published Padbrué's magnum opus, *De tranen Petri ende Pauli* [The tears of Peter and Paul], a work also based on texts by Van den Vondel and dedicated to Symon Felt. With this 'oratorio in the common language' he was the first to introduce this Italian genre to northern Europe.

In celebration of the Treaty of Westphalia in 1648 he composed another cantata, to his own texts, but the work has been lost. No trace has been found of Padbrué's musical activities in the last 22 years of his life. He died in 1670 and was buried in Haarlem's Saint Bavo Cathedral.

Padbrué was a versatile composer who kept abreast of the international musical developments of the seventeenth century. His *Kusjes*, for example, affects a virtuoso, sprightly counterpoint that closely corresponds with the erotic character of the verses. In a later edition of *Kusjes*, he replaced the strophic form with a through-composed version.

Text expression – 'madrigalisms' – was a constant feature in Padbrué's work. The poem *De Kruisbergh*, in which Van den Vondel likens Christ's bleeding head to a 'hat of roses', was the basis for Padbrué's first sacred composition. Here, too, he made use of tone painting and increasing melismatic writing, though to enhance the comprehensibility of the text the polyphonic style often gives way to homophonic, declamatory passages.

Contrasting with this madrigal cycle is his next work, the austere double motet *O vos omnes/O triste spectaculum*. The sustained lines of its Renaissance-like polyphony reveal an entirely new side of his style: a serene choral lyricism that does not shrink from 'modern' dissonant usage and abundant emotional upheavals.

Taking a special place among Dutch motets is the eight-voice *Da pacem, Domine super Ecce quam bonum* for double chorus; sounding above ('super') a classical, four-voice European-style motet (the peace antiphon *Da pacem*) is a four-voiced unison canon on the psalm text *Ecce quam bonum*. This can be seen as an attempt at least to reconcile the repertoires of the Reformation and the mother church.

Padbrué also employed the 'stile moderno' ('stile concertante'), for example in his *Cantate Domino canticum novum* and the *Eere-krans voor Constantin Sohier en Catharina Koymans* [Tribute to Constantin Sohier and Catharina Koymans], in which concertante coloraturas and milder consonant passages alternate in close accordance with the text.

Various surviving instrumental pieces refer back to his former life as a city musician; the pavanes and galliards of the 1640s bear witness to Padbrué's affinity with this style, as it was practiced throughout Europe. The pavane and galliard in the *Synphonia in nuptias J. Everswyn et Luciae Buys* refer to the English composer Peter Philips, who resided as a Catholic refugee in Brussels.

Padbrué's *De tranen Petri ende Pauli*, his largest and most important work, appears to have been directly motivically inspired by such works as Coprario's *Funeral Tears* (1606) and *Songs of Mourning* (1613). Significant differences in Padbrué's work, however, are its formal construction and passionate declamation. Frits Noske, the pioneer researcher into this 'Jubalist from Haarlem', called *De tranen Petri ende Pauli* a 'unique monument from our musical past'. The work is all the more important as it contains the only surviving polyphonic choruses by Joost van den Vondel.

BOB VAN ASPEREN

COMPOSITIONS

Kusjes in 't Latijn geschreven door Joannes Secundus ende in duytsche vaersen ghesteldt door Jacob Westerbaen ... [opus 1]. – Haarlem, 1631
Texts: Janus Secundus / J. Westerbaen, J. Brosterhuysen. Includes thirteen Kusjes (madrigals after Secundus' 'Basia') and two madrigals. For 3-4 voices and bc. Incomplete

O Kersnacht! schoonder dan de dagen. Christmas chorus in Gysbrecht van Aemstel (Vondel), 1637
Attributed to Padbrué in the monograph by De Klerk and the article by Van Asperen (which also includes a transcription) (see bibliography)

Kusjes... den tweeden Druck vermeerdert ende verbetert met 5, 4, ende 3 stemmen, met een basso continuo... [opus 1]. – Amsterdam, 1641
Texts: Janus Secundus / J. Westerbaen, Petrarca / J. Brosterhuysen, Salomon de Bray, P. Luidhenz, P. de Grebber. Modern ed. (without bc part): F. Noske, Amsterdam, VNM, 1962 (Monumenta Musica Neerlandica 5). Information concerning the bc in the article by Guillo (see bibliography)

J. v. Vondels Kruisbergh en Klaght over de tweedraght der Christe Princen...[opus 2]. – Amsterdam, 1640
For 3, 4, 5 v and bc. Includes: 1) *De kruisbergh*, madrigal cycle for 4-5 v and bc. Modern ed.: A. Smijers, Amsterdam, TVNM XLII, 1931. 2) *O vos omnes / O triste spectaculum*, motet for 4 v and bc. 3) *Klaght over de tweedraght der Christe Princen*, madrigal cycle for S, T, B and bc. 4) *Cantate Domino canticum novum*, motet for 2 S, B and bc. 5) *Da pacem, Domine super Ecce quam bonum*, motet canon for SATB, 4 T or S and bc. Modern ed.: F. Noske, 1989 (see bibliography)

Synphonia in nuptias... I. Everswyn ... sponsi et ... Luciae Buys, sponsae, celebrandas nono calendas May 1641 Harlemi Batavorum. – Amsterdam, 1641
Includes: Pavana and gaillarde, for 2 or 4-5 (?) v. Incomplete? Modern ed. (2 v): R. Rasch, Utrecht, The Diapason Press, 1985

Synphonia in nuptias... Mathaei Steyn ... sponsi et ... Mariae van Napels, sponsae, celebrandas Februarii IV. anno 1642 Harlemi Batavorum. – Amsterdam, 1642
Includes: Prima pars (pavana) en Secunda pars (gaillarde) for 5 v. Incomplete. Modern ed. (3 v): R. Rasch, Utrecht, The Diapason Press, 1985

Eere-krans voor Constantin Sohier en Catharina Koymans, echtelijck vereenight op den lesten May 1643. In Beverwijck. – Amsterdam, 1643
Includes: Madrigal '*Wat heeft den hemel hier zoo zoet gevoeght*' (for S, Bar and bc)

'T lof van Jubal. Eerste vinder der musijcke, en allerley musijck-instrumenten; door verscheyden poëten in duytsche, en latijnsche vaersen gestelt: nu eerst op musijck gebracht met vier, vijf, en ses stemmen, met de gemeene grontstem, ofte continuo... eerste boeck, derde werck. – Amsterdam, 1643
Includes: madrigals and motets: *O Jubal, die den eersten waert* (6 v); *O aldersoetste Lamechs-Soon* (6 v, text: Westerbaen); *De vinder van den sangh* (4/6 v, text: Cats); *Roert niet meer uw losse wieken* (5 v, text: Vondel); *Principio coelum & terras* (6 v, text: Barlaeus); *Domine Deus in simplicitate* (6 v); *Domus mea, domus orationis* (6 v); *Benedictus sit Deus Pater* (6 v); *Benedicimus Deum coeli* (6 v). Incomplete

'T lof Jubals... tweede boeck, vierde werck. –
Amsterdam, 1645
For 3, 4, 5 and 6 v and bc. Includes madrigals and motets: *O edele musijck* (4/6 v, text:
Swalmius); *Jubal, geen verzierde Apollen* (3-4
v, text: Vondel); *In laudem Jubalis. Laetitiae
primaeve dator* (3-6 v, text: Barlaeus); *Een
vryer neemt uw kunst* (3 v, text: Westerbaen);
De taelman van de Goon (4 v, text: Heere-
man); *In laudem Jubalis. Quem virum nos-
trae* (5 v, text: Boorten); *O zoete Jubal* (4 v,
text: Leenaerts); *Als Tubalcain met hamers* (3
or 4 v, 4 v, text: Van Kittenstein). Incomplete

De tranen Petri ende Pauli door J. v. Vondel. –
Amsterdam, 1646
Text: prologue, dialogues, monologues and
choruses from Vondel's tragedy 'Petrus en
Pauwels'. For 2, 3, 4 and 5 v and bc. Incom-
plete

Celebration cantata on the peace treaty of
Munster. – Haarlem, 1648
Text: Padbrué. Dedicated to the city of
Haarlem. Lost: mentioned in a letter fom
Padbrué to the local government of Haar-
lem

*Seneca's eerste Rey in Hyppolitus, gezongen ter
bruiloft van sr. Cornelis de Graet, en juffr.
Catharina Guldewagen*. – Haarlem, 1675
Text: Seneca / J. van Vlakveld. For 3 v. Includes madrigal '*Godin, geteelt uyt 't schuim
der zee*'. Attributed to Padbrué in the article
by Van Asperen (see bibliography)

BIBLIOGRAPHY
J.G.R. Acquoy: 'De zangwijze van het "O
kersnacht, schooner dan de daegen" ', *TVNM*,
4, 1894, p. 177 et seq.
B. van Asperen: 'Een 17de eeuwse Haarlemse bruiloftsbrochure', *Mens en Melodie*, vol.
43, 1988, p. 491-501
H.A. Bruinsma: 'An introduction to Vondel
and music', *TVNM*, 31/2, 1981, p. 95 et seq.
L. Guillo: 'Les deux recueils de musique
de Zuoz/Washington (1580-1643) : sur deux
témoins de la librairie musicale néerlandaise
au XVIIe siècle', *TVNM*, 46/2, 1996, p. 137-
151
J. de Klerk: *Haarlems muziekleven in de loop*

der tijden. Haarlem, Tjeenk Willink, 1965, p. 83
et seq.
A. van der Marel: *Cornelis Thymansz. Pad-
brué en zijn familie. Beroemd toonkunstenaar uit
de Gouden Eeuw* (typed genealogy (1961) in the
Public Library of Haarlem)
F. Noske: *C.Th. Padbrué : Nederlandse
madrigalen*. Amsterdam, VNM, 1962 (Monu-
menta Musica Neerlandica 5)
F. Noske: 'David Janszoon Padbrué : corael
– luytslager – vlascoper', *Renaissance-muziek
1400-1600 : donum natalicum René Bernard
Lenaerts*. Louvain, 1969, p. 179
F. Noske: *Music bridging divided religions*.
Wilhelmshaven, Noetzel, 1989
F. Noske: 'Padbrué en Vondel', *Organicae
voces : Festschrift Joseph Smits van Waesberghe*,
Amsterdam, 1963, p. 123-136
H.J. Pabbruwe: 'De herkomst van de fami-
lie Pabbruwe', *De Nederlandse Leeuw*, Feb.-
March 1985, p. 81 et seq.

DISCOGRAPHY
O kersnacht schoonder dan de dagen. Capella
Amsterdam (Attacca Babel 8636-5)
*De kruisbergh; Op de Tweedraght der Christe
Princen; Kusjes VII, XI en XII; Het Minne-net;
Aen Roosemonds oogen; Symphonia in nuptias
Joannis Everswyn et Luciae Buys; Symphonia in
nuptias Mathaei Steyn et Mariae van Napels*.
Camerata Trajectina (Globe 1997)
*Symphonia in nuptias ... I. Everswyn et Luciae
Buys*. M. Miessen (rec), B. van Asperen (hpd),
W. Möller (baroque vc) (BFO A-2)
*Symphonia in nuptias... I. Everswyn et Luciae
Buys*. B. van Asperen (hpd) (Vox Huma LC
2674)

David Petersen

LÜBECK, C.1650 – ?, 1737

Information on the life of David Petersen has only recently come to light. He came from the north German city of Lübeck and in the early 1670s worked as a university musician in the Swedish city of Lund. Around 1675 he took up residence in Amsterdam where, in 1679, he married Catharina Aertsen from Nijmegen. Baptismal records of their five children reveal that Petersen was a Lutheran, not unusual for a native of Lübeck.

Petersen may not have been a professional musician. He might have earned his living as a merchant, as indeed he was referred to in his marriage certificate. This would account for his apparent prosperity, lack of musical employment and his friendly relations with the prosperous poet Abraham Alewijn. There were, however, contacts with professional musicians. In 1704, for example, with the musicians Andreas Parcham, George Bingham and organist Evert Havercamp, he was called upon to appraise a carillon made in Amsterdam. The contract for this service indicates that he was apparently the committee's leader.

A few facts are known about other areas of Petersen's life: the city archives of Amsterdam indicate that he held various minor civil service positions, perhaps resulting from his dedication of the *Speelstukken* [Pieces] to Joan Hudde (1628-1704), who for many years was mayor of Amsterdam. In 1686 Petersen was named 'commissioner or registrar of the Gouda ferry' and in 1689 became an official at the New Fish Market (Mattheson, many years later, mistakenly attributed this post to Johan Schenck). In 1694 Petersen received permission to travel to England; he remained there until 1695, though the purpose of his journey is not known. It is from the records of his last civil post that we are informed that on 2 May 1737 Petersen was reported to have died; a successor was appointed on 19 May. Petersen apparently died outside of Amsterdam, although the place and date of his death are unknown.

As an amateur musician, Petersen was probably primarily a violinist, an assumption supported by the nature of his first compositions, the *Speelstukken* (1683) for violin and basso continuo. The twelve pieces in this collection, each a combination of a sonata and a suite, employ a rather virtuoso style that is clearly influenced by the work of the German composer of violin music Johann Jacob Walther. In fact there is such a striking resemblance between Pe-

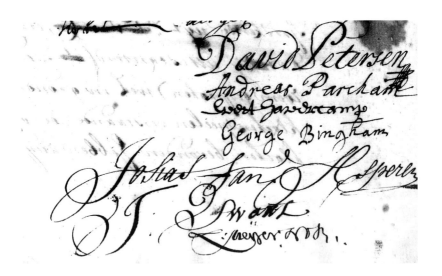

tersen's collection and Walther's *Scherzi da violino solo* (Dresden, 1676) that one is nearly compelled to conclude that Walther must have been Petersen's teacher. This hypothesis is supported to some extent by Walther's comment in the preface to his *Hortus chelicus* (Mainz, 1688) that the collection was initially to have been published in Amsterdam, at a time when Petersen lived in this city.

Each of the *Speelstukken* contains a sonata (in the general sense of an introductory, instrumental piece), some of which are followed by dance movements such as allemandes, courantes, sarabandes and gigues. There are slow movements with long melodic lines and passages with double stops, virtuoso and rapid passages, and fugues in which the violin plays at least two of the parts. The overall structures seem to foreshadow Corelli's famed op.5 sonatas (1700). In keeping with Walther's style, the pieces employ the typical violin techniques of arpeggiated chords, slurred staccatos, tremolos, piano-forte effects, and double stops.

The *Speelstukken* are the only published violin works of Petersen known to have survived. As far as we know, all of his later works are vocal compositions, including various songs with basso continuo accompaniment. The most important of these are his 24 songs to Abraham Alewijn's *Zede en harpgezangen* [Moralistic and harp songs] (1694). Alewijn (1664-1721) was one of the Netherlands' leading poets around the beginning of the eighteenth century, although his unwieldy and somewhat artificial style is little appreciated today. The collection contains eleven moralistic song texts ('zedegezangen') and thirteen psalm verses ('harpgezangen').

Apart from these and other lyrical works and occasional poems, Alewijn wrote a number of plays, some of which were performed in Amsterdam's City Theater. Alewijn, it seems, greatly appreciated Petersen, writing several panegyrics to him and dedicating the play *Amaryllis* to him.

There are a total of twelve songs by Petersen in the various editions of the collection *Boertige en ernstige minnezangen* [Jocular and serious love songs] (Amsterdam: 1705/3, 1705/4, 1709/5), settings of poems by Dirk Buysero (1644-1708), Kornelis Zweerts (1669-1742; Zweerts also wrote a panegyric to Petersen), and Alewijn. As was common in late seventeenth-century Dutch songs, as a consequence of the popularity of Jean-Baptiste Lully's French opera, Petersen's songs show strong French leanings.

Little is known about Petersen's contribution to music for the theater and vocal plays. Four songs to texts from Alewijn's *Amaryllis* have survived, but there is no evidence that Petersen composed music for the entire play. It is virtually certain, however, that he did compose the music for Frans Rijk's translation of Corneille's *Andromède*, which was performed in the Amsterdam Theater. After the premiere on 13 November 1730, the production had an additional eleven performances before Christmas and, judging by the receipts, it was very popular. Petersen, who by then was over 75 years old, received the not inconsiderable sum of 150 guilders for his work on this production, his last known compositions.

Petersen's music falls into two categories: instrumental music, as represented by the *Speelstukken*, and vocal music, such as the *Zede en harpgezangen* as well as other Dutch songs with basso continuo. In the *Speelstukken*, Petersen's contribution to the Dutch repertoire for the violin stands entirely on its own, lacking both predecessors and successors. The German influence on his violin music distinguishes his work from that of other early eighteenth-century Dutch composers, who were predominantely swayed by the music of the Italian masters: Henrico Albicastro by Corelli, Willem de Fesch by Vivaldi, and Pieter Hellendaal by Tartini. Petersen's songs are of the same high quality and show the same growing preference for Dutch texts as do the songs of Hendrik Anders and Servaas de Konink.

The *Zede en harpgezangen* was the first substantial collection of Dutch songs with basso continuo to appear in print, thus occupying a unique place in Dutch music history.

RUDOLF RASCH

COMPOSITIONS

*Speelstukken samengestelt door David Petersen,
dese stukken werden gespeelt met en viool en
bas continuo, waar by gevoegt kan werden een
theorbe, of viool da gamba.* – Amsterdam,
[Joan Philip Heus for the composer], 1683.
Facs. ed.: introd. by Rudolf Rasch. Utrecht.
STIMU 1989

A. *Alewyns Zede en harpgezangen, met zang-
kunst verrykt.* – Amsterdam, Katharijne
Lescailje for the composer, 1694. Repr.:
Haarlem, Hermanus van Hulkenroy, 1715.
For voice and bc

Twelve songs included in *Boertige en ernstige
minnezangen.* – Amsterdam, Joannes
Strander, 3, 4/1705, 5/1709. Texts by Abraham Alewijn, Kornelis Zweerts and Dirk
Buyzero

BIBLIOGRAPHY
R. Rasch: introd. in the facs. ed. of *Speel-
stukken* (see compositions)
J. Schröder: 'David Petersen : ein Geiger
im Amsterdam des 17. Jahrhunderts', *Alte
Musik : Praxis und Reflexion*. Winterthur, 1983

DISCOGRAPHY
Speelstuk no. 1. Trio Sonnerie (Teleac TEL
8901-8905)

Willem Pijper

ZEIST, 8 SEPTEMBER 1894 – LEIDSCHENDAM, 18 MARCH 1947

Like Matthijs Vermeulen, Willem Pijper is a composer about whom it still seems impossible to write without bias. Unlike Vermeulen, however, Pijper occupied a position at the center of Dutch musical life throughout his life. He was the spokesman for the younger generation of composers, the self-appointed figurehead of the avant-garde, and a strong opponent of what to his mind was the dully conservative, German-oriented public music making the Netherlands. He exerted enormous influence on Dutch music, not only through his compositions, but even more so through the polemics he was involved in and through his unmistakable charisma. This attracted a large group of students, among them Kees van Baaren, Henk Badings, Henriëtte Bosmans, Rudolf Escher, Hans Henkemans, Guillaume Landré, and Bertus van Lier.

Pijper was born on 8 September 1894 in Zeist, the son of a paperer. Music was of little importance to his family, although he did receive his first violin lessons from his father. Owing to his ill health, he was schooled at home and his thirst for learning revealed itself in music and biology in particular. From 1911, as a student at the Music School of the Society for the Advancement of Music in Utrecht, he took lessons in composition from Johan Wagenaar. Later, he would say: 'On the subject of composition, I have learned more from Freud than from Riemann – and also mutatis mutandis, from Nietzsche – from Kant, if you will, through the liberation of my soul. Seen in this light, composition is a process of deliberation.'

Pijper quickly rose to musical prominence and in his activities on three fronts (as a composer, teacher and polemicist) emerged as a distinct and often controversial personality. Soon after completing his studies, his first orchestral pieces were performed by the Concertgebouw Orchestra under Willem Mengelberg (Symphony no.1, written in 1917), and the Utrecht Municipal Orchestra under Jan van Gilse (*Fêtes galantes* for mezzo-soprano and orchestra, written in 1916). In 1918 he started teaching harmony and composition at the Amsterdam Conservatory, and from 1930 until his death in 1947 he was director of the Rotterdam Conservatory. In addition, he wrote essays and music reviews throughout his life: for the daily *Utrechts Dagblad* (1917-1923), for the journal *De Muziek* (1926-1933), and the weekly *De Groene Amsterdammer* (1934-1946).

In 1923 Pijper founded the Netherlands chapter of the International Soci-

ety for Contemporary Music. Attend-
ing this organization's annual festival,
he was able to keep well abreast of international developments in music
and maintain contact with foreign
musicians – for example, with Pierre
Monteux, to whom he dedicated his
Symphony no.3.

In the article 'An unharmonious
figure in an unharmonious age', the
musicologist Marius Flothuis distinguishes three periods in Pijper's relatively modest body of works. The first
(1914-1920) is characterized by the
influence of Mahler and Debussy.
His Symphony no.1, with the very revealing subtitle *Pan*, conjures up associations with the idyllic, pastoral
world of Mahler's Symphony no.4; in
Fêtes galantes, the relationship with Debussy, who also used texts from the similarly titled collection of poems by Paul Verlaine, is obvious.

The second, very productive period, in which Pijper composed most of his
chamber music, began with the Septet (1920) and the Symphony no.2 (1921).
It was in these pieces that he first employed his 'basic cell technique'. Analogous to the biological phenomenon in which an entire plant grows from a single seed, the music evolves organically through continuous variation of a
small melodic cell, usually consisting of four tones. This form of thematic
transformation actually existed as early as Beethoven, although Pijper's use of
the technique created the possibility of composing in various keys simultaneously (i.e. polytonality). This period reached its climax in *Zes symfonische epigrammen* [Six symphonic epigrams], in which broadly spun Mahlerian
rhetoric gives way to the much more concise style of Anton Webern.

The symphonic drama *Halewijn* (1933), set to a libretto by Pijper's wife
Emmy van Lokhorst, marks the transition to the third period. After 1930, Pijper seemed to have run out of steam. Concentrating on his organizational and
pedagogical duties as director of the Rotterdam Conservatory, he was decidedly less productive as a composer. Dating from the 1930s are the Violin and
Cello Concertos – in which Pijper's usual, dense orchestration occasionally demands the utmost from the performers – and the Piano Sonata. The essays he
wrote for *De Groene Amsterdammer* still demonstrate his characteristically crit-

ical tone and increasingly reveal his great cultural pessimism. Pijper's last important works – the incomplete symphonic drama *Merlijn*, set to a libretto by the famous novelist Simon Vestdijk, and the *Zes adagio's* [Six adagios] – betray his growing interest in esoteric matters such as astrology and freemasonry. The *Zes adagio's* in particular, music he composed for Masonic initiation rites, show a less complicated idiom containing tonal elements.

The outbreak of World War II and the bombing of Rotterdam, in which he lost everything but his scores, marked the end of his career. He fell seriously ill during the war and died in self-imposed solitude on 18 March 1947.

Pijper had a 'sharp, critical, caustic and combative intellect' (*Mensch en Melodie*, 1947); his character drove him to oppose the establishment. Through his literary gifts (Vestdijk said that he was primarily a man of letters) he developed into a venomous and fearless critic of pre-war musical life. His scathing reviews in the *Utrechtsch Dagblad* of the conductor Jan van Gilse, for example, earned him a reputation as a fiery polemicist for which he is remembered even today.

Writing was fundamentally important for Pijper. His reaction to the music of his time was sharp-witted; slowly he formulated his own aesthetics, finally postulating them in *De Quintencirkel* [The circle of fifths] (1929) and *De Stemvork* [The tuning fork] (1930). The primacy of melody, as formulated in his manifesto-like article 'Muzikale waarde' [Musical worth] (*De Muziek*, 1929) was central to his views: 'Music arises from melodic elements alone. [...] Counterpoint, harmony and structure are undoubtedly significant to the overall effect of a piece of music. But they are not the yardsticks by which the value of a musical creation may be determined. Musical worth is melodic worth.'

ARTHUR VAN DIJK

COMPOSITIONS

The K.-numbers in the list of compositions refer to Kloppenburg's thematic catalogue (see bibliography)

MUSIC FOR THE THEATRE: *De Bacchanten* (Euripides, Verhagen), sp.v, Bar, sp.chorus, orch. K. 63 (1924); *De cycloop* (Euripides, Verhagen), sp.v (Bar), boys' choir, sp.chorus, orch, K. 69 (1925); *Antigone* (3rd version) (Sophocles, Verhagen), sp.v (Bar), Bar, sp.chorus, orch, K. 72 (1926); *The Tempest* (Shakespeare), 3 Mez, 2 Bar, orch, K. 82 (1930)

OPERA: *Halewijn* (Van Lokhorst, Nijhoff), sp.v. (Mez), soloists, mix.choir, orch, K. 86 (1932-1933); *Merlijn* (Vestdijk), soloists, m.choir, orch, K. 102 (unfin.) (1939-1945)

OTHER VOCAL WORKS: *Fêtes galantes* (Verlaine), Mez, orch, K. 34 (1916); *Romances sans paroles* (Verlaine), Mez, orch, K. 40 (1919); *La maumariée I & II*, v, pf, K. 44 (1919, 1920); *Heer Halewijn*, 8-part mix.choir, K. 50 (1920); *Twee balladen van Paul Fort*, w.choir, pf, K. 51 (1921); *Twee liederen op Oud-Hollandse teksten*, v, pf, K. 61 (1923); *Hymne* (Boutens), Bar/B, orch, K. 100 (1943)

PIANO: *Drie aforismen*, K. 26 (1915); Three
Sonatinas, K. 36, 66, 67 (1917, 1925, 1925);
Sonata, K. 83 (1930); *Sonata*, 2 pf, K. 89
(1935)

CHAMBER MUSIC: *Piano Trio*, K. 20 (1914);
String Quartet, K. 23 (1914); *Sonata*, vl, pf,
K. 42 (1919); *Sonata*, vc, pf, K. 43 (1919);
Septet, pf, fl, ob, cl, bn, hn, db, K. 48
(1920); *String Quartet*, K. 49 (1920); *Piano
Trio*, K. 52 (1921); *Sonata*, vl, pf, K. 56
(1922); *Sextet*, pf, fl, ob, cl, bn, hn, K. 58
(1923); *String Quartet*, K. 59 (1923); *Sonata*,
vc, pf, K. 62 (1924); *Sonata*, fl, pf, K. 65
(1925); *Trio*, fl, cl, bn, K. 73 (1927); *String
Quartet*, K. 79 (1928); *Quintet*, fl, ob, cl, bn,
hn, K. 80 (1929); *Sonata*, vl, K. 84 (1931);
String Quartet, K. 103 (1946)

ORCHESTRA: Three Symphonies, K. 37, 53, 71
(1917, 1921, 1926); *Zes symfonische epigrammen*, K. 78 (1928); *Zes adagio's*, K. 96
(1940)

CONCERTOS: *Orkeststuk met piano*, K. 27
(1915); *Piano Concerto*, K. 75 (1927); *Cello
Concerto*, K. 92 (1936); *Violin Concerto*, K.
95 (1939)

PUBLICATIONS
De Quintencirkel. Amsterdam, Querido,
1929
De Stemvork, Amsterdam, Querido, 1930

Pijper wrote hundreds of articles for
Utrechtsch Dagblad (1917-1923), *Rotterdamsch
Nieuwsblad* (from 1925), *De Muziek* (1926-
1932), *De Groene Amsterdammer* (1934-1946)
and other newspapers and journals.

BIBLIOGRAPHY
H. Badings: *De hedendaagsche Nederland-
sche muziek*. Amsterdam, Bigot & Van
Rossum, 1936
R. de Beer: 'A phonographic portrait of
Willem Pijper', *Key Notes*, 23, 1986, p. 34-35
K.Ph. Bernet Kempers: *Inleiding tot de
opera Halewijn van Willem Pijper*. Rotterdam,
Brusse, 1950
H. van Dijk: *Jan van Gilse : strijder en idea-
list : een bijdrage tot de kennis van de Nederlandse
muziekgeschiedenis in de periode 1900 – 1944*.

Doctoral dissertation University of Utrecht,
1980. Abridged version: Buren, Knuf, 1988
M. Flothuis: 'Willem Pijper (1894-1947) :
an unharmonious figure in an unharmonious
age', *Key Notes* 3, 1976/1, p. 26-33
A. Haakman: 'Pijper on Pijper', *Key Notes*,
23, 1986, p. 36-40
F.W. Hoogerwerf: *The chamber music of
Willem Pijper (1894-1947)*. Doctoral disserta-
tion University of Michigan, 1977
W.C.M. Kloppenburg: *Thematisch-bibli-
ografische catalogus van de werken van Willem
Pijper (1894-1947)*. Assen, Van Gorcum, 1960
R. de Leeuw: 'Het einde van een mythe',
Muzikale anarchie. Amsterdam, De Bezige Bij,
1973
Mens en Melodie. Pijper memorial issues,
vol. 2, 1947, p. 161-209; vol. 12, 1957, p. 66-71
and p. 97-100; vol. 27, 1972, p. 65-81; vol. 49,
1994, p. 474-519
A. Ringer: 'The String Quartets of Willem
Pijper', *The Music Review*, 38, 1977, p. 44-64
H.C. Ryker: 'Closing the circle : Willem Pij-
per's music for theatre', *TVNM*, 43, 1993/1, p.
42-75
H.C. Ryker: *The symphonic music of Willem
Pijper (1894-1947)*. Doctoral dissertation Uni-
versity of Washington, 1971
L. Samama: *Zeventig jaar Nederlandse
muziek : 1915-1985 : voorspel tot een nieuwe dag*.
Amsterdam, Querido, 1986
P. Sanders: *Moderne Nederlandsche Com-
ponisten*. The Hague, Kruseman, 1930
S. Vestdijk: 'Willem Pijper', *Gestalten
tegenover mij*. Amsterdam, De Bezige Bij, 1975
S. Vestdijk en W. Pijper: *Merlijn : het
ontstaan van een opera in brieven en documenten*,
ed. A. van Dijk en M. Vestdijk. Amsterdam,
Nijgh & Van Ditmar, 1992
M.Vermeulen: *De muziek dat wonder*. The
Hague, Bert Bakker, 1958
J. Wouters: 'Willem Pijper', *Nederlandse
componisten galerij : negen portretten van Nederlandse componisten, vol. 1*. Amsterdam, Donemus, 1971

DISCOGRAPHY
Cello Concerto. H. Schiff (vc), Netherlands
Radio Chamber Orchestra, cond. E. Spanjaard
(NM Classics 92040)
Chamber Music for Strings and Piano. R.
Hoogeveen (vl), W. Mijnders (vc), P. Beijers-

bergen van Henegouwen (pf) (Composers'
Voice CVCD 15)
  Halewijn. Various soloists, Netherlands
Radio Orchestra, Small Omroep Choir, cond.
E. Downes (Composers' Voice CV 1987/2)
  La maumarieé. J. van Nes (Mez), G. van
Blerk (pf) (Globe GLO 6018)
  Merlijn. Various soloists, Netherlands
Radio Philharmonic Orchestra, men of the
Netherlands Radio Choir, cond. D. Porcelijn
(NM Classics 92055)
  Piano Concerto (1927). R. Brautigam (pf),
Residentie Orchestra, cond. R. van Driesten
(Olympia OCD 504)
  Piano Concerto (1927). R. Brautigam (pf),
Netherlands Radio Symphony Orchestra,
cond. J. van Steen (NM Classics 92058)
  Flute Sonata. J. Zoon (fl), B. Brackman (pf)
(NM Classics 92059)
  Sonata for piano. R. Brautigam (pf) (NM
Classics 92045)
  *Sonata for 2 pianos; Sonata for flute and
piano; Sonatinas no. 2 and 3; Violin Sonata no. 1;
Wind Quintet; String Quartet no. 5; Zes sym-
fonische epigrammen; Zes adagio's.* Various
soloists and ensembles, Concertgebouw Or-
chestra, cond. E. van Beinum, Residentie Or-
chestra, cond. E. Flipse (historical recording,
Composers' Voice CV/1987/1)
  String Quartets nos. 1-5. Schönberg Quartet
(Olympia OCD 457)
  *Symphonies nos. 1-3; Zes adagio's; Zes sym-
fonische epigrammen; Piano Concerto; Violin
Concerto; Cello Concerto.* Th. Bruins (pf), G.
Hettema (vl), M. van Staalen (vc), Rotterdam
Philharmonic Orchestra, cond. R. Dufallo, R.
van Driesten, L. Vis and S. Rattle (Composers'
Voice CV 1987/3)
  *Symphony no. 2; Piano Concerto; Zes ada-
gio's; String Quartets nos. 4 and 5.* Th. Bruins
(pf), Gaudeamus Quartet, Rotterdam Philhar-
monic Orchestra, cond. R. van Driesten (Com-
posers' Voice CVCD 1)
  Symphony no. 3. Concertgebouw Orchestra,
cond. P. Monteux (BFO A-6)

Dick Raaijmakers

MAASTRICHT, I SEPTEMBER 1930

For a composer Dick Raaijmakers has put remarkably few notes to paper. 'I am a composer without notes', he once said in an interview. 'I am fully aware that what I do has little to do with conventional music', he stated on another occasion. Raaijmakers's terrain embraces all that falls under the generation of sound between the two poles of music and technology, and could best be described as a form of applied music philosophy in which the visual arts and theater also play a role. In 1995 he was awarded the Ouborg Prize by the city of The Hague for his way of linking various artistic disciplines. Three years previously he received the Oeuvre Prize for Visual Arts. He is also a two-time winner of the Matthijs Vermeulen Prize: in 1985 for *Extase*, and in 1994 for *Der Fall/Dépons* and *Die glückliche Hand/geöffnet*.

Raaijmakers completed his piano studies at the Royal Conservatory in The Hague in 1953, but the idea of spending his life as a piano teacher held little appeal for him. After his final examination he returned to Eindhoven, where as a youth he had devoted his free time to tinkering with illegal radio installations and other electro-acoustic equipment. He was employed on the Philips production line from 1954 and in 1956 was named assistant to Henk Badings, Ton de Leeuw, Tom Dissevelt and professor A.D. Fokker, who had the electronics company's laboratory facilities at their disposal for musical experimentation. From 1960 to 1962 he was an academic assistant at the University of Utrecht; from 1963 to 1966 he and the composer Jan Boerman worked in their own electronic studio in The Hague, and from 1966 until his retirement in 1995 he was a professor of electronic and contemporary music at the Royal Conservatory in The Hague. During his last four years there he also taught a course on Electronic Music Theater.

Raaijmakers has provided the best overview of the versatility of his activities in a methodically detailed and categorized list of works. He distinguishes between compositional, theatrical, visual and educational projects and three 'lines' ('techniques and methods', 'models' and 'disciplines') that run through these categories. A systematic approach, also evidenced in his book *De methode* [The method], is typical of Raaijmakers's endeavors. Equally typical is that he applies his systems not with arid, blind precision, but as an unbiased inventor whose strict application of logic leads to absurd discoveries.

In his thoughts on art and technology, he always seeks the essence, the ger-

minating basic premise, the zero point. For his *Vijf canons* [Five canons] (1964-1967) he sought out the 'smallest sound', which he discovered in two pulses next to each other: 'tick-tick'. Though his preliminary research for electronic compositions as *Ballade Erlkönig, Plumes* and *Flux* (all composed in 1967) yielded more or less consistent, autonomous works of art, the questions he later researched led him to formulate principles and mechanisms of motion that inhabit a peripheral region of music making: 'the fall', 'the blow', 'the inversion', 'the imitation', and 'the reproduction'. By interpreting their significance as literally as possible and by dissecting them down to the bone, he attempted to 'rethink' these concepts and free them of misunderstandings that infected them.

'I always try to understand things from the perspective of someone from another planet', Raaijmakers said in 1982. In his role of alien, he redefines concepts according to existing meanings, but combines them differently. He reduces the word microphone, for example, to the basic elements 'small' (micro) and 'sound' (phone) and thus concludes that a microphone produces small sounds. While contradictory though it may seem, sounds are in fact enhanced by a microphone, by means of an amplifier.

Impurities in the use of language can almost always be traced back to impurities in the thought processes behind the terms. The miscomprehensions and problems thus arising over the relationship between technology and music are the very subject that Raaijmakers – using the widest range of forms – explores in all his work. One such miscomprehension is the generally accepted understanding that electronic instruments produce their own, real sound. No, counters Raaijmakers: an electronic sound is the mirror image of a physical sound because it is incorporeal. The tone produced by a violin is always influenced by the body of the instrument, but an electronic sound is variable because it is always housed in something else's body. The incorporeity of an electronic sound and its production through a 'borrowed' body (radio, amplifier, CD player, synthesizer) is something that Raaijmakers over-emphatically imitates and dramatizes in his work. He does this, for example, by stretching fleeting actions to durations of up to a half an hour, as in *De grafische methode tractor* [The graphic method tractor] (1976) and *De grafische methode fiets* [The graphic method bicycle] (1978), or by cleverly employing a combination of imitation and inversion, as in *Dépons/Der Fall* and *Der Fall/Dépons* – two music theater pieces he produced in 1992/1993 in collaboration with Theater Group Hollandia.

The ultimate disengagement arises when the body and sound uncontrollably set out in entirely different directions. Such moments are anchored, in Raaijmakers's oeuvre, in the term 'falling'. The fall is his metaphor for a loss of control, for 'making music while not being there', which is invariably the case with electronic music. One presses a button and a process is set in motion over which the performer at that moment has no influence. This is the essential discrepancy between technology and art.

'Technology stands for the unjustly gained energy and result', posits Raaijmakers. When the technology takes over and the performer is left powerless, the result is often the same sort of comic effect as the stumbling and fumbling of circus clowns with unwieldy suitcases, garden hoses, ladders and other objects. It is precisely in this manner that Raaijmakers subjects different figures to surrealistic falls: the French composer Ernest Chausson falls for half an hour in mechanized slow motion from his bicycle; Pierre Boulez tumbles seat and all with equal sloth; the Italian dictator Benito Mussolini spins on his axis and is literally turned upside-down.

However, the falling theme figures most prominently in a series of music theater pieces (*SHHH!, The Microman, The Soundmen, The Soundwall, Ow!* and *Come on!*) based on the Laurel and Hardy film *Night Owls*. This is the crux of Raaijmakers's art: not the advances made through technology, but the impotence of the sorcerer's apprentices who conjured it and the madness in this 'Zeitalter der technischen Reproduzierbarkeit' that obliterates the distinction between reality and reproduction.

PAY-UUN HIU

COMPOSITIONS

COMPOSITIONAL PROJECTS (ELECTRONIC COMPOSITIONS): *Song of the Second Moon* (1957); *Pianoforte* (1960); *Vijf plastieken* (1961); *Ster-Tune* (1966); *Vijf canons* (1964-1967); Three film compositions: *Mechanical Motions, Bekaert, Sidmar* (1960-1969); *Ballade Erlkönig* for loudspeakers (1967); *Plumes* (1967); *Flux* (1967); *Chairman Mao is our guide* (1970, withdrawn); *Mao leve!* for tape and slides (1977); *Ping-pong* (1983);

T-heo van Vel-zen (1986); *Du, Armer!* (1993); *Vier Fanfares* (1995)

SCENIC PROJECTS: *Kwartet* electr. circuit with 4 str.instr, 4 actors and 4 assistants (1967); *Nachtmuziek* for 4 electr. str., waterfall, 8 actors, electr. circuit, sound and light (1969); *Schaakmuziek* for 4 str.instr, 2 chess players, electr. circuit, clock system and sound (1969); *Gaman*, experimental music theatre (with M. Mengelberg)

(1970); *De lange mars,* 8 actors, 8 'Chinese violins', electr. circuit and artificial space-connection; *De grafische methode tractor* for 'international factory and slow motion film' (1976); *De grafische methode fiets* (1978); *SHHH!* version of *The Soundmen* for tape and projected moon (1981); *The Soundmen,* version for theatre (1982); *The Microman,* version for table theatre (1982); *Ow!* Hoketus version (1982); *Extase,* performance for 2 actors, machinery, light and tape (1982); *Come on!,* film version (1983); *Come on!,* version for chamber theatre (1984); *Ach ach!* elegy for 3 vl and cl (1987); *Music for Five Senses,* time-space plan for a multimedia performance (1988); *Intona,* 12 microphones (1991); *Der Fall Leiermann,* music theatre group(1991); *Dépons/Der Fall,* music theatre (1992); *Die glückliche Hand/geöffnet,* music theatre (1993); *Der Fall/Dépons,* music theatre (1993); *Probe,* performance (1993); *De promenoir van Mondriaan,* cooperation (1994); *Der Stein,* suitcase opera (1995); *Volta,* performance (1995); *De val van Mussolini,* music theatre (1995); *Hermans hand,* music theatre (1995); *Scheuer im Haag,* music theatre group (1996)

SCULPTURAL PROJECTS (MUSEUM PROJECTS AND PRODUCTIONS): *Drie ideofonen* (1970-1973);*The Soundwall* (1984); *Acht labielen* (1984-1985); *Kleurcirkel-licht-machine* (1985-1986); *Tombeau de Glenn Gould* (1989), *Fort-Klank* (with H. Rickels) (1993);*Volta,* an electro chemical construction (1995)

PUBLICATIONS
'De kunst van het machine lezen', *Raster 6,* Amsterdam, De Bezige Bij, 1978
'Is there such a thing as Dutch electronic music?'; 'Audio-kinetic art and electronics: three projects by dutch composers'; 'Electronics in music teaching; a question of supply and demand', *Key Notes,* 8, 1978/2
'A brief history of Dutch electronic music from 1966 to the present day'. Sleeve notes Composers' Voice CV 7803, 1978 (see discography)
'The electric method', *Dutch Art + Architecture Today,* Ministry of Culture, Recreation and

Social Work (CRM), 1981
De methode. Amsterdam, Bert Bakker, 1984
'De val van Mussolini, een vergeten Hollywood-project uit 1930', *Raster 29,* Amsterdam, De Bezige Bij, 1984
'Neo-plasticisme versus Neo-Bechstein', 'Snaar versus draad', *Elektrische Muziek,* The Hague, Gemeentemuseum, catalogue 1988
'Open muziekinstrument' and other articles, *Anti Qua Musica,* The Hague, Gemeentemuseum, catalogue 1989
'Over zitten voor elektrofonen', chapter 6 from 'Kleine Mechanica van de Open Vorm', *Raster 50,* Amsterdam, De Bezige Bij, 1992
'Stomme film', lemma in 'Vergeetwoordenboek', *Raster 58,* Amsterdam, De Bezige Bij, 1992
Fort-Klank, catalogue Stichting Fort Asperen, Acquoy, 1993
'De gecomponeerde stilte', *Theaterschrift* IV, 1993
'The future of electronic music', *Key Notes,* 29, 1995/3, p. 4-7. (also: 'De toekomst van de elektronische muziek, *Mens en Melodie,* Nov./Dec. 1995)
'Over tonale en atonale machines', *THD,* no. 1, 1996
'Het kleinste geluid', *THD,* no. 2, 1997
'Lichte muziek', *THD,* no. 3, 1997

BIBLIOGRAPHY
L. Andriessen en E. Schönberger: 'De verzonnen werkelijkheid', *Het apollinisch uurwerk. Over Stravinsky.* De Bezige Bij, Amsterdam, 1983
C. Blok: 'Dépons/Der Fall', *Notes,* vol. 7, no. 4, 1992
C. Blok: 'Het theater van het misverstand', *Notes* 7/8, 1993
K. Boehmer: 'Dick Raaijmakers, een open vorm, geen onbeschreven blad....Festival in de Branding,* Johan Wagenaar Stichting, The Hague, 1995
I. v.d. Burg [et al.]: *Interrelatie beeldende kunst en muziek.* University of Amsterdam, Faculty of Art History, 1978
G. Carl: 'Five canons by Dick Raaymakers. A method of repetition.', *Key Notes,* 14, 1981/2, p. 1-10
'De techniek van Dick Raaijmakers', *Kunst en Techniek,* io45-Magazine, Technical University Delft, faculty Industrial Design, 1987

J. Donker: 'Het denken van Dick Raaijmakers', *Beelding – Maandblad voor Kunsten*,
1989

H. Hartman en J. Roozenburg: *Dick Raaijmakers*. Dissertation University of Leiden,
Faculty of Art History

W.F. Hermans: 'Poetsen is niet stompzin-
niger dan wandelen', *NRC Handelsblad*, Cultural Supplement 10, Nov. 1978

P.-U. Hiu: 'Vallen, de vrijheid van angst en
extase', *Entr'acte* no.5 June 1996, p. 34-35

J. Oskamp: 'An artist without an oeuvre',
Key Notes, 30, 1996/1, p.10-14

W.J. Otten: *De Soundman in Frascatie*. Baal-
publication, 1984

W.J. Otten: 'How not to be trapped into
non-art. Notes towards a definition of Dick
Raaijmakers', *Key Notes*, 20, 1984/2, p. 2-10

K. Polling: 'Mijn werk is in wezen heel romantisch'. *Muziek en Dans*, May 1984, p. 62-67

E. Schönberger: 'Dick Raaijmakers en de
luisterhouding'. Sleeve notes cd box Done-
mus/NEAR, 1997 (see discography)

E. Schönberger: 'Het afsteken van een
band' (1980), *De wellustige tandarts & andere
componisten*, De Bezige Bij, Amsterdam, 1985

B. Spaan: 'Pioniers in elektronica : Dick
Raaijmakers en Jan Boerman op bezoek bij de
Concertzender', *Mens en Melodie* vol. 53, 1998,
p. 253-257

J. van Slooten: 'De commentator en de
componist', *Wolfsmond*, no. 13/14, 1985

E. de Visscher: 'Experimental Composer :
Dick Raaijmakers', *Logos*, Gent, 1991

DISCOGRAPHY

Ballade Erlkönig, Five Canons (Composers'
Voice CV 8103)

*The complete Dick Raaijmakers Edition.
Music for tape.* (cd box Composers' Voice
NEAR 9/10/11)

Piano-forte. Anthology of Dutch Electronic
Tape Music, vol. 1. (Composers' Voice CV 7803)

VIDEO

De val van Mussolini: direction Frank Alse-
ma, production Hank Onrust, VPRO, 1995

Volta: direction Kasper van der Horst, production STROOM, The Hague Center for
Sculptural Arts, 1995

Julius Röntgen

LEIPZIG, 9 MAY 1855 – BILTHOVEN, 13 SEPTEMBER 1932

Julius Röntgen was born in Leipzig into a musical family. His father, Engelbert Röntgen, was concertmaster of the Gewandhaus Orchestra and his mother, Pauline Klengel, the daughter of her husband's first violin teacher, was a talented pianist. Whereas Engelbert Röntgen left the Netherlands (Deventer) for Leipzig in 1848, Julius Röntgen left Leipzig to take up residence in the Netherlands. In 1878 he became a piano teacher at the music school of the Society for the Advancement of Music in Amsterdam. In 1880 he married Amanda Maier, one of his father's students, and lived with her on Amsterdam's Van Baerlestraat until her death in 1894.

Röntgen played an active role in Dutch music. In 1884 he became a piano teacher at the Amsterdam Conservatory, of which he was a co-founder, and conductor of the choral society Excelsior (as successor to G.A. Heinze). In 1886 he succeeded Johannes Verhulst as conductor of the Amsterdam Toonkunst choir, the local chapter of the Society for the Advancement of Music and as organizer of the concerts in Felix Meritis. When in 1888 the Society and the Concertgebouw began their collaboration, Röntgen was one of the first to conduct in the new hall.

Röntgen was also very active in chamber music. Of particular interest were the vocal recitals he organized with Johannes Messchaert from 1890. These recitals were well received both in the Netherlands and abroad and drew the enthusiastic praise of Johannes Brahms. In 1897 Röntgen remarried – with Abrahamina des Amorie van der Hoeven.

Röntgen became director of the Amsterdam Conservatory in 1913, a position he held until 1924, when he was succeeded by Sem Dresden. In 1925 the Röntgens moved to the Gaudeamus villa in Bilthoven, which was designed by the composer's son Frants Edvard. This villa became a gathering place for Röntgen's many famous musical friends, such as the cellist Pablo Casals. It remained a musical bastion even after World War II, when Walter Maas took up residence there and made it the home of the Gaudeamus Foundation, an organization dedicated to the advancement of modern music.

Röntgen had a close friendship with Edvard Grieg. He had come to know Grieg's music during his youth in Leipzig and later met the composer through Amanda Maier. When Grieg made his first visit to the Netherlands for the performance of his piano concerto, in 1883, he stayed with the Röntgen family.

The friendship, maintained by correspondence and marked by dedications of compositions, was sealed by their total agreement in questions of musical taste. The friendship with Edvard Grieg (and musician Frants Beier) went so far that at the birth of his son in 1902, Röntgen named the child Edvard Frants. Grieg found the rhythm of the names jarring and suggested their order would sound better reversed. Two years later, Röntgen named his second son Frants Edvard. After Grieg's death in 1907, his widow asked Röntgen to study the Norwegian composer's manuscripts and decide which of them would be suitable for publication. Röntgen was so taken by Grieg's unfinished String Quartet no.2 – only two movements were completed – that he decided to finish the work himself. It was performed in November 1907 by an *ad hoc* quartet, the pianist Harold Bauer and the cellist Pablo Casals playing first and second violins (Casals holding the violin upright on his lap, like a cello), Röntgen on the viola, and Casals's wife on the cello. The audience consisted solely of Röntgen's wife.

In the second half of the nineteenth century, Leipzig was a bastion of anti-Wagner criticism and Röntgen was full of antipathy toward the Wagnerian *Neutonerei*. His musical education, he would say, 'went no further than the Mendelssohn-Schumann period', and it was only after initial reserve that he came to admire the music of Johannes Brahms. Röntgen's enormous body of works – more than 900 compositions – reflects these aesthetics. He composed in every conceivable genre, and after retiring in 1924 increased his productivity. Aside rare exceptions, such as his somewhat Debussian bitonal symphony of 1930, he eschewed modernism in music.

Röntgen had a special interest in early Netherlands music. He made orchestral arrangements from this repertoire – for example the *Zes Oud-Nederlandsche dansen* [Six old-Dutch dances] – and borrowed melodies for new works, such as his songs for tenor, bass, men's choir and organ (1904), set to texts by the Dutch seventeenth-century writer Valerius. His attraction to folk music formed one of the pillars of his sympathy for Grieg. Although literal quotations from Norwegian folk music are rarely found in Grieg's works, his music was of enormous nationalistic significance. In his biography of Grieg, Röntgen opens with the comment: 'Edvard Grieg gave his countrymen a music of their own. This was his immortal accomplishment.' Röntgen and Grieg both shared an admiration for Brahms. In 1896 the two traveled together to Vienna to visit the old master, with whom Röntgen had been corresponding since 1884. Röntgen was not only interested in folk music of the Netherlands, but that of Norway, Ireland and Germany as well. In his later work he moved closer to the aesthetics of Max Reger.

JOHAN KOLSTEEG

COMPOSITIONS

Unpublished compositions are not included. An extensive list of compositions is included in the book by A. Röntgen-des Amorie van der Hoeven (see bibliography)

SONGS WITH PIANO: *Neun Lieder aus den Gedichten des Mirza Schaffy* (Bodenstedt), op. 15 (1876); *Oud-Nederlandsche amoureuse liedekens*, op. 29 (1889); *Das Kind von Oesterreich* (Von Gilm), op. 30 (1889); *Oud-Nederlandsche liederen naar Valerius*, op. 43; *Oud-Nederlandsche volksliederen* (F. van Duyse, P. van Duyse), op. 47; *Der Fasching zu Prag*, op. 52; *Liedeken van Jesuken ende S. Janneken die spelen met het lammeken* (Poirters), op. 53 (1911); *Deutsche Kriegslieder*, op. 61 (1915); *Die chinesische Flöte*, op. 66; *Bredero liederen*, op. 69 (1918); *Bethlehem*, op. 98; *Prometheus (Grenzen der Menschheit)* (Goethe), op. 99

OTHER VOCAL WORKS: *Toskanische Rispetti*, 4 v, pf, op. 9 (1874); *Frauenchöre aus 'Meine Ruh'*, op. 26; *Gebet*, mix.choir, orch, op. 27; *Sturmesmythe* (Lenau), mix.choir, orch, op. 31; *Oud-Nederlandsche liederen*, mix.choir, op. 42; *Oud-Nederlandsche liederen*, mix.choir, op. 44; *Zes kerstliederen* (F. van Duyse), mix.choir, op. 48; *Rei van edelingen* (Vondel), mix.choir, op. 49; *Kerstliederen*, v, pf, op. 57; *Two Songs*, mix.choir, op. 71; *Christelijke liederen voor de Protestantse Bond*, op. 82; *Fancies*, mix.choir, op. 92; *Metamorphoses*, mix.choir, op. 93; *Proöemion*, m.choir, op. 94; *David und Salomo*, m.choir, op. 95; *Spielmann*, m.choir, op. 96

PIANO (PIANO 2H UNLESS OTHERWISE STATED): *Sonata*, op. 2; *Aus der Jugendzeit*, pf 4h, op. 4; *Ein Cyclus von Phantasiestücken*, op. 5 (1871); *Ballade*, op. 6; *Suite in 4 Sätzen*, op. 7; *Phantasie*, op. 8 (1873); *Sonata*, op. 10; *Neckens Polska : Variationen über ein schwedisches Volkslied*, op. 11; *Julklapp (Weihnachtsgabe)*, op. 12; *Introduktion, Scherzo, Intermezzo und Finale*, pf 4h, op. 16; *Thema mit Variationen*, pf 4h, op. 17; *Improvisata über eine norwegische Volksweise*, op. 19 (1882); *Ballade*, op. 22; *Variationen über ein Czardas*, op. 25; *Fugen*, op. 28 (1888); *Drie romancen*, op. 32; *Scherzo*, 2 pf, op. 33; *Variationen über ein Thema von J.P. Hartmann*, op. 38; *Zes Oud-Nederlandsche dansen*, pf 4h, op. 46 (also arr. for orch); *Oud Hollandsche boerenliedjes*, op. 51; *Boerenliedjes*, op. 58; *Azzopardi-Studien*, op. 59; *Dolce far niente*, op. 60 (1909); *Sonatina*, op. 63; *Buiten*, op. 65; *Techniek en voordracht*, op. 67; *Uit Neerlands volksleven*, op. 81; *Uit Neerlands volksleven*, op. 91; *Cadenzen zu L. van Beethovens Clavierconcerten*

CHAMBER MUSIC: *Sonata*, vl, pf, op. 1; *Sonata*, vc, pf, op. 3; *Serenade für Blasinstrumente*, op. 14; *Sonata*, vl, pf, op. 20; *Nordisches Volkslied : Variationen*, vl, pf, op. 21 (1879); *Trio*, vl, vc, pf, op. 23; *Phantasie*, vl, pf, op. 24 (1884); *Sonata*, vl, pf, op. 40 (1900); *Sonata*, vc, pf, op. 41; *Piano Trio*, op. 50; *Sonata*, vc, op. 56; *Three Sonatas*, vl, op. 68b (1922); *Three Suites*, vl, op. 68a (1922); *Suite voor klokkenspel*, op. 70; *String Trio*, op. 76; *Schüler-Konzerte*, vl, pf, op. 85, 87, 88 (1926); *Trio*, fl, ob, bn, op. 86; *Sieben Vortragsstücke*, vl, pf, op. 89; *Piano Quintet*, op. 100

ORCHESTRA: *Concerto*, pf, orch, op. 18;
Ballade, orch, op. 36; *Liedje van de zee*, orch,
op. 45

PUBLICATIONS
*Brahms im Briefwechsel mit Th.W. Engel-
mann.* Berlin, 1918
Grieg. The Hague, 1930 (Beroemde musici
XIX)

BIBLIOGRAPHY
A. Averkamp: 'In Memoriam Julius
Röntgen (1855-1932)', *TVNM*, 14, 1932, p. 44-
47
J. de Boer: 'Julius Röntgen voelde zich
Nederlander maar was formeel Duitser', *Mens
en Melodie*, vol. 38, 1983, p. 82-85
L. Couturier: 'Julius Röntgen', *Symphonia*,
vol. 15, 1932, p. 183-186
H. Nolthenius: 'Julius Röntgen', *Weekblad
voor Muziek*, vol. 10, 1903, p. 51-52
A. Röntgen-des Amorie van der Hoeven:
Brieven van Julius Röntgen. Amsterdam, 1934
(includes an extensive list of compositions)
R. Schoute: 'Julius Röntgen (1855-1932)',
Preludium, vol. 41, 1982, p. 10-11
H. Viotta: 'Julius Röntgen', *Onze heden-
daagsche toonkunstenaars.* Amsterdam, [1892]

DISCOGRAPHY
Grieg – second string quartet (fin. by Julius
Röntgen). Raphael Quartet (Olympia OCD
432)
*Herders hij is geboren; Komt verwondert u
hier, menschen.* Quink Vocal Ensemble (Telarc
TE 80202)
Motetten. Netherlands Chamber Choir,
cond. U. Gronostay (NM Classics 92039)
Phantasie op. 24. J. Berkhemer (vl), R.
Mann (pf) (BFO A-1)
Rei van edelingen. Netherlands Chamber
Choir, cond. U. Gronostay (NM Classics
92065)
Serenade. Viotta Ensemble, members of the
Royal Concertgebouw Orchestra, cond. V.
Liberman (NM Classics 92035)
*Serenade, Thema mit Variationen, Motetten,
Symphony.* Various soloists, Viotta Ensemble,
Netherlands Chamber Choir, cond.
U. Gronostay, Netherlands Radio Chamber Or-
chestra, cond. J. van Steen (NM Classics
92096)

Sonata op. 41. G. Hoogeveen (vc), E. Grosz
(pf) (BFO A-2)
Sonata (1918). M. Karres (ob), A. Karres
(pf) (WVH 093)
Symphony C sharp minor. Utrecht Student
Orchestra, cond. B. de Greeve (CNM 95001)
Thema mit Variationen. W. Jordans (pf), L.
van Doeselaar (pf) (NM Classics 92014)
Zes Oud-Nederlandse dansen. Concertge-
bouw Orchestra, cond. W. Mengelberg (BFO
A-4 / Composers' Voice CVCD 7)

Christian Friedrich Ruppe

SALZUNGEN, 22 AUGUST 1753 – LEIDEN, 25 MAY 1826

Christian Friedrich Ruppe received his musical education from his father. He was enrolled on 25 February 1773 at Leiden University as a student of physics and mathematics, Classical literature, and the exegesis of the Gospel of St. Luke. It soon transpired that he had good prospects as a musician in Leiden, and his name is mentioned in that connection in the annals of the university's second centennial on 7 February 1775. By then he was also giving keyboard lessons.

In 1788 Ruppe was appointed organist of the Lutheran Church, in which capacity he supervised the construction of a new organ built by Andries Wolferts. Ruppe's German descent is reflected in the instrument's heavy pedal arrangement, with four independent stops including a 16' Posaune. On the occasion of the inauguration of the organ on 19 April 1790, Ruppe composed 'an elegant concerto, matched by a large and strong orchestra comprising a full complement of musical instruments.' Ruppe subsequently continued to provide professional advice for the construction of new organs and the restoration of older instruments.

Ruppe composed many works in connection with his appointment as church organist and performer. These compositions form an important part of his extensive body of work. They include *De zangwijzen van de Psalmen en gezangen bij de Hervormde Kerk in gebruik, XLV Praeludia en CCLXXVI Interludia, in alle gebruikelijke kerktoonen* [The melodies of the Psalms and hymns as used in the Dutch Reformed Church, 45 preludes and 276 interludes, arranged in all the common church modes] and *Zangwijzen der evangelischen gezangen, bij de Hervormde Kerk in gebruik* [Melodies of the evangelical hymns as used in the Dutch Reformed Church] for organ, pianoforte or keyboard. Shortly after his appointment as organist, he himself undertook the publication of a collection entitled *Dixhuit pièces pour l'orgue ou piano-forte* (op.10). An interesting aspect of the publication is the inclusion of a table containing proposals for register usage for both positive and church organs. These suggestions show Ruppe's preference for dramatic dynamic contrasts.

On 18 October 1790 Ruppe was appointed music director of Leiden University. The University Archives contain an interesting collection of letters from Ruppe, whose contents provide clues as to the forces used in various periods. In 1802, for instance, the orchestra included two flutes, two clarinets and two horns, eight violins, two violas, two double basses, two bassoons, and timpani. The vast majority of the works which Ruppe composed in his capacity as music director were either lost or never printed. His *Kerstmuziek* [Christmas Music], for large orchestra, dating from 1796, and the more intimate *Paasmuziek* [Easter Music] from 1797, both to Dutch texts, were recovered in 1987. Ruppe wrote these works for the choir of the Holy Spirit or Poor Orphans' and Children's Home in Leiden, which he conducted for several years.

Ruppe's wide acclaim resulted in 1802 in his appointment as Lecturer in Music Theory. The official description of his assignment was 'To Instruct the Reading Youngsters in the Theory of Music.' However, it took several years before Ruppe received his formal title, since 'the post was a novelty in this Country, even though it already exists in other Countries, e.g. in England, at the University of Oxford.' It was not until 22 May 1816 that the tenure of Lecturer in Music was officially ratified by Royal Decree. After several years' teaching experience, Ruppe summarized his teachings in a two-part treatise entitled *Theorie der hedendaagsche muzyk* [Treatise on contemporary music] (1809-1811).

Ruppe also had a busy private practice, teaching the keyboard, the violin and the cello, as is attested by a substantial volume of keyboard and chamber music surviving. In his private life, Ruppe was spared few hardships. In 1784 he married Christina Chalon, the daughter of the former director of the Amsterdamse Schouwburg. She bore him four children, all of whom died in infancy. His wife perished in 1808, after suffering from insanity for nine years, while Ruppe suffered from severe arthritis. Later he became immobile and had to be carried around in a litter.

In 1816 he married Johanna Pieternella Reyers. She bore him one daughter, who grew up to become an accomplished pianist, and it was for her that Ruppe at the end of his life composed his children's songs, set to lyrics by Hieronymus van Alphen. Ruppe died on 25 May 1826 and was buried in Katwijk near Leiden.

Ruppe is the most prolific exponent of the gallant and 'empfindsame' style in the Netherlands. He is not known to have composed any operatic music; his symphonic works, composed solely for the purpose of university celebrations, are largely lost. His programmatic works, such as *La grande bataille de Waterloo ou de la Belle-Alliance (Fait historique)* were composed immediately after the event boosting, no doubt, their popularity. From op.1 onwards, his harpsichord parts are complemented with violin and cello parts, though not in true polyphonic style. The extra two parts serve to fill the gaps of the basso continuo, virtually outdated by then, and impart color and structure to the harpsichord part. From op.2 onwards, the title page mentions the pianoforte alongside the harpsichord.

Presumably his *Romanzes door Mr. Rhynuis Feith* [Romances by Mr Rhynuis Feith], published by Cornelis van der Aa in Haarlem in 1787, earned him particular acclaim, as a second edition appeared in 1806 with Allart of Amsterdam. The *Oden en gedichten van Mr. J.P. Kleyn* [Odes and poems by Mr J.P. Kleyn] were published in 1788 in Leiden by A & J. Honkoop. From then on, a large number of sonatas, sonatinas and divertissements written for teaching purposes followed, initially published by Burchard/Hummel at The Hague, and from op.8 (1790) by the composer himself.

A sequence of vocal works followed several years later. Most of Ruppe's keyboard pieces composed after 1795 were given programmatic titles, such as *Chasse, Trois ballets caractéristiques, Ouverture turque*, etc. Perhaps there was no time for engravings like those adorning the works printed by the composer himself. Plattner of Rotterdam, Lotter of The Hague and Hummel of Amsterdam frequently published this 'consumer music'. The composer did not resume printing his own music until 1815-1816, after he remarried. The advent of the Romantic era emerges in the works he composed late in life. In this respect the title of op.31, *Six sérénades pour le piano forte, approprieés pour apprendre l'esprit ou l'expression de la musique* speaks volumes. The last edition of his *Tien stukjes uit de gedichtjes voor kinderen* [Ten pieces on children's poems], composed to texts by Hieronymus van Alphen (op.36, in sequence to op.33) was printed on the initiative of his widow.

GERT OOST

COMPOSITIONS

VOCAL:
Romanzes door Mr. Rhynuis Feith, naar den besten smaak op muziek gebracht. – Haarlem, Cornelis van der Aa, 1787
Oden en gedichten van Mr. J.P. Kleyn ... gecom- *poneerd voor de zang en het clavier, of fluit, viool, en bas.* – Leiden, A. & J. Honkoop, 1788
Kerstmuziek, 1796
Paasmuziek, 1797
Gezangen voor het feest van den 19 december 1799 ... *geschikt voor den zang en piano-forte*

*of orgel met accompagnement van twee violen
en bas ad libitum.* - Leiden, composer,
[1799]
*Twaalf gezangen, gekomponeerd voor drie stem-
men.* - Leiden, L. Herdingh & son, [1802]
For three voices and organ.
*Twaalf stukjes uit de gedichtjes voor kinderen door
Mr. H. van Alphen, op muzijk gebragt voor
den zang en piano-forte ... XXXIII werk.* –
Leiden, composer, J.G. van Terveen
*Tien stukjes uit de gedichtjes voor kinderen ... op
muzijk gebragt voor den zang en piano-forte
... XXXVI werk.* – Leiden, [Ruppes widow]

INSTRUMENTAL MUSIC (WITH OPUS
NUMBER):
*Quatre sonates pour le clavecin avec l'accompag-
nement d'un violon ... oeuvre première.* -
The Hague, Burchard Hummel & sons
*Six sonates pour le clavecin ou le piano forte avec
l'accompagnement d'un violon et violoncello ...*
oeuvre second. – The Hague, Burchard
Hummel & sons
Grand trio pour piano-forte, clarinette & basson ...
oeuvre 2. - Offenbach, Johann André
*Six divertissements pour le clavecin ou piano forte
avec l'accompagnement d'un violon ... oeuvre
III.* – Den Haag , Burchard Hummel & sons
*Trois sonates pour le clavecin ou piano forte avec
l'accompagnement d'un violon et violoncello
...oeuvre IV.* – The Hague, Burchard Hummel & sons
*Trois sonates à quatre mains pour le clavecin ou
piano forte ... oeuvre V.* – The Hague-Amsterdam, Burchard Hummel & sons
*Huit sonatines pour le clavecin ou piano forte
avec l'accompagnement d'un violon ... oeuvre
VI.* – Den Haag, Burchard Hummel & sons
*Air des ombres chinoises, varié pour le clavecin
(opus 7?).* – The Hague, Hummel et fils
*Trois sonates pour le clavecin ou piano forte avec
l'accompagnement d'un violon ... oeuvre
VIII.* -Leiden, composer, 1790
*Douze sonatines pour le clavecin ou piano forte
avec l'accompagnement d'un violon, à l'usage
des commençans ... oeuvre IX.* – Leiden,
composer, [1790]
*Dixhuit pièces pour l'orgue ou piano forte ... oeu-
vre 10.* - Leiden, composer
*Trois sonates pour le clavecin ou piano-forte avec
l'accompagnement d'une flûte ou violon ...*
oeuvre XI. - Leiden, composer

*Air Femmes voulez-vous éprouver, pour le clavecin
ou pianoforte avec l'accompagnement d'un violon (opus ?).* – The Hague, wid. Hummel
*Wilhelmus van Nassau, varié pour le clavecin ou
pianoforte avec l'accompagnement d'un violon
(opus 12?)* Leiden, Luzac & Co.
*Premières leçons pour apprendre le piano-forte
consistant en six sonatines très faciles et pro-
gressives ... oeuvre XIII.* – Leiden, composer
*Air favorit Où peut-on être mieux, varié pour le
pianoforte (opus 14?).*
*Chasse. Composée pour le piano-forte ... oeuvre
XV.* - Rotterdam, L. Plattner (also by Hummel, Berlin/Amsterdam)
Sonates à quatre mains pour le piano forte ...
oeuv. 16, no. 1. – Rotterdam, Plattner
Trois ballets caractéristiques pour le piano-forte ...
oeuvre XVII. - [Den Haag, Lotter & Co.]
*Sonate pour le piano forte avec accompagnement
de flûte et violoncelle ... oeuvre XVIII.* – The
Hague, Lotter & Co.
*Thème avec variations pour le pianoforte (opus
19?)* The Hague, Lotter & Co
*Ouverture turque pour le piano-forte avec accom-
pagnement de violon, violoncelle et tambour
ou contre-basse ... oeuvre XX.* – The Hague,
Lotter & Co.
*Thème avec variations pour le pianoforte ... [opus
21,1].* – The Hague, Lotter & Co.
*La grande bataille de Waterloo ou de la Belle-Al-
liance (Fait historique), composée pour le
piano-forte ...oeuvre XXIII.* - Leiden, com-
poser
*La paix universelle, conclue à Paris le 20 nov:
1815, entre les Puissances Alliées et la France.
Pièces caractéristique pour le piano-forte ...*
oeuvre XXIV. - Leiden, composer
*Sonate pour le piano forte avec accompagnement
de flûte ou violon et violoncelle ... oeuvre
XXV.* - Amsterdam, H.C. Steup
*Sonate pour le pianoforte avec accompagnement
de flûte ou violon et violoncelle ... oeuvre
XXVi.* - Amsterdam, H.C. Steup
*Sonate pour le piano forte avec accompagnement
de flûte ou violon et violoncelle ... oeuvre
XXVII.* - Amsterdam, H.C. Steup; Leiden,
composer
*Ouverture tartare pour le piano forte avec accom-
pagnement de violon et violoncelle ... oeuvre
XXVIII.* - Leiden, composer
Thème avec huit variations pour le piano-forte ...
oeuvre XXIX. - Leiden, composer

Potpourri (Variationen über Nel cor piu ..., Di tanti palpiti ..., Je suis né natif de Ferrara) ... oeuvre XXX. - Amsterdam, H.C. Steup
Six sérénades pour le piano forte, appropriées pour apprendre l'esprit ou l'expression de la musique ... oeuvre XXXI. - Leiden, composer
La Métamorphose ou le Changement des Chenilles et Papillons. Fantaisie pour le pianoforte avec l'accompagnement de flute ou violon ... oeuvre XXXII. - Leiden, composer
Ouverture grecque pour le pianoforte ... oeuvre 34. - Amsterdam, J. Vermaazen
Iö vivat. Air favori, varié pour le pianoforte ... oeuvre XXXV. - Leiden, composer

INSTRUMENTAL MUSIC (WITHOUT OPUS NUMBER):
Air. Enfant chéri des dames, etc. de l'opéra des Visitandines , varié pour le clavecin ou piano forte avec l'accompagnement d'un violon. - The Hague, Burchard Hummel & sons
Trio. Un militaire doit avoir, etc. de l'opéra L'amant statue [of Dalayrac], *varié pour le clavecin ou piano forte avec l'accompagnement d'un violon.* - The Hague-Amsterdam, Burchard Hummel & sons
Marche des Marseillois variées pour le clavecin ou piano forte avec l'accompagnement d'un violon. – The Hague, Burchard Hummel & sons
Organ Concerto, 1790
For the inauguration of the organ in the Lutheran Church of Leiden
XLV Praeludia en CCLXXVI Interludia, in alle gebruikelijke kerktoonen, ... - Leiden, L. Herdingh
De zangwijzen van de Psalmen en gezangen bij de Hervormde Kerk in gebruik, voor drie stemmen als ook voor het orgel of clavier. - Leiden, composer, 1801
Zangwijzen der evangelischen gezangen, bij de Hervormde Kerk in gebruik; geschikt voor het orgel, forte-piano of clavier. - Amsterdam, P. den Hengst & son, J. Brandt & son, Rutger Hoyman; Haarlem, Groningen, 1806

WRITINGS
Theorie der hedendaagsche muzyk. Amsterdam, J. Allart, 1809-1811
Over de muzyk. manuscript A.C.G. Vermeulen, Leiden, 1816/1817

BIBLIOGRAPHY
J.A.F. Doove: 'Christian Friedrich Rüppe : musicus en lector in de toonkunde', *Mens en Melodie,* vol. 33, 1978, p. 171 et seq.
J.A.F. Doove and J.L. Knödler: *Een ding van Parade.* Leiden, New Rhine Publishers, 1975
S.W.M.A. den Haan and P.M. Kann: *Zucht om zich te oefenen in de lieflijke zangkunst : het zangkoor van het Leidse weeshuis in de Bataafs-Franse tijd.* Alphen aan den Rijn, Canaletto, 1996
B. Kernfeld: 'Christian Friedrich Ruppe', *The New Grove dictionary of music and musicians*
F.C. Kist: 'Christian Frederik Ruppe', *Nederlandsch Muzikaal Tijdschrift,* 1841, p. 94 et seq.
J.H. van der Meer: 'Ruppe', *Die Musik in Geschichte und Gegenwart*

DISCOGRAPHY
Christmas Cantata; Easter Cantata. F. van der Heyden (S), K. van der Poel (Mez), O. Bouwknegt (T), M. Sandler (B), Ensemble Bouzignac, cond. J. Wentz (NM Classics 92067)
Duetto in F major. W. Jordans and L. van Doeselaar (pf) (NM Classics 92014)
Gezangen Voor het Feest van den 19 December 1799 : 'Hef aan! Bataaf!'; Largo con Espressione and Presto ma non troppo from *Dixhuit Pièces pour l'orgue* (op.10); *Odae Q. Horatii Flacci.* M. Beumer (S), L. van der Plas (T), G. Oost (org), Ensemble Pont de la Virtue (Erasmus WVH187/188)
Sonata op. 5, no. 1; Pièce op. 10, no. 9. H. van Nieuwkoop and J. van Oortmerssen (org) (Vanguard Classics 99060)

Daniel Ruyneman

AMSTERDAM, 8 AUGUST 1886 – AMSTERDAM, 25 JULY 1963

Daniel Ruyneman discovered his musical talents and creative gifts relatively late in life. He received piano lessons as a child, but was reluctant to practise and his lessons were suspended after six months. After leaving high school, he made several voyages as a ship's mate to the former Dutch East Indies and worked for some time at the French agency of the Netherlands Railways. At eighteen, he decided to devote his life to music. After a failed attempt to gain admission to the conservatory, he took private piano lessons with Karel de Jong and Ulfert Schults. Being of limited means, however, he was to a large extent forced to teach himself. Within a few years he attained a sufficiently high standard to be occasionally requested to perform as an accompanist. His earliest surviving composition dates from 1910. On the recommendation of Alphons Diepenbrock and with support from Julius Röntgen, he was admitted to the Amsterdam Conservatory as a piano and composition student in 1913, aged 27. He studied composition under Bernard Zweers and attained his degree in 1916.

Following World War I, Ruyneman was a pioneer and a driving force in Dutch musical life. He was the first and, for several decades, the only Dutch musician to consistently promote both Dutch and foreign contemporary music. He conceived various schemes to achieve this, including the establishment of concert societies devoted to contemporary music. In 1918 he was the principal founder of the Netherlands Society for the Advancement of Modern Music, with the objective of propagating Dutch contemporay music through concert performances and music publications both in the Netherlands and abroad. The Society's members included the composers Sem Dresden, Henri Zagwijn, Bernhard van den Sigtenhorst Meyer, Alexander Voormolen, and Willem Pijper.

In the early 1920s Ruyneman moved to Groningen, following a particlarly inflamed conflict between the Amsterdam Concertgebouw and the then music critic for the daily newspaper *De Telegraaf*, Matthijs Vermeulen. In 1918 Ruyneman had been co-signatory to a pamphlet protesting the decision of the Concertgebouw to refuse Vermeulen access to the building. As a result, the music of both Ruyneman and Vermeulen was boycotted in the series of concerts of international modern chamber music, held during the Mahler Festival of 1920.

Once settled in Groningen, Ruyneman became closely associated with a

group of painters called De Ploeg [The Plough], whose members included Jan Wiegers, Johan Dijkstra, Jan Altink and Hendrik Nikolaas Werkman. Ruyneman became the music editor for a magazine entitled *Blad voor Kunst* (1921-1922), published by Werkman. It ran articles on art, literature, drama and music. As musical director of the Groningen student consort Bragi, which he conducted from 1924 to 1929, Ruyneman directed in 1925 the first performance in the Netherlands of the ballet-pantomime *Le boeuf sur le toit* by Darius Milhaud and Jean Cocteau (the set and masks were created by Jan Wiegers). In 1928 Ruyneman established the Society for Contemporary Chamber Music in Groningen.

Around 1930, most of Ruyneman's activities gravitated towards Amsterdam, where he organized a concert series providing a complete overview of contemporary chamber music from Germany (Hindemith, Kaminski, Reutter, Toch), Czechoslovakia (Burian, Janáček, Schulhoff) and Austria (Schoenberg, Berg, Webern, Eisler, Wellesz, Hauer). These concerts provided the incentive for Ruyneman's foundation of the Netherlands Society for Contemporary Music. Between 1930 and 1962 Ruyneman was the moving spirit behind the organization, whose programming focused in particular on repertoire which was seldom heard in the traditional concert series. The Society's official mouthpiece, the monthly review *Maandblad voor Hedendaagsche Muziek*, appeared between 1931 and 1941.

Ruyneman continued his work as an organizer and composer during World War II. He accepted several national awards and composition assignments, while in addition securing funds for his society to continue promoting contemporary Dutch music.

From 1952 until his death in 1963, he was the artistic director of the Sunday afternoon concerts at the Amsterdam Stedelijk Museum, which included both Classical and contemporary repertoire. His final act of pioneering was a groundbreaking concert series entitled Experimental Music (1959-1961), paving the way for the next generation of composers: Boulez, Stockhausen, Henze, De Leeuw, and Schat.

The pieces Ruyneman composed during his conservatory studies clearly reflect the influence of composers such as Grieg and Skryabin but also, perhaps more notably, of Debussy and Ravel. At the same time, these works reflect the composer's search for a musical idiom of his own. The *Chineesche liederen* [Chinese Songs] (1917), signify a breakthrough, particularly in terms of his use of harmony, while expressing a newborn freedom in the deliberate omission of the customary bar lines.

With two compositions dating from 1918, *De Roep* [The Call] and *Hiëroglyphen* [Hieroglyphs] Ruyneman established himself at the forefront of Dutch avant-garde music. In both works, timbre and colouring play a dominant role. In *De Roep*, for unaccompanied mixed choir, the voices are treated as instruments: there is no text, only different vowels (bright and dark) and consonants. The vo-calized tone colours and their contrasting effect are associated by the composer with archetypal emotional values. The concept of a vocal 'color-polyphony' is later elaborated by Ruyneman in the *Sonata for chamber choir* (1931).

The scoring of *Hiëroglyphen* is as original as it is colourful; three flutes, ce-lesta, harp, piano, cup-bells, two mandolines and two guitars. With this small transparent ensemble, a most subtle and differentiated texture is created. A unique detail in the score are the cup-bells: twenty-five chromatically tuned, bowl-shaped brass bells with characteristic flageolet-like high notes. As in the *Chineesche liederen*, the stacking of fifths determines both the harmonic and melodic structure of the music. In addition, the composer frequently uses pentatonic scales and fragments of whole-tone sequences. Presumably, the oriental atmosphere of the work echoes the sound of the ethnic music as heard by the young Ruyneman during his seafaring days.

From the mid-1920s onwards, Ruyneman's work focuses less on sound ex-ploration than on the more formal and melodic-linear aspects of his style. This development can be heard, for instance, in his Sonata for solo violin (1925), the Divertimento for flute, clarinet, horn, viola and piano (1927), and the *Kleine sonate* [Small Sonata] for piano (1928). In the same period Ruyneman was involved with several projects combining music and drama; his opera *De Karamazovs* (1927-1928), based on the novel by Dostoyevsky and his comple-tion of Mussorgsky's opera *Le mariage* (1929) were, however, never published or performed.

Pronounced neo-Classicist aspects began to emerge in the mid-1930s, such as in the Partita for string orchestra (1943), the *Nightingales Quintet* (1949) and the Symphony (1953). Around 1960, Ruyneman changes his style for the last time; his enthusiasm for serial composition techniques, especially their stylis-tic consequences, is expressed in the four *Réflexions* for various chamber music ensembles (1959-1961).

PAUL OP DE COUL

COMPOSITIONS

SONGS: *Winterabend* (Mombert) (1914); *Trois mélodies* (Verlaine, Prud'homme) (1914); *Twee wij-zangen* (Tagore) (1915); *Chineesche liederen* (1917); *L'Absolu* (Pétronio) (1919); *Quatre poèmes* (Apollinaire) (1923); *Four Songs* (Leopold) (1937); *Seven Melodies* (Shakespeare, Wilde, Yeats, Rossetti) (1949); *Drei persische Lieder* (1950); *Trois chansons des maquisards condamnés* (1951, orchestr. 1957)

CHOIR: *De roep : kleurengamma voor gemengde stemmen* (1918); *Sonata for chamber choir* (1931)

OPERA: *De Karamazovs* (manuscript) (1927-1928); *Le mariage* (orchestr. and completion of Mussorgsky's opera) (manuscript) (1929)

PIANO: *Drie pathematologiën* (1914-1915); *Sonatina* (1917); *Kleine sonate* (1928); *Sonata no. 9* (1931); *Five nocturnes* (1947-1954); *Sonatina* (1954)

CHAMBER MUSIC: *Sonata no. 2*, vl, pf (1914); *Klaaglied van een slaaf*, vl, pf (1917); *Hiëroglyphen*, 3 fl, cel, hp, cup-bells (vibr), pf, 2 mand, 2 gui (1918); *Sonata*, vl (1925); *Divertimento*, fl, cl, hn, vla, pf (1927); *Sonata*, fl, pf (1942); *Quator à cordes* (1946); *Nightingales Quintet*, wind qnt (1949); *Sonata no. 3*, vl, pf (1956); *Réflexions no. 1*, S, fl, gui, xylophone, vibr, vla, perc (1958-1959); *Réflexions no. 2*, fl, gui, vla (1959); *Réflexions no. 3*, fl, vl, vla, vc, pf (1960-1961); *Réflexions no. 4*, wind qnt (1961)

ORCHESTRA: *Violin Concerto* (1940-1941); *Divertimento* (1936, rev. 1953: *Musica per una festa*); *Ouverture Amphitrion* (1943); *Partita*, str.orch (1943); *Amatarasu* (1952); *Symphony* (1953); *Gilgamesj* (1962)

PUBLICATIONS

De componist Jan Ingenhoven : beschouwingen in het licht van de hedendaagsche muziek. Amsterdam, De Spieghel, 1938

BIBLIOGRAPHY

P. Micheels: *Muziek in de schaduw van het Derde Rijk : de Nederlandse symfonie-orkesten 1933-1945.* Zutphen, Walburg Press, 1993, p. 214 et seq.

P. Op de Coul: 'Unveröffentlichte Briefe von Alban Berg und Anton Webern an Daniel Ruyneman', *TVNM* 22, 1972, p. 201-220

W. Paap: 'In memoriam Daniel Ruyneman', *Mens en Melodie*, vol. 18, 1963, p. 237-239

W. Paap: 'Nederlandse componisten van deze tijd, XIII : Daniel Ruyneman', *Mens en Melodie*, vol. 5, 1950, p. 75-80

E. Schoones: *Inventarislijst van het archief Daniel Ruyneman.* The Hague, 1983 (typoscr., The Hague, Gemeentemuseum, Music Archives)

K. Wieringa (ed.): *Daniel Ruyneman.* Groningen, 1987

DISCOGRAPHY

Hieroglyphs, Réflexions no. 4. Various performers (Donemus DAVS 6202)

Sonatina for piano. R. Brautigam (pf) (NM Classics 92045)

Dirk Schäfer

ROTTERDAM, 25 NOVEMBER 1873 – AMSTERDAM, 16 FEBRUARY 1931

Dirk Schäfer began studying the piano at an early age at the Music School of the Society for the Advancement of Music in his birthplace, Rotterdam. As he was also receiving private tuition in music theory, not much time remained for his general education. With the aid of a 'royal grant', Schäfer was able to continue his music studies at the conservatory of Cologne, where Willem Mengelberg, the future conductor of the Concertgebouw Orchestra, was one of his fellow students. Schäfer completed his studies in Cologne in 1894, attaining the highest distinctions in piano and composition. In the same year he won the Mendelssohn Prize for piano in Berlin. A year later, the young musician took up residence in The Hague, but moved to Amsterdam in 1904, where he continued to develop his career as a concert pianist. Schäfer was, first and foremost, a brilliant pianist, giving piano recitals and chamber music concerts with the cellist Gerard Hekking. Although he never accepted a teaching appointment at any conservatory, he had a private teaching practice until the age of forty.

Schäfer was a celebrated pianist, touring the international concert stages with the standard repertoire. He was particularly noted for his interpretations of Chopin, but his talent was not fully appreciated in the Netherlands until he had established an international reputation. His laborious quest for recognition in his native country reflects perhaps a misconception many Dutch musicians had to contend with and which was described by the music critic Willem Landré as follows: 'Audiences find it almost impossible to believe that a Dutch pianist can actually play the piano, or that a Dutch composer can actually compose music.'

Schäfer's uneasy relationship with Dutch music life was linked by the artist himself to an incident with the Concertgebouw Orchestra in 1916. Asked for the first time in sixteen years to perform with the orchestra, Schäfer declined the invitation on the grounds that 'his personal conception of art was incompatible with the views of the principal conductor', his former fellow-student Willem Mengelberg. The truth of the matter, according to music critic Paul F. Sanders, was that the two men were diametrically opposed. While Schäfer increasingly turned his back on the spectacular, virtuoso genre in favor of more reflective and meditative music, Mengelberg continued to aspire to virtuoso perfection.

But even the acclaim he earned as a concert pianist among a loyal group of

supporters could not, in the end, sat-
isfy Schäfer. Renouncing fame, he
continued to maintain that he was,
first and foremost, a composer, and
insisted that he deserved to be recognized as such. As a composer, however, Schäfer was considerably less successful.

In 1922, Schäfer's friend Leo Mossel offered to handle his concert book-
ings and business affairs. Mossel's involvement, however, did Schäfer's
career more harm than good, and the
relationship ended in 1924. A similar
friendship, sincere but ultimately un-
productive, was his relationship with
the writer Israël Querido. The latter
applauded Schäfer's compositions so
lavishly and on so many occasions that it exposed the composer to the mockery
of those taking a more discerning view, such as Willem Landré, describing
Querido's rave reviews as 'idle praise'.

Schäfer, however, was bent on achieving greatness. As a pianist, he aspired
no less than 'to give the very best of what the world's top composers had to
offer.' In April 1913 he conceived a plan for a concert series spanning ten his-
toric nights, providing a complete overview of keyboard and piano literature,
from William Byrd through to the contemporary composers of his day. During
the series, Schäfer introduced his audience to the music of Claude Debussy
and gave the first performance in the Netherlands of Arnold Schoenberg's
Drei Klavierstücke op.11.

Initially drawing a small audience, Schäfer's piano series grew more popular over time, and he received requests for performances all over the Netherlands. Although his agent was not pleased with Schäfer's progressive and
therefore risky programming, preferring him to stay with Chopin, Schäfer
himself was adamant that he should continue his work. 'I have an ideal, and I
shall continue to pursue it even if I stand to lose by it materially.' If Schäfer as
a composer never gained the recognition he felt he deserved, his piano performances contributed to fostering a sense of identity among Dutch musicians,
accustomed as they were to accepting the supremacy of foreign artists.
Schäfer recorded for Polydor and Columbia and made several player piano
rolls for Welte & Söhne, Freiburg.

Schäfer the composer was as prolific as he was critical. Only nineteen opus numbers withstood his fastidious criteria and were saved for posterity. These works were published during his lifetime, as were several of his early piano compositions without opus numbers.

Although his work was rarely seen on any music stand, Schäfer made few efforts to propagate his compositions. He composed from an inner need, and published his work because 'he felt compelled to do so.' He perceived a vast distance between himself and the material world, which, in his view, was 'superficial and shallow'.

Schäfer respected and loved contemporary music 'in as much as it deserves to be loved and respected', but he was essentially a classical musician who, in his role as a creative artist, could not match the courage he displayed as a pianist. The composer and music critic Sem Dresden described the composer in Schäfer as follows: 'As a pianist, he had a genius for performing the very same avant-garde music from which, as a composer, he shut himself off.' Paul F. Sanders, in a similar vein, wrote that Schäfer's compositions were 'outdated the very moment they were completed.'

As a composer, Schäfer felt most comfortable with chamber music, being himself a masterful performer in the genre. Although his harmonies evoke associations with the music of Richard Strauss, his music has a characteristic clarity and lightness which stands in stark contrast with the elaborate music of his contemporaries. Among Schäfer's best works are the String Quartet in C sharp minor op.14 and his piano suite *In de stilte* [In the silence] op.19, perfectly expressing his brilliant instrumental intuition. The String Quartet has a wonderful allure and is constructed expertly. That Schäfer also had a playful side is demonstrated by his virtuosic paraphrase on Johan Strauss's *Wiener Blut*, dating from 1929. If Schäfer never received complete recognition for his polished work, he was more optimistic with respect to his success as a concert pianist: 'I think it is fair to say that, as a performer, I have contributed to imparting a sense of national confidence in Dutch musicianship at a time when our own performers were denied the respect they deserved, in favor of anything imported from abroad.'

JOHAN KOLSTEEG/HUIB RAMAER

COMPOSITIONS

Zwei Lieder, mix.choir, orch, op. I (1894); *Zwei geistliche Gesänge*, mix.choir, op. 2 (1895); *Acht Etüden*, pf, op. 3 (dedicated to Busoni); *Violin Sonata no. 1*, op. 4; *Piano Quintet*, op. 5 (1901); *Violin Sonate no. 2*, op. 6; *Rhapsodie javanaise*, orch, op. 7 (1904); *Suite pastorale*, orch/pf, op. 8 (1903); *Sonate inaugurale*, pf, op. 9 (1905-1911); *Three Piano Pieces*, op. 10 (1901-1911); *Violin Sonata no. 3*, op. 11, no. 1 (1904); *Violin Sonata no. 4*, op. 11, no. 2 (1909); *Six Piano Pieces*, op. 12 (1893-1915); *Cello Sonata*, op. 13 (1909); *String Quartet*, op. 14; *Eight Piano Pieces*, op. 15 (1921); *Four Songs* (Bethge, after Wang-Seng-Yu, Keuls, Lenau, Weitbrecht), v, pf, op. 16; *Five Interludes*, pf, op. 17; *Toccata*, pf, op. 18 (1924); *Suite 'In de stilte'*, pf, op. 19 (1929); *Präludium und Fuge*, pf (1894); *Barcarolle*, pf (1897); *Quatre petits morceaux*, pf (1894-1899); *Scherzo, Impromptu, Valse di Bravura*, pf (1897, rev. 1917 and 1921); *Variationen auf eine Sequenz*, pf (1902); *Variaties op een wals [Wiener Blut] van Johann Strauss*, pf (1929)

PUBLICATIONS

'Aphorismen', *Caecilia*, vol. 68, 1911, p. 49-50
Het klavier. Samengesteld uit de nagelaten aanteekeningen door Ida Schäfer-Dumstorff. Amsterdam, Wereldbibliotheek, 1942

BIBLIOGRAPHY

L. Couturier: 'In memoriam Dirk Schäfer', *Symphonia*, vol. 14, March 1931, p. 45-47
W. Landré: 'Dirk Schäfer als componist', *Caecilia and De Muziek*, vol. 98 (15), 1941, p. 33-35
P. Sanders: 'In Memoriam Dirk Schäfer', *De Muziek*, vol. 5, 1931, p. 241
R. van Santen: *De piano en hare componisten*. The Hague, 1925
Ter herinnering aan Dirk Schäfer : 25 nov. 1873 – 16 febr. 1931. Amsterdam-Sloterdijk, Wereldbibliotheek, 1932

DISCOGRAPHY

Lente (op. 12, no. 4). F. van Ruth (pf) (Vara Gram VCD 477181-2)
Piano Quintet, op. 5. Raphael Quartet, J. Bogaart (pf) (Attacca Babel 8210-5)
Piano Quintet, op. 5. Orpheus Quartet, J. Bogaart (pf) (NM Classics 92046)
8 Piano Pieces, op. 15; Interludes, op. 17. D. Kuyken (pf) (NM Classics 92049)
Lente, op. 12, no. 4. F. van Ruth (pf) (Varagram VCD 4771812)
8 Piano Pieces, op. 15. J. de Bie (pf) (Koch Schwann CD 310077)
Piano Piece, op. 15, no. 1, 7, 8; Chant mélancholique; Sonate inaugurale. J. Bogaart (pf) (Attacca Babel 8201)

Peter Schat

UTRECHT, 5 JUNE 1935

Peter Schat is the son of a master baker who would return from his work in the evenings and play preludes and etudes of Chopin on the piano. It was in part through this circumstance that Schat developed early in life a great love of music. His father participated in the Dutch resistance during the German occupation of the Netherlands in World War II; Schat's experiences in this period had a crucial influence on his character and nurtured his lifelong sense of social responsibility and 'vigilance'.

In 1943, while still at primary school, he realized he wanted to become a composer. His first piece, the *Passacaglia en fuga* [Passacaglia and fugue] for organ, was premiered at Utrecht Cathedral during the Gaudeamus Music Week in 1954. He was then already a student at the Utrecht Conservatory and studied composition with Kees van Baaren (until 1958, transferring in his final year to the conservatory in The Hague), and piano with Jaap Callenbach (until 1957). Under Van Baaren's tutelage, Schat immersed himself in the twelve-tone technique of Schoenberg, Berg and Webern. He also developed an affinity for the music of Stravinsky, Bartók and Ravel. These composers all contributed to the development of his musical style, which had already begun to crystallize in such early works as the String Quartet (1954), his first twelve-tone composition.

Schat received his first international recognition in 1958 when his Septet was selected for performance at the ISCM Festival in Strasbourg. His first orchestral piece, *Mozaïeken* [Mosaics] (1960), was accorded the same honor. As a result, Schat became known as the most talented Dutch composer of his generation.

After gaining an early discharge from military service, he spent several years studying abroad – first in London (1959-1960) with the Hungarian pedagogue Mátyás Seiber, who helped him acquire a thorough knowledge of traditional counterpoint, and then at the Musikhochschule in Basel (1960-1962) with Pierre Boulez, who instructed him in analysis and serial techniques. These lessons led to compositions such as *Entelechie I* and *II* (1961), written according to strict serial principles. Schat experienced his time in Basel as an 'intellectual spring clean', although he considered that the iconoclasm of serial music had its drawbacks and that it could lead to mannerism and incomprehensibility. Nevertheless, he avidly studied its ideas and thoroughly re-

searched the artistic merits and compositional resources of serialism,
aleatoric methods, spatial deploy-
ment of musicians and electronic
music. In this regard, his work for
music theater, *Labyrint* (1960-1965)
is the first culmination of these experiences. This highly complex multimedia and multidimensional production combines all the arts: not
only various instrumental and vocal
techniques, but also dance, mime,
painting, drama and film.

The second half of the 1960s was
a period of social upheaval, in part
brought on by the war in Vietnam.
Schat's shock at the events in South-
East Asia nourished in him an anti-capitalistic attitude that found expression
not only in word and deed, but in music as well. In the 'combative' *On Escalation* (1968), for six percussionists and orchestra, the conductor gradually loses
authority as a consequence of an 'organized revolution' within the piece. The
work was written as a tribute to Che Guevara, as was the renowned morality
piece *Reconstructie* (1969), a music theater work written in collaboration with
Louis Andriessen, Reinbert de Leeuw, Misha Mengelberg, Jan van Vlijmen,
and the authors Hugo Claus and Harry Mulisch. Also significant in this regard were Schat's activities with the Amsterdam Elektrisch Circus, a mobile
concert podium founded under the motto 'Serve the people' and intended as
an alternative to the concert halls of institutionalized music.

Other compositions from this period are *Anathema* for piano, composed in
the summer of 1969, when the authorities initiated a heavy-handed crack-
down on the hippies at the Dam, a square in central Amsterdam; *Thema*
(1970) for oboe and orchestra, which conveys the hopelessness of that time;
and *To You* (1972) for soprano, guitars, keyboard instruments, spinning tops
and electronic instruments. To this list could be added *Canto General* (1974), a
lamentation for Salvador Allende; *Polonaise '81*, created at the time of the social uprising at the Lenin Pier in the Polish city of Gdánsk; and *De Hemel*
[Heaven] (1990), dedicated to 'the martyrs of democracy at the 'Square of
Heavenly Peace' in Beijing.

Despite the admiration aroused by his serial compositions, Schat became
increasingly convinced that the break with music history, brought on by mod-

ernism, had resulted primarily in 'barren, formal rhetoric', in one-dimensional music oriented solely to a single chromatic tone. He envisioned a more viable, harmonic music with chromatic depth. Its realization was preceded by years of critical (self-)investigation, divisible into four phases, each of which culminated in a music drama. The first was that of his apprenticeship itself (1953-1962), during which time he worked serially.

Clockwise and Anti-Clockwise (1967) for sixteen wind instruments and *Anathema* (1969) for piano are products of his second phase. Here Schat still focuses on the single tone which, through 'permuteration' (a combination of permutation/change and iteration/addition), is probed extensively before another tone is added. A work such as *Thema* (1970) might in this regard be understood as 'a ritual dance around the row'. But the serial structures of this phase were also combined with tonal elements which, whether exact quotations (*On Escalation*), stylistic quotations (*Anathema*) or diatonic constructions (*To You*), are decidedly at odds with his serial style.

The third period began with *Canto General* and came to a close with the song cycle *Kind en kraai* [Child and crow] (1977). Here Schat turns his attention from the row of individual tones to the mutual relationships between tones, the intervals. This phase reached a peak in *Houdini, een circus-opera* (1974-1977), based on a libretto by Adrian Mitchell. Each scene is governed by a specific constellation of intervals. Shortly afterwards, Schat realized that the most important element is the nature of the relationship between tones, or the depth that arises from it: that is, the difference between the two-dimensionality of an interval and the three-dimensionality of a tonality.

This depth was achieved in the Symphony no. 1 (1978), in the cartoon opera *Aap verslaat de knekelgeest* [Monkey subdues the White-Bone Demon] (1980) and in *Polonaise '81*, when he made the next logical step in this progression, arriving at the triad. It led in 1982 to his controversial 'tone clock'. At the root of this harmonic/melodic concept is the discovery that with the octave divided into twelve tones, precisely twelve different constellations of three tones (triads) may be formed. Schat calls these 'hours', analogous with the face of a clock, or 'tonalities', as each hour presents a different compilation, a different chromatic structure and its own characteristic sound. He developed this theory in a number of books, partially translated into English as *The Tone Clock*. In these books he coined the phrase 'chromatic tonality', complementing the traditional 'diatonic tonality', both being within the realm of the triad. He thus built a bridge over this century's notorious 'breach with history'.

Since then, and beginning with *Polonaise '81*, Schat has composed exclusively with the aid of the tone clock. Among the works written with this technique are his large-scale music drama *Symposion* (1982-1989) on the death of

Tchaikovsky, and the 45-minute orchestral variations *De Hemel*, both of which may be considered climaxes within his oeuvre. *De Hemel* was performed to great public and critical acclaim by the five major orchestras in the Netherlands, as well as by orchestras in Germany, Poland, Australia and the United States. Other major works from the 1990s are *An Indonesian Requiem* (1996), *Arch Music for St.Louis* (1997) for orchestra, and the Symphony no. 3 (1998-1999) for orchestra with a chromatic gamelan, commissioned by the Royal Concertgebouw Orchestra. Peter Schat remains a fascinating composer who to a large degree has helped determine the face of post-war Dutch music and the climate in which it exists.

ERIK VOERMANS

COMPOSITIONS

VOCAL: *Cryptogamen* (Achterberg), Bar, orch (1959); *The fall* (Joyce), 4 S, 4 A, 4 T, 4 B (1960); *Entelechie II* (Schierbeek), Mez, instr.ens (1961); *Improvisaties uit het Labyrint*, A, T, B, b-cl, perc, pf, db (1963); *Stemmen uit het Labyrint*, A, T, B, orch (1963); *Koren uit het Labyrint* (L. de Boer), choir SATB, orch (1964); *Scènes uit het Labyrint* (L. de Boer), sp.v., A, T, B, choir SATB, orch (1964); *To You* (Mitchell), Mez, instr.ens (1972); *Het vijfde seizoen* (Mitchell, Blake), S, inst.ens (1973); *Canto General* (Neruda, transl. N. Tarn), Mez, vl, pf (1974); *Mei '75 : een lied van bevrijding* (Mitchell), Mez, Bar, choir SATB, orch (1975); *Houdini Symphony* (Mitchell), S, Mez, T, Bar, choir SATB, orch (1976); *I am Houdini* (Mitchell), T, choir SATB, 2 pf (1976); *De briefscène* (Mitchell), S, T, pf (1976); *Kind en kraai* (Mulisch), S, pf (1977); *Adem*, choir SSAATTBB (1984); *For Lenny, at 70* (Kavafis, transl. R. Dalven), T, pf (1988); *An Indonesian Requiem* (1996)

MUSIC FOR THE THEATRE: *Labyrint* (a kind of opera) (1960-1965); *Reconstructie* (morality) (with L. Andriessen, H. Claus, R. de Leeuw, M. Mengelberg, H. Mulisch and J. van Vlijmen), v, 3 choirs, large ens (1969); *Houdini* (circus opera) (1974-1977); *Aap verslaat de knekelgeest* (cartoon opera) (1978-1980); *Symposion* (opera) (1982-1989)

ORCHESTRA: *Mozaïeken* (1960); *Concerto da camera* (1960); *Entelechie I* (1960-1961);

Dansen uit het Labyrint (1963); *Clockwise and Anti-Clockwise*, wind instr. (1967); *On Escalation* (1968); *Thema*, ob, orch (1970); *Symphony no. 1* (1978, rev. 1979); *Symphony no. 2* (1983, rev. 1984); *Serenade* (1984); *De Hemel* (1989-1990); *Opening* (1991); *Etudes*, pf, orch (1992); *Preludes* (1993); *Arch Music for St. Louis* (1997); *Symphony no. 3*, chromatic gamelan, orch (1998-1999)

OTHER INSTRUMENTAL WORKS: *Passacaglia en fuga*, org (1954); *Introductie en adagio in oude stijl*, str.qt (1954); *Septet*, fl, ob, b-cl, hn, vc, pf, perc (1956); *Octet*, fl, ob, cl, bn, hn, 2 tpt, trb (1958); *Inscripties*, pf (1959); *Two Pieces*, fl, vl, tpt, perc (1959); *Improvisations and Symphonies*, fl, ob, cl, bn, hn (1960); *Signalement*, 6 perc, 3 db (1961); *Banden uit het Labyrint* (1965); *The Aleph* (1965); *First Essay on Electrocution* (1966); *Anathema*, pf (1969); *Hypothema*, t-rec, tape (1969); *Polonaise '81*, pf (1981); *The Tone Clock*, mechanical clock (1987); *Alarm*, car, bells ad lib. (1994)

PUBLICATIONS

'On harmony and tonality', *Key Notes*, 19, 1984/1, p. 2-4
De Toonklok : essays en gesprekken over muziek. Amsterdam, Meulenhoff/Landshoff, 1984
De wereld chromatisch : een muzikaal reisverslag. Amsterdam, Meulenhoff/Landshoff, 1988
Adem : een vergelijking. Amsterdam, Bert Bakker, 1989

Requiem over het Hollands Diep : een nage-
zonden brief aan Rudolf Escher. Hilversum,
Centrum Nederlandse Muziek/Zutphen, Wal-
burg Press, 1993
The Tone Clock. Transl. and introd. by Jenny
McLeod. London, Harwood Academic Publish-
ers, 1993
Het componeren van de hemel. Amsterdam,
Donemus, 2000

BIBLIOGRAPHY

P. van Deurzen: 'Het uur van de waarheid :
analyse: De hemel van Peter Schat', *Mens en
Melodie*, vol. 48, 1993, p. 208-214
A. Douw: 'Gifmenger van het eerste uur :
Symposion, opera van Peter Schat', *Mens en
Melodie*, vol. 49, 1994, p. 210-217
A. Fransen: 'Herrie in de hemel', *HP/De
Tijd*, 4 Feb. 2000, p. 62-65
R. de Groot: 'The clockmaker as musician :
the Tone Clock in motion', *Key Notes*, 19,
1984/1, p. 22-28
R. de Groot: 'The wheels of the Tone
Clock : the musician as clockmaker', *Key Notes*,
19, 1984/1, p. 7-17
A. Porter: 'Houdini in America: Escape',
Key Notes, 10, 1979/2, p. 33-36
Peter Schat-Rudolf Escher: brieven 1958-1961,
ed. E. Voermans. Hilversum, Centrum Neder-
landse Muziek/Zutphen, Walburg Press, 1992
L. Samama: 'Peter Schat : profeet in eigen
land?', *Schat in Groningen : een festival rond de
componist Peter Schat*, ed. P. van Reijen.
Groningen, 1989
E. Schönberger: 'De pink van Beethoven',
De wellustige tandarts & andere componisten.
Amsterdam, De Bezige Bij, 1985, p. 197-202
S. Smit en J. Voeten: 'Peter Schat',
Entr'acte, Dec. 1990, p. 32-37
E. Voermans: *Peter Schat : dramatisch com-
ponist.* Brochure Donemus, Amsterdam 1993
E. Voermans: 'Peter Schat's search for chro-
matic order', *Key Notes*, 28, 1994/1, p. 16-17

DISCOGRAPHY

Aap verslaat de knekelgeest. Nationale
Reisopera, Ensemble Beestenboel, cond. V. de
'Kort (Composers' Voice CV 73)
Adem. Various soloists, Netherlands Cham-
ber Choir, cond. H. Kerstens (NM Classics
92025)

Anathema; Canto General; Thema; To you.
Various soloists and ensembles (Composers'
Voice Highlights, CVCD 19)
Etudes. J.-Y. Thibaudet (pf), Netherlands
Radio Philharmonic Orchestra, cond. E. de
Waart (Entr'acte CD 3)
De Hemel. Royal Concertgebouw Orches-
tra, cond. R. Chailly (NM Classcis 92033)
Houdini. Various soloists, Concertgebouw
Orchestra, Netherlands Opera Choir a.o.,
cond. H. Vonk (Composers' Voice Special
1977)
*Improvisations and symphonies; Inscripties;
Kind en kraai; Polonaise '81.* Van Gendt Quin-
tet, H. Austbö (pf), E. Schuring (S) (NM Clas-
sics 92027)
*Mosaics, Entelegy I, Dances from the
Labyrinth, On Escalation, Clockwise and Anti-
Clockwise.* Netherlands Ballet Orchestra, cond.
Th. Fischer (Composers' Voice Highlights CV
83)
Mozaïeken. Netherlands Radio Chamber
Orchestra, cond. E. Bour (BFO-A17)
Passacaglia and fugue. L. van der Vliet (org)
(Composers' Voice CVCD 16)
Polonaise '81. H. Austbö (pf) (NM Special
92093)
Serenade. Caecilia Consort, cond. D.
Porcelijn (Attacca Babel 8844-2)
Symphony no. 1; Septet. Concertgebouw Or-
chestra, cond. C. Davis, various soloists, cond.
H. Kerstens (Composers' Voice CV 7901)
Symphony no. 2. Concertgebouw Orchestra,
cond. B. Haitink (Composers' Voice Special
1986/1)

Johan Schenck

AMSTERDAM, BAPTIZED 3 JUNE 1660 – ?, C.1720

Johan Schenck was born in Amsterdam to German parents, Wienand Schenck and Catarina Cempies. He was baptized on 3 June 1660 in the Moses and Aaron Church. There are no known records of his youth and education, but it is assumed that he studied the viola da gamba with Philip or Carel Hacquart, both of whom lived and worked in Amsterdam in the 1670s. On Schenck's certificate of marriage, dated 13 April 1680, he is already referred to as the 'Musicant'. Among Amsterdam's affluent bourgeoisie, the young musician found an excellent environment in which to further his talents. It was with its support that he was able to publish an impressive collection of works, dating from 1687 onwards. With ten opus numbers to his name, Schenck was the most widely published of seventeenth-century Dutch composers.

Schenck enjoyed a considerable reputation as a virtuoso gamba player. 'Personne n'a touché a cet instrument avec plu de delicatesse que Lui' ['No one has ever played this instrument more delicately than he'], a contemporary wrote. Jan Snep, a fellow gamba player, in the preface to his suites for viola da gamba published around 1700, describes Schenck's talent as follows: 'Having listened for several years in enchantment to the captivating strokes with which the great Schenck caresses his viola di gamba, I have been encouraged by his masterful touch to take up this soulful instrument myself...'

Around 1696, Schenck's fame as a gamba player took him to Düsseldorf, where he accepted an appointment to the court of Elector Palatine Johann Wilhelm II, himself a gamba player. Here Schenck embarked on a double career, both as a musician and a court official, culminating in his appointment in 1710 as 'Hofkamerrat', in which capacity he attended the coronation of Emperor Charles VI in Frankfurt in 1711. He remained, however, an active musician, a fact attested to by a string of publications published under his name since that time. Late in life he also received keyboard and continuo lessons from the Düsseldorf conductor Feckler. It is assumed that Schenck remained in the service of Johann Wilhelm II until the latter's death on 8 June 1716, but no records of him exist after that date.

Schenck's work reveals that he was a typically Dutch composer. No fewer than three publications are devoted to vocal music, set to Dutch texts. Furthermore, his entire body of work was printed in Amsterdam, including the music which

EENIGE

GEZANGEN,

UIT DE OPERA VAN

BACCHUS, CERES en VENUS.

Gefteld door

JOAN SCHENK.

Voor den Autheur t'Amfteldam, by d'Erfg. Paulus Matthyfz., in 't Muzyc-boeck, 1687.

he composed while living in Düsseldorf. Op.1 (1687) comprises a collection of songs based on the score of the opera *Bacchus, Ceres en Venus*, which was set to a libretto by Govert Bidloo, an Amsterdam regent, physician and poet. The two other volumes containing vocal music are devoted to religious poetry. Unfortunately, the bulky *C. van Eekes koninklyke harpliederen* [C. van Eeke's Royal Harp Songs], published c.1694, has not survived intact, the two violin parts and the continuo part having been lost. Schenck's arrangement of the Song of Songs, *Zang-wyze op M:Gargons uitbreiding over 't Hooglied Salomons* from 1696 [Setting of M.Gargon's elaborations on the Song of Solomon], which has survived in its entirety, is less ambitious than the *Koninklyke harpliederen*. Schenck's vocal work has contributed significantly to the brief but intense flourishing of Dutch song in the late seventeenth century.

Schenck devoted two opus numbers to works for the violin. The only known copy to exist of *Il giardino armonico* (1691), a collection containing twelve sonatas for two violins, viola da gamba and continuo, was unfortunately lost in Berlin during World War II. From the preface to the *Suonate a violino e violone o cimbalo* op.7, published in 1699, it appears that Schenck had in fact composed the work much earlier. The publication contains a motley selection of suites, sonatas, capriccios, fantasias and variations for violin and continuo. The style of composition is an interesting blend of German (double stops, free passages in 'stile fantastico'), French (suites) and Italian (sonatas) elements, without making extraordinary demands on the virtuosity of the performer. It stands to reason that the crowning piece of Schenck's body of work is his gamba music, making up about half of the opus numbers. His first attempt in this genre is the *Uitgevondene tyd en konst oeffeningen* [Invented time and art exercises] (1688) op.2. Most of the fifteen 'sonatas' consist of a traditional suite, preceded by a free-style prelude. From a technical viewpoint, they are perhaps Schenck's most demanding works, containing virtuoso arpeggios, large intervals and frequent double stops. The most spectacular examples of this are found in the four sonatas in which dance movements are avoided, i.e. nos IV, VI, X and XV. Schenck's virtuoso style of composing borrows primarily from the English gamba school (Young, Butler), but the rich polyphony also traces back to the German violin music of the period. The *Uitgevondene tyd en konst oeffeningen* may reflect the influence of the *Speelstukken* [Pieces] for violin and continuo by David Petersen, published five years earlier, which in turn contain elements of the violin music of Johann Jacob Walther.

In view of the relatively large number of copies surviving, Schenck's op.6, *Scherzi musicali* (1698), probably was his most celebrated work. The collection contains fourteen suites for viola da gamba and continuo which, both in style and instrumentation, complement the *Uitgevondene tyd en konst oeffeningen*. In the *Scherzi*, the emphasis on the dance movements betrays a distinct French influence, while the writing is less exuberant.

Schenck's gamba music reaches its climax in his opp.8 and 9, *Le nymphe di Rheno* (1702) and *L'echo du Danube* (1704), i.e. from his German period. The first contains twelve duets for two gambas (suites and sonatas). Both parts are of equal difficulty, making no considerable demands on the player's virtuosity; apparently Schenck, in composing the work, was mindful of the ability of the person to whom the album was dedicated, namely his patron and employer Johann Wilhelm.

L'echo du Danube is generally considered to be Schenck's greatest work, restoring the gamba in full glory to its role as a virtuoso solo instrument. In these six sonatas, the instrument is increasingly treated as the 'soloist': the first two sonatas have an obligato continuo, nos.3 and 4 a continuo ad libitum, while the last two are composed 'senza basso'. An original manuscript of an earlier version of this work, kept by the Austrian National Library, shows that Schenck apparently substituted two of the sonatas before the work was published. In *L'echo du Danube*, the Italian style is predominant, reminiscent of Corelli in particular. In view of the consistent development of Schenck's talent as a composer, from his first published works through to the above opus number, it is regrettable that his last opus, *Les fantaisies bisarres de la goutte*, dating from 1711 or 1712, has largely disappeared. The surviving continuo part suggests that it might have been the crowning glory of his gamba music.

PIETER DIRKSEN

COMPOSITIONS

Eenige gezangen uit de opera van Bacchus, Ceres en Venus ... [opus 1]. – Amsterdam, heirs of Paul Matthysz, 1687
27 songs for voice and bc

Uitgevondene tyd en konst oeffeningen ... opera seconda. – Amsterdam, Estienne Roger, 1688
Fifteen sonatas for viola da gamba and bc

Il giardino armonico ... opera terza. – Amsterdam, Amadeo le Chevalier, 1691
Twelve sonatas for 2 violins, viola da gamba and bc. Lost

C[ornelis] van Eekes koninklyke harpliederen, ... opera quarta ... – Amsterdam, for the composer ... by the heirs of J. Lescailje, [c. 1694]
For soprano, bass, 2 violins and bc. Incomplete (only the vocal part has survived)

Zang-wyze op M: Gargons uitbreiding over 't Hooglied Salomons ... vyfde werk. – Amsterdam, heirs of Paul Matthysz, 1696
63 songs for voice and bc

Scherzi musicali per la viola di gamba con basso continuo ad libitum ... opera sesta. – Amsterdam, Estienne Roger, [1698]
Fourteen suites for viola da gamba and bc

Suonate a violino e violone o cimbalo ... opera 7ma. – Amsterdam, Estienne Roger, [1699]
Eightteen pieces (suites, sonatas, capriccios, fantasias and one air with variations) for violin and bc

Le nymphe di Rheno, per due viole di gamba sole ... opera ottava. – Amsterdam, Estienne Roger, [1702]
Twelve sonatas and suites for 2 viola da gambas

L'echo du Danube contenant six sonates ... IXe ouvrage. – Amsterdam, Estienne Roger, [1704]
Two sonatas for viola da gamba and bc, two for viola da gamba and bc ad lib., two for viola da gamba. The autograph Vienna, Österreichische Nationalbibliothek, cod.

nr. 16598 includes four sonatas, partly in a different version, and two unpublished sonatas

Les fantaisies bisarres de la goutte, contenant XII sonades pour un viole de gambe seule avec la basse continue, ou avec un autre viole de gambe ou théorbe ... dixième ouvrage. – Amsterdam, Estienne Roger & Michel Charles le Cène, [1711-1712]
Incomplete (only the bc part has survived)

BIBLIOGRAPHY

E. Hintermaier: 'Johannes Schenck', *The New Grove dictionary of music and musicians*
S. Luttman: 'The music of Johann Schenk : some observations', *Journal of the Viola da Gamba Society of America*, 18, 1981, p. 94-120
E.H. Meyer: 'Die Vorherrschaft der Instrumentalmusik im niederländischen Barock', *TVNM*, 15, 1936, p. 56-83 and 264-281
K.H. Pauls: 'Der kurpfalzische Kammermusikus Johannes Schenck', *Die Musikforschung*, 15, 1962, p. 157-171
K.H. Pauls: 'Ergänzungen zur Biographie des kurpfalzischen Kammermusikus Johannes Schenck', *Die Musikforschung*, 19, 1966, p. 288-289

DISCOGRAPHY

Fantasia no. 1 from op. 7 (arr.). R. Kanji (rec) a.o. (Globe GLO 5101)
Sonata op. 9, no. 2. Trio Sonnerie (Teleac TEL 8901-8905)
Sonata op. 9, no. 2. Trio Sonnerie (Emergo Classics EC 3984-2)

Leander Schlegel

OEGSTGEEST, 2 FEBRUARY 1844 – OVERVEEN, 20 OCTOBER 1913

Leander Schlegel grew up in the culturally stimulating international environment of Leiden University, where his father, a German from Thüringen, held a teaching position. A highly talented pianist and violinist, he was admitted as a student to the Royal Music School at The Hague in 1858. Three years later he moved to Leipzig to further his piano and composition studies. In 1871, after spending several years as a traveling performer with violinist August Wilhelmj, he accepted a post as director of the Music School of the Society for the Advancement of Music in Haarlem. Here he married Emma de Waal Malefijt. Their only daughter, Lydia, was an active piano teacher all her life.

Together with the organist Johan Bastiaans, the cellist Ernest Appy and several descendants of the Robert family, Schlegel was a driving force in lifting the quality of music making in Haarlem to professional standards. In the 'Séances for chamber music', he performed as a soloist, accompanist and chamber musician with such artists as the violinist Joseph Joachim.

As a piano teacher, Schlegel was active in the Society and supported the institution of a centralized national examination system. Among his piano pupils were Anna van Asbeck-Kluit, who also studied with Liszt, Louis Robert, the city organist of Haarlem and teacher of Hendrik Andriessen, and the composer Leo Michielsen, although this is not entirely certain. From 1890 onwards, Schlegel steadily decreased his performances to concentrate on composing, in addition to teaching at his own music school.

As a composer, Schlegel was a late developer. His first two opus numbers appeared only in 1880, and only after 1900 did he produce compositions with any regularity. Schlegel's cosmopolitan background never deflected him from following his own instincts, and he never once associated himself with the nationalist ramblings of many of his contemporaries. In essence, Leander Schlegel was an intimate and poetic composer. The critic Hugo Nolthenius, who formed part of an elite group of Schlegel admirers, formulated his enthusiasm for Schlegel's work as follows: 'He is an aristocrat in character, seemingly reserved, but only on the surface; those taking the trouble to understand him will find themselves amply rewarded.' Schlegel's work was perhaps most admired outside the Netherlands, notably in Vienna. Henri Marteau, Joachim's successor and an ardent advocate of Schlegel's chamber music, performed his Violin Concerto from manuscript in Berlin, Vienna, Munich and

Amsterdam. His Violin Sonata (1910), after its first performance by Charles Timner and Willem Andriessen, was also performed by Marteau and by Carl Flesch and Artur Schnabel. In Vienna, chiefly on the initiative of the piano professor Julius Epstein and music critic Max Kalbeck, several concerts were devoted to the music of Schlegel. In Haarlem too, an integral 'Schlegel Concert' was given in honor of the composer on 18 January 1910.

Due to some extent to the changed cultural ambience both in the Netherlands and in Vienna, Schlegel's music was practically forgotten after World War I. An article by the music critic Willem Landré in 1924, describing Schlegel as a 'representative of the old Leipzig aesthetes, a generation which has no affinity whatsoever with the new, French-oriented music', paints a caricature of Schlegel as a Schumann epigone. This view had already been contested by Kalbeck, who classed Schlegel's music 'to the left' of Brahms, implying a connection with Liszt, Wagner and Richard Strauss.

Likewise, Willem Andriessen's positive review in 1948 was unsuccessful in turning the tide in favor of Schlegel, whose music he defended as follows: 'There has been, in any case, a general misconception as to the authentic timbre, the personal harmony, and the quite progressive thinking which is evident in Schlegel's music; thus the essential value of his art has been denied the respect it deserves.' Thanks to the efforts of, among others, the famous promoter of Dutch music Willem Noske, there have been regular performances of Schlegel's songs and chamber music since 1980.

Among Schlegel's surviving publications there is a music booklet containing short piano pieces written in his youth. The first known performance of a Schlegel composition occurred in Leiden on 6 May 1859, when Leander Schleger himself, at thirteen years of age, performed his own *Nocturne voor viool* [Nocturne for violin]. From 1864 onwards, Schlegel's recitals often included several smaller piano compositions by the artist himself, but it was not until his performance of his Three Piano Pieces and *Ballade*, on 23 January 1877 in Rotterdam that opus numbers were appended, these two works becoming respectively opp.1 and 2, published in 1880 by Schott in Mainz. Notably, all his printed music except several of his early songs (printed in Amsterdam) and op.26 (published in Vienna by Universal Editions), were published by German music publishing houses, including Simrock. Schlegel's entire body of work comprises 35 opus numbers (eight of which never appeared in print), including eighteen piano collections, eight song anthologies, four chamber music compositions, one choral work, one piano concerto, one violin concerto, one symphony, and one symphonic poem.

The composer Schlegel appears to have been an extension of Schlegel the pianist: of the first thirteen opus numbers, eleven consist of piano works, while the remaining two are song collections composed for singers Schlegel himself accompanied at the piano. Most of these works are dedicated to fellow musicians and close friends, except for opp.2 and 5, which are dedicated to Brahms. Schlegel's intriguing opus 5, an interpretation in six parts of Heine's poem *Der arme Peter*, dating from 1886, is dedicated to Clara Schumann. As the work progresses, Schlegel's style increasingly betrays the influence of Liszt, and it is believed that Clara Schumann for that reason expressed only moderate appreciation of it. Opus 7, ending with 'Am Grabe Robert Schumanns', displays the utmost taste in dealing with the traditional idiom and signifies the composer's parting with Schumann as his closest influence.

Schlegel's Piano Quartet op.14 marks the beginning of the period in which the composer developed an authentic, identifiable musical language. It is the product of a long and arduous creative process, an early version of this composition having already been performed in 1886 as opus 6. Schlegel, however, was highly self critical and kept polishing his works even after they had been printed, as is attested by several private copies of his works. The Piano Quartet is dedicated to a German princess who financed its publication in 1908. Almost all his works were from then on dedicated to prominent foreigners, notably his friends in Vienna.

Nowhere else is Schlegel's music as progressive and as close to the young Schoenberg as in his songs, op.24. The *Deutsche Liebeslieder*, op.20, are his most monumental composition. Spanning some fifty minutes, the work is an amalgamation of twelve songs and three piano works, creating a song cycle based, once again, on the Leitmotiv of Heine's *Der arme Peter*. An interesting aspect of the work is that the voice and the piano are explicitly treated as equal protagonists. A perfect fusion of literary themes and harmonic coloring, Schlegel's latter work ranks among the best of the Dutch song repertoire.

FRANS VAN RUTH

COMPOSITIONS

SONGS: *Deutsche Liebeslieder*, op. 20 (1900);
Drei Lieder (Fiore della Neve/Osterwald,
Hölderlin, Hauser), op. 21; *Vier Lieder*
(Heine, Rückert), op. 22; *Drei Lieder* (Ver-
wey/Hauser, Nouhuys/Hauser, Lenau), op.
24 (1907); *Drei Lieder* (Marteau), op. 28
(1907)

PIANO (PIANO 2H UNLESS OTHERWISE
STATED): *Three Piano Pieces*, op. 1; *Ballade*, op. 2; *Suite*, op. 4 (1886; rev. 1903);
Der arme Peter, op. 5 (1886); *In's Album*, op.
7; *Drei Clavierstücke*, op. 10; *Sechs Phan-
tasien*, op. 15; *Drei Tonstücke*, op. 26 (1911);
Passacaglia, 2 pf, op. 31

CHAMBER MUSIC: *Piano Quartet in C major*,
op. 14; *String Quartet in F major/D major*,
op. 35 (autograph)

BIBLIOGRAPHY

W. Andriessen: *Mensen in de muziek*. Amsterdam, Arbeiderspers, 1962

W. Landré: 'Leander Schlegel', *De Verenigde
Tijdschriften*, 1924, p. 108-110

E. Reeser: *Een eeuw Nederlandse muziek :
1815-1915*. Amsterdam, Querido, 1950, 2/1986

DISCOGRAPHY

Deutsche Liebeslieder; Three Songs (op. 24);
Lieblich wallen durch die Lufte (op. 21, no. 2);
Three Songs (op. 28). B. Pierik (S), N. van der
Meel (T), A. van Wijk (Mez), T. Karlsen (S), F.
van Ruth (pf) (Attacca Babel 8951-4)

Dolorosa, ma non patetico (op. 5, no. 6). J.
de Bie (pf) (Koch Schwann 310 077)

Piano Quartet. J. Bingham (pf), E. Perry
(vl), P. Pacey (vla), D. Ferschtman (vc) (NM
Classics 92046)

Um Mitternacht (op. 24, no. 1); *Wo ich bin*
(op. 22, no. 1); *Sie haben heut' Abend* (op. 22,
no. 2). F. Fiselier (Bar), H.L. Meijer (pf), T. Sol
(Bar), F. van Ruth (pf) (Sweetlove SLR
9401255)

Wals (op. 30, no. 2); *Toonstuk* (op. 26,
no. 1). J. Bogaart (pf) (Attacca Babel 8101)

Cornelis Schuyt

LEIDEN, 1557 – LEIDEN, 9 JUNE 1616

Little is known about Cornelis Schuyt's early years, except that he was born between 30 January and 21 November 1557 as the fifth of six children of Floris Corneliszoon Schuyt and Maria Dirksdr. Floris Schuyt became the organist of the Peter's Church in Leiden one year after Cornelis was born, and was appointed town minstrel in 1560. Cornelis was the only child to receive an education in music, and presumably was a boy chorister in the choir of the Peter's Church.

When Schuyt published his *Il primo libro de madrigali* in 1600, he noted he was pleased at having returned to Leiden 'dopo molti travagli e peregrinationi per l'Italia ed altrove' – after having travelled and worked extensively in Italy and elsewhere. It is not known, however, where his travels took him nor what his work entailed. Since in the period between June 1572 and Christmas 1584 no entries in the city archives mention either Floris or Cornelis Schuyt, it may be presumed that both father and son lived and worked abroad during this period.

Floris Schuyt was, in any case, re-appointed as organist of the city of Leiden by Christmas 1584, both for the Peter's Church and the Hooglandse Church, also known as the Pancras Church. On 11 March 1593, Cornelis was appointed city organist alongside his father. Father and son switched between the two churches every week, albeit that Floris retained the privilege of playing the large organ of the Peter's Church every Sunday. Since the conversion of Leiden from Catholicism to Protestantism in 1572, organ music was banned from church services and the function of the organist had become a secular one, although Cornelis Schuyt himself retained his Catholic faith.

Cornelis Schuyt received a salary of two-hundred guilders per annum, which was to be increased to three-hundred guilders upon his marriage. This promise did not fall on deaf ears, as Cornelis was married on 7 August 1593 to Cecilia Pietersdr. Uytgeest. The couple remained childless.

Cornelis Schuyt was not only an organist, he was also expected to provide vocal and instrumental 'table music' at town festivities. His contract, furthermore, stipulated that he was to educate one or two boys in the art of music. Moreover, from 1 February 1598 it was his duty to change the pegs in the mechanical drum of the automatic carillon, both in the towers of the town hall and the tannery, a task of which he was acquitted three years later.

Cornelis' father was buried in the Peter's Church on 10 December 1601. As of that date, Cornelis was the city's first organist and principal performer on the organ of the Peter's Church. Cornelis Schuyt, by all accounts, was held in high esteem. The customary advice of the patron, instructing the appointee to study diligently, was omitted in Schuyt's contracts, nor was he required to take the oath, as custom required of public servants. Towards the end of his life he received a salary of 450 guilders per year, more than twice the amount he was hired for in 1593. Cornelis Schuyt died on 9 June 1616 and was buried three days later in the Peter's Church.

Four volumes of music by Cornelis Schuyt were published during the composer's lifetime, all of which were printed in Leiden. Three of these books contain madrigals: *Il primo Libro de madrigali a cinque voci*, published in 1600 by the Plantinian publishing house of Raphelengius (Van Ravelingen), *Hollandsche madrigalen met vijf, ses, ende acht stemmen* [Dutch madrigals with five, six, and eight voices], published in 1603 by Jan Janszoon Orlers, and, finally, *Hymeneo, overo madrigali nuptiali* in 1611, a collection of six-part matrimonial madrigals (Raphelengius).

Schuyt dedicated his first book of madrigals to the Leiden city council, and received an allowance of twenty-four guilders in return. *Il primo libro* contains fourteen madrigals, preceded by a four-part riddle canon entitled *Bewaert Heer Hollandt* [Keep Holland safe, O Lord]. The first madrigal, *O Leyda gratiosa*, is an ode to the city. The other works are composed to Italian texts of Torquato Tasso and anonymous poets. Some of the works were meant as occasional music, as were a number of works in the other collections dedicated to persons in Schuyt's close environment, often on the occasions of their weddings. As such, it is possible to ascertain the exact dates of some of the works.

The Dutch madrigals have not survived entirely, as two of the five partbooks are missing. The collection includes thirteen five-part madrigals, two six-part ones, and one in eight parts (double choir). Most of the texts are occasional poems of modest literary value. However, the madrigals include one song in praise of music to a text by Daniel Heinsius. Of special interest is a poem ascribed to Jan van Hout, in which the maxims of eleven rhetoric societies are incorporated. The third collection, *Hymeneo*, contains 21 six-part madrigals, followed by a double-choir, twelve-part *Echo doppio*. More than half of the madrigals were set to texts from the *Tre giardini de' madrigali* by Mauritio Moro (Venice, 1602), a copy of which Schuyt had in his possession. Others were settings of texts by Guarini, Petrarca, Tasso and anonymous poets.

Cornelis Schuyt composed his madrigals at a time when in Italy the monodic style was discovered as a more appropriate means of attaining the most individual textual expression, and while opera was making its entrance. Claudio Monteverdi was one of the most important innovators of the madrigal genre. Schuyt was far less progressive than Monteverdi in for example his use of dissonants. As a more traditional composer, he adhered to the Renaissance style. In the madrigal *Se non saetta Amore* from *Hymeneo*, for instance, the two upper voices are strictly canonical. Chromatism is sparsely used. The Dutch musicologist Alphons Annegarn describes Schuyt as 'a skilled composer in the tradition of the sixteenth-century masters', placing the composer alongside Luca Marenzio.

The only surviving instrumental works of Schuyt are the *Dodeci padovane, et altretante gagliarde, composte nelli dodeci modi, con due canzone fatte alla francese, per sonare à sei*. This collection of pieces for non-specified instruments was published at the same time the *Hymeneo* was issued, and by the same printer. The auction catalogue of Schuyt's private library (1617) indicates that these vocal and instrumental collections were paired, as they were found both in combination and 'separatum'. This implies that the *Padovane et altretante gagliarde* were meant as wedding music: similar pavane-gagliarde combinations by the Dutch composer Cornelis Thymanszoon Padbrué composed as wedding music have survived. Notably, the works are composed in an obviously preconceived format, as they follow a cyclic structure 'nelli dodeci modi' (in the twelve modi). The fact that Schuyt owned a consort of six viols suggests that these works were originally conceived for these instruments.

In addition to the works mentioned, a six-part motet has survived, entitled *Domine fiant anima mea*. Schuyt's legacy contained various of his own manuscripts of vocal and instrumental compositions, including a collection of madrigals entitled *Passioni amorose a cinque voci*. These works, however, are considered lost.

THIEMO WIND

COMPOSITIONS

Il primo libro de madrigali a cinque voci. – Leiden, 1600

Hollandsche madrigalen met vijf, ses, ende acht stemmen. – Leiden, 1603

Hymeneo overo madrigali nuptiali et altri amorosi, a sei voci con un echo doppio a dodeci. – Leiden, 1611

Dodeci padovane, et altretante gagliarde composte nelli dodeci modi, con due canzone fatte alla francese, per sonare à sei. – Leiden, 1611

Passioni amorose a cinque voci
Manuscript. Lost

Domine fiant anima mea (motet)
For 6 voices. Engraving

Modern ed. of the compositions: Opera, ed. Alfons Annegarn. Amsterdam, VNM, 1980, 1982, 1984 (Monumenta Musica Neerlandica, X-1, -2, -3)

BIBLIOGRAPHY

A. Annegarn: *Floris en Cornelis Schuyt : muziek in Leiden van de vijftiende tot het begin van de zeventiende eeuw.* Utrecht, VNM, 1973
R. Rasch and Th. Wind: 'The music library of Cornelis Schuyt', *From Ciconia to Sweelinck, Donum natalicium Willem Elders,* ed. A. Clement and E. Jas. Amsterdam [etc.], Rodopi

DISCOGRAPHY

Canzon 'Fortune Guida'; Dell'undecimo modo, padovana 11 and gagliarda 11; Canzon 'La barca'; Del primo modo, padovana 1 and gagliarda 1 (from: *Dodeci padovane et altretante gagliarde*). Members of the Residentie Orchestra, cond. T. Koopman (Olympia OCD 501)
Coronato d'alloro; O Leyda gratiosa (from: *Il primo libro de madrigali*). Ensemble dell'Anima Eterna, Vocal Ensemble Currende, various soloists, cond. J. van Immerseel (Emergo Classics EC 3984-2)
Voi bramate, ben mio. Netherlands Chamber Choir, cond. P. van Nevel (NM Classics 92064)

Bernhard van den Sigtenhorst Meyer

AMSTERDAM, 17 JUNE 1888 – THE HAGUE, 17 JULY 1953

Bernhard van den Sigtenhorst Meyer was born the son of Hendrik Diderik Bernhard Meyer, a merchant, and Anna Gerharda van den Sigtenhorst. After completing grammar school, he studied the piano, music theory and composition at the Amsterdam Conservatory, where Bernard Zweers was one of his teachers. In 1915 he met the poet and singer Rient van Santen (1882-1943), who became his lifetime companion. From that time on, Bernhard Meyer added his mother's maiden name, Van den Sigtenhorst, to his surname. In 1919 the couple moved to The Hague and their home became an artistic meeting place.

Until 1927 Sigtenhorst Meyer and Van Santen gave regular concerts, which included a concert tour of the Dutch East Indies in 1923. The duo's repertoire included contemporary music as well as a colorful array of folksongs, performed in their original languages. In the period following, Van den Sigtenhorst Meyer gave piano and theory tuition and for many years trained pupils for the state examinations in music. His introduction as a pianist to the work of Jan Pieterszoon Sweelinck (1562-1621) inspired him to carefully edit eight volumes of Sweelinck's keyboard compositions, all of which were published by G. Alsbach & Co. at Amsterdam. Van den Sigtenhorst Meyer's lack of formal training in musicology did not stop him from writing two monumental monographs on Sweelinck's vocal and instrumental music. Both publications received general acclaim among musicologists. In 1931 he became a member of the board of the Royal Society for Music History of the Netherlands (VNM) and in 1934 was invited to join the Royal Archaeological Society. In 1957 the VNM posthumously published his reviewed edition of the *Cantiones sacrae* for the Opera Omnia series of Sweelinck.

Van den Sigtenhorst Meyer was not a man to place himself in the foreground. He earned his living from private tuition and lectures. Although an inspired teacher, he never gathered a following of composition students. He was repeatedly requested to teach at the Amsterdam Conservatory, but consistently declined. On the few occasions that he participated in projects and organizations, it was not for personal gain but from idealism. In 1933, for instance, he agreed to act as musical adviser and co-ordinator of a film production on William of Orange by Jan Teunissen, and in 1935 he was among the founding members of the Society for Protestant Church Music.

327

During World War II Van den Sigtenhorst Meyer avoided all contacts with
the government; after 1945 he was active in the Netherlands Musicians'
Council and the Netherlands Federa-
tion of Artists' Associations. For one
season only, in 1948-1949, he taught
music theory at the Institute of Musicology of Utrecht University. In 1952,
Van den Sigtenhorst Meyer's *De lof der
jenever* [In praise of gin], a choral composition commissioned by the Ministry of Education, Arts and Science
resulted in a hilarious political discus-
sion, with questions raised in the
Lower House. Van den Sigtenhorst
Meyer's letter to State Secretary Cals,
in which he emphatically maintains
his stance, is still worthy of notice.

Several early works of Bernhard Meyer were performed during his studies
at the Amsterdam Conservatory, including a sonata for violin, a piano sonata
and a string quartet. With exception of the quartet, all compositions dating
from those years have been destroyed. His acquaintance with Rient van Santen and subsequent introduction to the latter's literary involvement and east-
ern-oriented philosophical and cultural interests inspired the composer to develop a more personal musical language and form. Thus, a sequence of eight
collections appeared in regular succession until 1923, including short mood
pieces for piano (*Zes gezichten op den Fuji* [Six views on Fuji], *Oude kasteelen*
[Ancient castles]), and twenty songs composed to texts of Van Santen (*Stemmingen* [Moods], *Doode steden* [Dead cities), Rabindranath Tagore, and the Javanese poet Noto Soeroto (*Fluisteringen* [Whisperings]). In essence, the structure of these compositions is built on a perpetual rhythmic impulse free of
metric complications, a modal melodic flow, and a phrasing in two bars or
multiples thereof. In the songs the melodic lines are subordinate to the text
declamation, revealing a kinship with the songs of Claude Debussy.

Both his solo piano compositions and song accompaniments are characteristically built upon traditional triads and seventh chords, principally arranged
in modal parallel movement; there are no fourth chords. The use of arpeggios,
broken triads and syncopated structures is frequent. Although these compositions were, at the time, experienced as modern and 'impressionist', they are in

fact quite pianistic, revealing influences of Schumann and Brahms. The music itself can be described as dreamlike and introverted, while perfectly shaped and structured.

After 1923, his music derives inspiration from more traditional forms: sonata and variation forms like the passacaglia, early dances and imitation techniques form the basis for both his vocal and instrumental compositions, with chamber music taking up a more prominent place. Two pieces for organ stem from the same period. Influenced by his studies of early polyphony, his piano music is increasingly dominated by two-part, and – to a lesser extent – three-part counterpoint, the melodic lines frequently emphasized by parallel intervals and the harmony becoming subordinate to the linear structure. In the vocal works, the composer's early preference for (at times mildly moralistic) lyric poetry 'in praise of nature' makes way for mystical-religious seventeenth-century Dutch poetry, a tendency which reaches its peak in his compositions to texts by the poet and etcher Jan Luyken (1649-1717), such as 5 Geestelijke liederen [Five spiritual songs] and Jesus en de Ziel [Jesus and the soul]. His arrangement for unaccompanied choir of P.N. van Eyck's poem De Tuinman en de Dood [The Gardener and Death] composed in the wake of the German invasion of Holland in May 1940, is impressive.

In the first half of the century Van den Sigtenhorst Meyer was considered one of the Netherlands' leading composers, although his music was never seen as avant-garde. His work is marked by a careful balance between artistic integrity and musical craftsmanship, and his talent was recognized and appreciated as such by his contemporaries. Many of his works evolved from his personal contacts with leading Dutch performing musicians and teachers, such as Cornelie van Zanten, Jaap Stotijn and Adriaan Engels.

JAAP VAN BENTHEM

COMPOSITIONS

SONGS (WITH PIANO UNLESS OTHERWISE STATED): Bij den tempel (Van Santen, Noto Soeroto), op. 3 (1916); Fluisteringen (Noto Soeroto), op. 5 (1917); Stemmingen (Van Santen), op. 6 (1918); Doode steden (Van Santen), op. 10 (1919); Veltdeuntjes (Hooft), op. 15 (1921); 5 Geestelijke liederen (Luyken), v, pf/org, op. 21 (1924); Lofzangen uit 'Jesus en de Ziel' (Luyken), v, pf/org, op. 35 (1932); Vier geestelijke liederen uit 'Jesus en de Ziel' (Luyken), v, pf/org, op. 37; Liederen van den Nijl (Van Santen), S, ob, op. 44 (1927); De stal (Adama van Scheltema) (1915); De witte

reiger (Van Santen) (1915); Het Naardermeer (Van Santen) (1916); Pulchri-lied (Gerritsen) (1952)

CHOIR: Stabat Mater, mix.choir/4 v, op. 7 (1918 or before); Canticum fratris solis (Francis of Assisi), mix.choir, op. 33 (1927); Psalm 150, mix.choir (1935); Erlkönig op het Buitenhof (Loeb), mix.choir (1950-1951); Een vrouw, die niet als singht en tuyt (A. Roemers Visscher), m.choir (1939?); De Tuinman en de Dood (Van Eyck), m.choir, op. 39 (1940); De lof der jenever (Hennebo), m.choir, op. 46 (1951); O land van mest en *mist* (De Genestet), m.choir, op 48 (1951); *Vijf geestelijke liederen*, w.choir, op. 31 (1929)

OTHER VOCAL WORKS: *De Bron van Badrah* (Van Santen), soloists, m.choir, hp, str (1917, new instrumentation 1918); *De verzoeking van Boeddha* (Van Santen), soloists, sp.v, w.choir, hp, cel, str.orch (1918); *Jesus en de Ziel* (Luyken), S, w.choir, org (1937)

PIANO: *Van de bloemen*, op. 1 (1916); *Het oude China*, op. 2 (1916); *Van de vogels*, op. 4; *Zes gezichten op den Fuji*, op. 9 (1919); *De Maas*, op. 11 (1920); *St. Quentin*, op. 12 (1920); *Oude kasteelen*, op. 14 (1920); *Prelude*, op. 16 (1923); *Eight Preludes*, op. 17 (1922); *Sonata no. 1*, op. 18 (1922); *Capri*, op. 19 (1923); *Variations*, op. 20 (1924); *Sonata no. 2*, op. 23 (1926); *Sprookjeswereld I* (also with English title *Spookland*), op. 27 (1926); *Sprookjeswereld II*, op. 29 (1928); *Sonatina no. 1*, op. 30 (1928), *Sonatina no. 2*, op. 32 (1930); *Two Capriccios*, op. 42 (1945); *Sonatina no. 3*, op. 43 (1948); *De wals van meester Cals oftewel Tweede Kamergeheimenissen*, pf 4h, op. 50 (1952); *De zeven intervallen*, pf 4h, op. 51

ORGAN: *Passacaglia en Fuga*, op. 36 (1935, also pf 4h); *Sweelinck-fantasie*, org/pf/hpd, op. 41 (1940)]

CHAMBER MUSIC: *Introductie, thema en variaties*, vl, op. 22 (1925); *Drie landelijke miniaturen*, vol. 1, ob/fl, op. 24 (1926); *Sonata*, vc, op. 25 (1926); *Sonata no. 1*, vl, pf, op. 26 (1926); *3 Hymnen*, vl, pf/org, op. 28 (1927?); *Sonatina*, ob, op. 34 (1930); *Sonata no. 2*, vl, pf, op. 38 (1938); *Drie landelijke miniaturen*, vol. 2, ob/fl, op. 40 (1946); *Drie landelijke miniaturen*, vol. 3, ob/fl, op. 45 (1950); *String Quartet no. 1*, op. 13 (1919); *String Quartet no. 2*, op. 47 (1944); *Trio*, 2 vl, vla or fl, vl, vla, op. 49 (1951)

IN MANUSCRIPT:
String Quartet (with annotations by B. Zweers) (1911); *The Eternal Melody* (Rabindranath Tagore), v, str (1919); *Het lied der wijsheid* (Van Santen), v, str (1923); *Voorspel en Tusschenspel* (prelude and entr'acte music for a performance of Rabindranath Tagore's

'Letter from a King'), str.qt (1927); *Klaere* (Hooft), S, Mez, pf (1930); *Rondo*, 2 ob, trb, bn (1936); *Grafschrift op een jong meisje en Grafschrift op Sweelinck* (Vondel), m.choir (1948); Seventeen songs composed between 1912 and 1923 (?)

PUBLICATIONS
'Naar aanleiding van een toccata van J.Pz. Sweelinck', *TVNM*, 13, 1932, p. 161-165
Jan P. Sweelinck en zijn instrumentale muziek. The Hague, Servire, 1934, 2/1946
'Jan Willemszoon Lossy, Sweelinck's leermeester', *TVNM*, 14, 1935, p. 237-251
'Sweelinckiana', *TVNM*, 14, 1935, p. 252-254
'Het pianowerk van Paul Dukas', *Orgaan der Federatie van Nederlandsche Toonkunstenaarsvereenigingen*, 1935
'De familie Swelinck : de voorouders van Jan Pieterszoon Sweelinck', *TVNM*, 14, 1935, p. 111-125
'Het pianowerk van Maurice Ravel', *Orgaan der Federatie van Nederlandsche Toonkunstenaarsvereenigingen*, 1938
'De familie Swelinck : de nakomelingen van Jan Pieterszoon Sweelinck', *TVNM*, 15, 1939, p. 234-251
'Een volledig exemplaar van het "Livre septieme" ', *TVNM*, 15, 1939, p. 252-263
De vocale muziek van Jan P. Sweelinck. The Hague, Servire, 1948
Jan P. Sweelinck. Amsterdam, Becht
R. van Santen: *Debussy*. rev., updated and completed by B. van den Sigtenhorst Meyer. The Hague, Kruseman

SWEELINCK EDITIONS
Chromatische fantasie; Echo fantasie; Hexachord fantasie; 3 Toccata's; Variaties op 'Est-ce Mars'; Ick voer al over Rhijn. Amsterdam, Alsbach (between 1928 and 1933)
Opera Omnia VI: Cantiones Sacrae. Amsterdam, VNM, 1957

BIBLIOGRAPHY
Archive Bernhard van den Sigtenhorst Meyer. The Hague, Gemeentemuseum, Music Archives
J.B. van Benthem: 'Bernhard van den Sigtenhorst Meyer', *Biografisch Woordenboek van Nederland*, 1979
[Necrology], *Mens en Melodie*, vol. 8, 1953,

p. 235-236

W. Paap: 'Bernhard van den Sigtenhorst Meyer', *Mens en Melodie*, vol. 3, 1948, p. 161-165

E. Reeser: 'Bernhard van den Sigtenhorst Meyer', *Jaarboek van de Maatschappij der Nederlandse Letterkunde te Leiden 1951-1953. Levensberichten*, p. 106-112

E. Reeser: *Stijlproeven van Nederlandse Muziek 1890-1960*, vol. 1. Amsterdam, 1963

P. Sanders: *Moderne Nederlandsche Componisten*. The Hague, Kruseman

R. Starreveld: 'Bernhard van den Sigtenhorst Meyer'. *The New Grove dictionary of music and musicians*

DISCOGRAPHY

Eight Preludes op. 17. M. van Paassen (pf) (Attacca Babel 8950-3)

Drie landelijke miniaturen. M. Karres (ob), A. Karres (pf) (Erasmus WVH 093)

Sonata no. 2; 6 gezichten op den Fuji. D. Kuyken (pf) (NM Classics 92049)

Waltz 1952. W. Jordans and L. van Doeselaar (pf 4h) (NM Classics 92014)

Leo Smit

AMSTERDAM, 14 MAY 1900 – SOBIBOR, 30 APRIL 1943

Leo Smit was trained at the Amsterdam Conservatory, where he studied composition subsequently with Bernard Zweers and Sem Dresden and piano with Ulfert Schults. He taught music theory at the same institute from 1924 to 1927. He then lived in Paris for nine years, and moved to Brussels before resettling in Amsterdam in 1937. As a Jew he was deported by the Nazis to the Polish concentration camp Sobibor in 1943. He was killed there on 30 April of the same year.

The value of Leo Smit's work, though not great in volume, perhaps lies most in his chamber music, revealing the composer's orientation to the French music of the period. The harp assumes an important role in two such works, presumably on account of the composer's association with Rosa Spier, the founder of modern harp playing in the Netherlands. It was for her that Smit composed a trio, a quintet and his Concertino for harp and orchestra.

After Debussy's Sonata for flute, viola and harp (1915) – undoubtedly one of the greatest masterpieces of the twentieth century – it took quite some courage to compose a trio for the same combination. Leo Smit had that courage, as well as the wisdom not to imitate Debussy, although his harmonies unmistakably reflect the influence of his French colleague. The work is technically quite demanding, especially for the harpist. The movements are performed without interruption: Allegro ma non troppo, Scherzando (rhythmically comparable to Debussy's *Jeux)*, and Molto lento, with recurring motivic elements of the Allegro.

Likewise, it took some courage to venture a Trio for clarinet, viola and piano, with Mozart's Trio (K. 498) setting the standard. This time, however, Smit had time on his side: with more than a century dividing the two, any comparison was hardly relevant. In this work too, the three movements merge into one another. The first movement, marked Allegretto in the rhythm of a siciliano, develops almost naturally into a Scherzando in 6/8 time, with some similarity to the Scherzando from the Harp Trio; a short intermediate section, reminiscent of the Allegretto, prepares the middle movement: a melodically rich Lento, the artistic centre-piece of the work. The closing Allegro vivace contains references to the Scherzi of Albert Roussel; the Coda reverts back to the Allegretto, though it is more powerful and virtuosic.

The Quintet for flute, violin, viola, cello and harp was written in 1928, presumably at the instigation of the Quintette Instrumental de Paris. By then, Smit had some experience in composing for harp. Mindful of the specific technical problems of the instrument, he succeeded in composing a demanding work of musical excellence.

Of the two works Smit composed for two instruments, the Suite for oboe and cello is the least typical of Smit's compositional style. Carried away by the neo-Classical waves that swept the period, and identifying with Bach, he reverts to titles such as Allemande, Courante, etc. without appearing to be totally comfortable with it. His last completed work, the Sonata for flute and piano (1943), is of a very different class. This is a perfectly balanced composition, in which the artist's creative imagination matches perfectly with the chosen form. Smit was in the prime of his life when he wrote this sonata, a work of superb quality, underscoring the tragic loss inflicted on Dutch society and culture by the ruthless Nazi regime.

Of the eight orchestral works composed by Leo Smit, four are solo concertos. In these works, the composer attains the clarity of his chamber music, which is not always the case in his purely orchestral works (*Silhouetten* [Silhouettes], Symphony). The orchestration of the solo concertos is carefully balanced, combining viola with a string orchestra, cello with six wind players, timpani and strings, and piano – apparently inspired by Stravinsky's Piano Concerto – with fifteen wind players, timpani, celli and double basses. An example of the composer's self-critical attitude is seen in the score of the Concertino for harp and orchestra, its surviving copy showing a number of changes made by the composer in the second phase – i.e. in reaction to a rehearsal or perhaps after a performance – where he has ruled out the third and fourth horns, the second and third trumpets, the second and third trombones, and the tuba.

While the relatively limited volume of Smit's surviving compositions suggests that some of his works might have been lost, this is not generally believed to be the case. Firstly, Smit was astutely aware of his precarious situation, and left his works in the custody of a friend shortly before his deportation. Secondly, when living in Paris he was compelled for material reasons to spend much of his time composing film music, leaving him less time to work on 'free' compositions.

For many years, Smit's work was seldom performed. As growing interest emerged in the work of concentration camp victims, his music was revived in the late 1980s. In the same context, his Sextet for piano and wind instruments was performed in Stuttgart on 17 October 1989 during a memorial manifestation for the victims of war, entitled *Den Opfern der Gewalt*. In this work, as in Smit's other compositions, ample French influences are evident, though not as a result of a lack of originality, as suggested by the author of this article in response to a performance in 1937. With the benefit of hindsight, a renewed acquaintance with Smit's work reveals that the composer felt a close affinity with the music of his French colleagues, while at the same time imparting to his compositions a unique and authentic sound quality, particularly through his use of fourth chords and his creation of a harmonic language containing polytonal elements, while retaining a tonal centre.

MARIUS FLOTHUIS

COMPOSITIONS
*Year of publication

VOCAL: *Kinderliedje*, S, pf (before 1916, lost); *Zigeunerleven* (Geibel, transl. M. Leopold), S, pf (1916, piano part lost, new piano part J. Hamburg, 1998); *Hobby-Trot (Bobby)*, 2 S, pf (*1921); *La mort (La mort des artistes, La mort des amants, La mort des pauvres)* (Baudelaire), S, A, pf (1938); *Kleine prelude van Ravel* (Nijhoff), A, pf (1938); *De bruid* (Prins), w.choir (1939)

PIANO: *Nocturne* (1919, lost); *Three Piano Pieces* (1919, lost); *Suite pour le piano* (*1926, part 2 and 3 orchestr. by G. De-vreese, c 1932); *Hommage à Czerny* (1928, lost); *Hommage à Sherlock Holmes* (1928); *Hommage à Remington* (1930); *Twintig eenvoudige oefeningen* (*1939); *Twaalf pianostukken voor vier handen*, pf 4h (*1941); *Divertimento*, pf 4h (1942)

CHAMBER MUSIC: *Trio*, fl, vla, hp (1926); *Quintet*, fl, vl, vla, vc, hp (1928); *Sextet*, fl, ob, cl, bn, hn, pf (1932); *Trio*, cl, vla, pf (1938); *Suite*, ob, vc (1938); *Sonata*, fl, pf (1943, orchestr. W. Strietman, 1989); *String Quartet* (1943, unfin.)

ORCHESTRA: *Nachtmuziek*, orch (unfin.); *Inleiding en Allegro*, orch (1921, lost); *Silhouetten*, orch (1922); *Voorspel tot Teirlincks 'De vertraagde film'*, chamb. orch (1923); *Lustrumspel A-Z*, wind band (1925); *Lustrumspel D. 16 M.M.*, wind band (1928); *Schemselnihar* (ballet), orch (1929); *Concertino*, hp, orch (1933); *Symphony*, orch (1936); *Concertino*, vc, orch (1937); *Concerto*, pf, wind orch (1937); *Concerto*, vla, str.orch (1940)

FILM MUSIC: *Strijdlied* for *Kentering* (J. Hin, 1932); *Schip in nood* (M. Franken, 1935); *Jonge Harten* (J.A. Huguenot van der Linden, 1936)

INSTRUMENTATIONS: *Carnaval* – Schumann, orch (1940); *Poème* – Algra, str. orch (1940); *Hulde aan den arbeid* – Algra, wind band (1940); *Requiem* – Algra, mix. choir, orch (1940)

BIBLIOGRAPHY
L. Samama: *Zeventig jaar Nederlandse muziek : 1915-1985 : voorspel tot een nieuwe dag.* Amsterdam, Querido, 1986
Documentation Leo Smit Foundation Amsterdam, Collection Hin Haarlem, Collection Vis Amsterdam, Collection Johan Algra, Musica Neerlandica The Hague, Gemeentemuseum The Hague

DISCOGRAPHY
Concerto. R. Brautigam (pf), Netherlands Radio Chamber Orchestra, cond. E. Spanjaard (NM Classics 92044)
Concerto; Concertino; Symphony in C major. R. Brautigam (pf), P. Wispelwey (vc), Netherlands Radio Chamber Orchestra, cond. E. Spanjaard and Th. Fischer (NM Special 92098)
Concertino. P. Wispelwey (vc), Netherlands Radio Chamber Orchestra, cond. E. Spanjaard (NM Classics 92040)
Sextuor. B. Pierweyer (pf), H. Zwart (fl), E. van Tright (ob), M. Hintzbergen (cl), T. Oldenkotte (bn), M. Ricanek (pf) (Twente Conservatory Enschede 1988-I)
Sonata. K. Verheul (fl), J. van der Meer (pf) (BFO A-I)

Sonata; Deux hommages. E. Pameijer (fl), F. van Ruth (pf) (Channel Classics CCS 7995)

Suite. R. Brautigam (pf) (NM Classics 92045)

Joep Straesser

AMSTERDAM, 11 MARCH 1934

In the post-war Amsterdam milieu in which Joep Straesser was raised, it was not an everyday matter to opt for an education in the arts. This was a 'no-nonsense' period of reconstruction. Nevertheless, in 1953 Straesser enrolled as a student of musicology in Amsterdam. In 1956 he began studying the organ at the conservatory in Amsterdam with Anthon van der Horst, through whom he became acquainted with the music of Debussy, Ravel and Pijper.

Straesser found the atmosphere at the conservatory somewhat old-fashioned and his motivation began to lag. This changed in 1959 when he began studying composition with Ton de Leeuw. Through De Leeuw, Straesser gained a thorough knowledge of the music of the Second Viennese School of composers and the progression through Webern to the serialism of the 1950s. De Leeuw opened his eyes to Messiaen, Boulez and Berio, composers of influential avant-garde music of the period. Through these composers he came to know the music of Stockhausen and Ligeti as well as the work of John Cage that is based on chance operations.

Upon graduating from the conservatory in 1965 Straesser was awarded the 'prix de composition' for his *22 Pages* for tenor, baritone, bass and large ensemble, a work based on the experimental text 'Two Pages' from John Cage's book *Silence*. That same year *22 Pages* was awarded the prize for the best Dutch composition at the Gaudeamus Music Week. Apart from his activities as a composer, Straesser also taught music theory at the Utrecht Conservatory from 1962 onwards. In 1975 he was also appointed professor of composition there. In 1989 he retired as a teacher and has since devoted all of his time to composition. In 1988 the city of Amsterdam awarded him the Matthijs Vermeulen Prize for his opera *Über Erich M.* (1986).

Straesser's extensive oeuvre falls roughly into two periods: an avant-garde period and the present period, which shows an increasingly intensive dialogue with tradition. The transition to the latter period, which came about gradually, was completed with the appearance of *Splendid Isolation* (1977).

During the first period Straesser experimented with the resources of serialism and aleatoric techniques in an attempt to distance himself from musical tradition. His successful synthesis of strict serial thought in parameters, at the same time leaving room for the personal contribution of the performers, is effectively demonstrated by *Ramasasiri* (1968) for soprano, flute, piano (or harpsichord) and three percussionists. With the exception of two measures, all pitches in the work are exactly notated. The rhythmic notation combines exact notation with approximate note values. In one passage, the percussionists are given the choice of several instruments. Straesser set himself the goal of creating a complex, multi-layered structure rising above its modest setting.

Straesser's strength as a composer lies in his virtuosity in coupling intuition with complicated structures or innovative playing techniques. He sets out to compose contemporary music with a 'human face', an effort perhaps emphasized in his predilection for the human voice. The clear, very singable soprano part (mostly with a limited range) in *Ramasasiri* serves as an oasis of calm in the rich vistas of the musical landscape. A decidedly humanist view permeates the dramatic *Musique pour l'homme* (1968), for four voices and large orchestra, a work based on the Declaration of Human Rights.

In the 1970s Straesser slowly but surely distanced himself from the modernistic trend to radically break with the musical past. Specifically, he no longer felt a need to control each musical parameter. *Spring Quartet* (1971) for string quartet was his last strictly serial piece, though here he already sought to bridge the gulf between the quartets of Beethoven and those of Webern. *Spring Quartet* is an homage to Beethoven: the form of the work germinates from a four-tone motif (G-sharp, B-sharp, C-sharp, A) from this composer's String Quartet in C-sharp minor (op.131). In the closing section, the musical styles of Beethoven and Webern are juxtaposed. In a technical sense, the penchant for multi-layered structures makes way for multiple significances of musical meaning in this work.

In the predominantly horizontal organization of serial procedures, harmony plays a lesser role. For *Splendid Isolation* (1977), for organ, Straesser designed a harmonic matrix of eight chords hierarchically ordered from consonance (a dominant-seventh chord) to jarring dissonance (a cluster). The third movement attains a high degree of complexity through the variation technique used: while the passacaglia theme is repeated in increasingly longer note values, the variations become increasingly shorter.

In the 1980s Straesser continued to follow his leaning toward the past with

Signals and Echoes (1982) for bass clarinet and eleven musicians — a recent musical past, in this case, with references to Edgar Varèse, one of the fathers of modern, twentieth-century music. Ten years later, in the Symphony no.3 (1992), Straesser employed motivic development techniques that reflect on the complexity of Beethoven's later work. The first movement, Sinfonia, is in sonata form, with a Mahlerian lyrical first theme in the woodwinds countered by a robust second theme in the brass. The theme of the second movement, Tombeau, is related to the opening movement's first theme. The third movement, Riflessione e Scherzo, and fourth, Finale, are also thematically related. Entirely in the tradition of Mahler, Straesser based the scherzo of this symphony on the third song of his song cycle *An die Musik* (1991), for mezzo-soprano and string quartet.

Straesser's evolution from his avant-garde work of the 1960s to his less radical work of the 1990s was an organic, gradual process. Over the years he has built an extensive oeuvre that is distinguished by its balance between sensuality, complexity and depth.

MICHAEL VAN EEKEREN

COMPOSITIONS

VOCAL: *En rade* (Engelman), school choir, school orch (1963); *Psalmus*, m.choir, wind band (1963); *Herfst der muziek* (Lucebert), mix.choir (1964, rev. 1966); *22 Pages* (Cage), T, Bar, B, large ens. (1965); *Ramasasiri*, S, instr. ens. (1968); *Blossom Songs*, mix.choir (1968); *Musique pour l'homme*, S, A, T, B, orch (1968); *Missa 1969*, mix.choir, 8 wind instr. (1969); *Rainsongs*, m.choir, pf (1971); *Eichenstadt und Abendstern* (Eichendorff, Morgenstern), S, pf (1972); *Intervals* (Basho), fl, vc, hp, mix.choir (1976); *Three psalms*, mix.choir, org (1976); *Three Songs* (Nijhoff), m.v, pf (1978); *Intervals II* (Goethe, Marlowe, Milton, Kellogg), Mez, mix.choir, instr.ens. (1979); *Nimm dir etwas Schönes*, S, cl, vl, pf (1979); *Longing for the Emperor (Intervals III)*, S, instr.ens.(1981); *Put up your Umbrella* (Basho, Joso, Kikaku, Hashin), mix.choir (1981); *Echoes Reversed*, S, fl, vl, vc, pf (1982, rev. 1983); *All Perishes* (Alkaios), fl, S (1985); *Über Erich M. : Prolog* (Mühsam), T, mix.choir, orch (1985); *Über Erich M. : ein komi-tragisches Singspiel* (Mühsam), soloists, mix.choir, orch (1986); *Longing for the Emperor*, version S, 9 instr.

(1986); *Drie liederen op Duitse tekst* - H. Bosmans, instrumentation Mez, orch (1986); *Verzauberte Lieder* (Lasker-Schüler), mix.choir, orch (1986); *Motetus* (Peters), mix.choir (1987); *From the Chinese Restaurant* (Confucius, Po Chu-I, Li T'ai Po, Chin Sheng-T'an), S, a-sax, acc, perc (1990); *Bienensegen* (in: *Tien vocale minuten*), Mez (1990); *Zynische Lieder* (Fried), Bar, pf (1991); *An die Musik* (Rilke), Mez, str.qt (1991); *Gedanken der Nacht* (Rilke), Mez, 3 cl, perc (1992); *Madrigals 1, 2 and 3* (Hammarskjöld), mix.choir (1994); *Madrigal 4* (Hammarskjöld), mix.choir, org (1995); *Madrigals 5 and 6* (Hammarskjöld), mix.choir, org, Bar (1996); *Fische* (Fried), Mez, fl, pf (1996)

CHAMBER MUSIC: *Sonatina*, pf (1957, rev. 1964); *Five Close-Ups*, pf (1961, rev. 1973); *Alliages no. 2*, instr.ens (1964); *Alliages no. 3*, vc, pf (1964); *Mouvements pour orgue* (1965); *Music for Brass*, hn, 2 tpt, trb (1965); *String Quartet no. 2* (1966); *Seismograms*, 2 perc (1967, rev. 1979); *Sightseeing I-II-III*, fl, pf (1969, rev. 1983); *Sightseeing IV*, db (1970); *Emergency Case*, (a-)fl, pf, 2 perc (1970); *Intersections III*, pf (1971); *Spring*

Quartet *(Sightseeing V)*, str.qt (1971); *Intersections IV*, ob, vl, vla, vc (1972, rev. 1984); *Encounters*, b-cl, 6 perc (1973, rev. 1975); *Intersections V*, sax.qt (1974, rev. 1979); *Intersections V-2*, b-cl, pf (1975); *Splendid Isolation*, org (1977, rev. 1983); *Duplum*, t-rec, vc (1977, rev. 1986); *Intersections V-1*, ob, cl, a-sax, bn (1977); *Just a Moment*, vl, vc, pf (1978); *Sonatiqua*, pf (1978) (in: *Neue niederländische Klaviermusik*, Heft I, Breitkopf & Härtel, Wiesbaden); *Fusion à six*, str.qt, b-cl, pf (1980); *Just for One*, vc (1981); *Roundabouts*, 4 mar (1981); *Just Signals*, pf (1982); *Chains*, 4 cl (1983); *Gran trio*, a-sax, hp, perc (1984); *Permanent Wave*, org (1985); *Duplum*, version vl, vc (1985); *A Solo for Alkaios*, fl (1985); Faites vos jeux, org (1986); *Triplum*, str.trio (1986); *It's All in the Air*, tpt, org (1987); *Points of Contact I*, t-rec, mar (1987); *Points of Contact II*, a-sax, perc (1988); *Intersections V-3*, b-cl, vc, pf (1988); *Quintuplum*, hn, 2 tpt, trb, tb (1988); *Quadruplum*, fl, vl, vla, vc (1988, rev. 1989); *Plain Language*, b-cl (1989); *Quasi una sonata*, 4 sax (1990); *Sonata a due*, 2 fl (1990); *Sonata a tre (Points of Contact III)*, fl, cl, pf (1990); *Fresh Air*, acc (1991, rev. 1992); *To the Point*, 2 mar (1993, rev.); *Bilder für Akkordeon* (1994); *Gran duo*, b-cl, acc (1994); *Music for Marimba*, (1994); *Duo piccolo*, fl, hp (1995); *Cinq études légères*, org (1995); *Duo festivo*, b-cl, mar (1995); *Briefings*, pf (1996); *Duetto sinfonico*, fl, vc (1997); *Romance*, vl, pf (1997)

ORCHESTRA, LARGE ENSEMBLE: *Chorai*, orch (1966); *Summerconcerto*, ob, chamb.orch (1967); *Intersections I*, wind qnt, large ens (1969); *Enclosures*, wind orch (1970); *Intersections II*, 100 or more musicians (1970); *Chorai Revisited*, orch (1975); *Canterbury Concerto*, chamb.orch, pf (1978); *Just a Moment Again*, str.orch, pf, 2 perc (1978); *Signals and Echoes*, b-cl, instr.ens (1982); *Winterconcerto*, s-sax, orch (1984); *The Wall* (ballet music) orch (1987); *Tableaux vivants* (from the opera *Über Erich M.*), orch (1988); *Symphony for Strings (Symphony no. 2)*, str.orch (1989); *Chamber Concerto no. 1*, vc, wind ens (1991); *Symphony III*, orch (1992); *Chamber Concerto no. 2*, hp,

chamb.orch (1993); *Chamber Concerto no. 3*, fl, chamb.orch (1993)

PUBLICATIONS

P. Schat and J. Straesser: 'Experiment en vakmanschap', *Mens en Melodie*, vol. 19, 1964, p. 354-355

'D.A.V. - Series 1965/1 : Quintetto a fiati (Soraposizioni 2)', *Sonorum Speculum*, no. 22, 1965, p. 12-19

G. Frid and J. Straesser: 'Gedachtenwisseling over tonaliteit', *Mens en Melodie*, vol. 24, 1969, p. 17-19

Ramasasiri. Sleeve notes Composers' Voice DAVS 1974/75 (see discography)

'Muziekte', *NRC Handelsblad*, 10 Jan. 1975

'Au, Rudolf Escher', *NRC Handelsblad*, Nov. 1976

'Webern en de herhaling', *Mens en Melodie*, vol. 31, 1976, p. 117-122

'Kleine analyses no. 1 : Preludium I uit Bachs 'Wohltemperierte Klavier', *Mens en Melodie*, vol. 31, 1976, p. 326-329

'Rêverie d'un après midi', *Mens en Melodie*, vol. 31, 1976, p. 245-247

'Kleine analyses no. 2 : Het variatiethema uit Mozart's KV 331', *Mens en Melodie*, vol. 33, 1978

'Kleine analyses no. 3 : Webern's Bagatel no. 5 opus 9', *Mens en Melodie*, vol. 33, 1978

'Canterbury Concerto', *Askokrant*, no. 21, Feb.1979

'Over Messiaen', *Het Orgel*, 10, 1979

'Mijn beste maten', *Oktaaf*, vol. 1, Feb. 1985

'The Narrow Path of Jacques Bank', *Key Notes*, 25, 1988/1989, p. 25-31

'De ongehoorde muziek en ongehoorde analyses van György Ligeti', *Muziek en Dans*, Feb. 1989

BIBLIOGRAPHY

B. Baas: 'Dutch 20th-century piano music', *Key Notes*, 14 1981/2, p. 36

B. Baas: 'Dutch 20th century piano music - Part II : catching up with international trends', *Key Notes*, 14, 1981/2, p. 39-41

H. Berkenkamp: 'Joep Straesser : expressivity and complexity as constants in a development', *Key Notes*, 17, 1983/1, p. 24-32

T. Hartsuiker: 'Joep Straesser', *Muziek en Dans*, Feb. 1986

K. Hoek: 'In gesprek met Joep Straesser',

Het Orgel, Oct. 1986

A. Huyerman: 'Drie nieuwe Nederlandse opera's : "Über Erich M.", "Een Tanthologie" en "Salto Mortale" ', *Muziek en Dans*, Oct./Nov. 1987

J.B. Klaster: 'De erftantes en haar neven in twee opera's', *Het Parool*, 5 Nov. 1987

R. Koning: 'Interview Joep Straesser', *Preludium*, Feb. 1981, p. 54

D. Manneke: 'About Joep Straesser's Intersections III for piano = Zu Joep Straessers Intersections III für Klavier', *Sonorum Speculum*, no. 53, 1973, p. 24-36

H. Mayer: 'Een nieuw orgelwerk van Joep Straesser', *Mens en Melodie*, vol. 33, 1978, p. 160-63

W. Paap: 'Composers' voice 7475/3', *Key Notes*, 1975/2, p. 48-55

L. Samama: 'Het is frustrerend als geen hond begrijpt wat je doet', *Haagse Post*, 9 Feb. 1980, p. 56-59

J. Sligter: *Joep Straesser : Tussen traditie en vernieuwing*. Brochure Donemus, Amsterdam, 1994

E. Vermeulen: '22 Pages by Joep Straesser', *Sonorum Speculum*, no. 31, 1967, p. 15-18

E. Vermeulen: 'Musique pour l'homme by Joep Straesser', *Sonorum Speculum*, no. 38, 1969, p.15-22

H. Visser: 'Peter Schat zuigt als een vampier de grootheid van anderen op', *De Tijd*, 4 May 1979, p. 56-58

DISCOGRAPHY

22 Pages. Netherlands Radio Philharmonic Orchestra, cond. B. Maderna (DAVS 1967 no. 2)

Blossom Songs. Pool for Modern Music in Utrecht, cond. J. Leussink (Composers' Voice CV 7902)

Fusion à six. Fusion Moderne, Gaudeamus Quartet (Composers' Voice CV Special 1981/2)

Herfst der muziek. NCRV vocal ensemble, cond. M. Voorberg (DAVS 1969 no. 3)

Intersections 5-2, H. Sparnaay (b-cl), P. de Haas (pf) (Composers' Voice CV 7801)

Intersections V. Netherlands Saxophone Quartet (Composers' Voice CV 8002)

Just for One. T. Kooistra (vc) (Attacca Babel 9369-1)

Madrigals I. II, & III; Madrigal IV; Splendid Isolation; Herfst der muziek; Cinq études légères; Motetus; Faites vos jeux. K. Vellinga (org), Monteverdi Chamber Choir Utrecht, cond. W. Brouwers (Erasmus WVH 211)

Nimm dir etwas Schönes. D. Aalbers (S), A. Ariens Kappers (cl), M. Krabbe (vl), Th. Bles(pf) (CBS LSP 14514)

Ramasasiri. L. Rottier (S) and ensemble, cond. H. Soudant (DAVS 1974/75 no. 3)

Ramasasiri; Spring Quartet; Intersections V-2; Signals and Echoes; A Solo for Alkaios; Gedanken der Nacht; Symfonie no.3. Various soloists and ensembles, cond. A. van Beek, J. Sligter and E. de Waart (Composers' Voice CV 44)

Signals and Echoes. Ensemble M, cond. D. Porcelijn (Composers' Voice Special 1984/2)

Sonate a tre (Points of contact III). Het Trio (NM Classics 92022)

Jan Pieterszoon Sweelinck

DEVENTER, MAY 1562 – AMSTERDAM, 16 OCTOBER 1621

Jan Pieterszoon Sweelinck was born in Deventer the son of Pieter Swybberts-zoon, the town organist. In 1564, Sweelinck's father was appointed to the more prestigious position of organist of the Old Church in Amsterdam. In 1580 – some believe as early as 1577 – Sweelinck succeeded his father, who died in 1573. He remained his entire life in Amsterdam, a period in which the city enjoyed an unprecedented cultural and economic growth. Sweelinck thrived in the liberal ambience of the rich merchant city, where he found his talents appreciated and stimulated by its prominent residents: his salary was frequently raised, he enjoyed special privileges and was able with the support of his patrons to publish his vocal works in expensive print. Amsterdam was in every respect the window to the world, and its lively trade and cultural exchanges provided Sweelinck with the opportunity to gain access to the important European music of the period. Sweelinck was a much sought-after expert, frequently hired to inspect organs throughout the Republic. Apart from these inspection visits he hardly travelled, and his sole journey abroad is believed to have been a trip to Antwerp in 1604 to purchase a harpsichord.

After 1600, Sweelinck's reputation must have spread far beyond the boundaries of the Republic, as a large group of Dutch and German pupils came to Amsterdam to study with him, including future celebrities such as Jacob Praetorius, Samuel Scheidt and Heinrich Scheidemann. As such, Sweelinck can arguably be seen as the patriarch of the North German school of organists, whose influence extended into the era of J.S. Bach. Sweelinck's period of intensive teaching coincided with a period of great productivity as a composer which lasted through to his untimely death on 16 October 1621.

It is not clear whether Sweelinck was a Catholic or a Protestant. It is certain, however, that he had a liberal attitude. His circle of friends included people of both denominations, and his German pupils were Lutheran. Furthermore, his music incorporates both Protestant and Catholic texts and melodies. Sweelinck's liberal stance also marked his outlook as a composer, deriving inspiration from all the important polyphonic traditions of the late sixteenth century. For this reason, he is justifiably considered the last great Dutch 'polyphonist'.

Sweelinck's work divides broadly into two sections: 252 vocal works, practically all of which have appeared in print, and some 65 compositions for key-

board, which have survived only in manuscript form. Although it is primarily his keyboard compositions that have been embraced in the repertoire, Swee-linck's vocal works are, nevertheless, of equal importance.

Sweelinck made his debut as a composer of chansons. It is believed that he produced three collections of five-part chansons (1592-1594), only the last of which has survived. His development as a composer seems to have begun after the turn of the century. In this context, his first book of fifty psalms, the *Cinquante pseaumes de David*, dating from 1604, signifies a milestone. Swee-linck not only used the melodies, but the original French texts of the Geneva Psalter as well. The work reveals the composer's complete mastery of late-Re-naissance polyphony and his stylistic diversity in bringing the texts to life in a highly varied and expressive manner. There are strict imitation techniques alongside homophonic passages, and complex canonical structures alternat-ing with picturesque textual treatment.

The setting of the complete 150 psalms was his life's work, the pinnacle of which is reached in the second and third books, dating from 1613 and 1614, each containing thirty psalms. The contrapuntal structures are still more bril-liant, and the psalms have gained in individual expression. Of special interest is the inclusion of many of the larger, multipartite psalms and the rich poly-phonic spectrum, with transparent four-part works on the one hand, and monumental seven-part or eight-part works on the other. Sweelinck's fourth and last collection of psalms was published posthumously in 1621.

The collection *Rimes françoises et italiennes*, dating from 1612, contains twelve songs and fifteen madrigals for two and three voices, a number of which are arrangements of Italian compositions. The work demonstrates Sweelinck's talent for transparent, imitative composition and playful melodic lines, qualities which also mark his keyboard music.

Sweelinck's *Cantiones sacrae* (1619) are the Catholic counterpart of the psalms. In this collection of thirty-seven five-part motets to Latin texts, the emphasis is no longer on complex polyphony. The compositions are transparent, the counterpoint more homophonic and the overall impression is one of melodic richness and subtle harmonic and rhythmical texture.

In contrast with his vocal music, Sweelinck's entire output of keyboard music has survived in manuscript form. Notably, the music is clearly keyboard-oriented in its polyphony and undeniably international in style, although distinctly different from that of his contemporaries. The compositions combine influences from all the important sixteenth-century European traditions (England, Italy, Spain, Germany and the Netherlands) to form an authentic, unique and convincing entity. The uniformity of style and consistent quality reflect perhaps the fact that Sweelinck took to composing for the keyboard relatively late in life: it is believed that all of his keyboard compositions were composed in his last fifteen years.

His keyboard music divides into three categories: toccatas, fantasias, and variations. The toccatas seem to be a rather individualized and, historically, somewhat isolated elaboration of the Venetian toccata, combined with English figuration techniques. In Sweelinck's fantasias, all conceivable forms of imitation technique are used, with two main forms emerging: the mono-thematic fantasia, and the echo fantasia. This first is probably the most ambitious: a single theme is presented in diminution, augmentation and division and combined with new countersubjects and effective keyboard figurations, resulting in elaborate and quite complex compositions. The echo fantasia is the playful counterpart of the monothematic fantasia: there is no central theme, and the emphasis is on figuration and canonical texture, the characteristic echo effect forming part of the latter.

Sweelinck's variation works can be grouped into variations for organ on ecclesiastical melodies, and secular variation pieces composed for the harpsichord. Those belonging to the first group – composed specifically for the classic Dutch organ – are characterized by the use of the traditional church modes and eclectic choice of melodies, including Calvinist psalms, Gregorian melodies and Lutheran chorales. The stylistic diversity in the sacred variations reveals Sweelinck's profound knowledge of all the important liturgical organ styles of Europe. The secular variations, in contrast, are principally oriented to the music of the English virginalists.

Sweelinck's keyboard music, by virtue of the composer's German pupils, exerted a major influence on the further development of keyboard music in Europe. Rooted in Renaissance tradition, his rich formal language found no significant resonance, lacking the connection with early Baroque trends. However, Sweelinck's idiomatic keyboard style, with its integration of counterpoint and figuration and its consistent polyphony, left an indelible imprint on seventeenth-century keyboard music.

PIETER DIRKSEN

COMPOSITIONS

PRINTED (VOCAL):

Chansons ... de M. Iean Pierre Svvelingh organiste, et Cornille Verdonq nouvellement composées... accomodées tant aux instruments, comme à la voix. – Antwerpen, Pierre Phalèse et Jean Bellète, 1594
For 5 voices

Cinquante pseaumes de David, mis en musique à 4, 5, 6 & 7 parties. – Amsterdam, s.n., 1604

Livre second des pseaumes de David ... à 4, 5, 6, 7, 8 parties ... contenant XXX pseaumes. – Amsterdam, Hendrik Barentsen, 1613

Livre troisième des pseaumes de David ... à 4, 5, 6, 7, 8 parties. – Amsterdam, Hendrik Barentsen, 1614

Livre quatriesme et conclusionnal des pseaumes de David, nouvellement mis en musique, à 4, 5, 6, 7, 8 parties. – Haarlem, David van Horenbeeck, 1621

Rimes françoises et italiennes, mises en musique, à deux et à trois parties, avec une chanson à quatre. – Leyden, 'Imprimerie Plantinienne de Raphelengius', 1612

Cantiones sacrae cum basso continuo ad organum quinque vocum. – Antwerpen, Pierre Phalèse, 1619

A small number of chansons and madrigals included in anthologies

IN MANUSCRIPT (ALL FOR ORGAN OR HARPSICHORD):
Twenty fantasias, Seventeen toccatas, Fifteen sacred variation works, Twelve secular variation works

BIBLIOGRAPHY

W. Breig: 'Der Umfang des choralgebundenen Orgelwerks von Jan Pieterszon Sweelinck', *Archiv für Musikwissenschaft*, 17, 1960, p. 258-276

A. Curtis: *Sweelinck's keyboard music.* Leiden [etc.], University Press [etc.], 1969, 2/1972, 3/1987 (Leiden, Brill)

P. Dirksen: *The keyboard music of Jan Pieterszoon Sweelinck : its style, significance and influence.* Utrecht, Koninklijke Vereniging voor Nederlandse Muziekgeschiedenis, 1997 (Muziekhistorische Monografieën 15)

F. Noske: *Sweelinck.* Oxford, Oxford University Press, 1988

L. Schierning: *Die Überlieferung der deutchen Orgel- und Klaviermusik aus der ersten Hälfte des 17. Jahrhunderts : eine quellenkundliche Studie.* Kassel, Bärenreiter, 1961

M. Seiffert: 'J.P. Sweelinck und seine direkten deutschen Schüler', *Vierteljahrshefte für Musikwissenschaft*, 7, 1891, p. 145-260

B. van den Sigtenhorst Meyer: *Jan P. Sweelinck en zijn instrumentale muziek.* The Hague, Servire, 1934, 2/1946

B. van den Sigtenhorst Meyer: *De vocale muziek van Jan P. Sweelinck.* The Hague, Servire, 1948

R.H. Tollefsen: 'Jan Pietersz. Sweelinck : a bio-bibliography : 1604-1842', *TVNM*, 22, 1971, p. 87-125

M.A. Vente: 'Sweelincks Orgelreisen',
TVNM, 22/2, 1971, p. 126-137

DISCOGRAPHY
The Choral Works of Sweelinck I. Nether-
lands Chamber Choir, cond. W. Christie, T.
Koopman and P. Phillips (NM Classics 92003)
The Choral Works of Sweelinck II. Nether-
lands Chamber Choir, cond. P. Phillips, Ph.
Herreweghe and J. Boeke (NM Classics
92010)
The Choral Works of Sweelinck III. Nether-
lands Chamber Choir, cond. P. van Nevel (NM
Classics 92015)
Courante; Psalm 23; Volte. T. Satoh (lt) (NM
Classics 92016)
*Onder de linde groen, More Palatino, Mein
junges Leben hat ein End.* Trio de L'Oustal, L.
Swarts (vc) (NM Classics 92101)
Orgelwerke. G. Leonhardt (Deutsche Har-
monia Mundi GD 77148)
*Pavana Lachrimae; Ballo del Granduca; Fan-
tasia cromatica.* B. van Asperen (Sony Classical
SK 46349)
Pseaume 90; Laudate Dominum. Nether-
lands Chamber Choir, cond. P. van Nevel (NM
Classics 92064)
Pseaumes de David (from livre 3). The Choir
of Trinity College Cambridge, cond. R. Marlow
(Conifer CDCF 205)
Pseaumes et Chorales. Ensemble Vocal
Sagittarius, cond. M. Laplénie; F. Eichelberger
(org) (Tempéraments 316006)
Werke für Tasteninstrumente. A. Uittenbosch
(Globe GLO 5030)
Works for harpsichord. P.-J. Belder (hpd)
(WVH 085)

Paul Termos

HILVERSUM, 15 JANUARY 1952

As well as being a composer, Paul Termos is an improviser on the saxophone, a double role in which he has significantly contributed to the developments characteristic of Dutch music since the 1970s. Like his soulmates Maarten Altena and Guus Janssen, Termos performs as an improviser with his own group (the Termos Tentet, founded in 1988) and composes for a divergent array of ensembles, orchestras and soloists.

Termos was born in Hilversum, moving with his family to Haarlem at the age of five. There he listened in fascination to the Saint Bavo choir at Mass on Sundays and gazed at the instruments in music store windows. He began taking guitar lessons at the age of ten. When he later moved to The Hague he played in various beat groups and came to know the music of Béla Bartók and Karlheinz Stockhausen through record stores and libraries. The performances of Willem Breuker and Misha Mengelberg at the Scheveningen Circus Theater and at the 'political experimental concert' on 30 May 1968 at the Carré Theater reinforced his desire to become a composer.

In 1971 Termos enrolled at the Sweelinck Conservatory in Amsterdam to study the guitar, but he soon switched to the saxophone and clarinet because the sound of these instruments was more compatible with his improvisations than the much softer guitar. He began his career as a performer in 1979 with the Maarten Altena Quartet, was a member of Misha Mengelberg's Instant Composers Pool from 1983 to 1986 and from 1985 to 1992 he played in a trio with the brothers Guus (piano) and Wim (percussion) Janssen.

From 1974 to 1980 he studied composition with Ton de Leeuw. In these lessons Termos developed his ability to compose with clarity and structural consistency, while De Leeuw was open-minded enough to stimulate and direct his improvisation-oriented methods. From this period dates his composition *Nieuw werk* [New work] (1976), for bass clarinet and piano, in which Termos already demonstrates the most essential characteristics of his style, such as the playfully derailing scalar figures and the clearly perceivable form. In an introduction to the work, Termos concisely formulates his artistic creed: '*Nieuw werk* is a good example of my passion for extremely simple material and my efforts to compose clear and yet ambiguous music.'

There are very few notes in Termos' music. Triads are never fully instrumented and the harmonies are never lush in sound. He concentrates mostly on musical narrative and its logical development. Termos strives to create music in which the entire concept of the piece is audible to the listener, free of basic principles that are not perceptible as such. He considers form the essence of the composed piece, and strives to accentuate it. The inner workings of his music are at the same time its most external factor.

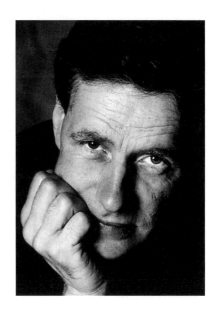

However, the form is not prefabricated. It develops organically, like a carefully nurtured plant, during the compositional process. Termos does not superimpose order on the notes, but strives to derive order from the notes themselves. His method as a composer reflects his work as an improviser. Termos preferably composes at the piano, literally feeling his way over the keys. His improvised ideas gradually solidify into the written work. 'You might say that my way of composing is like improvisation set in slow-motion', he explained in an interview.

He begins a composition by sketching out one or more motifs – archaic, brief and forceful motifs with a directly recognizable identity derived from such elementary features as a triad, a seventh, a see-sawing motion, a grating sound or a gripping melodic figure. Gradually, some of these motifs become 'personages' that serve as the building blocks of various works (composed and improvised) and that can serve various functions, sometimes as isolated elements, sometimes in conjunction with others, but always recognizable in themselves.

The piano piece *Carrara* (1985), for example, is characterized by a motif with large leaps; *Vuoto ossesso* (1989), for soprano recorder, leaves a lasting impression with its continued hammering of repeated notes in the high register; and in the String Quartet no.1 (1987, rev. 1991), grating string sounds play an important role. The number of motifs grows proportionately with the size of the forces used. *Expres(s)* (1984), for wind quintet, string trio, double bass and piano is in this regard exemplary of Termos' work and a display case of the characteristic motifs of his oeuvre: long-held notes, a see-sawing figure, an Arabian-tinted melodic figure, a motif with dotted rhythms, and the large leaps of *Carrara*.

These characteristic units form the most conspicuous contours in Termos' music, which is distinguished by the clear lines of a cartoon artist or boldly sprayed lines of a graffiti artist. However, his work has developed other signatures too. It is clearly tonally oriented, though he does put this tonality under pressure. In many works, too, a sharp contrast is drawn between restive and static textures in which all motion seems frozen. Using nearly obsessive, irregular repeats with unexpected variations (not to be confused with the process-like repeats in American minimal music, which are more regular and predictable), Termos breaks through the impasses.

The result is a sharply chiseled, monumental style that – particularly in *Linea recta* (1990), written for Orkest de Volharding, and *Groundwork* (1993) for brass quintet – reaches its peak in the way musical order is adhered to and then disrupted, and in the ambivalent relationship between simplicity – and at times even banality – of the material and its development.

PAY-UUN HIU

COMPOSITIONS

VOCAL: *Fortuna*, fl and pic (single performer), hp, vl, vc, mix.choir (1986, rev. 1987); *Vocalise X*, S, pf (1993); *Ensemblage*, Mez, b-cl, a-sax, hp, pf, db (1994); *The Book of Indians*, S, instr.ens (1996)

MUSIC FOR THE THEATRE: *Kans*, 5 dancers, instr.ens (1986); *Operatie Orpheus*, vocal ens (1989)

CHAMBER MUSIC: *Octavenlied*, pf (1975); *To Ben Hur*, 2 pf (1977); *Semantic Hedonism*, 3 cl (1976); *Nieuw werk*, b-cl, pf (1976); *Carrara*, pf (1985); *String Quartet I* (1987, rev. 1991); *Vuoto ossesso*, s-rec/pic (1989); *1991*, t-sax, pf, perc (1991); *Groundwork*, 2 trp, hn, trb, tb (1993)

ORCHESTRA, CHAMBER ORCHESTRA, LARGE ENSEMBLE: *Lustobject*, orch (1979, rev. 1980); *Buste*, 2 b-cl (1980); *Borstbeeld*, wind ens (1980, rev. 1984); *Bedankt maecenas*, ens (1982); *Concert*, a-sax, orch (1983); *Expres(s)*, ens (1984, rev. 1995); *Nagras*, orch (1988); *MM*, 4 perc (1988); *Kendang*, gamelan ens (1990); *Linea recta*, wind ens (1990); *As*, gamelan ens (1991); *Roma*, vc (1992); *Turgor*, wind ens, perc (1995); *KK*, perc (1995); *Concerto*, fl, chamb.orch (1995); *Octet*, wind ens, db (1996)

PUBLICATIONS

P. Termos and C. de Bondt: 'Kind regards: a musical correspondence', *Key Notes*, 23, 1986, p. 50-55

BIBLIOGRAPHY

E. v.d. Berg: 'Termos wil van iets banaals iets edels maken', *de Volkskrant*, 21 May 1988

T. Derks: 'Mijn muziek is authentiek en autobiografisch', *Entr'acte Muziekjournaal*, no. 4, May 1997 p. 10-12

P.-U. Hiu: 'Steve Martland & Paul Termos. Een barokke locomotief en een achttiende eeuwse botsauto', *Confrontaties*, Rotterdamse Kunststichting, 1993, p. 13-17

P.-U. Hiu: 'Why would I start doing sums as a composer?', *Key Notes*, 31, 1997/2, p. 10-14

P. Luttikhuis: 'Ik zoek naar het voor de hand liggende', *NRC Handelsblad*, 2 Feb. 1990

K. Polling: 'Het perfectionisme van Paul Termos', *Trouw*, 10 Aug. 1989

K. Stevens: 'Over het componeren of het schrijven voor improvisatoren', *Jazz Freak*, Jan 1989, p. 20-22

H. Visser: 'Eenvoud van Paul Termos', *De Tijd*, 23 Jan. 1981

DISCOGRAPHY

Carrara. G. Janssen (pf) (Composers' Voice CV 8703)

Concerto for Alto Saxophone and Chamber Orchestra; String Quartet I; Expres(s); Groundwork; Concerto for Flute and Chamber Orchestra. Various performers (Composers' Voice CV 60)

Death Dance of Principles. Termos Dubbel Expres, Termos Tentet (Geestgronden GG16)

Echos and Shadows. Maarten Altena Ensemble (Hat Hut Records)

Expres(s). Doelen Ensemble, cond. A. van Beek (Polygram 454 059-2)

For Sandy Nelson; Pok. Trio Janssen-Termos-Janssen (Geestgronden GG 3)

Kendang. Ensemble Gending, cond. J. Sligter (NM Classics 92062)

Linea Recta. Orkest de Volharding, cond. R. van Leyden (Volharding 009/Attacca Babel 9380)

Nieuw werk. H. Sparnaay (b-cl), P. de Haas (pf) (Composers' Voice CV7801)

Shakes & Sounds. Termos Tentet (Geestgronden GG 5)

Solo 84/85. P. Termos (a-sax) (Claxon 8617)

Klas Torstensson

NÄSSJÖ, 16 JANUARY 1951

Klas Torstensson studied music theory and composition from 1969 to 1973 at Folkliga Musikskolan Ingesund and musicology at the University of Göteborg. In 1973 he moved to the Netherlands, where for four years he composed electronic music at the Institute for Sonology in Utrecht. In 1974 he took up residence in Amsterdam, that year making his first contact with the Asko Ensemble, which was to have great significance for his development as a composer.

Torstensson has retained his Swedish nationality but in practice, certainly in musical practice, he is a Dutchman, although this does not mean that his music has a typically Dutch flavor. In as far as his complex music is related to a tradition, however, it is closer to that of Xenakis and Varèse than to contemporary Dutch music in which composers, regardless of their style, generally opt for a certain economy of means. Torstensson also works with other contemporary music ensembles. For example, he has composed for Orkest de Volharding (*Järn*) and the Hoketus ensemble (*Spåra*). During the 1986 Holland Festival Torstensson's grand 'intermedia' project *Barstend IJs* [Breaking ice] was staged. His next project in particular, the *Licks & Brains* trilogy, drew international attention. He was awarded the Matthijs Vermeulen Prize in 1991 for his large-scale orchestral piece *Stick on Stick* (1990). The work, which had not yet been performed at the time of the award, was premiered in 1993. Earlier that year, his *Urban Songs* for soprano, computers and ensemble, a work in part composed at the IRCAM, was performed by the soprano Charlotte Riedijk and Ensemble InterContemporain. Most of Torstensson's compositions have been published by Donemus, which has also issued LP and CD recordings of several of his works.

Torstensson thinks of composing as designing 'listening scenarios'. Regardless of the complexity of the work, his main concern is always what the finished product will sound like. It is because of this that he always strives to work with musicians, not only while the piece is being composed, but afterwards as well. Little is left to chance in his meticulously planned scores.

Torstensson strives to create multi-layered, labyrinthine textures: ensembles split into sub-ensembles, which then interact with each other. The listener may choose, so to speak, from various trajectories. 'I don't seek to give substance to thought, but direction', he explains.

The starting point in his music is often of nearly elementary simplicity, as

is the goal. How may a chord be reached from a single tone, velocity from sluggishness, unison from polyphony, agreement from conflict?

However it is the intervening motion, the different musical strategies and the – possibly unsuccessful – attempt at rapprochement that form the essence of his music. The image of an obstacle course is certainly applicable to Torstensson's work. The music repeatedly returns to its starting point, often given in the opening measures, only to set out again in a different manner. As new attempts progress new obstacles emerge, old strategies are given another chance, and new ingredients are gradually added. Thus the overall form takes on the semblance of a series of variations which, however, involve continual development, exploration, and extensions of the material.

From Torstensson's propensity for describing musical situations and processes in terms of such metaphors as 'tone clouds', 'evaporation' and 'granular structures' (metaphors that also turn up in many of the titles he gives his pieces) the supposition arises that he tends to approach musical material as though it were physical matter. This view is in part linked with his background as a composer of electronic music, but also with the great emphasis he places on the physical aspects of sound, a typical characteristic of his music. It is manifested in, among other things, his interest in the generally known and as yet unexplored acoustic resources of musical instruments. *Solo*, for bass saxophone, probes in its first pages into the sounds the instrument can make when played without the mouthpiece. *Koorde*, for two pianos, has a middle movement in which the instruments are prepared in various manners. In his orchestral piece *Stick on Stick* Torstensson employs iron pipes and metal plates, as well as the conventional percussion instruments, and he meticulously specifies their dimensions and the sounds he envisions.

The bodily activity of the performer also plays a large role. The physical exertions of playing in the previously mentioned *Solo* are further accentuated by breathing and throat noises the composer specifies. The accelerated breathing and sighs of the musician take on, aside from the theatricality of a literal illustration, an autonomous musical significance. The performer makes various attempts to move from one musical 'situation' to another and employs whatever tactics needed to reach this goal. Seen in this light, the musician's struggle to produce the notes is merely a component of the abstract, composed struggle that is enacted in the notes, or, more accurately, sound material.

Torstensson's music is decidedly aperiodic, for rhythm is also subjected to constant tension. Even synchronous playing, often a priori in other music, becomes part of the discourse. It requires constant exertion. Torstensson gives shape to the 'out-of-synch' playing coupled to that effort by spreading the succession of asynchronous notes through the ensemble in such a way as to give the illusion of motion through space. Literal, mechanical repetition is also employed, but then as a musical equivalent of stasis, of the contentless quality that surfaces when all energy has been consumed. Exemplary of this is a passage in *Stick on Stick* in which nearly the entire orchestra gets stuck in repetitive, rhythmic hand clapping.

Pitch and intervals are mere contributors to the scenario rather than its prime conveyers. At crucial moments, pitch is of great importance, but only as an element of color, for example when (quasi-) diatonic sounds in open spacing are placed in an atonal and dissonant environment. When Torstensson employs such contrasting material, he often consciously selects sounds calculated to evoke particular images. In *Barstend IJs*, for example, references are made to a kind of music – Indonesian ketjàk – that epitomizes a tropical atmosphere. Only in a more recent work like *Urban Songs* do quasi-quotations begin to come clearly to the forefront, with undisguised references to a Lebanese folk song and rap music, which are dissected into phonemes and fragments and interwoven like trace elements into an amalgamation of instrumental, electronic and vocal dimensions that blend and contrast with each other.

The Last Diary (1994), written for the Asko and Schönberg ensembles, closes with an exceptionally prolonged (by Torstensson's standards), gradually coagulating rallentando. In part through the declaimed solo part, this section makes a strong dramatic impact. The increasingly fragmented texts are taken from the recovered diary of the Swedish Arctic explorer Salomon August Andrée, who perished on the polar ice in an ill-fated balloon expedition in 1897. The same material served as a basis for his opera *Expeditionen*, the composition of which had occupied Torstensson since 1994. Plans for a staged performance fell through, and the work was finally premiered in concert form during the 1999 Holland Festival. In spite of this setback, things have gone well for Torstensson: his music has found its way to many venues and festivals in a variety of countries all over the world, making him one of the most successful and cosmopolitan composers of the Netherlands.

FRITS VAN DER WAA

COMPOSITIONS

VOCAL: *Isogloss*, 24 v, various perc instr (1985); *Urban solo*, S (1991); *Urban songs*, S, large ens, computers (1992), *The Last Diary*, sp.v, large ens (1994); *Intermezzo & Epilogue*, S, orch (1998)

OPERA: *Expeditionen* (Torstensson), S, T, Bar, B-Bar, orch, electr. (1994-1999)

ORCHESTRA, CHAMBER ORCHESTRA, LARGE ENSEMBLE: *Intros* (version 1980); *Järn* (1982, rev. 1987); *Fläka* (1983, rev. 1985); *Spåra* (1984); *Licks & Brains II* (1988); *Stick on Stick* (1990); *Kargt* (1994); *Intermezzo* (1998)

CHAMBER MUSIC: *Redskap*, 6 perc (1976, rev. 1981); *Pedaal*, vl (1979/1982); *Spans*, b-cl (1981); *Spans / Spännvidder*, b-cl, db-cl, 2 perc (1981); *Licks & Brains I*, sax.qt (1987); *Solo*, b-sax (1988); *Koorde*, 2 pf (1990); *Hamra*, s-sax (1991); *Urban Extra*, music box (1994)

MULTIMEDIA WORK: *Barstend IJs*, 24 v, 4 perc, tapes, light, laser beams, slides, video (1986)

BIBLIOGRAPHY

Th. Anderberg: 'Ett farväl till det lagoma', *Dagens Nyheter*, 21 March 1999

K. Arntzen: 'Torstensson maakt ijzig drama tot opera', *Trouw*, 9 June 1999

G. Bergendal: 'Klas Torstensson och islossningen', *Stockholm New Music Festival*, March 1999

M. Boldemann: 'Kontinental tonsättare återvänder', *Dagens Nyheter*, 26 Nov. 1995

H. Bosma: 'Composers and Computers in The Netherlands', *Key Notes*, 25, 1988/1989, p. 51-54

H. Brandin: 'Tragisk opera med förhinder', *Västerviks-Tidningen*, 23 Jule 1998

A. Brüggen: 'De waanzin van een poolexpeditie', *Haarlems Dagblad*, 10 June 1999

J. Dame: 'IJscomponist Klas Torstensson : het ambivalente geluk van een exil-Zweed', *Armada*, no. 4, Sept. 1996

J. Dame: *Verbreding*, Brochure Donemus, Amsterdam, 1999

J. Dame: 'Klas Torstensson', included in the publ. of the libretto *Expeditionen*, Holland Festival, June 1999

M. van Eekeren: 'Liefde is onmogelijk zonder tonaliteit', *de Volkskrant*, 12 June 1999

A. Fiumara: 'Torstensson and the sound of ice breaking', *Trackings 1*, Aug./Sept. 1999

M. Fuller: 'Shattering Music', *The Paper*, June 1986

H. van Gelder: 'Oe-wie-aa in rokkostuum', *NRC Handelsblad*, 23 May 1986

P. Gervasoni: 'Klas Torstensson', *Le magazine (Centre Georges Pompidou)*, Feb. 1993

R. Hazendonk: 'Componeren op floppy disk', *De Telegraaf*, 5 March 1993

W. Heijens: 'Kan mij dat ijs, kan mij die laser schelen! Ik ben uitgegaan van een totaal idee', *VPRO-gids*, June 1986

J. Huisman: 'Barstend ijs ken ik uit m'n jeugd', *de Volkskrant*, 30 May 1986

S. Jacobsson: 'Holländsk tonsättare med stuga i Småland', *Nutida Musik* no. 1/1991

W. van de Kamp: 'De klank van het noor-
derlicht', *Haagsche Courant*, 10 June 1999
C. Lundberg: 'En rauk i Amsterdam', *Ex-
pressen*, 1 Apr. 1997
T. Lundman: 'Expeditionens spår', *Nutida
Musik*, no. 1, 1999
P. Luttikhuis: ' De saxofonist moet kreu-
nen', *NRC Handelsblad*, 19 Feb. 1993
P. Luttikhuis: *Klas Torstensson : de fysieke
kracht van muziek*. Brochure Donemus, Am-
sterdam 1993
D. Nagan: 'Aan de slag met Barstend IJs',
Algemeen Handelsblad, 24 May 1986
G. van Oorschot: 'De klank van ijs',
Het Parool, 10 June 1999
E. Overbeeke: 'Opera van Klas Torstensson
in het Holland Festival', *Donemus Info*, June /
July 1999
K. Polling: 'Zoektocht naar contrasten',
Trouw, 28 June 1993
O. Roca: 'Oslo's Ultima Contemporary
Music festival', *The World and I (The Washing-
ton Times)*, Jan. 1993
A. Schaathun: 'As vague as this goal may
be...', *Ballade*, no. 3, 1992
A. van der Ven: 'The Oslo Festival of Con-
temporary Music', *Key Notes*, 1992/4
H. Visser: 'Luidruchtig verhaal van een
ijsvlakte', *Het Parool*, 5 June 1986
H. Visser: 'Mocht ik op m'n bek gaan, dan
hopelijk met veel kabaal', *Muziek & Dans*, June
1986
E. Voermans: 'Rauwe klanken zijn interes-
santer dan gepolijste', *Het Parool*, 23 Feb. 1993
E. Voermans: 'Music as a grim journey',
Key Notes 29, 1995/1, p.10
S. de Vries: 'IJs en sneeuw maken alles
zinloos en nietig', *Leeuwarder Courant*, Sept.
1996
F. van der Waa: 'Barstend IJs van Klas
Torstensson', *De Groene Amsterdammer*, 4 June
1986
F. van der Waa: 'Jag ger hellre riktning än
substans åt lyssnandet', *Nutida Musik*, no. 2,
1991
E. Wallrup: 'Så ljuder 90-talets symfoniska
musik', *Svenska Dagbladet*, 28 Sept. 1998
C. van Wijngaarden: 'De klank van het
noorderlicht', *Weekkrant 2*, Holland Festival,
June 1999
R. Zuidam: 'Noordpool-opera van Klas
Torstensson', *NRC Handelsblad*, 4 June 1999

DISCOGRAPHY
Redskap. Malmö Percussion Ensemble,
cond. K. Torstensson (Caprice CAP 1265)
Spans; Fläka. H. Sparnaay (b-cl/db-cl),
Asko Ensemble, cond. K. Torstensson (Com-
posers' Voice CV 8501)
Isogloss; Barstend IJs. Asko Choir a.o., cond.
K. Torstensson (cassette and book, Foundation
Isogloss 1986)
Järn. Orkest de Volharding, cond. K.
Torstensson (De Volharding 005/Donemus
Disk 002)
Järn. Orkest de Volharding, cond. K.
Torstensson (NM Classics 92021)
Koorde. C. van Zeeland and G. Bouwhuis
(pf) (NM Classics 92074)
Spåra. Hoketus, cond. K. Torstensson
(Composers' Voice Special 1986/2)
Solo; Licks & Brains I and II. L. van
Oostrom (b-sax), Netherlands Saxophone
Quartet, cond. K. Torstensson, Netherlands
Saxophone Quartet and Asko Ensemble, cond.
D. Porcelijn (Composers' Voice CV13)
Stick on Stick; Urban Solo; Urban Songs.
Netherlands Radio Symphony Orchestra,
cond. Z. Peskó, Ch. Riedijk (S), Asko Ensem-
ble, cond. S. Asbury (Composers' Voice CV 32)
Urban Extra. (Music Box VPRO EW 9413)
The Last Diary . P. Fuhr Jørgensen (sp.v.),
Asko Ensemble and Schönberg Ensemble,
cond. R. de Leeuw (Muziekpraktijk Donemus
CV 57)

Nicolaes Vallet

CORBÉNY, C.1583 – ?, C.1645

The lutenist Nicolaes Vallet was born in the village of Corbény, north of Paris. He settled in Amsterdam around 1613, and presumably remained there for the rest of his life. Vallet's emigration from France suggests that he may have been a Calvinist, which also explains the numerous Geneva psalm melodies which he transcribed for the lute.

Vallet's first years in Amsterdam reveal the makings of an ambitious musician. No less than four beautifully engraved lute books appeared in print in the period 1615-1620. Vallet earned his living as a freelance musician, performing at aubades, weddings and parties, for which purposes he formed a band with three musicians of English descent in 1626. He also founded a dance school.

In reconstructing Vallet's social network, it appears that he had many associates among foreign musicians. Vallet also had excellent relations with prominent local citizens, as attested by the names appearing in the dedications of his lute books, many of which refer to members of affluent Amsterdam families, who may have been among his students. His monumental psalm book *Regia pietas* was published with the aid of some of them, in return for which the coat of arms of each sponsor was engraved in the books by Michel le Blon, the renowned engraver and art dealer and a friend of Vallet's. Vallet also befriended the famous fencing master Girard Thibault, who lived in Amsterdam for some time. Nicolaes Vallet, by all accounts, was a gregarious artist who associated with the nobility of early seventeenth-century Amsterdam.

His rich connections notwithstanding, in 1633 he found himself in financial difficulties. He had accrued such enormous arrears that his possessions (including six lutes, one 'bass viol', several citterns and violins) had to be inventoried. It is not known when Vallet died, although it is presumed that he was still alive in the early 1640s, for two new volumes of his work were published in those years.

The four lute books published in the period 1615-1620 are the *Secretum musarum* (1615) containing secular music, *Een en twintich Psalmen Davids* [21 Psalms of David] or *Vingt et un pseaumes de David* for voice and lute (1615), the second part of the *Secretum musarum* (1616) and the *Regia pietas* (1620), containing lute arrangements of all 150 psalms. The three first-mentioned books are part of a trilogy, which was published in various versions, most notably in Dutch and French. The French version of *Secretum musarum,* for example, is entitled *Le secret des Muses,* while the Dutch equivalent appears as *Het gheheymenisse der zanggodinnen* [The secret of the Muses]. At first Vallet published the works himself, but was perhaps not a successful salesman, for he sold the remaining copies in 1618 to a book trader by the name of Jan Jansz, who changed the title engraving of *Secretum musarum* to *Paradisus musicus testudinis.* The proceeds of the transaction possibly provided Vallet with the means to finance his voluminous *Regia pietas.* The publications were of exceptional beauty, and probably as costly to produce, as the music for the first time in the history of Dutch printing was engraved in expensive copper plates. The notation is largely in tablature, a system indicating the stops on the fingerboard. This notation was preferred by most lute players in the period.

Secretum musarum opens with some notes of instruction, addressed to young players. Vallet's didactic 'secret' lies in the introduction of a fingering both for the left and right hands, and several instructions for the execution of ornaments. The music is broadly grouped according to genre. As is customary with collections of lute music, the first part begins with the author's own compositions: preludes and fantasies in semi-polyphonic style. This is followed by a selection of arrangements of older dances, such as pavanes, passamezzos and gaillardes. Of special importance are several sets of variations on popular songs. Finally, the more modern French dances are included: ballets, bourrées, courantes, and voltes.

The much shorter second volume follows the same pattern, as well as containing a group of lute quartets. This is a remarkable detail, since only a handful of such quartets have survived, almost all of which originate in the Netherlands. Presumably reflecting Vallet's own ensemble practice, the quartets are not perfectly finished polyphonic compositions, but notated improvisations in four parts – soprano, alto, tenor and bass – on a given melody. The book closes with a set of variations on *Onse Vader in Hemelryck* [Our Father in Heaven] for lute solo.

Many of the dances are originally French, or at least composed in the French style. However, it is difficult to determine which were composed by Vallet himself. The choice of the themes used for the variation pieces appears to reflect the popularity of the various melodies in the Netherlands: *Boerinneken* [Little farmer's wife], *Soet Robbert* [Sweet Robert], *Malle Symen* [Silly Simon, from the English 'Malsims'], *Slaep soete slaep* [Sleep sweet sleep], *Onder de Lindegroene* [Under the linden green] were best-loved tunes in the Netherlands, though often of foreign origin, and they were frequently given new Dutch lyrics.

The lute being typically considered a secular instrument, Vallet's psalm books

received much less attention than the *Secretum musarum.* They are, neverthe-less, of particular interest. Vallet's *Een en twintich Psalmen Davids,* from a mu-sical viewpoint, signifies the pinnacle of his oeuvre. The psalm melody is sung in long lines, the lute providing a semi-polyphonic, mostly three-part texture around it. This structure, in combination with short preludes and interludes, suggests that Vallet must have been inspired by the daily organ improvisations of Jan Pietersz Sweelinck and others. Vallet had set himself the task of tran-scribing the complete 150 psalms in the same elaborate fashion, but was com-pelled to abandon his ambitious scheme. In a second attempt he followed a simpler pattern, the lute playing variations around the psalm melody, along with an 'ad libitum' voice part. The effort resulted in *Regia pietas,* a work mod-elled after foreign examples, notably the *Testudo spiritualis* (Arnhem, 1617) by the German lawyer Daniël Laelius and the *Cythara spiritualis* (Cologne, 1613) by Matthias Reymann.

Vallet's *Secretum musarum* must have earned him international acclaim, as several of his compositions have been found abroad in print or manuscript form, most notably in Germany. The impact of Vallet's lute music in the Netherlands remained limited. Interestingly, his later collection *Apollinis süsse Leyr* [Apollo's sweet lyre] (1642) for violin and bass had a greater effect on Dutch instrumental music, leaving traces in particular in *Der Goden Fluit-Hemel* [The Gods' flute heaven] (1644), *'t Uitnement Kabinet* [The excellent cab-inet] (1649) and Jacob van Eyck's *Der Fluyten Lust-hof* [The flute's garden of de-light] (1644- c.1655).

LOUIS PETER GRIJP

COMPOSITIONS

Vingt et un pseaumes de David ...
> Also published as: *Een en twintich Psalmen
> Davids ghestelt om te singhen ende spelen
> 'tsamen.* – Amsterdam, s.n., (1615)

[Secretum musarum]
Le secret des muses
> Also published as: *Het gheheymenisse der
> zanggodinnen waer in levendich wort vertoont
> de rechte maniere om wel ende veerdichlijck op
> de luyt te spelen ...* – Amsterdam, Nicolaes
> Vallet, (1615)
> Later publisher Jan Janssz. replaced the
> Latin title by *Paradisus musicus testudinis*.

[Secretum musarum]
> *Het tweede boeck van de luyt-tablatuer ghe-
> noemt Het gheheymenisse der sangh-goddin-
> nen ...*
> *ettelijcke andere stukken op tablatuer ghestelt
> ... om te spelen op vier luyten van verscheyden
> acoord.* – Amsterdam, composer, 1616

*Regia pietas, hoc est Psalmi Davidici concinne ap-
tati ad modulantes fides ...* – Amsterdam,
composer, 1620

*Apollinis süsse Leyr. Das ist composition ... zu
spielen auff der Viol und Bass inhaltende
etliche pavannen ... und andere anmuthige
Stück...* – Amsterdam, Jan Janssz., 1642

DISCOGRAPHY

> *Gaillarde; Slaep, soete, slaep.* K. Ragossnig
(lt) (Deutsche Grammophon DG 447 727-2)
> *Helas seigneur.* D. Minter (Ct), P. O'Dette
(lt) (Harmonia Mundi USA HMU 90 7123)
> *Secretum musarum* (sel.). F. Mühlhölzer (lt)
(Ars Musici AM 1012-2)
> *Secretum musarum* (sel.). T. Satoh (lt) (NM
Classics 92016)
> *Suite.* J. Tyler (lt) (Emergo Classics EC
3350-2)
> *Suite.* Lauten Ensemble R. Goodman (BIS
CD 500 341)

Theo Verbey

DELFT, 5 JULY 1959

Theo Verbey began composing at the age of seven and was involved in a great variety of musical activities in his youth. Apart from composing, he played the recorder, the piano, trumpet and bassoon, he took lessons at the Delft Music School, and frequented the Public Music Library in The Hague, acquainting himself with much of the musical repertoire at an early age. When in 1977 he enrolled in the Royal Conservatory in The Hague, he already had a large number of youthful compositions to his credit.

From 1978 to 1984 Verbey studied music theory at the Royal Conservatory with Hein Kien, Ruud Koumans and Diderik Wagenaar, and from 1982 to 1986 composition with Peter Schat and Jan van Vlijmen. In 1987 he received the Prize for Composition at the Royal Conservatory. He began teaching music theory as early as 1979, first at the Music Center of the Delft University of Technology, then at the University of Utrecht, where he taught an extracurricular music theory course, and since 1984 at the Royal Conservatory. Since 1995 he has taught instrumentation and served as coordinator of the composition department at the Amsterdam Sweelinck Conservatory, where in 1997 he also became professor of composition. In 1993 and 1997 he was a member of the jury of the Queen Elisabeth International Competition for Composition.

Verbey's oeuvre, which began with the short *Nocturne* for piano (1980), comprises some twenty orchestral and chamber music works, a piece for soprano and orchestra, and various arrangements, all of which were written on commission.

The relatively modest dimensions of this body of works is a consequence of his meticulous compositional methods. Much of his music is finely crafted down to the smallest detail; in works such as the trilogy *Inversie-Contractie-Expulsie* (1987-1990), the wind septet *De Peryton* (1990), or the concertino for oboe *Notturno* (1995), the balanced structure and extraordinary clarity of instrumentation are immediately noticeable. In his carefully thought-out instrumentation, details come to the fore while his elegant melodies provide the listener with points of reference.

Some of his works, however, fall into a different category, having a more unruly sound, greater harmonic complexity and a less differentiated structure. Many of these are earlier works, such as the large-scale ensemble piece *Aura*

(1985) – for which Verbey was awarded the Encouragement Prize of the Amsterdam Fund for the Arts – *Tegenbeweging* [Countermovement] (1986), for symphony orchestra, and *De Simorq* (1989), for ensemble.

These two tendencies correspond with Verbey's rather broad definition of tonality and atonality: namely, the presence or absence of reference points. In his tonally conceived works the listener is given a certain guidance by more or less exact repeats of motifs, an indication of the tonal centers, regular phrasing, and a tendency for a periodic rhythmic pulse, which sometimes results in a characteristic swing. He avoids such symmetrical elements in his atonally conceived music.

Order, to Verbey, is the musical aspect that is most closely related to musical beauty. 'Beauty is the manner in which order is transformed into complexity', he writes in his 'Aesthetic premises', formulated on the occasion of a performance of his *Produkt*, for large ensemble, at the 1992 Donaueschinger Musiktage. Viewed in this light, the listener's activity is the reverse, namely the ordering of the complexity perceived.

Verbey effectively creates order by basing temporal structures on simple numerical proportions. In *Expulsie*, for large ensemble, the total lengths of the four movements and all further subdivisions are derived from the proportional series 4 : 5 : 6 : 7. This recursive technique (analogous with the *fractal* structures discovered in geometry) provides a means of creating musical depth, because the rhythmic processes refer to each other on various levels.

Verbey views sound and structure as separate entities. He strives in his music for both unity, for example through the use of mathematical methods, and diversity, through the realization of structure into sound. The relationship between sound and structure is dynamic, considering that structure, in Verbey's conception of it, is a product of the guidance imposed upon the spontaneous, natural tendencies of the musical material. In line with this is his love for Bach's *Kunst der Fuge* and Beethoven's late string quartets: music in which the balance between beauty of sound and the activity of structuring lies very much on the surface.

Verbey's interest in music history has been very fruitful, as evidenced for example by his orchestration of Alban Berg's Piano Sonata, which has been performed many times by the Royal Concertgebouw Orchestra on its international tours. *Triade* (1991/1994) for chamber orchestra, of which the most important structural aspects were directly derived from Mozart's Prague Symphony, is a successful work that has been performed in England by The London Sinfonietta and in the United States at the Tanglewood Music Festival.

Historical awareness, in Verbey's view, is a necessity if a composer is to effectively use the music of the past in a contemporary manner: 'I try to compose music that is influenced almost to the point of saturation: not by fifty years of tradition, but by hundreds of years. Everyone knows that that moment in 1914 when music was burst asunder is the most important moment of this century. But the further one looks back, the more insight one gains into the other side of the mirror', he said in an interview in the daily newspaper *de Volkskrant*.

JACO MIJNHEER

COMPOSITIONS

* Not printed

VOCAL: *Whitman* (Whitman), S, orch (1992)

CHAMBER MUSIC: *Nocturne*, pf (1980)*; *Random Symphonies*, electr. (1985)*; *Inversie*, a-fl, cl, vla, db, gui, hp, mand, pf, vibr (1987); *Contractie*, fl, b-cl, pf (1987); *De Peryton*, fl, ob, eh, cl, b-cl, bn, hn (1990); *Chaconne*, vl, vla, vc (1991); *Duet*, 2 tpt (1992); *Hommage*, fl (1993); *Passamezzo*, sax.qt (1991, rev. 1994)*

ORCHESTRA, LARGE ENSEMBLE: *Caprice symphonique*, orch (1976)*; *Triplum*, 3 bn, s-

sax, 2 a-sax, 2 hn, tpt, 3 trb (1982)*; *Aura*, instr.ens (1985, rev. 1989); *Tegenbeweging*, orch (1986); *Expulsie*, instr.ens (1988-1990); *De Simorq*, instr.ens (1989); *Triade*, chamb.orch (1991, rev. 1994); *Produkt*, chamb.ens (1991-1992); *Notturno*, ob, 2 hn, 4 vl, 2 vla, 2 vc, db (1995); *Pavane oubliée*, hp, str.orch (1995)*; *Conciso*, chamb.ens (1996)

ARRANGEMENTS: *Piano Sonata op. 101* – Beethoven, str.qt (1983)*; *Sonata for 2 pianos* – Stravinsky, fl, ob, cl, bn, vl, vc (1983)*; *Piano Sonata op. 1* – Berg, orch (1984); *Zonder Zon* – Mussorgsky, l.v, chamb.orch (1989); *Trois Chansons* – Ravel, fl, 2 cl, b-cl, hn, pf, hp, 2 vl, vla, vc, db (1990)*; *Liederen en Dansen van de Dood* – Mussorgsky, l.v, chamb.orch (1994); *De Kinderkamer* – Mussorgsky, S, chamb.orch (1994)

PUBLICATIONS
'Schönberg: Harmonielehre', *Van Aristoxenos tot Stockhausen*. Groningen, Wolters Noordhoff, 1990
Esthetisch uitgangspunt. Brochure Donemus Amsterdam, 1992
'Pre-composition in Passamezzo', *Key Notes*, 31 1997/1, p. 17-19

BIBLIOGRAPHY
P. van Deurzen: 'Water met een bruistablet : de twee gezichten van Theo Verbeys "Inversie" ', *Mens en Melodie*, vol. 49, 1994, p. 360-366
K. van Ingen Schenau: 'Componeren in stilte : Theo Verbey, componist', *Preludium*, Nov. 1995, p. 14-15
P. Luttikhuis: 'Componist Theo Verbey : "Het rekenwerk mag niet te horen zijn" ', *NRC Handelsblad*, 30 Nov. 1990
J. Oskamp: 'Composer Theo Verbey : a subtle innovator', *Key Notes*, 26, 1992/3, p. 17-19
J. Oskamp: *Theo Verbey*. Sleeve notes Composers' Voice CV 31 (see discography)
L. Samama: *Componeren is actie ondernemen : Theo Verbey*. Brochure Donemus, Amsterdam, 1992
O. Schoonderwoerd: 'Theo Verbey', *Lexicon Klassieke Muziek*. Utrecht/Antwerpen, Kosmos-Z&K Uitgevers, 1993
Theo Verbey. Brochure Donemus Amsterdam, 1992
F. van der Waa: 'Laveren in nauw vaarwater', *de Volkskrant* , 20 March 1992

DISCOGRAPHY
Duet; Inversie; Contractie; Expulsie; Hommage; Piano Sonata op.1 - Berg. P. Masseurs and H.J. Lindhout (tpt), Nieuw Ensemble, cond. E. Spanjaard, Het Trio, Asko Ensemble, cond. D. Porcelijn, E. Pameijer (fl), Royal Concertgebouw Orchestra, cond. R. Chailly (Composers' Voice Highlights CV 31)
Hommage. E. Pameijer (fl) (Attacca Babel 9478)
Hommage. E. Pameijer (fl) (Radio Nederland International: RN Classics 93003)
Passamezzo. Aurelia Saxophone Quartet (NM Classics 92053)
Piano Sonata op.1 - Berg. Royal Concertgebouw Orchestra, cond. R. Chailly (Decca 448 813-2)

Johannes Verhulst

Johannes Josephus Hermanus Verhulst showed an early aptitude for music, singing in a Catholic church choir when he was a boy. In 1826 he was admitted as a choral pupil to the newly founded music school in The Hague. The school's director, J.H. Lübeck, recognized his talent and enrolled him for violin and theory lessons. It was not long before Verhulst went on to become first violinist in the Royal Chapel of King William I, under the baton of Lübeck. In the meantime, Verhulst had already composed several works and received various incentive grants from the Society for the Advancement of Music.

During the summer of 1836, when Felix Mendelssohn Bartholdy was staying in Scheveningen, near The Hague, Lübeck seized the opportunity to show him an overture composed by Verhulst. Mendelssohn reacted with great enthusiasm and declared his willingness to accept Verhulst as a pupil. A stipendium from the Society enabled Verhulst to complete his studies in Leipzig. This period later proved decisive to his career. To what extent Verhulst actually studied with Mendelssohn is difficult to establish with any certainty. Of great significance, however, was his intimate friendship with Robert Schumann, who called Verhulst 'this quite unusual Dutchman'.

With effect from the season of 1838-39, Verhulst was appointed conductor of the Euterpe Orchestra in Leipzig. On January 24, 1842, he led the orchestra in a benefit concert featuring four of his own compositions, including his newly completed Symphony in E minor. This work was particularly well received. Soon afterwards, Verhulst visited his native Holland and gave a concert at The Hague in the presence of King William II, who subsequently decorated him as a Knight in the Order of the Dutch Lion, and appointed him as director of the Court Music. Verhulst settled in The Hague, dedicating himself chiefly to the composition of vocal music set to Dutch texts.

In 1848, Verhulst assumed the directorship of Toonkunst Rotterdam, the local chapter of the Society for the Advancement of Music. In that capacity, he enjoyed in 1854 one of his greatest successes ever, conducting a music festival held in the city on the occasion of the 25th anniversary of the Society. Numerous foreign celebrities were present, including Ferdinand Hiller, William Sterndale Bennett, Anton Rubinstein, and Franz Liszt.

In 1851, Verhulst married Johanna Elisabeth Rochussen, whose brother was Charles Rochussen, a renowned painter and book illustrator. The couple

had contact with Robert and Clara Schumann on several occasions.

After Lübeck's retirement in 1860, Verhulst assumed the conductorship of the Diligentia Concerts in The Hague. This was followed in 1864 by his appointment as director of both the Amsterdam Toonkunst choir and the Caecilia Orchestra. Furthermore, he took over the management of the concerts in Felix Meritis, a major concert hall in Amsterdam which boasted its own orchestra. He thus gained control over the country's most important musical institutions. Viewed in this context, his nickname 'the one and only' speaks volumes.

Verhulst revealed himself to be a conservative conductor, although it must be added that he conducted the first performance of Bach's St.Matthew Passion in Amsterdam, and that it was he who introduced Bruckner's Third Symphony to the Netherlands. However, his refusal to perform works by Wagner, Liszt and Berlioz led to increasing protests. A conflict over the issue with the Diligentia board of governors was settled with a compromise: Richard Hol from Utrecht was hired to come to The Hague several times a year to conduct the works so abhorred by Verhulst. Verhulst himself is said to have reacted with the words: 'Very well, the board behaves just like a woman in charge of a large household who takes on a full-time servant and, in addition, a charwoman who comes in twice a week to do the dirty work.'

In 1886, the year in which he celebrated his seventieth birthday, Verhulst was made an honorary member of the Diligentia board of governors, although he was simultaneously relieved of his duties. Shortly afterwards, he also resigned his posts in Amsterdam. The last years of his life were spent in the coastal town of Bloemendaal, where he died on January 17, 1891.

Verhulst's oeuvre consists of orchestral works, choral music (with and without orchestra), chamber music and songs, and was composed largely before 1850. Of his orchestral compositions, his only Symphony, op.46, is easily the most important, and it remained unequalled in the Netherlands for a long time. Although stylistically closely connected to the Leipzig school, the work reveals the young composer's individuality. Particularly worthy of mention is the fascinating way in which he develops relatively simple themes and the forward-looking use of harmonic progressions.

With regard to choral music, the Mass op.20 (1840-1843) for choir, four soloists and orchestra occupies a similar position. In this monumental work, Verhulst demonstrates his absolute mastery of polyphony and shows an understanding of how to build up dramatic tension. Given the forces it employs, the Requiem op.51 for male choir, organ, two trumpets, two horns, three trombones, tuba and tympani is also worth mentioning. The sacred music written after 1850 does not measure up to his earlier works.

As a composer of chamber music, Verhulst was not particularly productive, although his three string quartets should certainly not be passed over. The two Quartets op.6 were dedicated to Mendelssohn. In 1842, Schumann wrote a glowing review of these two pieces in the *Neue Zeitschrift für Musik*. Referring to the Quartet op.21, which was dedicated to him, Schumann wrote to Verhulst, 'For me it is the most precious music of yours that I know.'

Verhulst is probably most original in his over one hundred songs to Dutch texts, many of them by his contemporary Jan Pieter Heije, composed between 1844 and 1851. Although the poems are not really of the finest quality, Verhulst put his heart and soul into their musical settings. The use of chromaticism in the often extensive introductions and postludes is remarkable for its period. The declamatory melodic lines are also ahead of their time. Of particular interest is *Kinderleven* [Child's life], an anthology of forty songs in which Verhulst's power of imagination reaches a climax.

Considering the inhibiting influence exercised by Verhulst on the musical life of the Netherlands towards the end of his career, it is understandable that he became the butt of criticism by younger composers such as Alphons Diepenbrock. That does not, however, diminish in any way the quality of the compositions written during his earlier years, an oeuvre that is worthy of esteem.

MARCEL VENDERBOSCH

COMPOSITIONS

SONGS: *Eight Songs* (Heije, Broekhuyzen), op. 9; *Six Songs* (Heije), op. 16; *Zeven geestelijke liederen*, op. 22; *Songs* (Heije), op. 26; *Liederkrans* (Heije), op. 27; *Gezangen en psalmen* (Heije), op. 28; *Six Songs* (Heije), op. 29; *Kinderleven* (Heije), op. 30; *Two Songs*, op. 31; *Vergankelijkheid* (Heije), op. 33; *Kindertoonen* (Dusseau, Parson, Heije), op. 39; *Kerslied*; *Vaderlandsch lied* (Heije); *Der deutsche Rhein (Patriotisches Lied)* (Becker)

OTHER VOCAL WORKS: *Tantum ergo*, op. 5; *Koning en Vaderland*, m.choir, pf, op. 11; *Hymnus : Clemens est Dominus*, 2 mix.choirs, orch, op. 12; *Zes vierstemmige liederen*, mix.choir, op. 17; *Mis*, soloists, mix.choir, orch, op. 20; *Floris de Vijfde op het slot te Muiden*, T, mix.choir, orch. op. 23; *Concert Aria*, S, orch, op 24; *Vijfentwintig koren : voor grootere en kleinere zangvereenigingen* (Heije, Salis, Vondel), op. 32; *Vlaggelied*, m.choir, wind ens, op. 35; *Twaalf geestelijke gezangen* (Heije, Beets), mix.choir and mix.choir, org/pf, op. 38; *Psalm 145*, soloists, mix.choir, orch, op. 45; *Hymnus : Veni creator spiritus*, m.choir, org, op. 47; *Rembrandt feestzang* (Heije), m.choir, orch, op. 48; *Requiem : missa pro defunctis*, soloists, m.choir, orch op. 51 (1854); *Cantica in honorem sanctissimi sacramenti*, m.choir, org, op. 54; *Missa*, m.choir, org, op. 55; *Missa brevis*, boys' choir, m.choir, op. 58

CHAMBER MUSIC: *String Quartet no. 1*, op. 6, no. 1; *String Quartet no. 2*, op. 6, no. 2; *String Quartet no. 3*, op. 21; *Nocturne*, vl, pf (1840); *Arabesque : scherzo*, pf; *Romanze*, vl, pf (1840)

ORCHESTRA: *Overture*, op. 2; *Overture Gijsbrecht van Aemstel*, op. 3; *Gruss aus der Ferne*, op. 7; *Overture*, op. 8; *Symphony*, op. 46 (1841)

BIBLIOGRAPHY
A. Asselbergs: *Dr. Jan Pieter Heye of de kunst en het leven*. Utrecht, Oosthoek, 1966

E. Burnett-Elischer: 'Robert en Clara Schumann en Johannes Verhulst', *Mens en Melodie*, vol. 9, 1954, p. 284-287

J.D.C. van Dokkum: *Honderd jaar muziekleven in Nederland*. Amsterdam, Maatschappij tot Bevordering der Toonkunst, 1929

J. Hartog: *Felix Mendelssohn Bartholdy en zijne werken*. Leiden, Sijthoff, 1909

'Joh.J.H. Verhulst (1816-1886)', *Caecilia*, 43, 1886, p. 83-85

W.F.G. Nicolaï: 'Johannes Josephus Hermanus Verhulst', *Caecilia*, 48, 1891, p. 27-29

E. Reeser: *Een eeuw Nederlandse muziek : 1815-1915*. Amsterdam, Querido, 1950, 2/1986

E. Reeser: *Verzamelde geschriften van Alphons Diepenbrock*. Utrecht [etc.], Het Spectrum, 1950

J.C.M. van Riemsdijk: *Johannes Josephus Herman Verhulst*. Haarlem, Tjeenk Willink, 1886

E. van der Straeten: 'Mendelssohns und Schumanns Beziehungen zu J.H. Lübeck und Johann J.H. Verhulst', *Die Musik*, 3, 1903-1904, p. 8-20 and 95-102

M. Venderbosch: 'Opkomst en ondergang van Johannes Verhulst', *Entr'acte*, 8, 1992, p. 22-26

M. Venderbosch: 'De liederen van Verhulst : "eene nieuwe baan" ', *Muziek en Wetenschap*, III/4, 1993, p. 267-295

G. Werker (pseud. of W. Paap): 'Johannes Verhulst 1816-1891', *Mens en Melodie*, vol. 21, 1966, p. 70-72

J.P. Weyand: 'Rond Johan J.H.Verhulst : iets uit het Haagsche muziekleven in de 19e eeuw', *Die Haghe Jaarboek*, 1940, p. 134-215

W.L. Zalsma: 'J.J.H.Verhulst', *Caecilia* and *De Muziek* 98(15), 1941, p. 18-20

DISCOGRAPHY
De nevel dekt ons. Netherlands Chamber Choir, cond. U. Gronostay (NM Classics 92065)

Nocturne E flat major. M. Krücker (pf) (NM Extra 98011)

Overture Gijsbrecht van Aemstel. Netherlands Radio Symphony Orchestra, cond. J. van Steen (NM Classics 92090)

Songs. A. Stumphius (S), N. van der Meel (T), L. van Doeselaar (pf) (NM Classics 92029)

Symphony op. 46. Residentie Orchestra, cond. H. Vonk (Olympia OCD 502)

Matthijs Vermeulen

HELMOND, 8 FEBRUARY 1888 – LAREN, 26 JULY 1967

Having left primary school Matthijs Vermeulen initially wanted to follow in the footsteps of his father, who was a blacksmith. During a serious illness his inclination towards the spiritual gained the upper hand. Inspired by a God-fearing and thoroughly Catholic environment, he decided to become a priest. However, at the seminary, where he learned about the principles of counterpoint of the sixteenth-century polyphonic masters, his true calling – music – came to light. He abandoned his initial ideas and moved to Amsterdam, the country's musical capital. There he approached Daniël de Lange, the director of the conservatory, who recognized his talent and gave him free lessons for two years. In 1909 Vermeulen began to write for the Catholic daily newspaper *De Tijd*, where he soon distinguished himself with his personal, resolute tone, standing out in stark contrast to the usually long-winded music journalism of the day. The quality of his reviews also struck Alphons Diepenbrock. He warmly recommended Vermeulen to the progressive weekly *De Amsterdammer*. There Vermeulen revealed himself to be an advocate of the music of Debussy, Mahler and Diepenbrock, whom he later used to call his 'maître spirituel'.

In the years 1912-1914 Vermeulen composed his actual opus 1, the First Symphony. In this work, expressing the joys of summer and youth, he already employed the technique he would remain loyal to for the rest of his life: polymelodicism. The four songs Vermeulen wrote in 1917 display, each in its own special way, the composer's preoccupation with war. In the reviews for *De Telegraaf*, a daily newspaper he had worked for since 1915 as head of the Art and Literature department, he also showed just how much in his view politics and culture were inseparable.

Vermeulen's polemic against the unidirectional German orientation of Dutch musical life got him into trouble. After having presented his First Symphony to Willem Mengelberg, whom he much admired, it was disdainfully rejected after a one-year period of keen anticipation. Consequently, Vermeulen's orchestral work did not stand a chance in Amsterdam. The first performance, given by the Arnhem Orchestral Society in March 1919, took place under abominable circumstances and was a traumatic experience. Nonetheless, Vermeulen started work on his Second Symphony shortly after that, and a year later he gave up journalism in order to fully dedicate himself to composing, at

the same time receiving the financial backing of a few friends. After a last, fruitless appeal to Mengelberg, Vermeulen moved to France with his family in 1921 in the hope of finding a more favorable climate for his music. There he completed work on his Third Symphony, the String Trio and the Violin Sonata.

However, Vermeulen's symphonic works did not find their way into the French concert halls either. From sheer necessity Vermeulen returned to journalism. In 1926 he became the Paris correspondent for the *Soerabaiasch Handelsblad*. For fourteen years he wrote two extensive weekly articles on every possible, mostly non-musical topic. The commission, in 1930, to compose the incidental music to the play *De Vliegende Hollander* [The flying Dutchman] by Martinus Nijhoff was encouraging. Nine years later he received a new impetus with the first performance of his Third Symphony by the Concertgebouw Orchestra conducted by Eduard van Beinum. The long-awaited confrontation with the resounding notes confirmed the effectiveness of his concepts. In the years 1940-1944 he composed his Fourth and Fifth Symphonies, bearing the titles of *Les victoires* and *Les lendemains chantants* respectively, which symbolize Vermeulen's faith in the good outcome of World War II.

In the fall of 1944 Vermeulen took some severe blows. In a short space of time he lost his wife and his most cherished son, who was killed while serving in the French liberation army. The diary *Het enige hart* [The singular heart] gives a deeply moving account of his mourning process. Seeking the meaning of this loss, Vermeulen drew up a philosophical construction, which he further developed in his book *Het avontuur van den geest* [The adventure of the mind].

In 1946 Vermeulen remarried Thea Diepenbrock and went to work again for the weekly *De Groene Amsterdammer,* in the Netherlands. His articles on music rank, also internationally, among the most compelling in that area. His Fourth and Fifth Symphonies were performed in 1949.

Politics and society kept occupying Vermeulen passionately. He found the stifling atmosphere of the cold war increasingly depressing. Fearing a nuclear confrontation he spoke out against the arms race in several periodicals. During the first large-scale peace demonstrations of 1955 he said: 'The atomic bomb is an anti-life, anti-God, anti-man weapon.'

The performance of the Second Symphony (which was awarded a prize at the 1953 Queen Elisabeth Competition in Brussels) during the 1956 Holland Festival instigated a new period of creativity. Vermeulen moved to the village of Laren with his wife and child, where he composed the Sixth Symphony, followed by various songs and the String Quartet. His last work, the Seventh Symphony, entitled *Dithyrambes pour les temps à venir,* reveals unflagging optimism. The composer died after a wasting disease on 26 July 1967.

In his compositions Vermeulen always focused the attention on melody. A flow of melodies can be heard from beginning to end, quite diverse in form and character. The majority of the material is asymmetrical, based on the principle of 'free declamation', that is to say the melodic curve and length of two consecutive sentences usually vary. Frequently Vermeulen spins long melismas into ever continuous melodies, in which every reminiscence of period structure is absent. Particularly striking is the free rhythm of flowing lines, disengaged from a fixed classification of meter by antimetric figures and ties. Yet elsewhere we come across short and pithy melodies with a clear pulse. A characteristic feature of his music is the sophisticated handling of climaxes and the alternation of tension and relief, mostly supported by harmony.

In his writings Vermeulen always draws a parallel between melody and the individual: 'The melody is a frame of mind expressed in tones.' Seen in the light of Vermeulen's line of reasoning, a multi-voiced, polymelodic composition takes on the meaning of an aural representation of society. By combining several individual melodies, he reveals the wish he cherishes for society, namely that of every individual being able to freely express and develop himself without infringing upon other people's freedom to develop their abilities. Although Vermeulen's writings on music give the impression that he was completely consistent in applying his polymelodic concept, most of his compositions contain several passages with only one or two voices, embedded in marvellous harmonies. Open, simple textures alternate with very complex ones, as does quasi-tonality with wholly atonal constellations.

Early on, a spirit of freedom and urge for innovation prompted Vermeulen to abandon tonality and reject traditional formal schemes. In the First Cello Sonata free atonality breaks through in spurts, a method which from his Second Symphony onwards determines melody and harmony in his oeuvre. As opposed to Schoenberg, Vermeulen did not choose to build a new regulatory system, but proceeded purely in terms of thematic information and its (psycho-)logical development. His symphonies and chamber works consequently differ greatly as far as construction is concerned. But he always succeeded in creating architectonic cohesion. The Third Symphony is in a large A-B-A form, in which A develops linearly and B is reminiscent of a Classical rondo. The Fourth Symphony is built on six themes, three of which return just before the end; the long epilogue is counterbalanced by the hammering prologue, both on the pedal tone C. The large-scale Violin Sonata is based on the major seventh, omnipresent both in melody and harmony.

Vermeulen's compositions share a unique combination of overwhelming energy, power, lyricism, and tenderness. The vitality of his works is the result of the aim he had in mind: to compose as an ode to the beauty of the earth and in astonishment about life, creating music which appeals to the spirituality of man, bestowing feelings of happiness on him and making him acquainted with the source of life, the Creative Spirit. These lofty ambitions, put into words in the book titled *Princiepen der Europese muziek* [Principles of European music] and numerous articles, were at odds with the mainstream movements. Thus, Vermeulen did not have followers or disciples.

Apart from the aesthetic-ethical 'message', which is also the subject of most of his songs, Vermeulen's symphonies offer an ingenious interplay of melodies, a colorful orchestral sound with many felicitous instrumental ideas, fascinating soundscapes, innovative parallel harmony and a captivating canon technique.

TON BRAAS

COMPOSITIONS

VOCAL: *On ne passe pas*, T, pf (1917); *Les Filles du Roi d'Espagne*, Mez, pf (1917); *The Soldier*, Bar, pf (1917); *La Veille*, Mez, pf (1917; orchestr. 1932); *Trois salutations à Notre Dame*, Mez, pf (1941); *Le Balcon*, Mez/T, pf (1944); *Prélude des origines*, Bar, pf (1959); *Trois chants d'amour*, Mez, pf (1962)

INSTRUMENTAL: *Symphonia Carminum (Symphony no. 1)* (1912-1914); *Sonata*, vc, pf (1918); *Prélude à la nouvelle journée (Symphony no. 2)* (1919-1920); *Thrène et Péan (Symphony no. 3)* (1921-1922); *Trio à cordes* (1923); *Sonata*, pf, vl (1925); *Muziek bij het waterfeestspel De Vliegende Hollander van Martinus Nijhoff* (1930); *Sonata no. 2*, vc, pf (1927, 1937-1938); *Les victoires (Symphony no. 4)* (1940-1941); *Les lendemains chantants (Symphony no. 5)* (1941-1945); *Les minutes heureuses (Symphony no. 6)* (1956-1958); *Quatuor à cordes* (1960-1961); *Dithyrambes pour les temps à venir (Symphony no. 7)* (1963-1965)

PUBLICATIONS

De twee muzieken. Leiden, Sijthoff, 1919
Klankbord. Amsterdam / Mechelen, De Spieghel, 1929
De eene grondtoon. Amsterdam / Mechelen, De Spieghel, 1932
Het avontuur van den geest : de plaats van den mens in dat avontuur. Amsterdam, ABC, 1947
Princiepen der Europese muziek. Amsterdam, Uitgeversmaatschappij Holland, 1949
L'aventure de l'esprit. Parijs, Editions Lacoste, 1955
De muziek dat wonder. The Hague, Bert Bakker, 1957
De stem van levenden. Arnhem, Ravenberg Pers, 1981
Het enige hart (dagboek 1944-1945). Amsterdam, De Bezige Bij, 1991, 2/1993
Mijn geluk, mijn liefde (letters to Thea Diepenbrock). Amsterdam, De Bezige Bij, 1995

BIBLIOGRAPHY

T. Braas: *De symfonieën en de kamermuziek van Matthijs Vermeulen : poëtica en compositie.* Doctoral dissertation University of Utrecht. Amsterdam, Donemus, 1997 (includes an extensive bibliography)
T. Braas: *Door het geweld van zijn verlangen : een biografie van Matthijs Vermeulen.* Amsterdam, De Bezige Bij, 1997
T. Braas: 'Matthijs Vermeulen's symphonies', *Key Notes*, 25, 1988/89, p. 18-24
T. Braas: 'Negatieve impulsen worden niet toegelaten : Matthijs Vermeulen: idealist in woord en muziek', *Mens en Melodie*, vol. 47, 1992, p. 456-463
M. Brandt: 'The extraordinary musical language of an un-Dutch Dutchman', *Key Notes*, 31, 1997/4, p. 16-19
O. Ketting: 'Voorspel als naspel', *De ongeruste parapluie.* The Hague, Ulysses, 1981
W. Markus: 'De dwaalweg van het intellect : over de symfonieën van Matthijs Vermeulen (I)', *Mens en Melodie*, May 1997, p. 214-217
W. Markus: 'Het ideaal van de ongebroken inspiratie : over de symfonieën van Matthijs Vermeulen (II)', *Mens en Melodie*, June 1997, p. 270-277
Chr. van der Meulen: *Matthijs Vermeulen : zijn leven, zijn muziek, zijn proza.* Nieuwkoop, Heuff, 1982
P. Rapoport: 'Matthijs Vermeulen and his Symphony no. 2, Prélude à la Nouvelle Journée', *Opus Est. Six composers from Northern Europe.* London, Kahn & Averill, 1978
L. Samama: *Zeventig jaar Nederlandse muziek : 1915-1985 : voorspel tot een nieuwe dag.* Amsterdam, Querido, 1986

DISCOGRAPHY

Cello Sonatas no. 1 and 2. R. van Ast (vc), A. Vernède (pf) (BVHAAST 047)
The Complete Matthijs Vermeulen Edition : Orchestral Music. Various orchestras and conductors (Composers' Voice CV 36 t/m 38)
The Complete Matthijs Vermeulen Edition : Chamber Music. Various soloists and ensembles (Composers' Voice CV 39 t/m 41)
String Quartet. Schönberg Quartet (NM Classics 92078)
Symphony no. 3 Residentie Orchestra, cond. F. Leitner (Olympia OCD 504)
Symphony no. 4. Residentie Ochestra, cond. E. Bour (Olympia OCD 505)
Symphony no. 6. Rotterdam Philharmonic Orchestra, cond. E. de Waart (Teleac TEL 8905)

Jan Baptist Verrijt

OIRSCHOT, C.1600 – ROTTERDAM, BURIED 29 AUGUST 1650

Jan Baptist Verrijt's native town is known thanks to the addition 'Oirscotano' in the registration of one of his prints in a 1649 catalogue: it is the small town of Oirschot in Brabant. The exact date of his birth is unknown, but various indications lead to the assumption that it must have been around 1600. In 1627 he was a schoolmaster's assistant and organist in Weert, positions he held until All Saints' Day 1629. It is not clear what sort of activities he was engaged in during the five years after that. He may have been an organist in Oirschot during that time, for in 1634 he married Margareta Lenartsdochter Scherp there. He was to turn up again in Louvain in 1636, where he was appointed organist of the Saint Peter's Church and became one of the city's musicians. It was undoubtedly in the capacity of the latter that he published a collection of five-part dance music (op.3) in 1638.

Verrijt did not stay in the southern Netherlands very long, because in 1639 he became organist at the cathedral of 's-Hertogenbosch, the most important musical position in his native region of Brabant. Since this city had been a Protestant one since 1629, Verrijt was forced – at least nominally – to convert to the new faith in order to be able to accept this position. The large organ Verrijt now had at his disposal had a long history of construction which involved several organ builders. The instrument was completed only in 1635. In addition to being an organist, Verrijt was also appointed city carillonneur. This art form was probably new to him, for in 1642 he studied for a month with the famous carillon player Jacob van Eyck in Utrecht. Verrijt's stay there left its mark on an Almande melody that Van Eyck used for a series of variations in the second part of his *Fluyten Lust-hof* [The flute's garden of delight] (Amsterdam, 1646); this melody was probably derived from Verrijt's lost third opus of instrumental dances.

Verrijt did not stay in 's-Hertogenbosch for long either: in 1644 he became city organist in Rotterdam, a post that commanded a high salary. His acquaintance with Rotterdam probably stemmed from his inspection of the new organ of Saint Lawrence's Church two years earlier. Verrijt enjoyed a great reputation as an organ expert; about 1640 he was involved in many important organ building projects: in Rotterdam (1642, Hans Goldfuss), Arnhem (1645, Van Hagerbeer), Alkmaar (1646, Van Hagerbeer) and Leiden (1649, Van Hagerbeer). In Rotterdam Verrijt had a large, modern and remarkably versa-

tile instrument at his disposal and he
published two important collections
of vocal music there (in 1647 and
1649). This productive period was,
however, cut short prematurely (the
op.5 was expressly published as 'liber
primus') by Verrijt's death in 1650;
he was buried on 29 August in the
Prince's Church in Rotterdam.

It is inconceivable that the prominent organist Verrijt would not also
have been engaged in composing
organ music, yet nothing has survived. His printed works, normally
more likely to survive, have not fared
well either. Of the five published
opus numbers only the last from
1649 has been preserved. Entitled *Flammae divinae*, its high quality makes the
loss of the other books the more regrettable. The disappearance of the fourth
opus in particular, the *Divinae ac piae oblectiones*, which contained concertante
motets for four to eight voices and continuo with four instrumental parts ad libitum, is a painful loss to Dutch music. A short fragment of an eight-part
mass probably stemming from this collection has survived in manuscript.

Only the small-scale works from the *Flammae divinae* still exist to show Verrijt's ability as a composer, and they are gems indeed. The collection comprises-
es six two-part motets with basso continuo, as well as twelve motets and two
masses for three voices, also with continuo. The choice of text proves, just as
Sweelinck's *Cantiones sacrae* did thirty years earlier, the composer's strong
Catholic leanings. This is quite evident from the two masses, which were
probably intended for use at Catholic conventicles; the modest scoring also offers a clue to this.

Verrijt's motets show a remarkable control of the modern Italian concertato
style for solo voices and continuo. In the Netherlands it did not take much effort for one to become acquainted with it, thanks mainly to the activities of the
Antwerp publisher Phalèse, who issued many publications of the latest Italian
works in this genre. This must be the reason Verrijt also became familiar with
the music of composers such as Agazzari, Bernardi, Grandi, Rovetta, Donato,
Rigatti, and Monteverdi. In his motets Verrijt displays the same kind of sensitivity toward texts, fine, thoroughly vocally conceived lines and clear har-

monies as his renowned Italian examples. Furthermore, there is a strongly polyphonic bias: the expressive solo voices largely retain their independence and are closely interwoven in recitative-like phrases. Therefore, it is certainly no coincidence that Verrijt avoided genuine monody (for solo voice and basso continuo): he found its possibilities to be too constricted for him to give vent to his polyphonic talents. Verrijt was also fully familiar with the techniques of modal disposition and the application of rhetorical figures.

The majority of the motet texts are freely versified devotional texts, complemented by some texts from the Psalms and the Canticles. The free texts are clearly Catholic in character. Especially notable is the duet for two equal voices, *Vulnera cor meum*, with its splendid balance between vocal virtuosity and introspection, dance rhythms and chromaticism. *Fili, ego Salomon* is another fine example, belonging to the genre of spiritual dialogue which was particularly popular in Italy at the time. In this composition King Solomon (bass) interrogates his son (tenor and alto) about his sins. When the latter confesses – the dialogue growing increasingly intrusive – the King reassures him: he shall be forgiven. A dancing refrain and a final, richly contrasted chorus supply the drama with the necessary backing. Of an entirely different character is the Christmas duet *Currite pastores in Bethlehem*, in which the story of the adoration of the shepherds is told with a light touch. Verrijt continually relies on the texts and is able to turn almost any motet into an individual masterpiece.

PIETER DIRKSEN

COMPOSITIONS

Canzoni amorosi ... [opus 1]
For 4 voices and bc. Publ. before 1638. Lost

Canzoni amorosi ... [opus 2]
For 4 voices and bc. Publ. before 1638. Lost

Concentus harmonici ... [opus 3]. – Antwerpen, Pierre Phalèse, 1638
Dances for 5 instrumental voices. Lost

Divinae ac piae oblectiones ... [opus 4]. – Antwerpen, heirs of Pierre Phalèse, 1647
Motets for 4-8 voices and bc. Lost

Flammae divinae, binis, ternisque vocibus concinendae, cum basso generali ad organum, liber primus ... opus quintum. – Antwerpen, heirs of Pierre Phalèse, 1649
Eighteen motets and two masses for 2-3 voices and bc. Modern ed. (excluding the two masses): Flammae divinae, ed. F. Noske. Utrecht, VNM, 1985 (Monumenta Musica Neerlandica XVI)

IN MANUSCRIPT:
Missa fuge dilecti mi (fragment). Torún (Hungaria), University Library

BIBLIOGRAPHY

F. Noske: *Music bridging divided religions*. Wilhelmshaven, Noetzel, 1989

M.A. Vente: 'Jan Baptist Verrijt', *Die Musik in Geschichte und Gegenwart*

K. Vlaardingerbroek: 'Jan Baptist Verrijt : Rotterdams Monteverdi', *Mens en Melodie*, vol. 43, 1988, p. 289-298

DISCOGRAPHY

Currite pastores; Vulnera cor meum; Ave dulcis Iesu; O Jesu, splendor. Ensemble dell'Anima Eterna, cond. J. van Immerseel (Teleac TEL 8902)

Fili, ego Salomon. Ensemble Bouzignac, cond. E. van Nevel (Vanguard Classics 99126)

Jan van Vlijmen

ROTTERDAM, 11 OCTOBER 1935

One of Jan van Vlijmen's most remarkable characteristics is his organizational drive. As director of the Royal Conservatory in The Hague from 1970 to 1985, he initiated numerous new developments. As general manager of the Netherlands Opera (1984-1987) he fostered a number of ambitious plans. He was subsequently director of the Holland Festival, his crowning and final achievement being a grandly conceived project on the Dutch composer Matthijs Vermeulen in 1997. At his farewell he was made a Knight in the Order of the Netherlands Lion. Despite these time-consuming posts he was able to create an impressive body of works in his scarce free time, unlike his former composition teacher and predecessor at the conservatory in The Hague, Kees van Baaren, who owing to his pedagogical and organizational activities left behind a much smaller oeuvre.

Van Vlijmen was raised in 's-Hertogenbosch and studied the piano, the organ and – one year after Peter Schat – composition with Kees van Baaren at the conservatory in Utrecht. With the performance of the string quartets by Schat and Van Vlijmen during the 1956 Gaudeamus Music Week in Bilthoven, the two composers were introduced to the public. Both quartets were notably free of the then prevalent octatonic idioms derived from the work of Badings and Pijper.

Of the Van Baaren students who collaborated on the opera-morality play *Reconstructie* [Reconstruction], Van Vlijmen was the least rebellious. He was director of the Amersfoort Music School (1961-1965) and then taught music theory at the Utrecht Conservatory (until 1968). In 1967 he was appointed assistant director of the conservatory in The Hague and in 1970 he succeeded Van Baaren as its director. In his eighteen years at the helm of the Royal Conservatory he presided over its move to a new building, incorporating the ballet academy and a high school. Initiatives undertaken in the fields of pre-Classical and contemporary music led to special projects, such as one in 1972 devoted to Monteverdi led by the conductor Nikolaus Harnoncourt and another in 1982 centered on Karlheinz Stockhausen led by the composer himself.

As a composer, Van Vlijmen has shown his indebtedness to Stockhausen. A well-known example is his one-movement composition *Gruppi* (1962) for twenty instruments and percussion, with its references to Stockhausen's *Zeitmaße* for wind quintet, and *Gruppen* for three orchestras. In the central move-

ment ('Play of groups'), four spatially deployed instrumental groups are played off against each other. In the outer movements, a musical 'object' is distributed among the strongly heterogeneous groups, bringing timbre to the forefront as a structurally determinant element. Certain tones (in the harp) serve as structural hinges. A composition that has brought Van Vlijmen numerous awards, *Gruppi* is a key work of the new Dutch music. It was followed by similar spatially conceived works such as *Serenata I* and *II* (both from 1964) and the Sonata for piano and three instrumental groups (1966).

Van Vlijmen's most groundbreaking piece is *Interpolations*. It comprises twenty-five movements of various lengths, each based on its own cantus firmus. The score calls for two conductors, each operating in a different tempo, yielding a visual image that does justice to both the contrasting and synchronous playing of the groups. Most conspicuous is its rigorous treatment of the electronic distortions. Its performance erupted in a disturbance in which attempts were made literally to prevent Van Vlijmen from conducting. In reaction to this Van Vlijmen composed *Ommagio a Gesualdo* (1971). Taking the form of a concerto for violin, it sweeps away the aggression of the earlier works, traces one, long arc and is a strict and sober work marking a change in his aesthetics. The work is based on just one tone (D) which is sounded throughout its duration. Gesualdo's madrigal *Belta, poi che t'assenti*, incidentally, is quoted briefly.

After the Wind Quintet no.2 (1972), most notable for its strict adherence to vertical conception, Van Vlijmen fell silent for five years, only to re-emerge uproariously with the opera *Axel* (written in collaboration with Reinbert de Leeuw), a work that reflects the idioms of such contrasting natures as Satie and Wagner. Here, too, a slow-motion effect is employed, as is a form of pantonality (in the first act).

On 22 November 1990, Van Vlijmen's second opera received its premiere: *Un malheureux vêtu de noir*, based on a libretto by the critic and music historian Johan Thielemans on the life of Vincent van Gogh. Central to this opera is the complex relationship between Vincent van Gogh and his brother Theo in the years 1888-1890. Van Vlijmen employs in this opera a decidedly Expressionistic style that refers to the work of the Second Viennese School, in particular the music of Alban Berg. Dramaturgically, the short scenes flowing over into each other are reminiscent of Berg's *Wozzeck*. Of interest in this light is that Berg considered composing an opera on Van Gogh; he had already reserved the opus number 11 for the work.

The four-part cycle *Quaterni* (*I* for orchestra, *II* for violin, horn, piano and orchestra, and *III/IV* for soprano, choir and orchestra) is a remarkable work in which Van Vlijmen returns to serial techniques, with the qualification that the rows here are strictly conceived from tonal centers. *Quaterni*, in fact, consists of a single, continuous melody whose character is continuously transformed. The cycle is like a journey through the collective unconscious of the late Romantic and early Expressionistic tradition: mysterious, in dark colors, melancholy, autumnally reflective. The third movement is like an inscription on a gravestone, a musical 'tombeau' in memory of Kees van Baaren.

Not surprisingly, *Inferno* (1993), after Dante's similarly titled work, for three vocal and four instrumental groups, also explores dark colors, even though the 'bronze' hues often painted by the low brass instruments and strings seem characteristic of the composer in general. It is no coincidence that the solo parts for low instruments play an important role in Van Vlijmen's chamber music: viola (*Faithful*, 1984), clarinet (*Solo II*, 1986), cello (*Tombeau, Solo III*, 1991) and alto flute (*Solo IV*, 1994-1995). Other important chamber music works are: *Trimurti* (1980) for string quartet, *Nonet* (1985) and *Quintetto per Archi* (1995-1996).

Creating a strong impression in the recent past was Van Vlijmen's grand *Monumentum*, a symphony in two movements for orchestra and mezzo-soprano based on a poem by Wislawa Szymborska. *Monumentum* is an homage both to the Dutch designer Benno Premsela, who died on 27 March 1997, and to Bach – the row on which the work is based is inspired by Bach's Prelude in B-flat from *Das Wohltemperirte Clavier II*.

ERNST VERMEULEN

COMPOSITIONS

VOCAL: *Reconstructie* (with L. Andriessen, H. Claus, R. de Leeuw, M. Mengelberg, H. Mulisch and P. Schat), v, 3 choirs, large ens (1969); *Axel* (Mulisch) (opera, with R. de Leeuw); *Quaterni III/IV* (Pound), S, mix.choir, orch (1984); *Such a Day of Sweetness* (Auden), S, orch (1988); *Un malheureux vêtu de noir* (Thielemans) (opera) (1990); *Inferno* (Dante Alighieri), mix.choir, instr.ens (1993); *Monumentum* (after Szymborska), Mez, large orch (1998)

INSTRUMENTAL: *Costruzione*, 2 pf (1960); *Gruppi*, orch (1962); *Serenata I*, 2 fl, 2 ob, 2 cl, 2 bn, 2 hn, 2 trp, perc (1964); *Serenata II*, fl, orch (1964); *Sonata*, pf, 3 instr groups (1966); *Interpolations*, orch, electr. (1968, rev. 1981); *Per diciassette*, wind ens (1968); *Omaggio a Gesualdo*, vl, 6 instr groups (1971); *Wind Quintet no. 2* (1972); *Quaterni I*, orch (1979); *Quaterni II*, vl, hn, pf, orch (1982); *Faithful*, vla (1984); *Solo II*, cl (1986); *Tombeau (Solo III)*, vc (1991); *Piano Concerto* (1991); *Solo IV*, a-fl (1994-1995); *Quintetto per archi*, 2 vl, vla, vc (1995-1996); *Sei Pezzi*, vl, pf (1998); *Gestures I*, vl, pf (1998); *Gestures II*, vl, pf (1999)

ARRANGEMENTS: *Zwei Balladen op. 12* – Schönberg, Bar, orch (1994); *Sechs kleine Klavierstücke op. 19* – Schönberg, orch (1993); *Jane Grey (ballad)* – Zemlinsky, Bar, orch (1994); *Der verlorene Haufen (ballad)* – Zemlinsky, Bar, orch (1994); *Fünf Lieder auf Gedichte von Richard Dehmel* – Zemlinsky, Bar, orch (1994)

BIBLIOGRAPHY

M. Brandt: 'Jan van Vlijmen: "Serialism is not a spent force"', *Key Notes*, 30, 1996/2, p. 16-20

K. van Baaren: 'Costruzione van Van Vlijmen', *Sonorum Speculum*, no. 9, Dec. 1961

P. Janssen: 'Hoge ambities en fundamentele angst : de componist Jan van Vlijmen', *Mens en Melodie*, June 1997, p. 258-263

M. Legène and F.W. Andriessen: 'Axel : vraaggesprek met Jan van Vlijmen', *Muziek en Dans*, July 1977

W. Markus: 'Quaterni : theses', *Key Notes*, 15, 1982/1

C. Mueller: *The music of the contemporary Dutch composer Jan van Vlijmen*. University of Texas, Austin, 1989

E. Schönberger: 'Eigen huid : vraaggesprek met Jan van Vlijmen', *Vrij Nederland*, 26 Jan. 1980

J. Wouters: 'Jan van Vlijmen', *Nederlandse componisten galerij : negen portretten van Nederlandse componisten*, vol 1. Amsterdam, Donemus, 1971

DISCOGRAPHY

Wind Quintet II. Danzi Quintet (Composers' Voice CVS 1981/3)

Dialogue. P. Honigh (cl), R. de Leeuw (pf) (Attacca Babel 8531-6)

Faithful. N. Imai (vla) (Composers' Voice CV 8604)

Un malheureux vêtu de noir. Various soloists, male choir, Schönberg Ensemble, cond. R. de Leeuw (Composers' Voice CVCD 17/18)

Omaggio a Gesualdo. Th. Olof (vl), Netherlands Radio Chamber Orchestra, cond. H. Vonk (Composers' Voice CV 8602)

Piano Concerto. S. Grotenhuis (pf), Netherlands Radio Philharmonic Orchestra, cond. L. Vis (NM Classics 92070)

Quaterni I. Concertgebouw Orchestra, cond. L. Vis (Composers' Voice CVS 1981/3)

Quintetto per archi. Schönberg Quartet, N. Imai (vc) (NM Classics 92078)

Serenata II. Peter van Munster (fl), Netherlands Radio Philharmonic Orchestra, cond. B. Maderna (Fifty Years International Gaudeamus Music Week, Donemus CV45/46)

Sonata. Th. Bruins (pf), Residentie Orchestra, cond. E. Bour (W 6812.901/906)

Sonata per pianoforte e tre gruppi strumentali; Omaggio a Gesualdo per violini e sei gruppi strumentali; Inferno, cantata per tre gruppi vocali e quatro gruppi strumentali. Theo Bruins (pf), Residentie Orchestra, cond. E. Bour, V. Beths (vl), Netherlands Radio Philharmonic Orchestra, cond. J. van Steen, Netherlands Chamber Choir, Schönberg Ensemble, Asko Ensemble, cond. R. de Leeuw (Composers' Voice CV59)

Trimurti. Gaudeamus Quartet (Composers' Voice CV 8302)

Trimurti. Schönberg Quartet (Attacca Babel 9785)

Alexander Voormolen

ROTTERDAM, 3 MARCH 1895 – LEIDSCHENDAM, 12 NOVEMBER 1980

At the beginning of his career, Alexander (Nicolaas) Voormolen employed a musical idiom inspired by French modernists, placing him among the ranks of the most progressive composers of the Netherlands. After World War II his music soon became obsolete and was largely forgotten.

Voormolen had piano lessons from the age of eight and was admitted to the composition class of Johan Wagenaar in 1912. Willem Pijper and Bernard Wagenaar were among his fellow pupils. In 1914 Voormolen's *Valse triste* was printed in Utrecht and in 1916 the Prélude from his 'drame lyrique' *La mort de Tintagiles*, after Maeterlinck, was first performed in the Kurhaus in Scheveningen. However, Voormolen was never to finish this composition.

The conductor of this performance, the Frenchman Rhené-Bâton, was so enthusiastic about the work that he suggested the twenty-one-year-old composer try his luck in France. Here Voormolen became acquainted with composers such as Albert Roussel, subsequently taking classes with him. However, the Dutchman felt a closer affinity with the work of Maurice Ravel, with whom he became close friends. In musical respect the two composers shared an impressionistic idiom and an inclination toward a classical form. Thanks to Ravel's mediation, the publishing house of Rouart, Lerolle & Cie published seventeen of Voormolen's compositions between 1918 and 1927. These comprised mostly piano pieces, but also chamber music and songs.

In 1919 he retired to Veere, in the southern province of Zeeland. In spite of an excellent letter of recommendation by Ravel, Voormolen did not get a position with the Royal Conservatory in The Hague. In the mid-twenties he settled in The Hague, becoming a music reporter for the daily *Nieuwe Rotterdamsche Courant*.

With the premiere by the Haagsch Strijkkwartet of his *Quatuor à cordes* in July 1919, the star of composer Voormolen began to rise quite rapidly in the Netherlands. Willem Mengelberg conducted the *Symphonietta* on 21 December 1921 in Amsterdam's Concertgebouw, and Evert Cornelis conducted the first performance of the symphonic poem *Droomhuis* [Dream house] on 7 January 1925 in Utrecht. However, Voormolen withdrew all three works after their performances. The same fate befell many other compositions: almost half of the orchestral works disappeared from Voormolen's list of works, many of them immediately after their premieres. Dutch orchestras did, however, keep performing some of his scores (even on a regular basis), such as *De drie ruitertjes* [The three little horsemen] (1927) and both *Baron Hop suites* (1923-1924 and 1931). Becoming perhaps even more well known than these thoroughly Dutch compositions was the Concerto for two oboes and orchestra (1933), composed for Jaap and Haakon Stotijn, and the Concerto for oboe and orchestra, written five years later, in 1938.

In 1938 Voormolen accepted a position as a librarian at the Royal Conservatory in The Hague, and in 1955 the Ministry of Education, Culture and Science allowed him an honorary monetary award. Regarding the war years 1940-1945, the literature

on Voormolen is largely silent. During these years he was one of the most frequently performed Dutch composers and acquired more commissions than his colleagues. He was awarded a State Prize for Music in 1941, just as were Badings, Van Otterloo, Pijper, Willem Landré Sr., and Guillaume Landré. In 1944 he was granted a state subsidy. In the purges of the post-war years Voormolen was debarred from further participation in musical activities for three years by the Honorary Music Council.

In spite of this generally suppressed period, official authorities regularly paid him tribute at the end of his career. He was granted the ANV-Visserneerlandia Prize and the Johan Wagenaar Prize in 1961, the medallion of the 'Rotte' of the Rotterdam Art Foundation in 1976, and the honorary membership of the The Hague Art Society in 1978. But his post-war career as a composer largely took place in the sidelines of contemporary music. The slow movement ('Canzone') of his Oboe Concerto became popular as the signature tune for the television series *De kleine zielen* [The small souls] (1969), based on a novel by Louis Couperus.

In his early, French period in particular Voormolen employed an extremely well-developed, almost decadently refined harmonic language based on a broadened concept of tonality. Examples of this are early piano works such as *Le souper clandestin*, *Sonnet* and the *Tableaux des Pays-Bas*. The vocal works, such as *Nous n'irons plus au bois* and *Deux moralités*, were in stylistic terms

mounted in a significantly simpler frame than the instrumental compositions.

The First Violin Sonata is one of the high points of Voormolen's oeuvre. In
relation to other works, the varied piano part is remarkably active and rhythmically quite complex. As with his other sonatas, Voormolen applies traditional sonata forms in this work. Elsewhere (*Falbalas*, for example, a piano work
written in 1915) Voormolen displays his interest in eighteenth-century dance
forms (minuet, sarabande, gavotte). Unsurpisingly, the influence of Ravel and
his *Tombeau de Couperin* are evidently recognizable in those works.

Back in the Netherlands Voormolen increasingly allowed himself to be inspired by the ancient national music, especially the *Nederlantsche Gedenck-
clanck* (1626), a national song collection by Adriaen Valerius. Musical quotes
from this collection are to be found in both cycles of the *Tableaux des Pays-Bas*
and elsewhere. Other Dutch tunes worked their way into his works, for example in his orchestral variations *De drie ruitertjes*, the Second Violin Sonata and
the *Baron Hop suites*. The *Hop suites* were remnants of a plan for a comic opera
or pantomime about the eighteenth-century nobleman, diplomat and inventor
of the 'Haagse Hopje' (Hague toffees), on a libretto by Eduard Veterman; however, the plan was never realized. The ballet music to the *Kleine Haagsche suite*
[Small Hague suite] is an attempt to evoke the atmosphere of eighteenth- and
nineteenth-century life in The Hague, and a similar theme plays a key role in
the *Spiegel der Vaderlandsche kooplieden* [Mirror of Dutch Tradesmen]. Voormolen's idiom simplified; examples of this 'Dutch' style are the *Vier oud-Nederlandsche gedichten* [Four old-Dutch poems] (1921-1924) and *Appelona* (1933).

The post-war years once again saw a change of course in Voormolen's style.
The spiced harmonic idiom of his French period, now blended with a more
'German'-orientated command of form and orchestration, returned in
Arethuza (1947), the 'symphonic myth after Louis Couperus' and the *Sinfonia
concertante* for clarinet, horn and string orchestra, written in 1951.

ONNO SCHOONDERWOERD

COMPOSITIONS

SONGS: *Nous n'irons plus au bois* (Banville), v, pf (1915); *Claire de lune* (Verlaine) m.v, pf (1916, rev. 1969); *Deux moralités* (Perrault), Mez, pf (1919); *Veere* (Plasschaert), S, pf (1921); *Vier oud-Nederlandsche gedichten* (Luyken), v, pf (1921-1924); *Drie gedichten van Jan Luyken*, S, orch (1932); *Appelona* (1933; orchestr. 1950); *Een nieuwe lente op Hollands erf* (Boutens), S, orch (1936); *Drei Gedichte von Rainer Maria Rilke*, l.v, pf (1946); *Trois poèmes de Henri de Régnier*, m.v, pf (1947); *Three songs on British verse* (Stevenson, Suckling), B-Bar, pf (1948); *Angst* (Aafjes), S, pf (1948); *La sirène* (Von der Becke, after Yeats), h.v, orch (also version m.v/a-sax, orch, 1949); *Canzonetta* (Voormolen), Bar, pf (1950); *Herinnering aan Holland* (Marsman), m.v, b-cl, str.orch (also version m.v, pf, 1966); *Stanzas of Charles II*, Bar, orch (1966); *Amsterdam*, Mez/Bar, orch (1967); *Amsterdam* (Voormolen), m.v, orch (also version m.v, pf, 1967); *Kerstliedje* (Leopold), Mez/Bar, orch (1967); *Madrigal* (Jan I, Duke of Brabant), m.v, pf (1969); *From the recollection* (Shelley), m.v, pf (also version m.v, str.orch, cel, 1970); *Lofsang : Ex minimis patet ipse Deus*, m.v, pf/org (1970, version m.v, str.orch, cel, 1971); *Ave Maria*, v, pf/org (also version v, str.orch, 1973)

OTHER VOCAL WORKS: *Beatrijs* (declamatorio) (Boutens), sp.v, pf (1921); *Drie Nederlandse gedichten* (Van der Leeuw, Marsman), m.choir (1946); *Wanderers Nachtlied* (Goethe), mix.choir/4 v (1949); *Aux Baigneurs* (Chalupt), mix.choir (1967); *De jaargetijden* (Van der Leeuw), mix.choir (1967); *From the Recollection* (Shelley), mix.choir (1968); *Lofsang : Ex minimis patet ipse Deus*, mix.choir (1971); *Ave Maria*, mix.choir (1973); *Ave Maria*, mix.choir, hp, str.orch (1973)

PIANO: *Valse triste* (1914); *Falbalas, trois mouvements de danse* (1915); *Suite voor piano nr.1* (1914-1916); *Les éléphants* (1919); *Scène et danse érotique* (1920); *Tableaux des Pays-Bas (Taferelen uit de Lage Landen)*, (vol. 1: 1919-1920, vol. 2: 1924); *Le souper clandestin* (1921); *Suite de clavecin*, pf (1921); *Sonnet*

(1922); *Livre des enfants* (vol. 1: 1923, vol. 2: 1925); *Sonata* (1947); *Eline : notturno* (1951)

CHAMBER MUSIC: *Violin Sonata no.1* (1917); *Suite*, vc, pf (1917); *Piano Trio* (1918); *Quatuor à cordes* (1919, withdrawn); *Divertissement*, vc, pf (1922); *Romance*, vc, pf (1924); *Sicilienne et rigaudon*, vl, pf (1920); *Violin Sonata no.2* (1934); *Quartetto*, str.qt (1939); *Pastorale*, ob, pf (1940); *Viola Sonata* (1953)

ORCHESTRA: *La mort de Tintagiles* (after Maeterlinck) (1913-1915, only the Prélude fin.); *Valse de ballet* (1914, withdrawn); *Le Roi Grenouille* (ballet) (1916, withdrawn); *Symphonietta* (1919, withdrawn); *Droomhuis* (symphonic poem) (1919, withdrawn, later included in *Drie gedichten voor orchest*, also withdrawn); *Baron Hop suite I* (1923-1924); *De drie ruitertjes* (orchestra variations) (1927); *Een zomerlied* (1928); *Baron Hop suite II* (1931); *Concerto*, 2 ob, orch (1933); *Diana* (ballet) (1935-1936, withdrawn, music material later used for *Arethuza*); *Concerto*, ob, orch (1938); *Kleine Haagsche suite* (1939); *Sinfonia* (1939); *Pastorale*, ob, str.orch (1940); *Cello Concerto* (1941, withdrawn); *Spiegel-suite : balletmuziek bij Langendijk's Spiegel der Vaderlandsche kooplieden* (1943); *Arethuza : symfonische mythe naar Louis Couperus* (1947); *Concerto*, 2 pf/2 hpd, str.orch (1950); *Sinfonia concertante*, cl, hn, str.orch (1951); *Eline : notturno* (1957); *Ciacona e fuga* (1958)

BIBLIOGRAPHY

C. Backers: *Nederlandsche componisten van 1400 tot op onzen tijd*. The Hague, Kruseman, 1941

W.C.S. van Benthem Jutting: 'Een Engels madrigaal in taferelen uit de Lage Landen', *Mens en Melodie*, vol. 41, 1986, p. 18-23

R. du Bois: 'And there were others too', *Key notes*, 4, 1976/2

S. Dresden: *Het muziekleven in Nederland sinds 1880 : I. De componisten*. Amsterdam, 1923

P. Micheels: *Muziek in de schaduw van het Derde Rijk : de Nederlandse symfonie-orkesten 1933-1945*. Zutphen, Walburg Press, 1993

M. Monnikendam: *Nederlandse componisten*

van heden en verleden. Amsterdam, [1968]

P. Niessing: 'In memoriam Alexander Voormolen', *Mens en Melodie*, vol. 36, 1981, p. 82-84

E. Reeser: 'Alexander Voormolen', *Die Musik in Geschichte und Gegenwart*

E. Reeser: 'Alexander Voormolen', *Sonorum Speculum* no. 22, 1965, p. 11; no. 23, 1965 p. 18-25

E. Reeser: 'De drie Ruitertjes', *Caecilia* and *De Muziek* 91 (8), 1933-1934, p. 18-26

E. Reeser: *Stijlproeven van Nederlandse muziek 1890-1960*. Amsterdam, 1966

L. Samama: *Zeventig jaar Nederlandse muziek : 1915-1985 : voorspel tot een nieuwe dag*. Amsterdam, Querido, 1986

P.F. Sanders: *Moderne Nederlandsche componisten*. The Hague, Kruseman

R. van Santen: *De piano en hare componisten*. The Hague, [1925]

J.H. Speenhoff: *Daar komen de schutters*. The Hague, 1943

W.H. Thijsse: *Zeven eeuwen Nederlandse muziek*. Rijswijk, 1949

P.-J. Wagemans: 'Alexander Voormolen : From international avant garde to Hague conservatism', *Key Notes*, 15, 1982/1, p. 14-23

J. Wouters: 'Alexander Voormolen', *New Grove dictionary of music and musicians*

DISCOGRAPHY

Ave Maria. S. Buwalda (Ct), J. Harryvan (org) (Amsterdam Classics AC 19955)

Canzona. H. de Vries (ob), instr. ens (Arcade 01692062)

Canzona. H. de Vries (ob), London Studio Orchestra, cond. D. Bakker (Mercury 8421302)

Harpsichord Suite. L. Hoppen (hpd) (Arsis Classics 96006)

Les éléphants. M. van Paassen (pf) (Attacca Babel 83122)

Pastorale. M. Karres (ob), A. Karres (pf) (Erasmus WVH 093)

Songs on British Verse. M. van Egmond (Bar), Th. Bollen (pf) (CBS LSP 14514)

Wanderers Nachtlied. Netherlands Chamber Choir, cond. U. Gronostay (NM Classics 92065)

We Wandered to the Pine Forest. Netherlands Chamber Choir, cond. H. van den Hombergh (CBS 71110)

Een zomerlied; Ouverture Baron Hop and *Sarabande Fagel* (from *Baron Hop suite I*); *Eline* '*Notturno per orchestra*'; *De drie ruitertjes*; *Ouverture Viva Carolina* (from *Baron Hop suite II*). Netherlands Radio Orchestra, cond. H. Spruit, Netherlands Radio Philharmonic Orchestra, cond. W. van Otterloo (Editio Laran ST 707)

Jan Vriend

BENNINGBROEK, 10 NOVEMBER 1938

Jan Vriend began playing the piano at age five, the organ at nine, took clarinet lessons at eleven and violin lessons at fourteen. He studied the piano with Else Krijgsman, music theory with Anthon van der Horst and Jan Felderhof, and composition with Ton de Leeuw at the Amsterdam Conservatory (1960-1967). He followed a course in percussion instruments at the Utrecht Conservatory in 1965-1966, and in 1966-1967 another in the elements of electronic music at the Institute for Sonology in Utrecht, taught by Gottfried Michael Koenig, among others.

In 1967 Vriend was awarded the Prize for Composition by the Amsterdam Conservatory, which brought him his first commission for a composition – *Huantan* (1968), for organ and wind orchestra – and a stipend to further hone his skills in composition under the tutelage of Iannis Xenakis in Paris. Vriend lived in Paris during the student uprising of 1968, an event that influenced his ideals. Later, he learned to work with Xenakis's graphic, computerized system of composition UPIC at the Centre de Mathématique et Automatique Musicales (CEMAMU). With this system he composed the electronic piece *Albedo* in 1982. Vriend also studied electronic studio technique at the Groupe de Recherches Musicales (GRM).

In 1970 he won the International Gaudeamus Prize for Composition with *Huantan*. Since then he has systematically studied mathematics and exact sciences in search of ways to apply them to composition. He has published various articles on this subject and was inspirational in Jos Kunst's doctoral thesis in musicology *Making Sense in Music*.

From 1961 Vriend conducted various choirs, ensembles and orchestras, with whom he performed a repertoire ranging from the early fifteenth century to the twentieth-century avant-garde. In 1966 he cofounded the Amsterdam Student Chamber Orchestra (later the Asko Ensemble), which from the very beginning specialized in contemporary music. Vriend conducted this orchestra until 1971. From 1989 to 1994 he was the conductor of the New Stroud Orchestra in Gloucestershire, England. Vriend has resided in South Woodchester, in southern England, since 1984. In 1995 he began performing again as a concert pianist, showing a particular preference for the *Iberia Suite* by Albéniz, which he has also recorded.

Throughout the 1970s Vriend worked with Jos Kunst in various fields of

contemporary music in the Netherlands. This collaboration led in 1972
to the joint composition of *Elements
of Logic* for wind orchestra, their part-
nership having the purpose of 'objec-
tifying the production process as
much as possible'. Together, Vriend
and Kunst formed an idealistic and
iconoclastic composers' duo. Their approach to musical analysis and the
composition of complex, experimental works was founded on their conviction that the lower social classes could
not be emancipated with cheap, so-
called 'understandable' music.

Vriend's music stands in the tradi-
tion of such loners as Edgar Varèse and Iannis Xenakis. Varèse envisioned an
entirely new and experimental approach to 'the organization of sound', which
he believed was only possible if all acoustic musical instruments were replaced by electronic instruments. It was Xenakis who in the 1950s achieved
Varèse's vision of 'organizing sound' by describing the physical aspects of
music in mathematical and physical models.

Vriend unreservedly admired the theories and music of Xenakis, to whom
he dedicated *Huantan*. In *Making Sense in Music*, Vriend sought with Kunst a
formalization of aesthetics. Their attention shifted from the composition to
the perception of music. Using modern psychological theories of perception
and emotion, they attempted to discover how people become (aesthetically)
moved and whether this could be described in a formal system. Like Xenakis,
Vriend sought to playfully convey his findings to children. While Xenakis did
so with his UPIC system, Vriend crystallized his thoughts in the book *Leren
luisteren naar muziek* [Learning to listen to music] (1979).

Vriend's ideas found expression in a variety of ways in his compositions,
leading to highly variegated types of sounds. One common factor, however, is
his predilection for layered, atonal complexity. In his earliest work traces of
Webern and Schoenberg may be found, for example in the *Variations* for
piano, and of Berio and Stockhausen, in the performance-like *Introïtus*, for
choir and winds.

Vectorial is one of Vriend's very complex scores. In the original version
(1983), for wind instruments, (retuned) harp and piano – 'a monument for J.S.
Bach' – the incessant motion (Bach) creates an impenetrable entity of notes. In

the revised version (1987), Vriend sought to correct the problem of interference between the retuned harp and the tempered piano by replacing the harp with an extra trumpet and a bass clarinet. *Heterostase*, for flute, bass clarinet and piano, 'a trio of acrobats in a whirlwind of capricious change', is by contrast a mosaic of different 'musics' more easily followed by the listener.

Vriend's magnum opus is the monumental *Hallelujah I*, 'a symphony of the North' for bass clarinet and large orchestra, in which he seeks to paraphrase 'evolution'. The work opens on a single tone (B), which seems to hold all of the energy in balance. The equilibrium is disrupted, setting off a chain reaction that leads to a state of enormous chaos. The astonishing complexity of the double, fully divided orchestra with six percussionists far exceeds the most complex scores of Ligeti and Xenakis. Then, *Hallelujah I* goes on to portray in the dynamic struggle between chaos and order the evolution from primitive sound structures to higher forms of musical organization. *Hallelujah I* has proven a work in progress; in 1995 Vriend added an eighteen-minute movement and in 1997 he completed the finale. The four movements now have a total duration of about an hour. Despite its complexity, the drama of the work is its most prominent characteristic. Now that Vriend is allowing this dramatic dimension in his current composition, it seems that his complex techniques have found their logical place.

MICHAEL VAN EEKEREN

COMPOSITIONS

VOCAL: *Songs with intermezzi*, m.v, pf (1962); *Transformation I* ('On the Way to Hallelujah'), choir, orch (1967); *Introïtus*, choir, wind ens (1969); *Ensembles*, choir (1971); *Kri*, Mez, choir, instr.ens (1975); *Three songs* (Celan), (Mez)S, orch (1991)

INSTRUMENTAL: *Variations*, pf (1961); *String Quartet* (1963); *Deux pièces*, vl, pf (1963); *Paroesie*, 10 performers (1963, rev. 1967); *Herfst*, org (1965); *Watermuziek*, schl.orch, tape (1966); *Diamant*, orch (1967); *Huantan*, org, wind orch (1968); *Bau*, chamb. orch (1970); *Elements of Logic* (with J. Kunst), wind orch (1972); *Worlds*, orch (1978); *Heterostase (Eclipse III)*, fl, b-cl, pf (1981); *Toque por la tierra vacia*, 2 gui (1981, rev. 1983); *Albedo*, tape (1982); *Vectorial*, 6 wind instr, pf (1983, rev. 1987); *Gravity's Dance (Eclipse I)*, pf (1984, rev. 1986); *Jets d'orgue – part I*, org (1985); *Athena keramitis*

(Eclipse II), db-fl, b-cl (1985); *Wu li*, vc (1986, rev. 1987); *Hallelujah II*, large ens (1988); *Hallelujah I*, b-cl, orch (1990-1997); *Jets d'orgue – part II*, org (1990); *Jets d'orgue – part III*, org (1991); *Overture ... de origen volcánico*, orch (1992); *Symbiosis*, instr.ens. (1993); *Aura (Eclipse - Interlude)*, pf (1994); *Hallelujah I* (vol. 2) (1995); *Hallelujah I* (vol. 4) (1997)

PUBLICATIONS

Wiskunde & komponeren, vol. 1. Amsterdam, ASKO, 1977

J. Vriend a.o.: *Leren luisteren naar muziek*. Amsterdam, ASKO, 1979

'Nomos Alpha : analysis and comments', *Interface*, vol.10, 1981, p. 15-82

'Valse stochastique?', *Regards sur Iannis Xenakis*. Paris, Stock Musique, 1981

'Het muziekleven in Nederland', *Hollands Maandblad*, vol. 417/418, Aug./Sept. 1982, p. 3-24

'Een hypothese vanuit stilstand', *Bevrijding van de klank*. Amsterdam, ASKO, 1984
'Heterostase : trio voor fluit, basclarinet en piano (1980-81)', *Interface*, vol. 16, 1987, p. 97-111
'Le monde ouvert des sons et ses enemies - Ferneyhough versus Xenakis', *Entre temps*, vol. 6, Jan. 1988
'Jos Kunst, balling of kluizenaar?', *Mens en Melodie*, vol. 52, March 1997

BIBLIOGRAPHY

Th. Derks: '"Music reflects my attitude to life" : the multi-layered music of Jan Vriend', *Key Notes*, 31, 1997/1, p. 8-12
'Hallelujah in het labyrint : compositie van Jan Vriend op weg naar een uitvoering', ed. Entr'acte, *Entr'acte*, vol. 4, no. 3, 1992, p. 23-27
W. Paap: 'Composers' voice', *Key Notes*, 1975/2, p. 48-55
E. Vermeulen: 'Internationale Gaudeamus Muziekweek 1970', *Sonorum Speculum*, no. 44, 1970, p. 8
E. Vermeulen: '25 Jahre Gaudeamus in Bilthoven', *Melos*, vol. 37, Dec. 1970, p. 521-522
H. Visser: 'Componist Jan Vriend slaat weer toe : "Frustratie is de motor van mijn zwartgalligheid" ', *De Tijd,* 28 Jan. 1983, p. 60-63

DISCOGRAPHY

Huantan; Elements of Logic. J. Vriend (org), Netherlands Radio Wind Ensemble, Residentie Orchestra, cond. H. Vonk and E. Bour (Composers' Voice DAVS 7475/3)
Huantan. J. Vriend (org), Netherlands Radio Wind Ensemble, cond. H. Vonk (Composers' Voice CV 45/46)
Variations. B. Berman (pf) (Kunststichting Golf 6812 575)
Heterostase, Het Trio (Composers' Voice CV 8501)
Hallelujah II. Asko Ensemble, cond. D. Porcelijn (Composers' Voice CV 57)

Klaas de Vries

TERNEUZEN, 15 JULY 1944

Klaas de Vries, the son of a pianist and an engineer, began taking piano lessons at eight and in 1965 went on to study this instrument at the Rotterdam Conservatory with Christiaan Grootveld. After graduating as a soloist he worked for years as a performer, particularly in chamber music ensembles.

In his last years at the conservatory he also majored in composition, with Otto Ketting, and music theory. Among the compositions dating from his student period are *Organum* (1971) for four trombones and three pianos, and *Refrains* (1970) for orchestra and two piano soloists. These pieces reveal Ketting's influence on De Vries in a style, traceable back to Stravinsky, whose clarity of sound and form have earned it the name neo-Classical. They are also distinguished by their mostly diatonic structures and relatively simple rhythms and are built in a mosaic of homogeneous blocks. In those years, De Vries gave evidence of his constructivist penchant in the attention he gave to 'conceptual contrasts' and 'the relationship between the overall form and the material at hand'.

When in 1972 Ketting went to teach at the Royal Conservatory in The Hague, De Vries followed him and was awarded the prize for composition in 1974. On several occasions while still a student, he resided abroad for extended periods – in Stuttgart, for example, to study with Milko Kelemen.

De Vries has been teaching at conservatories since 1972: first as a choir rehearser and instructor of harmony, counterpoint and music history at the former Twente Conservatory, and from 1979 as an instructor of musical analysis, instrumentation and composition at the Rotterdam Conservatory. Among his former students are Andries van Rossem, Rob Zuidam and Jan van de Putte.

From 1972 to 1978 De Vries organized with Theo Loevendie the famed STAMP concerts, performances that included composed, improvised and traditional music.

In 1984 his *Discantus* (1982), composed for the Netherlands Student Orchestra, was selected for the award for the best new Dutch composition, the annual Matthijs Vermeulen Prize. He is regularly invited to serve as a guest teacher, lecturer and jury member in the Netherlands and abroad. In 1995, for example, he was guest composer and instructor at the Tanglewood Music Center (Massachusetts).

De Vries' attitude towards composition could be described as speculative; he is

conscious of and tries to take account of the fact that he cannot entirely envision what the effect of the written notes will be. He considers his Piano Sonata (1987) the work through which he was able to enter the universe of the unknown, the adventurous. Notable in this piece is the homogeneity of each of the two movements: 'Melancholie' and 'Peripetie'. This piece demonstrates that De Vries has found alternatives to his tried-and-tested montage techniques.

About compositions prior to this piece, De Vries says that he already had a very detailed image of the structure of each before actually composing them, an observation that indicates an objective approach characterized by a less personal relationship between the composer and a given composition. Parallel with the transition he underwent through the Piano Sonata is a change in the sources of his inspiration. Initially, these were derived exclusively from music (Stravinsky, Boulez and Berio); in his later work literary sources play an important role. The ideas he extracted from these deal primarily with form, structure and atmosphere.

The most conspicuous aspect of De Vries' oeuvre is nonetheless its remarkable continuity. Compositions from different periods – such as *Follia* (1973), for large ensemble, *Areas* (1980), for concert choir and orchestra, and ...*Sub nocte per umbras*... (1989), for large ensemble – typically have an energetic and often hard sound, with unisons, homophonic textures, and abrupt shifts between fast and slow tempos, in combination with a predilection for instrumentation in groups. Also characteristic is the contrast between chromatic and diatonic writing.

Two tendencies began to emerge in De Vries' music in the 1980s: larger dimensions (he composed less chamber music, showing a preference for longer pieces for large forces) and an increasing predilection for vocal music.

In the monumental trilogy *...Sub nocte per umbras...*, *Diafonía, la creación* (1989), and *De profundis* (1991) De Vries explicitly links the three pieces by including quotations from the first two in the last. This element is a consequence of an important consideration he entertains in his later work, the 'listening memory', which he seeks to stimulate through repeats of and variations on musical elements. But it remains important to him that in subsequent hearings the listener discovers new facets, which he believes can only occur when 'the form is placed under pressure', that is, when the musical progression is unpredictable.

This, in turn, explains his fascination with the Argentine author Jorge Luis Borges, in whose work a wide variety of mysterious repeats form a constantly recurring theme. Also similar to Borges is De Vries' interest for the link between events that take place at different times (the historical character of musical moments). Herein, De Vries shows himself to be a post-modern composer, for whom the linear progression and renewal concept has clear limitations and who sees the necessity of a non-nostalgic look at the past.

De Vries' staged oratorio *A King, Riding* was premiered in 1996 in Brussels and later that year performed at the Holland Festival. Its libretto, which he wrote himself, is based on Virginia Woolf's experimental novel *The Waves*, which is characterized by its lack of a clear plot. Each of the six characters is portrayed by a vocal and instrumental soloist, further filled out with an electronic pendant. The 'heterophonies' between each of the three movements are settings of poems by the Portuguese poet Fernando Pessoa.

In 1998 Klaas de Vries was once again awarded the Matthijs Vermeulen Prize, this time for *A King, Riding* and *Interludium* for string orchestra.

JACO MIJNHEER

COMPOSITIONS

VOCAL: *Tegenzangen* (Erasmus, Torres, Majakovsky), mix.choir, sp.chorus, perc, orch (1973); *Areas* (Neruda, Joyce, anonym), large mix.choir, small mix.choir, 6 instr. soloists, orch (1980); *Phrases* (Rimbaud), S, mix.choir, 6 instr. soloists, orch (1986); *Diafonía, la creación* (Galeano), S, Mez, instr.ens (1989)

DRAMATIC VOCAL: *Eréndira* (opera) (Te Nuyl, after García Márquez), 5 soloists, m.choir, instr. ens (1984); *A King, Riding* (scenic oratorio) (De Vries, after Woolf and Pessoa), 2 S, Mez, Ct, T, B-Bar, 7 instr. soloists, 3 instr.ens, live electr. (1996)

CHAMBER MUSIC: *Three Pieces for Wind Quintet* (1968); *Chain of Changes*, pf (1968); *Organum*, 4 trb, 3 (el.) pf (1971); *Five-part Fantasy*, fl.ens (or alternative instr.) (1971); *Mars*, t-sax, pf (1972); *Quartet*, 2 vla, vc, db, electr. (1973); *Toccata Americana*, pf (1974); *Echo* (1974); *Twee koralen*, sax.qt (1974); *Moeilijkheden*, wind ens, pf (1977); *Drie harpisten*, 3 small (Irish) hp (1979); *Kotz* (suite from Franssens' music theatre production with the same title), instr.ens (arr. Smit) (1979); *Das Lebewohl? oder...das Wiedersehen (deux petites pièces pour quatuor à cordes)*, str.qt (1979); *Rondo*, hn, pf (1979); *Instrumental Music from 'Eréndira'*, instr.ens (1984, rev. 1992); *Murder in the Dark (Five Quarter-Tone Pieces for Harpsichord)* (1985); *Sonata (Melancholie - Peripetie)*, pf (1987); *1'11"*, pf (1989); *Songs and Dances I-IV (vier eenvoudige stukken voor viool en piano)* (1989); *Berceuse*, b-cl, perc (1990); *Umbrae*, 2 fl, pf ad lib. (1992); *String Quartet no. 1* (1993)

ORCHESTRA, LARGE ENSEMBLE: *Refrains*, 2 pf, orch (1970); *Follia*, 16 brass instr, perc, el.gui, el.b-gui, el.pf, el.org, 3 vl, 2 vla (1973); *Kadens*, wind ens (1973); *Bewegingen*, instr.ens (1979); *Tombeau* (in memoriam Igor Stravinsky), str.orch (1980); *Discantus*, orch (1982); *Sub nocte per umbras*, instr.ens (1989); *De profundis*, wind ens (1991); *Sub nocte per umbras*, version chamb.orch (1992); *Eclips (hommage à Alexandre Scriabine)*, instr.ens (1992)

PUBLICATIONS

'The point of composing is to find out, again and again, what exactly you are after', *Key Notes*, 13 1981/1, p. 39-45

The Music of Theo Loevendie. Program notes 'Esmée', Holland Festival, 1995

'Een verzameling fossielen : over componisten en nationale identiteit', *Mens en Melodie* vol. 53, 1998, p. 196-199

BIBLIOGRAPHY

P. Janssen: ' "The moment someone starts to sing it immediately becomes a lot more interesting" : three composers in conversation about their new operas', *Key Notes*, 28, 1994/4, p. 18-23

J. Kasander: 'Via een novelle van film naar opera : "Eréndira" van Klaas de Vries op een libretto van Peter te Nuyl', *Mens en Melodie*, vol. 40, 1985, p. 94-101

G. Livingston: 'Klaas de Vries in conversation with Guy Livingston', *The Paris New Music Review*, vol. 1, no. 9, 1994, p. 7-9

J. Oskamp: 'De utopie van de identiteit', *Mens en Melodie*, vol. 47, 1992, p. 579-585

L. Samama: *Klaas de Vries*. Brochure Donemus Amsterdam, 1992

L. Samama: *Klaas de Vries*. Sleeve notes Composers' Voice CV 25 (see discography)

E. Schönberger: 'Klaas de Vries : "Componeren leer je niet door uitsluitend aan noten te denken" ', *Vrij Nederland* , 8 May 1982

O. Schneeweisz: 'Klaas de Vries : "Music must seduce the ear" ', *Key Notes*, 26, 1992/4, p. 8-12

A. van der Ven: 'Dutch opera in progress', *Key Notes*, 19, 1984/1, p. 30-31

E. Voermans: *De caleidoscopische blik*. Sleeve notes Composers' Voice CV 34 (see discography)

DISCOGRAPHY

Areas. Rotterdam Philharmonic Orchestra, Philharmonic Choir 'Toonkunst', cond. D. Zinman (Composers' Voice CV 8301)

Areas; Bewegingen; Discantus; Follia; Phrases. Various orchestras, Philharmonic Choir 'Toonkunst', various conductors (Composers' Voice Highlights CV 25)

Berceuse. Duo Contemporain (Globe GLO 5126)

Bewegingen. Members of the Residentie Orchestra, cond. O. Ketting (Composers' Voice CV 8004)

Diafonía, la Creación; Sub nocte per umbras; De profundis. G. de Vries and R. Boelens (S), various orchestras and conductors (Composers' Voice Highlights CV 34)

Discantus. Netherlands Radio Philharmonic Orchestra, cond. K. Montgomery (Composers' Voice CV 8602)

Echo. M. Copper (pf) (Attacca Babel 8421-6)

Follia. Rotterdam Philharmonic Orchestra, cond. O. Ketting (Composers' Voice CV 8004)

Moeilijkheden. Orkest de Volharding (De Volharding 003)

Murder in the Dark. A. de Man (hpd) (NM Classics 92038)

Toccata americana; Echo. B. Berman (pf) (Kunststichting Golf)

Toccata americana. A. de Man (hpd) (HGM CD 02)

Twee koralen. Netherlands Saxophone Quartet (Composers' Voice CV 8002)

Peter-Jan Wagemans

THE HAGUE, 7 SEPTEMBER 1952

If the term 'Dutch music' denotes music that is compressed, concise and exact, then the music of Peter-Jan Wagemans is un-Dutch. His works for large orchestra, in particular, consist of forceful chord blocks that take their time to resound, are extravagantly colorful, ecstatic like Messiaen, but more restless and capricious, and sooner related to Matthijs Vermeulen than Willem Pijper, to use pre-war points of reference.

Wagemans studied the organ (taking his final exam in 1974), composition (1975) and music theory (1977) at the Royal Conservatory in The Hague. He also worked in the conservatory's electronic studio. After concluding his studies in The Hague with the Prize for Composition, he studied with Klaus Huber in Freiburg. From 1978 to 1986 he taught music theory at the Royal Conservatory and since 1984 he has taught composition at the Rotterdam Conservatory. Since 1995 he has also been the artistic director of the Rotterdam Doelen Ensemble.

In 1971 Wagemans was overwhelmed by a performance he heard of Bernd-Alois Zimmermann's opera *Die Soldaten* at the Holland Festival. So much so, in fact, that even while he was studying composition with Jan van Vlijmen, he attempted to recompose the overture of this work in his own manner.

In an article in *Key Notes*, a journal aimed at promoting Dutch music abroad, the composer himself listed the music that has most influenced him: late-Romantic German works, Strauss, Skryabin (the last six piano sonatas), French Romantic organ music and film music (whose influence is evident in the first movements of *Romance*, *Muziek I*, as well as in the Two piano pieces op.5, plus jazz, improvised music and music in the Dutch style (in *Alla marcia*, *Fragmenten* and *As I Opened Fire*); then there is the music of Perotin, Bach, Stravinsky and Messiaen (in *Cantata*, *Octet* and *Irato*). The first group is emotional, using key words like 'beauty' and 'dream', the second is aggressive, and the third monumental and detached. Naturally, he also combines these influences, as in *Muziek I* and *II*.

Aside from his complex, austerely composed pieces, Wagemans has also written more spontaneous works, the smaller-scale chamber music in particular providing more relaxed moments. There is a conspicuous contrast between the colossal expansiveness of sound in the series of *Muzieken* and the mercurial cartoon style of the piano piece *As I Opened Fire*. In his later work, the con-

trast between orchestral and chamber music disappears.

Wagemans reserves a special role for such instruments as the tuba and trombone. In *Muziek I* (1974) low brass instruments are prominently featured (a characteristic shared with other of Wagemans' compositions) and in *Muziek II* (1977, rev. 1979) a group of brass instruments is pitted against a divided string ensemble. The premiere of this work was performed by the Südwestfunk Symphony Orchestra Baden-Baden, conducted by Ernest Bour, at the Donaueschinger Musiktage für Zeitgenössische Tonkunst in 1979. *Muziek IIIa*, for soloists, choir and instrumental ensemble, has a 'b' version for wind (1986, rev. 1987) in which two Wagner tubas, four horns and two bugles form an ensemble set against the ripieno of the rest of the wind instruments and percussion.

In *Irato* (1983, rev. 1990), for orchestra, five anvils are added to the percussion ensemble; in an unbridled expressionistic idiom, the orchestra is transformed into a furious machine. *Romance* (1981, rev. 1983), for violin and orchestra, by contrast, has a dreamy and tender sound in which the composer aspires to an accessible style that refers to the *Romances* of Beethoven. He came across an old, worn 45 rpm recording of these and sought to transform its dilapidated romanticism into a veritable 'Drama ohne Worte'.

In 1976 Wagemans discovered the twelfth-century organum style of Magister Perotin, music that had a strong influence on the *Cantata* (1979) and its arrangement in the *Octet* (1980) for two clarinets, two bassoons and string quartet. This marked the beginning of a period in which all of his music included long pedal points. *Viderunt omnes* (1988) is even more directly an homage to Perotin, without actually being a copy of its style.

However, musical sources are not the only catalysts of his work. He has also found inspiration in extra-musical sources such as the Gothic cathedral for *Muziek II*, and Orson Welles' film *Citizen Kane* for *Rosebud* (1988), for which he received the Matthijs Vermeulen Prize in 1990. *Walk on water* (1988), for piccolo trumpet and ensemble, originated in memories of Sunday school. From its position behind the ensemble, the high trumpet plays long, quasi-Gregorian melodies in which colorful fragments of chorales are left hanging like little bells. Wagemans explains: 'As I envisioned it, the trumpet walks on water and playing through the back of my mind was the distant memory of a color print I was given in Sunday school of Jesus walking on water.'

In *Klang* (1986) Wagemans quotes *Der ferne Klang* by Franz Schreker. 'I wanted to make a far-off sound', he says, 'that went beyond the late-Romantic music of Schreker and thus give life to the dream of the protagonist, the composer Fritz.'

Wagemans' most recent work takes a post-modern stance, with classical architecture as its central focus, but employing a variety of compositional means and aesthetics. A work of art, he believes, forms itself only in the listener's perception; hence, he does not predetermine the structure of the work, but rather the way it can be perceived. He presents an array of archetypes as a 'source' of memories, but the continuations of these may either confirm or disturb the images. This built-in variable in perception is particularly evident in his work of the 1990s for large forces, such as the *Requiem* (1992, rev. 1994), for string orchestra and percussion, *Panthalassa* (1994), for large wind ensemble, and the orchestral piece *De stad en de engel* [The city and the angel] (1996).

Particularly noteworthy is the Seventh Symphony, two movements of which were performed in 1998 by the Residentie Orchestra. The subject is Beethovian; the rhythm of the first movement refers to this composer's Seventh. The third movement is dedicated to the dying Goethe, a search for the light Goethe sought in his last moments. The work is rich in contrasts and all support is relative in the end.

ERNST VERMEULEN

COMPOSITIONS

VOCAL: *Nachts* (Kafka), Mez, orch, op. 2 (manuscript) (1971, rev. 1975); *Cantata* (Ecclesiastes 4:1-3), mix.choir, 2 cl, 2 bn, op. 14 (1979); *Muziek III, 'Europa na de regen'* (Apocalypse, Mallarmé, Tennyson), soloists, mix.choir, instr.ens, op. 19a (1984); *Wie* (Joyce/Franken), A, 2 cl, 2 hn, op. 27 (also version Mez, pf, 1987); *Al de stromen vrolijk handen* (after Psalm 98), mix.choir, fl (1989); *Four Songs* – Reger (Boelitz, Dehmel, Braungart, Bierbaum), instrumentation S, orch (1989)

CHAMBER MUSIC: *Twee kleine pianostukken*, op. 1 (1970); *Two Piano Pieces*, op. 5 (1972); *Wind Quintet*, op. 6 (1973); *Saxophone*

Quartet, op. 8 (1975, rev. 1976); *Drie kleine stukken*, 4 rec (1979); *Octet*, 2 cl, 2 bn, 2 vl, vla, vc, op. 16 (1980); *Muziek*, b-cl, pf, op. 18 (1981); *Ira*, 2 pf 8h, op. 20a (1983, rev. 1984); *Parade*, trb, 6 instr., op. 21 (1984); *As I Opened Fire*, pf, op. 22 (1985); *Trio*, cl, vl, pf, op. 23 (1985); *Great Expectations*, vl, pf, op. 26 (1986); *Het landschap*, pf (1989); *Trio*, hn, vl, pf (1992); *Lux*, org (1992); *Solo*, hn (1992); *Wind Quintet no. 2* (1993); *Quartet*, 4 rec (1993); *Concerto*, 2 pf (1993); *Ewig*, perc, pf (1994)

ORCHESTRA: *Symphony*, orch, op. 3 (1972); *Overture*, brass instr, perc, op. 4 (1972); *Muziek I*, wind instr, timp, op. 7 (1974); *Muziek II*, orch, op. 10 (1977, rev. 1979);

Alla marcia, tb, instr.ens, op. 11 (1977); *Romance*, vl, orch, op. 17 (1981, rev. 1983); *Irato*, orch, op. 20b (1983, rev. 1990); *Klang*, orch, op. 24 (1986); *Viderunt omnes*, instr.ens (1988); *Rosebud (The Last Forest)*, orch, w.choir ad lib. (1988); *Muziek IV*, instr.ens (1988); *Walk on water*, picc tpt, instr.ens (1988); *Piano Sonate no. 9 – Skrjabin*, instr.ens (1988); *De draak, het huis, de zon, de boom en de vijver*, brass qt, orch (1991); *Dreams, Four Pieces*, orch (1991); *Requiem*, str.orch, perc (1992, rev. 1994); *Panthalassa*, large wind ens (1994); *De stad en de engel*, orch (1996); *Symphony no. 7* (1998)

Saxophone Quartet. Netherlands Saxophone Quartet (Composers' Voice CV 8002)

PUBLICATIONS
'Requiem: a composer's analysis', *Key Notes*, 29, 1995/4, p. 16-19

BIBLIOGRAPHY
P. Luttikhuis: *Peter-Jan Wagemans : Het gaat om het mozaïek*. Brochure Donemus, Amsterdam

DISCOGRAPHY
Alla marcia. T. Oostendorp (tb), Residentie Orchestra, cond. H. Vonk (6814 781/786)
As I Opened Fire. G. Bouwhuis (pf) (Composers' Voice CVCD 8703)
Great Expectations. I. van Keulen (vl), R. Brautigam (pf) (NM Classics 92043)
Quartet. Amsterdam Loeki Stardust Quartet (CCS 8996)
Het landschap; Concerto. Tomoko Mukaiyama (pf), Fred Oldenburg (pf) (Attacca)
Panthalassa; Requiem; Alla marcia. W. Boeykens (cl), Symphonic Band of the Rotterdam Conservatory, cond. A. van beek, Netherlands Radio Chamber Orchestra, cond. R. de Leeuw, T. Oostendorp (tb), Residentie Orchestra, cond. H. Vonk (Composers' Voice CV 56)
Romance; Muziek I; Octet. Various soloists, Residentie Orchestra, cond. O. Mága, F. Layer and E. Bour (Composers' Voice 8503)
Rosebud; Muziek II; Viderunt omnes; Dreams. Residentie Orchestra, cond. J. van Steen, members of the Choir of the Royal Conservatory, cond. P.J. Wagemans, Südwestfunk Orchester, cond. E. Bour, Xenakis Ensemble, cond. H. Kerstens, Netherlands Ballet Orchestra, cond. L. Vis (Composers' Voice CV 28)

Diderik Wagenaar

UTRECHT, 10 MAY 1946

Quantitatively speaking, Diderik Wagenaar's oeuvre is not large. Over the thirty years since 1969, he has composed a mere 22 pieces, which breaks down to fourteen months expended per composition. Perhaps it is through this that his music makes such a well-considered impression and that each piece marks a stage in a development that carried him to various fronts, from one extreme to the other: from Igor Stravinsky to Alban Berg, from complexity to translucence, from rhythm to melody, and from a certain aggressiveness to lyricism. Along the way Wagenaar has bridged the gap between the rhythmically pulsating, anti-Romantic music of Stravinsky and the emotionally charged, expressionistic idiom of the Second Viennese School.

Wagenaar's early work is said to be a product of the The Hague School, a term that refers to the style of composers affiliated with the Royal Conservatory in the 1960s and 1970s. Their music was described by the composer Gene Carl – in an article about Wagenaar published in the music journal *Key Notes* – as 'loud, aggressive, rhythmically energetic music that shuns neo-Romantic sentiment and is often amplified or electronically manipulated.'

Strictly speaking, Wagenaar was not a composition student at the conservatory in The Hague. He studied the piano there, with Simon Admiraal, and music theory with Jan van Dijk, Hein Kien and Rudolf Koumans. His great hero was Thelonious Monk (whose music he would passionately play through on the piano from the time he was sixteen) and he so admired the new music of Pierre Boulez and Bruno Maderna that he never considered taking lessons in composition. Still, stimulated by the analysis lessons of Kees van Baaren, Wagenaar did begin to compose. And, since 1990 he has been teaching composition at the Royal Conservatory.

Tam Tam (1978-1979) is Wagenaar's only work that might be considered a true product of the The Hague School. He wrote this piece for the Hoketus ensemble, which was begun in 1976 by Louis Andriessen and students of the Royal Conservatory in response to American minimal music. *Tam Tam* is dominated by a strong rhythmic pulse (consciously peppered with irregularities) and a harmonically driven buildup working to a climax, all in combination with the process-like repetitive techniques of minimal music.

Among his compositions of this period, *Tam Tam* is stylistically speaking most clearly Wagenaar's work. The first piece of his recognized oeuvre, *Kalei-*

dofonen I (1969), for alto saxophone and piano, literally presents a kaleidoscopic view of different styles, employing such diverse ingredients as a sluggish jazz theme, clusters, harmonics, and pointillist, serial-sounding passages. In *Liederen* [Songs] (1976), for brass instruments, two pianos and double bass, a be-bopish opening theme and a melodic variant from Wagner's *Tristan und Isolde* are interwoven in a layered structure. Contrasting elements (such as chromaticism versus diatonicism, homophony set against polyphony and unison, and various forms of polyrhythm) alternate and are superimposed on each other. The energetic chord repetitions are a reference to the The Hague School, while the syncopated jazz melody in the beginning touches on the composer's background and the Wagner quotation presages his later work.

Complexity through structural layering reaches a peak in *Metrum* (1981-1984), for saxophone quartet and orchestra. It is an exciting, grandly conceived piece that builds for some twenty minutes, integrating all the techniques Wagenaar had at his disposal at the time. In 1989 *Metrum* was awarded the Kees van Baaren Prize.

The piece is based on a series of chords and from these are derived its melodies. The chords are sounded at certain points by the entire orchestra, like massive blocks of cast iron, and at other times are unraveled down to single notes plaintively offered by a muted trumpet or lone saxophone. These chords also echo through the various instrumental groups in lightly varied form, creating both harmonic and spatial depth. The various layers run at different speeds, thoroughly disorientating the perception of tempo.

After such complex, overloaded works like *Metrum* and *Limiet* (1985) Wagenaar turned to more translucent pieces, leaving more room for detail, and with drastically pared-down structures. *Tessituur* (1990) for orchestra, *Solenne* (1992) for six percussionists, and *Lent, vague, indécis* (1993) for ensemble, are typical of the transition. Rhythmic drive disappears; the iron-clad wind chorales make way for transparent timbres in *Solenne* and stationary expanses of string sound in the other two works. *Lent, vague, indécis* is an exceedingly contemplative interpretation of Skryabin's Prelude op.74 no.4, for piano. In

Tessituur, the oboe and English horn play a complementary melody, the oboe continually repeating a chromatic three-tone motif a tone higher and the music slowly ascending until it evaporates in the most rarefied of atmospheres.

With *Trois poèmes en prose* (1995) for soprano and orchestra and to texts by Baudelaire, for which Wagenaar was awarded the Matthijs Vermeulen Prize in 1996, his music definitively gravitated from its objective, energetic and somewhat aggressive sound toward a lyrical and more vulnerable one. The Baudelaire songs seem to mark the end of a phase, as was also the case with *Metrum*, and Wagenaar appears to have completed the synthesis of Stravinsky and the Second Viennese School. The work's instrumental accompaniment displays the clarity and superpersonal style propagated by Stravinsky, while the vocal part is characterized by a lyricism reminiscent of Alban Berg's *Altenberg-Lieder* (of which Wagenaar made a new arrangement in 1985 for soprano and ensemble). Like Berg in his opera *Lulu*, Wagenaar seeks in these songs to integrate tonality and atonality.

The persistence Wagenaar has shown for integration and synthesis while still maintaining his own sound is perhaps a remnant of the radicalness of the The Hague School. But just as one voice seeks the other in the complementary techniques for which he shows such affinity (hocket, alternating chordal treatment), synthesis in Wagenaar's music is an essential tool for balancing the contradictions in his musical character and uniting the Dionysian with the Apollonian.

PAY-UUN HIU

COMPOSITIONS
CHAMBER MUSIC: *Kaleidofonen*, a-sax, pf (1969); *Praxis*, 2 pf, ob ad lib. (1973, rev. 1990); *Canapé*, pf, cl, vl, vc (1980); *Stadium*, 2 pf (1981); *Limiet*, str.qt (1985); *La volta*, pf (1989); *Le chat*, Mez (1990); *Cat Music*, 2 vl (1994); *La caccia*, trb (1995, rev. 1996)

ENSEMBLE: *Liederen (Canzonas)*, 15 brass instr, 2 pf, db (1976, rev. 1978); *Tam Tam*, instr.ens (1978); *Solenne*, 6 perc (1992); *Lent, vague, indécis*, instr.ens (1993)

ORCHESTRA: *Metrum*, sax.qt, orch (1984, rev. 1986); *Crescent*, wind orch (1985); *Festina-lente*, tpt, brass orch, perc (1988); *Triforium*, wind band, perc (1988); *Tessituur*, orch (1990); *Trois poèmes en prose* (Baudelaire), S, orch (1995)

PUBLICATIONS
'Liederen : an analysis', *Key Notes*, 10, 1979/2, p. 28-32
'Tam Tam', *Key Notes*, 11, 1980/1, p. 5-6

BIBLIOGRAPHY
M. Altena: 'A fossilised abstraction', *Key Notes*, 23, 1986, p. 9
H. Calis: 'Rapidity creating the illusion of slowness', *Key Notes*, 22, 1985/2, p. 35
G. Carl: 'A sense of escalation : Diderik Wagenaar's discrete evolution', *Key Notes*, 24, 1987, p. 14-22
J. Kolsteeg: 'Alsof het hart overslaat : Diderik Wagenaar, componist van de Haagse

School', *Mens en Melodie*, vol. 49, 1994, p. 278-284

J. Kolsteeg: 'In dialogue with beauty', *Key Notes*, 28, 1994/2, p. 7

A. Roth: 'Ik zit vaak tot twaalf te tellen', *Mededelingenblad Vrienden van het Schönberg Ensemble*, no. 17, 1993, p. 5-9

L. Samama: Sleeve notes Composers' Voice CV 29 (see discography)

E. Schönberger: 'The hole in the Dome', *Key Notes*, 23, 1986, p. 4

DISCOGRAPHY

Cat Music. M. van Kooten (vl), M. Mars (vl) (Rumori 95/96)

Fünf Orchesterlieder nach Ansichtkarten-Texten von Peter Altenberg – op. 4, Alban Berg, arr. D. Wagenaar). A. Auger (S), Netherlands Radio Chamber Orchestra, cond. R. de Leeuw (Holland Festival Highlights 88 RNWO 88085/86)

Tessituur. Netherlands Radio Chamber Orchestra, cond. E. Spanjaard (BFO A-17)

La volta; Stadium; Solenne; Songs (Canzonas); Metrum. G.Bouwhuis, C. van Zeeland and H. Nijenhuis (pf), Percussion Group The Hague, Netherlands Wind Ensemble, cond. A. van Beek and G. van Keulen, Aurelia Saxophone Quartet, Netherlands Radio Symphony Orchestra, cond. L. Vis (Composers' Voice CV 29)

Johan Wagenaar

UTRECHT, I NOVEMBER 1862 – THE HAGUE, 17 JUNE 1941

Johan (Johannes) Wagenaar was the son of Johanna Wagenaar and Cypriaan Gerard Berger van Hengst. Social differences made a marriage between the two impossible, a circumstance which did not make the youth of the six Wagenaar children any easier.

Johan Wagenaar gained his first musical impressions via the church organ and the music of the civic guard ensemble; he was equally fascinated by the barrel organ he ran after on the streets in the company of the young Catharina van Rennes. When Wagenaar reached the age of fourteen he met Richard Hol, at that time the director of the Music School of the Society for the Advancement of Music. Wagenaar took violin and piano lessons from Martinus W. Petri and Gerrit Veerman, who later gave him organ lessons as well. Richard Hol taught him harmony and counterpoint, lessons probably paid for by his father. In 1885 Wagenaar was appointed piano tutor at the Utrecht Music School. From 1887 on he was in charge of a special class for advanced pianists and also taught music theory and composition. There are indications that Wagenaar had composition lessons for some time in 1892 with Heinrich von Herzogenberg in Berlin, but it is also possible that he made a study trip lasting some months to Germany and Austria.

In 1888 Wagenaar succeeded Richard Hol as the organist of the Utrecht Cathedral. Furthermore, he acquired the position of conductor of the Utrecht a cappella choir and became director of the Utrecht Male Choir Society in 1896. With Richard Hol falling seriously ill, Wagenaar became acting director of the music school during that same year. This temporary position was turned into a permanent one after the death of Hol in 1904. Occasionally, Wagenaar appeared as a conductor and in this capacity he introduced the symphonies of Mahler and others to Utrecht audiences. However, he remained first and foremost a pedagogue: many talented composers, such as Jacob van Domselaer, Alexander Voormolen, Peter van Anrooy and Willem Pijper, were molded by him.

In 1887 Wagenaar was admitted to the Shelfish Club, an association within the Utrecht Art Club that distinguished itself by its strong predilection for conviviality. For the members of this club he composed one of his most popular works, the 'humoristic cantata' *De Schipbreuk* [The Shipwreck] using texts by Gerrit van der Linden, writing under the pseudonym of 'De Schoolmeester'

[The Schoolmaster]. Within the circles of the Utrecht Art Club he also met Dina van Valkenburg, whom he married in 1897. She bore him two daughters, Nelly and Johanna, both of whom became pianists.

In 1916 Wagenaar received an honorary degree from the Senate of the State University of Utrecht. Shortly afterward, in 1919, he was appointed director of the Royal Conservatory in The Hague, a position he held until his retirement in 1937. As a pedagogue he devoted himself passionately to the cause of improving education. For example, he pressed for a thorough knowledge of music theory and did not allow practical exams to be taken before theoretical

knowledge had been tested and approved. In addition to modernizing educational forms, he also drew attention to the improvement of pension schemes for teaching staff and supporting personnel.

Although an extremely reserved human being, Wagenaar found in his music a way to express his feelings. His early compositions, especially *De Schipbreuk*, show a humorous streak. Wagenaar considered his sense of humor typically Dutch and consequently classified himself as a Dutch composer, unlike Diepenbrock, whom he called an international composer. All things considered, the text of *De Schipbreuk* is not merely nonsensical. De Schoolmeester lived in the first half of the nineteenth century, a time of rigid conventions and narrow-mindedness, and Wagenaar undoubtedly recognized a great deal in that which had moved De Schoolmeester to write this grotesque poem. Composed for soprano, tenor and bass soloists, mixed choir, piano, percussion and 'storm'-instruments, the music as an illustration of the text is characterized by a sequence of parodies. At the same time, the score contains a variety of modernist harmonies and modulations raising the entirety above the quality of an occasional piece.

His symphonic compositions can also be characterized as discerning and to the point. The overture *Cyrano de Bergerac*, dating from 1905, contains some seven themes, each of which can be traced back to a specific trait in the character of the central figure in Rostand's play. The symphonic poem *Saul en David* was composed in 1906 on the occasion of the Rembrandt celebrations. As far as orchestration techniques are concerned, Wagenaar's symphonic works are clearly influenced by Richard Strauss and to a lesser degree by those of Hector Berlioz. Wagenaar was able to give full vent to his art of musical characterization in Shakespearean roles in for example *De getemde feeks* [The Taming of the Shrew], *Driekoningenavond* [Twelfth Night] and *Koning Jan* [The Life and Death of King John]. Incidentally, Wagenaar did not get acquainted with these plays until 1888, when the first complete Dutch edition of Shakespeare's works was published, translated by Leendert A.J. Burgersdijk.

The few organ works of Wagenaar betray the influence of Bach as well as that of Mendelssohn, the latter especially in the *Introductie en fuga* op.3. The two operas composed by Wagenaar appear somewhat outdated, notably in terms of librettos. *De Doge van Venetië* [The Doge of Venice] and *De Cid* [The Cid] now hover on the verge of the ridiculous. And yet Wagenaar's orchestral, choral and organ works are distinguished by the composer's mastery of his craft and they exhibit an enthusiasm that has made him popular, not only during his lifetime, but after his death as well.

WILMA ROEST

COMPOSITIONS

SONGS: *Fünf Lieder*, v, pf, op. 6; *Aveux de Phèdre*, v, orch, op. 41 (1935)

CHOIR: *Drie canons*, w.choir, op. 28; *Des Winters als het regent*, w.choir, op. 31; *Chanson*, mix.choir, op. 30 (1917); *Canticum*, mix.choir, op. 33 (1923); *Zweedsche lucifermarsch*, w.choir, pf/orch, op. 16a; *Fantasie over een Oud-Nederlandsch lied*, w.choir, pf/orchk, op. 19 (1899); *Calme des nuits*, mix.choir, pf/orch, op. 16; *Ode aan de vriendschap*, mix.choir, pf/orch; *De vrolijke zangles*, mix.choir, pf/orch

CANTATA: *De Schipbreuk*, op. 8b (1889); *Proefzingen* (1904); *De fortuinlijke kist*, op. 29 (1916); *Jupiter Amans*, op. 35 (1924)

OPERA: *De Doge van Venetië*, op. 20 (1898); *De Cid*, op. 27 (1912-1913)

PIANO: *Impromptu a la Mazurka*, op. 2 (1880?); *Drie klavierstukken*; *Marche burlesque*; *Marcia Funebre* (1904); *Marsch van* de Utrechtse Shelfish-club (from: *De Schipbreuk*)

ORGAN: *Introductie en fuga op. 3* (1885); *Intrada* (1914); *Marcia Solemne*; *Koraalbewerking 'O Haupt voll Blut und Wunden'*, op.12, no. 1; *Inleiding en fuga over een Russisch thema*, op. 47 (1939)

CARILLON: *Utrechts jolijt*

WINDS: *Koraalfantasie 'Komt, dankt nu allen God'*, op. 33c (1923); *Intrada*, op. 43, no. 11 (1934); *Hymne voor Kor Kuiler* (1935); *Al uwe boos' aenslagen*, op. 43, no. 3; *Dubbelcanon in de Quart*, op. 43, no. 10 (1936); *Ein feste Burg*, op. 43, no. 5; *Gelukkig is het land*, op. 43, no. 17 (1936); *Grave*, op. 43, no. 1; *Hoort allegaar*, op. 43, no. 7; *Hymne* (1936); *Nobelman*, op. 43, no. 13 (1938); *Preludium solemne*, op. 43, no. 14 (1938); *Wilhelmus van Nassauwe*

STRINGS: *Andante*; *Andantino*; *String Quintet*

ORCHESTRA (WITHOUT SOLO INSTR., UN-
LESS OTHERWISE STATED): *Frithjof's Meer-*
fahrt, op. 5 (1886); *Fancy-Fair wals,* op. 8b;
Ouverture Koning Jan, op. 9 (1891); *Concert-*
ouverture Frühlingsgewalt, op. 11; *Levens-*
zomer, op. 21 (1903); *Ouverture Cyrano de*
Bergerac, op. 23 (1905); *Saul en David,* op.
24 (1906): *Ouverture De getemde feeks,* op.
25 (1909); *Marcia funebre,* op. 26 (1912);
Sinfonietta, op. 32 (1917); *Romantisch inter-*
mezzo, op. 13 (1923); *Avondfeest en mars,* op.
34 (1923); *Ouverture driekoningenavond,* op.
36 (1927); *Wiener Dreivierteltakt,* op. 38
(1929); *Ouverture De philosophische prinses,*
op. 39 (1932); *Intermezzo pastorale,* op. 37
(1933); *Larghetto,* ob, orch, op. 40 (1934);
Ouverture Amphitrion, op. 45 (1938); *Ko-*
raalfantasie 'Halleluja, eeuwig dank en eere',
op. 46 (1939); *Elverhoi,* op. 48 (1940);

BIBLIOGRAPHY
Archive Johan Wagenaar: The Hague,
Gemeentemuseum, Music Archives
    E. Reeser: *Een eeuw Nederlandse muziek :*
1815-1915. Amsterdam, Querido, 1950, 2/1986
    W. Roest: *Johan Wagenaar : biografische*
verkenning. Doctoral dissertation University of
Utrecht, 1988

DISCOGRAPHY
Concert Overture Frühlingsgewalt, Frithjof's
Meerfahrt. Netherlands Radio Symphony Orchestra, cond. J. van Steen (NM Classics
92090)
    Hymnus de ascensione Domine. Netherlands
Chamber Choir, cond. U. Gronostay (NM Clas-
sics 92065)
    Orchestral Works. Royal Concertgebouw Or-
chestra, cond. R. Chailly (includes: *Ouverture*
De getemde feeks; Saul en David; Driekoningen-
avond; Ouverture De Cid; Amphitrion, Wiener
Dreivierteltakt; Ouverture Cyrano de Bergerac)
(DECCA 425 833-2)
    Ouverture Cyrano de Bergerac. Residentie Or-
chestra, cond. A. Lombard (Olympia OCD 504)
    Ouverture De getemde feeks. Concertgebouw
Orchestra, cond. W. Mengelberg (BFO A-4)

Unico Wilhelm van Wassenaer

DELDEN, 9 NOVEMBER 1692 – THE HAGUE, 9 NOVEMBER 1766

Unico Wilhelm van Wassenaer (Unico Wilhelm, count of Wassenaer Obdam in full) was descended from the celebrated Dutch noble family of Van Wasse-naer. Unico Wilhelm (the first name is the Latin form of the Groningen male name Oene) was born at Twickel Castle near Delden (Overijssel), the son of Jacob van Wassenaer Obdam (son of the famous admiral of the same name) and Adriana Sophia van Raesfelt. Unico's father served his country as a general at first and later as a diplomat. For his activities in the latter position he was awarded the title of Count by Johann Wilhelm, Elector Palatine in Düsseldorf.

The Van Wassenaer family upheld a certain tradition of amateur music making in its residences in The Hague and Unico Wilhelm must surely have received his music lessons in the line of this very tradition. It is almost certain that Quirinus van Blankenburg (1654-1739), organist in The Hague, was one of his teachers, as well as Carlo Francesco Ricciotti detto Bacciccia (Bacciccia = Genoese; 1680-1756), also a musician from The Hague. The remote possibili-ty also exists that the musical serviceman Johann Heinrich von Weissenburg, alternatively known as Giovanni Henrico Albicastro (c.1660-1730), belonged to the above group of teachers.

Although Unico was not the only musically gifted member of the Van Wassenaer family, he certainly was the most susceptible one. As early as 1713, barely twenty years of age, he composed three very creditable recorder sonatas which he dedicated to the young German nobleman Friedrich Ludwig of Württemberg, a pupil of Van Blankenburg who lived in The Hague at the time. Around 1718 Unico Wilhelm made his *grand tour* of Europe, almost cer-tainly visiting both Paris and Italy. Undoubtedly he was receptive to any musi-cal influences he encountered. Back in the Netherlands, he conducted the life of an eighteenth-century Dutch regent-nobleman. He acquired several impor-tant official positions, was admitted into the knighthood of Overijssel, later on into that of 'Holland', accomplished several diplomatic missions (Cologne/ Bonn, Paris), committed himself to the administration of his country estates and manors (Wassenaar in Zuid-Holland, Obdam and bordering regions in Noord-Holland and Twickel in Overijssel, among other domains), and was an art collector and a musician. Presumably Unico Wilhelm played the violin and keyboard instruments, i.e. the harpsichord and organ.

In 1723 Unico Wilhelm married the Frisian Dodonea Lucia van Goslinga

(1702-1769). After the death of Johan Hendrik van Wassenaer Obdam (1683-1745), his elder brother, all titles and possessions of the Obdam-branch of the Van Wassenaer family passed to him. Of his five children (four sons and a daughter), only two sons lived long enough to become adults. These two, Jacob Jan (1724-1779) and Carel George (1733-1800), also enjoyed recognition as amateur musicians, as did the wife of the latter, the Amsterdam patrician's daughter Jacoba Elisabeth van Strijen (1741-1816), a pupil of, among others, the Amsterdam organist Conrad Friedrich Hurlebusch. Unico Wilhelm died on 9 November 1766, on his seventy-fourth birthday.

Van Wassenaer's musical pursuits were shaped by the context of the class to which he belonged, namely the upper echelons of Dutch society. In 1725 he joined a collegium musicum in The Hague. This association included members such as Willem Count Bentinck (son of Hans Willem Bentinck, the confidant of William III), his brother Carel Bentinck, Unico Wilhelm's brother-in-law Guido Pape (Marquis of Saint-Auban), and furthermore several high-ranking servicemen and rich members of the Walloon Reformed Church in The Hague. The group was chaired by the musician Carlo Ricciotti, referred to above.

Unico Wilhelm's principal composition, the six so-called *Concerti armonici*, composed for four violins, viola, violoncello and basso continuo, undoubtedly materialized within the context of this company. The instrumentation probably reflects the musical possibilities of Unico Wilhelm's circles. Although there is a constant interplay of soli and tutti in the four-part writing for the seven instruments, there is no distinct division between solo and tutti instruments as in the concerto grosso. The concertos are all in four movements (slow-fast-slow-fast, in keeping with the recorder sonatas). Generally, the first movement has a prefatory character, the second is a traditional ensemble fugue, often titled 'da capella' (church style), the third is an 'affettuoso', usually in a minor key, the fourth movement a lively and fast finale. Stylistically, the concertos display an abundance of mostly Italian influences.

Apart from the recorder sonatas and string concertos mentioned, Van Wassenaer definitely wrote the psalm motet *Laudate Dominum*, the autograph of which is still at Twickel Castle. Some instrumental works mentioned in old inventories have not been retraced.

As it happens, Unico Wilhelm van Wassenaer is a fairly recent addition to the canon of Dutch composers. Only in 1979 did the Dutch musicologist Albert Dunning discover that this nobleman was the composer of the six *Concertini* or *Concerti armonici*, until then usually attributed to Ricciotti, or to Giovanni Battista Pergolesi. The first attribution is a result of the fact that Ricciotti prepared the first (anonymous) edition of the VI *Concerti armonici* in The Hague in 1740, the latter as a result of the addition of the name of Pergolesi to a nineteenth-century copy of the score. Thanks to Dunning's discovery, the history of Dutch music has gained yet another important master.

RUDOLF RASCH

COMPOSITIONS

Sonate di flauto a solo et basso per il cembalo... (F major, G minor, G minor)
Autograph: Rostock, Universitätsbibliothek Mus. saec. XVIII 62
Modern ed.: Three sonatas for alto recorder and basso continuo – circa 1714 / ed. by Albert Dunning and Wim Brabants. Amsterdam, Groen, 1992

Six Concertini for four violins, violas, cello and bc
Autograph: Twickel (Overijssel, The Netherlands)
Facs. ed.: in the monograph by Dunning (see bibliography)
First ed.: *VI Concerti armonici a quattro violini obligati, alto viola, violoncello obligato e basso continuo.* – The Hague, Alexis Magito (Rotterdam) for Carlo [Francesco] Ricciotti detto Bacciccia, [1740]
Reprints: London, John Walsh, [1755]; London, John Johnson, [c 1757]
19th Century copies of the score: Washington (DC), Library of Congress, Ms. M712, A2 P44; Paris, Bibliothèque du Conservatoire, Ms. D 12.539
Modern ed.: 'Giovanni Battista Pergolesi' : Sei concertini per strumenti ad arco / ed. Filippo Caffarelli. Rome, Gli Amici della Musica da Camera, 1940; 'Carlo Ricciotti

(Pergolesi?)' : Concertini für vier Violinen, Viola, Violoncello und Basso continuo / ed. Philipp Hinnenthal. Kassel, Bärenreiter, 1951-1959

BIBLIOGRAPHY
A. Dunning: *Count Unico Wilhelm van Wassenaer (1692-1766) : a master unmasked or the Pergolesi-Ricciotti puzzle solved.* Buren, Knuf, 1980 (33 pages preface, followed by the Twickel autograph of the Concerti armonici in facsimile and the motet Laudate Dominum in facsimile and transcription)
Unico Wilhelm van Wassenaer 1692-1766 : componist en staatsman, ed. R. Rasch and K. Vlaardingerbroek. Hilversum, Centrum Nederlandse Muziek / Zutphen, Walburg Press, 1993

DISCOGRAPHY
Concerto armonico no. 1. Residentie Orchestra, cond. T. Koopman (Olympia OCD 501)
Sonata no. 1. Trio de L'Oustal (NM Classics 92101)
Sonatas for recorder and bc. R. Kanji (rec) a.o. (Globe GLO 5101)
Sonatas for recorder and bc. P. van Houwelingen (rec, tra-fl) a.o. (1993, Erasmus WVH 078)
Unico Wilhelm van Wassenaer : 6 concerti armonici (attrib. Pergolesi). Camerata Bern, cond.

Th. Füri (Archiv 427 138-2)

Unico Wilhelm van Wassenaer : Sei concerti armonici. Combattimento Consort Amsterdam, cond. J.W. de Vriend (NM Classics 92030)

Sei concerti armonici. Combattimento Consort Amsterdam, cond. J.W. de Vriend (NM Special 92097)

Wassenaer : Concerti armonici (formerly attributed to Pergolesi). Brandenburg Consort, cond. R. Goodman (Hyperion CDA 66670)

Van Wassenaer : 6 concerti armonici. Amsterdam Baroque Orchestra, cond. T. Koopman (Erato ECD 75395)

Henri Zagwijn

NIEUWER AMSTEL, 17 JULY 1878 – THE HAGUE, 25 OCTOBER 1954

Henri Zagwijn was born the son of an actor in Nieuwer Amstel. He received no systematic musical education, but acquired his knowledge from contacts with various professional musicians, such as Blumentritt, a conductor who had him make arrangements for wind bands. In 1912, Zagwijn completed his great work *Der Zauberlehrling*, the score and piano reduction of which were published in Germany. He submitted it for performance during the Netherlands Music Festival in 1912, but it was not selected. Its premiere was conducted by A.B.H. Verhey in January 1914, but the outbreak of World War I led to the cancellation of several performances scheduled to take place abroad. It was performed again in 1931 by the Rotterdam Toonkunst Choir, the local chapter of the Society for the Advancement of Music, under the baton of Willem Pijper.

Despite the large number of works he completed, composing was not Henri Zagwijn's profession. He taught at a primary school in Rotterdam and, in addition, held a number of organizational positions in the field of music. Together with, among others, Sem Dresden and Daniel Ruyneman, Zagwijn was one of the founders of the Netherlands Society for the Advancement of Modern Music in 1918. During this period he felt united with the more revolutionary musical minds of the time. He turned away from obsolete Romanticism, which for him 'clouded the emotional value of music', although he realized at the same time that a too extreme modernism 'could rigidify the element of feeling in music.' For him the essential issue was whether a twentieth-century sound idiom would still allow the creation of works 'capable of imparting new, moving experiences to people's spiritual lives.' In line with his anthroposophical convictions, he sought a solution to the dilemma that a radical choice for one of the two extremes would result in an inevitable impoverishment of the musical idiom: either in its emotional power to move or in its unavoidable desire for technical progress.

Between 1920 and 1930 he went through a period of contemplation during which he composed little. He wanted to complete his reflections before delving into a new world of sound. This came about with the composition in 1932 of his Sextet for strings, which Zagwijn himself regarded as a key work. It employs various modern compositional techniques without, he felt, 'losing the true nature of music.' The Sextet was described by the music critic Wouter

Paap as 'one of the most remarkable Dutch compositions of the 1930s.'

Of Zagwijn's remaining major works the following should be mentioned: *Vom Jahreslauf*, which received its first performance under the direction of Eduard Flipse in Rotterdam on 27 April 1940, and *Jaarkrans* [Year cycle], for which he received a government prize in 1947. Directly after the war, he became chairman of Geneco, the Society of Dutch Composers, and a member of the board of Donemus, the publishing house and documentation center of Dutch music, positions he held concurrently for several years. In his publication *De muziek in Nederland in het licht der anthroposophie* [Music in the Netherlands in the light of anthroposophy], Zagwijn takes as his point of departure the view that in

his time, 'Intellectually speaking, the Central European spirit has risen to being an all-embracing spirit of the age.' He noted a revival of the enriching influence of Dutch music on European music, comparable with developments in the sixteenth and seventeenth centuries. Zagwijn attached great importance to the aspiration towards cultural internationalism and anti-chauvinism.

He expressed his anthroposophical vision not only in speeches and writings, but also in music itself. This is evident from the considerable number of works he named after the seasons, or the times of day, such as *O Nacht* (1918), *Morgenzang* [Morning Song] (1937), *Vom Jahreslauf* (1938), *Frühling* (1941), *Winter* (1942), *Van de Jaargetijden* [Of the seasons] (1945), *Dagkrans* [Day cycle] (1946), *Jaarkrans* (1946) and *Zonnegang* [The sun's journey] (1952).

Der Zauberlehrling marks the conclusion of his first creative period. It is firmly anchored in the tonal tradition, despite 'a number of surprising modulations', noted by Wouter Paap. In this work Zagwijn uses the technique of the Leitmotif, as Wagner did in his operas. Instances are the 'motif of the master', the 'motif of the apprentice's joy' and the 'motif of the will'. In 1914, the critic H.W. de Ronde described Zagwijn's clear instrumentation and his instinct for instrumental colors as strong aspects of the work. He added, 'The best instrumental composers are usually the greatest color fantasts; it is also remarkable that these are most numerous among the so-called self-taught composers.' With regard to the art of instrumentation, which he had demonstrated in his Quintet for winds, Zagwijn clearly distinguished himself from his contemporaries.

If *Der Zauberlehrling* was the composer's final essay in the old style, his Suite for wind quintet and piano, written at the request of the Amsterdam Concertgebouw Sextet, was cast in an entirely new mold. Here Zagwijn was searching for a sacral element 'that should find its expression in the sound itself.' Over the course of time he developed polymeter in his music, and in later compositions demonstrated a preference for larger cyclical forms, counterpoint and fugue. In his a cappella works, he joined ranks with the early Dutch masters. He also wrote music for the stage.

JOHAN KOLSTEEG

COMPOSITIONS

SONGS (WITH PIANO UNLESS OTHERWISE STATED): *Galgenlieder* (Morgenstern) (1923); *Cyclus De eenzame wake* (Van de Woestijne); *Het avondgebed* (Greshoff); *Dichterleven* (Perk); *Dichterwijding* (Perk); *Geestelijk lied* (A. Roland Holst); *Ghasel* (Swarth); *Kleenliedjes op kleendichtjes* (Gezelle); *Het klokgebed* (Gezelle); *Het land van Kokanje* (Adama van Scheltema); *Lichtend ontwaken* (Leopold) (1922); *Two Songs* (Rodenbach); *Three Songs* (Wolfson); *Drie liedjes* (Perk); *Stervend licht* (Van Vriesland); *Vom Geisteslicht* (Morgenstern, Novalis); *Zangen der nacht* (Perk); *Weihe-Nacht* (Steiner, Morgenstern), v, harm, pf (1915-1916; *Auferstehung* (Steiner, Morgenstern, Novalis), 2 Mez, harm, pf

OTHER VOCAL WORKS: *Der Zauberlehrling* (Goethe), mix.choir, orch (1912*)*; *Vom Jahreslauf* (Steiner), mix.choir, orch (1938); *De geheime zee* (declamatorio) (A. Roland Holst) (1944); *Het hooglied van Salomo* (declamatorio) (1944); *Dagkrans, Jaarkrans* (Gezelle), GK (1946);

INSTRUMENTAL: *Fantasie in f*, orch (1903?); *Suite*, fl, ob, cl, bn, hn, pf (1912); *Van de daggetijden*, pf (1916); *Drie klankschetsen*, pf (1918); *Nocturne*, fl, eh, cl, hn, bn, hp, cel

(1918); *String Quartet* (1918); *Sylphes*, pf (1919); *Suite fantasque*, pf (1920); *Stemmen*, pf (1921); *Sextet*, 3 vl, vla, 2 vc (1932); *Harpkwintet* (1937); *Pastorale*, fl, ob, pf (1937); *Piano Concerto no. 1* (1939); *Flute Concerto* (1941); *Suite sinfonica*, 2 pf (1943); *Petite suite*, 2 pf (1944); *Suite*, pf (1945); *Trio*, vl, vla, vc (1946) *Piano Concerto no. 2 (Concertante II?)* (1946); *Musik zur Eurhythmie*, pf; *Ontwaken*, pf; *Vroolijke herinnering*, pf; *Lichte klanken*, pf 4h; *Image*, vl, pf; *Andante*, fl, pf

MUSIC FOR THE THEATRE: *Toneelmuziek bij Antigone* (Sophocles) (1946); *Lucifer* (Vondel) (1947); *Jephta* (Vondel) (1919)

PUBLICATIONS

Hedendaagsche stroomingen in de muziek. Rotterdam, [1921]

De muziek in Nederland in het licht der anthroposophie. Lecture for the Muziek Paedagogisch Verbond, section Amsterdam, 1 March 1927. Published in *De Muziek*

Was Goethe muzikaal? : een geesteswetenschappelijke studie. The Hague, [1930]

Debussy. The Hague, Kruseman, 1940

BIBLIOGRAPHY

W. Paap: 'Nederlandsche componisten van onzen tijd, X: Henri Zagwijn', *Mens en Melodie*, vol. 3, 1948, p. 263

H.W. de Ronde: 'Henri Zagwijn en zijn Zauberlehrling', *Caecilia*, 71, 1914, p. 54

DISCOGRAPHY

Galgenlieder. H. Meens (T), M. van Nieukerken (pf) (BFO A-1)

Bernard Zweers

AMSTERDAM, 18 MAY 1854 – AMSTERDAM, 9 DECEMBER 1924

Bernard Zweers was born on Amsterdam's Kalverstraat, near to the Munt, where his father ran a piano and music store. Zweers Jr. was predestined to succeed his father in the business, but decided at an early age to follow a different musical path. He received music lessons from Johan F. Kupers, and bought theory books in order to teach himself composition.

In 1880 Zweers' father closed his business and a year later, having finally received his parents' permission, Bernard was able to dedicate himself once and for all to composing. He left for Leipzig, studying with Salomon Jadassohn, and returned to his native city in 1883 as a fully qualified composer. He took on various appointments in order to make a living. These included the conductorships of several choirs, such as the Aemstel Male Choir and a Roman Catholic choir called 'Zelus pro domo Deï'. He later relinquished these posts to devote more time to composing and to a number of teaching positions in theory and composition. From 1888 he was attached to the Orchestral School, a training facility founded by Willem Kes, which was closely connected with the Concertgebouw Orchestra. He also taught at the Toonkunst Music School, the Amsterdam chapter of the Society for the Advancement of Music, and was appointed theory and composition teacher at the Amsterdam Conservatory in 1896. His innumerable students included composers who were to play major roles in Dutch musical life, such as Hendrik and Willem Andriessen, Sem Dresden, Daniel Ruyneman, Anthon van der Horst and Willem Landré.

Shortly after celebrating his seventieth birthday on 18 May 1924, Zweers was affected by heart problems and was ordered to 'take strict care of himself'. He died on December 9.

Despite his many students, Zweers never 'created a school'. In other words, his own style never had any recognizable influence on the work of younger composers. He permitted them too much freedom for that. Nevertheless, his importance as a teacher is difficult to overestimate: he instilled self-confidence in an entire generation of young composers, and the awareness that an independent Dutch musical art was perfectly justifiable. At the time, the work of Dutch composers was strongly influenced by musical developments in Germany.

413

Zweers was said to be a strict, though honest teacher, and he was revered by his students. As Willem Andriessen reminisced, 'Now Zweers may seem to you just like an old schoolmaster, a stuffed shirt, but just put that piece away for a few months. Take it out again and maybe you'll come round and say: that old Zweers was right after all.'

As early as 1876 (five years before going to study with Jadassohn), Zweers composed a Mass for male voices and organ. During the same year, he was present at a performance in Berlin of Wagner's *Der Ring des Nibelungen*, an experience that influenced his musical taste enormously. This is clear from his Second Symphony, composed in 1883, and he was not embarrassed: Wagner's music possessed a power from which few European composers could or wanted to escape.

Nevertheless, his own quest was for the key to Dutch music. He deliberately composed songs to Dutch texts (including those of P.C. Boutens) and performed a feat of virtually national importance when he named his Third Symphony (1887-89) *Aan mijn Vaderland* [To my Fatherland]. The work was premiered by the Concertgebouw Orchestra under Willem Kes on 10 April 1890. It was regarded as Zweers' 'principal composition', and simply because of its immensity, it was not until 1906 that both a full score and piano reduction were published on the initiative of A.A. Noske, a publisher in Middelburg. He, however, faced nothing but losses as sales were disappointingly poor. Nonetheless, the composer Alphons Diepenbrock assured him: 'Even if you never print anything again, you will still have fulfilled your task as a publisher.'

At the head of the manuscript Zweers had written, 'One's art is one's life'. The work is divided into four movements, each with a programmatic title: *In Neérland's wouden* [In the forests of the Netherlands], *Op het land, Aan het strand en op zee* [In the country, On the beach and at sea], *Ter hoofdstad* [In the capital]. The work's Dutch character has been pithily characterized by the renowned musicologist Eduard Reeser as 'partly folksong, partly ceremonious diatonic melodies, firmly rooted in a compact homophonic style with broad cadences, in which severe dissonances are added to the functional harmonies.' After the Third Symphony, Zweers' style showed little development. Other milestones in his oeuvre are the cantata *De Kosmos* (1883) and the music to Vondel's seventeenth-century play *Gysbrecht van Aemstel* (1892).

Instrumental chamber music is virtually absent from Zweers' output. He did, however, write an Andante for four violins, another for six violins, a Romance for violin and piano, and one for cello and piano. However, his interests were almost diametrically opposed. On the one hand he had a predilection for the intimacy of songs with nothing but piano accompaniment and, on the other, he wrote for large, occasionally unconventional, top-heavy forces. Examples of the latter are his *Veni, Creator* for tenor solo, male choir, organ and brass, and *Hoe ieder 't zoo wist* [How everyone came to know about it] for three children's choirs. Not to be omitted in this context is the children's cantata *Sinterklaasfeest* [Santa Claus' Feast] (1891), which he wrote for large orchestra, two soloists and a choir of six hundred children. Although the children's feast of Santa Claus is widely celebrated on the 5th of December, the work was performed by the Concertgebouw Orchestra on 19 and 26 April 1891.

Not entirely without reason, Zweers' Third Symphony is often referred to as an accomplishment of national consequence. During a period in which Dutch musical consciousness found expression chiefly in archaic and romanticized retrospects – for instance in the work of Julius Röntgen (1855-1932) and Cornelis Dopper (1870-1939) – Zweers cultivated the quotation of folk song into an individual style. He demonstrated the proof of the viability of homegrown symphonic music, and of the vitality of songs sung to Dutch texts. As Willem Landré put it: 'Thanks to his courageous advances, the disbelief in the idea of our own Music has evaporated, and Dutch song has undergone a restoration.'

JOHAN KOLSTEEG

COMPOSITIONS

VOCAL: *Mis*, m.choir, org (1876); *Winnend Verlies* (ballad), mix.choir, orch?; *De Kosmos* (cantata) (Ten Cate) (1883); *Voorspel en reien voor Gysbrecht van Aemstel* (1892); *Kroningscantate* (Beets) (1897); *Kroningscantate* (Fiore della Neve, pseud. of Van Loghem) (1898); *Leo-cantate* (Schaepman) (1902); *Aan de schoonheid* (Boutens), mix.choir (1909); *Rozen*, mix.choir, orch (1924); *Veni, creator*, T, m.choir, org, wind instr.; *Hoe ieder 't zoo wist*, 3 ch.choir

INSTRUMENTAL: *Symphony no. 1* (1881); *Symphony no. 2* (1883); *Symphony no. 3 (Aan mijn vaderland)* (1887-1889); *Saskia, concertstuk voor orkest* (1906)

PUBLICATIONS

Under pseud. Philomelus. *Vondels reizangen op muziek gezet*, Caecilia, 48, 1891, p. 175-178

BIBLIOGRAPHY

W. Andriessen: *Mensen in de muziek*. Amsterdam, 1962
H. Berckenhoff: *Kunstwerken en kunste-*

naars. Amsterdam, [1916]

T. Braas: 'Ik heb nu eindelijk het orchestreeren zoowat geleerd', *Harmonie en perspectief : zevenendertig bijdragen van Utrechtse musicologen voor Eduard Reeser*, ed. A. Annegarn [et al.]. Deventer, Sub Rosa, 1988 (includes information on Zweers' Vondelsettings)

J. Daniskas: *Nederlandsche Componisten in de XIXe en XXe eeuw*

E. Reeser: *Een eeuw Nederlandse muziek : 1815-1915.* Amsterdam, Querido, 1950, 2/1986

E. van Zoeren: *De muziekuitgeverij A.A. Noske (1896-1926) : een bijdrage tot dertig jaar Nederlandse muziekgeschiedenis.* Haarlemmerliede, Van Zoeren, 1987

DISCOGRAPHY

Een liedje. S. van Lier (S), N. van der Elst (pf) (Mirasound 4419830)

Symphony no. 3. Residentie Orchestra, cond. H. Vonk (Olympia OCD 503)

About the contributors

BOB VAN ASPEREN is harpsichordist and organist. A former professor of harpsichord at the Royal Conservatory in The Hague, he now leads an international harpsichord class at the Conservatorium van Amsterdam.

CASPAR BECX studied the saxophone and musicology at Utrecht University. He has published several articles on Dutch wind music. He is also active as a performing musician and saxophone teacher at the Utrecht Center for the Arts.

A musicologist and theorist, **JAAP VAN BENTHEM** taught music theory at the conservatories in Utrecht and Rotterdam, as well as the Sweelinck Conservatory in Amsterdam. From 1972 to 2001 he taught at Utrecht University. He has published articles on Renaissance music and early 20th-century Dutch composers.

JAN TEN BOKUM studied the piano at the Utrecht Conservatory and musicology at Utrecht University. He concluded his academic studies with a dissertation on J.G. Bastiaans. He is director of the Apeldoorn Music School.

TON BRAAS, musicologist, is active as conductor, writer, and staff member of the Foundation for Cooperating Dutch Choral Organizations (SNK). He taught history of Renaissance music at Utrecht University. 1997 saw the publication of his dissertation *De symfonieën en de kamermuziek van Matthijs Vermeulen: poëtica and compositie* as well as an extensive biography of Matthijs Vermeulen.

MICHIEL CLEIJ is a freelance musician and music journalist.

ALBERT CLEMENT studied the organ at the Brabant Conservatory in Tilburg, musicology at Utrecht University and theology at Leiden University. He concluded his studies *cum laude* with a dissertation on works of J.S. Bach. He works as a researcher and teacher in musicology at Utrecht University.

Musicologist **ARTHUR VAN DIJK** concluded his studies with a thesis on Willem Pijper's literary works. He is director of the Netherlands Youth Orchestra.

HANS VAN DIJK is a man of letters and a musicologist. He teaches musicology both at universities and institutions of higher professional education. In 1979 he obtained his doctorate with a dissertation entitled *Jan van Gilse, strijder en idealist*.

Musicologist, harpsichordist and organist PIETER DIRKSEN gained a doctorate with a dissertation on the keyboard music of Jan Pieterszn. Sweelinck and published a monograph on Bach's *Kunst der Fuge*. He frequently performs as a soloist, and with such ensembles as the Netherlands Bach Society and the Combattimento Consort Amsterdam.

MICHAEL VAN EEKEREN is musicologist and teaches music theory. He is also a freelance music journalist and producer with the AVRO broadcasting society.

ANTHONY FIUMARA is musicologist and music journalist. He teaches at the Conservatory of Amsterdam and is music editor with a.o. daily newspaper *Trouw*.

MARIUS FLOTHUIS studied the piano, music theory and musicology. He was artistic leader of the Royal Concertgebouw Orchestra and professor of musicology at Utrecht University, to name but a few of his numerous activities. He is the author of many publications, program notes and articles in newspapers and professional journals.

JEROEN VAN GESSEL studied the organ at the Utrecht Conservatory and musicology at Utrecht University. He works at the Centrale Discotheek (public CD library) in Rotterdam.

LOUIS PETER GRIJP, musicologist, is researcher at the P.J. Meertens Instituut in Amsterdam. He is also a lutist and artistic leader of the ensemble Camerata Trajectina, a group specialized in the performance of sixteenth- and seventeenth-century music from the Netherlands.

LUC VAN HASSELT studied musicology at the University of Amsterdam, piano at the conservatories of Amsterdam and Utrecht and harpsichord with Gustav Leonhardt. He has made radio programs and has published articles in several journals and books. He is currently editor of the monthly magazine *Preludium*.

MIEKE VAN HEIJSTER is trained as a music librarian at the Frederik Muller Akademie in Amsterdam. At Centrum Nederlandse Muziek she was engaged in cataloguing and managing the Alsbach Collectie. She is librarian at the Rotterdam Conservatory and Dance Academy.

CAECILE DE HOOG is a translator specializing in texts on classical music. She runs a small business called 'Muse Translations'.

PAY-UUN HIU is musicologist and music journalist. She is editor of the daily newspaper *de Volkskrant* and was one of the editors of the *HonderdComponistenBoek*, the Dutch version of *The Essential Guide to Dutch Music*.

Composer and musicologist WILLEM JETHS is the author of the chapter on Elisabeth Kuyper in *Zes vrouwelijke componisten*, a book on women composers published by Centrum Nederlandse Muziek/Walburg Pers.

TILLY JUMELET-VAN DOEVEREN is musicologist and piano teacher. Her special field of study is the music history of Rotterdam and she is currently working on her dissertation, at Leiden University, on choirs in Rotterdam. Her promoter is Dr. Jan Bank. She is the author of *Eene inrigting voor grondig en min kostbaar onderwijs*, a book about music schools in Rotterdam in the years 1844-1994.

JOLANDE VAN DER KLIS studied musicology at Utrecht University. She is the author of a book on the rise of the early music movement in the Netherlands and editor-in-chief of the *Tijdschrift Oude Muziek*. She also makes radio programs and was involved in the Dutch translation of Christoph Wolff's biography of J.S.Bach.

JOHAN KOLSTEEG, musicologist, works for NCRV radio. He is the author of *Eén groot oeuvre*, a book about the history of Donemus.

JEANINE LANDHEER studied musicology at Utrecht University and concluded her studies with a thesis on Anna Cramer which won her the Jan Pieter Heijeprijs, a prize awarded by the Royal Society for Music History of the Netherlands (VNM). She has worked as a music critic for *Klassiek* and the daily *Haagsche Courant*. She is currently active as a freelance writer.

HELEN METZELAAR, ph.D., is a freelance writer, musicologist, and flutist. She is currently writing a biography on the Dutch composer and pianist Henriëtte Bosmans. Last year her dissertation, *From Private to Public Spheres: Exploring*

Women's Role in Dutch Musical Life from c. 1700 to c. 1880 and *Three Case Studies* was published. She is director of the Dutch Women and Music Foundation and teaches flute at the Amsterdam Music School.

JACO MIJNHEER studied musicology at the University of Amsterdam and the Université de Montréal. He is active as writer, translator, program maker and organizer, for, among others, Holland Music Sessions in Alkmaar.

PAUL OP DE COUL is professor of post-1600 music history at Utrecht University. He gained a doctoral degree with a dissertation on Ferruccio Busoni's opera *Doktor Faust 1925*. His research focuses on opera and operatic theory in the first half of the twentieth century.

GERT OOST studied the organ at the Amsterdam Conservatory and was awarded the Prix d'Excellence. He also studied musicology at Utrecht University. He currently teaches musicology at the latter institution. He specializes in Dutch musical life in the eighteenth and nineteenth centuries. He is the author of a biography of Anthon van der Horst, his former teacher, which was published in 1994.

EMANUEL OVERBEEKE studied musicology at Utrecht University and then with Charles Rosen in New York. He is the author of several books, including *Muzikale dubbellevens, Igor Stravinsky in de spiegel van zijn tijd* and *Chopin: de man en zijn muziek*. He writes book reviews and is editor of music publications.

RENÉ RAKIER studied the piano, organ and choral conducting at the Royal Conservatory in The Hague. In the early 1960s he was awarded the Prix d'Excellence for piano and organ. He is active as a soloist, accompanist and chamber musician. He is also engaged in research on the history of Dutch music between 1850 and 1930.

HUIB RAMAER studies musicology at the University of Amsterdam and works as a freelance writer and compiler of programs. He is also associated with the Leo Smit Foundation.

RUDOLF RASCH studied musicology at the University of Amsterdam and is currently associated with the musicology department of Utrecht University. He specializes in the history of Dutch music from the seventeenth and eighteenth centuries. He is co-editor of *Unico Wilhelm van Wassenaer; componist en staats-*

man, which was published in 1993 by Centrum Nederlandse Muziek/Walburg Pers.

WILMA ROEST studied musicology at Utrecht University and concluded her studies with a thesis on Johan Wagenaar. She subsequently moved to London, where she still lives. After obtaining a post-graduate teaching qualification she worked as a teacher for a number of years. She currently works as an Anglican priest in Wimbledon.

CLEMENS ROMIJN, musicologist and harpsichordist, is active as a writer on music and teaches music history. His book *Oscar van Hemel: componist tussen klassiek en atonaal* appeared in 1992. He is the editor of the Dutch translation of Christoph Wolff's biography of J.S. Bach, and wrote the liner notes of a comlete new Dutch Bach edition on CD.

FRANS VAN ROSSUM's main activities are making radio programs and writing about music, with contemporary musical life as special field of interest.

FRANS VAN RUTH studied the piano with Hans Osieck and Herman Uhlhorn at the Utrecht Conservatory. He is coordinator of the chamber music department of the Conservatorium of Amsterdam. He is currently writing a biography of the composer Leander Schlegel.

ELMER SCHÖNBERGER is musicologist and composer. His articles on music have appeared in the weekly magazine *Vrij Nederland* since 1976. He is the author of *The Apollonian Clockwork, On Stravinsky* (in conjunction with Louis Andriessen), *De wellustige tandarts & andere componisten, De vrouw met de hamer & andere componisten* and *De kunst van het kruitverschieten*.

ONNO SCHOONDERWOERD is musicologist, freelance writer and editor-in-chief of various periodicals. He teaches the history of nineteenth- and twentieth-century music at Utrecht University.

JURRIEN SLIGTER studied the piano, composition and music theory at the Amsterdam Conservatory. He subsequently studied conducting with David Porcelijn and Lucas Vis. He teaches music theory at the Utrecht Conservatory, and conducts Ensemble Gending and the BASHO Ensemble. He is the editor of *Ton de Leeuw*, a book published by Centrum Nederlandse Muziek/Walburg Pers.

DÉSIRÉE STAVERMAN teaches music history at the Rotterdam Conservatory. She is engaged in research on Alphons Diepenbrock's theater music.

MARCEL VENDERBOSCH is musicologist and makes radio programs for the AVRO broadcasting society. He specializes in early music and the works of Johannes Verhulst.

REIN VERHAGEN studied the recorder in Haarlem and Amsterdam. He has edited several editions of sixteenth- and seventeenth-century music including a facsimile edition of the works of Sybrandus van Noordt. 1989 saw the publication of his monograph *Sybrandus van Noordt, organist van Amsterdam en Haarlem 1650-1705*. He is currently writing a monograph on Quirinus van Blankenburg.

ERNST VERMEULEN studied the flute and piano at the Utrecht Conservatory and ethnomusicology in Amsterdam. He has made radio programs and his articles have appeared in a variety of periodicals and newspapers including *NRC Handelsblad*. He teaches music and cultural history at the Rotterdam Conservatory.

ERIK VOERMANS is musicologist and music editor of daily newspaper *Het Parool*. He taught twentieth-century music history at the Utrecht Conservatory and was the editor of *Peter Schat–Rudolf Escher, brieven 1958-1961*, a book published by Centrum Nederlandse Muziek/Walburg Pers.

FRITS VAN DER WAA is musicologist, cartoonist and translator. He is editor of the periodical *Vrije Geluiden* and music editor with daily newspaper *de Volkskrant*. *De slag van Andriessen*, a book published by De Bezige Bij, appeared under his editorship.

EMILE WENNEKES is professor of post-1600 Dutch music history at Utrecht University and is artistic advisor of MuziekGroep Nederland. He was active as a music critic for the daily newspapers *NRC Handelsblad* and *de Volkskrant*. He was (co)author of books on Mahler, Bach, and the former Paleis voor Volksvlijt in Amsterdam.

KEES WIERINGA studied the piano at the Sweelinck Conservatory in Amsterdam. He has made several CD-recordings with music by Simeon ten Holt. He is a member of various ensembles (including the Lemniscaat Ensemble, Ingenhovenproject, Ruynemanproject), and is also active as a freelance radio and television maker.

THIEMO WIND studied musicology at Utrecht University, oboe and recorder at the conservatories of Utrecht and Hilversum respectively. He is music editor of daily newspaper *De Telegraaf.* He has edited a modern text edition of Jacob van Eyk's *Der Fluyten Lust-hof.*

Index